P9-ECS-597

שערי תפלה

GATES OF PRAYER

The New Union Prayerbook

Weekdays, Sabbaths, and Festivals

Services and Prayers

for Synagogue and Home

CENTRAL CONFERENCE OF AMERICAN RABBIS

5735 New York 1975

EIGHTH PRINTING, 1984

LIBRARY OF CONGRESS CATALOGUE CARD NUMBER: 75-13752

PRINTED IN U.S.A.

LITURGY COMMITTEE

OF THE

CENTRAL CONFERENCE OF AMERICAN RABBIS

Robert I. Kahn,
Chairman 1967–1973

A. Stanley Dreyfus,
Chairman 1973–

HERBERT BRONSTEIN

A. STANLEY DREYFUS

HARVEY J. FIELDS

ALBERT A. GOLDMAN

LEONARD S. KRAVITZ

RICHARD N. LEVY

EUGENE MIHALY

JOSEPH R. NAROT

NATHAN A. PERILMAN

CHAIM STERN

DUDLEY WEINBERG

JOSEPH B. GLASER, *ex-officio*

MALCOLM H. STERN, *ex-officio*

JACK BEMPORAD, *ex-officio*

SIDNEY L. REGNER, *ex-officio*

EDWARD GRAHAM, *for the American Conference of Cantors*

◆ ◆

Chaim Stern, *Editor of the Prayerbook*

Contents

Page

Introduction xi הקדמה

A Note on Usage xiv

Acknowledgments xv

Meditations and Readings 3 הגיונות

From Chapters of the Fathers 16 לקוטים מפרקי אבות

Weekday Services תפלות לימות החול

Evening Service 31
Morning Service 51
Evening or Morning Service I 72
Evening or Morning Service II 82
Evening or Morning Service III 92
Evening or Morning Service IV 102
Afternoon Service 111

Sabbath Evening Services תפלות ערבית לשבת

Service I 117
Service II 142
Service III 158
Service IV 176
Service V 189
Service VI 204
Service VII 219
Service VIII 244
Service IX 260
Service X 269

Sabbath Morning Services תפלות שחרית לשבת

Service I 283
Service II 318
Service III 332
Service IV 348
Service V 364
Service VI 378

Prayers and Readings for Special Occasions תפלות וקריאות שונות

The Sabbath of Repentance 391
The Sabbath in Sukkot 395
The Sabbath in Chanukah 397
Shabbat Zachor 400
Purim 403
The Sabbath in Pesach 405
In Remembrance of Jewish Suffering 407
The Sabbath before Yom Ha-atsma-ut 412

For the Reading of the Torah — סדר קריאת התורה

I 417
II 425
III 431
IV 437
V 442
Special Prayers 449

Services for the Festivals — תפלות ליום טוב

Evening Service 455
Morning Service 489
Hallel 525
For the Reading of the Torah 531
For the Reading of the Torah on Atzeret-Simchat Torah 538
Memorial Service 546

Afternoon Service for the Sabbath and Festivals 554 — תפלת מנחה לשבת וליום טוב

Service for Tish'a be-Av and Yom Hasho-ah 573 — תפלות לתשעה באב וליום השואה

Service for Yom Ha-atsma-ut 590 — תפלות ליום העצמאות

Concluding Prayers — עלינו

Aleinu I 615
Aleinu II 617
Aleinu III 618
Aleinu IV 620
Before the Kaddish 622
Kaddish 629

For Synagogue and Home — תפלות בבית ובבית הכנסת

Havdalah I 633
Havdalah II 637
Chanukah 642
At a House of Mourning 645

Special Themes — לקוטים

Nature 651
Omnipresence 658
Quest 663
Humanity 667
Loneliness 670
Trust 673
Sincerity 677
Righteousness 681
Justice 685
Unity 689
Peace 692
Revelation 696
The Ten Commandments 701
Israel's Mission 703
Redemption 707
Doubt 711

Kiddush for Shabbat and Yom Tov

סדר קדוש לשבת וליום טוב

For Sabbath Evening 719
For Sabbath Morning 720
For Yom Tov Evening 721
For Yom Tov Morning 723

Songs and Transliterations

שירים וזמירות

Index to Songs and Hymns 726
Songs and Hymns 729
Transliterations of Recurring Passages 766

Index to Psalms

This index cites Psalms appearing in whole or in substantial part

Psalm	*Page*	*Psalm*	*Page*
1	559	98	121
8	668	99	122
15	177	100	506
16	549	104	652
19	290/424	105	463
23	546	107	591
24	442	111	499
29	122	113	525
33	291	114	526
42/3	663	115	526
57	497	117	527
63	664	118	528
67/8	505	121	546
84	144	122	491
85	102	124	400
90	548	126	608
91	673	131	674
92	125	136	558
93	127	137	606
95	118	139	658
96	119	145	111
97	120	150	297

Introduction

In the liturgy of the synagogue the Jewish people has written its spiritual autobiography. For a score of centuries, each generation has, in turn, added its own distinctive chapter to this book, which contains memories of time past and promises for the future, praise and lamentation, ethical teaching, and mystical vision. A people possessed by its God is the author of this book.

We are that people still. There are divisions among us; some are matters of principle and others relate to style. And yet, at root, we remain united in our yearning for transcendence, in our hope for peace and human friendship. All of us, in our reflective moments, continue to look beneath the surface of our lives, hoping for light, strength, eternal — or at least durable — purpose. Our people's modes of worship are many and various, but we are at one in attempting, through worship, to express our deepest selves.

Worship is more than an act of cognition; it is a turning of the whole being toward that which we affirm as ultimately real and valuable. Humble in the face of a spiritual reality whose essence we cannot 'know', we speak in metaphors. Our 'truth' is a truth of the heart no less than of the mind. The 'facts' we assert are those of the hopeful spirit. But we believe that the spiritual reality within us corresponds to a spiritual Reality beyond us, and in worship we hope to bring the two realities into communion. *Shaarei Tefillah* will be, we pray, a means to that end. As Jews have done since the twilight days of the Second Temple, we have sought, in our own way, to express our people's soul: our joys and our sorrows, our sense of wonder, our longing for God, our hopes for humanity.

We are a diversified people. Within our Reform community are proponents of many viewpoints. There is disagreement among us on many issues. It is our hope that *Gates of Prayer* will unite us all in worship. We do not assume that all controversy is harmful; we do not presume to judge which controversy is not "for the sake of Heaven"; still less do we wish to stifle the expression of views sincerely held. Therefore in this prayerbook we have followed the principle that there are many paths to heaven's gates, that this prayer and that one, this service and that one, may both have the power to lead us to the living God. Faithful to this view, we have tried to provide room for many ways of worship. We have included many old songs to God, and we have attempted new ones that seem appropriate to our time and condition. So it is that while our themes are the ageless ones of our tradition, the manner of their expression reflects our own day. The result is variety of mood and thought and style. We offer all these songs, old and new, with reverence.

Ours has been a time of almost perpetual strife. By reason of our technological prowess in the art of warfare, the very continuance of human life on this planet is by no means assured. Our civilization is unstable; information has grown exponentially, without an equivalent growth in wisdom; we have experienced tremendous changes, material and intellectual. Some have been harmful, others beneficial, but all of them have had their impact upon us. And we Jews have also experienced the Holocaust and the rebirth of Israel — events that loom large in our consciousness. To these, in particular, have we attempted a response. We have also been keenly aware of the changing status of women in our society. Our commitment in the Reform movement to the equality of the sexes is of long standing. In this book, it takes the form of avoiding the use of masculine terminology exclusively, when we are referring to the human race in general.

Gates of Prayer replaces *The Union Prayerbook*, last revised in 1940. The Central Conference of American Rabbis offers *Gates of Prayer* with gratitude for the rich liturgical heritage that made it possible. All Jewish liturgy begins with the Siddur, whose profound influence on the present volume will be immediately apparent. *The Union Prayerbook*, which served American Reform Jewry for eighty years, has contributed much of its contents to its successor. And *Gates of Prayer* as a whole is modelled after, and borrows much from, *Service of the Heart* (London, 1967), the first comprehensive post-World War II prayerbook of Reform Jewry. Finally, many new prayers and meditations have been incorporated into this volume, for faith and aspiration live on. The result is a new prayerbook profoundly rooted in Jewish tradition, and one that expresses that tradition within the context of Reform Judaism.

We have called this volume *Shaarei Tefillah*, mindful of the Rabbinic dictum that the gates of prayer are never barred. We feel privileged to present this prayerbook to the House of Israel, and pray that many will seek to enter the gates, to find their way to the presence of the Eternal.

קרוב יי לכל־קראיו, לכל אשר יקראהו באמת.

ערב שבת קדש ׳בהעלתך׳ תשל״ה
20 Sivan 5735

Chaim Stern
CHAPPAQUA, NEW YORK

A Note on Usage

For the most part, in place of the conventional rubrics, 'Reader,' 'All Reading,' 'Singing,' and the like, the type-face is intended to suggest how the service might be conducted. We employ Roman type for 'Reader', *italics* for 'All Reading', and sans-serif (in the English) for Hebrew passages that will usually be sung. However, congregations may continue to follow their established custom, or they may choose to experiment with different patterns.

This prayerbook affords congregations the widest latitude in worship. It provides many optional prayers and meditations. Some are included at the beginning of the volume; these are entitled 'Meditations and Readings' and 'From Chapters of the Fathers'. Others include 'Prayers and Readings for Special Occasions' and 'Special Themes'. Still others are found in the body of the services themselves, especially in the Kabbalat Shabbat sections on Sabbath evenings, and in the introductory sections of the services for Sabbath mornings and for Festivals. At a Sabbath evening service, special readings might replace the Kabbalat Shabbat, or they might be inserted after the Tefillah. Even when no additional readings are included, it is not contemplated that, in each service, every English and Hebrew passage will be read. And although certain passages will surely always be sung others will be sung less frequently. Therefore, the presence of sans-serif alongside a Hebrew passage should not be taken as an indication that it *must* be sung.

Shabbat Evening Services IX and X, and Shabbat Morning Service VI are offered for those occasions when many children will attend.

Acknowledgments

The Central Conference of American Rabbis wishes to express its gratitude to all who helped shape the contents of this volume. Many suggestions, comments, and criticisms were received during the course of its preparation. All were carefully considered. They came from individuals and from congregations in North America, Europe, and Israel. We thank those who shared their love of Jewish prayer with us.

The Conference takes this opportunity to record its special indebtedness to a number of individuals in particular. Rabbi Chaim Stern served as Editor of *Gates of Prayer*. In that capacity, he prepared the various drafts for circulation, compiling and shaping all the material in them, translating the Hebrew, writing many new prayers, and adapting many others. In addition, he prepared the manuscript for the printer, and participated in the process of design and correction. Rabbi Stern wishes here to record his great sense of indebtedness to Rabbi A. Stanley Dreyfus (Chairman of the Liturgy Committee since 1973). Rabbi Dreyfus devoted much time and effort to a painstaking scrutiny of the manuscript. His suggestions and corrections resulted in great improvements in the text, and in the avoidance of many errors, both of content and design. Rabbi Robert I. Kahn, who preceded Rabbi Dreyfus as Chairman of the Committee, also gave the work much time, insight, and devotion. Under his farsighted leadership of the Committee, the arduous process of translating the dream of a new prayerbook into a reality began.

The Liturgy Committee published and distributed four experimental services to the Conference. Reactions to these pamphlets helped determine the direction of our new liturgy. They were prepared by Rabbis Harvey J. Fields, Robert I. Kahn, Leonard S. Kravitz, Joseph Rudavsky, and Richard N. Levy. Rabbi Malcolm H. Stern served as Secretary to the Committee and as an invaluable counsellor on many difficult problems. There is no phase of the work to which he did not make a contribution. Dr. Edward Graham (who as delegate from the American Conference of Cantors served as an active member of the Committee) was most helpful in every aspect of the work. Rabbi John D. Rayner (London) read much of the final draft and made many valuable suggestions. Mr. Abraham Rothberg, the distinguished novelist, read the entire manuscript. His feeling for the niceties of English style enhanced the text at many points. Mr. Andor Braun brought a sensitive mind and a wealth of experience to bear on the difficult problems of design. His creative work is responsible for much of the beauty of this volume. We are indebted to Mr. Ismar David for his Hebrew caligraphy. We thank Professor Jakob J. Petuchowski for his advice, and for permission to include his moving liturgy for Yom Ha-atsma-ut, which we use as a supplement to the service for that day. Professors Abraham Aaroni and Werner Weinberg of the Hebrew Union College - Jewish Institute of Religion graciously helped on specific matters pertaining to the Hebrew texts. Rabbi James R. Michaels assisted the Editor and Rabbi Dreyfus with the proofreading. His work was meticulous and scholarly, and his helpful suggestions are incorporated in the text and in the Notes, which appear in the companion-volume *Shaarei Habayit, Gates of the House*. Finally, we thank Rabbi Joseph B. Glaser, Executive Vice-President of the Conference, whose energy and vision helped give birth to this project, and whose help and counsel smoothed its path from inception to completion.

* *

The Conference records its thanks to the following persons, all of whom offered detailed suggestions: Rabbis Albert A. Axelrad, Sidney Ballon ז״ל, Bernard J. Bamberger, Henry Bamberger, Terry R. Bard, Jack Bemporad, H. Philip Berkowitz, Haskell M. Bernat, Sheldon H. Blank, Bernard H. Bloom, Herman J. Blumberg, William G. Braude, Jay R. Brickman, Herbert Bronstein, Sidney H. Brooks, Henry Cohen, William C. Cutter, Stanley M. Davids, Herbert E. Drooz, Arnold C. Fink, Frank A. Fisher, Leon C. Fram, Roland B. Gittelsohn, Albert S. Goldstein, David S. Goldstein, Albert A. Gordon, Norman D. Hirsch, Gunter Hirschberg, Lawrence A. Hoffman, Walter Jacob, David Jacobson, Wolli Kaelter, Ralph P. Kingsley, Leonard S. Kravitz, William J. Leffler, Richard N. Levy, Theodore N. Lewis, Allen S. Maller, Samuel H. Markowitz, Ronald Millstein, Isaac Neuman, Norman R. Patz, W. Gunther Plaut, Albert Plotkin, David Polish, H. Leonard Poller, Fredric S. Pomerantz, Morton H. Pomerantz, Sally J. Priesand, Robert A. Raab, Michael A. Robinson, James B. Rosenberg, Harry A. Roth, Martin B. Ryback, Marc Saperstein,

Herman E. Schaalman, Bernard Schachtel, Sanford Seltzer, Mordecai I. Soloff, Martin I. Silverman, William B. Silverman, Ezra Z. Spicehandler (Jerusalem), Samuel M. Stahl, Arthur Z. Steinberg, Leo J. Stillpass, Frank N. Sundheim, Roy D. Tanenbaum, Edward S. Treister, Leo E. Turitz, Stephen E. Weisberg, Leonard Winograd, H. Richard White, Meir Ydit (Rehovot), Andre Zaoui (Jerusalem), Edward Zerin; Cantors Barry Hyams, Samuel Kligfeld, Paul Kwartin, Murray E. Simon, and Raymond Smolover. It is impossible to mention the names of the many lay persons who contributed valuable suggestions to this volume, but their assistance is here most gratefully noted. It is, however, appropriate that we express our particular gratitude to Mr. Seymour Phillips and Mr. Daniel Koshland for their generous support of this project.

⋆ ⋆

Although *Gates of Prayer* breaks new ground in the liturgy of Reform Judaism, its roots include the *Union Prayerbook*, whose last edition (1940) has exerted much influence on its successor. We pay tribute to the distinguished members of the Conference's Liturgy Committee, who brought that edition into being: Solomon B. Freehof, Chairman; Isaac E. Marcuson, Secretary; Israel Bettan, Edward N. Calisch, Samuel S. Cohon, Abraham J. Feldman, James G. Heller, and Louis Witt. Although they were not members of the Committee at the time when the Prayerbook was completed, Joseph L. Baron, Hyman G. Enelow, and Gerson B. Levi served during part of the time during which it was prepared.

⋆ ⋆

Every effort has been made to ascertain the owners of copyrights for the selections used in this volume, and its companion-volume, *Gates of the House*, and to obtain permission to reprint copyrighted passages. For the use of the passages indicated, the Central Conference of American Rabbis expresses its gratitude to those whose names appear below. The Conference will be pleased, in subsequent editions, to correct any inadvertent errors or omissions that may be pointed out.

A. S. BARNES AND COMPANY, INC.: From *The Golden Peacock: A Worldwide Treasury of Yiddish Poetry*, compiled, translated and edited by Dr. Joseph Leftwich. Reprinted by permission.

ASSOCIATION PRESS, INC.: From "The Moral Outrage of Vietnam," by Abraham Joshua Heschel, in *Vietnam: Crisis of Conscience*, copyright © 1967.

ATHENEUM PUBLISHERS: From *The Hard Hours*, by Anthony Hecht. Copyright © 1967 by Anthony E. Hecht. Reprinted by permission of Atheneum Publishers.

BLANK, AMY K.: "I will lift my hands unto thee, O my God!" Used by permission.

BLOCH PUBLISHING COMPANY, INC.: From *The Hasidic Anthology*, Edited by Louis I. Newman, copyright © 1944.

CAMBRIDGE UNIVERSITY PRESS: From *The New English Bible*. Copyright © The Delegates of the Oxford University Press and the Syndics of the Cambridge University Press 1961, 1970. Reprinted by permission.

CHARLES SCRIBNER'S SONS: "This Quiet Dust" is reprinted by permission of Charles Scribner's Sons from *The Bright Doom* by John Hall Wheelock. Copyright 1927 Charles Scribner's Sons.

COLLINS PUBLISHERS, LTD.: From *Ardours and Endurance*, by Robert Nichols, 1917.

EDWARD ARNOLD, LTD.: From *The Human Situation*, by W. MacNeile Dixon.

EISENSTEIN, JUDITH K.: From *The Gateway to Jewish Song*, the song "In the Wilderness." Behrman House, Inc., New York. Reprinted by permission.

FARRAR, STRAUSS & GIROUX, INC.: From *O The Chimneys*, by Nelly Sachs, Copyright, 1967, poems on pp. 3, 9, 29–30, 61, 65–66.

HAMISH HAMILTON, LTD.: "Message from Home," by Kathleen Raine. From *Collected Poems of Kathleen Raine*, © by Kathleen Raine, 1956, London.

HARCOURT BRACE JOVANOVITCH, INC.: "i thank you god." Copyright, 1950, by E. E. Cummings. Reprinted from his volume, *Complete Poems 1913–1962*, by permission of Harcourt Brace Jovanovitch, Inc.

HARVARD UNIVERSITY PRESS: Reprinted by permission of the publishers from Theodore Spencer, *An Act Of Life*, Cambridge, Mass.: Harvard University Press, Copyright 1944, by the President and Fellows of Harvard College; © 1972, by Eloise Spencer Bender.

HOLT, RINEHART AND WINSTON, INC.: From *The Poetry of Robert Frost*, edited by Edward Connery Lathem. Copyright 1928. © 1969 by Holt, Rinehart and Winston Inc. Copyright © 1956, by Robert Frost. Reprinted by permission of Holt, Rinehart and Winston, Inc.

HOUGHTON MIFFLIN COMPANY, INC.: From *The Human Season: Selected Poems, 1926–1972*, by Archibald MacLeish. Reprinted by permission.

THE JEWISH PUBLICATION SOCIETY OF AMERICA: From *Poems*, by A. M. Klein, Copyright © 1944, reprinted by permission, and from *The Torah* and *Psalms* for occasional use of the translation.

THE JEWISH RECONSTRUCTIONIST FOUNDATION, INC., New York, publishers of *Sabbath Prayer Book*, 1965.

Judaism, VOLUME 16, NUMBER 3 (SUMMER, 1967), p. 299; the short passage by Elie Weisel is reprinted by permission of the American Jewish Congress.

KNOPF, ALFRED A., INC.: "Now from the world the light of God is gone . . ." is reprinted from *A Winter Tide*, by Robert Nathan, by permission of Alfred A. Knopf, Inc., 1939.

ACKNOWLEDGMENTS

MACMILLAN PUBLISHING CO. INC.: From *Poems* by John Masefield. Copyright 1916 by John Masefield, renewed 1944 by John Masefield; and from *Science and the Modern World* by Alfred North Whitehead. Copyright 1925 by Macmillan Publishing Co. Inc., renewed 1953 by Evelyn Whitehead. Both selections reprinted by permission of Macmillan Publishing Co. Inc.

MCGRAW-HILL, INC.: From *I Never Saw Another Butterfly*, copyright © 1964 by McGraw-Hill, Inc. Used by permission of McGraw-Hill, Inc.

MONICA MCCALL, INC., New York, by whose permission *Letter to the Front*, by Muriel Rukeyser (Copyright 1944 and 1962, Muriel Rukeyser) is reprinted.

THE NATIONAL COUNCIL OF CHURCHES: *Revised Standard Version of the Bible*, for occasional use of the translation.

NEW DIRECTIONS PUBLISHING CORPORATION: Denise Levertov, *The Jacob's Ladder*. Copyright 1961 by Denise Levertov Goodman, and Charles Reznikoff, *By the Waters of Manhattan*. Copyright 1951 by Charles Reznikoff. Both selections reprinted by permission of New Directions Publishing Corporation and the San Francisco Review.

THE RABBINICAL ASSEMBLY: "This Is My Prayer," by Hillel Bavli, translated by Norman Tarnor, in *Selihot*, copyright © 1964 by The Rabbinical Assembly, reprinted by permission of The Rabbinical Assembly.

RANDOM HOUSE, INC.: "I think continually of those . . ." is reprinted from *Selected Poems*, by Stephen Spender, by permission of Random House, Inc., 1934.

SCHOCKEN BOOKS, INC.: From *Tales of the Hasidim, Early Masters*, by Martin Buber. Copyright © 1947; from *Ten Rungs, Hasidic Sayings*, edited by Martin Buber. Copyright © 1947; from *The Way of Response*, by Martin Buber. Copyright © 1966; from *Zohar, The Book of Splendor*, edited by Gershom G. Scholem. Copyright © 1949; from *Language of Faith*, edited by Nahum N. Glatzer. Copyright © 1947. All of the above are copyright by Schocken Books Inc. and reprinted by permission of Schocken Books Inc.

SIFRIAT POALIM: "A Vow," by Abraham Shlonsky.

SIMON AND SCHUSTER, INC.: From *On a Note of Triumph*, by Norman Corwin, published by permission of Simon and Schuster.

TUPPER AND LOVE, INC.: "As The Moon Sinks," translated by Ishii and Obata, in *A Thousand And One Poems Of Mankind*, Edited by H. W. Wells.

UNION OF AMERICAN HEBREW CONGREGATIONS: From *This People Israel*, by Leo Baeck, translated by Albert H. Friedlander, copyright © 1964. Reprinted by permission.

THE UNIVERSITY OF CALIFORNIA PRESS: From *Modern Hebrew Poetry*, selected and translated by Ruth Finer Mintz, copyright © 1966. Originally published by the University of California Press; reprinted by permission of The Regents of the University of California.

VICTOR GOLLANCZ, LTD.: From "Why I Am A Jew" by Edmund Fleg.

THE VIKING PRESS, INC.: From *Selected Poems 1956–1968*, by Leonard Cohen.

WEATHERHEAD, LESLIE D.: From *A Private House of Prayer*. Reprinted by permission.

YALE UNIVERSITY PRESS: From *Belief Unbound*, by William Pepperell Montague.

GATES OF PRAYER

הגיונות

Meditations and Readings for Worship

1

THE PIOUS ONES of old used to wait a whole hour before praying, the better to concentrate their minds on God.

2

THE REBBE of Tsanz was asked by a Chasid: What does the Rabbi do before praying? I pray, was the reply, that I may be able to pray properly.

3

IF I KNEW that I had answered a single 'Amen' as it ought to be said, I would be contented.

4

ONCE the Baal Shem stopped on the threshold of a House of Prayer and refused to go in. I cannot enter, he said. It is crowded with teachings and prayers from wall to wall and from floor to ceiling. How could there be room for me? When he saw that those around him were staring, unable to understand, he added: The words of those whose teaching and praying does not come from hearts lifted to heaven, cannot rise to heaven; instead, their words fill the house from wall to wall and from floor to ceiling.

5

I HAVE always found prayer difficult. So often it seems like a fruitless game of hide-and-seek where we seek and God hides. . . . Yet I cannot leave prayer alone for long. My need drives me to Him. And I have a feeling that He has His own reasons for hiding Himself, and that finally all my seeking will prove infinitely worthwhile. And I am not sure what I mean by 'finding'. Some days my very seeking seems a kind of 'finding'. And, of course, if 'finding' means the *end* of 'seeking', it were better to go on seeking.

6

MAKE EVERY effort to pray from the heart. Even if you do not succeed, in the eyes of the Lord the effort is precious.

7

THE LORD will scatter you among the peoples . . . but if you search there for the Lord your God, if you seek Him with all your heart and soul, you will find Him.

8

KNOW THE GOD of your ancestors, and serve Him with a whole heart and a willing mind; for the Lord searches all hearts, and understands the impulse behind every thought. If you seek Him, He will allow you to find Him.

9

THE LORD is near to all who call upon Him, to all who call upon Him in truth.

10

CONSIDER how high God is above the world! Yet if one enters the synagogue and stands behind a pillar and prays in a whisper, the Holy One, blessed be He, listens to that prayer. . . . Can there be a God nearer than this, who is as near to His creatures as the mouth is to the ear?

11

I DO NOT pretend to understand how the divine Creator influences the human child. I feel as if spiritual forces were pouring constantly from the infinite source which is never poorer for all it gives forth. . . . Yet the influences of spirit make their way in different degrees, or not at all, to different souls. The windows of some are perhaps nearly shut. The windows of others have open only a few chinks and crevices. At some seasons — the seasons of prayer — those chinks and crevices may open a little wider so that a little more of God's light may enter in.

12

TRUE PRAYER is the opening of our hearts Godward, and the answer is a flow of light and influence from Him.

Prayer means a consciousness full of God's presence and of our relation with Him.

His aim is the increase of spiritual and moral goodness in the world, to lead the universe toward perfection. His laws are in their workings organized toward this end. Those who are loyal to Him must organize their own lives to be within the sphere of the workings of these laws.

13

PRAYER gives us the guidance we need. It opens the mind to the illumination of God. The prophets made their whole life an act of prayer — so they received the inspiration of God. Our humbler minds, standing much below the heights in which they stood, receiving for the most part only a reflected illumination, may now and then by climbing a little higher catch a glimpse of the direct light. Through prayer, we can receive the guidance of God to strengthen our hold on truth, goodness, righteousness and purity which are the laws for humanity emanating from the nature of God.

14

"OUT OF the depths I have called to You, O Lord." (*Psalm* 130:1)

All people of all generations can take this Psalm for their very own. Anyone praying before the Holy King must pray from the depths of his soul, for then his heart will be entirely directed to God, and his mind entirely bent on his prayer.

15

CHIEF among the duties of the heart is the attuning of the soul into such perfect harmony with God that all right conduct and right thought must follow without effort on our part, because our will is one with His, through love.

16

PRAYER is speech, but not 'mere' speech. The word is not to be despised. Words have power over the soul. "Hear, O Israel!" is a cry and an affirmation, a reminder of glory and martyrdom, a part of the very essence of our people's history. Our prayerbooks are but words on paper; they can mean little or nothing. Yet the searching spirit and questing heart may find great power in their words. Through them we link ourselves to all the generations of our people, pouring out our souls in prayer with those of our brothers and sisters. These words, laden with the tears and joys of centuries, have the power to bring us into the very presence of God. Not easily, not all at once, not every time, but somehow, sometimes, the worshipper who offers up his heart and mind without reservation will know that he has touched the Throne of Glory.

17

I REGARD the old Jewish *Siddur* as the most important single Jewish book — a more personal expression, a closer record, of Jewish sufferings, Jewish needs, Jewish hopes and aspirations, than the Bible itself. For one thing the Bible is too grand and universal to be exclusively Jewish (as Shakespeare is not the typical Englishman), and for another, whatever is quintessentially needed for daily use has been squeezed out of it into the prayerbook and so made our daily own. And if you want to know what Judaism is — the question which has no answer if debated on the plane of intellectual argument — you can find it by absorbing that book. The Jewish soul is mirrored there as nowhere else, mirrored or rather embodied there: the individual's soul in his private sorrows, and the people's soul in its historic burdens, its heroic passion and suffering, its unfaltering faith, through the ages.

18

IF ANYONE comes to public worship and leaves with the feeling that he has got nothing out of it, let him ask: Did I bring anything to it? Most often the answer to the second will supply the cause of the first. A stubborn heart, a rebellious heart, a cold heart that cherishes its coldness, a critical mind that looks for objects of criticism, will not profit. It is true of public worship in a high degree that only they receive who give. The influence of public worship, like that of electricity, is felt only where there is a capacity for receiving it. Stone and ice are spiritual non-conductors.

19

NORMALLY, we are compelled to pass from one task to another in quick succession; one duty is completed only to be followed immediately by the next; a difficulty surmounted, a problem solved is replaced with such rapidity by further worries and by other cares that we have no choice, in daily life, but to live from one minute to another, to eliminate from our minds everything but that which is immediately ahead of us and which demands immediate attention.

In worship, however, we are freed from the pressure of life. There are no immediate tasks to be performed: no insistent needs clamoring for immediate satisfaction. For once, we are guaranteed Time and Quietude — the rarest possessions in life today. For once, we can escape from the tyranny of the next minute with its worries, tasks and duties.

And when, as now, we do have time to take a larger view of life; when, in calm reflection, we enlarge our vision until we see life in its entirety, considerations come before us which tend to be excluded in the rush of everyday experience. Elements in life which at other times can receive but little of our attention now come into the forefront of our thought. We can now allow our spiritual needs to take precedence over those material satisfactions to which, usually, we pay such high regard and to which, normally, we devote so large a measure of our effort. In worship, the foremost place in our consideration is given to that which develops character, all that which lends nobility and dignity to human life, all wherein we can express the greatness of the human spirit. We consider what it means to us and for our lives that we have been endowed by God with reason, with a power to love, with a sense of the beautiful, and with a knowledge of righteousness.

20

PUBLIC WORSHIP draws out the latent life in the human spirit. Those who, when alone, do not, or cannot, pray, find an impulse to prayer when they worship with others; and some will pray together who cannot pray alone, as many will sing in chorus who would not sing solos. As two walking together in some dark wood feel the stronger and braver each for the other's near presence, so many who are spiritually weak in themselves will find spiritual strength in a common spiritual effort. That is the value of public worship for the individual. It has also a social value.

Public worship expresses the sanctity we feel in the social bond. A congregation at worship is a society declaring its devotion to God, a community forged by faith in Him. Here is an experience that can deepen the social spirit and strengthen the bond of sympathy among men and women. If in public worship I realize that my prayers are also the prayers of the one by my side, it will make us more effectively aware of our common humanity and implant a spirit which will be potent for social good. They who worship God together bring Him into their mutual relations. If public worship does not produce this result, then it is but private worship in a public place. If it does bring men and women closer together under the influence of God, then it is a way to the sanctification of human society.

21

WHY FIXED PRAYERS? To learn what we should value, what we should pray for. To be at one with our people, the household of Israel. To ensure that the ideals painfully learned and purified, and for which many have lived and died, shall not perish from the community, and shall have a saving influence upon the individual.

22

IT IS NOT you alone who pray, or we, or those others; all things pray, and all things pour forth their souls. The heavens pray, the earth prays, every creature and every living thing. In all life, there is longing. Creation is itself but a longing, a kind of prayer to the Almighty. What are the clouds, the rising and the setting of the sun, the soft radiance of the moon and the gentleness of the night? What are the flashes of the human mind and the storms of the human heart? They are all prayers — the outpouring of boundless longing for God.

23

UNLESS WE believe that God renews the work of creation every day, our prayers grow old and stale.

In *Lamentations* (3.23) it is written: "They are new every morning: great is Your faithfulness." The fact that the world is new to us every morning — that is Your great faithfulness!

24

WHO RISE from prayer better persons, their prayer is answered.

25

WHERE IS GOD? Wherever you let Him in.

26

THERE is no room for God in those who are full of themselves.

27

WHEREVER you find God's footsteps, there is God before you.

28

TO LOVE GOD truly, one must first love people. And if anyone tells you that he loves God and does not love his fellow humans, you will know that he is lying.

29

A FATHER complained to the Baal Shem that his son had forsaken God. 'Rabbi, what shall I do?' 'Love him more than ever,' was the reply.

30

IF GOD IS NOT, then the existence of all that is beautiful and ... good, is but the accidental ... by-product of blindly swirling atoms, or of the equally unpurposeful ... mechanisms of present-day physics. A man may believe that this dreadful thing is true. But only the fool will say in his heart that he is glad that it is true. For to wish there should be no God is to wish that the things which we love and strive to realize and make permanent, should be only temporary and doomed to frustration and destruction. ... Atheism leads not to badness but only to an incurable sadness and loneliness.

31

RELIGION is not merely a belief in an ultimate reality or in an ultimate ideal. These beliefs are worse than false; they are platitudes, truisms, that nobody will dispute. Religion is a momentous possibility, the possibility namely that what is highest in spirit is also deepest in nature — that there is something at the heart of nature, something akin to us, a conserver and increaser of values ... that the things that matter most are not at the mercy of the things that matter least.

32

ONE WHO has never been bewildered, who has never looked upon life and his own existence as phenomena which require answers and yet, paradoxically, for which the only answers are new questions, can hardly understand what religious experience is.

33

WHETHER or not we know it, what we really mean when we say that a god is dead is that the images of God vanish, and that therefore an image which up to now was regarded and worshipped as God, can no longer be so regarded and so worshipped. For what we call gods are nothing but images of God and must suffer the fate of such images. But Nietzsche manifestly wished to say something different, and that something different is terribly wrong in a way characteristic of our time. For it means confusing an image, confusing one of the many images of God that are born and perish, with the real God whose reality men could never shake with any one of these images, no matter what forms they might honestly invent for the objects of their particular adoration.

Time after time, the images must be broken, the iconoclasts must have their way. For the iconoclast is the human soul which rebels against having an image that can no longer be believed in, elevated above the heads of humanity as a thing that demands to be worshipped. In our longing for a god, we try again and again to set up a greater, a more genuine and more just image, which is intended to be more glorious than the last and only proves the more unsatisfactory.

The commandment, "Thou shalt not make unto thee an image," means at the same time, "Thou canst not make an image." This does not, of course, refer merely to sculptured or painted images, but to our fantasy, to all the power of our imagination as well. But we are forced time and again to make images, and forced to destroy them when we realize that we have not succeeded.

The images topple, but the voice is never silenced.... The voice speaks in the guise of everything that happens, in the guise of all world events; it speaks to the men of all generations, makes demands upon them, and summons them to accept their responsibility.... It is of the utmost importance not to lose one's openness. But to be open means not to shut out the voice — call it what you will. It does not matter what you call it. All that matters is that you hear it.

34

RELIGION is essentially the act of holding fast to God. And that does not mean holding fast to an image that one has made of God, nor even holding fast to the faith in God that one has conceived. It means holding fast to the existing God. The earth would not hold fast to its conception of the sun (if it had one) nor to its connection with it, but to the sun itself.

35

THE DESCRIPTION of God as a Person is indispensable for everyone who like myself means by 'God' not a principle . . . and not an idea . . . but who rather means by 'God', as I do, Him who — whatever else He may be — enters in a direct relation with us in creative, revealing, and redeeming acts, and thus makes it possible for us to enter into a direct relation with Him. . . . The concept of personal being is indeed completely incapable of declaring what God's essential being is, but it is both permitted and necessary to say that God is also a Person.

36

SOMETIMES WE have a personal experience related to those recorded as revelations and capable of opening the way for them. We may unexpectedly grow aware of a certain apperception within ourselves, which was lacking but a moment ago, and whose origin we are unable to discover. The attempt to derive such apperception from the famous 'unconscious' stems from the widespread superstition that the soul can do everything by itself, and it fundamentally means nothing but this: what you have just experienced always was in you. Such notions build up a temporary construction which is useful for psychological orientation, but collapses when I try to stand upon it. But what occurred to me was 'otherness', was the touch of the other. Nietzsche says it more honestly, "You take, you do not ask who it is that gives." But I think that as we take, it is of the utmost importance to know that someone is giving. He who takes what is given him and does not experience it as a gift, is not really receiving; and so the gift turns into theft. But when we do experience the giving, we find out that revelation exists.

37

IN GENUINE dialogue the turning to the partner takes place in all truth, that is, it is a turning of the being. . . . He receives him as his partner, and that means that he confirms this other being, so far as it is for him to confirm. The true turning of his person to the other includes this confirmation, this acceptance. Of course, such a confirmation does not mean approval; but no matter in what I am against the other, by accepting him as my partner in genuine dialogue I have affirmed him as a person.

38

WHAT IS IT TO BE A JEW? What are the pains and the joys, the price paid and the distinction, of being born into the ironically styled Chosen People? The popular answer, on the surface, seems to take a cynical view. "*Shver tzu zein ein yid,*" says the Yiddish-speaking Jew, "Hard to be a Jew," though at bottom he is rooted and embedded in it, and at bottom, at home and content. It is just a manner of speaking.

But there is an element of truth in such cynicism which comes home especially to those of us who, like you and me, having cast off the warmth and protection of the ghetto, materially and spiritually, are now subject to all the wind and weather, all the tides and currents, all the impact and erosion of the great outside world, washing away the old loyalties and subtly tempting and seducing us to conformity with the general type.

For the old-timers it was easy, despite the terrible pressure of persecution. They were padded and buttressed with an armor that made them impregnable in a world of enemies. They had that within them which made them proud, and they actually looked down with pity on the gross, crude creatures who did not have the *Zechut*, the privilege of being Jews, and who hated and killed them. They had faith, belief, of being partners of God, of being the central figure in the whole economy of history.

But some of us today have no beliefs at all. Everything is eroded. Our inner forces have evaporated, and the inner resistance being reduced to nil, the outer impact crushes our chest. We have been flattened out by an inferiority complex — disembowelled, emasculated. The desire to be like others, the gregarious animal's fear to be unlike the powerful, fashionable ruling majority, leaving us out in the cold, is a pain than which there can be no greater pain for one who is without inner resources.

And indeed, the question arises for the reflective mood — why the suffering? What is it for? And for the same reflective mood, there are two answers — one on a simple plane of decency, and the other on a deeper plane of religion.

Even on the most elementary and unpretending plane, without much knowledge and emotion as to the values involved, it is an act of decency. Not to be a slacker, not to welch, not to cringe; it is an act of decency to brighten the corner where you are, to stick it out where ineluctable fate has put you. We are all born, all of us, specifically — not as human beings but as Chinese, Negro, Jew. That is our fate and destiny, and we must make the best and most of it. Running away does not help you with the outside world, and it inoculates you with the worst of all poisons — secret self-contempt.

But there is a deeper ground of loyalty for the reflective soul. The company into which we Jews are born is of the grandest. The word 'company' is too loose; every great historic people is like a single person extending through the ages, and every single human being born within that people takes part in all that people's grandeur. To be of that people enlarges the individual soul to immensity. Every Jew has a part in Moses and Sinai, in prophets and psalmists, in the genius that gave religion to the world, in every great man who lifted his peak to the sky; he has part in a unique, heroic, and tragic destiny. And even though in his daily life he has to go on making a living, and be for the most part oblivious of these high, transcendent things — and even though in common decency he cannot regard himself as individually better than his neighbor — he knows in his bones that by some mysterious fate, the Jewish People was called to high things, and that there is an arch spanning time from Sinai to the furthest future, when, as we confidently hope, the Messianic Kingdom will truly begin.

All of that we can consciously make our own. All these great men and all this greatness are my potential me — now and here. We can make it ours by filling our minds and hearts with knowledge and love — we can appropriate it by a grand resolve to enrich our inner beings.

And so we say: Stand firm. Free yourself from externals, yes. But enrich your inner life — assured that where the best names are named, ours will be among the first.

39

IF WE were only one nation among others, we should long ago have perished from the earth. Paradoxically we exist only because we dared to be serious about the unity of God and His undivided, absolute sovereignty. If we give up God, He will give us up. And we do give Him up when we profess Him in synagogue and deny Him when we come together for discussion, when we do His commands in our personal life, and set up other norms for the life of the group we belong to. What is wrong for the individual cannot be right for the community; for if it were, then God, the God of Sinai, would no longer be the Lord of peoples, but only of individuals. If we really are Jews, we believe that God gives His commands to men and women to observe throughout their whole life, and that whether or not life has a meaning depends on the fulfillment of those commands.

40

A PEOPLE which seriously calls God Himself its King must become a true people, a community where all members are ruled by honesty without compulsion, kindness without hypocrisy, and the brotherliness of those who are passionately devoted to their divine leader. When social inequality, distinction between the free and the unfree, splits the community and creates chasms between its members, there can be no true people, there can be no 'God's people'.

41

PROPHETIC criticism and demand are directed toward every individual whom other individuals depend upon, toward everyone who has a hand in shaping the destinies of others; that means directed toward every one of us. When Isaiah speaks of justice, he is not thinking of institutions but of you and me, because without you and me the most glorious institution becomes a lie.

42

THE WORD of the One God penetrated this people from its beginning. When the commandment of God awakes in us, freedom also opens its eyes; and where freedom commences, history begins. A difficult task was assigned this people in its history. It is so easy to listen to the voices of idols, and it is so hard to receive the word of the One God into oneself. It is so easy to remain a slave, and it is so difficult to become free. But this people can only exist in the full seriousness of its task. It can only exist in this freedom which reaches beyond all other freedoms. Its history began when it heard the word, rising out of the mystery, and emerging into clarity: "I am 'He-Who-Is' your God, who brought you out of the land of Egypt, out of the house of bondage." (*Exodus* 20.2)

43

A RELIGIOUS search is a lonely labor. It is like a flight over an ocean or a desert. Its main preoccupation is not the collecting of interesting episodes as one floats along, but the keeping of one's wings aloft and the reading of one's course by constant sun and steadfast stars. And at the end one's concern is to leave a few words of guidance, if one can, for other voyagers soon to take off upon a like adventure.

44

RELIGION is the vision of something which stands beyond, behind, and within the passing flux of immediate things; something which is real, and yet waiting to be realized; something which is a remote possibility, and yet the greatest of present facts; something that gives meaning to all that passes, and yet eludes apprehension; something whose possession is the final good, and yet is beyond all reach; something which is the ultimate ideal, and the hopeless quest.

45

THE RELIGIOUS feeling of the scientist takes the form of rapturous amazement at the harmony of the natural law, which reveals an intelligence of such superiority that, compared with it, all the systematic thinking and acting of human beings is an utterly insignificant reflection. This feeling is the guiding principle of his life and work in so far as he succeeds in keeping himself from the shackles of selfish desire.... It is beyond question closely akin to that which has possessed the religious geniuses of all ages.... It is to know that what is impenetrable to us really exists, revealing itself to us as the highest truth and the most radiant beauty.

46

WE ARE encompassed by questions to which we can only respond with awe.

47

I CANNOT be religious without belonging to a particular religion any more than I can talk without using a particular language.

48

THERE ARE eight degrees in the giving of *Tsedakah*, each one higher than the next:

to give grudgingly, reluctantly, or with regret;
to give less than one should, but with grace;
to give what one should, but only after being asked;
to give before one is asked;
to give without knowing who will receive it, although the recipient knows the identity of the giver;
to give without making known one's identity;
to give so that neither giver nor receiver knows the identity of the other;
to help another to become self-supporting, by means of a gift, a loan, or by finding employment for the one in need.

49

YOU SHALL be to Me a kingdom of priests, a holy people.

לקוטים מפרקי אבות

from Chapters of the Fathers

1.2

שִׁמְעוֹן הַצַּדִּיק הָיָה מִשְּׁיָרֵי כְנֶסֶת הַגְּדוֹלָה. הוּא הָיָה אוֹמֵר: עַל־שְׁלֹשָׁה דְבָרִים הָעוֹלָם עוֹמֵד: עַל הַתּוֹרָה וְעַל הָעֲבוֹדָה וְעַל גְּמִילוּת חֲסָדִים.

Simon the Just: The world is sustained by three things: by the Torah, by worship, and by loving deeds.

1.3

אַנְטִיגְנוֹס אִישׁ סוֹכוֹ קִבֵּל מִשִּׁמְעוֹן הַצַּדִּיק. הוּא הָיָה אוֹמֵר: אַל־תִּהְיוּ כַּעֲבָדִים הַמְשַׁמְּשִׁין אֶת־הָרַב עַל מְנָת לְקַבֵּל פְּרָס, אֶלָּא הֱווּ כַּעֲבָדִים הַמְשַׁמְּשִׁין אֶת־הָרַב שֶׁלֹּא עַל־מְנָת לְקַבֵּל פְּרָס, וִיהִי מוֹרָא שָׁמַיִם עֲלֵיכֶם.

Antigonos of Socho: Be not like servants who work for their master only on condition that they receive payment, but be like servants who work for their master without looking for any reward; and be filled with reverence for God.

1.4

יוֹסֵי בֶּן יוֹעֶזֶר, אִישׁ צְרֵדָה, אוֹמֵר: יְהִי בֵיתְךָ בֵּית וַעַד לַחֲכָמִים, וֶהֱוֵי מִתְאַבֵּק בַּעֲפַר רַגְלֵיהֶם, וֶהֱוֵי שׁוֹתֶה בְצָמָא אֶת דִּבְרֵיהֶם.

Yosei ben Yoezer: Let your house be a meeting place for the wise, sit at their feet always, and drink in their words with thirst.

1.5

יוֹסֵי בֶּן יוֹחָנָן, אִישׁ יְרוּשָׁלַיִם, אוֹמֵר: יְהִי בֵיתְךָ פָּתוּחַ לִרְוָחָה, וְיִהְיוּ עֲנִיִּים בְּנֵי בֵיתֶךָ.

Yosei ben Yochanan: Let your house be open wide, and let the poor be members of your household.

1.6

יְהוֹשֻׁעַ בֶּן פְּרַחְיָה אוֹמֵר: עֲשֵׂה לְךָ רַב, וּקְנֵה לְךָ חָבֵר, וֶהֱוֵי דָן אֶת־כָּל־הָאָדָם לְכַף זְכוּת.

Joshua ben Perachya: Get yourself a teacher; acquire a friend to study with you. When you judge people, give them the benefit of the doubt.

1.7

נִתַּאי הָאַרְבֵּלִי אוֹמֵר: הַרְחֵק מִשָּׁכֵן רָע, וְאַל־תִּתְחַבֵּר לְרָשָׁע, וְאַל־תִּתְיָאֵשׁ מִן הַפֻּרְעָנוּת.

Nitai the Arbelite: Keep away from an evil neighbor; do not associate with the lawless; and do not suppose that no price is paid for wickedness.

1.8

יְהוּדָה בֶּן טַבַּאי אוֹמֵר: אַל תַּעַשׂ עַצְמְךָ כְּעוֹרְכֵי הַדַּיָּנִים; וּכְשֶׁיִּהְיוּ בַּעֲלֵי הַדִּין עוֹמְדִים לְפָנֶיךָ, יִהְיוּ בְעֵינֶיךָ כִּרְשָׁעִים; וּכְשֶׁנִּפְטָרִים מִלְּפָנֶיךָ, יִהְיוּ בְעֵינֶיךָ כְּזַכָּאִין, כְּשֶׁקִּבְּלוּ עֲלֵיהֶם אֶת־הַדִּין.

Judah ben Tabai: A judge must not act as an advocate; in a dispute, view both sides as potentially in the wrong; but when judgment has been given, consider both parties cleared, since they have accepted the judges' decision.

1.10

שְׁמַעְיָה אוֹמֵר: אֱהַב אֶת־הַמְּלָאכָה, וּשְׂנָא אֶת־הָרַבָּנוּת.

Shemayah: Love work; hate tyranny.

1.12

הִלֵּל אוֹמֵר: הֱוֵי מִתַּלְמִידָיו שֶׁל אַהֲרֹן: אוֹהֵב שָׁלוֹם וְרוֹדֵף שָׁלוֹם אוֹהֵב אֶת־הַבְּרִיּוֹת וּמְקָרְבָן לַתּוֹרָה.

Hillel: Be of the disciples of Aaron, loving peace and pursuing it, loving your fellow creatures, and drawing them near to the Torah.

1.*13*

הוּא הָיָה אוֹמֵר: נְגַד שְׁמָא אֲבַד שְׁמֵהּ, וּדְלָא מוֹסִיף יְסוּף, וּדְלָא
יָלֵף קַטְלָא חַיָּב, וּדְאִשְׁתַּמַּשׁ בְּתָגָא חֲלָף.

Hillel: When you seek fame, it flees; when you do not add, you detract; when you do not learn, you earn destruction; when you make selfish use of the crown of Torah, you drive yourself out of the world.

1.*14*

הוּא הָיָה אוֹמֵר: אִם אֵין אֲנִי לִי, מִי לִי? וּכְשֶׁאֲנִי לְעַצְמִי, מָה אֲנִי?
וְאִם לֹא עַכְשָׁו, אֵימָתַי?

Hillel: If I am not for myself, who will be for me? But if I am only for myself, what am I? And if not now, when?

1.*15*

שַׁמַּאי אוֹמֵר: עֲשֵׂה תוֹרָתְךָ קֶבַע. אֱמֹר מְעַט וַעֲשֵׂה הַרְבֵּה, וֶהֱוֵי
מְקַבֵּל אֶת־כָּל־הָאָדָם בְּסֵבֶר פָּנִים יָפוֹת.

Shammai: Make your study of Torah a fixed habit. Say little and do much, and greet all people with a cheerful smile.

1.*18*

רַבָּן שִׁמְעוֹן בֶּן גַּמְלִיאֵל אוֹמֵר: עַל־שְׁלֹשָׁה דְבָרִים הָעוֹלָם קַיָּם:
עַל־הָאֱמֶת, וְעַל־הַדִּין, וְעַל־הַשָּׁלוֹם.

Rabban Shimon ben Gamaliel: The world is sustained by three things: by truth, by justice, and by peace.

2.*1*

רַבִּי אוֹמֵר: אֵיזוֹ הִיא דֶּרֶךְ יְשָׁרָה שֶׁיָּבֹר לוֹ הָאָדָם? כָּל שֶׁהִיא
תִּפְאֶרֶת לְעֹשֶׂהָ וְתִפְאֶרֶת לוֹ מִן הָאָדָם.

'Rabbi': Which is the right path to choose? One that is honorable in itself and also wins honor from others.

2.*4*

רַבָּן גַּמְלִיאֵל בְּנוֹ שֶׁל רַבִּי יְהוּדָה הַנָּשִׂיא הָיָה אוֹמֵר: עֲשֵׂה רְצוֹנוֹ
כִּרְצוֹנֶךָ, כְּדֵי שֶׁיַּעֲשֶׂה רְצוֹנְךָ כִּרְצוֹנוֹ.

Rabban Gamaliel, son of 'Rabbi': Make God's will your will, so that He may make your will His will.

2.5

הִלֵּל אוֹמֵר: אַל תִּפְרוֹשׁ מִן הַצִּבּוּר; וְאַל תַּאֲמֵן בְּעַצְמְךָ עַד יוֹם מוֹתְךָ; וְאַל תָּדִין אֶת־חֲבֵרְךָ עַד שֶׁתַּגִּיעַ לִמְקוֹמוֹ . . . וְאַל תֹּאמַר "לִכְשֶׁאֶפָּנֶה אֶשְׁנֶה", שֶׁמָּא לֹא תִפָּנֶה.

Hillel: Do not separate yourself from the community; do not be certain of yourself until the day you die; do not judge another until you are in his position . . . and do not say: "When I have leisure I shall study" — you may never have any leisure.

2.6

הוּא הָיָה אוֹמֵר: לֹא הַבַּיְשָׁן לָמֵד, וְלֹא הַקַּפְּדָן מְלַמֵּד.

Hillel: The reticent do not learn; the hot-tempered do not teach.

2.6

בִּמְקוֹם שֶׁאֵין אֲנָשִׁים, הִשְׁתַּדֵּל לִהְיוֹת אִישׁ!

Hillel: In a place where no one behaves like a human being, you must strive to be human!

2.8

הוּא הָיָה אוֹמֵר: מַרְבֶּה תוֹרָה, מַרְבֶּה חַיִּים; מַרְבֶּה עֵצָה, מַרְבֶּה תְבוּנָה; מַרְבֶּה צְדָקָה, מַרְבֶּה שָׁלוֹם.

Hillel: . . . the more Torah, the more life; the more counsel, the more understanding; the more justice, the more peace. . . .

2.13

רַבָּן יוֹחָנָן בֶּן זַכַּאי אָמַר לָהֶם: "צְאוּ וּרְאוּ אֵיזוֹ הִיא דֶרֶךְ טוֹבָה שֶׁיִּדְבַּק בָּהּ הָאָדָם." רַבִּי אֱלִיעֶזֶר אוֹמֵר: 'עַיִן טוֹבָה.' רַבִּי יְהוֹשֻׁעַ אוֹמֵר: 'חָבֵר טוֹב.' רַבִּי יוֹסֵי אוֹמֵר: 'שָׁכֵן טוֹב.' רַבִּי שִׁמְעוֹן אוֹמֵר: 'הָרוֹאֶה אֶת־הַנּוֹלָד.' רַבִּי אֶלְעָזָר אוֹמֵר: 'לֵב טוֹב.' אָמַר לָהֶם: "רוֹאֶה אֲנִי אֶת־דִּבְרֵי אֶלְעָזָר בֶּן עֲרָךְ מִדִּבְרֵיכֶם, שֶׁבִּכְלַל דְּבָרָיו דִּבְרֵיכֶם."

Rabban Yochanan ben Zakkai said to his disciples: "Consider well the good that one should always seek." Rabbi Eliezer said: 'A kindly eye.' Rabbi Joshua said: 'A good friend.' Rabbi Yosei said: 'A good neighbor.' Rabbi Shimon said: 'Foresight.' Rabbi Elazar said: 'A good heart.' Then he said to them: "I prefer the words of Rabbi Elazar ben Arach to yours, because his words include yours as well."

2.15

רַבִּי אֱלִיעֶזֶר אוֹמֵר: יְהִי כְבוֹד חֲבֵרְךָ חָבִיב עָלֶיךָ כְּשֶׁלָּךְ, וְאַל תְּהִי נוֹחַ לִכְעוֹס, וְשׁוּב יוֹם אֶחָד לִפְנֵי מִיתָתְךָ!

Rabbi Eliezer: Let your neighbor's honor be as dear to you as your own; do not be easily angered; and repent one day before your death!

2.17

רַבִּי יוֹסֵי אוֹמֵר: יְהִי מָמוֹן חֲבֵרְךָ חָבִיב עָלֶיךָ כְּשֶׁלָּךְ, וְהַתְקֵן עַצְמְךָ לִלְמֹד תּוֹרָה, שֶׁאֵינָהּ יְרֻשָּׁה־לָךְ, וְכָל־מַעֲשֶׂיךָ יִהְיוּ לְשֵׁם שָׁמָיִם.

Rabbi Yosei: Let your neighbor's property be as dear to you as your own; train yourself to study Torah, for the knowledge of it is not inherited; and let all your deeds be for the sake of God.

2.18

רַבִּי שִׁמְעוֹן אוֹמֵר: כְּשֶׁאַתָּה מִתְפַּלֵּל, אַל תַּעַשׂ תְּפִלָּתְךָ קֶבַע, אֶלָּא רַחֲמִים וְתַחֲנוּנִים לִפְנֵי הַמָּקוֹם, שֶׁנֶּאֱמַר: "כִּי־חַנּוּן וְרַחוּם הוּא, אֶרֶךְ אַפַּיִם וְרַב־חֶסֶד וְנִחָם עַל־הָרָעָה." וְאַל תְּהִי רָשָׁע בִּפְנֵי עַצְמֶךָ.

Rabbi Shimon: When you pray, let not your prayer become routine, but let it be a sincere supplication for God's mercy, as it says: "For He is gracious and merciful, endlessly patient, overflowing in love, and eager to forgive." And never condemn yourself as totally wicked.

2.20

רַבִּי טַרְפוֹן אוֹמֵר: הַיּוֹם קָצֵר, וְהַמְּלָאכָה מְרֻבָּה, וְהַפּוֹעֲלִים עֲצֵלִים, וְהַשָּׂכָר הַרְבֵּה, וּבַעַל הַבַּיִת דּוֹחֵק.

Rabbi Tarfon: The day is short, and the task is great, and the workers are sluggish, and the wages are high, and the Master of the house is pressing.

2.21

הוּא הָיָה אוֹמֵר: לֹא עָלֶיךָ הַמְּלָאכָה לִגְמֹר, וְלֹא אַתָּה בֶן־חוֹרִין לְהִבָּטֵל מִמֶּנָּה.

Rabbi Tarfon: You are not required to complete the work, but neither are you at liberty to abstain from it.

3.3

רַבִּי חֲנַנְיָא בֶּן תְּרַדְיוֹן אוֹמֵר: שְׁנַיִם שֶׁיּוֹשְׁבִים וְיֵשׁ בֵּינֵיהֶם דִּבְרֵי תוֹרָה, שְׁכִינָה שְׁרוּיָה בֵינֵיהֶם.

Rabbi Chananya ben Teradion: When two people sit and words of Torah pass between them, the Divine Presence rests between them.

3.8

רַבִּי אֶלְעָזָר, אִישׁ בַּרְתּוֹתָא, אוֹמֵר: תֶּן־לוֹ מִשֶּׁלוֹ, שֶׁאַתָּה וְשֶׁלְּךָ שֶׁלוֹ.

Rabbi Elazar of Bartota: Render to God what is His, for all that you are and have is His.

3.11

רַבִּי חֲנִינָא בֶּן דּוֹסָא אוֹמֵר: כֹּל שֶׁיִּרְאַת חֶטְאוֹ קוֹדֶמֶת לְחָכְמָתוֹ, חָכְמָתוֹ מִתְקַיֶּמֶת; וְכֹל שֶׁחָכְמָתוֹ קוֹדֶמֶת לְיִרְאַת חֶטְאוֹ, אֵין חָכְמָתוֹ מִתְקַיֶּמֶת.

Rabbi Chanina ben Dosa: When conscience takes precedence over learning, learning endures; but when learning takes precedence over conscience, learning does not endure.

3.12

הוּא הָיָה אוֹמֵר: כֹּל שֶׁמַּעֲשָׂיו מְרֻבִּים מֵחָכְמָתוֹ, חָכְמָתוֹ מִתְקַיֶּמֶת; וְכֹל שֶׁחָכְמָתוֹ מְרֻבָּה מִמַּעֲשָׂיו, אֵין חָכְמָתוֹ מִתְקַיֶּמֶת.

Rabbi Chanina ben Dosa: When deeds exceed learning, learning endures; but when learning exceeds deeds, it does not endure.

3.13

הוּא הָיָה אוֹמֵר: כֹּל שֶׁרוּחַ הַבְּרִיּוֹת נוֹחָה הֵימֶנּוּ, רוּחַ הַמָּקוֹם נוֹחָה הֵימֶנּוּ; וְכֹל שֶׁאֵין רוּחַ הַבְּרִיּוֹת נוֹחָה הֵימֶנּוּ, אֵין רוּחַ הַמָּקוֹם נוֹחָה הֵימֶנּוּ.

Rabbi Chanina ben Dosa: Those who bring serenity to others please God; but those who do not bring serenity to others do not please God.

3.18

רַבִּי עֲקִיבָא הָיָה אוֹמֵר: חָבִיב אָדָם שֶׁנִּבְרָא בְּצֶלֶם; חִבָּה יְתֵרָה נוֹדַעַת לוֹ שֶׁנִּבְרָא בְּצֶלֶם.

Rabbi Akiva: How greatly God must have loved us to create us in His image; yet even greater love did He show us in making us conscious that we are created in His image.

3.21

רַבִּי אֶלְעָזָר בֶּן עֲזַרְיָה אוֹמֵר: אִם אֵין תּוֹרָה, אֵין דֶּרֶךְ אֶרֶץ; אִם אֵין דֶּרֶךְ אֶרֶץ, אֵין תּוֹרָה. אִם אֵין חָכְמָה, אֵין יִרְאָה; אִם אֵין יִרְאָה, אֵין חָכְמָה. אִם אֵין דַּעַת, אֵין בִּינָה; אִם אֵין בִּינָה, אֵין דַּעַת. אִם אֵין קֶמַח, אֵין תּוֹרָה; אִם אֵין תּוֹרָה, אֵין קֶמַח.

Rabbi Elazar ben Azarya: Without Torah, there is no social order; without the social order, there is no Torah. Without wisdom, there is no conscience; without conscience, there is no wisdom. Without knowledge, there is no understanding; without understanding, there is no knowledge. Without sustenance, there is no Torah; without Torah, there is no sustenance

3.22

הוּא הָיָה אוֹמֵר: כָּל־שֶׁחָכְמָתוֹ מְרֻבָּה מִמַּעֲשָׂיו, לְמָה הוּא דוֹמֶה? לְאִילָן שֶׁעֲנָפָיו מְרֻבִּין וְשָׁרָשָׁיו מוּעָטִין: וְהָרוּחַ בָּאָה וְעוֹקַרְתּוֹ וְהוֹפַכְתּוֹ עַל פָּנָיו . . . אֲבָל כָּל־שֶׁמַּעֲשָׂיו מְרֻבִּין מֵחָכְמָתוֹ, לְמָה הוּא דוֹמֶה? לְאִילָן שֶׁעֲנָפָיו מוּעָטִין וְשָׁרָשָׁיו מְרֻבִּין, שֶׁאֲפִילוּ כָּל־הָרוּחוֹת שֶׁבָּעוֹלָם בָּאוֹת וְנוֹשְׁבוֹת בּוֹ, אֵין מְזִיזִין אוֹתוֹ מִמְּקוֹמוֹ.

Rabbi Elazar ben Azarya: When our learning exceeds our deeds we are like trees whose branches are many but whose roots are few: the wind comes and uproots them. . . . But when our deeds exceed our learning we are like trees whose branches are few but whose roots are many, so that even if all the winds of the world were to come and blow against them, they would be unable to move them.

4.1

בֶּן זוֹמָא אוֹמֵר: אֵיזֶהוּ חָכָם? הַלּוֹמֵד מִכָּל־אָדָם . . . אֵיזֶהוּ גִבּוֹר? הַכּוֹבֵשׁ אֶת־יִצְרוֹ . . . אֵיזֶהוּ עָשִׁיר? הַשָּׂמֵחַ בְּחֶלְקוֹ . . . אֵיזֶהוּ מְכֻבָּד? הַמְכַבֵּד אֶת־הַבְּרִיּוֹת.

Ben Zoma: Who are wise? Those who learn from all people.... Who are strong? Those who control their passions.... Who are rich? Those who rejoice in their lot.... Who are honorable? Those who honor others.

4.2

בֶּן עַזַּי אוֹמֵר: הֱוֵי רָץ לְמִצְוָה קַלָּה כְּבַחֲמוּרָה, וּבוֹרֵחַ מִן הָעֲבֵרָה. שֶׁמִּצְוָה גוֹרֶרֶת מִצְוָה וַעֲבֵרָה גוֹרֶרֶת עֲבֵרָה, שֶׁשְּׂכַר מִצְוָה מִצְוָה וּשְׂכַר עֲבֵרָה עֲבֵרָה.

Ben Azai: Be as quick to obey a minor Mitzvah as a major one, and flee from transgression: for one Mitzvah performed leads to another, and one transgression leads to another; moreover, the reward of one Mitzvah is another, and the price of one transgression is another.

4.3

הוּא הָיָה אוֹמֵר: אַל תְּהִי בָז לְכָל־אָדָם וְאַל תְּהִי מַפְלִיג לְכָל־דָּבָר, שֶׁאֵין לְךָ אָדָם שֶׁאֵין לוֹ שָׁעָה וְאֵין לְךָ דָבָר שֶׁאֵין לוֹ מָקוֹם.

Ben Azai: Despise no one, and call nothing useless, for there is no one whose hour does not come, and there is no thing that does not have its place.

4.14

רַבִּי יוֹחָנָן הַסַּנְדְּלָר אוֹמֵר: כָּל־כְּנֵסִיָּה שֶׁהִיא לְשֵׁם שָׁמַיִם סוֹפָהּ לְהִתְקַיֵּם, וְשֶׁאֵינָהּ לְשֵׁם שָׁמַיִם אֵין סוֹפָהּ לְהִתְקַיֵּם.

Rabbi Jochanan the Sandalmaker: Every assembly that is for the sake of Heaven shall in the end bear fruit; but any which is not for the sake of Heaven shall not bear fruit.

4.15

רַבִּי אֶלְעָזָר בֶּן שַׁמּוּעַ אוֹמֵר: יְהִי כְבוֹד תַּלְמִידְךָ חָבִיב עָלֶיךָ כְּשֶׁלָּךְ, וּכְבוֹד חֲבֵרְךָ כְּמוֹרָא רַבָּךְ, וּמוֹרָא רַבְּךָ כְּמוֹרָא שָׁמָיִם.

Rabbi Elazar ben Shamua: Let your pupil's honor be as dear to you as your own; and your concern for your colleague's honor as great as your reverence for your teacher; and your reverence for your teacher as your reverence for God.

4.*17*

רַבִּי שִׁמְעוֹן אוֹמֵר: שְׁלשָׁה כְתָרִים הֵן: כֶּתֶר תּוֹרָה וְכֶתֶר כְּהֻנָּה וְכֶתֶר מַלְכוּת; וְכֶתֶר שֵׁם טוֹב עוֹלֶה עַל גַּבֵּיהֶן.

Rabbi Shimon: There are three crowns: the crown of Torah, the crown of priesthood, and the crown of royalty; but the crown of a good name excels them all.

4.*21*

רַבִּי יַעֲקֹב אוֹמֵר: הָעוֹלָם הַזֶּה דּוֹמֶה לִפְרוֹזְדוֹר בִּפְנֵי הָעוֹלָם הַבָּא; הַתְקֵן עַצְמְךָ בַּפְּרוֹזְדוֹר, כְּדֵי שֶׁתִּכָּנֵס לַטְּרַקְלִין.

Rabbi Jacob: This world is like an anteroom before the world-to-come; prepare yourself in the anteroom that you may enter into the banquet hall.

4.*22*

הוּא הָיָה אוֹמֵר: יָפָה שָׁעָה אַחַת בִּתְשׁוּבָה וּמַעֲשִׂים טוֹבִים בָּעוֹלָם הַזֶּה מִכָּל־חַיֵּי הָעוֹלָם הַבָּא; וְיָפָה שָׁעָה אַחַת שֶׁל קֹרַת רוּחַ בָּעוֹלָם הַבָּא מִכָּל־חַיֵּי הָעוֹלָם הַזֶּה.

Rabbi Jacob: Better one hour of repentance and good works in this world than all the life of the world-to-come; and better one hour of serenity in the world-to-come than all the life of this world.

4.*23*

רַבִּי שִׁמְעוֹן בֶּן אֶלְעָזָר אוֹמֵר: אַל תְּרַצֶּה אֶת־חֲבֵרְךָ בִּשְׁעַת כַּעְסוֹ, וְאַל תְּנַחֲמֵהוּ בְּשָׁעָה שֶׁמֵּתוֹ מֻטָּל לְפָנָיו, וְאַל תִּשְׁאַל לוֹ בִּשְׁעַת נִדְרוֹ, וְאַל תִּשְׁתַּדֵּל לִרְאוֹתוֹ בִּשְׁעַת קַלְקָלָתוֹ.

Rabbi Shimon ben Elazar: Do not try to placate your friends at the height of their anger; do not attempt to comfort them in the first shock of bereavement; do not question their sincerity at the moment when they make a solemn promise; do not be overeager to visit them in the hour of their disgrace.

4.*27*

רַבִּי אוֹמֵר: אַל תִּסְתַּכֵּל בַּקַּנְקַן אֶלָּא בְּמַה שֶּׁיֵּשׁ בּוֹ. יֵשׁ קַנְקַן חָדָשׁ מָלֵא יָשָׁן, וְיָשָׁן שֶׁאֲפִילוּ חָדָשׁ אֵין בּוֹ.

Rabbi: Do not look at the flask but at what it contains; a new flask may be full of old wine, and an old flask may not even contain new wine.

5.13

אַרְבַּע מִדּוֹת בָּאָדָם: הָאוֹמֵר 'שֶׁלִּי שֶׁלִּי וְשֶׁלְּךָ שֶׁלָּךְ,' זוֹ מִדָּה בֵּינוֹנִית, וְיֵשׁ אוֹמְרִים זוֹ מִדַּת סְדוֹם. 'שֶׁלִּי שֶׁלָּךְ וְשֶׁלְּךָ שֶׁלִּי,' עַם הָאָרֶץ. 'שֶׁלִּי שֶׁלָּךְ וְשֶׁלְּךָ שֶׁלָּךְ,' חָסִיד. 'שֶׁלְּךָ שֶׁלִּי וְשֶׁלִּי שֶׁלִּי,' רָשָׁע.

There are four types of character among human beings: some say: 'What is mine is mine and what is yours is yours'— they are the average type, though some consider them callous, like the citizens of Sodom. Some say: 'What is mine is yours and what is yours is mine' — they are stupid. Some say: 'What is mine is yours and what is yours is yours' — they are saints. Some say: 'What is yours is mine and what is mine is mine' — they are wicked.

5.14

אַרְבַּע מִדּוֹת בְּדֵעוֹת: נוֹחַ לִכְעוֹס וְנוֹחַ לִרְצוֹת – יָצָא הֶפְסֵדוֹ בִּשְׂכָרוֹ. קָשֶׁה לִכְעוֹס וְקָשֶׁה לִרְצוֹת – יָצָא שְׂכָרוֹ בְּהֶפְסֵדוֹ. קָשֶׁה לִכְעוֹס וְנוֹחַ לִרְצוֹת – חָסִיד. נוֹחַ לִכְעוֹס וְקָשֶׁה לִרְצוֹת – רָשָׁע.

There are four temperaments: easily angered, easily appeased — the loss is offset by the gain; hard to anger, hard to appease — the gain is offset by the loss; hard to anger, easily appeased — a saint; easily angered, hard to appease — wicked.

5.17

אַרְבַּע מִדּוֹת בְּהוֹלְכֵי בֵית הַמִּדְרָשׁ: הוֹלֵךְ וְאֵינוֹ עוֹשֶׂה, שְׂכַר הֲלִיכָה בְּיָדוֹ; עוֹשֶׂה וְאֵינוֹ הוֹלֵךְ, שְׂכַר מַעֲשֶׂה בְּיָדוֹ; הוֹלֵךְ וְעוֹשֶׂה, חָסִיד; לֹא הוֹלֵךְ וְלֹא עוֹשֶׂה, רָשָׁע.

There are four types among those who attend or fail to attend the house of study: some attend but do not practice what they learn — they are rewarded for attending; some practice but do not attend — they are rewarded for practicing; some attend and practice — they are the devout; some neither attend nor practice — they are the wicked.

5.18

אַרְבַּע מִדּוֹת בְּיוֹשְׁבִים לִפְנֵי חֲכָמִים: סְפוֹג, וּמַשְׁפֵּךְ, מְשַׁמֶּרֶת, וְנָפָה. סְפוֹג, שֶׁהוּא סוֹפֵג אֶת־הַכֹּל. וּמַשְׁפֵּךְ, שֶׁמַּכְנִיס בְּזוֹ וּמוֹצִיא

בְזוֹ. מְשַׁמֶּרֶת, שֶׁמּוֹצִיאָה אֶת־הַיַּיִן וְקוֹלֶטֶת אֶת־הַשְּׁמָרִים. וְנָפָה, שֶׁמּוֹצִיאָה אֶת־הַקֶּמַח וְקוֹלֶטֶת אֶת־הַסֹּלֶת.

Four types of minds sit before the wise: a sponge, a funnel, a strainer, and a sieve. A sponge takes in all things. A funnel receives at one end and lets out at the other. A strainer lets out the wine and retains the dregs. A sieve lets out the coarse meal and retains the fine flour.

5.*20*

כָּל־מַחֲלֹקֶת שֶׁהִיא לְשֵׁם שָׁמַיִם סוֹפָהּ לְהִתְקַיֵּם; וְשֶׁאֵינָהּ לְשֵׁם שָׁמַיִם אֵין סוֹפָהּ לְהִתְקַיֵּם.

Every controversy conducted for God's sake will in the end prove fruitful; every controversy not conducted for God's sake will in the end prove fruitless.

5.*23*

יְהוּדָה בֶּן תֵּימָא אוֹמֵר: הֱוֵי עַז כַּנָּמֵר וְקַל כַּנֶּשֶׁר, רָץ כַּצְּבִי וְגִבּוֹר כָּאֲרִי לַעֲשׂוֹת רְצוֹן אָבִיךָ שֶׁבַּשָּׁמָיִם.

Judah ben Tema: Be strong as a leopard, swift as an eagle, fleet as a gazelle, and brave as a lion to do the will of your divine Creator.

5.*25*

בֶּן בַּג בַּג אוֹמֵר: הֲפָךְ־בַּהּ וַהֲפָךְ־בַּהּ דְּכֹלָּא בַהּ. וּבַהּ תֶּחֱזֵא, וְסִיב וּבְלֵה בַהּ. וּמִנַּהּ לָא תְזוּעַ, שֶׁאֵין לְךָ מִדָּה טוֹבָה הֵימֶנָּה.

Ben Bag Bag: Turn it [the Torah] over and over, for it contains everything. Keep your eyes riveted to it. Spend yourself in its study. Never budge from it, for there is no better way of life than that.

5.*26*

בֶּן הֵא הֵא אוֹמֵר: לְפֻם צַעֲרָא אַגְרָא.

Ben Hei Hei: According to the labor is the reward.

תפלות לימות החול

WEEKDAY SERVICES

Evening Service ערבית לחול

The synagogue is the sanctuary of Israel. Born out of our longing for the living God, it has been to Israel, throughout our wanderings, a visible token of the presence of God in His people's midst. Its beauty is the beauty of holiness; steadfast it has stood as the champion of justice, mercy, and peace.

Its truths are true for all people. Its love is a love for all people. Its God is the God of all people, as it has been said: "My house shall be called a house of prayer for all peoples."

Let all the family of Israel, all who hunger for righteousness, all who seek the Eternal find Him here — and here find life!

◆ ◆

All rise

שמע וברכותיה

בָּרְכוּ אֶת־יְיָ הַמְבֹרָךְ!

Praise the Lord, to whom our praise is due!

בָּרוּךְ יְיָ הַמְבֹרָךְ לְעוֹלָם וָעֶד!

Praised be the Lord, to whom our praise is due,
now and for ever!

◆ ◆

CREATION מעריב ערבים

בָּרוּךְ אַתָּה, יְיָ אֱלֹהֵינוּ, מֶלֶךְ הָעוֹלָם, אֲשֶׁר בִּדְבָרוֹ מַעֲרִיב עֲרָבִים. בְּחָכְמָה פּוֹתֵחַ שְׁעָרִים, וּבִתְבוּנָה מְשַׁנֶּה עִתִּים, וּמַחֲלִיף אֶת־הַזְּמַנִּים, וּמְסַדֵּר אֶת־הַכּוֹכָבִים בְּמִשְׁמְרוֹתֵיהֶם בָּרָקִיעַ כִּרְצוֹנוֹ.

Praised be the Lord our God, Ruler of the universe, whose word brings on the evening. His wisdom opens heaven's gates; His understanding makes the ages pass and the seasons alternate; and His will controls the stars as they travel through the skies.

בּוֹרֵא יוֹם וָלָיְלָה, גּוֹלֵל אוֹר מִפְּנֵי חֹשֶׁךְ וְחֹשֶׁךְ מִפְּנֵי אוֹר, וּמַעֲבִיר יוֹם וּמֵבִיא לָיְלָה, וּמַבְדִּיל בֵּין יוֹם וּבֵין לָיְלָה, יְיָ צְבָאוֹת שְׁמוֹ.

He is Creator of day and night, rolling light away from darkness, and darkness from light; He causes day to pass and brings on the night; He sets day and night apart: He is the Lord of Hosts.

אֵל חַי וְקַיָּם, תָּמִיד יִמְלוֹךְ עָלֵינוּ, לְעוֹלָם וָעֶד. בָּרוּךְ אַתָּה, יְיָ, הַמַּעֲרִיב עֲרָבִים.

May the living and eternal God rule us always, to the end of time! Blessed is the Lord, whose word makes evening fall.

◆ ◆

REVELATION אהבת עולם

אַהֲבַת עוֹלָם בֵּית יִשְׂרָאֵל עַמְּךָ אָהָבְתָּ: תּוֹרָה וּמִצְוֹת, חֻקִּים וּמִשְׁפָּטִים אוֹתָנוּ לִמַּדְתָּ.

Unending is Your love for Your people, the House of Israel: Torah and Mitzvot, laws and precepts have You taught us.

עַל־כֵּן, יְיָ אֱלֹהֵינוּ, בְּשָׁכְבֵנוּ וּבְקוּמֵנוּ נָשִׂיחַ בְּחֻקֶּיךָ, וְנִשְׂמַח בְּדִבְרֵי תוֹרָתְךָ וּבְמִצְוֹתֶיךָ לְעוֹלָם וָעֶד.

Therefore, O Lord our God, when we lie down and when we rise up, we will meditate on Your laws and rejoice in Your Torah and Mitzvot for ever.

כִּי הֵם חַיֵּינוּ וְאֹֽרֶךְ יָמֵינוּ, וּבָהֶם נֶהְגֶּה יוֹמָם וָלָֽיְלָה. וְאַהֲבָתְךָ
אַל־תָּסִיר מִמֶּֽנּוּ לְעוֹלָמִים! בָּרוּךְ אַתָּה, יְיָ, אוֹהֵב עַמּוֹ יִשְׂרָאֵל.

*Day and night we will reflect on them, for they are our life
and the length of our days. Then Your love shall never depart
from our hearts! Blessed is the Lord, who loves His people Israel.*

◆ ◆

שְׁמַע יִשְׂרָאֵל: יְיָ אֱלֹהֵינוּ, יְיָ אֶחָד!

Hear, O Israel: the Lord is our God, the Lord is One!

בָּרוּךְ שֵׁם כְּבוֹד מַלְכוּתוֹ לְעוֹלָם וָעֶד!

Blessed is His glorious kingdom for ever and ever!

All are seated

וְאָהַבְתָּ אֵת יְיָ אֱלֹהֶיךָ בְּכָל־לְבָבְךָ וּבְכָל־נַפְשְׁךָ וּבְכָל־מְאֹדֶךָ.
וְהָיוּ הַדְּבָרִים הָאֵֽלֶּה, אֲשֶׁר אָנֹכִי מְצַוְּךָ הַיּוֹם, עַל־לְבָבֶךָ.
וְשִׁנַּנְתָּם לְבָנֶֽיךָ, וְדִבַּרְתָּ בָּם בְּשִׁבְתְּךָ בְּבֵיתֶֽךָ, וּבְלֶכְתְּךָ
בַדֶּֽרֶךְ, וּבְשָׁכְבְּךָ וּבְקוּמֶֽךָ.

*You shall love the Lord your God with all your mind, with
all your strength, with all your being.
Set these words, which I command you this day, upon your
heart. Teach them faithfully to your children; speak of them
in your home and on your way, when you lie down and when
you rise up.*

וּקְשַׁרְתָּם לְאוֹת עַל־יָדֶֽךָ, וְהָיוּ לְטֹטָפֹת בֵּין עֵינֶֽיךָ, וּכְתַבְתָּם
עַל־מְזֻזוֹת בֵּיתֶֽךָ, וּבִשְׁעָרֶֽיךָ.

*Bind them as a sign upon your hand; let them be a symbol
before your eyes; inscribe them on the doorposts of your
house, and on your gates.*

לְמַֽעַן תִּזְכְּרוּ וַעֲשִׂיתֶם אֶת־כָּל־מִצְוֺתָי, וִהְיִיתֶם קְדֹשִׁים
לֵאלֹהֵיכֶם. אֲנִי יְיָ אֱלֹהֵיכֶם, אֲשֶׁר הוֹצֵֽאתִי אֶתְכֶם מֵאֶֽרֶץ
מִצְרַֽיִם לִהְיוֹת לָכֶם לֵאלֹהִים. אֲנִי יְיָ אֱלֹהֵיכֶם.

*Be mindful of all My mitzvot, and do them: so shall you
consecrate yourselves to your God. I, the Lord, am your God*

who led you out of Egypt to be your God; I, the Lord, am your God.

◆ ◆

REDEMPTION גאולה

אֱמֶת וֶאֱמוּנָה כָּל־זֹאת, וְקַיָּם עָלֵינוּ כִּי הוּא יְיָ אֱלֹהֵינוּ וְאֵין זוּלָתוֹ, וַאֲנַחְנוּ יִשְׂרָאֵל עַמּוֹ.
הַפּוֹדֵנוּ מִיַּד מְלָכִים, מַלְכֵּנוּ הַגּוֹאֲלֵנוּ מִכַּף כָּל־הֶעָרִיצִים.

All this we hold to be true and sure: He alone is our God; there is none else, and we are Israel His people.
He is our King: He delivers us from the hand of oppressors, and saves us from the fist of tyrants.

הָעֹשֶׂה גְדֹלוֹת עַד אֵין חֵקֶר, וְנִפְלָאוֹת עַד־אֵין מִסְפָּר.
הַשָּׂם נַפְשֵׁנוּ בַּחַיִּים, וְלֹא־נָתַן לַמּוֹט רַגְלֵנוּ.

He does wonders without number, marvels that pass our understanding.
He gives us our life; by His help we survive all who seek our destruction.

הָעֹשֶׂה לָנוּ נִסִּים בְּפַרְעֹה, אוֹתוֹת וּמוֹפְתִים בְּאַדְמַת בְּנֵי חָם.
וַיּוֹצֵא אֶת־עַמּוֹ יִשְׂרָאֵל מִתּוֹכָם לְחֵרוּת עוֹלָם.

He did wonders for us in the land of Egypt, miracles and marvels in the land of Pharaoh.
He led His people Israel out, for ever to serve Him in freedom.

וְרָאוּ בָנָיו גְּבוּרָתוֹ; שִׁבְּחוּ וְהוֹדוּ לִשְׁמוֹ. וּמַלְכוּתוֹ בְּרָצוֹן קִבְּלוּ עֲלֵיהֶם. מֹשֶׁה וּבְנֵי יִשְׂרָאֵל לְךָ עָנוּ שִׁירָה בְּשִׂמְחָה רַבָּה, וְאָמְרוּ כֻלָּם:

When His children witnessed His power, they extolled Him and gave Him thanks; freely they acclaimed Him King; and full of joy, Moses and all Israel sang this song:

Who is like You, Eternal One, among the gods that are worshipped?	מִי־כָמֹכָה בָּאֵלִם, יְיָ?
Who is like You, majestic in holiness,	מִי כָּמֹכָה, נֶאְדָּר בַּקֹּדֶשׁ,
awesome in splendor, doing wonders?	נוֹרָא תְהִלֹּת, עֹשֵׂה פֶלֶא?

מַלְכוּתְךָ רָאוּ בָנֶיךָ, בּוֹקֵעַ יָם לִפְנֵי מֹשֶׁה; "זֶה אֵלִי!" עָנוּ וְאָמְרוּ: "יְיָ יִמְלֹךְ לְעֹלָם וָעֶד!"

In their escape from the sea, Your children saw Your sovereign might displayed. "This is my God!" they cried. "The Eternal will reign for ever and ever!"

וְנֶאֱמַר: "כִּי־פָדָה יְיָ אֶת־יַעֲקֹב, וּגְאָלוֹ מִיַּד חָזָק מִמֶּנּוּ." בָּרוּךְ אַתָּה, יְיָ, גָּאַל יִשְׂרָאֵל.

And it has been said: "The Eternal delivered Jacob, and redeemed him from the hand of one stronger than himself." Blessed is the Lord, the Redeemer of Israel.

◆ ◆

DIVINE PROVIDENCE השכיבנו

הַשְׁכִּיבֵנוּ, יְיָ אֱלֹהֵינוּ, לְשָׁלוֹם וְהַעֲמִידֵנוּ, מַלְכֵּנוּ, לְחַיִּים. וּפְרוֹשׂ עָלֵינוּ סֻכַּת שְׁלוֹמֶךָ, וְתַקְּנֵנוּ בְּעֵצָה טוֹבָה מִלְּפָנֶיךָ, וְהוֹשִׁיעֵנוּ לְמַעַן שְׁמֶךָ, וְהָגֵן בַּעֲדֵנוּ. וְהָסֵר מֵעָלֵינוּ אוֹיֵב, דֶּבֶר וְחֶרֶב וְרָעָב וְיָגוֹן; וְהָסֵר שָׂטָן מִלְּפָנֵינוּ וּמֵאַחֲרֵינוּ; וּבְצֵל כְּנָפֶיךָ תַּסְתִּירֵנוּ, כִּי אֵל שׁוֹמְרֵנוּ וּמַצִּילֵנוּ אָתָּה, כִּי אֵל מֶלֶךְ חַנּוּן וְרַחוּם אָתָּה. וּשְׁמוֹר צֵאתֵנוּ וּבוֹאֵנוּ לְחַיִּים וּלְשָׁלוֹם, מֵעַתָּה וְעַד עוֹלָם. בָּרוּךְ אַתָּה, יְיָ, שׁוֹמֵר עַמּוֹ יִשְׂרָאֵל לָעַד.

Grant, O Eternal God, that we may lie down in peace, and raise us up, O Sovereign, to life renewed. Spread over us the shelter of Your peace; guide us with Your good counsel; and for Your name's sake, be our Help.

Shield us from hatred and plague; keep us from war and famine and anguish; subdue our inclination to evil. O God our Guardian and Helper, our gracious and merciful Ruler, give us refuge in the shadow of Your wings. O guard our coming and our going, that now and always we have life and peace.

Blessed is the Lord, Guardian of His people Israel for ever.

READER'S KADDISH — חצי קדיש

יִתְגַּדַּל וְיִתְקַדַּשׁ שְׁמֵהּ רַבָּא בְּעָלְמָא דִּי־בְרָא כִרְעוּתֵהּ,
וְיַמְלִיךְ מַלְכוּתֵהּ בְּחַיֵּיכוֹן וּבְיוֹמֵיכוֹן וּבְחַיֵּי דְכָל־בֵּית
יִשְׂרָאֵל, בַּעֲגָלָא וּבִזְמַן קָרִיב, וְאִמְרוּ: אָמֵן.

יְהֵא שְׁמֵהּ רַבָּא מְבָרַךְ לְעָלַם וּלְעָלְמֵי עָלְמַיָּא.

יִתְבָּרַךְ וְיִשְׁתַּבַּח, וְיִתְפָּאַר וְיִתְרוֹמַם וְיִתְנַשֵּׂא, וְיִתְהַדַּר
וְיִתְעַלֶּה וְיִתְהַלָּל שְׁמֵהּ דְּקוּדְשָׁא, בְּרִיךְ הוּא, לְעֵלָּא מִן
כָּל־בִּרְכָתָא וְשִׁירָתָא, תֻּשְׁבְּחָתָא וְנֶחֱמָתָא דַּאֲמִירָן בְּעָלְמָא,
וְאִמְרוּ: אָמֵן.

Let the glory of God be extolled, let His great name be hallowed in the world whose creation He willed. May His kingdom soon prevail, in our own day, our own lives, and the life of all Israel, and let us say: Amen.

Let His great name be blessed for ever and ever.

Let the name of the Holy One, blessed is He, be glorified, exalted and honored, though He is beyond all the praises, songs, and adorations that we can utter, and let us say: Amen.

◆ ◆

All rise

תפלה

אֲדֹנָי, שְׂפָתַי תִּפְתָּח, וּפִי יַגִּיד תְּהִלָּתֶךָ.

Eternal God, open my lips, that my mouth may declare Your glory.

GOD OF ALL GENERATIONS — אבות

בָּרוּךְ אַתָּה, יְיָ אֱלֹהֵינוּ וֵאלֹהֵי אֲבוֹתֵינוּ, אֱלֹהֵי אַבְרָהָם, אֱלֹהֵי יִצְחָק, וֵאלֹהֵי יַעֲקֹב: הָאֵל הַגָּדוֹל, הַגִּבּוֹר וְהַנּוֹרָא, אֵל עֶלְיוֹן.

We praise You, Lord our God and God of all generations: God of Abraham, God of Isaac, God of Jacob; great, mighty, and awesome God, God supreme.

גּוֹמֵל חֲסָדִים טוֹבִים, וְקוֹנֵה הַכֹּל, וְזוֹכֵר חַסְדֵי אָבוֹת, וּמֵבִיא גְאֻלָּה לִבְנֵי בְנֵיהֶם, לְמַעַן שְׁמוֹ, בְּאַהֲבָה.*

Master of all the living, Your ways are ways of love. You remember the faithfulness of our ancestors, and in love bring redemption to their children's children for the sake of Your name.*

מֶלֶךְ עוֹזֵר וּמוֹשִׁיעַ וּמָגֵן. בָּרוּךְ אַתָּה, יְיָ, מָגֵן אַבְרָהָם.

You are our King and our Help, our Savior and our Shield. Blessed is the Lord, the Shield of Abraham.

* *On the Ten Days of Repentance insert:*

זָכְרֵנוּ לְחַיִּים, מֶלֶךְ חָפֵץ בַּחַיִּים,
וְכָתְבֵנוּ בְּסֵפֶר הַחַיִּים, לְמַעַנְךָ אֱלֹהִים חַיִּים.

Remember us unto life, for You are the King who delights in life, and inscribe us in the Book of Life, that Your will may prevail, O God of life.

◆ ◆

GOD'S POWER גבורות

אַתָּה גִּבּוֹר לְעוֹלָם, אֲדֹנָי, מְחַיֵּה הַכֹּל אַתָּה, רַב לְהוֹשִׁיעַ.

Eternal is Your might, O Lord; all life is Your gift; great is Your power to save!

מְכַלְכֵּל חַיִּים בְּחֶסֶד, מְחַיֵּה הַכֹּל בְּרַחֲמִים רַבִּים. סוֹמֵךְ נוֹפְלִים, וְרוֹפֵא חוֹלִים, וּמַתִּיר אֲסוּרִים, וּמְקַיֵּם אֱמוּנָתוֹ לִישֵׁנֵי עָפָר.

With love You sustain the living, with great compassion give life to all. You send help to the falling and healing to the sick; You bring freedom to the captive and keep faith with those who sleep in the dust.

מִי כָמוֹךָ, בַּעַל גְּבוּרוֹת, וּמִי דּוֹמֶה לָּךְ, מֶלֶךְ מֵמִית וּמְחַיֶּה וּמַצְמִיחַ יְשׁוּעָה?*

וְנֶאֱמָן אַתָּה לְהַחֲיוֹת הַכֹּל. בָּרוּךְ אַתָּה, יְיָ, מְחַיֵּה הַכֹּל.

Who is like You, Master of Might? Who is Your equal, O Lord of life and death, Source of salvation? Blessed is the Lord, the Source of life.*

** On the Ten Days of Repentance insert:*

מִי כָמוֹךָ, אַב הָרַחֲמִים, זוֹכֵר יְצוּרָיו לְחַיִּים בְּרַחֲמִים?

Who is like You, Source of mercy, who in compassion sustains the life of His children?

◆ ◆

GOD'S HOLINESS קדושת השם

אַתָּה קָדוֹשׁ וְשִׁמְךָ קָדוֹשׁ, וּקְדוֹשִׁים בְּכָל־יוֹם יְהַלְלוּךָ סֶּלָה.*

בָּרוּךְ אַתָּה, יְיָ, הָאֵל הַקָּדוֹשׁ.

You are holy, Your name is holy, and those who strive to be holy declare Your glory day by day.* Blessed is the Lord, the holy God.

** On the Ten Days of Repentance conclude:*

Blessed is the Lord, the holy King. בָּרוּךְ אַתָּה, יְיָ, הַמֶּלֶךְ הַקָּדוֹשׁ.

All are seated

◆ ◆

FOR UNDERSTANDING — בינה

אַתָּה חוֹנֵן לְאָדָם דַּעַת וּמְלַמֵּד לֶאֱנוֹשׁ בִּינָה. חָנֵּנוּ מֵאִתְּךָ
דֵּעָה, בִּינָה וְהַשְׂכֵּל.
בָּרוּךְ אַתָּה, יְיָ, חוֹנֵן הַדָּעַת.

You favor us with knowledge and teach mortals understanding. May You continue to favor us with knowledge, understanding, and insight.

Blessed is the Lord, gracious Giver of knowledge.

◆ ◆

FOR REPENTANCE — תשובה

הֲשִׁיבֵנוּ אָבִינוּ לְתוֹרָתֶךָ, וְקָרְבֵנוּ מַלְכֵּנוּ לַעֲבוֹדָתֶךָ,
וְהַחֲזִירֵנוּ בִּתְשׁוּבָה שְׁלֵמָה לְפָנֶיךָ.
בָּרוּךְ אַתָּה, יְיָ, הָרוֹצֶה בִּתְשׁוּבָה.

Help us to return, our Maker, to Your Torah; draw us near, O Sovereign God, to Your service; and bring us back into Your presence in perfect repentance.

Blessed is the Lord, who calls for repentance.

◆ ◆

FOR FORGIVENESS — סליחה

סְלַח־לָנוּ אָבִינוּ כִּי חָטָאנוּ, מְחַל־לָנוּ מַלְכֵּנוּ כִּי פָשָׁעְנוּ, כִּי
מוֹחֵל וְסוֹלֵחַ אָתָּה.
בָּרוּךְ אַתָּה, יְיָ, חַנּוּן הַמַּרְבֶּה לִסְלוֹחַ.

Forgive us, our Creator, when we have sinned; pardon us, our King, when we transgress; for You are a forgiving God.

Blessed is the Lord, the gracious God, whose forgiveness is abundant.

◆ ◆

FOR REDEMPTION גאולה

רְאֵה בְעָנְיֵנוּ וְרִיבָה רִיבֵנוּ, וּגְאָלֵנוּ מְהֵרָה לְמַעַן שְׁמֶךָ, כִּי גוֹאֵל חָזָק אָתָּה.

בָּרוּךְ אַתָּה, יְיָ, גּוֹאֵל יִשְׂרָאֵל.

Look upon our affliction and help us in our need; O mighty Redeemer, redeem us speedily for Your name's sake.

Blessed is the Lord, the Redeemer of Israel.

◆ ◆

FOR HEALTH רפואה

רְפָאֵנוּ יְיָ וְנֵרָפֵא, הוֹשִׁיעֵנוּ וְנִוָּשֵׁעָה, וְהַעֲלֵה רְפוּאָה שְׁלֵמָה לְכָל־מַכּוֹתֵינוּ.

בָּרוּךְ אַתָּה, יְיָ, רוֹפֵא הַחוֹלִים.

Heal us, O Lord, and we shall be healed; save us, and we shall be saved; grant us a perfect healing from all our wounds.

Blessed is the Lord, Healer of the sick.

◆ ◆

FOR ABUNDANCE ברכת השנים

בָּרֵךְ עָלֵינוּ, יְיָ אֱלֹהֵינוּ, אֶת־הַשָּׁנָה הַזֹּאת וְאֶת־כָּל־מִינֵי תְבוּאָתָהּ לְטוֹבָה. וְתֵן בְּרָכָה עַל־פְּנֵי הָאֲדָמָה, וְשַׂבְּעֵנוּ מִטּוּבֶךָ.

בָּרוּךְ אַתָּה, יְיָ, מְבָרֵךְ הַשָּׁנִים.

Bless this year, O Lord our God, and let its produce bring us well-being. Bestow Your blessing on the earth and satisfy us with Your goodness.

Blessed is the Lord, from whom all blessings flow.

◆ ◆

FOR FREEDOM — חרות

תְּקַע בְּשׁוֹפָר גָּדוֹל לְחֵרוּתֵנוּ, וְשָׂא נֵס לִפְדּוֹת עֲשׁוּקֵינוּ, וְקוֹל דְּרוֹר יִשָּׁמַע בְּאַרְבַּע כַּנְפוֹת הָאָרֶץ.

בָּרוּךְ אַתָּה, יְיָ, פּוֹדֶה עֲשׁוּקִים.

Sound the great horn to proclaim freedom, inspire us to strive for the liberation of the oppressed, and let the song of liberty be heard in the four corners of the earth.

Blessed is the Lord, Redeemer of the oppressed.

◆ ◆

FOR JUSTICE — משפט

עַל שׁוֹפְטֵי אֶרֶץ שְׁפוֹךְ רוּחֶךָ, וְהַדְרִיכֵם בְּמִשְׁפְּטֵי צִדְקֶךָ, וּמְלוֹךְ עָלֵינוּ אַתָּה לְבַדֶּךָ, בְּחֶסֶד וּבְרַחֲמִים!

בָּרוּךְ אַתָּה, יְיָ, מֶלֶךְ אוֹהֵב צְדָקָה וּמִשְׁפָּט.

Pour Your spirit upon the rulers of all lands; guide them, that they may govern justly. O may You alone reign over us in steadfast love and compassion!

Blessed is the Sovereign Lord, who loves righteousness and justice.

◆ ◆

FOR RIGHTEOUSNESS — צדיקים

עַל־הַצַּדִּיקִים וְעַל־הַחֲסִידִים וְעָלֵינוּ יֶהֱמוּ רַחֲמֶיךָ, יְיָ אֱלֹהֵינוּ, וְתֵן שָׂכָר טוֹב לְכֹל הַבּוֹטְחִים בְּשִׁמְךָ בֶּאֱמֶת, וְשִׂים חֶלְקֵנוּ עִמָּהֶם לְעוֹלָם.

בָּרוּךְ אַתָּה, יְיָ, מִשְׁעָן וּמִבְטָח לַצַּדִּיקִים.

Have mercy, O Lord our God, upon the righteous and faithful of all peoples, and upon all of us. Uphold all who faithfully put their trust in You, and grant that we may always be numbered among them.

Blessed is the Lord, the Staff and Support of the righteous.

◆ ◆

FOR JERUSALEM

שלום ירושלים

וְלִירוּשָׁלַיִם עִירְךָ בְּרַחֲמִים תִּפְנֶה, וִיהִי שָׁלוֹם בִּשְׁעָרֶיהָ, וְשַׁלְוָה בְּלֵב יוֹשְׁבֶיהָ, וְתוֹרָתְךָ מִצִּיּוֹן תֵּצֵא וּדְבָרְךָ מִירוּשָׁלָיִם.

בָּרוּךְ אַתָּה, יְיָ, נוֹתֵן שָׁלוֹם בִּירוּשָׁלָיִם.

And turn in compassion to Jerusalem, Your city. Let there be peace in her gates, quietness in the hearts of her inhabitants. Let Your Torah go forth from Zion and Your word from Jerusalem.

Blessed is the Lord, who gives peace to Jerusalem.

◆ ◆

FOR DELIVERANCE

ישועה

אֶת־צֶמַח צְדָקָה מְהֵרָה תַצְמִיחַ, וְקֶרֶן יְשׁוּעָה תָּרוּם כִּנְאֻמֶךָ, כִּי לִישׁוּעָתְךָ קִוִּינוּ כָּל־הַיּוֹם.

בָּרוּךְ אַתָּה, יְיָ, מַצְמִיחַ קֶרֶן יְשׁוּעָה.

Cause the plant of justice to spring up soon. Let the light of deliverance shine forth according to Your word, for we await Your deliverance all the day.

Blessed is the Lord, who will cause the light of deliverance to dawn for all the world.

◆ ◆

FOR ACCEPTANCE OF PRAYER

שומע תפלה

שְׁמַע קוֹלֵנוּ, יְיָ אֱלֹהֵינוּ, חוּס וְרַחֵם עָלֵינוּ, וְקַבֵּל בְּרַחֲמִים וּבְרָצוֹן אֶת תְּפִלָּתֵנוּ, כִּי אֵל שׁוֹמֵעַ תְּפִלּוֹת וְתַחֲנוּנִים אָתָּה.

בָּרוּךְ אַתָּה, יְיָ, שׁוֹמֵעַ תְּפִלָּה.

Hear our voice, O Lord our God; have compassion upon us, and accept our prayer with favor and mercy, for You are a God who hears prayer and supplication.

Blessed is the Lord, who hearkens to prayer.

◆ ◆

WORSHIP — עבודה

רְצֵה, יְיָ אֱלֹהֵינוּ, בְּעַמְּךָ יִשְׂרָאֵל, וּתְפִלָּתָם בְּאַהֲבָה תְקַבֵּל, וּתְהִי לְרָצוֹן תָּמִיד עֲבוֹדַת יִשְׂרָאֵל עַמֶּךָ.
אֵל קָרוֹב לְכָל־קֹרְאָיו, פְּנֵה אֶל עֲבָדֶיךָ וְחָנֵּנוּ; שְׁפוֹךְ רוּחֲךָ עָלֵינוּ, וְתֶחֱזֶינָה עֵינֵינוּ בְּשׁוּבְךָ לְצִיּוֹן בְּרַחֲמִים.

בָּרוּךְ אַתָּה, יְיָ, הַמַּחֲזִיר שְׁכִינָתוֹ לְצִיּוֹן.

Be gracious, O Lord our God, to Your people Israel, and receive our prayers with love. O may our worship always be acceptable to You.
Fill us with the knowledge that You are near to all who seek You in truth. Let our eyes behold Your presence in our midst and in the midst of our people in Zion.

Blessed is the Lord, whose presence gives life to Zion and all Israel.

◆ ◆

ON ROSH CHODESH AND CHOL HAMO-EID

אֱלֹהֵינוּ וֵאלֹהֵי אֲבוֹתֵינוּ, יַעֲלֶה וְיָבֹא וְיִזָּכֵר זִכְרוֹנֵנוּ וְזִכְרוֹן כָּל־עַמְּךָ בֵּית יִשְׂרָאֵל לְפָנֶיךָ, לְטוֹבָה לְחֵן לְחֶסֶד וּלְרַחֲמִים, לְחַיִּים וּלְשָׁלוֹם בְּיוֹם

Our God and God of all ages, be mindful of Your people Israel on this

first day of the new month,	רֹאשׁ הַחֹדֶשׁ הַזֶּה.
day of Pesach,	חַג הַמַּצּוֹת הַזֶּה.
day of Sukkot,	חַג הַסֻּכּוֹת הַזֶּה.

and renew in us love and compassion, goodness, life and peace.

This day remember us for well-being. *Amen.*	זָכְרֵנוּ, יְיָ אֱלֹהֵינוּ, בּוֹ לְטוֹבָה. אָמֵן.
This day bless us with Your nearness. *Amen.*	וּפָקְדֵנוּ בוֹ לִבְרָכָה. אָמֵן.
This day help us to a fuller life. *Amen.*	וְהוֹשִׁיעֵנוּ בוֹ לְחַיִּים. אָמֵן.

◆ ◆

THANKSGIVING **הודאה**

מוֹדִים אֲנַחְנוּ לָךְ, שָׁאַתָּה הוּא יְיָ אֱלֹהֵינוּ וֵאלֹהֵי אֲבוֹתֵינוּ לְעוֹלָם וָעֶד. צוּר חַיֵּינוּ, מָגֵן יִשְׁעֵנוּ, אַתָּה הוּא לְדוֹר וָדוֹר. נוֹדֶה לְּךָ וּנְסַפֵּר תְּהִלָּתֶךָ, עַל־חַיֵּינוּ הַמְּסוּרִים בְּיָדֶךָ, וְעַל־נִשְׁמוֹתֵינוּ הַפְּקוּדוֹת לָךְ, וְעַל־נִסֶּיךָ שֶׁבְּכָל־יוֹם עִמָּנוּ, וְעַל־נִפְלְאוֹתֶיךָ וְטוֹבוֹתֶיךָ שֶׁבְּכָל־עֵת, עֶרֶב וָבֹקֶר וְצָהֳרָיִם. הַטּוֹב: כִּי לֹא־כָלוּ רַחֲמֶיךָ, וְהַמְרַחֵם: כִּי־לֹא תַמּוּ חֲסָדֶיךָ, מֵעוֹלָם קִוִּינוּ לָךְ.

We gratefully acknowledge that You are the Lord our God and God of our people, the God of all generations. You are the Rock of our life, the Power that shields us in every age. We thank You and sing Your praises: for our lives, which are in Your hand; for our souls, which are in Your keeping; for the signs of Your presence we encounter every day; and for Your wondrous gifts at all times, morning, noon, and night. You are Goodness: Your mercies never end; You are Compassion: Your love will never fail. You have always been our hope.

וְעַל כֻּלָּם יִתְבָּרַךְ וְיִתְרוֹמַם שִׁמְךָ, מַלְכֵּנוּ, תָּמִיד לְעוֹלָם וָעֶד.

For all these things, O Sovereign God, let Your name be for ever exalted and blessed.

On the Ten Days of Repentance insert:

וּכְתוֹב לְחַיִּים טוֹבִים כָּל־בְּנֵי בְרִיתֶךָ.

Let life abundant be the heritage of all Your children.

וְכֹל הַחַיִּים יוֹדוּךָ סֶּלָה, וִיהַלְלוּ אֶת שִׁמְךָ בֶּאֱמֶת, הָאֵל יְשׁוּעָתֵנוּ וְעֶזְרָתֵנוּ סֶלָה. בָּרוּךְ אַתָּה, יְיָ, הַטּוֹב שִׁמְךָ וּלְךָ נָאֶה לְהוֹדוֹת.

O God our Redeemer and Helper, let all who live affirm You and praise Your name in truth. Lord, whose nature is Goodness, we give You thanks and praise.

◆ ◆

ON CHANUKAH

עַל הַנִּסִּים וְעַל הַפֻּרְקָן, וְעַל הַגְּבוּרוֹת וְעַל הַתְּשׁוּעוֹת, וְעַל הַמִּלְחָמוֹת, שֶׁעָשִׂיתָ לַאֲבוֹתֵינוּ בַּיָּמִים הָהֵם בַּזְּמַן הַזֶּה.

בִּימֵי מַתִּתְיָהוּ בֶּן־יוֹחָנָן כֹּהֵן גָּדוֹל, חַשְׁמוֹנַי וּבָנָיו, כְּשֶׁעָמְדָה מַלְכוּת יָוָן הָרְשָׁעָה עַל־עַמְּךָ יִשְׂרָאֵל לְהַשְׁכִּיחָם תּוֹרָתֶךָ, וּלְהַעֲבִירָם מֵחֻקֵּי רְצוֹנֶךָ.

וְאַתָּה בְּרַחֲמֶיךָ הָרַבִּים עָמַדְתָּ לָהֶם בְּעֵת צָרָתָם. רַבְתָּ אֶת־רִיבָם, דַּנְתָּ אֶת־דִּינָם, מָסַרְתָּ גִבּוֹרִים בְּיַד חַלָּשִׁים, וְרַבִּים בְּיַד מְעַטִּים, וּטְמֵאִים בְּיַד טְהוֹרִים, וּרְשָׁעִים בְּיַד צַדִּיקִים, וְזֵדִים בְּיַד עוֹסְקֵי תוֹרָתֶךָ.

וּלְךָ עָשִׂיתָ שֵׁם גָּדוֹל וְקָדוֹשׁ בְּעוֹלָמֶךָ, וּלְעַמְּךָ יִשְׂרָאֵל עָשִׂיתָ תְּשׁוּעָה גְדוֹלָה וּפֻרְקָן כְּהַיּוֹם הַזֶּה.

וְאַחַר כֵּן בָּאוּ בָנֶיךָ לִדְבִיר בֵּיתֶךָ, וּפִנּוּ אֶת־הֵיכָלֶךָ, וְטִהֲרוּ אֶת־מִקְדָּשֶׁךָ, וְהִדְלִיקוּ נֵרוֹת בְּחַצְרוֹת קָדְשֶׁךָ, וְקָבְעוּ שְׁמוֹנַת יְמֵי חֲנֻכָּה אֵלּוּ לְהוֹדוֹת וּלְהַלֵּל לְשִׁמְךָ הַגָּדוֹל.

We give thanks for the redeeming wonders and the mighty deeds by which, at this season, our people was saved in days of old.

In the days of the Hasmoneans, a tyrant arose against our ancestors, determined to make them forget Your Torah, and to turn them away from obedience to Your will. But You were at their side in time of trouble. You gave them strength to struggle and to triumph, that they might serve You in freedom.

Through the power of Your spirit the weak defeated the strong, the few prevailed over the many, and the righteous were triumphant. Then Your children returned to Your house, to purify the sanctuary and kindle its lights. And they dedicated these days to give thanks and praise to Your great name.

◆ ◆

ON PURIM

עַל הַנִּסִּים וְעַל הַפֻּרְקָן, וְעַל הַגְּבוּרוֹת וְעַל הַתְּשׁוּעוֹת, וְעַל הַמִּלְחָמוֹת, שֶׁעָשִׂיתָ לַאֲבוֹתֵינוּ בַּיָּמִים הָהֵם בַּזְּמַן הַזֶּה.
בִּימֵי מָרְדְּכַי וְאֶסְתֵּר בְּשׁוּשַׁן הַבִּירָה, כְּשֶׁעָמַד עֲלֵיהֶם הָמָן הָרָשָׁע, בִּקֵּשׁ לְהַשְׁמִיד לַהֲרוֹג וּלְאַבֵּד אֶת־כָּל־הַיְּהוּדִים, מִנַּעַר וְעַד־זָקֵן, טַף וְנָשִׁים, בְּיוֹם אֶחָד, בִּשְׁלוֹשָׁה עָשָׂר לְחֹדֶשׁ שְׁנֵים־עָשָׂר, הוּא־חֹדֶשׁ אֲדָר, וּשְׁלָלָם לָבוֹז.
וְאַתָּה בְּרַחֲמֶיךָ הָרַבִּים הֵפַרְתָּ אֶת־עֲצָתוֹ, וְקִלְקַלְתָּ אֶת־מַחֲשַׁבְתּוֹ.

We give thanks for the redeeming wonders and the mighty deeds by which, at this season, our people was saved in days of old.
In the days of Mordecai and Esther, the wicked Haman arose in Persia, plotting the destruction of all the Jews. He planned to destroy them in a single day, the thirteenth of Adar, and to permit the plunder of their possessions.
But through Your great mercy his plan was thwarted, his scheme frustrated. We therefore thank and bless You, O great and gracious God!

◆ ◆

PEACE — ברכת שלום

שָׁלוֹם רָב עַל־יִשְׂרָאֵל עַמְּךָ תָּשִׂים לְעוֹלָם, כִּי אַתָּה הוּא מֶלֶךְ אָדוֹן לְכָל הַשָּׁלוֹם. וְטוֹב בְּעֵינֶיךָ לְבָרֵךְ אֶת־עַמְּךָ יִשְׂרָאֵל בְּכָל־עֵת וּבְכָל־שָׁעָה בִּשְׁלוֹמֶךָ.*

בָּרוּךְ אַתָּה, יְיָ, הַמְבָרֵךְ אֶת־עַמּוֹ יִשְׂרָאֵל בַּשָּׁלוֹם.

O Sovereign Lord of peace, let Israel Your people know enduring peace, for it is good in Your sight continually to bless Israel with Your peace. Praised be the Lord, who blesses His people Israel with peace.*

* *On the Ten Days of Repentance conclude:*

בְּסֵפֶר חַיִּים וּבְרָכָה נִכָּתֵב לְחַיִּים טוֹבִים וּלְשָׁלוֹם.
בָּרוּךְ אַתָּה, יְיָ, עוֹשֵׂה הַשָּׁלוֹם.

Teach us then to find our happiness in the search for righteousness and peace. Blessed is the Lord, the Source of peace.

◆ ◆

SILENT PRAYER

אֱלֹהַי, נְצֹר לְשׁוֹנִי מֵרָע, וּשְׂפָתַי מִדַּבֵּר מִרְמָה, וְלִמְקַלְלַי
נַפְשִׁי תִדֹּם, וְנַפְשִׁי כֶּעָפָר לַכֹּל תִּהְיֶה. פְּתַח לִבִּי בְּתוֹרָתֶךָ,
וּבְמִצְוֹתֶיךָ תִּרְדּוֹף נַפְשִׁי, וְכֹל הַחוֹשְׁבִים עָלַי רָעָה, מְהֵרָה
הָפֵר עֲצָתָם וְקַלְקֵל מַחֲשַׁבְתָּם. עֲשֵׂה לְמַעַן שְׁמֶךָ, עֲשֵׂה לְמַעַן
יְמִינֶךָ, עֲשֵׂה לְמַעַן קְדֻשָּׁתֶךָ, עֲשֵׂה לְמַעַן תּוֹרָתֶךָ. לְמַעַן
יֵחָלְצוּן יְדִידֶיךָ, הוֹשִׁיעָה יְמִינְךָ וַעֲנֵנִי.

O God, keep my tongue from evil and my lips from deceit. Help me to be silent in the face of derision, humble in the presence of all. Open my heart to Your Torah, and I will hasten to do Your Mitzvot. Save me with Your power; in time of trouble be my answer, that those who love You may rejoice.

◆ ◆

יִהְיוּ לְרָצוֹן אִמְרֵי־פִי וְהֶגְיוֹן לִבִּי לְפָנֶיךָ, יְיָ, צוּרִי וְגוֹאֲלִי.

May the words of my mouth, and the meditations of my heart, be acceptable to You, O Lord, my Rock and my Redeemer.

or

עֹשֶׂה שָׁלוֹם בִּמְרוֹמָיו, הוּא יַעֲשֶׂה שָׁלוֹם עָלֵינוּ וְעַל כָּל־
יִשְׂרָאֵל, וְאִמְרוּ אָמֵן.

May He who causes peace to reign in the high heavens let peace descend on us, on all Israel, and all the world.

◆ ◆

Prayers at a House of Mourning begin on page 645.

Concluding Prayers begin on page 613.

Havdalah for the conclusion of Shabbat is on page 633.

For Weekday Mornings

For those who wear the Tallit

בָּרְכִי נַפְשִׁי אֶת יְיָ!
יְיָ אֱלֹהַי, גָּדַלְתָּ מְּאד!
הוד וְהָדָר לָבָשְׁתָּ,
עֹטֶה אור כַּשַּׂלְמָה,
נוטֶה שָׁמַיִם כַּיְרִיעָה.

Praise the Lord, O my soul!
O Lord my God, You are very great!
Arrayed in glory and majesty,
You wrap Yourself in light as with a garment,
You stretch out the heavens like a curtain.

בָּרוּךְ אַתָּה, יְיָ אֱלֹהֵינוּ, מֶלֶךְ הָעוֹלָם,
אֲשֶׁר קִדְּשָׁנוּ בְּמִצְוֹתָיו וְצִוָּנוּ לְהִתְעַטֵּף בַּצִּיצִת.

Blessed is the Lord our God, Ruler of the universe, who hallows us with His Mitzvot, and teaches us to wrap ourselves in the fringed Tallit.

◆ ◆

For those who wear Tefillin

הִנְנִי מְכַוֵּן בְּהַנָּחַת תְּפִלִּין לְקַיֵּם מִצְוַת בּוֹרְאִי שֶׁצִּוָּנוּ לְהַנִּיחַ תְּפִלִּין,
כַּכָּתוּב בַּתּוֹרָה: וּקְשַׁרְתָּם לְאוֹת עַל יָדֶךָ, וְהָיוּ לְטֹטָפֹת בֵּין עֵינֶיךָ.

In the Torah it is written: "Bind them as a sign upon your hand; let them be a symbol before your eyes."

וְהֵם אַרְבַּע פָּרָשִׁיּוֹת אֵלּוּ: שְׁמַע, וְהָיָה אִם שָׁמֹעַ, קַדֶּשׁ, וְהָיָה כִּי
יְבִיאֲךָ, שֶׁיֵּשׁ בָּהֶם יִחוּדוֹ וְאַחְדוּתוֹ יִתְבָּרַךְ שְׁמוֹ.
וְצִוָּנוּ לְהַנִּיחַ עַל הַיָּד לְזִכְרוֹן זְרוֹעוֹ הַנְּטוּיָה; וְשֶׁהִיא נֶגֶד הַלֵּב, לְשַׁעְבֵּד
בָּזֶה תַּאֲוֹת וּמַחְשְׁבוֹת לִבֵּנוּ לַעֲבוֹדָתוֹ, יִתְבָּרַךְ שְׁמוֹ; וְעַל הָרֹאשׁ נֶגֶד
הַמֹּחַ, שֶׁהַנְּשָׁמָה שֶׁבְּמֹחִי עִם שְׁאָר חוּשַׁי וְכֹחוֹתַי כֻּלָּם יִהְיוּ מְשֻׁעְבָּדִים
לַעֲבוֹדָתוֹ, יִתְבָּרַךְ שְׁמוֹ.

By this we proclaim the unity and uniqueness of the Blessed One; we recall the wonder of the Exodus; and we acclaim His power in all the universe.
By this symbol we bind hand, heart, and mind to the service of the Blessed One.

FOR THE HAND

בָּרוּךְ אַתָּה, יְיָ אֱלֹהֵינוּ, מֶלֶךְ הָעוֹלָם,
אֲשֶׁר קִדְּשָׁנוּ בְּמִצְוֹתָיו וְצִוָּנוּ לְהַנִּיחַ תְּפִלִּין.

Blessed is the Lord our God, Ruler of the universe, who hallows us with His Mitzvot, and teaches us to wear Tefillin.

FOR THE HEAD

בָּרוּךְ אַתָּה, יְיָ אֱלֹהֵינוּ, מֶלֶךְ הָעוֹלָם,
אֲשֶׁר קִדְּשָׁנוּ בְּמִצְוֹתָיו וְצִוָּנוּ עַל־מִצְוַת תְּפִלִּין.
בָּרוּךְ שֵׁם כְּבוֹד מַלְכוּתוֹ לְעוֹלָם וָעֶד!

Blessed is the Lord our God, Ruler of the universe, who hallows us with His Mitzvot, and teaches us concerning the Mitzvah of Tefillin.

Blessed is His glorious kingdom for ever and ever!

UPON WINDING THE RETSUAH ON THE FINGER

וְאֵרַשְׂתִּיךְ לִי לְעוֹלָם,
וְאֵרַשְׂתִּיךְ לִי בְּצֶדֶק וּבְמִשְׁפָּט וּבְחֶסֶד וּבְרַחֲמִים.
וְאֵרַשְׂתִּיךְ לִי בֶּאֱמוּנָה, וְיָדַעַתְּ אֶת־יְיָ.

"I will betroth you to Me for ever; I will betroth you to Me in righteousness and justice, in love and compassion; I will betroth you to Me in faithfulness, and you shall know the Lord."

◆ ◆

ברכות השחר

FOR THE BLESSING OF WORSHIP מה טבו

מַה־טֹּבוּ אֹהָלֶיךָ, יַעֲקֹב, מִשְׁכְּנֹתֶיךָ, יִשְׂרָאֵל!

How lovely are Your tents, O Jacob, your dwelling-places, O Israel!

וַאֲנִי, בְּרֹב חַסְדְּךָ אָבוֹא בֵיתֶךָ,
אֶשְׁתַּחֲוֶה אֶל־הֵיכַל קָדְשְׁךָ בְּיִרְאָתֶךָ.

In Your abundant lovingkindness, O God, let me enter Your house, reverently to worship in Your holy temple.

יְיָ, אָהַבְתִּי מְעוֹן בֵּיתֶךָ, וּמְקוֹם מִשְׁכַּן כְּבוֹדֶךָ.
וַאֲנִי אֶשְׁתַּחֲוֶה וְאֶכְרָעָה, אֶבְרְכָה לִפְנֵי־יְיָ עֹשִׂי.

Lord, I love Your house, the place where Your glory dwells.
So I would worship with humility, I would seek blessing in the presence of God, my Maker.

וַאֲנִי תְפִלָּתִי לְךָ, יְיָ, עֵת רָצוֹן.
אֱלֹהִים, בְּרָב־חַסְדֶּךָ, עֲנֵנִי בֶּאֱמֶת יִשְׁעֶךָ.

To You, then, Lord, does my prayer go forth. May this be a time of joy and favor.
In Your great love, O God, answer me with Your saving truth.

◆ ◆

FOR HEALTH אשר יצר

בָּרוּךְ אַתָּה, יְיָ אֱלֹהֵינוּ, מֶלֶךְ הָעוֹלָם, אֲשֶׁר יָצַר אֶת־הָאָדָם בְּחָכְמָה, וּבָרָא בוֹ נְקָבִים נְקָבִים, חֲלוּלִים חֲלוּלִים.

Blessed is our Eternal God, Creator of the universe, who has made our bodies with wisdom, combining veins, arteries, and vital organs into a finely balanced network.

גָּלוּי וְיָדוּעַ לִפְנֵי כִסֵּא כְבוֹדֶךָ, שֶׁאִם יִפָּתֵחַ אֶחָד מֵהֶם, אוֹ יִסָּתֵם אֶחָד מֵהֶם, אִי אֶפְשָׁר לְהִתְקַיֵּם וְלַעֲמוֹד לְפָנֶיךָ.

בָּרוּךְ אַתָּה, יְיָ, רוֹפֵא כָל־בָּשָׂר וּמַפְלִיא לַעֲשׂוֹת.

Wondrous Fashioner and Sustainer of life, Source of our health and our strength, we give You thanks and praise.

◆ ◆

FOR TORAH — לעסוק בדברי תורה

בָּרוּךְ אַתָּה, יְיָ אֱלֹהֵינוּ, מֶלֶךְ הָעוֹלָם, אֲשֶׁר קִדְּשָׁנוּ בְּמִצְוֹתָיו וְצִוָּנוּ לַעֲסוֹק בְּדִבְרֵי תוֹרָה.

Blessed is the Eternal, our God, Ruler of the universe, who hallows us with His Mitzvot, and commands us to engage in the study of Torah.

וְהַעֲרֶב־נָא, יְיָ אֱלֹהֵינוּ, אֶת־דִּבְרֵי תוֹרָתְךָ בְּפִינוּ, וּבְפִי עַמְּךָ בֵּית יִשְׂרָאֵל, וְנִהְיֶה אֲנַחְנוּ וְצֶאֱצָאֵינוּ, וְצֶאֱצָאֵי עַמְּךָ בֵּית יִשְׂרָאֵל, כֻּלָּנוּ יוֹדְעֵי שְׁמֶךָ וְלוֹמְדֵי תוֹרָתֶךָ לִשְׁמָהּ. בָּרוּךְ אַתָּה, יְיָ, הַמְלַמֵּד תּוֹרָה לְעַמּוֹ יִשְׂרָאֵל.

Eternal our God, make the words of Your Torah sweet to us, and to the House of Israel, Your people, that we and our children may be lovers of Your name and students of Your Torah.

Blessed is the Eternal, the Teacher of Torah to His people Israel.

◆

אֵלּוּ דְבָרִים שֶׁאֵין לָהֶם שִׁעוּר, שֶׁאָדָם אוֹכֵל פֵּרוֹתֵיהֶם בָּעוֹלָם הַזֶּה וְהַקֶּרֶן קַיֶּמֶת לוֹ לָעוֹלָם הַבָּא, וְאֵלּוּ הֵן:

These are the obligations without measure, whose reward, too, is without measure;

To honor father and mother; — כִּבּוּד אָב וָאֵם,

to perform acts of love and kindness; — וּגְמִילוּת חֲסָדִים,

to attend the house of study daily; — וְהַשְׁכָּמַת בֵּית הַמִּדְרָשׁ שַׁחֲרִית וְעַרְבִית,

to welcome the stranger;	וְהַכְנָסַת אוֹרְחִים,
to visit the sick;	וּבִקּוּר חוֹלִים,
to rejoice with bride and groom;	וְהַכְנָסַת כַּלָּה,
to console the bereaved;	וּלְוָיַת הַמֵּת,
to pray with sincerity;	וְעִיּוּן תְּפִלָּה,
to make peace when there is strife.	וַהֲבָאַת שָׁלוֹם בֵּין אָדָם לַחֲבֵרוֹ;
And the study of Torah is equal to them all, because it leads to them all.	וְתַלְמוּד תּוֹרָה כְּנֶגֶד כֻּלָּם.

◆ ◆

FOR THE SOUL — אלהי נשמה

אֱלֹהַי, נְשָׁמָה שֶׁנָּתַתָּ בִּי טְהוֹרָה הִיא! אַתָּה בְרָאתָהּ, אַתָּה יְצַרְתָּהּ, אַתָּה נְפַחְתָּהּ בִּי, וְאַתָּה מְשַׁמְּרָהּ בְּקִרְבִּי. כָּל־זְמַן שֶׁהַנְּשָׁמָה בְקִרְבִּי, מוֹדֶה אֲנִי לְפָנֶיךָ, יְיָ אֱלֹהַי וֵאלֹהֵי אֲבוֹתַי, רִבּוֹן כָּל־הַמַּעֲשִׂים, אֲדוֹן כָּל־הַנְּשָׁמוֹת.

בָּרוּךְ אַתָּה, יְיָ, אֲשֶׁר בְּיָדוֹ נֶפֶשׁ כָּל־חָי, וְרוּחַ כָּל־בְּשַׂר־אִישׁ.

The soul that You have given me, O God, is a pure one! You have created and formed it, breathed it into me, and within me You sustain it. So long as I have breath, therefore, I will give thanks to You, O Lord my God and God of all ages, Master of all creation, Lord of every human spirit.

Blessed is the Lord, in whose hands are the souls of all the living and the spirits of all flesh.

◆ ◆

FOR LIFE — ברוך שאמר

בָּרוּךְ שֶׁאָמַר וְהָיָה הָעוֹלָם, בָּרוּךְ הוּא.
בָּרוּךְ עוֹשֶׂה בְרֵאשִׁית.

Blessed is the One who spoke, and the world came to be.
Blessed is the Source of creation.

בָּרוּךְ אוֹמֵר וְעוֹשֶׂה, בָּרוּךְ גּוֹזֵר וּמְקַיֵּם.

Blessed is the One whose word is deed, whose thought is fact.

בָּרוּךְ מְרַחֵם עַל הָאָרֶץ, בָּרוּךְ מְרַחֵם עַל הַבְּרִיּוֹת.
בָּרוּךְ מְשַׁלֵּם שָׂכָר טוֹב לִירֵאָיו.
בָּרוּךְ חַי לָעַד וְקַיָּם לָנֶצַח, בָּרוּךְ פּוֹדֶה וּמַצִּיל, בָּרוּךְ שְׁמוֹ.

Blessed is the One whose compassion covers the earth and all its creatures.

Blessed is the living and eternal God, Ruler of the universe, divine Source of deliverance and help.

בְּשְׁבָחוֹת וּבִזְמִרוֹת נְגַדֶּלְךָ וּנְשַׁבֵּחֲךָ וּנְפָאֶרְךָ, וְנַזְכִּיר שִׁמְךָ וְנַמְלִיכְךָ, מַלְכֵּנוּ, אֱלֹהֵינוּ. יָחִיד, חֵי הָעוֹלָמִים, מֶלֶךְ, מְשֻׁבָּח וּמְפֹאָר עֲדֵי־עַד שְׁמוֹ הַגָּדוֹל.

בָּרוּךְ אַתָּה, יְיָ, מֶלֶךְ מְהֻלָּל בַּתִּשְׁבָּחוֹת.

With songs of praise we extol You and proclaim Your sovereignty, our God and King, for You are the source of life in the universe.

Blessed is the Eternal King, to whom our praise is due.

READER'S KADDISH — חצי קדיש

יִתְגַּדַּל וְיִתְקַדַּשׁ שְׁמֵהּ רַבָּא בְּעָלְמָא דִּי־בְרָא כִרְעוּתֵהּ, וְיַמְלִיךְ מַלְכוּתֵהּ בְּחַיֵּיכוֹן וּבְיוֹמֵיכוֹן וּבְחַיֵּי דְכָל־בֵּית יִשְׂרָאֵל, בַּעֲגָלָא וּבִזְמַן קָרִיב, וְאִמְרוּ: אָמֵן.

יְהֵא שְׁמֵהּ רַבָּא מְבָרַךְ לְעָלַם וּלְעָלְמֵי עָלְמַיָּא.

יִתְבָּרַךְ וְיִשְׁתַּבַּח, וְיִתְפָּאַר וְיִתְרוֹמַם וְיִתְנַשֵּׂא, וְיִתְהַדַּר וְיִתְעַלֶּה וְיִתְהַלַּל שְׁמֵהּ דְּקוּדְשָׁא, בְּרִיךְ הוּא, לְעֵלָּא מִן כָּל־בִּרְכָתָא וְשִׁירָתָא, תֻּשְׁבְּחָתָא וְנֶחֱמָתָא דַּאֲמִירָן בְּעָלְמָא, וְאִמְרוּ: אָמֵן.

Let the glory of God be extolled, let His great name be hallowed in the world whose creation He willed. May His kingdom soon prevail, in our own day, our own lives, and the life of all Israel, and let us say: Amen.

Let His great name be blessed for ever and ever.

Let the name of the Holy One, blessed is He, be glorified, exalted and honored, though He is beyond all the praises, songs, and adorations that we can utter, and let us say: Amen.

◆ ◆

All rise

שמע וברכותיה

בָּרְכוּ אֶת־יְיָ הַמְבֹרָךְ!

Praise the Lord, to whom our praise is due!

בָּרוּךְ יְיָ הַמְבֹרָךְ לְעוֹלָם וָעֶד!

Praised be the Lord, to whom our praise is due, now and for ever!

◆ ◆

CREATION יוצר

בָּרוּךְ אַתָּה, יְיָ אֱלֹהֵינוּ, מֶלֶךְ הָעוֹלָם, יוֹצֵר אוֹר וּבוֹרֵא חֹשֶׁךְ, עֹשֶׂה שָׁלוֹם וּבוֹרֵא אֶת־הַכֹּל.

Praised be the Lord our God, Ruler of the universe, who makes light and creates darkness, who ordains peace and fashions all things.

הַמֵּאִיר לָאָרֶץ וְלַדָּרִים עָלֶיהָ בְּרַחֲמִים, וּבְטוּבוֹ מְחַדֵּשׁ בְּכָל־יוֹם תָּמִיד מַעֲשֵׂה בְרֵאשִׁית.

With compassion He gives light to the earth and all who dwell there; with goodness He renews the work of creation continually, day by day.

מָה רַבּוּ מַעֲשֶׂיךָ, יְיָ! כֻּלָּם בְּחָכְמָה עָשִׂיתָ, מָלְאָה הָאָרֶץ קִנְיָנֶךָ.

How manifold are Your works, O Lord; in wisdom You have made them all; the earth is full of Your creations.

תִּתְבָּרַךְ, יְיָ אֱלֹהֵינוּ, עַל־שֶׁבַח מַעֲשֵׂה יָדֶיךָ, וְעַל־מְאוֹרֵי־אוֹר שֶׁעָשִׂיתָ: יְפָאֲרוּךָ. סֶּלָה.

בָּרוּךְ אַתָּה, יְיָ, יוֹצֵר הַמְּאוֹרוֹת.

Let all bless You, O Lord our God, for the excellence of Your handiwork, and for the glowing stars that You have made: let them glorify You for ever. Blessed is the Lord, the Maker of light.

◆ ◆

REVELATION — אהבה רבה

אַהֲבָה רַבָּה אֲהַבְתָּנוּ, יְיָ אֱלֹהֵינוּ, חֶמְלָה גְדוֹלָה וִיתֵרָה חָמַלְתָּ עָלֵינוּ. אָבִינוּ מַלְכֵּנוּ, בַּעֲבוּר אֲבוֹתֵינוּ שֶׁבָּטְחוּ בְךָ וַתְּלַמְּדֵם חֻקֵּי חַיִּים, כֵּן תְּחָנֵּנוּ וּתְלַמְּדֵנוּ.

Deep is Your love for us, O Lord our God, and great is Your compassion. Our Maker and King, our ancestors trusted You, and You taught them the laws of life: be gracious now to us, and teach us.

אָבִינוּ, הָאָב הָרַחֲמָן, הַמְרַחֵם, רַחֵם עָלֵינוּ וְתֵן בְּלִבֵּנוּ לְהָבִין וּלְהַשְׂכִּיל, לִשְׁמֹעַ לִלְמֹד וּלְלַמֵּד, לִשְׁמֹר וְלַעֲשׂוֹת וּלְקַיֵּם אֶת־כָּל־דִּבְרֵי תַלְמוּד תּוֹרָתֶךָ בְּאַהֲבָה.

Have compassion upon us, O Source of mercy, and guide us to know and understand, learn and teach, observe and uphold with love all the teachings of Your Torah.

וְהָאֵר עֵינֵינוּ בְּתוֹרָתֶךָ, וְדַבֵּק לִבֵּנוּ בְּמִצְוֹתֶיךָ, וְיַחֵד לְבָבֵנוּ לְאַהֲבָה וּלְיִרְאָה אֶת־שְׁמֶךָ. וְלֹא־נֵבוֹשׁ לְעוֹלָם וָעֶד, כִּי בְשֵׁם קָדְשְׁךָ הַגָּדוֹל וְהַנּוֹרָא בָּטָחְנוּ. נָגִילָה וְנִשְׂמְחָה בִּישׁוּעָתֶךָ, כִּי אֵל פּוֹעֵל יְשׁוּעוֹת אָתָּה. וּבָנוּ בָחַרְתָּ וְקֵרַבְתָּנוּ לְשִׁמְךָ הַגָּדוֹל סֶלָה בֶּאֱמֶת, לְהוֹדוֹת לְךָ וּלְיַחֶדְךָ בְּאַהֲבָה.

בָּרוּךְ אַתָּה, יְיָ, הַבּוֹחֵר בְּעַמּוֹ יִשְׂרָאֵל בְּאַהֲבָה.

Enlighten us with Your Teaching, help us to hold fast to Your Mitzvot, and unite our hearts to love and revere Your name.

Then shall we never be shamed, for we shall put our trust in You, the great, holy, and awesome One. We shall rejoice and be glad in Your salvation, for You, O God, are the Author of many deliverances. In love You have chosen us and drawn us near to You to serve You in faithfulness and to proclaim Your unity.

Blessed is the Lord, who in love has chosen His people Israel to serve Him.

◆ ◆

שְׁמַע יִשְׂרָאֵל: יְיָ אֱלֹהֵינוּ, יְיָ אֶחָד!

Hear, O Israel: the Lord is our God, the Lord is One!

בָּרוּךְ שֵׁם כְּבוֹד מַלְכוּתוֹ לְעוֹלָם וָעֶד!

Blessed is His glorious kingdom for ever and ever!

All are seated

וְאָהַבְתָּ אֵת יְיָ אֱלֹהֶיךָ בְּכָל־לְבָבְךָ וּבְכָל־נַפְשְׁךָ וּבְכָל־מְאֹדֶךָ.
וְהָיוּ הַדְּבָרִים הָאֵלֶּה, אֲשֶׁר אָנֹכִי מְצַוְּךָ הַיּוֹם, עַל־לְבָבֶךָ.
וְשִׁנַּנְתָּם לְבָנֶיךָ, וְדִבַּרְתָּ בָּם בְּשִׁבְתְּךָ בְּבֵיתֶךָ, וּבְלֶכְתְּךָ
בַדֶּרֶךְ, וּבְשָׁכְבְּךָ וּבְקוּמֶךָ.

You shall love the Lord your God with all your mind, with all your strength, with all your being.
Set these words, which I command you this day, upon your heart. Teach them faithfully to your children; speak of them in your home and on your way, when you lie down and when you rise up.

וּקְשַׁרְתָּם לְאוֹת עַל־יָדֶךָ, וְהָיוּ לְטֹטָפֹת בֵּין עֵינֶיךָ, וּכְתַבְתָּם
עַל־מְזֻזוֹת בֵּיתֶךָ, וּבִשְׁעָרֶיךָ.

Bind them as a sign upon your hand; let them be a symbol before your eyes; inscribe them on the doorposts of your house, and on your gates.

לְמַעַן תִּזְכְּרוּ וַעֲשִׂיתֶם אֶת־כָּל־מִצְוֹתָי, וִהְיִיתֶם קְדֹשִׁים
לֵאלֹהֵיכֶם. אֲנִי יְיָ אֱלֹהֵיכֶם, אֲשֶׁר הוֹצֵאתִי אֶתְכֶם מֵאֶרֶץ
מִצְרַיִם לִהְיוֹת לָכֶם לֵאלֹהִים. אֲנִי יְיָ אֱלֹהֵיכֶם.

Be mindful of all My Mitzvot, and do them: so shall you consecrate yourselves to your God. I, the Lord, am your God who led you out of Egypt to be your God; I, the Lord, am your God.

◆ ◆

REDEMPTION גאולה

אֱמֶת וְיַצִּיב, וְאָהוּב וְחָבִיב, וְנוֹרָא וְאַדִּיר, וְטוֹב וְיָפֶה הַדָּבָר הַזֶּה עָלֵינוּ לְעוֹלָם וָעֶד.
אֱמֶת, אֱלֹהֵי עוֹלָם מַלְכֵּנוּ, צוּר יַעֲקֹב מָגֵן יִשְׁעֵנוּ.

True and enduring, beloved and precious, awesome, good, and beautiful is this eternal teaching.
This truth we hold to be for ever certain: the Eternal God is our King. He is the Rock of Jacob, our protecting Shield.

לְדֹר וָדֹר הוּא קַיָּם, וּשְׁמוֹ קַיָּם, וְכִסְאוֹ נָכוֹן, וּמַלְכוּתוֹ וֶאֱמוּנָתוֹ לָעַד קַיֶּמֶת. וּדְבָרָיו חָיִים וְקַיָּמִים, נֶאֱמָנִים וְנֶחֱמָדִים, לָעַד וּלְעוֹלְמֵי עוֹלָמִים.

He abides through all generations; His name is Eternal. His throne stands firm; His sovereignty and faithfulness are everlasting.
His words live and endure, true and precious to all eternity.

מִמִּצְרַיִם גְּאַלְתָּנוּ, יְיָ אֱלֹהֵינוּ, וּמִבֵּית עֲבָדִים פְּדִיתָנוּ.

Lord our God, You redeemed us from Egypt;
You set us free from the house of bondage.

עַל־זֹאת שִׁבְּחוּ אֲהוּבִים וְרוֹמְמוּ אֵל, וְנָתְנוּ יְדִידִים זְמִירוֹת, שִׁירוֹת וְתִשְׁבָּחוֹת, בְּרָכוֹת וְהוֹדָאוֹת לַמֶּלֶךְ, אֵל חַי וְקַיָּם.

For this the people who felt Your love sang songs of praise to You:
The living God, high and exalted, mighty and awesome,

רָם וְנִשָּׂא, גָּדוֹל וְנוֹרָא, מַשְׁפִּיל גֵּאִים וּמַגְבִּיהַּ שְׁפָלִים, מוֹצִיא אֲסִירִים וּפוֹדֶה עֲנָוִים, וְעוֹזֵר דַּלִּים, וְעוֹנֶה לְעַמּוֹ בְּעֵת שַׁוְּעָם אֵלָיו.

Who humbles the proud and raises the lowly, who frees the captive and redeems the oppressed,
who is the Answer to all who cry out to Him.

תְּהִלּוֹת לְאֵל עֶלְיוֹן, בָּרוּךְ הוּא וּמְבֹרָךְ. מֹשֶׁה וּבְנֵי יִשְׂרָאֵל לְךָ עָנוּ שִׁירָה בְּשִׂמְחָה רַבָּה, וְאָמְרוּ כֻלָּם:

All praise to God Most High, the Source of blessing! Like Moses and Israel, we sing to Him this song of rejoicing:

מִי־כָמֹכָה בָּאֵלִם, יְיָ?

Who is like You, Eternal One, among the gods that are worshipped?

מִי כָּמֹכָה, נֶאְדָּר בַּקֹּדֶשׁ,

Who is like You, majestic in holiness,

נוֹרָא תְהִלֹּת, עֹשֵׂה פֶלֶא?

awesome in splendor, doing wonders?

שִׁירָה חֲדָשָׁה שִׁבְּחוּ גְאוּלִים לְשִׁמְךָ עַל־שְׂפַת הַיָּם; יַחַד כֻּלָּם הוֹדוּ וְהִמְלִיכוּ וְאָמְרוּ: "יְיָ יִמְלֹךְ לְעוֹלָם וָעֶד!"

A new song the redeemed sang to Your name. At the shore of the Sea, saved from destruction, they proclaimed Your sovereign power: "The Eternal will reign for ever and ever!"

צוּר יִשְׂרָאֵל, קוּמָה בְּעֶזְרַת יִשְׂרָאֵל, וּפְדֵה כִנְאֻמֶךָ יְהוּדָה וְיִשְׂרָאֵל. גֹּאֲלֵנוּ, יְיָ צְבָאוֹת שְׁמוֹ, קְדוֹשׁ יִשְׂרָאֵל.

בָּרוּךְ אַתָּה, יְיָ, גָּאַל יִשְׂרָאֵל.

O Rock of Israel, come to Israel's help. Fulfill Your promise of redemption for Judah and Israel. Our Redeemer is the Lord of Hosts, the Holy One of Israel. Blessed is the Lord, the Redeemer of Israel.

◆ ◆

All rise

תפלה

אֲדֹנָי, שְׂפָתַי תִּפְתָּח, וּפִי יַגִּיד תְּהִלָּתֶךָ.

Eternal God, open my lips, that my mouth may declare Your glory.

GOD OF ALL GENERATIONS — אבות

בָּרוּךְ אַתָּה, יְיָ אֱלֹהֵינוּ וֵאלֹהֵי אֲבוֹתֵינוּ, אֱלֹהֵי אַבְרָהָם, אֱלֹהֵי יִצְחָק, וֵאלֹהֵי יַעֲקֹב: הָאֵל הַגָּדוֹל, הַגִּבּוֹר וְהַנּוֹרָא, אֵל עֶלְיוֹן.

We praise You, Lord our God and God of all generations: God of Abraham, God of Isaac, God of Jacob; great, mighty, and awesome God, God supreme.

גּוֹמֵל חֲסָדִים טוֹבִים, וְקוֹנֵה הַכֹּל, וְזוֹכֵר חַסְדֵי אָבוֹת, וּמֵבִיא גְאֻלָּה לִבְנֵי בְנֵיהֶם, לְמַעַן שְׁמוֹ, בְּאַהֲבָה.*

Master of all the living, Your ways are ways of love. You remember the faithfulness of our ancestors, and in love bring redemption to their children's children for the sake of Your name.*

מֶלֶךְ עוֹזֵר וּמוֹשִׁיעַ וּמָגֵן. בָּרוּךְ אַתָּה, יְיָ, מָגֵן אַבְרָהָם.

You are our King and our Help, our Savior and our Shield. Blessed is the Lord, the Shield of Abraham.

* *On the Ten Days of Repentance insert:*

זָכְרֵנוּ לְחַיִּים, מֶלֶךְ חָפֵץ בַּחַיִּים,
וְכָתְבֵנוּ בְּסֵפֶר הַחַיִּים, לְמַעַנְךָ אֱלֹהִים חַיִּים.

Remember us unto life, for You are the King who delights in life, and inscribe us in the Book of Life, that Your will may prevail, O God of life.

◆ ◆

GOD'S POWER — גבורות

אַתָּה גִּבּוֹר לְעוֹלָם, אֲדֹנָי, מְחַיֵּה הַכֹּל אַתָּה, רַב לְהוֹשִׁיעַ.

Eternal is Your might, O Lord; all life is Your gift; great is Your power to save!

מְכַלְכֵּל חַיִּים בְּחֶסֶד, מְחַיֵּה הַכֹּל בְּרַחֲמִים רַבִּים. סוֹמֵךְ נוֹפְלִים, וְרוֹפֵא חוֹלִים, וּמַתִּיר אֲסוּרִים, וּמְקַיֵּם אֱמוּנָתוֹ לִישֵׁנֵי עָפָר.

With love You sustain the living, with great compassion give life to all. You send help to the falling and healing to the sick; You bring freedom to the captive and keep faith with those who sleep in the dust.

מִי כָמוֹךָ, בַּעַל גְּבוּרוֹת, וּמִי דּוֹמֶה לָּךְ, מֶלֶךְ מֵמִית וּמְחַיֶּה וּמַצְמִיחַ יְשׁוּעָה?*

וְנֶאֱמָן אַתָּה לְהַחֲיוֹת הַכֹּל. בָּרוּךְ אַתָּה, יְיָ, מְחַיֵּה הַכֹּל.

Who is like You, Master of Might? Who is Your equal, O Lord of life and death, Source of salvation? Blessed is the Lord, the Source of life.*

**On the Ten Days of Repentance insert:*

מִי כָמוֹךָ, אַב הָרַחֲמִים, זוֹכֵר יְצוּרָיו לְחַיִּים בְּרַחֲמִים?

Who is like You, Source of mercy, who in compassion sustains the life of His children?

◆ ◆

SANCTIFICATION קדושה

נְקַדֵּשׁ אֶת־שִׁמְךָ בָּעוֹלָם, כְּשֵׁם שֶׁמַּקְדִּישִׁים אוֹתוֹ בִּשְׁמֵי מָרוֹם, כַּכָּתוּב עַל־יַד נְבִיאֶךָ: וְקָרָא זֶה אֶל־זֶה וְאָמַר:

We sanctify Your name on earth, even as all things, to the ends of time and space, proclaim Your holiness; and in the words of the prophet we say:

קָדוֹשׁ, קָדוֹשׁ, קָדוֹשׁ יְיָ צְבָאוֹת, מְלֹא כָל־הָאָרֶץ כְּבוֹדוֹ.

Holy, Holy, Holy is the Lord of Hosts; the fullness of the whole earth is His glory!

לְעֻמָּתָם בָּרוּךְ יֹאמֵרוּ:

They respond to Your glory with blessing:

בָּרוּךְ כְּבוֹד יְיָ מִמְּקוֹמוֹ.

Blessed is the glory of God in heaven and earth.

וּבְדִבְרֵי קָדְשְׁךָ כָּתוּב לֵאמֹר:

And this is Your sacred word:

יִמְלֹךְ יְיָ לְעוֹלָם, אֱלֹהַיִךְ צִיּוֹן, לְדֹר וָדֹר, הַלְלוּיָהּ.

The Lord shall reign for ever; your God, O Zion, from generation to generation. Halleluyah!

לְדוֹר וָדוֹר נַגִּיד גָּדְלֶךָ, וּלְנֵצַח נְצָחִים קְדֻשָּׁתְךָ נַקְדִּישׁ. וְשִׁבְחֲךָ, אֱלֹהֵינוּ, מִפִּינוּ לֹא יָמוּשׁ לְעוֹלָם וָעֶד.*

בָּרוּךְ אַתָּה, יְיָ, הָאֵל הַקָּדוֹשׁ.

To all generations we will make known Your greatness, and to all eternity proclaim Your holiness. Your praise, O God, shall never depart from our lips.*

Blessed is the Lord, the holy God.

** On the Ten Days of Repentance conclude:*

Blessed is the Lord, the holy King. בָּרוּךְ אַתָּה, יְיָ, הַמֶּלֶךְ הַקָּדוֹשׁ.

All are seated

◆ ◆

FOR UNDERSTANDING בינה

אַתָּה חוֹנֵן לְאָדָם דַּעַת וּמְלַמֵּד לֶאֱנוֹשׁ בִּינָה. חָנֵּנוּ מֵאִתְּךָ דֵּעָה, בִּינָה וְהַשְׂכֵּל.

בָּרוּךְ אַתָּה, יְיָ, חוֹנֵן הַדָּעַת.

You favor us with knowledge and teach mortals understanding. May You continue to favor us with knowledge, understanding, and insight.

Blessed is the Lord, gracious Giver of knowledge.

◆ ◆

FOR REPENTANCE תשובה

הֲשִׁיבֵנוּ אָבִינוּ לְתוֹרָתֶךָ, וְקָרְבֵנוּ מַלְכֵּנוּ לַעֲבוֹדָתֶךָ, וְהַחֲזִירֵנוּ בִּתְשׁוּבָה שְׁלֵמָה לְפָנֶיךָ.

בָּרוּךְ אַתָּה, יְיָ, הָרוֹצֶה בִּתְשׁוּבָה.

Help us to return, our Maker, to Your Torah; draw us near, O Sovereign God, to Your service; and bring us back into Your presence in perfect repentance.

Blessed is the Lord, who calls for repentance.

◆ ◆

FOR FORGIVENESS סליחה

סְלַח־לָנוּ אָבִינוּ כִּי חָטָאנוּ, מְחַל־לָנוּ מַלְכֵּנוּ כִּי פָשָׁעְנוּ, כִּי מוֹחֵל וְסוֹלֵחַ אָתָּה.

בָּרוּךְ אַתָּה, יְיָ, חַנּוּן הַמַּרְבֶּה לִסְלוֹחַ.

Forgive us, our Creator, when we have sinned; pardon us, our King, when we transgress; for You are a forgiving God.

Blessed is the Lord, the gracious God, whose forgiveness is abundant.

◆ ◆

FOR REDEMPTION גאולה

רְאֵה בְעָנְיֵנוּ וְרִיבָה רִיבֵנוּ, וּגְאָלֵנוּ מְהֵרָה לְמַעַן שְׁמֶךָ, כִּי גוֹאֵל חָזָק אָתָּה.

בָּרוּךְ אַתָּה, יְיָ, גּוֹאֵל יִשְׂרָאֵל.

Look upon our affliction and help us in our need; O mighty Redeemer, redeem us speedily for Your name's sake.

Blessed is the Lord, the Redeemer of Israel.

◆ ◆

FOR HEALTH רפואה

רְפָאֵנוּ יְיָ וְנֵרָפֵא, הוֹשִׁיעֵנוּ וְנִוָּשֵׁעָה, וְהַעֲלֵה רְפוּאָה שְׁלֵמָה לְכָל־מַכּוֹתֵינוּ.

בָּרוּךְ אַתָּה, יְיָ, רוֹפֵא הַחוֹלִים.

Heal us, O Lord, and we shall be healed; save us, and we shall be saved; grant us a perfect healing from all our wounds.

Blessed is the Lord, the Healer of the sick.

◆ ◆

FOR ABUNDANCE — ברכת השנים

בָּרֵךְ עָלֵינוּ, יְיָ אֱלֹהֵינוּ, אֶת־הַשָּׁנָה הַזֹּאת וְאֶת־כָּל־מִינֵי תְבוּאָתָהּ לְטוֹבָה. וְתֵן בְּרָכָה עַל־פְּנֵי הָאֲדָמָה, וְשַׂבְּעֵנוּ מִטּוּבֶךָ.

בָּרוּךְ אַתָּה, יְיָ, מְבָרֵךְ הַשָּׁנִים.

Bless this year, O Lord our God, and let its produce bring us well-being. Bestow Your blessing on the earth and satisfy us with Your goodness.

Blessed is the Lord, from whom all blessings flow.

◆ ◆

FOR FREEDOM — חרות

תְּקַע בְּשׁוֹפָר גָּדוֹל לְחֵרוּתֵנוּ, וְשָׂא נֵס לִפְדּוֹת עֲשׁוּקֵינוּ, וְקוֹל דְּרוֹר יִשָּׁמַע בְּאַרְבַּע כַּנְפוֹת הָאָרֶץ.

בָּרוּךְ אַתָּה, יְיָ, פּוֹדֶה עֲשׁוּקִים.

Sound the great horn to proclaim freedom, inspire us to strive for the liberation of the oppressed, and let the song of liberty be heard in the four corners of the earth.

Blessed is the Lord, Redeemer of the oppressed.

◆ ◆

FOR JUSTICE — משפט

עַל שׁוֹפְטֵי אֶרֶץ שְׁפוֹךְ רוּחֶךָ, וְהַדְרִיכֵם בְּמִשְׁפְּטֵי צִדְקֶךָ, וּמְלוֹךְ עָלֵינוּ אַתָּה לְבַדֶּךָ, בְּחֶסֶד וּבְרַחֲמִים!

בָּרוּךְ אַתָּה, יְיָ, מֶלֶךְ אוֹהֵב צְדָקָה וּמִשְׁפָּט.

Pour Your spirit upon the rulers of all lands; guide them, that they may govern justly. O may You alone reign over us in steadfast love and compassion!

Blessed is the Sovereign Lord, who loves righteousness and justice.

◆ ◆

FOR RIGHTEOUSNESS צדיקים

עַל־הַצַּדִּיקִים וְעַל־הַחֲסִידִים וְעָלֵינוּ יֶהֱמוּ רַחֲמֶיךָ, יְיָ אֱלֹהֵינוּ, וְתֵן שָׂכָר טוֹב לְכֹל הַבּוֹטְחִים בְּשִׁמְךָ בֶּאֱמֶת, וְשִׂים חֶלְקֵנוּ עִמָּהֶם לְעוֹלָם.

בָּרוּךְ אַתָּה, יְיָ, מִשְׁעָן וּמִבְטָח לַצַּדִּיקִים.

Have mercy, O Lord our God, upon the righteous and faithful of all peoples, and upon all of us. Uphold all who faithfully put their trust in You, and grant that we may always be numbered among them.

Blessed is the Lord, the Staff and Support of the righteous.

◆ ◆

FOR JERUSALEM שלום ירושלים

וְלִירוּשָׁלַיִם עִירְךָ בְּרַחֲמִים תִּפְנֶה, וִיהִי שָׁלוֹם בִּשְׁעָרֶיהָ, וְשַׁלְוָה בְּלֵב יוֹשְׁבֶיהָ, וְתוֹרָתְךָ מִצִּיּוֹן תֵּצֵא וּדְבָרְךָ מִירוּשָׁלָיִם.

בָּרוּךְ אַתָּה, יְיָ, נוֹתֵן שָׁלוֹם בִּירוּשָׁלָיִם.

And turn in compassion to Jerusalem, Your city. Let there be peace in her gates, quietness in the hearts of her inhabitants. Let Your Torah go forth from Zion and Your word from Jerusalem.

Blessed is the Lord, who gives peace to Jerusalem.

◆ ◆

FOR DELIVERANCE ישועה

אֶת־צֶמַח צְדָקָה מְהֵרָה תַצְמִיחַ, וְקֶרֶן יְשׁוּעָה תָּרוּם כִּנְאֻמֶךָ, כִּי לִישׁוּעָתְךָ קִוִּינוּ כָּל־הַיּוֹם.

בָּרוּךְ אַתָּה, יְיָ, מַצְמִיחַ קֶרֶן יְשׁוּעָה.

Cause the plant of justice to spring up soon. Let the light of deliverance shine forth according to Your word, for we await Your deliverance all the day.

Blessed is the Lord, who will cause the light of deliverance to dawn for all the world.

◆ ◆

FOR ACCEPTANCE OF PRAYER — שומע תפלה

שְׁמַע קוֹלֵנוּ, יְיָ אֱלֹהֵינוּ, חוּס וְרַחֵם עָלֵינוּ, וְקַבֵּל בְּרַחֲמִים
וּבְרָצוֹן אֶת תְּפִלָּתֵנוּ, כִּי אֵל שׁוֹמֵעַ תְּפִלּוֹת וְתַחֲנוּנִים אָתָּה.
בָּרוּךְ אַתָּה, יְיָ, שׁוֹמֵעַ תְּפִלָּה.

Hear our voice, O Lord our God; have compassion upon us, and accept our prayer with favor and mercy, for You are a God who hears prayer and supplication.

Blessed is the Lord, who hearkens to prayer.

◆ ◆

WORSHIP — עבודה

רְצֵה, יְיָ אֱלֹהֵינוּ, בְּעַמְּךָ יִשְׂרָאֵל, וּתְפִלָּתָם בְּאַהֲבָה תְקַבֵּל,
וּתְהִי לְרָצוֹן תָּמִיד עֲבוֹדַת יִשְׂרָאֵל עַמֶּךָ.
אֵל קָרוֹב לְכָל־קֹרְאָיו, פְּנֵה אֶל עֲבָדֶיךָ וְחָנֵּנוּ; שְׁפוֹךְ רוּחֲךָ
עָלֵינוּ, וְתֶחֱזֶינָה עֵינֵינוּ בְּשׁוּבְךָ לְצִיּוֹן בְּרַחֲמִים.
בָּרוּךְ אַתָּה, יְיָ, הַמַּחֲזִיר שְׁכִינָתוֹ לְצִיּוֹן.

Be gracious, O Lord our God, to Your people Israel, and receive our prayers with love. O may our worship always be acceptable to You.
Fill us with the knowledge that You are near to all who seek You in truth. Let our eyes behold Your presence in our midst and in the midst of our people in Zion.

Blessed is the Lord, whose presence gives life to Zion and all Israel.

◆ ◆

ON ROSH CHODESH, CHOL HAMO-EID, AND YOM HA-ATSMA-UT

אֱלֹהֵינוּ וֵאלֹהֵי אֲבוֹתֵינוּ, יַעֲלֶה וְיָבֹא וְיִזָּכֵר זִכְרוֹנֵנוּ וְזִכְרוֹן כָּל־עַמְּךָ בֵּית יִשְׂרָאֵל לְפָנֶיךָ, לְטוֹבָה לְחֵן לְחֶסֶד וּלְרַחֲמִים, לְחַיִּים וּלְשָׁלוֹם בְּיוֹם

Our God and God of all ages, be mindful of Your people Israel on this

first day of the new month,	רֹאשׁ הַחֹדֶשׁ הַזֶּה.
day of Pesach,	חַג הַמַּצּוֹת הַזֶּה.
day of Sukkot,	חַג הַסֻּכּוֹת הַזֶּה.
day of Independence,	הָעַצְמָאוּת הַזֶּה.

and renew in us love and compassion, goodness, life and peace.

This day remember us for well-being. *Amen.*	זָכְרֵנוּ, יְיָ אֱלֹהֵינוּ, בּוֹ לְטוֹבָה. אָמֵן.
This day bless us with Your nearness. *Amen.*	וּפָקְדֵנוּ בוֹ לִבְרָכָה. אָמֵן.
This day help us to a fuller life. *Amen.*	וְהוֹשִׁיעֵנוּ בוֹ לְחַיִּים. אָמֵן.

◆ ◆

THANKSGIVING — הודאה

מוֹדִים אֲנַחְנוּ לָךְ, שָׁאַתָּה הוּא יְיָ אֱלֹהֵינוּ וֵאלֹהֵי אֲבוֹתֵינוּ לְעוֹלָם וָעֶד. צוּר חַיֵּינוּ, מָגֵן יִשְׁעֵנוּ, אַתָּה הוּא לְדוֹר וָדוֹר. נוֹדֶה לְךָ וּנְסַפֵּר תְּהִלָּתֶךָ, עַל־חַיֵּינוּ הַמְּסוּרִים בְּיָדֶךָ, וְעַל־נִשְׁמוֹתֵינוּ הַפְּקוּדוֹת לָךְ, וְעַל־נִסֶּיךָ שֶׁבְּכָל־יוֹם עִמָּנוּ, וְעַל־נִפְלְאוֹתֶיךָ וְטוֹבוֹתֶיךָ שֶׁבְּכָל־עֵת, עֶרֶב וָבֹקֶר וְצָהֳרָיִם. הַטּוֹב: כִּי לֹא־כָלוּ רַחֲמֶיךָ, וְהַמְרַחֵם: כִּי־לֹא תַמּוּ חֲסָדֶיךָ, מֵעוֹלָם קִוִּינוּ לָךְ.

We gratefully acknowledge that You are the Lord our God and God of our people, the God of all generations. You are the Rock of our life, the Power that shields us in every age. We thank You and sing Your praises: for our lives, which are in Your hand; for our souls, which are in Your keeping; for the signs of Your presence we encounter every day; and for

Your wondrous gifts at all times, morning, noon, and night. You are Goodness: Your mercies never end; You are Compassion: Your love will never fail. You have always been our hope.

וְעַל כֻּלָּם יִתְבָּרַךְ וְיִתְרוֹמַם שִׁמְךָ, מַלְכֵּנוּ, תָּמִיד לְעוֹלָם וָעֶד.

For all these things, O Sovereign God, let Your name be for ever exalted and blessed.

On the Ten Days of Repentance insert:

וּכְתוֹב לְחַיִּים טוֹבִים כָּל־בְּנֵי בְרִיתֶךָ.

Let life abundant be the heritage of all Your children.

וְכֹל הַחַיִּים יוֹדוּךָ סֶּלָה, וִיהַלְלוּ אֶת שִׁמְךָ בֶּאֱמֶת, הָאֵל יְשׁוּעָתֵנוּ וְעֶזְרָתֵנוּ סֶלָה. בָּרוּךְ אַתָּה, יְיָ, הַטּוֹב שִׁמְךָ, וּלְךָ נָאֶה לְהוֹדוֹת.

O God our Redeemer and Helper, let all who live affirm You and praise Your name in truth. Lord, whose nature is Goodness, we give You thanks and praise.

◆ ◆

ON CHANUKAH

עַל הַנִּסִּים וְעַל הַפֻּרְקָן, וְעַל הַגְּבוּרוֹת וְעַל הַתְּשׁוּעוֹת, וְעַל הַמִּלְחָמוֹת, שֶׁעָשִׂיתָ לַאֲבוֹתֵינוּ בַּיָּמִים הָהֵם בַּזְּמַן הַזֶּה.

בִּימֵי מַתִּתְיָהוּ בֶּן־יוֹחָנָן כֹּהֵן גָּדוֹל, חַשְׁמוֹנַי וּבָנָיו, כְּשֶׁעָמְדָה מַלְכוּת יָוָן הָרְשָׁעָה עַל־עַמְּךָ יִשְׂרָאֵל לְהַשְׁכִּיחָם תּוֹרָתֶךָ, וּלְהַעֲבִירָם מֵחֻקֵּי רְצוֹנֶךָ.

וְאַתָּה בְּרַחֲמֶיךָ הָרַבִּים עָמַדְתָּ לָהֶם בְּעֵת צָרָתָם. רַבְתָּ אֶת־רִיבָם, דַּנְתָּ אֶת־דִּינָם, מָסַרְתָּ גִבּוֹרִים בְּיַד חַלָּשִׁים, וְרַבִּים בְּיַד מְעַטִּים, וּטְמֵאִים בְּיַד טְהוֹרִים, וּרְשָׁעִים בְּיַד צַדִּיקִים, וְזֵדִים בְּיַד עוֹסְקֵי תוֹרָתֶךָ.

וּלְךָ עָשִׂיתָ שֵׁם גָּדוֹל וְקָדוֹשׁ בְּעוֹלָמֶךָ, וּלְעַמְּךָ יִשְׂרָאֵל עָשִׂיתָ תְּשׁוּעָה גְדוֹלָה וּפֻרְקָן כְּהַיּוֹם הַזֶּה.

וְאַחַר כֵּן בָּאוּ בָנֶיךָ לִדְבִיר בֵּיתֶךָ, וּפִנּוּ אֶת־הֵיכָלֶךָ, וְטִהֲרוּ אֶת־מִקְדָּשֶׁךָ, וְהִדְלִיקוּ נֵרוֹת בְּחַצְרוֹת קָדְשֶׁךָ, וְקָבְעוּ שְׁמוֹנַת יְמֵי חֲנֻכָּה אֵלּוּ לְהוֹדוֹת וּלְהַלֵּל לְשִׁמְךָ הַגָּדוֹל.

We give thanks for the redeeming wonders and the mighty deeds by which, at this season, our people was saved in days of old.

In the days of the Hasmoneans, a tyrant arose against our ancestors, determined to make them forget Your Torah, and to turn them away from obedience to Your will. But You were at their side in time of trouble. You gave them strength to struggle and to triumph, that they might serve You in freedom.

Through the power of Your spirit the weak defeated the strong, the few prevailed over the many, and the righteous were triumphant.

Then Your children returned to Your house, to purify the sanctuary and kindle its lights. And they dedicated these days to give thanks and praise to Your great name.

◆ ◆

ON PURIM

עַל הַנִּסִּים וְעַל הַפֻּרְקָן, וְעַל הַגְּבוּרוֹת וְעַל הַתְּשׁוּעוֹת, וְעַל הַמִּלְחָמוֹת, שֶׁעָשִׂיתָ לַאֲבוֹתֵינוּ בַּיָּמִים הָהֵם בַּזְּמַן הַזֶּה.

בִּימֵי מָרְדְּכַי וְאֶסְתֵּר בְּשׁוּשַׁן הַבִּירָה, כְּשֶׁעָמַד עֲלֵיהֶם הָמָן הָרָשָׁע, בִּקֵּשׁ לְהַשְׁמִיד לַהֲרוֹג וּלְאַבֵּד אֶת־כָּל־הַיְּהוּדִים, מִנַּעַר וְעַד־זָקֵן, טַף וְנָשִׁים, בְּיוֹם אֶחָד, בִּשְׁלוֹשָׁה עָשָׂר לְחֹדֶשׁ שְׁנֵים־עָשָׂר, הוּא־חֹדֶשׁ אֲדָר, וּשְׁלָלָם לָבוֹז.

וְאַתָּה בְּרַחֲמֶיךָ הָרַבִּים הֵפַרְתָּ אֶת־עֲצָתוֹ, וְקִלְקַלְתָּ אֶת־מַחֲשַׁבְתּוֹ.

We give thanks for the redeeming wonders and the mighty deeds by which, at this season, our people was saved in days of old.

In the days of Mordecai and Esther, the wicked Haman arose in Persia, plotting the destruction of all the Jews. He planned to destroy them in a single day, the thirteenth of Adar, and to permit the plunder of their possessions.

But through Your great mercy his plan was thwarted, his scheme frustrated. We therefore thank and bless You, O great and gracious God!

◆ ◆

PEACE **ברכת שלום**

שִׂים שָׁלוֹם, טוֹבָה וּבְרָכָה, חֵן וָחֶסֶד וְרַחֲמִים, עָלֵינוּ וְעַל־כָּל־יִשְׂרָאֵל עַמֶּךָ.

Peace, happiness, and blessing; grace and love and mercy: may these descend on us, on all Israel, and all the world.

בָּרְכֵנוּ אָבִינוּ, כֻּלָּנוּ כְּאֶחָד, בְּאוֹר פָּנֶיךָ, כִּי בְאוֹר פָּנֶיךָ נָתַתָּ לָּנוּ, יְיָ אֱלֹהֵינוּ, תּוֹרַת חַיִּים, וְאַהֲבַת חֶסֶד, וּצְדָקָה וּבְרָכָה וְרַחֲמִים, וְחַיִּים וְשָׁלוֹם.

Bless us, our Creator, one and all, with the light of Your presence; for by that light, O God, You have revealed to us the law of life: to love kindness and justice and mercy, to seek blessing, life, and peace.

וְטוֹב בְּעֵינֶיךָ לְבָרֵךְ אֶת־עַמְּךָ יִשְׂרָאֵל בְּכָל־עֵת וּבְכָל־שָׁעָה בִּשְׁלוֹמֶךָ.*

בָּרוּךְ אַתָּה, יְיָ, הַמְבָרֵךְ אֶת־עַמּוֹ יִשְׂרָאֵל בַּשָּׁלוֹם.

O bless Your people Israel and all peoples with enduring peace!*

Praised be the Lord, who blesses His people Israel with peace.

On the Ten Days of Repentance conclude:

בְּסֵפֶר חַיִּים וּבְרָכָה נִכָּתֵב לְחַיִּים טוֹבִים וּלְשָׁלוֹם.

בָּרוּךְ אַתָּה, יְיָ, עוֹשֵׂה הַשָּׁלוֹם.

Teach us then to find our happiness in the search for righteousness and peace. Blessed is the Lord, the Source of peace.

◆ ◆

SILENT PRAYER

אֱלֹהַי, נְצֹר לְשׁוֹנִי מֵרָע, וּשְׂפָתַי מִדַּבֵּר מִרְמָה, וְלִמְקַלְלַי נַפְשִׁי תִדּוֹם, וְנַפְשִׁי כֶּעָפָר לַכֹּל תִּהְיֶה. פְּתַח לִבִּי בְּתוֹרָתֶךָ, וּבְמִצְוֹתֶיךָ תִּרְדּוֹף נַפְשִׁי, וְכֹל הַחוֹשְׁבִים עָלַי רָעָה, מְהֵרָה

הָפֵר עֲצָתָם וְקַלְקֵל מַחֲשַׁבְתָּם. עֲשֵׂה לְמַעַן שְׁמֶךָ, עֲשֵׂה לְמַעַן יְמִינֶךָ, עֲשֵׂה לְמַעַן קְדֻשָּׁתֶךָ, עֲשֵׂה לְמַעַן תּוֹרָתֶךָ. לְמַעַן יֵחָלְצוּן יְדִידֶיךָ. הוֹשִׁיעָה יְמִינְךָ וַעֲנֵנִי.

O God, keep my tongue from evil and my lips from deceit. Help me to be silent in the face of derision, humble in the presence of all. Open my heart to Your Torah, and I will hasten to do Your Mitzvot. Save me with Your power; in time of trouble be my answer, that those who love You may rejoice.

◆ ◆

יִהְיוּ לְרָצוֹן אִמְרֵי־פִי וְהֶגְיוֹן לִבִּי לְפָנֶיךָ, יְיָ, צוּרִי וְגוֹאֲלִי.

May the words of my mouth, and the meditations of my heart, be acceptable to You, O Lord, my Rock and my Redeemer.

or

עֹשֶׂה שָׁלוֹם בִּמְרוֹמָיו, הוּא יַעֲשֶׂה שָׁלוֹם עָלֵינוּ וְעַל כָּל־יִשְׂרָאֵל, וְאִמְרוּ אָמֵן.

May He who causes peace to reign in the high heavens let peace descend on us, on all Israel, and all the world.

◆ ◆

For Rosh Chodesh, Chol Hamo-eid, Chanukah, and Purim, a short form of Hallel is on page 487.

For Yom Ha-atsma-ut, continue with Hallel (page 487), Supplementary reading (pages 605–611), the Reading of the Torah (page 531), and Concluding Prayers.

Prayers at a House of Mourning begin on page 645.

The Ritual for the Reading of Torah begins on page 415.

Concluding Prayers begin on page 613.

וְעַתָּה, יִשְׂרָאֵל, מָה יְיָ אֱלֹהֶיךָ שֹׁאֵל מֵעִמָּךְ?

And now, O Israel, what is it that the Lord your God demands of you?

כִּי אִם־לְיִרְאָה אֶת־יְיָ אֱלֹהֶיךָ, לָלֶכֶת בְּכָל־דְּרָכָיו, וּלְאַהֲבָה אֹתוֹ וְלַעֲבֹד אֶת־יְיָ אֱלֹהֶיךָ בְּכָל־לְבָבְךָ וּבְכָל־נַפְשֶׁךָ.

To revere the Lord our God, to walk always in His ways, to love and serve Him with heart and soul.

וְעַתָּה אִם־שָׁמוֹעַ תִּשְׁמְעוּ בְּקֹלִי וּשְׁמַרְתֶּם אֶת־בְּרִיתִי, וְאַתֶּם תִּהְיוּ־לִי מַמְלֶכֶת כֹּהֲנִים, וְגוֹי קָדוֹשׁ.

Now therefore if you will truly keep My covenant, you shall be to Me a kingdom of priests, a holy people:

לִפְקֹחַ עֵינַיִם עִוְרוֹת, לְהוֹצִיא מִמַּסְגֵּר אַסִּיר, מִבֵּית כֶּלֶא יֹשְׁבֵי חֹשֶׁךְ.

To open blind eyes, to bring out of prison the captive, and from their dungeons those who sit in darkness.

◆ ◆

All rise

שמע וברכותיה

בָּרְכוּ אֶת־יְיָ הַמְבֹרָךְ!

Praise the Lord, to whom our praise is due!

בָּרוּךְ יְיָ הַמְבֹרָךְ לְעוֹלָם וָעֶד!

Praised be the Lord, to whom our praise is due, now and for ever!

◆ ◆

Morning

בָּרוּךְ אַתָּה, יְיָ אֱלֹהֵינוּ, מֶלֶךְ הָעוֹלָם, יוֹצֵר אוֹר וּבוֹרֵא חֹשֶׁךְ, עֹשֶׂה שָׁלוֹם וּבוֹרֵא אֶת־הַכֹּל.

הַמֵּאִיר לָאָרֶץ וְלַדָּרִים עָלֶיהָ בְּרַחֲמִים, וּבְטוּבוֹ מְחַדֵּשׁ בְּכָל־יוֹם תָּמִיד מַעֲשֵׂה בְרֵאשִׁית.

מָה רַבּוּ מַעֲשֶׂיךָ, יְיָ! כֻּלָּם בְּחָכְמָה עָשִׂיתָ, מָלְאָה הָאָרֶץ קִנְיָנֶךָ.

תִּתְבָּרַךְ, יְיָ אֱלֹהֵינוּ, עַל־שֶׁבַח מַעֲשֵׂה יָדֶיךָ, וְעַל־מְאוֹרֵי־אוֹר שֶׁעָשִׂיתָ: יְפָאֲרוּךָ. סֶּלָה.

בָּרוּךְ אַתָּה, יְיָ, יוֹצֵר הַמְּאוֹרוֹת.

Evening

בָּרוּךְ אַתָּה, יְיָ אֱלֹהֵינוּ, מֶלֶךְ הָעוֹלָם, אֲשֶׁר בִּדְבָרוֹ מַעֲרִיב עֲרָבִים. בְּחָכְמָה פּוֹתֵחַ שְׁעָרִים, וּבִתְבוּנָה מְשַׁנֶּה עִתִּים, וּמַחֲלִיף אֶת־הַזְּמַנִּים, וּמְסַדֵּר אֶת־הַכּוֹכָבִים בְּמִשְׁמְרוֹתֵיהֶם בָּרָקִיעַ כִּרְצוֹנוֹ. בּוֹרֵא יוֹם וָלָיְלָה, גּוֹלֵל אוֹר מִפְּנֵי חֹשֶׁךְ וְחֹשֶׁךְ מִפְּנֵי אוֹר, וּמַעֲבִיר יוֹם וּמֵבִיא לָיְלָה, וּמַבְדִּיל בֵּין יוֹם וּבֵין לָיְלָה, יְיָ צְבָאוֹת שְׁמוֹ. אֵל חַי וְקַיָּם, תָּמִיד יִמְלוֹךְ עָלֵינוּ, לְעוֹלָם וָעֶד. בָּרוּךְ אַתָּה, יְיָ, הַמַּעֲרִיב עֲרָבִים.

Eternal God, Your majesty is proclaimed by the marvels of earth and sky. Sun, moon, and stars testify to Your power and wisdom. Day follows day in endless succession, and the years vanish, but Your sovereignty endures. Though all things pass, let not Your glory depart from us. Help us to become co-workers with You, and endow our fleeting days with abiding worth.

◆ ◆

Morning

אַהֲבָה רַבָּה אֲהַבְתָּנוּ, יְיָ אֱלֹהֵינוּ, חֶמְלָה גְדוֹלָה וִיתֵרָה חָמַלְתָּ עָלֵינוּ. אָבִינוּ מַלְכֵּנוּ, בַּעֲבוּר אֲבוֹתֵינוּ שֶׁבָּטְחוּ בְךָ וַתְּלַמְּדֵם חֻקֵּי חַיִּים, כֵּן תְּחָנֵּנוּ וּתְלַמְּדֵנוּ.

Evening

אַהֲבַת עוֹלָם בֵּית יִשְׂרָאֵל עַמְּךָ אָהָבְתָּ: תּוֹרָה וּמִצְוֹת, חֻקִּים וּמִשְׁפָּטִים אוֹתָנוּ לִמַּדְתָּ.

עַל־כֵּן, יְיָ אֱלֹהֵינוּ, בְּשָׁכְבֵנוּ וּבְקוּמֵנוּ נָשִׂיחַ בְּחֻקֶּיךָ, וְנִשְׂמַח

Morning

אָבִינוּ, הָאָב הָרַחֲמָן, הַמְרַחֵם, רַחֵם עָלֵינוּ וְתֵן בְּלִבֵּנוּ לְהָבִין וּלְהַשְׂכִּיל, לִשְׁמֹעַ לִלְמֹד וּלְלַמֵּד, לִשְׁמֹר וְלַעֲשׂוֹת וּלְקַיֵּם אֶת־כָּל־דִּבְרֵי תַלְמוּד תּוֹרָתֶךָ בְּאַהֲבָה. וְהָאֵר עֵינֵינוּ בְּתוֹרָתֶךָ, וְדַבֵּק לִבֵּנוּ בְּמִצְוֹתֶיךָ, וְיַחֵד לְבָבֵנוּ לְאַהֲבָה וּלְיִרְאָה אֶת־

Evening

בְּדִבְרֵי תוֹרָתְךָ וּבְמִצְוֹתֶיךָ לְעוֹלָם וָעֶד.
כִּי הֵם חַיֵּינוּ וְאֹרֶךְ יָמֵינוּ, וּבָהֶם נֶהְגֶּה יוֹמָם וָלָיְלָה. וְאַהֲבָתְךָ אַל־תָּסִיר מִמֶּנּוּ לְעוֹלָמִים!
בָּרוּךְ אַתָּה, יְיָ, אוֹהֵב עַמּוֹ יִשְׂרָאֵל.

שְׁמֶךָ. וְלֹא־נֵבוֹשׁ לְעוֹלָם וָעֶד, כִּי בְשֵׁם קָדְשְׁךָ הַגָּדוֹל וְהַנּוֹרָא בָּטָחְנוּ. נָגִילָה וְנִשְׂמְחָה בִּישׁוּעָתֶךָ, כִּי אֵל פּוֹעֵל יְשׁוּעוֹת אָתָּה, וּבָנוּ בָחַרְתָּ וְקֵרַבְתָּנוּ לְשִׁמְךָ הַגָּדוֹל סֶלָה בֶּאֱמֶת, לְהוֹדוֹת לְךָ וּלְיַחֶדְךָ בְּאַהֲבָה. בָּרוּךְ אַתָּה, יְיָ, הַבּוֹחֵר בְּעַמּוֹ יִשְׂרָאֵל בְּאַהֲבָה.

You are our God, the Source of life and its blessings. Wherever we turn our gaze we behold signs of Your goodness and love. The whole universe proclaims Your glory. Your loving spirit hovers over all Your works, guiding and sustaining them. The harmony and grandeur of nature speak to us of You; the beauty and truth of Torah reveal Your will to us. You are the One and Eternal God of time and space!

◆ ◆

שְׁמַע יִשְׂרָאֵל: יְיָ אֱלֹהֵינוּ, יְיָ אֶחָד!

Hear, O Israel: the Lord is our God, the Lord is One!

בָּרוּךְ שֵׁם כְּבוֹד מַלְכוּתוֹ לְעוֹלָם וָעֶד!

Blessed is His glorious kingdom for ever and ever!

All are seated

וְאָהַבְתָּ אֵת יְיָ אֱלֹהֶיךָ בְּכָל־לְבָבְךָ וּבְכָל־נַפְשְׁךָ וּבְכָל־מְאֹדֶךָ.
וְהָיוּ הַדְּבָרִים הָאֵלֶּה, אֲשֶׁר אָנֹכִי מְצַוְּךָ הַיּוֹם, עַל־לְבָבֶךָ.
וְשִׁנַּנְתָּם לְבָנֶיךָ, וְדִבַּרְתָּ בָּם בְּשִׁבְתְּךָ בְּבֵיתֶךָ, וּבְלֶכְתְּךָ בַדֶּרֶךְ, וּבְשָׁכְבְּךָ וּבְקוּמֶךָ.

You shall love the Lord your God with all your mind, with all your strength, with all your being.
Set these words, which I command you this day, upon your heart. Teach them faithfully to your children; speak of them in your home and on your way, when you lie down and when you rise up.

וּקְשַׁרְתָּם לְאוֹת עַל־יָדֶךָ, וְהָיוּ לְטֹטָפֹת בֵּין עֵינֶיךָ, וּכְתַבְתָּם עַל־מְזֻזוֹת בֵּיתֶךָ, וּבִשְׁעָרֶיךָ.

Bind them as a sign upon your hand; let them be a symbol before your eyes; inscribe them on the doorposts of your house, and on your gates.

לְמַעַן תִּזְכְּרוּ וַעֲשִׂיתֶם אֶת־כָּל־מִצְוֹתָי, וִהְיִיתֶם קְדֹשִׁים לֵאלֹהֵיכֶם. אֲנִי יְיָ אֱלֹהֵיכֶם, אֲשֶׁר הוֹצֵאתִי אֶתְכֶם מֵאֶרֶץ מִצְרַיִם לִהְיוֹת לָכֶם לֵאלֹהִים. אֲנִי יְיָ אֱלֹהֵיכֶם.

Be mindful of all My Mitzvot, and do them: so shall you consecrate yourselves to your God. I, the Lord, am your God who led you out of Egypt to be your God; I, the Lord, am your God.

◆ ◆

אֲנִי, יְיָ, קְרָאתִיךָ בְצֶדֶק וְאַחְזֵק בְּיָדֶךָ, וְאֶצָּרְךָ; וְאֶתֶּנְךָ לִבְרִית עָם, לְאוֹר גּוֹיִם.

I, the Eternal, have called you to righteousness, and taken you by the hand, and kept you; I have made you a covenant people, a light to the nations.

We are Israel: witness to the covenant between God and His children.

כִּי זֹאת הַבְּרִית אֲשֶׁר אֶכְרֹת אֶת־בֵּית יִשְׂרָאֵל: נָתַתִּי אֶת־תּוֹרָתִי בְּקִרְבָּם, וְעַל־לִבָּם אֶכְתֲּבֶנָּה. וְהָיִיתִי לָהֶם לֵאלֹהִים, וְהֵמָּה יִהְיוּ־לִי לְעָם.

This is the covenant I make with Israel: I will place My Torah in your midst, and write it upon your hearts. I will be your God, and you will be My people.

We are Israel: our Torah forbids the worship of race or nation, possessions or power.

You who worship gods that cannot save you, hear the words of the Eternal: "I am God, there is none else!"

הַמִּתְפַּלְלִים אֶל־אֵל לֹא־יוֹשִׁיעַ,
שִׁמְעוּ דְבַר־יְיָ: "הֲלוֹא אֲנִי יְיָ,
וְאֵין־עוֹד אֱלֹהִים מִבַּלְעָדַי!"

We are Israel: our prophets proclaimed an exalted vision for the world.

Hate evil, and love what is good. Let justice well up as waters and righteousness as a mighty stream.

שִׂנְאוּ־רָע וְאֶהֱבוּ טוֹב. וְיִגַּל
כַּמַּיִם מִשְׁפָּט וּצְדָקָה כְּנַחַל
אֵיתָן.

We are Israel: schooled in the suffering of the oppressed.

You shall not oppress your neighbors nor rob them. You shall not stand idle while your neighbor bleeds.

לֹא־תַעֲשֹׁק אֶת־רֵעֲךָ וְלֹא תִגְזֹל.
לֹא תַעֲמֹד עַל־דַּם רֵעֶךָ.

We are Israel, taught to beat swords into plowshares, commanded to pursue peace.

Violence shall no longer be heard in your land, desolation and destruction within your borders. All your children shall be taught of the Lord, and great shall be the peace of your children.

לֹא־יִשָּׁמַע עוֹד חָמָס בְּאַרְצֵךְ,
שֹׁד וָשֶׁבֶר בִּגְבוּלָיִךְ. וְכָל־בָּנַיִךְ
לִמּוּדֵי יְיָ, וְרַב שְׁלוֹם בָּנָיִךְ.

We are Israel, O God, when we are witness to Your will and messengers of Your truth.

You are My witnesses, says the Eternal, and My servant whom I have chosen; know Me, therefore, and put your trust in Me.

אַתֶּם עֵדַי, נְאֻם יְיָ, וְעַבְדִּי אֲשֶׁר
בָּחָרְתִּי; לְמַעַן תֵּדְעוּ וְתַאֲמִינוּ
לִי.

We are Israel, O Lord, when we proclaim You the God of freedom, as did our ancestors on the shores of the sea:

Who is like You, Eternal One, among the gods that are worshipped?	מִי־כָמֹכָה בָּאֵלִם, יְיָ?
Who is like You, majestic in holiness,	מִי כָּמֹכָה, נֶאְדָּר בַּקֹּדֶשׁ,
awesome in splendor, doing wonders?	נוֹרָא תְהִלֹּת, עֹשֵׂה פֶלֶא?

Morning

שִׁירָה חֲדָשָׁה שִׁבְּחוּ גְאוּלִים לְשִׁמְךָ עַל־שְׂפַת הַיָּם; יַחַד כֻּלָּם הוֹדוּ וְהִמְלִיכוּ וְאָמְרוּ:

"יְיָ יִמְלֹךְ לְעוֹלָם וָעֶד!"

צוּר יִשְׂרָאֵל, קוּמָה בְּעֶזְרַת יִשְׂרָאֵל, וּפְדֵה כִנְאֻמֶךָ יְהוּדָה וְיִשְׂרָאֵל. גֹּאֲלֵנוּ, יְיָ צְבָאוֹת שְׁמוֹ, קְדוֹשׁ יִשְׂרָאֵל.

בָּרוּךְ אַתָּה, יְיָ, גָּאַל יִשְׂרָאֵל.

Evening

מַלְכוּתְךָ רָאוּ בָנֶיךָ, בּוֹקֵעַ יָם לִפְנֵי מֹשֶׁה; "זֶה אֵלִי!" עָנוּ וְאָמְרוּ:

"יְיָ יִמְלֹךְ לְעֹלָם וָעֶד!"

וְנֶאֱמַר: "כִּי־פָדָה יְיָ אֶת־יַעֲקֹב, וּגְאָלוֹ מִיַּד חָזָק מִמֶּנּוּ."

בָּרוּךְ אַתָּה, יְיָ, גָּאַל יִשְׂרָאֵל.

When Your children perceive Your power they exclaim: "This is my God!" "The Eternal will reign for ever and ever!"

◆ ◆

All rise

תפלה

אֲדֹנָי, שְׂפָתַי תִּפְתָּח, וּפִי יַגִּיד תְּהִלָּתֶךָ.

Eternal God, open my lips, that my mouth may declare Your glory.

בָּרוּךְ אַתָּה, יְיָ אֱלֹהֵינוּ וֵאלֹהֵי אֲבוֹתֵינוּ, אֱלֹהֵי אַבְרָהָם, אֱלֹהֵי יִצְחָק, וֵאלֹהֵי יַעֲקֹב: הָאֵל הַגָּדוֹל, הַגִּבּוֹר וְהַנּוֹרָא, אֵל עֶלְיוֹן.

Blessed is the Lord our God and God of all generations, God of Abraham, God of Isaac, and God of Jacob, great, mighty, and exalted.

גּוֹמֵל חֲסָדִים טוֹבִים, וְקוֹנֵה הַכֹּל, וְזוֹכֵר חַסְדֵי אָבוֹת, וּמֵבִיא גְאֻלָּה לִבְנֵי בְנֵיהֶם, לְמַעַן שְׁמוֹ, בְּאַהֲבָה.

He bestows love and kindness on all His children. He remembers the devotion of ages past. In His love, He brings redemption to their descendants for the sake of His name. He is our Ruler and Helper, our Savior and Protector.

מֶלֶךְ עוֹזֵר וּמוֹשִׁיעַ וּמָגֵן. בָּרוּךְ אַתָּה, יְיָ, מָגֵן אַבְרָהָם.

Blessed is the Eternal God, the Shield of Abraham.

◆ ◆

אַתָּה גִּבּוֹר לְעוֹלָם, אֲדֹנָי, מְחַיֵּה הַכֹּל אַתָּה, רַב לְהוֹשִׁיעַ.

Eternal is Your might, O Lord, and great is Your saving power.

מְכַלְכֵּל חַיִּים בְּחֶסֶד, מְחַיֵּה הַכֹּל בְּרַחֲמִים רַבִּים. סוֹמֵךְ נוֹפְלִים, וְרוֹפֵא חוֹלִים, וּמַתִּיר אֲסוּרִים, וּמְקַיֵּם אֱמוּנָתוֹ לִישֵׁנֵי עָפָר.

In love You sustain the living; in Your great mercy, You sustain us all. You uphold the falling and heal the sick; free the captives and keep faith with Your children in death as in life.

מִי כָמְוֹךָ, בַּעַל גְּבוּרוֹת, וּמִי דְוֹמֶה לָּךְ, מֶלֶךְ מֵמִית וּמְחַיֶּה וּמַצְמִיחַ יְשׁוּעָה?

וְנֶאֱמָן אַתָּה לְהַחֲיוֹת הַכֹּל. בָּרוּךְ אַתָּה, יְיָ, מְחַיֵּה הַכֹּל.

Who is like You, Almighty God, Author of life and death, Source of salvation?
Blessed is the Eternal God, the Source of life.

• •

For an Evening Service

אַתָּה קָדוֹשׁ וְשִׁמְךָ קָדוֹשׁ, וּקְדוֹשִׁים בְּכָל־יוֹם יְהַלְלְוּךָ סֶּלָה.
בָּרוּךְ אַתָּה, יְיָ, הָאֵל הַקָּדוֹשׁ.

You are holy, Your name is holy, and Your worshippers proclaim Your holiness. Blessed is the Eternal One, the holy God.

• •

For a Morning Service

SANCTIFICATION — קדושה

נְקַדֵּשׁ אֶת־שִׁמְךָ בָּעוֹלָם, כְּשֵׁם שֶׁמַּקְדִּישִׁים אוֹתוֹ בִּשְׁמֵי מָרוֹם,
כַּכָּתוּב עַל־יַד נְבִיאֶךָ: וְקָרָא זֶה אֶל־זֶה וְאָמַר:

We sanctify Your name on earth, even as all things, to the ends of time and space, proclaim Your holiness; and in the words of the prophet we say:

קָדוֹשׁ, קָדוֹשׁ, קָדוֹשׁ יְיָ צְבָאוֹת, מְלֹא כָל־הָאָרֶץ כְּבוֹדוֹ.

Holy, Holy, Holy is the Lord of Hosts; the fullness of the whole earth is His glory!

לְעֻמָּתָם בָּרוּךְ יֹאמֵרוּ:

They respond to Your glory with blessing:

בָּרוּךְ כְּבוֹד יְיָ מִמְּקוֹמוֹ.

Blessed is the glory of God in heaven and earth.

וּבְדִבְרֵי קָדְשְׁךָ כָּתוּב לֵאמֹר:

And this is Your sacred word:

יִמְלֹךְ יְיָ לְעוֹלָם, אֱלֹהַיִךְ צִיּוֹן, לְדֹר וָדֹר, הַלְלוּיָהּ.

The Lord shall reign for ever; your God, O Zion, from generation to generation. Halleluyah!

לְדוֹר וָדוֹר נַגִּיד גָּדְלֶךָ, וּלְנֵצַח נְצָחִים קְדֻשָּׁתְךָ נַקְדִּישׁ.
וְשִׁבְחֲךָ, אֱלֹהֵינוּ, מִפִּינוּ לֹא יָמוּשׁ לְעוֹלָם וָעֶד.

בָּרוּךְ אַתָּה, יְיָ, הָאֵל הַקָּדוֹשׁ.

To all generations we will make known Your greatness, and to all eternity proclaim Your holiness. Your praise, O God, shall never depart from our lips.

Blessed is the Lord, the holy God.

All are seated

◆ ◆

Eternal Source of knowledge, You have endowed us with reason and understanding. We pray now for the light of Your truth, for insight into Your ways, and for the strength to banish from our hearts every desire and thought of evil.

Forgive our sins, pardon our failings, and help us to remove suffering and sorrow from our midst.

May those who have lost their way come again to know Your love, and turn to You in newness of heart; and let those who love goodness and do justly rejoice in the knowledge of Your favor.

Bless our land with plenty and our nation with peace. May righteousness abide with us, and virtue bring us happiness. Blessed is the Lord, the Eternal God, who hearkens to prayer.

Lord our God, Creator of all the world, You have blessed us with noble powers: teach us to make wise use of them. You have called us to be Your partners in the work of creation, and we thank You for the power to choose a life devoted to Your service, dedicated to the well-being of those around us. May all that we do bring nearer the coming of Your kingdom on earth.

May all peoples find their way to establish peace on earth. Let them cultivate that good will which alone can bring enduring peace.

Let the nations realize that the triumphs of war turn to ashes, that justice and right are better than conquest and dominion.

May they come to see that it is not by might nor by power, but by Your spirit that life prevails.

◆ ◆

MEDITATION

◆ ◆

יִהְיוּ לְרָצוֹן אִמְרֵי־פִי וְהֶגְיוֹן לִבִּי לְפָנֶיךָ, יְיָ, צוּרִי וְגוֹאֲלִי.

May the words of my mouth, and the meditations of my heart, be acceptable to You, O Lord, my Rock and my Redeemer.

or

עֹשֶׂה שָׁלוֹם בִּמְרוֹמָיו, הוּא יַעֲשֶׂה שָׁלוֹם עָלֵינוּ וְעַל כָּל־יִשְׂרָאֵל, וְאִמְרוּ אָמֵן.

May He who causes peace to reign in the high heavens let peace descend on us, on all Israel, and all the world.

◆ ◆

Prayers at a House of Mourning begin on page 645.

The Rituals for the Reading of Torah begin on page 415.

Concluding Prayers begin on page 613.

Havdalah for the conclusion of Shabbat is on page 633.

Evening or Morning Service II

The greatness of the Eternal One surpasses our understanding, and yet at times we feel His nearness.

Overwhelmed by awe and wonder as we behold the signs of His presence, still we feel within us a kinship with the divine.

And so we turn to You, O God, looking at the world about us, and inward to the world within us, there to find You, and from Your presence gain life and strength.

◆ ◆

All rise

שמע וברכותיה

בָּרְכוּ אֶת־יְיָ הַמְבֹרָךְ!

Praise the Lord, to whom our praise is due!

בָּרוּךְ יְיָ הַמְבֹרָךְ לְעוֹלָם וָעֶד!

Praised be the Lord, to whom our praise is due,
now and for ever!

◆ ◆

Evening

בָּרוּךְ אַתָּה, יְיָ אֱלֹהֵינוּ, מֶלֶךְ
הָעוֹלָם, אֲשֶׁר בִּדְבָרוֹ מַעֲרִיב
עֲרָבִים. בְּחָכְמָה פּוֹתֵחַ שְׁעָרִים,
וּבִתְבוּנָה מְשַׁנֶּה עִתִּים, וּמַחֲלִיף
אֶת־הַזְּמַנִּים, וּמְסַדֵּר אֶת־
הַכּוֹכָבִים בְּמִשְׁמְרוֹתֵיהֶם בָּרָקִיעַ

Morning

בָּרוּךְ אַתָּה, יְיָ אֱלֹהֵינוּ, מֶלֶךְ
הָעוֹלָם, יוֹצֵר אוֹר וּבוֹרֵא חֹשֶׁךְ,
עֹשֶׂה שָׁלוֹם וּבוֹרֵא אֶת־הַכֹּל.
הַמֵּאִיר לָאָרֶץ וְלַדָּרִים עָלֶיהָ
בְּרַחֲמִים, וּבְטוּבוֹ מְחַדֵּשׁ בְּכָל־
יוֹם תָּמִיד מַעֲשֵׂה בְרֵאשִׁית.

Morning

מָה רַבּוּ מַעֲשֶׂיךָ, יְיָ! כֻּלָּם בְּחָכְמָה עָשִׂיתָ, מָלְאָה הָאָרֶץ קִנְיָנֶךָ. תִּתְבָּרַךְ, יְיָ אֱלֹהֵינוּ, עַל־שֶׁבַח מַעֲשֵׂה יָדֶיךָ, וְעַל־מְאוֹרֵי־אוֹר שֶׁעָשִׂיתָ: יְפָאֲרוּךָ. סֶּלָה.

בָּרוּךְ אַתָּה, יְיָ, יוֹצֵר הַמְּאוֹרוֹת.

Evening

כִּרְצוֹנוֹ. בּוֹרֵא יוֹם וָלָיְלָה, גּוֹלֵל אוֹר מִפְּנֵי חֹשֶׁךְ וְחֹשֶׁךְ מִפְּנֵי אוֹר, וּמַעֲבִיר יוֹם וּמֵבִיא לָיְלָה, וּמַבְדִּיל בֵּין יוֹם וּבֵין לָיְלָה, יְיָ צְבָאוֹת שְׁמוֹ. אֵל חַי וְקַיָּם, תָּמִיד יִמְלוֹךְ עָלֵינוּ, לְעוֹלָם וָעֶד.

בָּרוּךְ אַתָּה, יְיָ, הַמַּעֲרִיב עֲרָבִים.

Heaven and earth, O Lord, are the work of Your hands. The roaring seas and the life within them issue forth from Your creative will. The universe is one vast wonder proclaiming Your wisdom and singing Your greatness.

The mysteries of life and death, of growth and decay, alike display the miracle of Your creative power. O God of life, the whole universe is Your dwelling-place, all being a hymn to Your glory!

◆ ◆

Morning

אַהֲבָה רַבָּה אֲהַבְתָּנוּ, יְיָ אֱלֹהֵינוּ, חֶמְלָה גְדוֹלָה וִיתֵרָה חָמַלְתָּ עָלֵינוּ. אָבִינוּ מַלְכֵּנוּ, בַּעֲבוּר אֲבוֹתֵינוּ שֶׁבָּטְחוּ בְךָ וַתְּלַמְּדֵם חֻקֵּי חַיִּים, כֵּן תְּחָנֵּנוּ וּתְלַמְּדֵנוּ. אָבִינוּ, הָאָב הָרַחֲמָן, הַמְרַחֵם, רַחֵם עָלֵינוּ וְתֵן בְּלִבֵּנוּ לְהָבִין וּלְהַשְׂכִּיל, לִשְׁמֹעַ לִלְמֹד וּלְלַמֵּד, לִשְׁמֹר וְלַעֲשׂוֹת וּלְקַיֵּם אֶת־כָּל־דִּבְרֵי תַלְמוּד תּוֹרָתֶךָ

Evening

אַהֲבַת עוֹלָם בֵּית יִשְׂרָאֵל עַמְּךָ אָהָבְתָּ: תּוֹרָה וּמִצְוֹת, חֻקִּים וּמִשְׁפָּטִים אוֹתָנוּ לִמַּדְתָּ.

עַל־כֵּן, יְיָ אֱלֹהֵינוּ, בְּשָׁכְבֵנוּ וּבְקוּמֵנוּ נָשִׂיחַ בְּחֻקֶּיךָ, וְנִשְׂמַח בְּדִבְרֵי תוֹרָתְךָ וּבְמִצְוֹתֶיךָ לְעוֹלָם וָעֶד.

כִּי הֵם חַיֵּינוּ וְאֹרֶךְ יָמֵינוּ, וּבָהֶם נֶהְגֶּה יוֹמָם וָלָיְלָה. וְאַהֲבָתְךָ אַל־תָּסִיר מִמֶּנּוּ לְעוֹלָמִים!

Morning

בְּאַהֲבָה. וְהָאֵר עֵינֵינוּ בְּתוֹרָתֶךָ,
וְדַבֵּק לִבֵּנוּ בְּמִצְוֹתֶיךָ, וְיַחֵד
לְבָבֵנוּ לְאַהֲבָה וּלְיִרְאָה אֶת־
שְׁמֶךָ. וְלֹא־נֵבוֹשׁ לְעוֹלָם וָעֶד, כִּי בְשֵׁם קָדְשְׁךָ הַגָּדוֹל וְהַנּוֹרָא
בָּטָחְנוּ. נָגִילָה וְנִשְׂמְחָה בִּישׁוּעָתֶךָ, כִּי אֵל פּוֹעֵל יְשׁוּעוֹת אָתָּה,
וּבָנוּ בָחַרְתָּ וְקֵרַבְתָּנוּ לְשִׁמְךָ הַגָּדוֹל סֶלָה בֶּאֱמֶת, לְהוֹדוֹת לְךָ
וּלְיַחֶדְךָ בְּאַהֲבָה. בָּרוּךְ אַתָּה, יְיָ, הַבּוֹחֵר בְּעַמּוֹ יִשְׂרָאֵל בְּאַהֲבָה.

Evening

בָּרוּךְ אַתָּה, יְיָ, אוֹהֵב עַמּוֹ
יִשְׂרָאֵל.

In the human heart, too, You reign supreme. Above the storms of passion and hate that shake our world, we hear Your voice proclaim the law of justice and love.

May our eyes be open to Your truth, our spirits alive to Your teaching, our hearts united to serve You.

May we find the will to consecrate ourselves anew to the task of all the generations: to speed the dawn of the new day when all will be united in friendship and peace, and with one accord acclaim You their Eternal God.

◆ ◆

שְׁמַע יִשְׂרָאֵל: יְיָ אֱלֹהֵינוּ, יְיָ אֶחָד!

Hear, O Israel: the Lord is our God, the Lord is One!

בָּרוּךְ שֵׁם כְּבוֹד מַלְכוּתוֹ לְעוֹלָם וָעֶד!

Blessed is His glorious kingdom for ever and ever!

All are seated

וְאָהַבְתָּ אֵת יְיָ אֱלֹהֶיךָ בְּכָל־לְבָבְךָ וּבְכָל־נַפְשְׁךָ וּבְכָל־מְאֹדֶךָ.
וְהָיוּ הַדְּבָרִים הָאֵלֶּה, אֲשֶׁר אָנֹכִי מְצַוְּךָ הַיּוֹם, עַל־לְבָבֶךָ.
וְשִׁנַּנְתָּם לְבָנֶיךָ, וְדִבַּרְתָּ בָּם בְּשִׁבְתְּךָ בְּבֵיתֶךָ, וּבְלֶכְתְּךָ
בַדֶּרֶךְ, וּבְשָׁכְבְּךָ וּבְקוּמֶךָ.

You shall love the Lord your God with all your mind, with all your strength, with all your being.
Set these words, which I command you this day, upon your heart. Teach them faithfully to your children; speak of them in your home and on your way, when you lie down and when you rise up.

וּקְשַׁרְתָּם לְאוֹת עַל־יָדֶךָ, וְהָיוּ לְטֹטָפֹת בֵּין עֵינֶיךָ, וּכְתַבְתָּם עַל־מְזֻזוֹת בֵּיתֶךָ, וּבִשְׁעָרֶיךָ.

Bind them as a sign upon your hand; let them be a symbol before your eyes; inscribe them on the doorposts of your house, and on your gates.

לְמַעַן תִּזְכְּרוּ וַעֲשִׂיתֶם אֶת־כָּל־מִצְוֹתָי, וִהְיִיתֶם קְדֹשִׁים לֵאלֹהֵיכֶם. אֲנִי יְיָ אֱלֹהֵיכֶם, אֲשֶׁר הוֹצֵאתִי אֶתְכֶם מֵאֶרֶץ מִצְרַיִם לִהְיוֹת לָכֶם לֵאלֹהִים. אֲנִי יְיָ אֱלֹהֵיכֶם.

Be mindful of all My Mitzvot, and do them: so shall you consecrate yourselves to your God. I, the Lord, am your God who led you out of Egypt to be your God; I, the Lord, am your God.

◆ ◆

Morning

עַל־הָרִאשׁוֹנִים וְעַל־הָאַחֲרוֹנִים דָּבָר טוֹב וְקַיָּם לְעוֹלָם וָעֶד.
אֱמֶת וֶאֱמוּנָה, חֹק וְלֹא יַעֲבוֹר.
אֱמֶת שָׁאַתָּה הוּא יְיָ אֱלֹהֵינוּ וֵאלֹהֵי אֲבוֹתֵינוּ, מַלְכֵּנוּ מֶלֶךְ אֲבוֹתֵינוּ, גּוֹאֲלֵנוּ גּוֹאֵל אֲבוֹתֵינוּ, יוֹצְרֵנוּ, צוּר יְשׁוּעָתֵנוּ. פּוֹדֵנוּ וּמַצִּילֵנוּ מֵעוֹלָם הוּא שְׁמֶךָ, אֵין אֱלֹהִים זוּלָתֶךָ.

Evening

אֱמֶת וֶאֱמוּנָה כָּל־זֹאת, וְקַיָּם עָלֵינוּ כִּי הוּא יְיָ אֱלֹהֵינוּ וְאֵין זוּלָתוֹ, וַאֲנַחְנוּ יִשְׂרָאֵל עַמּוֹ.
הַפּוֹדֵנוּ מִיַּד מְלָכִים, מַלְכֵּנוּ הַגּוֹאֲלֵנוּ מִכַּף כָּל־הֶעָרִיצִים.
הָעֹשֶׂה גְדֹלוֹת עַד אֵין חֵקֶר, וְנִפְלָאוֹת עַד־אֵין מִסְפָּר.
הָעֹשֶׂה לָּנוּ נִסִּים בְּפַרְעֹה, אוֹתוֹת וּמוֹפְתִים בְּאַדְמַת בְּנֵי חָם.

Morning

עֶזְרַת אֲבוֹתֵינוּ אַתָּה הוּא
מֵעוֹלָם, מָגֵן וּמוֹשִׁיעַ לִבְנֵיהֶם
אַחֲרֵיהֶם בְּכָל־דּוֹר וָדוֹר. בְּרוּם
עוֹלָם מוֹשָׁבֶךָ וּמִשְׁפָּטֶיךָ
וְצִדְקָתְךָ עַד אַפְסֵי־אָרֶץ.
אַשְׁרֵי אִישׁ שֶׁיִּשְׁמַע לְמִצְוֹתֶיךָ,
וְתוֹרָתְךָ וּדְבָרְךָ יָשִׂים עַל־לִבּוֹ.

Evening

וַיּוֹצֵא אֶת־עַמּוֹ יִשְׂרָאֵל מִתּוֹכָם
לְחֵרוּת עוֹלָם.
וְרָאוּ בָנָיו גְּבוּרָתוֹ; שִׁבְּחוּ וְהוֹדוּ
לִשְׁמוֹ.
וּמַלְכוּתוֹ בְּרָצוֹן קִבְּלוּ עֲלֵיהֶם.
מֹשֶׁה וּבְנֵי יִשְׂרָאֵל לְךָ עָנוּ שִׁירָה
בְּשִׂמְחָה רַבָּה, וְאָמְרוּ כֻלָּם:

Infinite God, Creator and Redeemer of all being, You are Most High, Most Near. In all generations we have cried out to You; we have put our trust in You; we have borne witness to Your truth before the nations! O now let Your light and Your truth appear to us and lead us; let them bring us to Your holy mountain.

We shall not fear, then, though earth itself should shake, though the mountains fall into the heart of the sea, though its waters thunder and rage, though the winds lift its waves to the very vault of heaven.

We shall not fear, for You are with us; we shall rejoice in Your deliverance. Then shall we know You, our Redeemer and our God, and in the shadow of Your wings we shall sing with joy:

מִי־כָמֹכָה בָּאֵלִם, יְיָ?
מִי כָּמֹכָה, נֶאְדָּר בַּקֹּדֶשׁ,
נוֹרָא תְהִלֹּת, עֹשֵׂה פֶלֶא?

Who is like You, Eternal One, among the gods that are worshipped?
Who is like You, majestic in holiness,
awesome in splendor, doing wonders?

Morning

שִׁירָה חֲדָשָׁה שִׁבְּחוּ גְאוּלִים
לְשִׁמְךָ עַל־שְׂפַת הַיָּם; יַחַד כֻּלָּם
הוֹדוּ וְהִמְלִיכוּ וְאָמְרוּ:
"יְיָ יִמְלֹךְ לְעוֹלָם וָעֶד!"
צוּר יִשְׂרָאֵל, קוּמָה בְּעֶזְרַת

Evening

מַלְכוּתְךָ רָאוּ בָנֶיךָ, בּוֹקֵעַ יָם
לִפְנֵי מֹשֶׁה; "זֶה אֵלִי!" עָנוּ
וְאָמְרוּ:
"יְיָ יִמְלֹךְ לְעֹלָם וָעֶד!"
וְנֶאֱמַר: "כִּי־פָדָה יְיָ אֶת־יַעֲקֹב,

Evening

וּגְאָלוֹ מִיַּד חָזָק מִמֶּנּוּ."
בָּרוּךְ אַתָּה, יְיָ, גָּאַל יִשְׂרָאֵל.

Morning

יִשְׂרָאֵל, וּפְדֵה כִנְאֻמֶךָ יְהוּדָה
וְיִשְׂרָאֵל. גֹּאֲלֵנוּ, יְיָ צְבָאוֹת שְׁמוֹ,
קְדוֹשׁ יִשְׂרָאֵל.
בָּרוּךְ אַתָּה, יְיָ, גָּאַל יִשְׂרָאֵל.

When your children perceive Your power they exclaim: "This is my God!" "The Lord will reign for ever and ever!"

◆ ◆

For an Evening Service

הַשְׁכִּיבֵנוּ, יְיָ אֱלֹהֵינוּ, לְשָׁלוֹם, וְהַעֲמִידֵנוּ, מַלְכֵּנוּ, לְחַיִּים. וּפְרוֹשׂ עָלֵינוּ סֻכַּת שְׁלוֹמֶךָ, וְתַקְּנֵנוּ בְּעֵצָה טוֹבָה מִלְּפָנֶיךָ, וְהוֹשִׁיעֵנוּ לְמַעַן שְׁמֶךָ, וְהָגֵן בַּעֲדֵנוּ. וְהָסֵר מֵעָלֵינוּ אוֹיֵב, דֶּבֶר וְחֶרֶב וְרָעָב וְיָגוֹן; וְהָסֵר שָׂטָן מִלְּפָנֵינוּ וּמֵאַחֲרֵינוּ; וּבְצֵל כְּנָפֶיךָ תַּסְתִּירֵנוּ, כִּי אֵל שׁוֹמְרֵנוּ וּמַצִּילֵנוּ אָתָּה, כִּי אֵל מֶלֶךְ חַנּוּן וְרַחוּם אָתָּה. וּשְׁמוֹר צֵאתֵנוּ וּבוֹאֵנוּ לְחַיִּים וּלְשָׁלוֹם, מֵעַתָּה וְעַד עוֹלָם. בָּרוּךְ אַתָּה, יְיָ, שׁוֹמֵר עַמּוֹ יִשְׂרָאֵל לָעַד.

Let there be love and understanding among us; let peace and friendship be our shelter from life's storms. Eternal God, help us to walk with good companions, to live with hope in our hearts and eternity in our thoughts, that we may lie down in peace and rise up to find our hearts waiting to do Your will.

Blessed is the Eternal One, Guardian of Israel, whose love gives light to all the world.

◆ ◆

All rise

תפלה

אֲדֹנָי, שְׂפָתַי תִּפְתָּח, וּפִי יַגִּיד תְּהִלָּתֶךָ.

Eternal God, open my lips, that my mouth may declare Your glory.

בָּרוּךְ אַתָּה, יְיָ אֱלֹהֵינוּ וֵאלֹהֵי אֲבוֹתֵינוּ, אֱלֹהֵי אַבְרָהָם, אֱלֹהֵי יִצְחָק, וֵאלֹהֵי יַעֲקֹב: הָאֵל הַגָּדוֹל, הַגִּבּוֹר וְהַנּוֹרָא, אֵל עֶלְיוֹן.

God of ages past and future, God of this day, as You were with our fathers and mothers, be with us as well.

As You strengthened them, strengthen us.

גּוֹמֵל חֲסָדִים טוֹבִים, וְקוֹנֵה הַכֹּל, וְזוֹכֵר חַסְדֵי אָבוֹת, וּמֵבִיא גְאֻלָּה לִבְנֵי בְנֵיהֶם, לְמַעַן שְׁמוֹ, בְּאַהֲבָה.

As You were their Guide, be ours as well.

Grant that we too may be bearers of Your teaching, teachers of Your truth.

Then our tradition shall endure, and Israel live: from mother and father to daughter and son, and all who follow them.

One generation comes, one generation passes. Daughters become mothers, and sons, fathers.

מֶלֶךְ עוֹזֵר וּמוֹשִׁיעַ וּמָגֵן. בָּרוּךְ אַתָּה, יְיָ, מָגֵן אַבְרָהָם.

Students of Torah become teachers. The people and its tradition endure.

The people and its tradition will live.

◆ ◆

אַתָּה גִּבּוֹר לְעוֹלָם, אֲדֹנָי, מְחַיֵּה הַכֹּל אַתָּה, רַב לְהוֹשִׁיעַ. מְכַלְכֵּל חַיִּים בְּחֶסֶד, מְחַיֵּה הַכֹּל בְּרַחֲמִים רַבִּים. סוֹמֵךְ נוֹפְלִים, וְרוֹפֵא חוֹלִים, וּמַתִּיר אֲסוּרִים, וּמְקַיֵּם אֱמוּנָתוֹ לִישֵׁנֵי עָפָר.

מִי כָמְוֹךָ, בַּעַל גְּבוּרוֹת, וּמִי דְּוֹמֶה לָּךְ, מֶלֶךְ מֵמִית וּמְחַיֶּה
וּמַצְמִיחַ יְשׁוּעָה?
וְנֶאֱמָן אַתָּה לְהַחֲיוֹת הַכֹּל. בָּרוּךְ אַתָּה, יְיָ, מְחַיֵּה הַכֹּל.

Your might, O God, is everlasting;
Help us to use our strength for good and not for evil.

You are the Source of life and blessing;
Help us to choose life for ourselves and our children.

You are the Support of the falling;
Help us to lift up the fallen.

You are the Author of freedom;
Help us to set free the captive.

You are our Hope in death as in life;
Help us to keep faith with those who sleep in the dust.

Your might, O God, is everlasting;
Help us to use our strength for good.

◆ ◆

For an Evening Service

אַתָּה קָדוֹשׁ וְשִׁמְךָ קָדוֹשׁ, וּקְדוֹשִׁים בְּכָל־יוֹם יְהַלְלְוּךָ סֶּלָה.
בָּרוּךְ אַתָּה, יְיָ, הָאֵל הַקָּדוֹשׁ.

You are holy, Your name is holy, and those who strive to be holy declare Your glory day by day. Blessed is the Lord, the holy God.

◆ ◆

For a Morning Service

SANCTIFICATION — קדושה

נְקַדֵּשׁ אֶת־שִׁמְךָ בָּעוֹלָם, כְּשֵׁם שֶׁמַּקְדִּישִׁים אוֹתוֹ בִּשְׁמֵי מָרוֹם,
כַּכָּתוּב עַל־יַד נְבִיאֶךָ: וְקָרָא זֶה אֶל־זֶה וְאָמַר:

We sanctify Your name on earth, even as all things, to the ends of time and space, proclaim Your holiness; and in the words of the prophet we say:

קָדוֹשׁ, קָדוֹשׁ, קָדוֹשׁ יְיָ צְבָאוֹת, מְלֹא כָל־הָאָרֶץ כְּבוֹדוֹ.

Holy, Holy, Holy is the Lord of Hosts; the fullness of the whole earth is His glory!

לְעֻמָּתָם בָּרוּךְ יֹאמֵרוּ:

They respond to Your glory with blessing:

בָּרוּךְ כְּבוֹד יְיָ מִמְּקוֹמוֹ.

Blessed is the glory of God in heaven and earth.

וּבְדִבְרֵי קָדְשְׁךָ כָּתוּב לֵאמֹר:

And this is Your sacred word:

יִמְלֹךְ יְיָ לְעוֹלָם, אֱלֹהַיִךְ צִיּוֹן, לְדֹר וָדֹר, הַלְלוּיָהּ.

The Lord shall reign for ever; your God, O Zion, from generation to generation. Halleluyah!

לְדוֹר וָדוֹר נַגִּיד גָּדְלֶךָ, וּלְנֵצַח נְצָחִים קְדֻשָּׁתְךָ נַקְדִּישׁ.
וְשִׁבְחֲךָ, אֱלֹהֵינוּ, מִפִּינוּ לֹא יָמוּשׁ לְעוֹלָם וָעֶד.
בָּרוּךְ אַתָּה, יְיָ, הָאֵל הַקָּדוֹשׁ.

To all generations we will make known Your greatness, and to all eternity proclaim Your holiness. Your praise, O God, shall never depart from our lips.

Blessed is the Lord, the holy God.

All are seated

◆ ◆

A spark of the divine flame glows within us all. We give thanks for the gift of reason that enables us to search after knowledge. May our use of this gift make Your light burn ever more brightly within us.

Blessed is the Eternal Source of wisdom and knowledge.

May our pride of intellect never be an idol turning us away from You. And as we grow in knowledge, may we remain aware of our own limitations.

Blessed is the God of forgiveness and understanding.

May the beauty and mystery of the world move us to reverence and humility. O let the tree of knowledge bear good fruit for us and our children.

Blessed is our God from whom all blessings flow.

And let the consciousness of Your Presence be the glory of our lives, making joyous our days and years, and leading us to a clearer understanding of Your will.

Blessed is our God who hearkens to prayer.

◆ ◆

MEDITATION

◆ ◆

יִהְיוּ לְרָצוֹן אִמְרֵי־פִי וְהֶגְיוֹן לִבִּי לְפָנֶיךָ, יְיָ, צוּרִי וְגוֹאֲלִי.

May the words of my mouth, and the meditations of my heart, be acceptable to You, O Lord, my Rock and my Redeemer.

or

עֹשֶׂה שָׁלוֹם בִּמְרוֹמָיו, הוּא יַעֲשֶׂה שָׁלוֹם עָלֵינוּ וְעַל כָּל־יִשְׂרָאֵל, וְאִמְרוּ אָמֵן.

May He who causes peace to reign in the high heavens let peace descend on us, on all Israel, and all the world.

◆ ◆

Prayers at a House of Mourning begin on page 645.

The Rituals for the Reading of Torah begin on page 415.

Concluding Prayers begin on page 613.

Havdalah for the conclusion of Shabbat is on page 633.

Evening or Morning Service III

Lord, You give meaning to our hopes, to our struggles and our strivings. Without You we are lost, our lives empty. And so when all else fails us, we turn to You! In the stillness of night, when the outer darkness enters the soul; in the press of the crowd, when we walk alone though yearning for companionship; and when in agony we are bystanders to our own confusion, we look to You for hope and peace.

Lord, we do not ask for a life of ease, for happiness without alloy. Instead we ask You to teach us to be uncomplaining and unafraid. In our darkness help us to find Your light, and in our loneliness to discover the many spirits akin to our own. Give us strength to face life with hope and courage, that even from its discords and conflicts we may draw blessing. Make us understand that life calls us not merely to enjoy the richness of the earth, but to exult in heights attained after the toil of climbing.

Let our darkness be dispelled by Your love, that we may rise above fear and failure, our steps sustained by faith.

Lord, You give meaning to our lives; You are our support and our trust.

◆ ◆

All rise

שמע וברכותיה

בָּרְכוּ אֶת־יְיָ הַמְבֹרָךְ!

Praise the Lord, to whom our praise is due!

בָּרוּךְ יְיָ הַמְבֹרָךְ לְעוֹלָם וָעֶד!

Praised be the Lord, to whom our praise is due,
now and for ever!

◆ ◆

Can we imagine a world without color, a world without the grace of blue, the life of green?

We give thanks for eyes that see, for the sublime gift of beauty.

בָּרוּךְ אַתָּה, יְיָ אֱלֹהֵינוּ, מֶלֶךְ הָעוֹלָם, זוֹכֵר הַבְּרִית.

Blessed is the Eternal One, for the rainbow's brilliant colors.

Can we imagine a world without sound, never knowing the joy of song?

We give thanks for words that speak to the mind, for hymns of joy and songs of sorrow, and for souls that know how to listen.

בָּרוּךְ אַתָּה, יְיָ אֱלֹהֵינוּ, מֶלֶךְ הָעוֹלָם, שֶׁכֹּחוֹ וּגְבוּרָתוֹ מָלֵא עוֹלָם.

Blessed is the Eternal One, whose strength and might pervade the world.

Can we imagine a world without law, where flowing of tide or coming of dawn could not be counted on?

We give thanks for the wondrous order that governs stars and dust, and our own heart's beating.

בָּרוּךְ אַתָּה, יְיָ אֱלֹהֵינוּ, מֶלֶךְ הָעוֹלָם, עֹשֶׂה מַעֲשֵׂה בְרֵאשִׁית.

Blessed is the Eternal One, Creative Source of all being.

Can we imagine a world without love, where the spirit is shackled in the prison of the self?

We give thanks for the godlike spirit within us we call love, which binds life to life and heart to heart.

בָּרוּךְ אַתָּה, יְיָ אֱלֹהֵינוּ, מֶלֶךְ הָעוֹלָם, שֶׁנָּתַן מֵחָכְמָתוֹ לְבָשָׂר וָדָם.

Blessed is the Eternal One, who shares His glory with flesh and blood.

◆ ◆

שְׁמַע יִשְׂרָאֵל: יְיָ אֱלֹהֵינוּ, יְיָ אֶחָד!

Hear, O Israel: the Lord is our God, the Lord is One!

בָּרוּךְ שֵׁם כְּבוֹד מַלְכוּתוֹ לְעוֹלָם וָעֶד!

Blessed is His glorious kingdom for ever and ever!

All are seated

וְאָהַבְתָּ אֵת יְיָ אֱלֹהֶיךָ בְּכָל־לְבָבְךָ וּבְכָל־נַפְשְׁךָ וּבְכָל־מְאֹדֶךָ.
וְהָיוּ הַדְּבָרִים הָאֵלֶּה, אֲשֶׁר אָנֹכִי מְצַוְּךָ הַיּוֹם, עַל־לְבָבֶךָ.
וְשִׁנַּנְתָּם לְבָנֶיךָ, וְדִבַּרְתָּ בָּם בְּשִׁבְתְּךָ בְּבֵיתֶךָ, וּבְלֶכְתְּךָ
בַדֶּרֶךְ, וּבְשָׁכְבְּךָ וּבְקוּמֶךָ.

You shall love the Lord your God with all your mind, with all your strength, with all your being.
Set these words, which I command you this day, upon your heart. Teach them faithfully to your children; speak of them in your home and on your way, when you lie down and when you rise up.

וּקְשַׁרְתָּם לְאוֹת עַל־יָדֶךָ, וְהָיוּ לְטֹטָפֹת בֵּין עֵינֶיךָ, וּכְתַבְתָּם
עַל־מְזֻזוֹת בֵּיתֶךָ, וּבִשְׁעָרֶיךָ.

Bind them as a sign upon your hand; let them be a symbol before your eyes; inscribe them on the doorposts of your house, and on your gates.

לְמַעַן תִּזְכְּרוּ וַעֲשִׂיתֶם אֶת־כָּל־מִצְוֹתָי, וִהְיִיתֶם קְדֹשִׁים
לֵאלֹהֵיכֶם. אֲנִי יְיָ אֱלֹהֵיכֶם, אֲשֶׁר הוֹצֵאתִי אֶתְכֶם מֵאֶרֶץ
מִצְרַיִם לִהְיוֹת לָכֶם לֵאלֹהִים. אֲנִי יְיָ אֱלֹהֵיכֶם.

Be mindful of all My mitzvot, and do them: so shall you consecrate yourselves to your God. I, the Lord, am your God who led you out of Egypt to be your God; I, the Lord, am your God.

◆ ◆

Morning

עַל־הָרִאשׁוֹנִים וְעַל־הָאַחֲרוֹנִים
דָּבָר טוֹב וְקַיָּם לְעוֹלָם וָעֶד.
אֱמֶת וֶאֱמוּנָה, חֹק וְלֹא יַעֲבוֹר.
אֱמֶת שָׁאַתָּה הוּא יְיָ אֱלֹהֵינוּ
וֵאלֹהֵי אֲבוֹתֵינוּ, מַלְכֵּנוּ מֶלֶךְ
אֲבוֹתֵינוּ, גּוֹאֲלֵנוּ גּוֹאֵל אֲבוֹתֵינוּ,
יוֹצְרֵנוּ, צוּר יְשׁוּעָתֵנוּ. פּוֹדֵנוּ
וּמַצִּילֵנוּ מֵעוֹלָם הוּא שְׁמֶךָ, אֵין
אֱלֹהִים זוּלָתֶךָ.
עֶזְרַת אֲבוֹתֵינוּ אַתָּה הוּא
מֵעוֹלָם, מָגֵן וּמוֹשִׁיעַ לִבְנֵיהֶם
אַחֲרֵיהֶם בְּכָל־דּוֹר וָדוֹר. בְּרוּם
עוֹלָם מוֹשָׁבֶךָ וּמִשְׁפָּטֶיךָ
וְצִדְקָתְךָ עַד אַפְסֵי־אָרֶץ.
אַשְׁרֵי אִישׁ שֶׁיִּשְׁמַע לְמִצְוֹתֶיךָ,
וְתוֹרָתְךָ וּדְבָרְךָ יָשִׂים עַל־לִבּוֹ.

Evening

אֱמֶת וֶאֱמוּנָה כָּל־זֹאת, וְקַיָּם
עָלֵינוּ כִּי הוּא יְיָ אֱלֹהֵינוּ וְאֵין
זוּלָתוֹ, וַאֲנַחְנוּ יִשְׂרָאֵל עַמּוֹ.
הַפּוֹדֵנוּ מִיַּד מְלָכִים, מַלְכֵּנוּ
הַגּוֹאֲלֵנוּ מִכַּף כָּל־הֶעָרִיצִים.
הָעֹשֶׂה גְדֹלוֹת עַד אֵין חֵקֶר,
וְנִפְלָאוֹת עַד־אֵין מִסְפָּר.
הָעֹשֶׂה לָנוּ נִסִּים בְּפַרְעֹה, אוֹתוֹת
וּמוֹפְתִים בְּאַדְמַת בְּנֵי חָם.
וַיּוֹצֵא אֶת־עַמּוֹ יִשְׂרָאֵל מִתּוֹכָם
לְחֵרוּת עוֹלָם.
וְרָאוּ בָנָיו גְּבוּרָתוֹ; שִׁבְּחוּ וְהוֹדוּ
לִשְׁמוֹ.
וּמַלְכוּתוֹ בְּרָצוֹן קִבְּלוּ עֲלֵיהֶם.
מֹשֶׁה וּבְנֵי יִשְׂרָאֵל לְךָ עָנוּ שִׁירָה
בְּשִׂמְחָה רַבָּה, וְאָמְרוּ כֻלָּם:

There lives a God:
Our sages beheld Him when they looked up to the heavens.

There lives a God:
Our poets saw Him when they looked into the soul.

Our people found Him in their liberation from bondage.
In the wilderness of Sinai they met Him.

Through long years of wandering they put their trust in Him.
Through bitter times of oppression they kept faith in Him.

There lives a God:
In love He summoned us to bear witness to Him; in love He has preserved us to this day; and in love we declare:

מִי־כָמֹכָה בָּאֵלִם, יְיָ? מִי כָּמֹכָה, נֶאְדָּר בַּקֹּדֶשׁ, נוֹרָא תְהִלֹּת, עֹשֵׂה פֶלֶא?

Morning

שִׁירָה חֲדָשָׁה שִׁבְּחוּ גְאוּלִים לְשִׁמְךָ עַל־שְׂפַת הַיָּם; יַחַד כֻּלָּם הוֹדוּ וְהִמְלִיכוּ וְאָמְרוּ:

"יְיָ יִמְלֹךְ לְעוֹלָם וָעֶד!"

צוּר יִשְׂרָאֵל, קוּמָה בְּעֶזְרַת יִשְׂרָאֵל, וּפְדֵה כִנְאֻמֶךָ יְהוּדָה וְיִשְׂרָאֵל. גֹּאֲלֵנוּ יְיָ צְבָאוֹת שְׁמוֹ, קְדוֹשׁ יִשְׂרָאֵל.

בָּרוּךְ אַתָּה, יְיָ, גָּאַל יִשְׂרָאֵל.

Evening

מַלְכוּתְךָ רָאוּ בָנֶיךָ, בּוֹקֵעַ יָם לִפְנֵי מֹשֶׁה; "זֶה אֵלִי!" עָנוּ וְאָמְרוּ:

"יְיָ יִמְלֹךְ לְעֹלָם וָעֶד!"

וְנֶאֱמַר: "כִּי־פָדָה יְיָ אֶת־יַעֲקֹב, וּגְאָלוֹ מִיַּד חָזָק מִמֶּנּוּ."

בָּרוּךְ אַתָּה, יְיָ, גָּאַל יִשְׂרָאֵל.

You are the Redeemer of Israel and all the oppressed. Blessed is the Eternal One, the God of Israel, the Source of freedom.

◆ ◆

For an Evening Service

הַשְׁכִּיבֵנוּ, אָבִינוּ, לְשָׁלוֹם, וְהַעֲמִידֵנוּ, מַלְכֵּנוּ, לְחַיִּים טוֹבִים וּלְשָׁלוֹם.

Cause us, our Creator, to lie down in peace, and raise us up, O Sovereign God, to renewed life and peace.

וּפְרוֹשׂ עָלֵינוּ סֻכַּת שְׁלוֹמֶךָ, וְתַקְּנֵנוּ בְּעֵצָה טוֹבָה מִלְּפָנֶיךָ. וְהוֹשִׁיעֵנוּ מְהֵרָה לְמַעַן שְׁמֶךָ, וְהָגֵן בַּעֲדֵנוּ. וּפְרוֹשׂ עָלֵינוּ סֻכַּת רַחֲמִים וְשָׁלוֹם.

בָּרוּךְ אַתָּה, יְיָ, שׁוֹמֵר עַמּוֹ יִשְׂרָאֵל לָעַד.

Spread over us the shelter of Your peace; guide us with Your good counsel; be our Shield of mercy and peace.

Blessed is the Lord, Guardian of His people Israel for ever.

◆ ◆

All rise

תפלה

אֲדֹנָי, שְׂפָתַי תִּפְתָּח, וּפִי יַגִּיד תְּהִלָּתֶךָ.

Eternal God, open my lips, that my mouth may declare Your glory.

בָּרוּךְ אַתָּה, יְיָ אֱלֹהֵינוּ וֵאלֹהֵי אֲבוֹתֵינוּ, אֱלֹהֵי אַבְרָהָם, אֱלֹהֵי יִצְחָק, וֵאלֹהֵי יַעֲקֹב: הָאֵל הַגָּדוֹל, הַגִּבּוֹר וְהַנּוֹרָא, אֵל עֶלְיוֹן. גּוֹמֵל חֲסָדִים טוֹבִים, וְקוֹנֵה הַכֹּל, וְזוֹכֵר חַסְדֵי אָבוֹת, וּמֵבִיא גְאֻלָּה לִבְנֵי בְנֵיהֶם, לְמַעַן שְׁמוֹ, בְּאַהֲבָה.

מֶלֶךְ עוֹזֵר וּמוֹשִׁיעַ וּמָגֵן. בָּרוּךְ אַתָּה, יְיָ, מָגֵן אַבְרָהָם.

Our God and God of our fathers, God of Abraham, Isaac, and Jacob, Amos, Isaiah, and Micah, a heritage has come down to us along all the painful paths our people has travelled.

Our God and God of our mothers, God of Sarah, Rebekah, Leah, and Rachel, Deborah, Hannah, and Ruth, a heritage has come down to us.

When others worshipped gods indifferent to goodness, our mothers and fathers found the One whose law unites all people in justice and love.

A heritage of faith has come down to us out of the life of our people.

When knowledge was the secret lore of princes and priests, our sages opened their doors to all who sought understanding.

A heritage of learning has come down to us out of the life of our people.

◆ ◆

אַתָּה גִּבּוֹר לְעוֹלָם, אֲדֹנָי, מְחַיֵּה הַכֹּל אַתָּה, רַב לְהוֹשִׁיעַ. מְכַלְכֵּל חַיִּים בְּחֶסֶד, מְחַיֵּה הַכֹּל בְּרַחֲמִים רַבִּים. סוֹמֵךְ נוֹפְלִים, וְרוֹפֵא חוֹלִים, וּמַתִּיר אֲסוּרִים, וּמְקַיֵּם אֱמוּנָתוֹ לִישֵׁנֵי עָפָר. מִי כָמוֹךָ, בַּעַל גְּבוּרוֹת, וּמִי דּוֹמֶה לָּךְ, מֶלֶךְ

מֵמִית וּמְחַיֶּה וּמַצְמִיחַ יְשׁוּעָה? וְנֶאֱמָן אַתָּה לְהַחֲיוֹת הַכֹּל.
בָּרוּךְ אַתָּה, יְיָ, מְחַיֵּה הַכֹּל.

In a world where the weak were tormented by oppressors, our Torah taught us to love the poor and the stranger.
A heritage of justice has come down to us.

Where the sword was sovereign, we were commanded to seek peace and pursue it.
A heritage of peace has come down to us.

All this now is ours. Ours the teaching, ours the task, to make the heritage live.
For it is our life, and the length of our days!

◆ ◆

For an Evening Service

אַתָּה קָדוֹשׁ וְשִׁמְךָ קָדוֹשׁ, וּקְדוֹשִׁים בְּכָל־יוֹם יְהַלְלוּךָ סֶּלָה.
בָּרוּךְ אַתָּה, יְיָ, הָאֵל הַקָּדוֹשׁ.

You are holy, Your name is holy, and those who strive to be holy declare Your glory day by day. Blessed is the Lord, the holy God.

◆ ◆

For a Morning Service

SANCTIFICATION קדושה

נְקַדֵּשׁ אֶת־שִׁמְךָ בָּעוֹלָם, כְּשֵׁם שֶׁמַּקְדִּישִׁים אוֹתוֹ בִּשְׁמֵי מָרוֹם,
כַּכָּתוּב עַל־יַד נְבִיאֶךָ: וְקָרָא זֶה אֶל־זֶה וְאָמַר:

We sanctify Your name on earth, even as all things, to the ends of time and space, proclaim Your holiness; and in the words of the prophet we say:

קָדוֹשׁ, קָדוֹשׁ, קָדוֹשׁ יְיָ צְבָאוֹת, מְלֹא כָל־הָאָרֶץ כְּבוֹדוֹ.

Holy, Holy, Holy is the Lord of Hosts; the fullness of the whole earth is His glory!

לְעֻמָּתָם בָּרוּךְ יֹאמֵרוּ:

They respond to Your glory with blessing:

בָּרוּךְ כְּבוֹד יְיָ מִמְּקוֹמוֹ.

Blessed is the glory of God in heaven and earth.

וּבְדִבְרֵי קָדְשְׁךָ כָּתוּב לֵאמֹר:

And this is Your sacred word:

יִמְלֹךְ יְיָ לְעוֹלָם, אֱלֹהַיִךְ צִיּוֹן, לְדֹר וָדֹר, הַלְלוּיָהּ.

The Lord shall reign for ever; your God, O Zion, from generation to generation. Halleluyah!

לְדוֹר וָדוֹר נַגִּיד גָּדְלֶךָ, וּלְנֵצַח נְצָחִים קְדֻשָּׁתְךָ נַקְדִּישׁ.
וְשִׁבְחֲךָ, אֱלֹהֵינוּ, מִפִּינוּ לֹא יָמוּשׁ לְעוֹלָם וָעֶד.
בָּרוּךְ אַתָּה, יְיָ, הָאֵל הַקָּדוֹשׁ.

To all generations we will make known Your greatness, and to all eternity proclaim Your holiness. Your praise, O God, shall never depart from our lips.

Blessed is the Lord, the holy God.

All are seated

◆ ◆

O fill our minds with knowledge and our hearts with wisdom;
Praised be the Mind that unifies all creation.

Remind us of the best that is in us:
Praised be the Will that gives us power to choose our way.

Help us to feel the anguish of the afflicted and oppressed;
Praised be the Heart that inspires in us a vision of justice and love.

Make us bring knowledge and skill to help the infirm;
Praised be the Power that brings healing to the sick.

Teach us to stand in awe before the mystery of being.
Praised be the One who is present in the miracle of prayer.

◆ ◆

Evening	*Morning*
שָׁלוֹם רָב עַל־יִשְׂרָאֵל עַמְּךָ תָּשִׂים לְעוֹלָם, כִּי אַתָּה הוּא מֶלֶךְ אָדוֹן לְכָל הַשָּׁלוֹם. וְטוֹב בְּעֵינֶיךָ לְבָרֵךְ אֶת־עַמְּךָ יִשְׂרָאֵל בְּכָל־עֵת וּבְכָל־שָׁעָה בִּשְׁלוֹמֶךָ. בָּרוּךְ אַתָּה, יְיָ, הַמְבָרֵךְ אֶת־ עַמּוֹ יִשְׂרָאֵל בַּשָּׁלוֹם.	שִׂים שָׁלוֹם, טוֹבָה וּבְרָכָה, חֵן וָחֶסֶד וְרַחֲמִים, עָלֵינוּ וְעַל־כָּל־ יִשְׂרָאֵל עַמֶּךָ. בָּרְכֵנוּ אָבִינוּ, כֻּלָּנוּ כְּאֶחָד, בְּאוֹר פָּנֶיךָ, כִּי בְאוֹר פָּנֶיךָ נָתַתָּ לָּנוּ, יְיָ אֱלֹהֵינוּ, תּוֹרַת חַיִּים, וְאַהֲבַת חֶסֶד, וּצְדָקָה וּבְרָכָה וְרַחֲמִים, וְחַיִּים וְשָׁלוֹם.

וְטוֹב בְּעֵינֶיךָ לְבָרֵךְ אֶת־עַמְּךָ יִשְׂרָאֵל בְּכָל־עֵת וּבְכָל־שָׁעָה
בִּשְׁלוֹמֶךָ. בָּרוּךְ אַתָּה, יְיָ, הַמְבָרֵךְ אֶת־עַמּוֹ יִשְׂרָאֵל בַּשָּׁלוֹם.

We pray for the peace of Israel and all the nations. Our prophets envisioned an age of blessing. Still we yearn for it and work for it. As we have learned:

Let justice dwell in the wilderness, righteousness in the fruitful field.	וְשָׁכַן בַּמִּדְבָּר מִשְׁפָּט, וּצְדָקָה בַּכַּרְמֶל תֵּשֵׁב.
For righteousness shall lead to peace; *it shall bring quietness and confidence* *for ever.*	וְהָיָה מַעֲשֵׂה הַצְּדָקָה שָׁלוֹם; וַעֲבֹדַת הַצְּדָקָה הַשְׁקֵט וָבֶטַח עַד־עוֹלָם.
Then all shall sit under their vines and under their fig-trees, *and none shall make them afraid.*	וְיָשְׁבוּ אִישׁ תַּחַת גַּפְנוֹ וְתַחַת תְּאֵנָתוֹ, וְאֵין מַחֲרִיד.

◆ ◆

◆ ◆

MEDITATION

◆ ◆

יִהְיוּ לְרָצוֹן אִמְרֵי־פִי וְהֶגְיוֹן לִבִּי לְפָנֶיךָ, יְיָ, צוּרִי וְגוֹאֲלִי.

May the words of my mouth, and the meditations of my heart, be acceptable to You, O Lord, my Rock and my Redeemer.

or

עֹשֶׂה שָׁלוֹם בִּמְרוֹמָיו, הוּא יַעֲשֶׂה שָׁלוֹם עָלֵינוּ וְעַל כָּל־יִשְׂרָאֵל, וְאִמְרוּ אָמֵן.

May He who causes peace to reign in the high heavens let peace descend on us, on all Israel, and all the world.

◆ ◆

Prayers at a House of Mourning begin on page 645.

The Rituals for the Reading of Torah begin on page 415.

Concluding Prayers begin on page 613.

Havdalah for the conclusion of Shabbat is on page 633.

From Psalm 85

אֶשְׁמְעָה מַה־יְדַבֵּר הָאֵל יְיָ, כִּי יְדַבֵּר שָׁלוֹם אֶל־עַמּוֹ, וְאֶל־
חֲסִידָיו, וְאַל יָשׁוּבוּ לְכִסְלָה.

אַךְ קָרוֹב לִירֵאָיו יִשְׁעוֹ, לִשְׁכֹּן כָּבוֹד בְּאַרְצֵנוּ.

Let us listen to the words of God the Eternal, for they are words of peace to His people, to His faithful ones, to those who turn their hearts to Him.

Help is near to those who revere Him, that glory may abide in our land.

חֶסֶד וֶאֱמֶת נִפְגָּשׁוּ, צֶדֶק וְשָׁלוֹם נָשָׁקוּ.

אֱמֶת מֵאֶרֶץ תִּצְמָח, וְצֶדֶק מִשָּׁמַיִם נִשְׁקָף.

Love and truth shall meet, justice and peace shall embrace.

Truth shall spring up from the earth, and justice look down from the sky.

גַּם־יְיָ יִתֵּן הַטּוֹב, וְאַרְצֵנוּ תִּתֵּן יְבוּלָהּ.

צֶדֶק לְפָנָיו יְהַלֵּךְ, וְיָשֵׂם לְדֶרֶךְ פְּעָמָיו.

The Lord shall give of His goodness, the earth shall yield its harvest.

Justice shall go before Him, paving the way for our steps.

◆ ◆

MEDITATION

There are moments when we hear the call of our higher selves, the call that links us to the divine. Then we know how blessed we are with life and love. May this be a moment of such vision, a time of deeper attachment to the godlike in us and in our world: for which we shall give thanks and praise!

◆ ◆

O give thanks to the Lord, for He is good;	הוֹדוּ לַייָ כִּי־טוֹב,
for His love is everlasting!	כִּי לְעוֹלָם חַסְדּוֹ!

◆ ◆

All rise

שמע וברכותיה

בָּרְכוּ אֶת־יְיָ הַמְבֹרָךְ!

Praise the Lord, to whom our praise is due!

בָּרוּךְ יְיָ הַמְבֹרָךְ לְעוֹלָם וָעֶד!

Praised be the Lord, to whom our praise is due,
now and for ever!

◆ ◆

O God, the keenest eye sees only a minute portion of Your greatness. Even the mind of genius perceives but little of Your glory. Poets labor to express Your splendor, sages stammer in their effort to describe You, but in vain. All our learning is but a grain of sand on the shores of an infinite sea of knowledge.

We cannot comprehend or name You. The mystery of Your works is a riddle we cannot solve. We can only stand in awe of the Infinite. And yet we reach out, hoping to grow toward Your light!

◆ ◆

דְּרָכֶיךָ, יְיָ, הוֹדִיעֵנִי; אָרְחוֹתֶיךָ לַמְּדֵנִי, הַדְרִיכֵנִי בַאֲמִתֶּךָ, וְלַמְּדֵנִי.

כִּי חֶסֶד חָפַצְתִּי, וְלֹא זָבַח; וְדַעַת אֱלֹהִים מֵעֹלוֹת.

Help me to know Your ways, O Lord; teach me Your paths, lead me in Your truth, and guide me.
I desire love, and not sacrifices; the knowledge of God rather than burnt-offerings.

הוֹי בֹּנֶה בֵיתוֹ בְּלֹא־צֶדֶק וַעֲלִיּוֹתָיו בְּלֹא מִשְׁפָּט;

בְּרֵעֵהוּ יַעֲבֹד חִנָּם, וּפֹעֲלוֹ לֹא יִתֶּן־לוֹ.

Woe to those who build their house by unjust means and their upper rooms by injustice;
who make their neighbors work for nothing, and withhold their rightful wages.

אָבִיךָ הֲלֹא אָכַל וְשָׁתָה, וְעָשָׂה מִשְׁפָּט וּצְדָקָה? אָז טוֹב לוֹ.

הֲלוֹא־הִיא הַדַּעַת אֹתִי? נְאֻם־יְיָ.

Did not those who came before you eat and drink, like you, yet do justice and right? Then it was well.
Is this not what it means to know Me? says the Lord.

◆ ◆

שְׁמַע יִשְׂרָאֵל: יְיָ אֱלֹהֵינוּ, יְיָ אֶחָד!

Hear, O Israel: the Lord is our God, the Lord is One!

בָּרוּךְ שֵׁם כְּבוֹד מַלְכוּתוֹ לְעוֹלָם וָעֶד!

Blessed is His glorious kingdom for ever and ever!

All are seated

וְאָהַבְתָּ אֵת יְיָ אֱלֹהֶיךָ בְּכָל־לְבָבְךָ וּבְכָל־נַפְשְׁךָ וּבְכָל־מְאֹדֶךָ.
וְהָיוּ הַדְּבָרִים הָאֵלֶּה, אֲשֶׁר אָנֹכִי מְצַוְּךָ הַיּוֹם, עַל־לְבָבֶךָ.
וְשִׁנַּנְתָּם לְבָנֶיךָ, וְדִבַּרְתָּ בָּם בְּשִׁבְתְּךָ בְּבֵיתֶךָ, וּבְלֶכְתְּךָ
בַדֶּרֶךְ, וּבְשָׁכְבְּךָ וּבְקוּמֶךָ.

You shall love the Lord your God with all your mind, with all your strength, with all your being.
Set these words, which I command you this day, upon your heart. Teach them faithfully to your children; speak of them in your home and on your way, when you lie down and when you rise up.

וּקְשַׁרְתָּם לְאוֹת עַל־יָדֶךָ, וְהָיוּ לְטֹטָפֹת בֵּין עֵינֶיךָ, וּכְתַבְתָּם עַל־מְזֻזוֹת בֵּיתֶךָ, וּבִשְׁעָרֶיךָ.

Bind them as a sign upon your hand; let them be a symbol before your eyes; inscribe them on the doorposts of your house, and on your gates.

לְמַעַן תִּזְכְּרוּ וַעֲשִׂיתֶם אֶת־כָּל־מִצְוֹתָי, וִהְיִיתֶם קְדֹשִׁים לֵאלֹהֵיכֶם. אֲנִי יְיָ אֱלֹהֵיכֶם, אֲשֶׁר הוֹצֵאתִי אֶתְכֶם מֵאֶרֶץ מִצְרַיִם לִהְיוֹת לָכֶם לֵאלֹהִים. אֲנִי יְיָ אֱלֹהֵיכֶם.

Be mindful of all My Mitzvot, and do them: so shall you consecrate yourselves to your God. I, the Lord, am your God who led you out of Egypt to be your God; I, the Lord, am your God.

◆ ◆

Morning

עַל־הָרִאשׁוֹנִים וְעַל־הָאַחֲרוֹנִים דָּבָר טוֹב וְקַיָּם לְעוֹלָם וָעֶד. אֱמֶת וֶאֱמוּנָה, חֹק וְלֹא יַעֲבוֹר. אֱמֶת שָׁאַתָּה הוּא יְיָ אֱלֹהֵינוּ וֵאלֹהֵי אֲבוֹתֵינוּ, מַלְכֵּנוּ מֶלֶךְ אֲבוֹתֵינוּ, גּוֹאֲלֵנוּ גּוֹאֵל אֲבוֹתֵינוּ, יוֹצְרֵנוּ, צוּר יְשׁוּעָתֵנוּ. פּוֹדֵנוּ וּמַצִּילֵנוּ מֵעוֹלָם הוּא שְׁמֶךָ, אֵין אֱלֹהִים זוּלָתֶךָ.

עֶזְרַת אֲבוֹתֵינוּ אַתָּה הוּא מֵעוֹלָם, מָגֵן וּמוֹשִׁיעַ לִבְנֵיהֶם אַחֲרֵיהֶם בְּכָל־דּוֹר וָדוֹר. בְּרוּם עוֹלָם מוֹשָׁבֶךָ וּמִשְׁפָּטֶיךָ וְצִדְקָתְךָ עַד אַפְסֵי־אָרֶץ. אַשְׁרֵי אִישׁ שֶׁיִּשְׁמַע לְמִצְוֹתֶיךָ, וְתוֹרָתְךָ וּדְבָרְךָ יָשִׂים עַל־לִבּוֹ.

Evening

אֱמֶת וֶאֱמוּנָה כָּל־זֹאת, וְקַיָּם עָלֵינוּ כִּי הוּא יְיָ אֱלֹהֵינוּ וְאֵין זוּלָתוֹ, וַאֲנַחְנוּ יִשְׂרָאֵל עַמּוֹ.

הַפּוֹדֵנוּ מִיַּד מְלָכִים, מַלְכֵּנוּ הַגּוֹאֲלֵנוּ מִכַּף כָּל־הֶעָרִיצִים.

הָעֹשֶׂה גְדֹלוֹת עַד אֵין חֵקֶר, וְנִפְלָאוֹת עַד־אֵין מִסְפָּר.

הָעֹשֶׂה לָנוּ נִסִּים בְּפַרְעֹה, אוֹתוֹת וּמוֹפְתִים בְּאַדְמַת בְּנֵי חָם.

וַיּוֹצֵא אֶת־עַמּוֹ יִשְׂרָאֵל מִתּוֹכָם לְחֵרוּת עוֹלָם.

וְרָאוּ בָנָיו גְּבוּרָתוֹ; שִׁבְּחוּ וְהוֹדוּ לִשְׁמוֹ.

וּמַלְכוּתוֹ בְּרָצוֹן קִבְּלוּ עֲלֵיהֶם.

מֹשֶׁה וּבְנֵי יִשְׂרָאֵל לְךָ עָנוּ שִׁירָה בְּשִׂמְחָה רַבָּה, וְאָמְרוּ כֻלָּם:

True and enduring are the words spoken by our prophets.
You are the living God; Your word brings life and light to the soul.

You are the First and the Last:
besides You there is no redeemer or savior.

You are the strength of our life, the Power that saves us.
Your kingdom and Your truth abide for ever.

You have been the help of our people in time of trouble;
You are our Refuge in all generations.

Your power was manifest when we went free out of Egypt;
in every liberation from bondage we see it.

May Your law of freedom rule the hearts of all Your children,
and Your law of justice unite them in friendship.

May the righteous of all nations rejoice in Your love and triumph by Your power.
O God, our Refuge and our Hope, we glorify You now as did our people in ancient days:

מִי־כָמֹכָה בָּאֵלִם, יְיָ? מִי כָּמֹכָה, נֶאְדָּר בַּקֹּדֶשׁ, נוֹרָא תְהִלֹּת,
עֹשֵׂה פֶלֶא?

Morning

שִׁירָה חֲדָשָׁה שִׁבְּחוּ גְאוּלִים
לְשִׁמְךָ עַל־שְׂפַת הַיָּם; יַחַד כֻּלָּם
הוֹדוּ וְהִמְלִיכוּ וְאָמְרוּ:
"יְיָ יִמְלֹךְ לְעוֹלָם וָעֶד!"
צוּר יִשְׂרָאֵל, קוּמָה בְּעֶזְרַת
יִשְׂרָאֵל, וּפְדֵה כִנְאֻמֶךָ יְהוּדָה
וְיִשְׂרָאֵל. גֹּאֲלֵנוּ יְיָ צְבָאוֹת שְׁמוֹ,
קְדוֹשׁ יִשְׂרָאֵל.
בָּרוּךְ אַתָּה, יְיָ, גָּאַל יִשְׂרָאֵל.

Evening

מַלְכוּתְךָ רָאוּ בָנֶיךָ, בּוֹקֵעַ יָם
לִפְנֵי מֹשֶׁה; "זֶה אֵלִי!" עָנוּ
וְאָמְרוּ:
"יְיָ יִמְלֹךְ לְעֹלָם וָעֶד!"
וְנֶאֱמַר: "כִּי־פָדָה יְיָ אֶת־יַעֲקֹב,
וּגְאָלוֹ מִיַּד חָזָק מִמֶּנּוּ."
בָּרוּךְ אַתָּה, יְיָ, גָּאַל יִשְׂרָאֵל.

◆ ◆

All rise

תפלה

בָּרוּךְ אַתָּה, יְיָ אֱלֹהֵינוּ וֵאלֹהֵי אֲבוֹתֵינוּ, אֱלֹהֵי אַבְרָהָם, אֱלֹהֵי יִצְחָק, וֵאלֹהֵי יַעֲקֹב, הָאֵל הַגָּדוֹל, הַגִּבּוֹר, וְהַנּוֹרָא, אֵל עֶלְיוֹן, קוֹנֵה שָׁמַיִם וָאָרֶץ.

Be praised, O Lord, God of all generations, of Abraham, of Isaac, and of Jacob; our God. Your wondrous creative power fills heaven and earth.

◆ ◆

אַתָּה גִּבּוֹר לְעוֹלָם, אֲדֹנָי, מְחַיֵּה הַכֹּל אַתָּה, רַב לְהוֹשִׁיעַ.

For Your many blessings, O God, we give thanks. From You comes our life, and in Your great love You sustain it within us.

מְכַלְכֵּל חַיִּים בְּחֶסֶד, מְחַיֵּה הַכֹּל בְּרַחֲמִים רַבִּים. סוֹמֵךְ נוֹפְלִים, וְרוֹפֵא חוֹלִים, וּמַתִּיר אֲסוּרִים, וּמְקַיֵּם אֱמוּנָתוֹ לִישֵׁנֵי עָפָר.

You give strength to the weak, courage to those who are afraid, and light to all who dwell in darkness.

מִי כָמוֹךָ, בַּעַל גְּבוּרוֹת, וּמִי דּוֹמֶה לָּךְ, מֶלֶךְ מֵמִית וּמְחַיֶּה וּמַצְמִיחַ יְשׁוּעָה?
וְנֶאֱמָן אַתָּה לְהַחֲיוֹת הַכֹּל. בָּרוּךְ אַתָּה, יְיָ, מְחַיֵּה הַכֹּל.

O Source of all that we are and have, teach us to use our gifts in Your service, for the well-being of our nation and our world. Then will our lives give glory to Your name.

◆ ◆

For an Evening Service

אַתָּה קָדוֹשׁ וְשִׁמְךָ קָדוֹשׁ, וּקְדוֹשִׁים בְּכָל־יוֹם יְהַלְלוּךָ סֶּלָה.
בָּרוּךְ אַתָּה, יְיָ, הָאֵל הַקָּדוֹשׁ.

You are holy, Your name is holy, and those who strive to be holy declare Your glory day by day. Blessed is the Lord, the holy God.

◆ ◆

For a Morning Service

SANCTIFICATION — קדושה

נְקַדֵּשׁ אֶת־שִׁמְךָ בָּעוֹלָם, כְּשֵׁם שֶׁמַּקְדִּישִׁים אוֹתוֹ בִּשְׁמֵי מָרוֹם,
כַּכָּתוּב עַל־יַד נְבִיאֶךָ: וְקָרָא זֶה אֶל־זֶה וְאָמַר:

We sanctify Your name on earth, even as all things, to the ends of time and space, proclaim Your holiness; and in the words of the prophet we say:

קָדוֹשׁ, קָדוֹשׁ, קָדוֹשׁ יְיָ צְבָאוֹת, מְלֹא כָל־הָאָרֶץ כְּבוֹדוֹ.

Holy, Holy, Holy is the Lord of Hosts; the fullness of the whole earth is His glory!

לְעֻמָּתָם בָּרוּךְ יֹאמֵרוּ:

They respond to Your glory with blessing:

בָּרוּךְ כְּבוֹד יְיָ מִמְּקוֹמוֹ.

Blessed is the glory of God in heaven and earth.

וּבְדִבְרֵי קָדְשְׁךָ כָּתוּב לֵאמֹר:

And this is Your sacred word:

יִמְלֹךְ יְיָ לְעוֹלָם, אֱלֹהַיִךְ צִיּוֹן, לְדֹר וָדֹר, הַלְלוּיָהּ.

The Lord shall reign for ever; your God, O Zion, from generation to generation. Halleluyah!

לְדוֹר וָדוֹר נַגִּיד גָּדְלֶךָ, וּלְנֵצַח נְצָחִים קְדֻשָּׁתְךָ נַקְדִּישׁ.
וְשִׁבְחֲךָ, אֱלֹהֵינוּ, מִפִּינוּ לֹא יָמוּשׁ לְעוֹלָם וָעֶד.
בָּרוּךְ אַתָּה, יְיָ, הָאֵל הַקָּדוֹשׁ.

To all generations we will make known Your greatness, and to all eternity proclaim Your holiness. Your praise, O God, shall never depart from our lips.

Blessed is the Lord, the holy God.

All are seated

◆ ◆

הֲבִינֵנוּ, יְיָ אֱלֹהֵינוּ, לָדַעַת דְּרָכֶיךָ, וּמוֹל אֶת־לְבָבֵנוּ לְיִרְאָתֶךָ. וְתִסְלַח לָנוּ לִהְיוֹת גְּאוּלִים; וְרַחֲקֵנוּ מִמַּכְאוֹב.

Give us insight, Lord our God, to understand Your ways, and consecrate our hearts to revere You.
From our sins redeem us with forgiveness; from pain and sorrow keep us far.

וְדַשְּׁנֵנוּ בִּנְאוֹת אַרְצֶךָ, וּנְפוּצוֹתֵינוּ מֵאַרְבַּע כַּנְפוֹת הָאָרֶץ תְּקַבֵּץ. וְהַתּוֹעִים עַל דַּעְתְּךָ יִשָּׁפֵטוּ; וְעַל הָרְשָׁעִים תָּנִיף יָדֶךָ.

Bestow upon us Your earth's abundance, and gather our exiles from earth's four corners.
To those who stray, bring correction; upon the lawless, place Your hand.

וְיִשְׂמְחוּ צַדִּיקִים בְּבִנְיַן עִירֶךָ, וּבִצְמִיחַת קֶרֶן יְשׁוּעָתֶךָ. טֶרֶם נִקְרָא אַתָּה תַעֲנֶה. בָּרוּךְ אַתָּה, יְיָ, שׁוֹמֵעַ תְּפִלָּה.

Let the righteous rejoice in the building of Your city and the flowering of Your redemption.
Before we call comes Your reply. Blessed is the Lord, who hearkens to prayer.

◆ ◆

Our God, the Guide of humanity, let Your spirit rule this nation and its citizens, that their deeds may be prompted by a love of justice and right, and bear fruit in goodness and peace.
Bless our people with love of righteousness.

Teach us to work for the welfare of all, to diminish the evils that beset us, and to enlarge our nation's virtues.
Bless our people with civic courage.

Bless our striving to make real the dream of Your kingdom, when we shall put an end to the suffering we now inflict upon each other.
Bless our people with a vision of Your kingdom on earth.

For You have endowed us with noble powers; help us to use them wisely, and with compassion.
Bless our people with a wise and feeling heart.

You have given us freedom to choose between good and evil, life and death. May we choose life and good, that our children may inherit from us the blessings of dignity and freedom, prosperity and peace.

◆ ◆

MEDITATION

◆ ◆

יִהְיוּ לְרָצוֹן אִמְרֵי־פִי וְהֶגְיוֹן לִבִּי לְפָנֶיךָ, יְיָ, צוּרִי וְגוֹאֲלִי.

May the words of my mouth, and the meditations of my heart, be acceptable to You, O Lord, my Rock and my Redeemer.

or

עֹשֶׂה שָׁלוֹם בִּמְרוֹמָיו, הוּא יַעֲשֶׂה שָׁלוֹם עָלֵינוּ וְעַל כָּל־יִשְׂרָאֵל וְאִמְרוּ אָמֵן.

May He who causes peace to reign in the high heavens let peace descend on us, on all Israel, and all the world.

◆ ◆

Prayers at a House of Mourning begin on page 645.

The Rituals for the Reading of Torah begin on page 415.

Concluding Prayers begin on page 613.

Havdalah for the conclusion of Shabbat is on page 633.

אשרי

אַשְׁרֵי יוֹשְׁבֵי בֵיתֶךָ; עוֹד יְהַלְלוּךָ סֶּלָה.
אַשְׁרֵי הָעָם שֶׁכָּכָה לוֹ; אַשְׁרֵי הָעָם שֶׁיְיָ אֱלֹהָיו.

Happy are those who dwell in Your house;
they will sing Your praise for ever.
Happy the people to whom such blessing falls;
happy the people whose God is the Lord.

Psalm 145

תְּהִלָּה לְדָוִד.

אֲרוֹמִמְךָ, אֱלֹהַי הַמֶּלֶךְ, וַאֲבָרְכָה שִׁמְךָ לְעוֹלָם וָעֶד.
בְּכָל־יוֹם אֲבָרְכֶךָּ, וַאֲהַלְלָה שִׁמְךָ לְעוֹלָם וָעֶד.

I will exalt You, my Sovereign God;
I will bless Your name for ever.
Every day will I bless You;
I will extol Your name for ever.

גָּדוֹל יְיָ וּמְהֻלָּל מְאֹד, וְלִגְדֻלָּתוֹ אֵין חֵקֶר.
דּוֹר לְדוֹר יְשַׁבַּח מַעֲשֶׂיךָ, וּגְבוּרֹתֶיךָ יַגִּידוּ.

Great is the Lord and worthy of praise;
His greatness is infinite.
One generation shall acclaim Your work to the next;
they shall tell of Your mighty acts.

הֲדַר כְּבוֹד הוֹדֶךָ,
וְדִבְרֵי נִפְלְאֹתֶיךָ אָשִׂיחָה.

They shall consider Your radiant glory;
they shall reflect on Your wondrous works.

וְעֱזוּז נוֹרְאוֹתֶֽיךָ יֹאמֵֽרוּ, וּגְדֻלָּתְךָ אֲסַפְּרֶֽנָּה.
זֵֽכֶר רַב־טוּבְךָ יַבִּֽיעוּ, וְצִדְקָתְךָ יְרַנֵּֽנוּ.

They shall speak of Your awesome might,
and make known Your greatness.
They shall tell the world of Your great goodness,
and sing of Your righteousness.

חַנּוּן וְרַחוּם יְיָ, אֶֽרֶךְ אַפַּֽיִם וּגְדָל־חָֽסֶד.
טוֹב־יְיָ לַכֹּל, וְרַחֲמָיו עַל־כָּל־מַעֲשָׂיו.

"The Lord is gracious and compassionate,
endlessly patient, overflowing with love."
"The Lord is good to all; His compassion
shelters all His creatures."

יוֹדֽוּךָ יְיָ כָּל מַעֲשֶֽׂיךָ,
וַחֲסִידֶֽיךָ יְבָרְכֽוּכָה.

All Your works, O Lord, shall thank You;
Your faithful shall bless You.

כְּבוֹד מַלְכוּתְךָ יֹאמֵֽרוּ, וּגְבוּרָתְךָ יְדַבֵּֽרוּ,
לְהוֹדִֽיעַ לִבְנֵי הָאָדָם גְּבוּרֹתָיו, וּכְבוֹד הֲדַר מַלְכוּתוֹ.

They shall speak of the glory of Your kingdom,
and tell of Your strength:
to reveal Your power to the world, and
the glorious splendor of Your kingdom.

מַלְכוּתְךָ מַלְכוּת כָּל־עֹלָמִים,
וּמֶמְשַׁלְתְּךָ בְּכָל־דּוֹר וָדֹר.

Your kingdom is an everlasting kingdom;
Your dominion endures through all generations.

סוֹמֵךְ יְיָ לְכָל־הַנֹּפְלִים, וְזוֹקֵף לְכָל־הַכְּפוּפִים.
עֵינֵי כֹל אֵלֶֽיךָ יְשַׂבֵּֽרוּ, וְאַתָּה נוֹתֵן־לָהֶם אֶת־אָכְלָם בְּעִתּוֹ.

Lord, You support the falling;
You raise up all who are bowed down.
The eyes of all are turned to You;
You sustain them in time of need.

פּוֹתֵחַ אֶת־יָדֶךָ וּמַשְׂבִּיעַ לְכָל־חַי רָצוֹן.
צַדִּיק יְיָ בְּכָל־דְּרָכָיו, וְחָסִיד בְּכָל־מַעֲשָׂיו.

You open Your hand to fulfill the needs of all the living.
Lord, You are just in all Your paths, loving in all Your deeds.

קָרוֹב יְיָ לְכָל־קֹרְאָיו, לְכֹל אֲשֶׁר יִקְרָאֻהוּ בֶאֱמֶת.
רְצוֹן־יְרֵאָיו יַעֲשֶׂה, וְאֶת־שַׁוְעָתָם יִשְׁמַע וְיוֹשִׁיעֵם.

The Lord is near to all who call upon Him,
to all who call upon Him in truth.
He will fulfill the hope of all who revere Him;
He will hear their cry and help them.

שׁוֹמֵר יְיָ אֶת־כָּל־אֹהֲבָיו,
וְאֵת כָּל־הָרְשָׁעִים יַשְׁמִיד.

The Lord preserves those who love Him,
but the lawless He brings to grief.

תְּהִלַּת יְיָ יְדַבֶּר־פִּי
וִיבָרֵךְ כָּל־בָּשָׂר שֵׁם קָדְשׁוֹ לְעוֹלָם וָעֶד.
וַאֲנַחְנוּ נְבָרֵךְ יָהּ מֵעַתָּה וְעַד־עוֹלָם. הַלְלוּיָהּ.

My lips shall declare the glory of the Lord;
let all flesh bless His holy name for ever and ever.
We will bless the Lord now and always. Halleluyah!

◆ ◆

READER'S KADDISH — חצי קדיש

יִתְגַּדַּל וְיִתְקַדַּשׁ שְׁמֵהּ רַבָּא בְּעָלְמָא דִּי־בְרָא כִרְעוּתֵהּ, וְיַמְלִיךְ מַלְכוּתֵהּ בְּחַיֵּיכוֹן וּבְיוֹמֵיכוֹן וּבְחַיֵּי דְכָל־בֵּית יִשְׂרָאֵל, בַּעֲגָלָא וּבִזְמַן קָרִיב, וְאִמְרוּ: אָמֵן.

יְהֵא שְׁמֵהּ רַבָּא מְבָרַךְ לְעָלַם וּלְעָלְמֵי עָלְמַיָּא.

יִתְבָּרַךְ וְיִשְׁתַּבַּח, וְיִתְפָּאַר וְיִתְרוֹמַם וְיִתְנַשֵּׂא, וְיִתְהַדַּר וְיִתְעַלֶּה וְיִתְהַלַּל שְׁמֵהּ דְּקוּדְשָׁא, בְּרִיךְ הוּא, לְעֵלָּא מִן כָּל־בִּרְכָתָא וְשִׁירָתָא, תֻּשְׁבְּחָתָא וְנֶחֱמָתָא דַּאֲמִירָן בְּעָלְמָא, וְאִמְרוּ: אָמֵן.

Let the glory of God be extolled, let His great name be hallowed in the world whose creation He willed. May His kingdom soon prevail, in our own day, our own lives, and the life of all Israel, and let us say: Amen.

Let His great name be blessed for ever and ever.

Let the name of the Holy One, blessed is He, be glorified, exalted and honored, though He is beyond all the praises, songs, and adorations that we can utter, and let us say: Amen.

◆ ◆

The Tefillah is on page 60.

Alternative forms of the Tefillah are on pages 78, 88, 97, 107.

תפלות ערבית לשבת

SABBATH EVENING SERVICES

א I א

For congregations where the lights are kindled in the synagogue

הדלקת הנרות

אַב הָרַחֲמִים, אָנָּא מְשֹׁךְ חַסְדְּךָ עָלֵינוּ וְעַל קְרוֹבֵינוּ הָאֲהוּבִים. וְזַכֵּנוּ לָלֶכֶת בְּדַרְכֵי יְשָׁרִים לְפָנֶיךָ, דְּבֵקִים בַּתּוֹרָה וּבְמַעֲשִׂים טוֹבִים.

Source of mercy, continue Your loving care for us and our loved ones. Give us strength to walk in Your presence on the paths of the righteous, loyal to Your Torah, steadfast in goodness.

הַרְחֵק מֵעָלֵינוּ כָּל־חֶרְפָּה, תּוּגָה, וְיָגוֹן. וְשִׂים שָׁלוֹם, אוֹרָה, וְשִׂמְחָה בִּמְעוֹנֵינוּ. כִּי עִמְּךָ מְקוֹר הַחַיִּים. בְּאוֹרְךָ נִרְאֶה אוֹר. אָמֵן.

Keep far from us all shame, grief, and anguish; fill our homes with peace, light, and joy. O God, fountain of life, by Your light do we see light.

◆ ◆

בָּרוּךְ אַתָּה, יְיָ אֱלֹהֵינוּ, מֶלֶךְ הָעוֹלָם,
אֲשֶׁר קִדְּשָׁנוּ בְּמִצְוֹתָיו וְצִוָּנוּ לְהַדְלִיק נֵר שֶׁל שַׁבָּת.

Blessed is the Lord our God, Ruler of the universe,
who hallows us with His Mitzvot, and commands us
to kindle the lights of Shabbat.

◆ ◆

May God bless us with Shabbat joy.
May God bless us with Shabbat holiness.
May God bless us with Shabbat peace.

◆ ◆

Welcoming Shabbat קבלת שבת

One or more of the following passages may be read or chanted

From Psalm 95

Come, let us sing to the Lord:	לְכוּ נְרַנְּנָה לַייָ,
let our song ring out to our sheltering Rock.	נָרִֽיעָה לְצוּר יִשְׁעֵנוּ.
Let us approach Him with thanksgiving,	נְקַדְּמָה פָנָיו בְּתוֹדָה,
our voices loud with song.	בִּזְמִירוֹת נָרִֽיעַ לוֹ.
For the Lord is a great God,	כִּי אֵל גָּדוֹל יְיָ,
a Ruler high above the idols of every age.	וּמֶֽלֶךְ גָּדוֹל עַל־כָּל־אֱלֹהִים.
In His hands are the depths of the earth;	אֲשֶׁר בְּיָדוֹ מֶחְקְרֵי־אָֽרֶץ,
His are the mountain-peaks.	וְתוֹעֲפוֹת הָרִים לוֹ.
He made the sea, it is His;	אֲשֶׁר־לוֹ הַיָּם, וְהוּא עָשָֽׂהוּ,
the dry land is the work of His hands.	וְיַבֶּֽשֶׁת יָדָיו יָצָֽרוּ.
He is our God and our Shepherd;	כִּי הוּא אֱלֹהֵֽינוּ,
we are His people and His flock:	וַאֲנַֽחְנוּ עַם מַרְעִיתוֹ וְצֹאן יָדוֹ:
if only today	הַיּוֹם–
we would listen to His voice!	אִם־בְּקֹלוֹ תִשְׁמָֽעוּ!

◆ ◆

From Psalm 96

שִׁירוּ לַייָ שִׁיר חָדָשׁ; שִׁירוּ לַייָ, כָּל־הָאָרֶץ!
שִׁירוּ לַייָ, בָּרְכוּ שְׁמוֹ; בַּשְּׂרוּ מִיּוֹם־לְיוֹם יְשׁוּעָתוֹ.

Sing a new song to the Lord;
all the earth sing to the Lord!
Sing to the Lord, bless His name,
tell of His power day after day.

סַפְּרוּ בַגּוֹיִם כְּבוֹדוֹ, בְּכָל הָעַמִּים נִפְלְאוֹתָיו.
כִּי גָדוֹל יְיָ, וּמְהֻלָּל מְאֹד, נוֹרָא הוּא עַל־כָּל־אֱלֹהִים.

Declare His glory among the nations,
His wonders among the peoples.
For great is God, beyond all praise,
and awesome, far above the gods that are worshipped!

כִּי כָּל־אֱלֹהֵי הָעַמִּים אֱלִילִים – וַייָ שָׁמַיִם עָשָׂה.
הוֹד־וְהָדָר לְפָנָיו, עֹז וְתִפְאֶרֶת בְּמִקְדָּשׁוֹ.

All the other gods are merely idols:
it is the Lord who made the heavens.
Honor and beauty attend Him,
strength and splendor are in His presence.

הָבוּ לַייָ, מִשְׁפְּחוֹת עַמִּים, הָבוּ לַייָ כָּבוֹד וָעֹז.
הָבוּ לַייָ כְּבוֹד שְׁמוֹ; הִשְׁתַּחֲווּ לַייָ בְּהַדְרַת קֹדֶשׁ.

Give honor to God, all races and peoples,
give honor to God for His glory and might.
Give honor to God for the glory of His name;
worship the Lord in the beauty of holiness.

חִילוּ מִפָּנָיו כָּל־הָאָרֶץ. אִמְרוּ בַגּוֹיִם: "יְיָ מָלָךְ;
אַף תִּכּוֹן תֵּבֵל, בַּל־תִּמּוֹט: יָדִין עַמִּים בְּמֵישָׁרִים."
יִשְׂמְחוּ הַשָּׁמַיִם וְתָגֵל הָאָרֶץ; יִרְעַם הַיָּם וּמְלֹאוֹ.

Let all the earth tremble at His presence.
Declare to the nations: "God reigns;

now the world is secure and firmly based:
He will judge the peoples with integrity."
Let the heavens be glad and the earth rejoice;
let the sea roar, and all that fills it.

יַעֲלֹז שָׂדַי וְכָל־אֲשֶׁר־בּוֹ;
אָז יְרַנְּנוּ כָּל־עֲצֵי־יָעַר לִפְנֵי יְיָ.

Let the field and all its creatures exult;
let the trees of the forest sing for joy before the Lord.

כִּי בָא, כִּי בָא לִשְׁפֹּט הָאָרֶץ:
יִשְׁפֹּט־תֵּבֵל בְּצֶדֶק, וְעַמִּים בֶּאֱמוּנָתוֹ.

For He comes to rule the earth:
He will rule the world with justice,
and the peoples with His truth.

◆ ◆

From Psalm 97

יְיָ מָלָךְ: תָּגֵל הָאָרֶץ, יִשְׂמְחוּ אִיִּים רַבִּים.
עָנָן וַעֲרָפֶל סְבִיבָיו; צֶדֶק וּמִשְׁפָּט מְכוֹן כִּסְאוֹ.

God reigns:
let the earth rejoice,
the many nations be glad.
Cloud and mist surround Him,
right and justice are the foundation of His throne.

הִגִּידוּ הַשָּׁמַיִם צִדְקוֹ, וְרָאוּ כָל־הָעַמִּים כְּבוֹדוֹ.
שָׁמְעָה וַתִּשְׂמַח צִיּוֹן; וַתָּגֵלְנָה בְּנוֹת יְהוּדָה, לְמַעַן מִשְׁפָּטֶיךָ, יְיָ.

The heavens tell of His righteousness,
the peoples witness His glory.
Zion hears and is glad;
the cities of Judah rejoice, O God, over Your judgments.

כִּי אַתָּה, יְיָ, עֶלְיוֹן עַל־כָּל־הָאָֽרֶץ:
מְאֹד נַעֲלֵיתָ עַל־כָּל־אֱלֹהִים.

For You, Lord, are supreme over all the earth,
You are exalted far above the gods that are worshipped.

אֹהֲבֵי יְיָ שִׂנְאוּ רָע!
אוֹר זָרֻעַ לַצַּדִּיק, וּלְיִשְׁרֵי־לֵב שִׂמְחָה.

The Lord loves those who hate evil!
Light dawns for the righteous,
gladness for the upright in heart.

שִׂמְחוּ צַדִּיקִים בַּייָ,
וְהוֹדוּ לְזֵכֶר קָדְשׁוֹ.

Let the righteous rejoice in God,
and give thanks to His holy name.

◆ ◆

From Psalm 98

מִזְמוֹר. שִׁירוּ לַייָ שִׁיר חָדָשׁ, כִּי נִפְלָאוֹת עָשָׂה.
הוֹדִיעַ יְיָ יְשׁוּעָתוֹ; לְעֵינֵי הַגּוֹיִם גִּלָּה צִדְקָתוֹ.

Sing a new song to God, for He has done wonders.
God has made known His power,
He has revealed His justice for all to see.

זָכַר חַסְדּוֹ וֶאֱמוּנָתוֹ לְבֵית יִשְׂרָאֵל.
רָאוּ כָל־אַפְסֵי־אָֽרֶץ אֵת יְשׁוּעַת אֱלֹהֵֽינוּ.

He has remembered His love for Jacob,
His faithfulness to Israel.
All the ends of the earth have seen the power of God.

הָרִֽיעוּ לַייָ כָּל־הָאָֽרֶץ; פִּצְחוּ וְרַנְּנוּ וְזַמֵּֽרוּ!
בַּחֲצֹצְרוֹת וְקוֹל שׁוֹפָר הָרִֽיעוּ לִפְנֵי הַמֶּֽלֶךְ יְיָ.

Let the earth ring out in song to God;
break forth, sing aloud, shout praise!
Sound trumpet and horn
before the Sovereign God.

יִרְעַם הַיָּם וּמְלֹאוֹ; תֵּבֵל וְיֹשְׁבֵי בָהּ.
נְהָרוֹת יִמְחֲאוּ־כָף! יַחַד הָרִים יְרַנֵּנוּ לִפְנֵי יְיָ;

Let the sea roar, and all that fills it;
the world and all who dwell there.
Let the rivers clap hands!
Let all the mountains sing for joy before God.

כִּי בָא לִשְׁפֹּט הָאָרֶץ:
יִשְׁפֹּט תֵּבֵל בְּצֶדֶק, וְעַמִּים בְּמֵישָׁרִים.

For He comes to rule the earth:
He will rule the world with justice,
and the peoples with integrity.

◆ ◆

From Psalm 99

יְיָ מָלָךְ: יִרְגְּזוּ עַמִּים. יֹשֵׁב כְּרוּבִים, תָּנוּט הָאָרֶץ. יְיָ בְּצִיּוֹן
גָּדוֹל, וְרָם הוּא עַל־כָּל־הָעַמִּים. יוֹדוּ שִׁמְךָ: גָּדוֹל וְנוֹרָא,
קָדוֹשׁ הוּא. וְעֹז מֶלֶךְ, מִשְׁפָּט אָהֵב: אַתָּה כּוֹנַנְתָּ מֵישָׁרִים,
מִשְׁפָּט וּצְדָקָה בְּיַעֲקֹב אַתָּה עָשִׂיתָ. רוֹמְמוּ יְיָ אֱלֹהֵינוּ,
וְהִשְׁתַּחֲווּ לְהַר קָדְשׁוֹ, כִּי קָדוֹשׁ יְיָ אֱלֹהֵינוּ.

Adonai reigns: let the peoples shake with awe. He sits enthroned, and the earth trembles. Adonai is exalted in Zion, high above all the peoples. Let them praise Your name, great and awesome and holy. Your power, O Sovereign, is Your love of justice. You make righteousness stand firm; justice and right take root in Jacob. We will exalt Adonai our God, and worship at His holy mountain, for our God Adonai is holy.

◆ ◆

Psalm 29

מִזְמוֹר לְדָוִד. הָבוּ לַיְיָ, בְּנֵי אֵלִים, הָבוּ לַיְיָ כָּבוֹד וָעֹז! הָבוּ
לַיְיָ כְּבוֹד שְׁמוֹ, הִשְׁתַּחֲווּ לַיְיָ בְּהַדְרַת־קֹדֶשׁ.

A Song of David.
Praise the Lord, all celestial beings, praise the Lord for His glory and strength! Praise the Lord, whose name is great; worship the Lord in the beauty of holiness.

קוֹל יְיָ עַל־הַמָּיִם! אֵל־הַכָּבוֹד הִרְעִים! יְיָ עַל־מַיִם רַבִּים! קוֹל יְיָ בַּכֹּחַ, קוֹל יְיָ בֶּהָדָר, קוֹל יְיָ שֹׁבֵר אֲרָזִים, וַיְשַׁבֵּר יְיָ אֶת־אַרְזֵי הַלְּבָנוֹן. וַיַּרְקִידֵם כְּמוֹ־עֵגֶל לְבָנוֹן וְשִׂרְיוֹן כְּמוֹ בֶן־רְאֵמִים.

The Eternal's voice above the waters! The God of glory thunders! The Eternal's voice, with power—the Eternal's voice, majestic—the Eternal's voice breaks cedars, He shatters Lebanon's cedars, till Lebanon skips like a calf, Sirion like a wild young ox.

קוֹל־יְיָ חֹצֵב לַהֲבוֹת אֵשׁ; קוֹל יְיָ יָחִיל מִדְבָּר; יָחִיל יְיָ מִדְבַּר קָדֵשׁ; קוֹל יְיָ יְחוֹלֵל אַיָּלוֹת, וַיֶּחֱשֹׂף יְעָרוֹת, וּבְהֵיכָלוֹ כֻּלּוֹ אֹמֵר: 'כָּבוֹד!'

The Lord: His voice sparks fiery flames; the Lord: His voice makes the desert spin; the Lord: His voice shakes the Kadesh desert; the Lord: His voice uproots the oaks, and strips the forests bare, while in His temple all cry: 'Glory!'

יְיָ לַמַּבּוּל יָשָׁב, וַיֵּשֶׁב יְיָ מֶלֶךְ לְעוֹלָם. יְיָ עֹז לְעַמּוֹ יִתֵּן, יְיָ יְבָרֵךְ אֶת־עַמּוֹ בַשָּׁלוֹם.

The Lord, enthroned above the flood, the Lord will reign for ever. The Lord will give strength to His people, the Lord will bless His people with peace.

◆ ◆

לכה דודי

לְכָה דוֹדִי לִקְרַאת כַּלָּה, פְּנֵי שַׁבָּת נְקַבְּלָה.
לְכָה דוֹדִי לִקְרַאת כַּלָּה, פְּנֵי שַׁבָּת נְקַבְּלָה.

Beloved, come to meet the bride; beloved, come to greet Shabbat.

"שָׁמוֹר" וְ"זָכוֹר" בְּדִבּוּר אֶחָד, הִשְׁמִיעָנוּ אֵל הַמְיֻחָד.
יְיָ אֶחָד וּשְׁמוֹ אֶחָד, לְשֵׁם וּלְתִפְאֶרֶת וְלִתְהִלָּה.
לְכָה . . .

"Keep" and "Remember": a single command the Only God caused us to hear; the Eternal is One, His name is One; His are honor and glory and praise

Beloved . . .

לִקְרַאת שַׁבָּת לְכוּ וְנֵלְכָה, כִּי הִיא מְקוֹר הַבְּרָכָה.
מֵרֹאשׁ מִקֶּדֶם נְסוּכָה, סוֹף מַעֲשֶׂה, בְּמַחֲשָׁבָה תְּחִלָּה.
לְכָה . . .

Come with me to meet Shabbat, for ever a fountain of blessing. Still it flows, as from the start: the last of days, for which the first was made.

Beloved . . .

מִקְדַּשׁ מֶלֶךְ, עִיר מְלוּכָה, קוּמִי צְאִי מִתּוֹךְ הַהֲפֵכָה.
רַב לָךְ שֶׁבֶת בְּעֵמֶק הַבָּכָא – וְהוּא יַחֲמֹל עָלַיִךְ חֶמְלָה.
לְכָה . . .

Royal shrine, city of kings, rise up and leave your ravaged state. You have dwelt long enough in the valley of tears — now God will shower His mercy upon you.

Beloved . . .

הִתְנַעֲרִי! מֵעָפָר קוּמִי! לִבְשִׁי בִּגְדֵי תִפְאַרְתֵּךְ, עַמִּי!
עַל־יַד בֶּן־יִשַׁי, בֵּית הַלַּחְמִי, קָרְבָה אֶל־נַפְשִׁי גְאָלָהּ.
לְכָה . . .

Lift yourself up! Shake off the dust! Array yourself in beauty, O my people! At hand is Bethlehem's David, Jesse's son, bringing deliverance into my life.

Beloved . . .

הִתְעוֹרְרִי, הִתְעוֹרְרִי, כִּי בָא אוֹרֵךְ! קוּמִי, אוֹרִי,
עוּרִי עוּרִי, שִׁיר דַּבֵּרִי; כְּבוֹד יְיָ עָלַיִךְ נִגְלָה.
לְכָה . . .

Awake, awake, your light has come! Arise, shine, awake and sing: the Eternal's glory dawns upon you.

Beloved . . .

לֹא תֵבֹשִׁי וְלֹא תִכָּלְמִי; מַה תִּשְׁתּוֹחֲחִי, וּמַה תֶּהֱמִי?
בָּךְ יֶחֱסוּ עֲנִיֵּי עַמִּי, וְנִבְנְתָה עִיר עַל־תִּלָּהּ.
לְכָה . . .

An end to shame and degradation; forget your sorrow; quiet your groans. The afflicted of my people find respite in you, the city renewed upon its ancient ruins.

Beloved . . .

וְהָיוּ לִמְשִׁסָּה שֹׁאסָיִךְ, וְרָחֲקוּ כָּל־מְבַלְּעָיִךְ;
יָשִׂישׂ עָלַיִךְ אֱלֹהָיִךְ, כִּמְשׂוֹשׂ חָתָן עַל־כַּלָּה.
לְכָה . . .

The scavengers are scattered, your devourers have fled; as a bridegroom rejoices in his bride, your God will take joy in you.

Beloved . . .

יָמִין וּשְׂמֹאל תִּפְרֹוצִי, וְאֶת־יְיָ תַּעֲרִיצִי:
עַל־יַד אִישׁ בֶּן פַּרְצִי, וְנִשְׂמְחָה וְנָגִילָה!
לְכָה . . .

Your space will be broad, your worship free: await the promised one; we will exult, we will sing for joy!

Beloved . . .

בּוֹאִי בְשָׁלוֹם, עֲטֶרֶת בַּעְלָהּ, גַּם בְּשִׂמְחָה וּבְצָהֳלָה,
תּוֹךְ אֱמוּנֵי עַם סְגֻלָּה. בּוֹאִי כַלָּה! בּוֹאִי כַלָּה!
לְכָה . . .

Enter in peace, O crown of your husband; enter in gladness, enter in joy. Come to the people that keeps its faith. Enter, O bride! Enter, O bride!

Beloved . . .

◆ ◆

Psalm 92

A SONG FOR THE SABBATH DAY

מִזְמוֹר שִׁיר לְיוֹם הַשַּׁבָּת.

טוֹב לְהֹדוֹת לַייָ, וּלְזַמֵּר לְשִׁמְךָ, עֶלְיוֹן,
לְהַגִּיד בַּבֹּקֶר חַסְדֶּךָ, וֶאֱמוּנָתְךָ בַּלֵּילוֹת,
עֲלֵי־עָשׂוֹר וַעֲלֵי־נָבֶל, עֲלֵי הִגָּיוֹן בְּכִנּוֹר.

It is good to give thanks to the Lord,
to sing hymns to Your name, O Most High!
To tell of Your love in the morning,

to sing at night of Your faithfulness;
to pluck the strings, to sound the lute,
to make the harp vibrate.

כִּי שִׂמַּחְתַּנִי, יְיָ, בְּפָעֳלֶךָ, בְּמַעֲשֵׂי יָדֶיךָ אֲרַנֵּן.
מַה־גָּדְלוּ מַעֲשֶׂיךָ, יְיָ! מְאֹד עָמְקוּ מַחְשְׁבֹתֶיךָ.

Your deeds, O Lord, fill me with gladness,
Your work moves me to song.
How great are Your works, O Lord!
How profound Your design!

אִישׁ־בַּעַר לֹא יֵדָע, וּכְסִיל לֹא־יָבִין אֶת־זֹאת:
בִּפְרֹחַ רְשָׁעִים כְּמוֹ־עֵשֶׂב, וַיָּצִיצוּ כָּל־פֹּעֲלֵי אָוֶן,
לְהִשָּׁמְדָם עֲדֵי־עַד.
וְאַתָּה מָרוֹם לְעֹלָם, יְיָ.

The fool will never learn,
the dullard never grasp this:
the wicked may flourish like grass,
all who do evil may blossom,
yet they are doomed to destruction,
while You, O Lord, are exalted for all time.

כִּי הִנֵּה אֹיְבֶיךָ, יְיָ, כִּי־הִנֵּה אֹיְבֶיךָ יֹאבֵדוּ,
יִתְפָּרְדוּ כָּל־פֹּעֲלֵי אָוֶן.
וַתָּרֶם כִּרְאֵים קַרְנִי, בַּלֹּתִי בְּשֶׁמֶן רַעֲנָן.
וַתַּבֵּט עֵינִי בְּשׁוּרָי, בַּקָּמִים עָלַי מְרֵעִים,
תִּשְׁמַעְנָה אָזְנָי:

See how Your enemies, O Lord,
see how Your enemies shall perish,
how all who do evil shall be scattered.
You lift up my head in pride,
I am bathed in freshening oil.
I shall see the defeat of my foes,
my ears shall hear of their fall.

צַדִּיק כַּתָּמָר יִפְרָח, כְּאֶרֶז בַּלְּבָנוֹן יִשְׂגֶּה.
שְׁתוּלִים בְּבֵית יְיָ, בְּחַצְרוֹת אֱלֹהֵינוּ יַפְרִיחוּ.
עוֹד יְנוּבוּן בְּשֵׂיבָה, דְּשֵׁנִים וְרַעֲנַנִּים יִהְיוּ,
לְהַגִּיד כִּי־יָשָׁר יְיָ, צוּרִי, וְלֹא־עַוְלָתָה בּוֹ.

The righteous shall flourish like palms,
grow tall like cedars in Lebanon.
Rooted in the house of the Lord,
they shall be ever fresh and green,
proclaiming that the Lord is just,
my Rock, in whom there is no wrong.

◆ ◆

Psalm 93

יְיָ מָלָךְ, גֵּאוּת לָבֵשׁ;
לָבֵשׁ יְיָ, עֹז הִתְאַזָּר;
אַף־תִּכּוֹן תֵּבֵל, בַּל־תִּמּוֹט.
נָכוֹן כִּסְאֲךָ מֵאָז,
מֵעוֹלָם אָתָּה.

The Eternal is enthroned,
He is robed in grandeur;
the Eternal is robed,
He is girded with strength.
And He founded the solid earth
to be unmoving.
Ageless is Your throne,
endless Your being.

נָשְׂאוּ נְהָרוֹת, יְיָ,
נָשְׂאוּ נְהָרוֹת קוֹלָם,
יִשְׂאוּ נְהָרוֹת דָּכְיָם;
מִקֹּלוֹת מַיִם רַבִּים,
אַדִּירִים מִשְׁבְּרֵי־יָם,
אַדִּיר בַּמָּרוֹם יְיָ.

The oceans cry out, O Eternal God,
the oceans cry out their thunder,
the oceans rage in their fury;
but greater than the thunder of the torrents,
mightier than the breakers of the sea,
is the Lord's majesty on high!

עֵדֹתֶיךָ נֶאֶמְנוּ מְאֹד;
לְבֵיתְךָ נַאֲוָה־קֹדֶשׁ,
יְיָ, לְאֹרֶךְ יָמִים.

Your law stands firm;
and in Your temple, O Eternal God,
holiness reigns to the end of time!

◆ ◆

READER'S KADDISH — חצי קדיש

יִתְגַּדַּל וְיִתְקַדַּשׁ שְׁמֵהּ רַבָּא בְּעָלְמָא דִּי־בְרָא כִרְעוּתֵהּ,
וְיַמְלִיךְ מַלְכוּתֵהּ בְּחַיֵּיכוֹן וּבְיוֹמֵיכוֹן וּבְחַיֵּי דְכָל־בֵּית
יִשְׂרָאֵל, בַּעֲגָלָא וּבִזְמַן קָרִיב, וְאִמְרוּ: אָמֵן.

יְהֵא שְׁמֵהּ רַבָּא מְבָרַךְ לְעָלַם וּלְעָלְמֵי עָלְמַיָּא.

יִתְבָּרַךְ וְיִשְׁתַּבַּח, וְיִתְפָּאַר וְיִתְרוֹמַם וְיִתְנַשֵּׂא, וְיִתְהַדַּר
וְיִתְעַלֶּה וְיִתְהַלַּל שְׁמֵהּ דְּקוּדְשָׁא, בְּרִיךְ הוּא, לְעֵלָּא מִן
כָּל־בִּרְכָתָא וְשִׁירָתָא, תֻּשְׁבְּחָתָא וְנֶחֱמָתָא דַּאֲמִירָן בְּעָלְמָא,
וְאִמְרוּ: אָמֵן.

Let the glory of God be extolled, let His great name be hallowed in the world whose creation He willed. May His kingdom soon prevail, in our own day, our own lives, and the life of all Israel, and let us say: Amen.

Let His great name be blessed for ever and ever.

Let the name of the Holy One, blessed is He, be glorified, exalted and honored, though He is beyond all the praises, songs, and adorations that we can utter, and let us say: Amen.

◆ ◆

All rise

שמע וברכותיה

בָּרְכוּ אֶת־יְיָ הַמְבֹרָךְ!

Praise the Lord, to whom our praise is due!

בָּרוּךְ יְיָ הַמְבֹרָךְ לְעוֹלָם וָעֶד!

Praised be the Lord, to whom our praise is due,
now and for ever!

◆ ◆

CREATION — מעריב ערבים

בָּרוּךְ אַתָּה, יְיָ אֱלֹהֵינוּ, מֶלֶךְ הָעוֹלָם, אֲשֶׁר בִּדְבָרוֹ מַעֲרִיב עֲרָבִים. בְּחָכְמָה פּוֹתֵחַ שְׁעָרִים, וּבִתְבוּנָה מְשַׁנֶּה עִתִּים, וּמַחֲלִיף אֶת־הַזְּמַנִּים, וּמְסַדֵּר אֶת־הַכּוֹכָבִים בְּמִשְׁמְרוֹתֵיהֶם בָּרָקִיעַ כִּרְצוֹנוֹ.

Praised be the Lord our God, Ruler of the universe, whose word brings on the evening. His wisdom opens heaven's gates; his understanding makes the ages pass and the seasons alternate; and His will controls the stars as they travel through the skies.

בּוֹרֵא יוֹם וָלָיְלָה, גּוֹלֵל אוֹר מִפְּנֵי חֹשֶׁךְ וְחֹשֶׁךְ מִפְּנֵי אוֹר, וּמַעֲבִיר יוֹם וּמֵבִיא לָיְלָה, וּמַבְדִּיל בֵּין יוֹם וּבֵין לָיְלָה, יְיָ צְבָאוֹת שְׁמוֹ.

He is Creator of day and night, rolling light away from darkness, and darkness from light; He causes day to pass and brings on the night; He sets day and night apart: He is the Lord of Hosts.

אֵל חַי וְקַיָּם, תָּמִיד יִמְלוֹךְ עָלֵינוּ, לְעוֹלָם וָעֶד. בָּרוּךְ אַתָּה, יְיָ, הַמַּעֲרִיב עֲרָבִים.

May the living and eternal God rule us always, to the end of time! Blessed is the Lord, whose word makes evening fall.

◆ ◆

REVELATION

אהבת עולם

אַהֲבַת עוֹלָם בֵּית יִשְׂרָאֵל עַמְּךָ אָהָבְתָּ: תּוֹרָה וּמִצְוֹת, חֻקִּים וּמִשְׁפָּטִים אוֹתָנוּ לִמַּדְתָּ.

Unending is Your love for Your people, the House of Israel: Torah and Mitzvot, laws and precepts have You taught us.

עַל־כֵּן, יְיָ אֱלֹהֵינוּ, בְּשָׁכְבֵנוּ וּבְקוּמֵנוּ נָשִׂיחַ בְּחֻקֶּיךָ, וְנִשְׂמַח בְּדִבְרֵי תוֹרָתְךָ וּבְמִצְוֹתֶיךָ לְעוֹלָם וָעֶד.

Therefore, O Lord our God, when we lie down and when we rise up, we will meditate on Your laws and rejoice in Your Torah and Mitzvot for ever.

כִּי הֵם חַיֵּינוּ וְאֹרֶךְ יָמֵינוּ, וּבָהֶם נֶהְגֶּה יוֹמָם וָלָיְלָה. וְאַהֲבָתְךָ אַל־תָּסִיר מִמֶּנּוּ לְעוֹלָמִים! בָּרוּךְ אַתָּה, יְיָ, אוֹהֵב עַמּוֹ יִשְׂרָאֵל.

Day and night we will reflect on them, for they are our life and the length of our days. Then Your love shall never depart from our hearts! Blessed is the Lord, who loves His people Israel.

◆ ◆

שְׁמַע יִשְׂרָאֵל: יְיָ אֱלֹהֵינוּ, יְיָ אֶחָד!

Hear, O Israel: the Lord is our God, the Lord is One!

בָּרוּךְ שֵׁם כְּבוֹד מַלְכוּתוֹ לְעוֹלָם וָעֶד!

Blessed is His glorious kingdom for ever and ever!

All are seated

וְאָהַבְתָּ אֵת יְיָ אֱלֹהֶיךָ בְּכָל־לְבָבְךָ וּבְכָל־נַפְשְׁךָ וּבְכָל־מְאֹדֶךָ.
וְהָיוּ הַדְּבָרִים הָאֵלֶּה, אֲשֶׁר אָנֹכִי מְצַוְּךָ הַיּוֹם, עַל־לְבָבֶךָ.
וְשִׁנַּנְתָּם לְבָנֶיךָ, וְדִבַּרְתָּ בָּם בְּשִׁבְתְּךָ בְּבֵיתֶךָ, וּבְלֶכְתְּךָ בַדֶּרֶךְ, וּבְשָׁכְבְּךָ וּבְקוּמֶךָ.

You shall love the Lord your God with all your mind, with all your strength, with all your being.

Set these words, which I command you this day, upon your heart. Teach them faithfully to your children; speak of them in your home and on your way, when you lie down and when you rise up.

וּקְשַׁרְתָּם לְאוֹת עַל־יָדֶךָ, וְהָיוּ לְטֹטָפֹת בֵּין עֵינֶיךָ, וּכְתַבְתָּם עַל־מְזֻזוֹת בֵּיתֶךָ, וּבִשְׁעָרֶיךָ.

Bind them as a sign upon your hand; let them be a symbol before your eyes; inscribe them on the doorposts of your house, and on your gates.

לְמַעַן תִּזְכְּרוּ וַעֲשִׂיתֶם אֶת־כָּל־מִצְוֹתָי, וִהְיִיתֶם קְדֹשִׁים לֵאלֹהֵיכֶם. אֲנִי יְיָ אֱלֹהֵיכֶם, אֲשֶׁר הוֹצֵאתִי אֶתְכֶם מֵאֶרֶץ מִצְרַיִם לִהְיוֹת לָכֶם לֵאלֹהִים. אֲנִי יְיָ אֱלֹהֵיכֶם.

Be mindful of all My Mitzvot, and do them: so shall you consecrate yourselves to your God. I, the Lord, am your God who led you out of Egypt to be your God; I, the Lord, am your God.

◆ ◆

REDEMPTION — גאולה

אֱמֶת וֶאֱמוּנָה כָּל־זֹאת, וְקַיָּם עָלֵינוּ כִּי הוּא יְיָ אֱלֹהֵינוּ וְאֵין זוּלָתוֹ, וַאֲנַחְנוּ יִשְׂרָאֵל עַמּוֹ.

הַפּוֹדֵנוּ מִיַּד מְלָכִים, מַלְכֵּנוּ הַגּוֹאֲלֵנוּ מִכַּף כָּל־הֶעָרִיצִים.

All this we hold to be true and sure: He alone is our God; there is none else, and we are Israel His people.

He is our King: He delivers us from the hand of oppressors, and saves us from the fist of tyrants.

הָעֹשֶׂה גְדֹלוֹת עַד אֵין חֵקֶר, וְנִפְלָאוֹת עַד־אֵין מִסְפָּר.

הַשָּׂם נַפְשֵׁנוּ בַּחַיִּים, וְלֹא־נָתַן לַמּוֹט רַגְלֵנוּ.

He does wonders without number, marvels that pass our understanding.

He gives us our life; by His help we survive all who seek our destruction.

הָעֹשֶׂה לָּנוּ נִסִּים בְּפַרְעֹה, אוֹתוֹת וּמוֹפְתִים בְּאַדְמַת בְּנֵי חָם.
וַיּוֹצֵא אֶת־עַמּוֹ יִשְׂרָאֵל מִתּוֹכָם לְחֵרוּת עוֹלָם.

He did wonders for us in the land of Egypt, miracles and marvels in the land of Pharaoh.
He led his people Israel out, forever to serve Him in freedom.

וְרָאוּ בָנָיו גְּבוּרָתוֹ; שִׁבְּחוּ וְהוֹדוּ לִשְׁמוֹ. וּמַלְכוּתוֹ בְּרָצוֹן
קִבְּלוּ עֲלֵיהֶם. מֹשֶׁה וּבְנֵי יִשְׂרָאֵל לְךָ עָנוּ שִׁירָה בְּשִׂמְחָה
רַבָּה, וְאָמְרוּ כֻלָּם:

When His children witnessed His power they extolled Him and gave Him thanks; freely they acclaimed Him King; and full of joy, Moses and all Israel sang this song:

Who is like You, Eternal One, among the gods that are worshipped?	מִי־כָמֹכָה בָּאֵלִם, יְיָ?
Who is like You, majestic in holiness,	מִי כָּמֹכָה, נֶאְדָּר בַּקֹּדֶשׁ,
awesome in splendor, doing wonders?	נוֹרָא תְהִלֹּת, עֹשֵׂה פֶלֶא?

מַלְכוּתְךָ רָאוּ בָנֶיךָ, בּוֹקֵעַ יָם לִפְנֵי מֹשֶׁה; "זֶה אֵלִי!" עָנוּ
וְאָמְרוּ: "יְיָ יִמְלֹךְ לְעֹלָם וָעֶד!"

In their escape from the sea, Your children saw Your sovereign might displayed. "This is my God!" they cried. "The Eternal will reign for ever and ever!"

וְנֶאֱמַר: "כִּי־פָדָה יְיָ אֶת יַעֲקֹב, וּגְאָלוֹ מִיַּד חָזָק מִמֶּנּוּ." בָּרוּךְ
אַתָּה, יְיָ, גָּאַל יִשְׂרָאֵל.

And it has been said: "The Eternal delivered Jacob, and redeemed him from the hand of one stronger than himself." Blessed is the Lord, the Redeemer of Israel.

◆ ◆

השכיבנו

DIVINE PROVIDENCE

הַשְׁכִּיבֵנוּ, יְיָ אֱלֹהֵינוּ, לְשָׁלוֹם, וְהַעֲמִידֵנוּ, מַלְכֵּנוּ, לְחַיִּים. וּפְרוֹשׂ עָלֵינוּ סֻכַּת שְׁלוֹמֶךָ, וְתַקְּנֵנוּ בְּעֵצָה טוֹבָה מִלְּפָנֶיךָ, וְהוֹשִׁיעֵנוּ לְמַעַן שְׁמֶךָ, וְהָגֵן בַּעֲדֵנוּ. וְהָסֵר מֵעָלֵינוּ אוֹיֵב, דֶּבֶר וְחֶרֶב וְרָעָב וְיָגוֹן; וְהָסֵר שָׂטָן מִלְּפָנֵינוּ וּמֵאַחֲרֵינוּ; וּבְצֵל כְּנָפֶיךָ תַּסְתִּירֵנוּ, כִּי אֵל שׁוֹמְרֵנוּ וּמַצִּילֵנוּ אָתָּה, כִּי אֵל מֶלֶךְ חַנּוּן וְרַחוּם אָתָּה. וּשְׁמוֹר צֵאתֵנוּ וּבוֹאֵנוּ לְחַיִּים וּלְשָׁלוֹם, מֵעַתָּה וְעַד עוֹלָם, וּפְרוֹשׂ עָלֵינוּ סֻכַּת שְׁלוֹמֶךָ. בָּרוּךְ אַתָּה, יְיָ, הַפּוֹרֵשׂ סֻכַּת שָׁלוֹם עָלֵינוּ, וְעַל־כָּל־עַמּוֹ יִשְׂרָאֵל וְעַל יְרוּשָׁלָיִם.

Grant, O Eternal God, that we may lie down in peace, and raise us up, O Sovereign, to life renewed. Spread over us the shelter of Your peace; guide us with Your good counsel; and for Your name's sake, be our Help.

Shield us from hatred and plague; keep us from war and famine and anguish; subdue our inclination to evil. O God, our Guardian and Helper, our gracious and merciful Ruler, give us refuge in the shadow of Your wings. O guard our coming and our going, that now and always we have life and peace.

Blessed is the Lord, whose shelter of peace is spread over us, over all His people Israel, and over Jerusalem.

ושמרו

THE COVENANT OF SHABBAT

וְשָׁמְרוּ בְנֵי־יִשְׂרָאֵל אֶת־הַשַּׁבָּת, לַעֲשׂוֹת אֶת־הַשַּׁבָּת לְדֹרֹתָם בְּרִית עוֹלָם. בֵּינִי וּבֵין בְּנֵי יִשְׂרָאֵל אוֹת הִיא לְעֹלָם, כִּי שֵׁשֶׁת יָמִים עָשָׂה יְיָ אֶת־הַשָּׁמַיִם וְאֶת־הָאָרֶץ, וּבַיּוֹם הַשְּׁבִיעִי שָׁבַת וַיִּנָּפַשׁ.

The people of Israel shall keep the Sabbath, observing the Sabbath in every generation as a covenant for all time. It is a sign for ever between Me and the people of Israel, for in six days the Eternal God made heaven and earth, and on the seventh day He rested from His labors.

◆ ◆

All rise

תפלה

אֲדֹנָי, שְׂפָתַי תִּפְתָּח, וּפִי יַגִּיד תְּהִלָּתֶךָ.

Eternal God, open my lips, that my mouth may declare Your glory.

GOD OF ALL GENERATIONS — אבות

בָּרוּךְ אַתָּה, יְיָ אֱלֹהֵינוּ וֵאלֹהֵי אֲבוֹתֵינוּ, אֱלֹהֵי אַבְרָהָם, אֱלֹהֵי
יִצְחָק, וֵאלֹהֵי יַעֲקֹב: הָאֵל הַגָּדוֹל, הַגִּבּוֹר וְהַנּוֹרָא, אֵל עֶלְיוֹן.

We praise You, Lord our God and God of all generations: God of Abraham, God of Isaac, God of Jacob; great, mighty, and awesome God, God supreme.

גּוֹמֵל חֲסָדִים טוֹבִים, וְקוֹנֵה הַכֹּל, וְזוֹכֵר חַסְדֵי אָבוֹת, וּמֵבִיא
גְאֻלָּה לִבְנֵי בְנֵיהֶם, לְמַעַן שְׁמוֹ, בְּאַהֲבָה.*

Master of all the living, Your ways are ways of love. You remember the faithfulness of our ancestors, and in love bring redemption to their children's children for the sake of Your name.*

מֶלֶךְ עוֹזֵר וּמוֹשִׁיעַ וּמָגֵן. בָּרוּךְ אַתָּה, יְיָ, מָגֵן אַבְרָהָם.

You are our King and our Help, our Savior and our Shield. Blessed is the Lord, the Shield of Abraham.

** On Shabbat Shuvah insert:*

זָכְרֵנוּ לְחַיִּים, מֶלֶךְ חָפֵץ בַּחַיִּים,
וְכָתְבֵנוּ בְּסֵפֶר הַחַיִּים, לְמַעַנְךָ אֱלֹהִים חַיִּים.

Remember us unto life, for You are the King who delights in life, and inscribe us in the Book of Life, that Your will may prevail, O God of life.

◆ ◆

GOD'S POWER — גבורות

אַתָּה גִּבּוֹר לְעוֹלָם, אֲדֹנָי, מְחַיֵּה הַכֹּל אַתָּה, רַב לְהוֹשִׁיעַ.
מְכַלְכֵּל חַיִּים בְּחֶסֶד, מְחַיֵּה הַכֹּל בְּרַחֲמִים רַבִּים. סוֹמֵךְ

נוֹפְלִים, וְרוֹפֵא חוֹלִים, וּמַתִּיר אֲסוּרִים, וּמְקַיֵּם אֱמוּנָתוֹ לִישֵׁנֵי עָפָר.

Eternal is Your might, O Lord; all life is Your gift; great is Your power to save! With love You sustain the living, with great compassion give life to all. You send help to the falling and healing to the sick; You bring freedom to the captive and keep faith with those who sleep in the dust.

מִי כָמוֹךָ, בַּעַל גְּבוּרוֹת, וּמִי דּוֹמֶה לָּךְ, מֶלֶךְ מֵמִית וּמְחַיֶּה וּמַצְמִיחַ יְשׁוּעָה?*

וְנֶאֱמָן אַתָּה לְהַחֲיוֹת הַכֹּל. בָּרוּךְ אַתָּה, יְיָ, מְחַיֵּה הַכֹּל.

Who is like You, Master of Might? Who is Your equal, O Lord of life and death, Source of salvation? Blessed is the Lord, the Source of life.*

** On Shabbat Shuvah insert:*

מִי כָמוֹךָ, אַב הָרַחֲמִים, זוֹכֵר יְצוּרָיו לְחַיִּים בְּרַחֲמִים?

Who is like You, Source of mercy, who in compassion sustains the life of His children?

◆ ◆

GOD'S HOLINESS
קדושת השם

אַתָּה קָדוֹשׁ וְשִׁמְךָ קָדוֹשׁ, וּקְדוֹשִׁים בְּכָל־יוֹם יְהַלְלוּךָ סֶּלָה.* בָּרוּךְ אַתָּה, יְיָ, הָאֵל הַקָּדוֹשׁ.

You are holy, Your name is holy, and those who strive to be holy declare Your glory day by day.* Blessed is the Lord, the holy God.

** On Shabbat Shuvah conclude:*

Blessed is the Lord, the holy King. בָּרוּךְ אַתָּה, יְיָ, הַמֶּלֶךְ הַקָּדוֹשׁ.

All are seated

◆ ◆

THE HOLINESS OF SHABBAT

קדושת היום

אַתָּה קִדַּשְׁתָּ אֶת־יוֹם הַשְּׁבִיעִי לִשְׁמֶךָ; תַּכְלִית מַעֲשֵׂה שָׁמַיִם וָאָרֶץ, וּבֵרַכְתּוֹ מִכָּל הַיָּמִים וְקִדַּשְׁתּוֹ מִכָּל־הַזְּמַנִּים, וְכֵן כָּתוּב בְּתוֹרָתֶךָ:

You set the seventh day apart for Your service; it is the goal of creation, more blessed than other days, more sacred than other times, as we read in the story of creation:

וַיְכֻלּוּ הַשָּׁמַיִם וְהָאָרֶץ וְכָל־צְבָאָם. וַיְכַל אֱלֹהִים בַּיּוֹם הַשְּׁבִיעִי מְלַאכְתּוֹ אֲשֶׁר עָשָׂה; וַיִּשְׁבֹּת בַּיּוֹם הַשְּׁבִיעִי מִכָּל־מְלַאכְתּוֹ אֲשֶׁר עָשָׂה. וַיְבָרֶךְ אֱלֹהִים אֶת־יוֹם הַשְּׁבִיעִי וַיְקַדֵּשׁ אֹתוֹ, כִּי בוֹ שָׁבַת מִכָּל־מְלַאכְתּוֹ אֲשֶׁר־בָּרָא אֱלֹהִים לַעֲשׂוֹת.

Now the whole universe – sky, earth, and all their array – was completed. With the seventh day God ended His work of creation; on the seventh day He rested, with all His work completed. Then God blessed the seventh day and called it holy, for with this day He had completed the work of creation.

◆

אֱלֹהֵינוּ וֵאלֹהֵי אֲבוֹתֵינוּ, רְצֵה בִמְנוּחָתֵנוּ. קַדְּשֵׁנוּ בְּמִצְוֹתֶיךָ, וְתֵן חֶלְקֵנוּ בְּתוֹרָתֶךָ. שַׂבְּעֵנוּ מִטּוּבֶךָ, וְשַׂמְּחֵנוּ בִּישׁוּעָתֶךָ, וְטַהֵר לִבֵּנוּ לְעָבְדְּךָ בֶּאֱמֶת. וְהַנְחִילֵנוּ, יְיָ אֱלֹהֵינוּ, בְּאַהֲבָה וּבְרָצוֹן שַׁבַּת קָדְשֶׁךָ, וְיָנוּחוּ בָהּ יִשְׂרָאֵל מְקַדְּשֵׁי שְׁמֶךָ. בָּרוּךְ אַתָּה, יְיָ, מְקַדֵּשׁ הַשַּׁבָּת.

Our God and God of ages past, may our rest on this day be pleasing in Your sight. Sanctify us with Your Mitzvot, and let Your Torah be our way of life. Satisfy us with Your goodness, gladden us with Your salvation, and purify our hearts to serve You in truth. In Your gracious love, O Lord our God, let Your holy Sabbath remain our heritage, that all Israel, hallowing Your name, may find rest and peace. Blessed is the Lord, for the Sabbath and its holiness.

◆ ◆

WORSHIP

עבודה

רְצֵה, יְיָ אֱלֹהֵינוּ, בְּעַמְּךָ יִשְׂרָאֵל, וּתְפִלָּתָם בְּאַהֲבָה תְקַבֵּל, וּתְהִי לְרָצוֹן תָּמִיד עֲבוֹדַת יִשְׂרָאֵל עַמֶּךָ. אֵל קָרוֹב לְכָל-קֹרְאָיו, פְּנֵה אֶל עֲבָדֶיךָ וְחָנֵּנוּ; שְׁפוֹךְ רוּחֲךָ עָלֵינוּ, וְתֶחֱזֶינָה עֵינֵינוּ בְּשׁוּבְךָ לְצִיּוֹן בְּרַחֲמִים.

בָּרוּךְ אַתָּה, יְיָ, הַמַּחֲזִיר שְׁכִינָתוֹ לְצִיּוֹן.

Be gracious, O Lord our God, to Your people Israel, and receive our prayers with love. O may our worship always be acceptable to You.

Fill us with the knowledge that You are near to all who seek You in truth. Let our eyes behold Your presence in our midst and in the midst of our people in Zion. Blessed is the Lord, whose presence gives life to Zion and all Israel.

◆ ◆

ON ROSH CHODESH AND CHOL HAMO-EID

אֱלֹהֵינוּ וֵאלֹהֵי אֲבוֹתֵינוּ, יַעֲלֶה וְיָבֹא וְיִזָּכֵר זִכְרוֹנֵנוּ וְזִכְרוֹן כָּל-עַמְּךָ בֵּית יִשְׂרָאֵל לְפָנֶיךָ, לְטוֹבָה לְחֵן לְחֶסֶד וּלְרַחֲמִים, לְחַיִּים וּלְשָׁלוֹם בְּיוֹם

Our God and God of all ages, be mindful of Your people Israel on this

first day of the new month,	רֹאשׁ הַחֹדֶשׁ הַזֶּה.
day of Pesach,	חַג הַמַּצּוֹת הַזֶּה.
day of Sukkot,	חַג הַסֻּכּוֹת הַזֶּה.

and renew in us love and compassion, goodness, life and peace.

This day remember us for well-being. *Amen.*	זָכְרֵנוּ, יְיָ אֱלֹהֵינוּ, בּוֹ לְטוֹבָה. אָמֵן.
This day bless us with Your nearness. *Amen.*	וּפָקְדֵנוּ בוֹ לִבְרָכָה. אָמֵן.
This day help us to a fuller life. *Amen.*	וְהוֹשִׁיעֵנוּ בוֹ לְחַיִּים. אָמֵן.

◆ ◆

THANKSGIVING

הודאה

מוֹדִים אֲנַחְנוּ לָךְ, שָׁאַתָּה הוּא יְיָ אֱלֹהֵינוּ וֵאלֹהֵי אֲבוֹתֵינוּ לְעוֹלָם וָעֶד. צוּר חַיֵּינוּ, מָגֵן יִשְׁעֵנוּ, אַתָּה הוּא לְדוֹר וָדוֹר. נוֹדֶה לְךָ וּנְסַפֵּר תְּהִלָּתֶךָ, עַל־חַיֵּינוּ הַמְּסוּרִים בְּיָדֶךָ, וְעַל־נִשְׁמוֹתֵינוּ הַפְּקוּדוֹת לָךְ, וְעַל־נִסֶּיךָ שֶׁבְּכָל־יוֹם עִמָּנוּ, וְעַל־נִפְלְאוֹתֶיךָ וְטוֹבוֹתֶיךָ שֶׁבְּכָל־עֵת, עֶרֶב וָבֹקֶר וְצָהֳרָיִם. הַטּוֹב: כִּי לֹא־כָלוּ רַחֲמֶיךָ, וְהַמְרַחֵם: כִּי־לֹא תַמּוּ חֲסָדֶיךָ, מֵעוֹלָם קִוִּינוּ לָךְ.

We gratefully acknowledge that You are the Lord our God and God of our people, the God of all generations. You are the Rock of our life, the Power that shields us in every age. We thank You and sing Your praises: for our lives, which are in Your hand; for our souls, which are in Your keeping; for the signs of Your presence we encounter every day; and for Your wondrous gifts at all times, morning, noon, and night. You are Goodness: Your mercies never end; You are Compassion: Your love will never fail. You have always been our hope.

וְעַל כֻּלָּם יִתְבָּרַךְ וְיִתְרוֹמַם שִׁמְךָ, מַלְכֵּנוּ, תָּמִיד לְעוֹלָם וָעֶד.

For all these things, O Sovereign God, let Your name be forever exalted and blessed.

On Shabbat Shuvah insert:

וּכְתוֹב לְחַיִּים טוֹבִים כָּל־בְּנֵי בְרִיתֶךָ.

Let life abundant be the heritage of all Your children.

וְכֹל הַחַיִּים יוֹדוּךָ סֶּלָה, וִיהַלְלוּ אֶת שִׁמְךָ בֶּאֱמֶת, הָאֵל יְשׁוּעָתֵנוּ וְעֶזְרָתֵנוּ סֶלָה. בָּרוּךְ אַתָּה, יְיָ, הַטּוֹב שִׁמְךָ וּלְךָ נָאֶה לְהוֹדוֹת.

O God our Redeemer and Helper, let all who live affirm You and praise Your name in truth. Lord, whose nature is Goodness, we give You thanks and praise.

◆ ◆

ON CHANUKAH

עַל הַנִּסִּים וְעַל הַפֻּרְקָן, וְעַל הַגְּבוּרוֹת וְעַל הַתְּשׁוּעוֹת, וְעַל הַמִּלְחָמוֹת, שֶׁעָשִׂיתָ לַאֲבוֹתֵינוּ בַּיָּמִים הָהֵם בַּזְּמַן הַזֶּה.

בִּימֵי מַתִּתְיָהוּ בֶּן־יוֹחָנָן כֹּהֵן גָּדוֹל, חַשְׁמוֹנַי וּבָנָיו, כְּשֶׁעָמְדָה מַלְכוּת יָוָן הָרְשָׁעָה עַל־עַמְּךָ יִשְׂרָאֵל לְהַשְׁכִּיחָם תּוֹרָתֶךָ, וּלְהַעֲבִירָם מֵחֻקֵּי רְצוֹנֶךָ.

וְאַתָּה בְּרַחֲמֶיךָ הָרַבִּים עָמַדְתָּ לָהֶם בְּעֵת צָרָתָם. רַבְתָּ אֶת־רִיבָם, דַּנְתָּ אֶת־דִּינָם, מָסַרְתָּ גִבּוֹרִים בְּיַד חַלָּשִׁים, וְרַבִּים בְּיַד מְעַטִּים, וּטְמֵאִים בְּיַד טְהוֹרִים, וּרְשָׁעִים בְּיַד צַדִּיקִים, וְזֵדִים בְּיַד עוֹסְקֵי תוֹרָתֶךָ.

וּלְךָ עָשִׂיתָ שֵׁם גָּדוֹל וְקָדוֹשׁ בְּעוֹלָמֶךָ, וּלְעַמְּךָ יִשְׂרָאֵל עָשִׂיתָ תְּשׁוּעָה גְדוֹלָה וּפֻרְקָן כְּהַיּוֹם הַזֶּה.

וְאַחַר כֵּן בָּאוּ בָנֶיךָ לִדְבִיר בֵּיתֶךָ, וּפִנּוּ אֶת־הֵיכָלֶךָ, וְטִהֲרוּ אֶת־מִקְדָּשֶׁךָ, וְהִדְלִיקוּ נֵרוֹת בְּחַצְרוֹת קָדְשֶׁךָ, וְקָבְעוּ שְׁמוֹנַת יְמֵי חֲנֻכָּה אֵלּוּ לְהוֹדוֹת וּלְהַלֵּל לְשִׁמְךָ הַגָּדוֹל.

We give thanks for the redeeming wonders and the mighty deeds by which at this season our people was saved in days of old.

In the days of the Hasmoneans, a tyrant arose against our ancestors, determined to make them forget Your Torah, and to turn them away from obedience to Your will. But You were at their side in time of trouble. You gave them strength to struggle and to triumph, that they might serve You in freedom.

Through the power of Your spirit the weak defeated the strong, the few prevailed over the many, and the righteous were triumphant. Then Your children returned to Your house, to purify the sanctuary and kindle its lights. And they dedicated these days to give thanks and praise to Your great name.

◆ ◆

PEACE

ברכת שלום

שָׁלוֹם רָב עַל־יִשְׂרָאֵל עַמְּךָ תָּשִׂים לְעוֹלָם, כִּי אַתָּה הוּא מֶלֶךְ אָדוֹן לְכָל הַשָּׁלוֹם. וְטוֹב בְּעֵינֶיךָ לְבָרֵךְ אֶת־עַמְּךָ יִשְׂרָאֵל בְּכָל־עֵת וּבְכָל־שָׁעָה בִּשְׁלוֹמֶךָ.*

בָּרוּךְ אַתָּה, יְיָ, הַמְבָרֵךְ אֶת־עַמּוֹ יִשְׂרָאֵל בַּשָּׁלוֹם.

O Sovereign Lord of peace, let Israel Your people know enduring peace, for it is good in Your sight continually to bless Israel with Your peace. Praised be the Lord, who blesses His people Israel with peace.*

On Shabbat Shuvah conclude:

בְּסֵפֶר חַיִּים וּבְרָכָה נִכָּתֵב לְחַיִּים טוֹבִים וּלְשָׁלוֹם.

בָּרוּךְ אַתָּה, יְיָ, עוֹשֵׂה הַשָּׁלוֹם.

Teach us then to find our happiness in the search for righteousness and peace. Blessed is the Lord, the Source of peace.

◆ ◆

SILENT PRAYER

אֱלֹהַי, נְצֹר לְשׁוֹנִי מֵרָע, וּשְׂפָתַי מִדַּבֵּר מִרְמָה, וְלִמְקַלְלַי נַפְשִׁי תִדּוֹם, וְנַפְשִׁי כֶּעָפָר לַכֹּל תִּהְיֶה. פְּתַח לִבִּי בְּתוֹרָתֶךָ, וּבְמִצְוֹתֶיךָ תִּרְדּוֹף נַפְשִׁי, וְכֹל הַחוֹשְׁבִים עָלַי רָעָה, מְהֵרָה הָפֵר עֲצָתָם וְקַלְקֵל מַחֲשַׁבְתָּם. עֲשֵׂה לְמַעַן שְׁמֶךָ, עֲשֵׂה לְמַעַן יְמִינֶךָ, עֲשֵׂה לְמַעַן קְדֻשָּׁתֶךָ, עֲשֵׂה לְמַעַן תּוֹרָתֶךָ. לְמַעַן יֵחָלְצוּן יְדִידֶיךָ, הוֹשִׁיעָה יְמִינְךָ וַעֲנֵנִי.

O God, keep my tongue from evil and my lips from deceit. Help me to be silent in the face of derision, humble in the presence of all. Open my heart to Your Torah, and I will hasten to do Your Mitzvot. Save me with Your power; in time of trouble be my answer, that those who love You may rejoice.

◆ ◆

יִהְיוּ לְרָצוֹן אִמְרֵי־פִי וְהֶגְיוֹן לִבִּי לְפָנֶיךָ, יְיָ, צוּרִי וְגוֹאֲלִי.

May the words of my mouth, and the meditations of my heart, be acceptable to You, O Lord, my Rock and my Redeemer.

or

עֹשֶׂה שָׁלוֹם בִּמְרוֹמָיו, הוּא יַעֲשֶׂה שָׁלוֹם עָלֵינוּ וְעַל כָּל־יִשְׂרָאֵל, וְאִמְרוּ אָמֵן.

May He who causes peace to reign in the high heavens let peace descend on us, on all Israel, and all the world.

◆ ◆

ESSENCE OF THE TEFILLAH — מעין שבע

בָּרוּךְ אַתָּה, יְיָ אֱלֹהֵינוּ וֵאלֹהֵי אֲבוֹתֵינוּ, אֱלֹהֵי אַבְרָהָם, אֱלֹהֵי יִצְחָק, וֵאלֹהֵי יַעֲקֹב: הָאֵל הַגָּדוֹל, הַגִּבּוֹר וְהַנּוֹרָא, אֵל עֶלְיוֹן, קֹנֵה שָׁמַיִם וָאָרֶץ.

We praise You, Lord our God and God of all generations: God of Abraham, God of Isaac, God of Jacob; great, mighty, and awesome God, God supreme, Maker of heaven and earth.

מָגֵן אָבוֹת בִּדְבָרוֹ, מְחַיֵּה הַכֹּל בְּמַאֲמָרוֹ. הָאֵל הַקָּדוֹשׁ, שֶׁאֵין כָּמוֹהוּ, הַמֵּנִיחַ לְעַמּוֹ בְּיוֹם שַׁבַּת קָדְשׁוֹ, כִּי בָם רָצָה לְהָנִיחַ לָהֶם. לְפָנָיו נַעֲבוֹד בְּיִרְאָה וָפַחַד, וְנוֹדֶה לִשְׁמוֹ בְּכָל־יוֹם תָּמִיד מֵעֵין הַבְּרָכוֹת. אֵל הַהוֹדָאוֹת, אֲדוֹן הַשָּׁלוֹם, מְקַדֵּשׁ הַשַּׁבָּת וּמְבָרֵךְ שְׁבִיעִי, וּמֵנִיחַ בִּקְדֻשָּׁה לְעַם מְדֻשְּׁנֵי עֹנֶג, זֵכֶר לְמַעֲשֵׂה בְרֵאשִׁית.

His word was a shield to our ancestors. He is the Source of all life. He is the holy God, beyond compare. He gives rest to His people on His holy Sabbath day. Him will we serve with awe and trembling, Him affirm day after day. To Him, the Lord of Peace, our thanks are due. In remembrance of the work of creation, He hallows and blesses the Sabbath. In its rest our people finds abounding joy.

◆ ◆

Prayers for Special Occasions begin on page 389.
The Rituals for the Reading of Torah begin on page 415.
Concluding Prayers begin on page 613.

ב II ב

For congregations where the lights are kindled in the synagogue

הדלקת הנרות

As these Shabbat candles give light to all who behold them, so may we, by our lives, give light to all who behold us.

As their brightness reminds us of the generations of Israel who have kindled light, so may we, in our own day, be among those who kindle light.

◆ ◆

בָּרוּךְ אַתָּה, יְיָ אֱלֹהֵינוּ, מֶלֶךְ הָעוֹלָם,
אֲשֶׁר קִדְּשָׁנוּ בְּמִצְוֹתָיו וְצִוָּנוּ לְהַדְלִיק נֵר שֶׁל שַׁבָּת.

Blessed is the Lord our God, Ruler of the universe,
who hallows us with His Mitzvot, and commands us
to kindle the lights of Shabbat.

◆ ◆

Let there be joy!
Let there be peace!

Let there be light!
Let there be Shabbat!

◆ ◆

MEDITATION

In this quiet hour of worship we reflect upon the meaning of our lives.

I harbor within — we all do — a vision of my highest self, a dream of what I could and should become. May I pursue this vision, labor to make real my dream. Thus will I give meaning to my life.

An artist in the course of painting will pause, lay aside the brush, step back from the canvas, and consider what needs to be done, what direction is to be taken. So does each of us on this Sabbath eve pause to reflect. As I hope to make my life a work of art, so may this hour of worship help me to turn back to the canvas of life to paint the portrait of my highest self.

May my efforts to grow in moral stature bring me the joy of achievement. And may I always hold before my eyes the vision of perfection we call by the name of God — and grow toward Him.

◆ ◆

A PRAYER

O Source of light and truth, Creator of the eternal law of goodness, and of the impulse within us for justice and mercy, we pray that this hour of worship may be one of vision and inspiration. Help us to find knowledge by which to live; lead us to take the words we shall speak into our hearts and our lives.

Bless all who enter this sanctuary in search and in need; all who bring to this place the offering of their hearts. May our worship here lead us to fulfill our words and our hopes with acts of kindness, peace, and love. Amen.

◆ ◆

Welcoming Shabbat קבלת שבת

From Psalm 84

מַה־יְּדִידוֹת מִשְׁכְּנוֹתֶיךָ, יְיָ צְבָאוֹת!
נִכְסְפָה וְגַם־כָּלְתָה נַפְשִׁי לְחַצְרוֹת יְיָ, לִבִּי וּבְשָׂרִי יְרַנְּנוּ אֶל אֵל־חָי.

How lovely are Your dwelling places, O Lord of Hosts!

My soul longs and yearns for the courts of the Lord; my heart and my flesh sing for joy to the living God.

גַּם־צִפּוֹר מָצְאָה בַיִת, וּדְרוֹר קֵן לָהּ אֲשֶׁר־שָׁתָה אֶפְרֹחֶיהָ,
אֶת־מִזְבְּחוֹתֶיךָ, יְיָ צְבָאוֹת, מַלְכִּי וֵאלֹהָי.

As the sparrow finds a home, and the swallow has a nest where she rears her young,

So do I seek out Your altars, O Lord of Hosts, my Sovereign God.

אַשְׁרֵי יוֹשְׁבֵי בֵיתֶךָ, עוֹד יְהַלְלוּךָ. סֶּלָה.
אַשְׁרֵי אָדָם עוֹז־לוֹ בָךְ, מְסִלּוֹת בִּלְבָבָם.

Happy are those who dwell in Your house: they will sing Your praise for ever.

Happy are those who find strength in You: their hearts are highways leading to Your presence.

עֹבְרֵי בְּעֵמֶק הַבָּכָא מַעְיָן יְשִׁיתוּהוּ, גַּם־בְּרָכוֹת יַעְטֶה מוֹרֶה.
יֵלְכוּ מֵחַיִל אֶל־חָיִל, יֵרָאֶה אֶל־אֱלֹהִים בְּצִיּוֹן.

When they pass through the driest of valleys, they find it a place of springs; the rain blesses it with pools.

They go from strength to strength; they behold God in Zion.

כִּי טוֹב־יוֹם בַּחֲצֵרֶיךָ מֵאָלֶף.
בָּחַרְתִּי הִסְתּוֹפֵף בְּבֵית אֱלֹהַי, מִדּוּר בְּאָהֳלֵי־רֶשַׁע.

One day in Your courts is better than a thousand elsewhere.

And better it is to wait at the doorstep of Your house than to be an honored guest among the wicked.

כִּי שֶׁמֶשׁ וּמָגֵן יְיָ אֱלֹהִים, חֵן וְכָבוֹד יִתֵּן יְיָ.
לֹא יִמְנַע־טוֹב לַהֹלְכִים בְּתָמִים.
יְיָ צְבָאוֹת, אַשְׁרֵי אָדָם בֹּטֵחַ בָּךְ!

For the Lord God is a sun and a shield;

the Lord gives grace and glory.

No good is withheld from those who walk uprightly.

O Lord of Hosts, happy is the one who trusts in You!

◆ ◆

We have come together to strengthen our bonds with our people Israel. Like Jews of generations past, we celebrate the grandeur of creation. Like Jews of every age, we echo our people's ancient call for justice.

Our celebration is a sharing of memory and hope.

We are Jews, but each of us is unique. We stand apart and alone, with differing feelings and insights. And yet we are not entirely alone and separate, for we are children of one people and one heritage.

Our celebration unites many separate selves into a single chorus.

And we are one in search of life's meaning. All of us know despair and exaltation; all bear burdens; all have moments of weakness and times of strength; all sing songs of sorrow and love.

May our celebration bring us strength along our way.

In this circle of hope, in the presence of the sacred, may the heart come to know itself and its best, finding a fresh impulse to love the good.

May our celebration lead us to work for the good; and may this Shabbat give strength to us and to our people Israel.

◆ ◆

הִנֵּה מַה־טּוֹב וּמַה־נָּעִים
שֶׁבֶת אַחִים גַּם־יָחַד.

How good it is, and how pleasant,
when brethren dwell together in unity.

◆ ◆

Many are the generations of our people, and in every age Israel has sought the living God through Sabbath rest and worship. This time and place hold the power to increase our joy in the Eternal. O God, even as we seek You in the sanctuary, help us to know that Your glory fills all space; make us understand that You are with us at all times, if we but open our minds to You.

We feel the presence of Your spirit in our homes and on our ways; we see the beauty of Your creation in mountain, sea, and sky, and in the human form; we hear You in the silence of our own hearts speaking the truths the heart knows.

May we be Your witness to the world, Your messenger to all the earth.

May we show forth Your image within us, the divine spark that makes us human.

READER'S KADDISH **חצי קדיש**

יִתְגַּדַּל וְיִתְקַדַּשׁ שְׁמֵהּ רַבָּא בְּעָלְמָא דִּי־בְרָא כִרְעוּתֵהּ, וְיַמְלִיךְ מַלְכוּתֵהּ בְּחַיֵּיכוֹן וּבְיוֹמֵיכוֹן וּבְחַיֵּי דְכָל־בֵּית יִשְׂרָאֵל, בַּעֲגָלָא וּבִזְמַן קָרִיב, וְאִמְרוּ: אָמֵן.

יְהֵא שְׁמֵהּ רַבָּא מְבָרַךְ לְעָלַם וּלְעָלְמֵי עָלְמַיָּא.

יִתְבָּרַךְ וְיִשְׁתַּבַּח, וְיִתְפָּאַר וְיִתְרוֹמַם וְיִתְנַשֵּׂא, וְיִתְהַדַּר וְיִתְעַלֶּה וְיִתְהַלַּל שְׁמֵהּ דְּקוּדְשָׁא, בְּרִיךְ הוּא, לְעֵלָּא מִן כָּל־בִּרְכָתָא וְשִׁירָתָא, תֻּשְׁבְּחָתָא וְנֶחֱמָתָא דַּאֲמִירָן בְּעָלְמָא, וְאִמְרוּ: אָמֵן.

Let the glory of God be extolled, let His great name be hallowed in the world whose creation He willed. May His kingdom soon prevail, in our own day, our own lives, and the life of all Israel, and let us say: Amen.

Let His great name be blessed for ever and ever.

Let the name of the Holy One, blessed is He, be glorified, exalted and honored, though He is beyond all the praises, songs, and adorations that we can utter, and let us say: Amen.

◆ ◆

All rise

שמע וברכותיה

בָּרְכוּ אֶת־יְיָ הַמְבֹרָךְ!

Praise the Lord, to whom our praise is due!

בָּרוּךְ יְיָ הַמְבֹרָךְ לְעוֹלָם וָעֶד!

Praised be the Lord, to whom our praise is due,
now and for ever!

❖ ❖

WE LIFT OUR EYES   מעריב ערבים

בָּרוּךְ אַתָּה, יְיָ אֱלֹהֵֽינוּ, מֶֽלֶךְ הָעוֹלָם, אֲשֶׁר בִּדְבָרוֹ מַעֲרִיב
עֲרָבִים. בְּחָכְמָה פּוֹתֵֽחַ שְׁעָרִים, וּבִתְבוּנָה מְשַׁנֶּה עִתִּים,
וּמַחֲלִיף אֶת־הַזְּמַנִּים, וּמְסַדֵּר אֶת־הַכּוֹכָבִים בְּמִשְׁמְרוֹתֵיהֶם
בָּרָקִיעַ כִּרְצוֹנוֹ.

As day departs, as the dark of night descends, we lift our eyes
to the heavens. In awe and wonder our hearts cry out:

Eternal God, how majestic is Your name in all the earth!

בּוֹרֵא יוֹם וָלָֽיְלָה, גּוֹלֵל אוֹר מִפְּנֵי חֹֽשֶׁךְ וְחֹֽשֶׁךְ מִפְּנֵי אוֹר,
וּמַעֲבִיר יוֹם וּמֵֽבִיא לָֽיְלָה, וּמַבְדִּיל בֵּין יוֹם וּבֵין לָֽיְלָה, יְיָ
צְבָאוֹת שְׁמוֹ.

A vast universe: who can know it? What mind can fathom it?
We look out to the endless suns and ask: What are we, what
are our dreams and our hopes?

*What are we, that You are mindful of us? What are we, that
You should care for us?*

אֵל חַי וְקַיָּם, תָּמִיד יִמְלוֹךְ עָלֵֽינוּ, לְעוֹלָם וָעֶד. בָּרוּךְ אַתָּה,
יְיָ, הַמַּעֲרִיב עֲרָבִים.

And yet within us abides a measure of Your spirit. You are remote, but, oh, how near! Ordering the stars in the vast solitudes of the dark, yet whispering in the mind that You are

closer than the air we breathe. With love and awe we turn to You, and in the dark of evening seek the light of Your presence.

For You have made us little less than divine, and crowned us with glory and honor!

◆ ◆

YOUR POWER AND YOUR LOVE — אהבת עולם

אַהֲבַת עוֹלָם בֵּית יִשְׂרָאֵל עַמְּךָ אָהָבְתָּ: תּוֹרָה וּמִצְוֹת, חֻקִּים
וּמִשְׁפָּטִים אוֹתָנוּ לִמַּדְתָּ.
עַל־כֵּן, יְיָ אֱלֹהֵינוּ, בְּשָׁכְבֵנוּ וּבְקוּמֵנוּ נָשִׂיחַ בְּחֻקֶּיךָ, וְנִשְׂמַח
בְּדִבְרֵי תוֹרָתְךָ וּבְמִצְוֹתֶיךָ לְעוֹלָם וָעֶד.

O One and Only God, You have made each of us unique, and formed us to be united in one family of life. Be with us, Eternal One, as we seek to unite our lives with Your power and Your love.

כִּי הֵם חַיֵּינוּ וְאֹרֶךְ יָמֵינוּ, וּבָהֶם נֶהְגֶּה יוֹמָם וָלָיְלָה. וְאַהֲבָתְךָ
אַל־תָּסִיר מִמֶּנּוּ לְעוֹלָמִים! בָּרוּךְ אַתָּה, יְיָ, אוֹהֵב עַמּוֹ יִשְׂרָאֵל.

We proclaim now Your Oneness and our own hope for unity; we acclaim Your creative power in the universe and in ourselves, the Law that binds world to world and heart to heart:

שְׁמַע יִשְׂרָאֵל: יְיָ אֱלֹהֵינוּ, יְיָ אֶחָד!

Hear, O Israel: the Lord is our God, the Lord is One!

בָּרוּךְ שֵׁם כְּבוֹד מַלְכוּתוֹ לְעוֹלָם וָעֶד!

Blessed is His glorious kingdom for ever and ever!

All are seated

וְאָהַבְתָּ אֵת יְיָ אֱלֹהֶיךָ בְּכָל־לְבָבְךָ וּבְכָל־נַפְשְׁךָ וּבְכָל־מְאֹדֶךָ.
וְהָיוּ הַדְּבָרִים הָאֵלֶּה, אֲשֶׁר אָנֹכִי מְצַוְּךָ הַיּוֹם, עַל־לְבָבֶךָ.

וְשִׁנַּנְתָּם לְבָנֶיךָ, וְדִבַּרְתָּ בָּם בְּשִׁבְתְּךָ בְּבֵיתֶךָ, וּבְלֶכְתְּךָ בַדֶּרֶךְ, וּבְשָׁכְבְּךָ וּבְקוּמֶךָ.

You shall love the Lord your God with all your mind, with all your strength, with all your being.
Set these words, which I command you this day, upon your heart. Teach them faithfully to your children; speak of them in your home and on your way, when you lie down and when you rise up.

וּקְשַׁרְתָּם לְאוֹת עַל־יָדֶךָ, וְהָיוּ לְטֹטָפֹת בֵּין עֵינֶיךָ, וּכְתַבְתָּם עַל־מְזֻזוֹת בֵּיתֶךָ, וּבִשְׁעָרֶיךָ.

Bind them as a sign upon your hand; let them be a symbol before your eyes; inscribe them on the doorposts of your house, and on your gates.

לְמַעַן תִּזְכְּרוּ וַעֲשִׂיתֶם אֶת־כָּל־מִצְוֹתָי, וִהְיִיתֶם קְדֹשִׁים לֵאלֹהֵיכֶם. אֲנִי יְיָ אֱלֹהֵיכֶם, אֲשֶׁר הוֹצֵאתִי אֶתְכֶם מֵאֶרֶץ מִצְרַיִם לִהְיוֹת לָכֶם לֵאלֹהִים. אֲנִי יְיָ אֱלֹהֵיכֶם.

Be mindful of all My Mitzvot, and do them: so shall you consecrate yourselves to your God. I, the Lord, am your God who led you out of Egypt to be your God; I, the Lord, am your God.

◆ ◆

THE VISION OF A WORLD REDEEMED — גאולה

אֱמֶת וֶאֱמוּנָה כָּל־זֹאת, וְקַיָּם עָלֵינוּ כִּי הוּא יְיָ אֱלֹהֵינוּ וְאֵין זוּלָתוֹ, וַאֲנַחְנוּ יִשְׂרָאֵל עַמּוֹ.

In a world torn by violence and pain, a world far from wholeness and peace, a world waiting still to be redeemed, give us, Lord, the courage to say: There is One God in heaven and earth.

The high heavens declare His glory; may earth reveal His justice and His love.

הַפּוֹדֵנוּ מִיַּד מְלָכִים, מַלְכֵּנוּ הַגּוֹאֲלֵנוּ מִכַּף כָּל־הֶעָרִיצִים.
הָעֹשֶׂה גְדֹלוֹת עַד אֵין חֵקֶר, וְנִפְלָאוֹת עַד־אֵין מִסְפָּר.
הַשָּׂם נַפְשֵׁנוּ בַּחַיִּים, וְלֹא־נָתַן לַמּוֹט רַגְלֵנוּ.
הָעֹשֶׂה לָנוּ נִסִּים בְּפַרְעֹה, אוֹתוֹת וּמוֹפְתִים בְּאַדְמַת בְּנֵי חָם.
וַיּוֹצֵא אֶת־עַמּוֹ יִשְׂרָאֵל מִתּוֹכָם לְחֵרוּת עוֹלָם.

From Egypt, the house of bondage, we were delivered; at Sinai, amid peals of thunder, we bound ourselves to His purpose. Inspired by prophets and instructed by sages, we survived oppression and exile, time and again overcoming the forces that would have destroyed us.

Our failings are many — our faults are great — yet it has been our glory to bear witness to our God, and to keep alive in dark ages the vision of a world redeemed.

וְרָאוּ בָנָיו גְּבוּרָתוֹ; שִׁבְּחוּ וְהוֹדוּ לִשְׁמוֹ. וּמַלְכוּתוֹ בְּרָצוֹן קִבְּלוּ עֲלֵיהֶם. מֹשֶׁה וּבְנֵי יִשְׂרָאֵל לְךָ עָנוּ שִׁירָה בְּשִׂמְחָה רַבָּה, וְאָמְרוּ כֻלָּם:

May this vision never fade; let us continue to work for the day when the nations will be one and at peace. Then shall we sing with one accord, as Israel sang at the shores of the Sea:

Who is like You, Eternal One, among the gods that are worshipped?	מִי־כָמֹכָה בָּאֵלִם, יְיָ?
Who is like You, majestic in holiness,	מִי כָּמֹכָה, נֶאְדָּר בַּקֹּדֶשׁ,
awesome in splendor, doing wonders?	נוֹרָא תְהִלֹּת, עֹשֵׂה פֶלֶא?

מַלְכוּתְךָ רָאוּ בָנֶיךָ, בּוֹקֵעַ יָם לִפְנֵי מֹשֶׁה; "זֶה אֵלִי!" עָנוּ וְאָמְרוּ: "יְיָ יִמְלֹךְ לְעֹלָם וָעֶד!"

In their escape from the sea, Your children saw Your sovereign might displayed. "This is my God!" they cried. "The Eternal will reign for ever and ever!"

וְנֶאֱמַר: "כִּי־פָדָה יְיָ אֶת יַעֲקֹב, וּגְאָלוֹ מִיַּד חָזָק מִמֶּנּוּ." בָּרוּךְ אַתָּה, יְיָ, גָּאַל יִשְׂרָאֵל.

Now let all come to say: The Eternal has redeemed Israel and all the oppressed. Blessed is the Eternal God.

◆ ◆

TO FIND OUR HEARTS WAITING — השכיבנו

הַשְׁכִּיבֵֽנוּ, יְיָ אֱלֹהֵֽינוּ, לְשָׁלוֹם, וְהַעֲמִידֵֽנוּ, מַלְכֵּֽנוּ, לְחַיִּים.
וּפְרוֹשׂ עָלֵֽינוּ סֻכַּת שְׁלוֹמֶֽךָ, וְתַקְּנֵֽנוּ בְּעֵצָה טוֹבָה מִלְּפָנֶֽיךָ,
וְהוֹשִׁיעֵֽנוּ לְמַֽעַן שְׁמֶֽךָ, וְהָגֵן בַּעֲדֵֽנוּ. וְהָסֵר מֵעָלֵֽינוּ אוֹיֵב,
דֶּֽבֶר וְחֶֽרֶב וְרָעָב וְיָגוֹן; וְהָסֵר שָׂטָן מִלְּפָנֵֽינוּ וּמֵאַחֲרֵֽינוּ;
וּבְצֵל כְּנָפֶֽיךָ תַּסְתִּירֵֽנוּ, כִּי אֵל שׁוֹמְרֵֽנוּ וּמַצִּילֵֽנוּ אָֽתָּה, כִּי
אֵל מֶֽלֶךְ חַנּוּן וְרַחוּם אָֽתָּה. וּשְׁמוֹר צֵאתֵֽנוּ וּבוֹאֵֽנוּ לְחַיִּים
וּלְשָׁלוֹם, מֵעַתָּה וְעַד עוֹלָם, וּפְרוֹשׂ עָלֵֽינוּ סֻכַּת שְׁלוֹמֶֽךָ.
בָּרוּךְ אַתָּה, יְיָ, הַפּוֹרֵשׂ סֻכַּת שָׁלוֹם עָלֵֽינוּ, וְעַל־כָּל־עַמּוֹ
יִשְׂרָאֵל וְעַל יְרוּשָׁלָֽיִם.

Let there be love and understanding among us; let peace and friendship be our shelter from life's storms. Eternal God, help us to walk with good companions, to live with hope in our hearts and eternity in our thoughts, that we may lie down in peace and rise up to find our hearts waiting to do Your will.

Blessed is the Eternal One, Guardian of Israel, whose love gives light to all the world.

◆ ◆

O God of Israel, may our worship on this day help us to grow in loyalty to our covenant with You and to the way of life it demands: the way of gentleness and justice, the path of truth and of peace.

THE COVENANT OF SHABBAT — ושמרו

וְשָׁמְרוּ בְנֵי־יִשְׂרָאֵל אֶת־הַשַּׁבָּת, לַעֲשׂוֹת אֶת־הַשַּׁבָּת לְדֹרֹתָם
בְּרִית עוֹלָם. בֵּינִי וּבֵין בְּנֵי יִשְׂרָאֵל אוֹת הִיא לְעֹלָם, כִּי שֵֽׁשֶׁת
יָמִים עָשָׂה יְיָ אֶת־הַשָּׁמַֽיִם וְאֶת־הָאָֽרֶץ, וּבַיּוֹם הַשְּׁבִיעִי שָׁבַת
וַיִּנָּפַשׁ.

The people of Israel shall keep the Sabbath, observing the Sabbath in every generation as a covenant for all time. It is a sign for ever between Me and the people of Israel, for in six days the Eternal God made heaven and earth, and on the seventh day He rested from His labors.

◆ ◆

MEDITATION

Prayer invites God to let His presence suffuse our spirits, to let His will prevail in our lives. Prayer cannot bring water to parched fields, nor mend a broken bridge, nor rebuild a ruined city; but prayer can water an arid soul, mend a broken heart, and rebuild a weakened will.

◆ ◆

All rise

תפלה

אֲדֹנָי, שְׂפָתַי תִּפְתָּח, וּפִי יַגִּיד תְּהִלָּתֶךָ.

Eternal God, open my lips, that my mouth may declare Your glory.

THEIR QUEST IS OURS אבות

בָּרוּךְ אַתָּה, יְיָ אֱלֹהֵינוּ וֵאלֹהֵי אֲבוֹתֵינוּ, אֱלֹהֵי אַבְרָהָם, אֱלֹהֵי יִצְחָק, וֵאלֹהֵי יַעֲקֹב: הָאֵל הַגָּדוֹל, הַגִּבּוֹר וְהַנּוֹרָא, אֵל עֶלְיוֹן.

Source of all being, we turn to You as did our people in ancient days. They beheld You in the heavens; they felt You in their hearts; they sought You in their lives.

גּוֹמֵל חֲסָדִים טוֹבִים, וְקוֹנֵה הַכֹּל, וְזוֹכֵר חַסְדֵי אָבוֹת, וּמֵבִיא גְאֻלָּה לִבְנֵי בְנֵיהֶם, לְמַעַן שְׁמוֹ, בְּאַהֲבָה.

מֶלֶךְ עוֹזֵר וּמוֹשִׁיעַ וּמָגֵן. בָּרוּךְ אַתָּה, יְיָ, מָגֵן אַבְרָהָם.

Now their quest is ours. Help us, O God, to see the wonder of being. Give us the courage to search for truth. Teach us the path to a better life. So shall we, by our lives and our labors, bring nearer to realization the great hope inherited from ages past, for a world transformed by liberty, justice, and peace.

• •

HELP US TO USE OUR STRENGTH גבורות

אַתָּה גִּבּוֹר לְעוֹלָם, אֲדֹנָי, מְחַיֵּה הַכֹּל אַתָּה, רַב לְהוֹשִׁיעַ.
מְכַלְכֵּל חַיִּים בְּחֶסֶד, מְחַיֵּה הַכֹּל בְּרַחֲמִים רַבִּים. סוֹמֵךְ
נוֹפְלִים, וְרוֹפֵא חוֹלִים, וּמַתִּיר אֲסוּרִים, וּמְקַיֵּם אֱמוּנָתוֹ
לִישֵׁנֵי עָפָר.
מִי כָמוֹךָ, בַּעַל גְּבוּרוֹת, וּמִי דּוֹמֶה לָּךְ, מֶלֶךְ מֵמִית וּמְחַיֶּה
וּמַצְמִיחַ יְשׁוּעָה?
וְנֶאֱמָן אַתָּה לְהַחֲיוֹת הַכֹּל. בָּרוּךְ אַתָּה, יְיָ, מְחַיֵּה הַכֹּל.

Your might, O God, is everlasting;
Help us to use our strength for good and not for evil.

You are the Source of life and blessing;
Help us to choose life for ourselves and our children.

You are the support of the falling;
Help us to lift up the fallen.

You are the Author of freedom;
Help us to set free the captive.

You are our hope in death as in life;
Help us to keep faith with those who sleep in the dust.

Your might, O God, is everlasting;
Help us to use our strength for good.

• •

O WORLD ABLAZE קדושת השם

אַתָּה קָדוֹשׁ וְשִׁמְךָ קָדוֹשׁ, וּקְדוֹשִׁים בְּכָל־יוֹם יְהַלְלוּךָ סֶּלָה.
בָּרוּךְ אַתָּה, יְיָ, הָאֵל הַקָּדוֹשׁ.

A time can come to us when our hearts are filled with awe: suddenly the noise of life will be stilled, as our eyes open to a world just beyond the border of our minds. All at once there is a glory in our souls! הָאֵל הַקָּדוֹשׁ!—The Holy God! O majestic Presence! O world ablaze with splendor!

Holy, Holy, Holy is the Lord of Hosts; the fullness of the whole earth is His glory!

All are seated

◆ ◆

MOST PRECIOUS OF DAYS

קדושת היום

יִשְׂמְחוּ בְמַלְכוּתְךָ שׁוֹמְרֵי שַׁבָּת וְקוֹרְאֵי עֹנֶג. עַם מְקַדְּשֵׁי שְׁבִיעִי כֻּלָּם יִשְׂבְּעוּ וְיִתְעַנְּגוּ מִטּוּבֶךָ. וְהַשְּׁבִיעִי רָצִיתָ בּוֹ וְקִדַּשְׁתּוֹ. חֶמְדַּת יָמִים אוֹתוֹ קָרָאתָ, זֵכֶר לְמַעֲשֵׂה בְרֵאשִׁית.

Those who keep the Sabbath and call it a delight shall rejoice in Your kingdom. All who hallow the seventh day shall be gladdened by Your goodness. This day is Israel's festival of the spirit, sanctified and blessed by You, the most precious of days, a symbol of the joy of creation.

◆

ALL THAT IS HIGH AND HOLY

אֱלֹהֵינוּ וֵאלֹהֵי אֲבוֹתֵינוּ, רְצֵה בִמְנוּחָתֵנוּ. קַדְּשֵׁנוּ בְּמִצְוֹתֶיךָ וְתֵן חֶלְקֵנוּ בְּתוֹרָתֶךָ. שַׂבְּעֵנוּ מִטּוּבֶךָ, וְשַׂמְּחֵנוּ בִּישׁוּעָתֶךָ, וְטַהֵר לִבֵּנוּ לְעָבְדְּךָ בֶּאֱמֶת. וְהַנְחִילֵנוּ, יְיָ אֱלֹהֵינוּ, בְּאַהֲבָה וּבְרָצוֹן שַׁבַּת קָדְשֶׁךָ, וְיָנוּחוּ בָהּ יִשְׂרָאֵל מְקַדְּשֵׁי שְׁמֶךָ. בָּרוּךְ אַתָּה, יְיָ, מְקַדֵּשׁ הַשַּׁבָּת.

God of Israel, may our worship on this Sabbath bring us nearer to all that is high and holy. May it bind the generations in bonds of love and sharing, and unite us with our people in common hope and faith. And through Sabbath rest and worship, may we learn to find fulfillment and joy in the vision of peace for all the world.

◆ ◆

NEW STRENGTH FOR YOUR SERVICE עבודה

רְצֵה, יְיָ אֱלֹהֵינוּ, בְּעַמְּךָ יִשְׂרָאֵל, וּתְפִלָּתָם בְּאַהֲבָה תְקַבֵּל, וּתְהִי לְרָצוֹן תָּמִיד עֲבוֹדַת יִשְׂרָאֵל עַמֶּךָ.

בָּרוּךְ אַתָּה, יְיָ, שֶׁאוֹתְךָ לְבַדְּךָ בְּיִרְאָה נַעֲבוֹד.

You are with us in our prayer, in our love and our doubt, in our longing to feel Your presence and do Your will. You are the still, clear voice within us. Therefore, O God, when doubt troubles us, when anxiety makes us tremble, and pain clouds the mind, we look inward for the answer to our prayers. There may we find You, and there find courage, insight, and endurance. And let our worship bring us closer to one another, that all Israel, and all who seek You, may find new strength for Your service.

◆ ◆

GIFTS AND BLESSINGS הודאה

מוֹדִים אֲנַחְנוּ לָךְ, שָׁאַתָּה הוּא יְיָ אֱלֹהֵינוּ וֵאלֹהֵי אֲבוֹתֵינוּ, אֱלֹהֵי כָל־בָּשָׂר, יוֹצְרֵנוּ יוֹצֵר בְּרֵאשִׁית.
בְּרָכוֹת וְהוֹדָאוֹת לְשִׁמְךָ הַגָּדוֹל וְהַקָּדוֹשׁ עַל־שֶׁהֶחֱיִיתָנוּ וְקִיַּמְתָּנוּ.

Eternal Source of good, we thank You for the numberless gifts and blessings that fill our days: for life itself and its endless variety; for all that sustains body and mind; for love and friendship; for the delights of the senses; and for the excellence of Your Torah, which deepens our life and enriches our days.

כֵּן תְּחַיֵּנוּ וּתְקַיְּמֵנוּ, יְיָ אֱלֹהֵינוּ, וּתְאַמְּצֵנוּ לִשְׁמֹר חֻקֶּיךָ, לַעֲשׂוֹת רְצוֹנֶךָ, וּלְעָבְדְּךָ בְּלֵבָב שָׁלֵם. בָּרוּךְ אֵל הַהוֹדָאוֹת.

Help us, O God, to work for a just and compassionate society, where all may share Your gifts in the joy of freedom.

◆ ◆

KNOW PEACE FOR EVER ברכת שלום

שָׁלוֹם רָב עַל־יִשְׂרָאֵל עַמְּךָ, וְעַל־כָּל־הָעַמִּים, תָּשִׂים לְעוֹלָם.

Let Israel Your people, and all peoples, know peace for ever.

Let the great shofar of freedom be sounded for us and all peoples.

Let peace and freedom reign in all the world.

Let every wanderer come home from the bitterness of exile.

And may our eyes behold Your return to Zion in mercy.

Then will Jerusalem, the city of David, be the city of peace,
the joy of all the world.

The land of Israel and its people will see freedom and peace.

בָּרוּךְ אַתָּה, יְיָ, עוֹשֵׂה הַשָּׁלוֹם.

Blessed is the Lord, the Source of peace.

◆ ◆

MEDITATION

These quiet moments of Shabbat open my soul. Blessed with another week of life, I give thanks to Him who creates and sustains us.

For all the good I have known during the days that have passed, I am very grateful. I know I have not always responded with my best effort, but often I did earnestly try. I have tried to give my family love and devotion, and I pray that I may grow more loving as the years pass.

Even as I regret my weakness, I rejoice in my accomplishments. Let these achievements, O God, lead to many others. May I be blessed on each Shabbat with the sense of having grown in goodness and compassion. There have been times when I endeavored to help those in need. Now I ask only that I may be able to do yet more. Let my actions testify to my worth as Your partner in creation; more and more let me find my life's meaning in working with others to bless our lives by making this a better world.

◆ ◆

יִהְיוּ לְרָצוֹן אִמְרֵי־פִי וְהֶגְיוֹן לִבִּי לְפָנֶיךָ, יְיָ, צוּרִי וְגוֹאֲלִי.

May the words of my mouth, and the meditations of my heart, be acceptable to You, O Lord, my Rock and my Redeemer.

or

עֹשֶׂה שָׁלוֹם בִּמְרוֹמָיו, הוּא יַעֲשֶׂה שָׁלוֹם עָלֵינוּ וְעַל כָּל־יִשְׂרָאֵל, וְאִמְרוּ אָמֵן.

May He who causes peace to reign in the high heavens let peace descend on us, on all Israel, and all the world.

◆ ◆

Pray as if everything depended on God; act as if everything depended on you.

Who rise from prayer better persons, their prayer is answered.

◆ ◆

Prayers for Special Occasions begin on page 389.

The Rituals for the Reading of Torah begin on page 415.

Concluding Prayers begin on page 613.

ג III ג

For congregations where the lights are kindled in the synagogue

הדלקת הנרות

On this day
we would see the world
in a new light.

On this day
we would add new spirit
to our lives.

On this day
we would taste
a new time of peace.

We would rest
from desire for gain,
ambition for things.

We would raise our eyes
to look beyond time and space
toward eternity.

O may we
come to see the world
in a new light.

As it is written:
"Let a new light shine upon Zion,
and may it be our blessing
to see its splendor."

◆ ◆

בָּרוּךְ אַתָּה, יְיָ אֱלֹהֵינוּ, מֶלֶךְ הָעוֹלָם,
אֲשֶׁר קִדְּשָׁנוּ בְּמִצְוֹתָיו וְצִוָּנוּ לְהַדְלִיק נֵר שֶׁל שַׁבָּת.

Blessed is the Lord our God, Ruler of the universe,
who hallows us with His Mitzvot, and commands us
to kindle the lights of Shabbat.

◆ ◆

Welcoming Shabbat קבלת שבת

HEART'S DELIGHT	ידיד נפש
Heart's delight, Source of mercy,	יְדִיד נֶפֶשׁ, אָב הָרַחֲמָן,
draw Your servant into Your arms:	מְשׁוֹךְ עַבְדְּךָ אֶל רְצוֹנֶךָ:
I leap like a deer	יָרוּץ עַבְדְּךָ כְּמוֹ אַיָּל
to stand in awe before You.	יִשְׁתַּחֲוֶה אֶל מוּל הֲדָרֶךָ.
Your love is sweeter to me	יֶעֱרַב לוֹ יְדִידוֹתֶיךָ
than the taste of honey.	מִנֹּפֶת צוּף וְכָל טָעַם.
World's light, shining glory,	הָדוּר נָאֶה, זִיו הָעוֹלָם,
my heart is faint for love of You:	נַפְשִׁי חוֹלַת אַהֲבָתֶךָ:
heal it, Lord, help my heart,	אָנָּא אֵל נָא רְפָא נָא לָהּ,
show me Your radiant splendor.	בְּהַרְאוֹת לָהּ נֹעַם זִיוֶךָ.
Let me return to strength	אָז תִּתְחַזֵּק וְתִתְרַפֵּא,
and have joy for ever.	וְהָיְתָה לָהּ שִׂמְחַת עוֹלָם.
Have compassion, O Faithful One,	וָתִיק, יֶהֱמוּ נָא רַחֲמֶיךָ,
pity for Your loved child:	וְחוּסָה נָא עַל בֵּן אֲהוּבֶךָ:
how long have I hoped	כִּי זֶה כַּמָּה נִכְסוֹף נִכְסַפְתִּי
to see Your glorious might.	לִרְאוֹת בְּתִפְאֶרֶת עֻזֶּךָ.
O God, my heart's desire,	אָנָּא, אֵלִי, חֶמְדַּת לִבִּי,
have pity, hold back no more.	חוּסָה נָא וְאַל תִּתְעַלָּם.
Show Yourself, Beloved, and cover me	הִגָּלֶה נָא, וּפְרוֹס, חֲבִיבִי,
with the shelter of Your peace.	עָלַי אֶת סֻכַּת שְׁלוֹמָךְ.
Light up the world with Your presence,	תָּאִיר אֶרֶץ מִכְּבוֹדֶךָ;
that we may exult and rejoice in You.	נָגִילָה וְנִשְׂמְחָה בָּךְ.
Hurry, Loved One, the holy day has come:	מַהֵר, אָהוּב, כִּי בָא מוֹעֵד,
show us grace as long ago.	וְחָנֵּנוּ כִּימֵי עוֹלָם.

◆ ◆

MEDITATION

O God, may this hour help us to an awareness of Your presence. We are seekers after the One whose name we cannot utter. We cannot truly know You, we cannot see You, and yet You are known and named and seen. As it is said: "Did not those who came before you eat and drink, like you, yet do justice and right? They defended the poor and the needy; then it was well. Is not this to know Me? says the Lord." We will look then to truth and to right, follow the path of beauty and love: these bear witness to You; by them shall we know You.

◆ ◆

Perfect truth, O God, is far beyond us; and yet we pray that our love of truth may never falter.
"I have chosen the path of truth, setting my heart upon Your laws."

Though we cannot hope to be wholly righteous, yet may our ruling passion be the desire for righteousness.
"By righteousness shall you be made secure; you shall not fear."

Perfect love, we know, is too hard for us to reach; yet would we have love become our guiding light.
"You shall love your neighbor as yourself: I am the Lord."

And though we can never experience the full joy of beauty, yet may we learn more and more to see the beautiful in the world and in ourselves.
"He has made everything beautiful in its time; He has put the world into our hearts."

Open our hearts, O High and Hidden God, to the light of Your presence and the joy of Your love. Help us to seek goodness and truth, for this is Your Way and Your Teaching, and thus do we meet You in human life.
Endow us, O God, with a Sabbath spirit, that we may come to serve You in faithfulness and in love.

◆ ◆

NOTE: The mystics of Israel conceived of the Sabbath as entering the world as Israel's bride, and they welcomed her with ecstatic joy. They saw Shabbat, especially hallowed by God, as the day when Israel may unite with God in love. They sang the Song of Songs as a love song of God and Israel, and they sang Lecha Dodi:

לְכָה דוֹדִי לִקְרַאת כַּלָּה, פְּנֵי שַׁבָּת נְקַבְּלָה.
לְכָה דוֹדִי לִקְרַאת כַּלָּה, פְּנֵי שַׁבָּת נְקַבְּלָה.

Beloved, come to meet the bride; beloved, come to greet Shabbat.

"שָׁמוֹר" וְ"זָכוֹר", בְּדִבּוּר אֶחָד, הִשְׁמִיעָנוּ אֵל הַמְיֻחָד.
יְיָ אֶחָד וּשְׁמוֹ אֶחָד, לְשֵׁם וּלְתִפְאֶרֶת וְלִתְהִלָּה.
לְכָה . . .

"Keep" and "Remember": a single command the Only God caused us to hear; the Eternal is One, His name is One; His are honor and glory and praise.

Beloved . . .

לִקְרַאת שַׁבָּת לְכוּ וְנֵלְכָה, כִּי הִיא מְקוֹר הַבְּרָכָה.
מֵרֹאשׁ מִקֶּדֶם נְסוּכָה, סוֹף מַעֲשֶׂה, בְּמַחֲשָׁבָה תְּחִלָּה.
לְכָה . . .

Come with me to meet Shabbat, for ever a fountain of blessing. Still it flows, as from the start: the last of days, for which the first was made.

Beloved . . .

הִתְעוֹרְרִי, הִתְעוֹרְרִי, כִּי בָא אוֹרֵךְ! קוּמִי, אוֹרִי,
עוּרִי עוּרִי, שִׁיר דַּבֵּרִי; כְּבוֹד יְיָ עָלַיִךְ נִגְלָה.
לְכָה . . .

Awake, awake, your light has come! Arise, shine, awake and sing; the Eternal's glory dawns upon you.

Beloved . . .

בּוֹאִי בְשָׁלוֹם, עֲטֶרֶת בַּעְלָהּ, גַּם בְּשִׂמְחָה וּבְצָהֳלָה,
תּוֹךְ אֱמוּנֵי עַם סְגֻלָּה. בּוֹאִי כַלָּה! בּוֹאִי כַלָּה!
לְכָה . . .

Enter in peace, O crown of your husband; enter in gladness, enter in joy. Come to the people that keeps its faith. Enter, O bride! Enter, O bride!

Beloved . . .

◆ ◆

Sing a new song to the Lord!
Sing to the Lord, all the earth!

שִׁירוּ לַייָ שִׁיר חָדָשׁ!
שִׁירוּ לַייָ כָּל־הָאָרֶץ!

Let the earth ring out in song to God.
Sing to the Lord a new song!

הָרִיעוּ לַייָ, כָּל־הָאָרֶץ.
שִׁירוּ לַייָ שִׁיר חָדָשׁ!

Break forth, sing aloud, shout praise!
Sing to the Lord, all the earth!

פִּצְחוּ וְרַנְּנוּ וְזַמֵּרוּ!
הָרִיעוּ לַייָ, כָּל־הָאָרֶץ!

Let the heavens be glad
and the earth rejoice.
Let the sea roar, and all that fills it.

יִשְׂמְחוּ הַשָּׁמַיִם, וְתָגֵל הָאָרֶץ.
יִרְעַם הַיָּם, וּמְלֹאוֹ.

Let the field exult, and all its creatures.
Let the trees of the forest sing for joy.

יַעֲלֹז שָׂדַי, וְכָל־אֲשֶׁר־בּוֹ.
אָז יְרַנְּנוּ כָּל־עֲצֵי־יָעַר.

Sing to the Lord, all the earth!
Sing to the Lord a new song!

שִׁירוּ לַייָ, כָּל־הָאָרֶץ!
שִׁירוּ לַייָ שִׁיר חָדָשׁ!

Let the rivers clap hands.
Let the mountains sing for joy.

נְהָרוֹת יִמְחֲאוּ־כָף.
יַחַד הָרִים יְרַנֵּנוּ.

Sing to the Lord, all the earth!
Break forth, sing aloud, shout praise!

שִׁירוּ לַייָ, כָּל־הָאָרֶץ!
פִּצְחוּ וְרַנְּנוּ וְזַמֵּרוּ!

◆ ◆

This might be read in place of the preceding

How can I sing of day and night,
when it is God who formed them?

אֵיכָה אָשִׁיר עַל־יוֹם וָלַיְלָה—
וֵאלֹהִים הוּא יְצָרָם!

How can I sing of heaven and earth,
when it is God who decreed them?

אֵיכָה אָשִׁיר עַל־שָׁמַיִם וָאָרֶץ—
וֵאלֹהִים הוּא יְסָדָם!

How can I sing of mountains and hills, when it is God who planted them?	אֵיכָה אָשִׁיר עַל־הָרִים וּגְבָעוֹת – וֵאלֹהִים הוּא טְבָעָם!
How can I sing of seas and deserts, when it is God who begot them?	אֵיכָה אָשִׁיר עַל־יַמִּים וְצִיּוֹת – וֵאלֹהִים הוּא חוֹלְלָם!
And how can I sing of earth and its fullness, when it is God who bade them be?	אֵיכָה אָשִׁיר עַל־תֵּבֵל וּמְלוֹאָהּ – וֵאלֹהִים הוּא צִוָּהּ!
I shall sing to Him who fashioned all and is beyond all — it is to God I shall sing!	אָשִׁיר לְיוֹצֵר הַכֹּל וְנַעֲלֶה עַל־כֹּל – לֵאלֹהִים אָשִׁירָה!

READER'S KADDISH
חצי קדיש

יִתְגַּדַּל וְיִתְקַדַּשׁ שְׁמֵהּ רַבָּא בְּעָלְמָא דִּי־בְרָא כִרְעוּתֵהּ, וְיַמְלִיךְ מַלְכוּתֵהּ בְּחַיֵּיכוֹן וּבְיוֹמֵיכוֹן וּבְחַיֵּי דְכָל־בֵּית יִשְׂרָאֵל, בַּעֲגָלָא וּבִזְמַן קָרִיב, וְאִמְרוּ: אָמֵן.

יְהֵא שְׁמֵהּ רַבָּא מְבָרַךְ לְעָלַם וּלְעָלְמֵי עָלְמַיָּא.

יִתְבָּרַךְ וְיִשְׁתַּבַּח, וְיִתְפָּאַר וְיִתְרוֹמַם וְיִתְנַשֵּׂא, וְיִתְהַדַּר וְיִתְעַלֶּה וְיִתְהַלַּל שְׁמֵהּ דְּקוּדְשָׁא, בְּרִיךְ הוּא, לְעֵלָּא מִן כָּל־בִּרְכָתָא וְשִׁירָתָא, תֻּשְׁבְּחָתָא וְנֶחֱמָתָא דַּאֲמִירָן בְּעָלְמָא, וְאִמְרוּ: אָמֵן.

Let the glory of God be extolled, let His great name be hallowed in the world whose creation He willed. May His kingdom soon prevail, in our own day, our own lives, and the life of all Israel, and let us say: Amen.

Let His great name be blessed for ever and ever.

Let the name of the Holy One, blessed is He, be glorified, exalted and honored, though He is beyond all the praises, songs, and adorations that we can utter, and let us say: Amen.

◆ ◆

All rise

שמע וברכותיה

בָּרְכוּ אֶת־יְיָ הַמְבֹרָךְ!

Praise the Lord, to whom our praise is due!

בָּרוּךְ יְיָ הַמְבֹרָךְ לְעוֹלָם וָעֶד!

Praised be the Lord, to whom our praise is due,
now and for ever!

• •

WISDOM AND POWER

מעריב ערבים

בָּרוּךְ אַתָּה, יְיָ אֱלֹהֵינוּ, מֶלֶךְ הָעוֹלָם, אֲשֶׁר בִּדְבָרוֹ מַעֲרִיב עֲרָבִים. בְּחָכְמָה פּוֹתֵחַ שְׁעָרִים, וּבִתְבוּנָה מְשַׁנֶּה עִתִּים, וּמַחֲלִיף אֶת־הַזְּמַנִּים, וּמְסַדֵּר אֶת־הַכּוֹכָבִים בְּמִשְׁמְרוֹתֵיהֶם בָּרָקִיעַ כִּרְצוֹנוֹ.

We praise You, Lord our God, Ruler of the universe, Creator of all things. You have made the moon to mark the seasons, and the sun knows its time of setting.

בּוֹרֵא יוֹם וָלָיְלָה, גּוֹלֵל אוֹר מִפְּנֵי חֹשֶׁךְ וְחֹשֶׁךְ מִפְּנֵי אוֹר, וּמַעֲבִיר יוֹם וּמֵבִיא לָיְלָה, וּמַבְדִּיל בֵּין יוֹם וּבֵין לָיְלָה, יְיָ צְבָאוֹת שְׁמוֹ.

O Lord our God, exalted far above the heavens, You are robed in majesty and honor. When the sun rises and when it sets, let Your great name be praised.

אֵל חַי וְקַיָּם, תָּמִיד יִמְלוֹךְ עָלֵינוּ, לְעוֹלָם וָעֶד. בָּרוּךְ אַתָּה, יְיָ, הַמַּעֲרִיב עֲרָבִים.

How manifold are Your works, O Lord! In wisdom have You made them all. Blessed is the Lord, whose wisdom and power are revealed in creation.

• •

TEACH US YOUR WAY אהבת עולם

אַהֲבַת עוֹלָם בֵּית יִשְׂרָאֵל עַמְּךָ אָהָבְתָּ: תּוֹרָה וּמִצְוֹת, חֻקִּים וּמִשְׁפָּטִים אוֹתָנוּ לִמַּדְתָּ.

Give us understanding, O God, that we may hold fast to Your Teaching, and observe it with a whole heart.
Teach us Your way, that we may walk in Your truth; unite our hearts, that we may revere Your name.

עַל־כֵּן, יְיָ אֱלֹהֵינוּ, בְּשָׁכְבֵּנוּ וּבְקוּמֵנוּ נָשִׂיחַ בְּחֻקֶּיךָ, וְנִשְׂמַח בְּדִבְרֵי תוֹרָתְךָ וּבְמִצְוֹתֶיךָ לְעוֹלָם וָעֶד.

Then we shall walk in liberty; mercy and truth shall meet, justice and peace shall embrace.
And we will give thanks to You, O God, and honor Your name for ever.

כִּי הֵם חַיֵּינוּ וְאֹרֶךְ יָמֵינוּ, וּבָהֶם נֶהְגֶּה יוֹמָם וָלָיְלָה. וְאַהֲבָתְךָ אַל־תָּסִיר מִמֶּנּוּ לְעוֹלָמִים! בָּרוּךְ אַתָּה, יְיָ, אוֹהֵב עַמּוֹ יִשְׂרָאֵל.

Blessed is the Lord our God, who hallows us with His Mitzvot, and calls us to acclaim His kingdom with a whole heart, to serve Him with a willing spirit, and with a pure mind to proclaim His unity.

◆ ◆

שְׁמַע יִשְׂרָאֵל: יְיָ אֱלֹהֵינוּ, יְיָ אֶחָד!

Hear, O Israel: the Lord is our God, the Lord is One!

בָּרוּךְ שֵׁם כְּבוֹד מַלְכוּתוֹ לְעוֹלָם וָעֶד!

Blessed is His glorious kingdom for ever and ever!

All are seated

וְאָהַבְתָּ אֵת יְיָ אֱלֹהֶיךָ בְּכָל־לְבָבְךָ וּבְכָל־נַפְשְׁךָ וּבְכָל־מְאֹדֶךָ.

You shall love the Lord your God with all your mind, with all your strength, with all your being.
For You are with us: the God of the stars and planets is with us.

וְהָיוּ הַדְּבָרִים הָאֵלֶּה, אֲשֶׁר אָנֹכִי מְצַוְּךָ הַיּוֹם, עַל־לְבָבֶךָ.

Set these words, which I command you this day, upon your heart.

The God of springing grass and the loving heart is with us.

וְשִׁנַּנְתָּם לְבָנֶיךָ, וְדִבַּרְתָּ בָּם בְּשִׁבְתְּךָ בְּבֵיתֶךָ, וּבְלֶכְתְּךָ בַדֶּרֶךְ, וּבְשָׁכְבְּךָ וּבְקוּמֶךָ.

Teach them faithfully to your children; speak of them in your home and on your way, when you lie down and when you rise up.

We are grains of sand warmed by You on the wide shore of the world.

וּקְשַׁרְתָּם לְאוֹת עַל־יָדֶךָ, וְהָיוּ לְטֹטָפֹת בֵּין עֵינֶיךָ,

Bind them as a sign upon your hand; let them be a symbol before your eyes.

And in You we are great as all the stars, and all the souls that were ever born.

וּכְתַבְתָּם עַל־מְזֻזוֹת בֵּיתֶךָ, וּבִשְׁעָרֶיךָ.

Inscribe them on the doorposts of your house, and on your gates.

Hold our hands in Yours, O Lord, that those who take our loving hands may find You there.

לְמַעַן תִּזְכְּרוּ וַעֲשִׂיתֶם אֶת־כָּל־מִצְוֹתָי, וִהְיִיתֶם קְדֹשִׁים לֵאלֹהֵיכֶם. אֲנִי יְיָ אֱלֹהֵיכֶם, אֲשֶׁר הוֹצֵאתִי אֶתְכֶם מֵאֶרֶץ מִצְרַיִם לִהְיוֹת לָכֶם לֵאלֹהִים. אֲנִי יְיָ אֱלֹהֵיכֶם.

Be mindful of all My Mitzvot, and do them: so shall you consecrate yourselves to your God. I, the Lord, am your God who led you out of Egypt to be your God; I, the Lord, am your God.

◆ ◆

FREEDOM TO THOSE IN SHACKLES — גאולה

אֱמֶת וֶאֱמוּנָה כָּל־זֹאת, וְקַיָּם עָלֵינוּ כִּי הוּא יְיָ אֱלֹהֵינוּ וְאֵין זוּלָתוֹ, וַאֲנַחְנוּ יִשְׂרָאֵל עַמּוֹ. הַפּוֹדֵנוּ מִיַּד מְלָכִים, מַלְכֵּנוּ

הַגּוֹאֲלֵנוּ מִכַּף כָּל־הֶעָרִיצִים. הָעֹשֶׂה גְדֹלוֹת עַד אֵין חֵקֶר, וְנִפְלָאוֹת עַד־אֵין מִסְפָּר. הַשָּׂם נַפְשֵׁנוּ בַּחַיִּים, וְלֹא־נָתַן לַמּוֹט רַגְלֵנוּ. הָעֹשֶׂה לָנוּ נִסִּים בְּפַרְעֹה, אוֹתוֹת וּמוֹפְתִים בְּאַדְמַת בְּנֵי חָם. וַיּוֹצֵא אֶת־עַמּוֹ יִשְׂרָאֵל מִתּוֹכָם לְחֵרוּת עוֹלָם. וְרָאוּ בָנָיו גְּבוּרָתוֹ; שִׁבְּחוּ וְהוֹדוּ לִשְׁמוֹ. וּמַלְכוּתוֹ בְּרָצוֹן קִבְּלוּ עֲלֵיהֶם. מֹשֶׁה וּבְנֵי יִשְׂרָאֵל לְךָ עָנוּ שִׁירָה בְּשִׂמְחָה רַבָּה, וְאָמְרוּ כֻלָּם:

Happy is the one whose trust is in God, who draws hope from hope's own Source.
God keeps faith for ever: He will do justice for the oppressed, and give bread to the hungry.

He will set free the captive, and open the blind eye.
He will lift up the fallen, and take care of the stranger.

The Lord's spirit is in us, the Eternal has called us.
To bring hope to the oppressed, to bring healing to the broken, to proclaim liberty to the enslaved, freedom to those in shackles.

When Israel saw Your might displayed in Egypt, they put their faith in You, and in Moses Your servant. Now let all be free, and let them sing as Israel did at the shore of freedom's sea:

מִי־כָמֹכָה בָּאֵלִם, יְיָ?
מִי כָּמֹכָה, נֶאְדָּר בַּקֹּדֶשׁ,
נוֹרָא תְהִלֹּת, עֹשֵׂה פֶלֶא?

Who is like You, Eternal One, among the gods that are worshipped?
Who is like You, majestic in holiness,
awesome in splendor, doing wonders?

מַלְכוּתְךָ רָאוּ בָנֶיךָ, בּוֹקֵעַ יָם לִפְנֵי מֹשֶׁה; "זֶה אֵלִי!" עָנוּ וְאָמְרוּ: "יְיָ יִמְלֹךְ לְעֹלָם וָעֶד!"

Your children saw Your saving power, and they said: "This is my God!" "The Eternal will reign for ever and ever!"

וְנֶאֱמַר: "כִּי־פָדָה יְיָ אֶת־יַעֲקֹב, וּגְאָלוֹ מִיַּד חָזָק מִמֶּנּוּ." בָּרוּךְ אַתָּה, יְיָ, גָּאַל יִשְׂרָאֵל.

◆ ◆

MEDITATION

"And God said: 'Let there be light.' " This first light God made before He made the sun and stars. He showed it to David, who burst into song. This was the light Moses saw on Sinai! At the creation, the universe from end to end radiated light — but it was withdrawn. . . . And now it is stored away for the righteous, until all the worlds will be in harmony again and all will be united and whole. But until this future world is established, this light, coming out of darkness and formed by the Most Secret, is hidden: "Light is sown for the righteous."

◆ ◆

THE SUDDEN LIGHT THAT LIFTS THE HEART — השכיבנו

הַשְׁכִּיבֵנוּ, יְיָ אֱלֹהֵינוּ, לְשָׁלוֹם, וְהַעֲמִידֵנוּ, מַלְכֵּנוּ, לְחַיִּים.
וּפְרוֹשׂ עָלֵינוּ סֻכַּת שְׁלוֹמֶךָ, וְתַקְּנֵנוּ בְּעֵצָה טוֹבָה מִלְּפָנֶיךָ,
וְהוֹשִׁיעֵנוּ לְמַעַן שְׁמֶךָ, וְהָגֵן בַּעֲדֵנוּ. וְהָסֵר מֵעָלֵינוּ אוֹיֵב,
דֶּבֶר וְחֶרֶב וְרָעָב וְיָגוֹן; וְהָסֵר שָׂטָן מִלְּפָנֵינוּ וּמֵאַחֲרֵינוּ;
וּבְצֵל כְּנָפֶיךָ תַּסְתִּירֵנוּ, כִּי אֵל שׁוֹמְרֵנוּ וּמַצִּילֵנוּ אָתָּה, כִּי
אֵל מֶלֶךְ חַנּוּן וְרַחוּם אָתָּה. וּשְׁמוֹר צֵאתֵנוּ וּבוֹאֵנוּ לְחַיִּים
וּלְשָׁלוֹם, מֵעַתָּה וְעַד עוֹלָם, וּפְרוֹשׂ עָלֵינוּ סֻכַּת שְׁלוֹמֶךָ.
בָּרוּךְ אַתָּה, יְיָ, הַפּוֹרֵשׂ סֻכַּת שָׁלוֹם עָלֵינוּ, וְעַל־כָּל־עַמּוֹ
יִשְׂרָאֵל וְעַל יְרוּשָׁלָיִם.

The shadows fall, but end of day fills the eye with brightness; the infinite heavens glow, and all creation sings its hymn of glory. With hope, therefore, we pray for light within: O God, reveal Yourself; hide no more; let Your face shine on all who seek You.

Eternal and infinite God, banish our darkness! Be present to us as the sudden light that lifts the heart and brings us joy.

Then shall we be at peace, O God, whose peaceful shelter we seek through all the days and nights of our lives.

◆ ◆

THE COVENANT OF SHABBAT ושמרו

וְשָׁמְרוּ בְנֵי־יִשְׂרָאֵל אֶת־הַשַּׁבָּת, לַעֲשׂוֹת אֶת־הַשַּׁבָּת לְדֹרֹתָם בְּרִית עוֹלָם. בֵּינִי וּבֵין בְּנֵי יִשְׂרָאֵל אוֹת הִיא לְעֹלָם, כִּי שֵׁשֶׁת יָמִים עָשָׂה יְיָ אֶת־הַשָּׁמַיִם וְאֶת־הָאָרֶץ, וּבַיּוֹם הַשְּׁבִיעִי שָׁבַת וַיִּנָּפַשׁ.

The people of Israel shall keep the Sabbath, observing the Sabbath in every generation as a covenant for all time. It is a sign for ever between Me and the people of Israel, for in six days the Eternal God made heaven and earth, and on the seventh day He rested from His labors.

◆ ◆

All rise

תפלה

אֲדֹנָי, שְׂפָתַי תִּפְתָּח, וּפִי יַגִּיד תְּהִלָּתֶךָ.

Eternal God, open my lips, that my mouth may declare Your glory.

A COVENANT PEOPLE, ETERNAL . . . אבות

בָּרוּךְ אַתָּה, יְיָ אֱלֹהֵינוּ וֵאלֹהֵי אֲבוֹתֵינוּ, אֱלֹהֵי אַבְרָהָם, אֱלֹהֵי יִצְחָק, וֵאלֹהֵי יַעֲקֹב: הָאֵל הַגָּדוֹל, הַגִּבּוֹר וְהַנּוֹרָא, אֵל עֶלְיוֹן.

Lord, You are the God of all generations: the ones that are past, and those yet unborn. You are our God.
You are the First; You are the Last; You are the Only One.

גּוֹמֵל חֲסָדִים טוֹבִים, וְקוֹנֵה הַכֹּל, וְזוֹכֵר חַסְדֵי אָבוֹת, וּמֵבִיא גְאֻלָּה לִבְנֵי בְנֵיהֶם, לְמַעַן שְׁמוֹ, בְּאַהֲבָה.

You made the earth and brought us forth to dwell in it.
You called Abraham to righteousness, his children to bear witness to Your glory.

מֶלֶךְ עוֹזֵר וּמוֹשִׁיעַ וּמָגֵן. בָּרוּךְ אַתָּה, יְיָ, מָגֵן אַבְרָהָם.

You formed us to be a covenant people, eternal as the hosts of heaven.
O God, You are the Shield of our people, our everlasting light!

◆ ◆

TO PLANT SEEDS OF LOVE גבורות

אַתָּה גִּבּוֹר לְעוֹלָם, אֲדֹנָי, מְחַיֵּה הַכֹּל אַתָּה, רַב לְהוֹשִׁיעַ. מְכַלְכֵּל חַיִּים בְּחֶסֶד, מְחַיֵּה הַכֹּל בְּרַחֲמִים רַבִּים. סוֹמֵךְ נוֹפְלִים, וְרוֹפֵא חוֹלִים, וּמַתִּיר אֲסוּרִים, וּמְקַיֵּם אֱמוּנָתוֹ לִישֵׁנֵי עָפָר.

Great is the power of Your love. You have made us in Your image and raised us high above all other creatures.

You have exalted us to struggle against evil, to strive for holiness, to plant seeds of love in all our dwellings.

And You, the Eternal One, help us to face death with the trust that what is good and lovely shall not perish.

מִי כָמוֹךָ, בַּעַל גְּבוּרוֹת, וּמִי דּוֹמֶה לָּךְ, מֶלֶךְ מֵמִית וּמְחַיֶּה וּמַצְמִיחַ יְשׁוּעָה?

וְנֶאֱמָן אַתָּה לְהַחֲיוֹת הַכֹּל. בָּרוּךְ אַתָּה, יְיָ, מְחַיֵּה הַכֹּל.

Lord and Creator, joyfully we embrace Your call to life. Help us to live with courage, that we may hallow our lives as we sanctify Your name.

◆ ◆

HOW FILLED WITH AWE קדושת השם

אַתָּה קָדוֹשׁ וְשִׁמְךָ קָדוֹשׁ, וּקְדוֹשִׁים בְּכָל־יוֹם יְהַלְלוּךָ סֶּלָה.
בָּרוּךְ אַתָּה, יְיָ, הָאֵל הַקָּדוֹשׁ.

Days pass and the years vanish, and we walk sightless among miracles. Lord, fill our eyes with seeing and our minds with knowing; let there be moments when Your Presence, like lightning, illumines the darkness in which we walk.

Help us to see, wherever we gaze, that the bush burns unconsumed.

And we, clay touched by God, will reach out for holiness, and exclaim in wonder:

How filled with awe is this place, and we did not know it! Blessed is the Eternal One, the holy God!

All are seated

◆ ◆

MOST PRECIOUS OF DAYS

קדושת היום

יִשְׂמְחוּ בְמַלְכוּתְךָ שׁוֹמְרֵי שַׁבָּת וְקוֹרְאֵי עֹנֶג. עַם מְקַדְּשֵׁי שְׁבִיעִי כֻּלָּם יִשְׂבְּעוּ וְיִתְעַנְּגוּ מִטּוּבֶךָ. וְהַשְּׁבִיעִי רָצִיתָ בּוֹ וְקִדַּשְׁתּוֹ. חֶמְדַּת יָמִים אוֹתוֹ קָרָאתָ, זֵכֶר לְמַעֲשֵׂה בְרֵאשִׁית.

Those who keep the Sabbath and call it a delight shall rejoice in Your kingdom. All who hallow the seventh day shall be gladdened by Your goodness. This day is Israel's festival of the spirit, sanctified and blessed by You, the most precious of days, a symbol of the joy of creation.

◆

A GARLAND OF GLORY

אַתָּה אֶחָד וְשִׁמְךָ אֶחָד, וּמִי כְּעַמְּךָ יִשְׂרָאֵל, גּוֹי אֶחָד בָּאָרֶץ? תִּפְאֶרֶת גְּדֻלָּה וַעֲטֶרֶת יְשׁוּעָה, יוֹם מְנוּחָה וּקְדֻשָּׁה לְעַמְּךָ נָתָתָּ:

You are One, Your name is One, and there is none like Your people Israel, a people unique on the earth. A garland of glory have You given us, a crown of salvation: a day of rest and holiness.

אַבְרָהָם יָגֵל, יִצְחָק יְרַנֵּן, יַעֲקֹב וּבָנָיו יָנוּחוּ בוֹ. מְנוּחַת אַהֲבָה וּנְדָבָה, מְנוּחַת אֱמֶת וֶאֱמוּנָה, מְנוּחַת שָׁלוֹם וְשַׁלְוָה וְהַשְׁקֵט וָבֶטַח. מְנוּחָה שְׁלֵמָה שָׁאַתָּה רוֹצֶה בָּהּ.

Abraham rejoiced in it, Isaac sang, Jacob and his children were refreshed by its rest. In this rest are love and sharing, truth and faithfulness and peace, quiet and safety. It is the perfect rest that You have willed.

יַכִּירוּ בָנֶיךָ וְיֵדְעוּ כִּי מֵאִתְּךָ הִיא מְנוּחָתָם, וְעַל־מְנוּחָתָם יַקְדִּישׁוּ אֶת־שְׁמֶךָ.

May your children come to understand that this Sabbath rest links them to You, that by it they may hallow Your name.

◆ ◆

TO THE GOD OF MY LIFE — עבודה

רְצֵה, יְיָ אֱלֹהֵינוּ, בְּעַמְּךָ יִשְׂרָאֵל, וּתְפִלָּתָם בְּאַהֲבָה תְקַבֵּל, וּתְהִי לְרָצוֹן תָּמִיד עֲבוֹדַת יִשְׂרָאֵל עַמֶּךָ. אֵל קָרוֹב לְכָל־קֹרְאָיו, פְּנֵה אֶל עֲבָדֶיךָ וְחָנֵּנוּ; שְׁפוֹךְ רוּחֲךָ עָלֵינוּ, וְתֶחֱזֶינָה עֵינֵינוּ בְּשׁוּבְךָ לְצִיּוֹן בְּרַחֲמִים.

בָּרוּךְ אַתָּה, יְיָ, הַמַּחֲזִיר שְׁכִינָתוֹ לְצִיּוֹן.

O God enthroned by Israel's praise, O God my hope, for You alone my soul waits in silence. By day extend Your steadfast love, and at night I shall sing to You, a prayer to the God of my life. Blessed is the Lord who day by day upholds me, the God who is my Help.

◆ ◆

FOR ALL THESE GIFTS — הודאה

מוֹדִים אֲנַחְנוּ לָךְ, שָׁאַתָּה הוּא יְיָ אֱלֹהֵינוּ וֵאלֹהֵי אֲבוֹתֵינוּ,
אֱלֹהֵי כָל־בָּשָׂר, יוֹצְרֵנוּ יוֹצֵר בְּרֵאשִׁית.
בְּרָכוֹת וְהוֹדָאוֹת לְשִׁמְךָ הַגָּדוֹל וְהַקָּדוֹשׁ עַל־שֶׁהֶחֱיִיתָנוּ וְקִיַּמְתָּנוּ.
כֵּן תְּחַיֵּנוּ וּתְקַיְּמֵנוּ, יְיָ אֱלֹהֵינוּ, וּתְאַמְּצֵנוּ לִשְׁמֹר חֻקֶּיךָ, לַעֲשׂוֹת רְצוֹנֶךָ, וּלְעָבְדְךָ בְּלֵבָב שָׁלֵם. בָּרוּךְ אֵל הַהוֹדָאוֹת.

Eternal God, we give thanks for the gift of life, wonder beyond words; the awareness of soul, our light within; the world around us, so filled with beauty; and the richness of the earth, which day by day sustains us. For all these gifts and more, we thank and bless You, the Source of all goodness.

◆ ◆

MEDITATION

How can we give thanks when we remember Treblinka? Only silence speaks loudly enough for our millions who were marched into the abyss.

We have been where we did not find You, O Hidden One! Yet even there, even there, our people sang: I believe in redemption. *Ani Ma-amin.* And they sang again:

זאָג ניט קיינמאָל אַז דו גייסט דעם לעצטן וועג.

Never say you walk the final road!

And even then this deathless people was renewing itself, its life.

Whose faith is equal to this people's? Whose will to live? The storm ends. In the sky, a rainbow signals hope and new life. Again, and yet again, there is a song to sing.

◆ ◆

A PEACE PROFOUND AND TRUE
ברכת שלום

שָׁלוֹם רָב עַל־יִשְׂרָאֵל עַמְּךָ תָּשִׂים לְעוֹלָם, כִּי אַתָּה הוּא מֶלֶךְ אָדוֹן לְכָל הַשָּׁלוֹם. וְטוֹב בְּעֵינֶיךָ לְבָרֵךְ אֶת־עַמְּךָ יִשְׂרָאֵל בְּכָל־עֵת וּבְכָל־שָׁעָה בִּשְׁלוֹמֶךָ.

בָּרוּךְ אַתָּה, יְיָ, הַמְבָרֵךְ אֶת־עַמּוֹ יִשְׂרָאֵל בַּשָּׁלוֹם.

Let the day come when we turn to the Lord of peace, when all are a single family doing His will with a perfect heart.

O Source of peace, lead us to peace, a peace profound and true; lead us to a healing, to mastery of all that drives us to war within ourselves and with others.

O Lord of peace, bless us with peace.

◆ ◆

MEDITATION

You are the world's beginning: this world
bears witness to
You — alone, apart,
the Only God,
the Mind we glimpse in all —
Hills wrenched from earth
and skies spread out before our humbled eyes.

Inexhaustible God: You flow, burst out,
overflow: You have poured Yourself
into universes beyond thought
and they cannot contain You.
You fill the endless worlds.
Deep beyond our guess, the Deep itself,
hidden, hiding, abyss, shadow, friend, 'Illusion':
What shall we call You whom we do not know?
How shall we speak to You?
We are lonely, afraid to hope:
Is the ground firm under our feet?
Or do they tremble upon a precipice?
Are You the bridge across that fearful fall?
In this dark world we search for You,
with anxious lines about our eyes,
and even for the pure the light is dim.
Our ears hear sounds from afar —
music is it? Lifeless noise?

Is there — surely there is? — an echo of love?
We look, and listen, and struggle
to gaze upon Your world
in joy in awe in love in praise:

holy, holy, holy:
the hidden God
the One who speaks —
and there is light!

◆ ◆

יִהְיוּ לְרָצוֹן אִמְרֵי־פִי וְהֶגְיוֹן לִבִּי לְפָנֶיךָ, יְיָ, צוּרִי וְגוֹאֲלִי.

May the words of my mouth, and the meditations of my heart, be acceptable to You, O Lord, my Rock and my Redeemer.

or

עֹשֶׂה שָׁלוֹם בִּמְרוֹמָיו, הוּא יַעֲשֶׂה שָׁלוֹם עָלֵינוּ וְעַל כָּל־יִשְׂרָאֵל, וְאִמְרוּ אָמֵן.

May He who causes peace to reign in the high heavens let peace descend on us, on all Israel, and all the world.

◆ ◆

Prayers for Special Occasions begin on page 389.

The Rituals for the Reading of Torah begin on page 415.

Concluding Prayers begin on page 613.

ד IV ד

For congregations where the lights are kindled in the synagogue

הדלקת הנרות

These lights
are only flickering flames.

Yet flames
illumine
our uncertain steps.

Flames purify and renew,
soften and refine;
they brighten and make warm.
Flames remind us
of Sabbaths long past,
and of their beauty
that delighted our hearts.

May they inspire us
to work
for the Great Sabbath of peace.

◆ ◆

בָּרוּךְ אַתָּה, יְיָ אֱלֹהֵינוּ, מֶלֶךְ הָעוֹלָם,
אֲשֶׁר קִדְּשָׁנוּ בְּמִצְוֹתָיו וְצִוָּנוּ לְהַדְלִיק נֵר שֶׁל שַׁבָּת.

Blessed is the Lord our God, Ruler of the universe,
who hallows us with His Mitzvot, and commands us
to kindle the lights of Shabbat.

◆ ◆

Psalm 15

יְיָ, מִי־יָגוּר בְּאָהֳלֶךָ, מִי־יִשְׁכֹּן בְּהַר קָדְשֶׁךָ?

הוֹלֵךְ תָּמִים וּפֹעֵל צֶדֶק וְדֹבֵר אֱמֶת בִּלְבָבוֹ.

Lord, who may abide in Your house? Who may dwell in Your holy mountain?

Those who are upright; who do justly; who speak the truth within their hearts.

לֹא־רָגַל עַל־לְשֹׁנוֹ, לֹא־עָשָׂה לְרֵעֵהוּ רָעָה,
וְחֶרְפָּה לֹא נָשָׂא עַל־קְרֹבוֹ.

נִבְזֶה בְּעֵינָיו נִמְאָס, וְאֶת־יִרְאֵי יְיָ יְכַבֵּד.

Who do not slander others, or wrong them, or bring shame upon them.

Who scorn the lawless, but honor those who revere the Lord.

נִשְׁבַּע לְהָרַע וְלֹא יָמִיר.

כַּסְפּוֹ לֹא־נָתַן בְּנֶשֶׁךְ וְשֹׁחַד עַל־נָקִי לֹא לָקָח.

Who give their word, and, come what may, do not retract.

Who do not exploit others, who never take bribes.

עֹשֵׂה אֵלֶּה לֹא יִמּוֹט לְעוֹלָם.

Those who live in this way shall never be shaken.

◆ ◆

There are days
when we seek things for ourselves and measure failure by what we do not gain.

On the Sabbath
we seek not to acquire but to share.

There are days
when we exploit nature as if it were a horn of plenty that can never be exhausted.

On the Sabbath
we stand in wonder before the mystery of creation.

There are days
when we act as if we cared nothing for the rights of others.

On the Sabbath
we are reminded that justice is our duty and a better world our goal.

Therefore we welcome Shabbat —

Day of rest,
day of wonder,
day of peace.

◆ ◆

שלום עליכם

שָׁלוֹם עֲלֵיכֶם, מַלְאֲכֵי הַשָּׁרֵת, מַלְאֲכֵי עֶלְיוֹן,
מִמֶּלֶךְ מַלְכֵי הַמְּלָכִים, הַקָּדוֹשׁ בָּרוּךְ הוּא.

Peace be to you, O ministering angels, messengers of the Most High, the supreme King of kings, the Holy One, blessed is He.

בּוֹאֲכֶם לְשָׁלוֹם, מַלְאֲכֵי הַשָּׁלוֹם, מַלְאֲכֵי עֶלְיוֹן,
מִמֶּלֶךְ מַלְכֵי הַמְּלָכִים, הַקָּדוֹשׁ בָּרוּךְ הוּא.

Enter in peace, O messengers of peace, messengers of the Most High, the supreme King of kings, the Holy One, blessed is He.

בָּרְכוּנִי לְשָׁלוֹם, מַלְאֲכֵי הַשָּׁלוֹם, מַלְאֲכֵי עֶלְיוֹן,
מִמֶּלֶךְ מַלְכֵי הַמְּלָכִים, הַקָּדוֹשׁ בָּרוּךְ הוּא.

Bless me with peace, O messengers of peace, messengers of the Most High, the supreme King of kings, the Holy One, blessed is He.

צְאתְכֶם לְשָׁלוֹם, מַלְאֲכֵי הַשָּׁלוֹם, מַלְאֲכֵי עֶלְיוֹן,
מִמֶּלֶךְ מַלְכֵי הַמְּלָכִים, הַקָּדוֹשׁ בָּרוּךְ הוּא.

Depart in peace, O messengers of peace, messengers of the Most High, the supreme King of kings, the Holy One, blessed is He.

◆ ◆

The synagogue is the sanctuary of Israel, born of Israel's longing for God. Throughout our wanderings it has endured as a stronghold of hope and inspiration, teaching us the holiness of life and inspiring in us a love of all humanity. Come, then, all who are children of Israel, all who strive for righteousness, all who seek to do the will of God, let us affirm our faith.

READER'S KADDISH

חצי קדיש

יִתְגַּדַּל וְיִתְקַדַּשׁ שְׁמֵהּ רַבָּא בְּעָלְמָא דִּי־בְרָא כִרְעוּתֵהּ, וְיַמְלִיךְ מַלְכוּתֵהּ בְּחַיֵּיכוֹן וּבְיוֹמֵיכוֹן וּבְחַיֵּי דְכָל־בֵּית יִשְׂרָאֵל, בַּעֲגָלָא וּבִזְמַן קָרִיב, וְאִמְרוּ: אָמֵן.

יְהֵא שְׁמֵהּ רַבָּא מְבָרַךְ לְעָלַם וּלְעָלְמֵי עָלְמַיָּא.

יִתְבָּרַךְ וְיִשְׁתַּבַּח, וְיִתְפָּאַר וְיִתְרוֹמַם וְיִתְנַשֵּׂא, וְיִתְהַדַּר וְיִתְעַלֶּה וְיִתְהַלַּל שְׁמֵהּ דְּקוּדְשָׁא, בְּרִיךְ הוּא, לְעֵלָּא מִן כָּל־בִּרְכָתָא וְשִׁירָתָא, תֻּשְׁבְּחָתָא וְנֶחֱמָתָא דַּאֲמִירָן בְּעָלְמָא, וְאִמְרוּ: אָמֵן.

Let the glory of God be extolled, let His great name be hallowed in the world whose creation He willed. May His kingdom soon prevail, in our own day, our own lives, and the life of all Israel, and let us say: Amen.

Let His great name be blessed for ever and ever.

Let the name of the Holy One, blessed is He, be glorified, exalted and honored, though He is beyond all the praises, songs, and adorations that we can utter, and let us say: Amen.

◆ ◆

All rise

שמע וברכותיה

בָּרְכוּ אֶת־יְיָ הַמְבֹרָךְ!

Praise the Lord, to whom our praise is due!

בָּרוּךְ יְיָ הַמְבֹרָךְ לְעוֹלָם וָעֶד!

Praised be the Lord, to whom our praise is due,
now and for ever!

◆ ◆

AS CLOSE TO US AS BREATHING — מעריב ערבים

בָּרוּךְ אַתָּה, יְיָ אֱלֹהֵינוּ, מֶלֶךְ הָעוֹלָם, אֲשֶׁר בִּדְבָרוֹ מַעֲרִיב עֲרָבִים. בְּחָכְמָה פּוֹתֵחַ שְׁעָרִים, וּבִתְבוּנָה מְשַׁנֶּה עִתִּים, וּמַחֲלִיף אֶת־הַזְּמַנִּים, וּמְסַדֵּר אֶת־הַכּוֹכָבִים בְּמִשְׁמְרוֹתֵיהֶם בָּרָקִיעַ כִּרְצוֹנוֹ.

בּוֹרֵא יוֹם וָלָיְלָה, גּוֹלֵל אוֹר מִפְּנֵי חֹשֶׁךְ וְחֹשֶׁךְ מִפְּנֵי אוֹר, וּמַעֲבִיר יוֹם וּמֵבִיא לָיְלָה, וּמַבְדִּיל בֵּין יוֹם וּבֵין לָיְלָה, יְיָ צְבָאוֹת שְׁמוֹ.

אֵל חַי וְקַיָּם, תָּמִיד יִמְלוֹךְ עָלֵינוּ, לְעוֹלָם וָעֶד. בָּרוּךְ אַתָּה, יְיָ, הַמַּעֲרִיב עֲרָבִים.

O God, how can we know You? Where can we find You? You are as close to us as breathing, yet You are farther than the farthermost star.

You are as mysterious as the vast solitudes of night, yet as familiar to us as the light of the sun. To Moses You said: "You cannot see My face, but I will make all My goodness pass before you."

Even so does Your goodness pass before us: in the realm of nature, and in the joys and sorrows of life.

◆ ◆

YOUR GOODNESS ENTERS OUR LIVES אהבת עולם

אַהֲבַת עוֹלָם בֵּית יִשְׂרָאֵל עַמְּךָ אָהָבְתָּ: תּוֹרָה וּמִצְוֹת, חֻקִּים וּמִשְׁפָּטִים אוֹתָנוּ לִמַּדְתָּ.
עַל־כֵּן, יְיָ אֱלֹהֵינוּ, בְּשָׁכְבֵנוּ וּבְקוּמֵנוּ נָשִׂיחַ בְּחֻקֶּיךָ, וְנִשְׂמַח בְּדִבְרֵי תוֹרָתְךָ וּבְמִצְוֹתֶיךָ לְעוֹלָם וָעֶד.
כִּי הֵם חַיֵּינוּ וְאֹרֶךְ יָמֵינוּ, וּבָהֶם נֶהְגֶּה יוֹמָם וָלָיְלָה. וְאַהֲבָתְךָ אַל־תָּסִיר מִמֶּנּוּ לְעוֹלָמִים! בָּרוּךְ אַתָּה, יְיָ, אוֹהֵב עַמּוֹ יִשְׂרָאֵל.

When justice burns within us like a flaming fire, when love evokes willing sacrifice from us, when, to the last full measure of selfless devotion, we demonstrate our belief in the ultimate triumph of truth and righteousness, then Your goodness enters our lives and we can begin to change the world; and then You live within our hearts, and we through righteousness behold Your presence.

◆ ◆

שְׁמַע יִשְׂרָאֵל: יְיָ אֱלֹהֵינוּ, יְיָ אֶחָד!

Hear, O Israel: the Lord is our God, the Lord is One!

בָּרוּךְ שֵׁם כְּבוֹד מַלְכוּתוֹ לְעוֹלָם וָעֶד!

Blessed is His glorious kingdom for ever and ever!

All are seated

וְאָהַבְתָּ אֵת יְיָ אֱלֹהֶיךָ בְּכָל־לְבָבְךָ וּבְכָל־נַפְשְׁךָ וּבְכָל־מְאֹדֶךָ.
וְהָיוּ הַדְּבָרִים הָאֵלֶּה, אֲשֶׁר אָנֹכִי מְצַוְּךָ הַיּוֹם, עַל־לְבָבֶךָ.
וְשִׁנַּנְתָּם לְבָנֶיךָ, וְדִבַּרְתָּ בָּם בְּשִׁבְתְּךָ בְּבֵיתֶךָ, וּבְלֶכְתְּךָ בַדֶּרֶךְ, וּבְשָׁכְבְּךָ וּבְקוּמֶךָ.

You shall love the Lord your God with all your mind, with all your strength, with all your being.
Set these words, which I command you this day, upon your heart. Teach them faithfully to your children; speak of them

in your home and on your way, when you lie down and when you rise up.

וּקְשַׁרְתָּם לְאוֹת עַל־יָדֶךָ, וְהָיוּ לְטֹטָפֹת בֵּין עֵינֶיךָ, וּכְתַבְתָּם עַל־מְזֻזוֹת בֵּיתֶךָ, וּבִשְׁעָרֶיךָ.

Bind them as a sign upon your hand; let them be a symbol before your eyes; inscribe them on the doorposts of your house, and on your gates.

לְמַעַן תִּזְכְּרוּ וַעֲשִׂיתֶם אֶת־כָּל־מִצְוֹתָי, וִהְיִיתֶם קְדשִׁים לֵאלֹהֵיכֶם. אֲנִי יְיָ אֱלֹהֵיכֶם, אֲשֶׁר הוֹצֵאתִי אֶתְכֶם מֵאֶרֶץ מִצְרַיִם לִהְיוֹת לָכֶם לֵאלֹהִים. אֲנִי יְיָ אֱלֹהֵיכֶם.

Be mindful of all My Mitzvot, and do them: so shall you consecrate yourselves to your God. I, the Lord, am your God who led you out of Egypt to be your God; I, the Lord, am your God.

◆ ◆

THE GOD OF FREEDOM — גאולה

I, the Eternal, have called you to righteousness, and taken you by the hand, and kept you; I have made you a covenant people, a light to the nations.

אֲנִי, יְיָ, קְרָאתִיךָ בְצֶדֶק וְאַחְזֵק בְּיָדֶךָ, וְאֶצָּרְךָ; וְאֶתֶּנְךָ לִבְרִית עָם, לְאוֹר גּוֹיִם.

We are Israel: witness to the covenant between God and His children.

This is the covenant I make with Israel: I will place My Torah in your midst, and write it upon your hearts. I will be your God, and you will be My people.

כִּי זֹאת הַבְּרִית אֲשֶׁר אֶכְרֹת אֶת־בֵּית יִשְׂרָאֵל: נָתַתִּי אֶת־תּוֹרָתִי בְּקִרְבָּם, וְעַל־לִבָּם אֶכְתֲּבֶנָּה. וְהָיִיתִי לָהֶם לֵאלֹהִים, וְהֵמָּה יִהְיוּ־לִי לְעָם.

We are Israel: our Torah forbids the worship of race or nation, possessions or power.

הַמִּתְפַּלְלִים אֶל־אֵל לֹא־יוֹשִׁיעַ,
שִׁמְעוּ דִּבְרֵי־יְיָ: "הֲלוֹא אֲנִי יְיָ,
וְאֵין־עוֹד אֱלֹהִים מִבַּלְעָדַי!"

You who worship gods that cannot save you, hear the words of the Eternal: "I am God, there is none else!"

We are Israel: our prophets proclaimed an exalted vision for the world.

שִׂנְאוּ־רָע, וְאֶהֱבוּ טוֹב. וְיִגַּל
כַּמַּיִם מִשְׁפָּט וּצְדָקָה כְּנַחַל
אֵיתָן.

Hate evil, and love what is good. Let justice well up as waters and righteousness as a mighty stream.

We are Israel, schooled in the suffering of the oppressed.

לֹא־תַעֲשֹׁק אֶת־רֵעֲךָ וְלֹא תִגְזֹל.
לֹא תַעֲמֹד עַל־דַּם רֵעֶךָ.

You shall not oppress your neighbors nor rob them. You shall not stand idle while your neighbor bleeds.

We are Israel, taught to beat swords into plowshares, commanded to pursue peace.

לֹא־יִשָּׁמַע עוֹד חָמָס בְּאַרְצֵךְ,
שֹׁד וָשֶׁבֶר בִּגְבוּלָיִךְ. וְכָל־בָּנַיִךְ
לִמּוּדֵי יְיָ, וְרַב שְׁלוֹם בָּנָיִךְ.

Violence shall no longer be heard in your land, desolation and destruction within your borders. All your children shall be taught of the Lord, and great shall be the peace of your children.

We are Israel, O God, when we are witnesses to Your will and messengers of Your truth.

אַתֶּם עֵדַי, נְאֻם יְיָ, וְעַבְדִּי אֲשֶׁר
בָּחָרְתִּי; לְמַעַן תֵּדְעוּ וְתַאֲמִינוּ
לִי.

You are My witnesses, says the Eternal, and My servant whom I have chosen; know Me, therefore, and put your trust in Me.

We are Israel, O Lord, when we proclaim You the God of freedom, as did our ancestors on the shores of the sea:

Who is like You, Eternal One, among the gods that are worshipped?	מִי־כָמֹכָה בָּאֵלִם, יְיָ?
Who is like You, majestic in holiness,	מִי כָּמֹכָה, נֶאְדָּר בַּקֹּדֶשׁ,
awesome in splendor, doing wonders?	נוֹרָא תְהִלֹּת, עֹשֵׂה פֶלֶא?

מַלְכוּתְךָ רָאוּ בָנֶיךָ, בּוֹקֵעַ יָם לִפְנֵי מֹשֶׁה; "זֶה אֵלִי!" עָנוּ וְאָמְרוּ: "יְיָ יִמְלֹךְ לְעֹלָם וָעֶד!"

When Your children perceive Your power they exclaim: "This is my God!" "The Eternal will reign for ever and ever!"

◆ ◆

THE SHELTER OF YOUR PEACE — השכיבנו

הַשְׁכִּיבֵנוּ, אָבִינוּ, לְשָׁלוֹם, וְהַעֲמִידֵנוּ, מַלְכֵּנוּ, לְחַיִּים טוֹבִים וּלְשָׁלוֹם. וּפְרוֹשׂ עָלֵינוּ סֻכַּת שְׁלוֹמֶךָ, וְתַקְּנֵנוּ בְּעֵצָה טוֹבָה מִלְּפָנֶיךָ. וְהוֹשִׁיעֵנוּ מְהֵרָה לְמַעַן שְׁמֶךָ. וְהָגֵן בַּעֲדֵנוּ. וּפְרוֹשׂ עָלֵינוּ סֻכַּת רַחֲמִים וְשָׁלוֹם.

Cause us, our Creator, to lie down in peace, and raise us up, O Sovereign God, to renewed life and peace. Spread over us the shelter of Your peace; guide us with Your good counsel; and be our shield of mercy and of peace.

בָּרוּךְ אַתָּה, יְיָ, הַפּוֹרֵשׂ סֻכַּת שָׁלוֹם עָלֵינוּ, וְעַל־עַמּוֹ יִשְׂרָאֵל, וְעַל־יְרוּשָׁלָיִם.

Blessed is the Lord, whose shelter of peace is spread over us, over all His people Israel, and over Jerusalem.

◆ ◆

THE COVENANT OF SHABBAT — ושמרו

וְשָׁמְרוּ בְנֵי־יִשְׂרָאֵל אֶת־הַשַּׁבָּת, לַעֲשׂוֹת אֶת־הַשַּׁבָּת לְדֹרֹתָם בְּרִית עוֹלָם. בֵּינִי וּבֵין בְּנֵי יִשְׂרָאֵל אוֹת הִיא לְעֹלָם, כִּי שֵׁשֶׁת יָמִים עָשָׂה יְיָ אֶת־הַשָּׁמַיִם וְאֶת־הָאָרֶץ, וּבַיּוֹם הַשְּׁבִיעִי שָׁבַת וַיִּנָּפַשׁ.

The people of Israel shall keep the Sabbath, observing the Sabbath in every generation as a covenant for all time. It is a sign for ever between Me and the people of Israel, for in six days the Eternal God made heaven and earth, and on the seventh day He rested from His labors.

◆ ◆

MEDITATION

Each of us is a battleground for the struggle of sacred with profane. At times the profane seems to win the day. Love and truth are debased. Reason, our chief glory, is turned to evil ends. And in us the divine gift of compassion lies dormant; we fail to feel the anguish of others.

How much we need You, O God, in days of trial! We need faith to live, faith in Your creative power that overcomes chaos and stirs all life toward a new and better world. We seek You, O God: thereby we grow in vision, as we elevate our souls beyond the sordid to the sacred.

Your presence is the light piercing the darkness on our way, lighting our steps, making us see beauty and worth in all human beings.

May our lips and our lives
be one in serving You.

אֲדֹנָי, שְׂפָתַי תִּפְתָּח,
וּפִי יַגִּיד תְּהִלָּתֶךָ.

◆ ◆

All rise

תפלה

BE PRAISED

אבות

בָּרוּךְ אַתָּה, יְיָ אֱלֹהֵינוּ וֵאלֹהֵי אֲבוֹתֵינוּ, אֱלֹהֵי אַבְרָהָם, אֱלֹהֵי יִצְחָק, וֵאלֹהֵי יַעֲקֹב: הָאֵל הַגָּדוֹל, הַגִּבּוֹר וְהַנּוֹרָא, אֵל עֶלְיוֹן, קוֹנֵה שָׁמַיִם וָאָרֶץ.

Be praised, O Lord, God of all generations, of Abraham, of Isaac and Jacob; our God. Your wondrous creative power fills heaven and earth.

◆ ◆

GOD OF ETERNAL MIGHT — גבורות

אַתָּה גִּבּוֹר לְעוֹלָם, יְיָ, סוֹמֵךְ נוֹפְלִים וְרוֹפֵא חוֹלִים וּמַתִּיר אֲסוּרִים, וּמְקַיֵּם אֱמוּנָתוֹ לִישֵׁנֵי עָפָר. בָּרוּךְ אַתָּה, יְיָ, מְחַיֵּה הַכֹּל.

God of eternal might, through us send help to the falling, healing to the sick, freedom to the captive: confirm Your faithfulness to those who sleep in the dust. We praise You, the Source of life.

◆ ◆

BE HOLY — קדושת השם

נְקַדֵּשׁ אֶת־שִׁמְךָ בָּעוֹלָם, כַּכָּתוּב עַל־יַד נְבִיאֶךָ: ״קְדוֹשִׁים תִּהְיוּ, כִּי־קָדוֹשׁ אֲנִי יְיָ אֱלֹהֵיכֶם.״ בָּרוּךְ אַתָּה, יְיָ, הָאֵל הַקָּדוֹשׁ.

With acts of love, of sharing, and of truth, we sanctify You, O God. As it is written: "Be holy, for I the Lord your God am holy." We praise You, our holy God.

◆ ◆

READY TO SERVE YOU — קדושת היום

אֱלֹהֵינוּ וֵאלֹהֵי אֲבוֹתֵינוּ, רְצֵה בִמְנוּחָתֵנוּ, קַדְּשֵׁנוּ בְּמִצְוֹתֶיךָ, וְתֵן חֶלְקֵנוּ בְּתוֹרָתֶךָ, וְשַׂמְּחֵנוּ בִּישׁוּעָתֶךָ. וְטַהֵר לִבֵּנוּ לְעָבְדְּךָ בֶּאֱמֶת. בָּרוּךְ אַתָּה, יְיָ, מְקַדֵּשׁ הַשַּׁבָּת.

God of all ages, enable us through Sabbath rest to learn, impart, and uphold the commandments of Your Torah. Let us rejoice to strive for the triumph of Your will. Make our hearts ready to serve You. We thank You, O Lord, for the Sabbath and its holiness.

◆ ◆

IN OUR DEEDS AND OUR PRAYER — עבודה

רְצֵה, יְיָ אֱלֹהֵינוּ, בְּעַמְּךָ יִשְׂרָאֵל, וּתְפִלָּתָם בְּאַהֲבָה תְקַבֵּל, וּתְהִי לְרָצוֹן תָּמִיד עֲבוֹדַת יִשְׂרָאֵל עַמֶּךָ. שְׁפוֹךְ רוּחֲךָ עָלֵינוּ, וְתֶחֱזֶינָה עֵינֵינוּ בְּשׁוּבְךָ לְצִיּוֹן בְּרַחֲמִים. בָּרוּךְ אַתָּה, יְיָ, שֶׁאוֹתְךָ לְבַדְּךָ בְּיִרְאָה נַעֲבוֹד.

O Lord our God, may we, Your people Israel, be worthy in our deeds and our prayer. Wherever we live, wherever we seek You — in this land, in Zion restored, in all lands — You are our God, whom alone we serve in reverence.

◆ ◆

FOR THE GLORY OF LIFE — הודאה

מוֹדִים אֲנַחְנוּ לָךְ עַל־חַיֵּינוּ הַמְּסוּרִים בְּיָדֶךָ, וְעַל־נִפְלְאוֹתֶיךָ וְטוֹבוֹתֶיךָ. הַטּוֹב: כִּי לֹא־כָלוּ רַחֲמֶיךָ, וְהַמְרַחֵם: כִּי לֹא־תַמּוּ חֲסָדֶיךָ. בָּרוּךְ אַתָּה, יְיָ, הַטּוֹב שִׁמְךָ, וּלְךָ נָאֶה לְהוֹדוֹת.

For the glory of life, O Lord, and for its wonder, we give thanks. You are Goodness, You are Compassion. We give thanks to You for ever.

◆ ◆

ONE HUMAN FAMILY — ברכת שלום

שִׂים שָׁלוֹם, טוֹבָה וּבְרָכָה, חֵן וָחֶסֶד וְרַחֲמִים עַל־כָּל־יִשְׂרָאֵל וְעַל־כָּל־יִרְאֵי שְׁמֶךָ. יְהִי רָצוֹן מִלְּפָנֶיךָ שֶׁתְּבַטֵּל מִלְחָמוֹת וּשְׁפִיכוּת דָּמִים מִן הָעוֹלָם. וְיֵעָשׂוּ כֻלָּם אֲגֻדָּה אַחַת, לַעֲשׂוֹת רְצוֹנְךָ בְּלֵבָב שָׁלֵם. יְיָ שָׁלוֹם, בָּרְכֵנוּ בְשָׁלוֹם!

Grant peace to our world, goodness and blessing, mercy and compassion, life and love. Inspire us to banish for ever hatred, war, and bloodshed. Help us to establish for ever one human family doing Your will in love and peace. O God of peace, bless us with peace.

All are seated

◆ ◆

MEDITATION

Looking inward, I see that all too often I fail to use time and talent to improve myself and to serve others. And yet there is in me much goodness, and a yearning to use my gifts for the well-being of those around me. This Sabbath calls me to renew my vision, to fulfill the best that is within me. For this I look to God for help.

Give meaning to my life and substance to my hopes; help me understand those about me and fill me with the desire to serve them. Let me not forget that I depend on others as they depend on me; quicken my heart and hand to lift them up; make fruitful my words of prayer, that they may fulfill themselves in deeds.

◆ ◆

יִהְיוּ לְרָצוֹן אִמְרֵי־פִי וְהֶגְיוֹן לִבִּי לְפָנֶיךָ, יְיָ, צוּרִי וְגוֹאֲלִי.

May the words of my mouth, and the meditations of my heart, be acceptable to You, O Lord, my Rock and my Redeemer.

or

עֹשֶׂה שָׁלוֹם בִּמְרוֹמָיו, הוּא יַעֲשֶׂה שָׁלוֹם עָלֵינוּ וְעַל כָּל־יִשְׂרָאֵל, וְאִמְרוּ אָמֵן.

May He who causes peace to reign in the high heavens let peace descend on us, on all Israel, and all the world.

◆ ◆

Prayers for Special Occasions begin on page 389.

The Rituals for the Reading of Torah begin on page 415.

Concluding Prayers begin on page 613.

For congregations where the lights are kindled in the synagogue

הדלקת הנרות

Come, let us welcome Shabbat.
May its radiance illumine our hearts.

Light is the symbol of the divine.
"The Lord is my light and my salvation."

Light is the symbol of the divine within us.
"The human spirit is the light of the Lord."

Light is the symbol of the divine law.
"For the Mitzvah is a lamp and the Torah a light."

Light is the symbol of Israel's mission.
"I, the Lord, have made you a covenant people, a light to the nations."

◆ ◆

בָּרוּךְ אַתָּה, יְיָ אֱלֹהֵינוּ, מֶלֶךְ הָעוֹלָם,
אֲשֶׁר קִדְּשָׁנוּ בְּמִצְוֹתָיו וְצִוָּנוּ לְהַדְלִיק נֵר שֶׁל שַׁבָּת.

Blessed is the Lord our God, Ruler of the universe,
who hallows us with His Mitzvot, and commands us
to kindle the lights of Shabbat.

◆ ◆

May God bless us with Shabbat joy.
May God bless us with Shabbat holiness.
May God bless us with Shabbat peace.

◆ ◆

Welcoming Shabbat קבלת שבת

Lord of the universe, we lift up our hearts to You, the Maker of heaven and earth. The infinite heavens and the quiet stars tell of Your endless power. We turn from our daily toil, from its clamor and its weariness, to meditate on the serene calm of Your presence that pervades all creation and hallows our life with the blessing of Sabbath peace.

Author of peace, bless our worship on this Sabbath day. Enlighten our eyes to behold Your guiding power in all nature, from the remotest star to our inmost thought. Incline our hearts to love You and to make Your will the law of our life. Be with us as our comfort in sorrow, our strength in trial; give us courage to serve You in all our ways. May our words of prayer and our unspoken meditations unite us in the love of Your name, O God, our Creator and Redeemer. Amen.

◆ ◆

הַחַמָּה מֵרֹאשׁ הָאִילָנוֹת נִסְתַּלְּקָה,
בֹּאוּ וְנֵצֵא לִקְרַאת שַׁבָּת הַמַּלְכָּה.
הִנֵּה הִיא יוֹרֶדֶת, הַקְּדוֹשָׁה הַבְּרוּכָה,
וְעִמָּהּ מַלְאָכִים, צְבָא שָׁלוֹם וּמְנוּחָה.
בֹּאִי, בֹּאִי הַמַּלְכָּה!
בֹּאִי, בֹּאִי הַכַּלָּה!
שָׁלוֹם עֲלֵיכֶם מַלְאֲכֵי הַשָּׁלוֹם.

The sun on the treetops no longer is seen,
Come gather to welcome the Sabbath, our queen.
Behold her descending, the holy, the blessed,
And with her the angels of peace and of rest.
Draw near, draw near, and here abide,
Draw near, draw near, O Sabbath bride.
Peace also to you, you angels of peace.

◆ ◆

We give thanks to You, O God, for this Sabbath day, which unites us as a community of faith and hope.

For the holiness of the Sabbath, which can lead us to fulfill the best that is in us, we give thanks.

For the memories of the Sabbath, enriched by generations of our people who observed it and from it drew courage to face hardship, and light to banish darkness, we are grateful.

We offer thanks for the peace of the Sabbath, the day consecrated to family love.

O God, our turning to You exalts our humanity. You are the joy of our life, the Source of its greatness, its power, and its beauty.

Help us, O God, to find inspiration for the coming week; help us to find peace within ourselves and one another.

✦ ✦

MEDITATION

This Shabbat sheds light upon us — light for the days to come. We have leisure by which to see the world with new and grateful eyes. We have time now to look inward. And now we are free to embrace family and friends, to make our lives simpler and more complete.

We think of our homes and those we love. When we call to mind the duties and affections of home, how greatly are all blessings enriched, all cares and sorrows softened. May the hearts of parents and children always be turned to one another, that our homes may be sanctuaries of love and devotion. May we use this Shabbat to bring happiness to our family life, and blessing to our people.

✦ ✦

Blessed is the Sabbath, the queen of days, which adds new soul to Israel's life.

More than Israel has kept the Sabbath, has the Sabbath kept Israel.

Happy are those who remember the Sabbath, who hallow it with prayer and song.

Happy are those who rejoice in the Eternal, who take delight in the heritage of their people.

Their homes are filled with light and gladness;

The joy of the Eternal is their strength.

READER'S KADDISH — חצי קדיש

יִתְגַּדַּל וְיִתְקַדַּשׁ שְׁמֵהּ רַבָּא בְּעָלְמָא דִּי־בְרָא כִרְעוּתֵהּ,
וְיַמְלִיךְ מַלְכוּתֵהּ בְּחַיֵּיכוֹן וּבְיוֹמֵיכוֹן וּבְחַיֵּי דְכָל־בֵּית
יִשְׂרָאֵל, בַּעֲגָלָא וּבִזְמַן קָרִיב, וְאִמְרוּ: אָמֵן.

יְהֵא שְׁמֵהּ רַבָּא מְבָרַךְ לְעָלַם וּלְעָלְמֵי עָלְמַיָּא.

יִתְבָּרַךְ וְיִשְׁתַּבַּח וְיִתְפָּאַר וְיִתְרוֹמַם וְיִתְנַשֵּׂא, וְיִתְהַדַּר
וְיִתְעַלֶּה וְיִתְהַלַּל שְׁמֵהּ דְּקוּדְשָׁא, בְּרִיךְ הוּא, לְעֵלָּא מִן
כָּל־בִּרְכָתָא וְשִׁירָתָא, תֻּשְׁבְּחָתָא וְנֶחֱמָתָא דַּאֲמִירָן בְּעָלְמָא,
וְאִמְרוּ: אָמֵן.

Let the glory of God be extolled, let His great name be hallowed in the world whose creation He willed. May His kingdom soon prevail, in our own day, our own lives, and the life of all Israel, and let us say: Amen.

Let His great name be blessed for ever and ever.

Let the name of the Holy One, blessed is He, be glorified, exalted and honored, though He is beyond all the praises, songs, and adorations that we can utter, and let us say: Amen.

◆ ◆

All rise

שמע וברכותיה

בָּרְכוּ אֶת־יְיָ הַמְבֹרָךְ!

Praise the Lord, to whom our praise is due!

בָּרוּךְ יְיָ הַמְבֹרָךְ לְעוֹלָם וָעֶד!

Praised be the Lord, to whom our praise is due,
now and for ever!

◆ ◆

THE MARVELS OF EARTH AND SKY — מעריב ערבים

בָּרוּךְ אַתָּה, יְיָ אֱלֹהֵינוּ, מֶלֶךְ הָעוֹלָם, אֲשֶׁר בִּדְבָרוֹ מַעֲרִיב עֲרָבִים. בְּחָכְמָה פּוֹתֵחַ שְׁעָרִים, וּבִתְבוּנָה מְשַׁנֶּה עִתִּים, וּמַחֲלִיף אֶת־הַזְּמַנִּים, וּמְסַדֵּר אֶת־הַכּוֹכָבִים בְּמִשְׁמְרוֹתֵיהֶם בָּרָקִיעַ כִּרְצוֹנוֹ.

בּוֹרֵא יוֹם וָלָיְלָה, גּוֹלֵל אוֹר מִפְּנֵי חֹשֶׁךְ וְחֹשֶׁךְ מִפְּנֵי אוֹר, וּמַעֲבִיר יוֹם וּמֵבִיא לָיְלָה, וּמַבְדִּיל בֵּין יוֹם וּבֵין לָיְלָה, יְיָ צְבָאוֹת שְׁמוֹ.

אֵל חַי וְקַיָּם, תָּמִיד יִמְלוֹךְ עָלֵינוּ, לְעוֹלָם וָעֶד. בָּרוּךְ אַתָּה, יְיָ, הַמַּעֲרִיב עֲרָבִים.

Eternal God, Your majesty is proclaimed by the marvels of earth and sky. Sun, moon, and stars testify to Your power and wisdom.

Day follows day in endless succession, and the years vanish, but Your sovereignty endures.

Though all things pass, let not Your glory depart from us. Help us to become co-workers with You, and endow our fleeting days with abiding worth.

◆ ◆

YOUR GOODNESS AND LOVE

אהבת עולם

אַהֲבַת עוֹלָם בֵּית יִשְׂרָאֵל עַמְּךָ אָהָבְתָּ: תּוֹרָה וּמִצְוֹת, חֻקִּים וּמִשְׁפָּטִים אוֹתָנוּ לִמַּדְתָּ.
עַל־כֵּן, יְיָ אֱלֹהֵינוּ, בְּשָׁכְבֵנוּ וּבְקוּמֵנוּ נָשִׂיחַ בְּחֻקֶּיךָ, וְנִשְׂמַח בְּדִבְרֵי תוֹרָתְךָ וּבְמִצְוֹתֶיךָ לְעוֹלָם וָעֶד.
כִּי הֵם חַיֵּינוּ וְאֹרֶךְ יָמֵינוּ, וּבָהֶם נֶהְגֶּה יוֹמָם וָלָיְלָה. וְאַהֲבָתְךָ אַל־תָּסִיר מִמֶּנּוּ לְעוֹלָמִים! בָּרוּךְ אַתָּה, יְיָ, אוֹהֵב עַמּוֹ יִשְׂרָאֵל.

You are our God, the Source of life and its blessings. Wherever we turn our gaze, we behold signs of Your goodness and love.

The whole universe proclaims Your glory. Your loving spirit hovers over all Your works, guiding and sustaining them.

The harmony and grandeur of nature speak to us of You; the beauty and truth of Torah reveal Your will to us. You are the One and Eternal God of time and space!

◆ ◆

שְׁמַע יִשְׂרָאֵל: יְיָ אֱלֹהֵינוּ, יְיָ אֶחָד!

Hear, O Israel: the Lord is our God, the Lord is One!

בָּרוּךְ שֵׁם כְּבוֹד מַלְכוּתוֹ לְעוֹלָם וָעֶד!

Blessed is His glorious kingdom for ever and ever!

All are seated

וְאָהַבְתָּ אֵת יְיָ אֱלֹהֶיךָ בְּכָל־לְבָבְךָ וּבְכָל־נַפְשְׁךָ וּבְכָל־מְאֹדֶךָ.
וְהָיוּ הַדְּבָרִים הָאֵלֶּה, אֲשֶׁר אָנֹכִי מְצַוְּךָ הַיּוֹם, עַל־לְבָבֶךָ.
וְשִׁנַּנְתָּם לְבָנֶיךָ, וְדִבַּרְתָּ בָּם בְּשִׁבְתְּךָ בְּבֵיתֶךָ, וּבְלֶכְתְּךָ בַדֶּרֶךְ, וּבְשָׁכְבְּךָ וּבְקוּמֶךָ.

You shall love the Lord your God with all your mind, with all your strength, with all your being.

Set these words, which I command you this day, upon your heart. Teach them faithfully to your children; speak of them in your home and on your way, when you lie down and when you rise up.

וּקְשַׁרְתָּם לְאוֹת עַל־יָדֶךָ, וְהָיוּ לְטֹטָפֹת בֵּין עֵינֶיךָ, וּכְתַבְתָּם עַל־מְזֻזוֹת בֵּיתֶךָ, וּבִשְׁעָרֶיךָ.

Bind them as a sign upon your hand; let them be a symbol before your eyes; inscribe them on the doorposts of your house, and on your gates.

לְמַעַן תִּזְכְּרוּ וַעֲשִׂיתֶם אֶת־כָּל־מִצְוֹתָי, וִהְיִיתֶם קְדֹשִׁים לֵאלֹהֵיכֶם. אֲנִי יְיָ אֱלֹהֵיכֶם, אֲשֶׁר הוֹצֵאתִי אֶתְכֶם מֵאֶרֶץ מִצְרַיִם לִהְיוֹת לָכֶם לֵאלֹהִים. אֲנִי יְיָ אֱלֹהֵיכֶם.

Be mindful of all My Mitzvot, and do them: so shall you consecrate yourselves to your God. I, the Lord, am your God who led you out of Egypt to be your God; I, the Lord, am your God.

◆ ◆

FREE TO SING — גאולה

אֱמֶת וֶאֱמוּנָה כָּל־זֹאת, וְקַיָּם עָלֵינוּ כִּי הוּא יְיָ אֱלֹהֵינוּ וְאֵין זוּלָתוֹ, וַאֲנַחְנוּ יִשְׂרָאֵל עַמּוֹ.

Eternal truth it is that You alone are God,
and there is none else.

May the righteous of all nations rejoice in Your love
and exult in Your justice.

הַפּוֹדֵנוּ מִיַּד מְלָכִים, מַלְכֵּנוּ הַגּוֹאֲלֵנוּ מִכַּף כָּל־הֶעָרִיצִים.
הָעֹשֶׂה גְדֹלוֹת עַד אֵין חֵקֶר, וְנִפְלָאוֹת עַד־אֵין מִסְפָּר.

Let them beat their swords into plowshares;
Let them beat their spears into pruninghooks.

הַשָּׂם נַפְשֵׁנוּ בַּחַיִּים, וְלֹא־נָתַן לַמּוֹט רַגְלֵנוּ.
הָעֹשֶׂה לָנוּ נִסִּים בְּפַרְעֹה, אוֹתוֹת וּמוֹפְתִים בְּאַדְמַת בְּנֵי חָם.
וַיּוֹצֵא אֶת־עַמּוֹ יִשְׂרָאֵל מִתּוֹכָם לְחֵרוּת עוֹלָם.

Let nation not lift up sword against nation;
let them study war no more.

You shall not hate another in your heart;
you shall love your neighbor as yourself.

וְרָאוּ בָנָיו גְּבוּרָתוֹ; שִׁבְּחוּ וְהוֹדוּ לִשְׁמוֹ. וּמַלְכוּתוֹ בְּרָצוֹן
קִבְּלוּ עֲלֵיהֶם. מֹשֶׁה וּבְנֵי יִשְׂרָאֵל לְךָ עָנוּ שִׁירָה בְּשִׂמְחָה
רַבָּה, וְאָמְרוּ כֻלָּם:

Let the stranger in your midst be to you as the native;
for you were strangers in the land of Egypt.

From the house of bondage we went forth to freedom;
so let all be free to sing with joy:

מִי־כָמֹכָה בָּאֵלִם, יְיָ?
מִי כָּמֹכָה, נֶאְדָּר בַּקֹּדֶשׁ,
נוֹרָא תְהִלֹּת, עֹשֵׂה פֶלֶא?

Who is like You, Eternal One, among
the gods that are worshipped?
Who is like You, majestic in holiness,
awesome in splendor, doing wonders?

מַלְכוּתְךָ רָאוּ בָנֶיךָ, בּוֹקֵעַ יָם לִפְנֵי מֹשֶׁה; "זֶה אֵלִי!" עָנוּ
וְאָמְרוּ: "יְיָ יִמְלֹךְ לְעֹלָם וָעֶד!"

Your people acknowledged Your sovereign power: "This is my God!" they sang; "The Eternal will reign for ever and ever!"

וְנֶאֱמַר: "כִּי־פָדָה יְיָ אֶת־יַעֲקֹב, וּגְאָלוֹ מִיַּד חָזָק מִמֶּנּוּ." בָּרוּךְ
אַתָּה, יְיָ, גָּאַל יִשְׂרָאֵל.

As You redeemed Israel and saved us from arms stronger than our own, so may You redeem all the oppressed and persecuted. Blessed is the Lord, the Redeemer of Israel.

◆ ◆

THE SHADOW OF YOUR WINGS השכיבנו

הַשְׁכִּיבֵנוּ, יְיָ אֱלֹהֵינוּ, לְשָׁלוֹם, וְהַעֲמִידֵנוּ, מַלְכֵּנוּ, לְחַיִּים.
וּפְרוֹשׂ עָלֵינוּ סֻכַּת שְׁלוֹמֶךָ.
וְתַקְּנֵנוּ בְּעֵצָה טוֹבָה מִלְּפָנֶיךָ, וְהוֹשִׁיעֵנוּ לְמַעַן שְׁמֶךָ, וְהָגֵן
בַּעֲדֵנוּ. וְהָסֵר מֵעָלֵינוּ אוֹיֵב, דֶּבֶר וְחֶרֶב וְרָעָב וְיָגוֹן.

Cause us, O Lord our God, to lie down in peace, and to awaken each morning to renewed life and strength. Spread over us the shelter of Your peace.

Help us to order our lives by Your counsel, and lead us in the paths of righteousness. Be a shield about us, protecting us from hate and war, from pestilence and sorrow.

וְהָסֵר שָׂטָן מִלְּפָנֵינוּ וּמֵאַחֲרֵינוּ; וּבְצֵל כְּנָפֶיךָ תַּסְתִּירֵנוּ, כִּי
אֵל שׁוֹמְרֵנוּ וּמַצִּילֵנוּ אָתָּה, כִּי אֵל מֶלֶךְ חַנּוּן וְרַחוּם אָתָּה.
וּשְׁמוֹר צֵאתֵנוּ וּבוֹאֵנוּ לְחַיִּים וּלְשָׁלוֹם, מֵעַתָּה וְעַד עוֹלָם,
וּפְרוֹשׂ עָלֵינוּ סֻכַּת שְׁלוֹמֶךָ.
בָּרוּךְ אַתָּה, יְיָ, הַפּוֹרֵשׂ סֻכַּת שָׁלוֹם עָלֵינוּ, וְעַל־כָּל־עַמּוֹ
יִשְׂרָאֵל וְעַל יְרוּשָׁלָיִם.

Curb also within us the inclination to do evil, and shelter us beneath the shadow of Your wings. Guard our going out and our coming in unto life and peace, from this time forth and for ever.

Blessed is the Lord, whose shelter of peace is spread over us, over all His people Israel, and over Jerusalem.

◆ ◆

THE COVENANT OF SHABBAT ושמרו

וְשָׁמְרוּ בְנֵי־יִשְׂרָאֵל אֶת־הַשַּׁבָּת, לַעֲשׂוֹת אֶת־הַשַּׁבָּת לְדֹרֹתָם
בְּרִית עוֹלָם. בֵּינִי וּבֵין בְּנֵי יִשְׂרָאֵל אוֹת הִיא לְעֹלָם, כִּי שֵׁשֶׁת

יָמִים עָשָׂה יְיָ אֶת־הַשָּׁמַיִם וְאֶת־הָאָרֶץ, וּבַיּוֹם הַשְּׁבִיעִי שָׁבַת וַיִּנָּפַשׁ.

The people of Israel shall keep the Sabbath, observing the Sabbath in every generation as a covenant for all time. It is a sign for ever between Me and the people of Israel, for in six days the Eternal God made heaven and earth, and on the seventh day He rested from His labors.

◆ ◆

All rise

תפלה

אֲדֹנָי, שְׂפָתַי תִּפְתָּח, וּפִי יַגִּיד תְּהִלָּתֶךָ.

Eternal God, open my lips, that my mouth may declare Your glory.

THE SHIELD OF ABRAHAM — אבות

בָּרוּךְ אַתָּה, יְיָ אֱלֹהֵינוּ וֵאלֹהֵי אֲבוֹתֵינוּ, אֱלֹהֵי אַבְרָהָם, אֱלֹהֵי יִצְחָק, וֵאלֹהֵי יַעֲקֹב: הָאֵל הַגָּדוֹל, הַגִּבּוֹר וְהַנּוֹרָא, אֵל עֶלְיוֹן.

Blessed is the Lord our God and God of all generations, God of Abraham, God of Isaac, and God of Jacob, great, mighty, and exalted.

גּוֹמֵל חֲסָדִים טוֹבִים, וְקוֹנֵה הַכֹּל, וְזוֹכֵר חַסְדֵי אָבוֹת, וּמֵבִיא גְאֻלָּה לִבְנֵי בְנֵיהֶם, לְמַעַן שְׁמוֹ, בְּאַהֲבָה.

He bestows love and kindness on all His children. He remembers the devotion of ages past. In His love, He brings redemption to their descendants for the sake of His name.

מֶלֶךְ עוֹזֵר וּמוֹשִׁיעַ וּמָגֵן. בָּרוּךְ אַתָּה, יְיָ, מָגֵן אַבְרָהָם.

He is our Ruler and Helper, our Savior and Protector.

Blessed is the Eternal God, the Shield of Abraham.

◆ ◆

THE SOURCE OF LIFE

גבורות

אַתָּה גִּבּוֹר לְעוֹלָם, אֲדֹנָי, מְחַיֵּה הַכֹּל אַתָּה, רַב לְהוֹשִׁיעַ.

Eternal is Your might, O Lord, and great is Your saving power.

מְכַלְכֵּל חַיִּים בְּחֶסֶד, מְחַיֵּה הַכֹּל בְּרַחֲמִים רַבִּים. סוֹמֵךְ נוֹפְלִים, וְרוֹפֵא חוֹלִים, וּמַתִּיר אֲסוּרִים, וּמְקַיֵּם אֱמוּנָתוֹ לִישֵׁנֵי עָפָר.

In love You sustain the living; in Your great mercy, You sustain us all. You uphold the falling and heal the sick; free the captives and keep faith with Your children in death as in life.

מִי כָמוֹךָ, בַּעַל גְּבוּרוֹת, וּמִי דּוֹמֶה לָּךְ, מֶלֶךְ מֵמִית וּמְחַיֶּה וּמַצְמִיחַ יְשׁוּעָה?

וְנֶאֱמָן אַתָּה לְהַחֲיוֹת הַכֹּל. בָּרוּךְ אַתָּה, יְיָ, מְחַיֵּה הַכֹּל.

Who is like You, Almighty God, Author of life and death, Source of salvation?

Blessed is the Eternal God, the Source of life.

◆ ◆

THE HOLY GOD

קדושת השם

אַתָּה קָדוֹשׁ וְשִׁמְךָ קָדוֹשׁ, וּקְדוֹשִׁים בְּכָל־יוֹם יְהַלְלוּךָ סֶּלָה. בָּרוּךְ אַתָּה, יְיָ, הָאֵל הַקָּדוֹשׁ.

You are holy, Your name is holy, and Your worshippers proclaim Your holiness. Blessed is the Eternal One, the holy God.

All are seated

◆ ◆

MOST PRECIOUS OF DAYS

קדושת היום

יִשְׂמְחוּ בְמַלְכוּתְךָ שׁוֹמְרֵי שַׁבָּת וְקוֹרְאֵי עֹנֶג. עַם מְקַדְּשֵׁי שְׁבִיעִי כֻּלָּם יִשְׂבְּעוּ וְיִתְעַנְּגוּ מִטּוּבֶךָ. וְהַשְּׁבִיעִי רָצִיתָ בּוֹ וְקִדַּשְׁתּוֹ. חֶמְדַּת יָמִים אוֹתוֹ קָרָאתָ, זֵכֶר לְמַעֲשֵׂה בְרֵאשִׁית.

Those who keep the Sabbath and call it a delight shall rejoice in Your kingdom. All who hallow the seventh day shall be gladdened by Your goodness. This day is Israel's festival of the spirit, sanctified and blessed by You, the most precious of days, a symbol of the joy of creation.

◆

THE SABBATH AND ITS HOLINESS

אֱלֹהֵינוּ וֵאלֹהֵי אֲבוֹתֵינוּ, רְצֵה בִמְנוּחָתֵנוּ. קַדְּשֵׁנוּ בְּמִצְוֹתֶיךָ וְתֵן חֶלְקֵנוּ בְּתוֹרָתֶךָ. שַׂבְּעֵנוּ מִטּוּבֶךָ, וְשַׂמְּחֵנוּ בִּישׁוּעָתֶךָ, וְטַהֵר לִבֵּנוּ לְעָבְדְּךָ בֶּאֱמֶת. וְהַנְחִילֵנוּ, יְיָ אֱלֹהֵינוּ, בְּאַהֲבָה וּבְרָצוֹן שַׁבַּת קָדְשֶׁךָ, וְיָנוּחוּ בָהּ יִשְׂרָאֵל מְקַדְּשֵׁי שְׁמֶךָ. בָּרוּךְ אַתָּה, יְיָ, מְקַדֵּשׁ הַשַּׁבָּת.

Our God and God of all Israel, grant that our worship on this Sabbath be acceptable in Your sight. Sanctify us with Your Mitzvot that we may share in the blessings of Your word. Teach us to be satisfied with the gifts of Your goodness and gratefully to rejoice in all Your mercies. Purify our hearts that we may serve You in truth. O help us to preserve the Sabbath from generation to generation, that it may bring rest and joy, peace and comfort to the dwellings of our people, and through it Your name be hallowed in all the earth. We thank You, O God, for the Sabbath and its holiness.

◆ ◆

WHOM ALONE WE SERVE IN REVERENCE

עבודה

רְצֵה, יְיָ אֱלֹהֵינוּ, בְּעַמְּךָ יִשְׂרָאֵל, וּתְפִלָּתָם בְּאַהֲבָה תְקַבֵּל, וּתְהִי לְרָצוֹן תָּמִיד עֲבוֹדַת יִשְׂרָאֵל עַמֶּךָ. בָּרוּךְ אַתָּה, יְיָ, שֶׁאוֹתְךָ לְבַדְּךָ בְּיִרְאָה נַעֲבוֹד.

Look with favor, O Lord, upon us, and may our service be acceptable to You. Blessed is the Eternal God, whom alone we serve with reverence.

◆ ◆

MEDITATION

Lord, we give thanks for the freedom that is ours, and we pray for those in other lands who are persecuted and oppressed. Help them to bear their burdens, and keep alive in them the love of freedom and the hope of deliverance. Uphold also the hands of our brothers and sisters in the land of Israel. Cause a new light to shine upon Zion and upon us all, that the time may come again when Your Torah will go forth from the House of Israel, Your word from the tents of Jacob. Blessed is our God, whose presence gives life to His people Israel.

◆ ◆

TO WHOM OUR THANKS ARE DUE הודאה

מוֹדִים אֲנַחְנוּ לָךְ, שָׁאַתָּה הוּא יְיָ אֱלֹהֵינוּ וֵאלֹהֵי אֲבוֹתֵינוּ לְעוֹלָם וָעֶד. צוּר חַיֵּינוּ, מָגֵן יִשְׁעֵנוּ, אַתָּה הוּא לְדוֹר וָדוֹר.

We gratefully acknowledge, O Lord our God, that You are our Creator and Preserver, the Rock of our life and our protecting Shield.

נוֹדֶה לְּךָ וּנְסַפֵּר תְּהִלָּתֶךָ, עַל־חַיֵּינוּ הַמְּסוּרִים בְּיָדֶךָ, וְעַל־נִשְׁמוֹתֵינוּ הַפְּקוּדוֹת לָךְ, וְעַל־נִסֶּיךָ שֶׁבְּכָל־יוֹם עִמָּנוּ, וְעַל־נִפְלְאוֹתֶיךָ וְטוֹבוֹתֶיךָ שֶׁבְּכָל־עֵת, עֶרֶב וָבֹקֶר וְצָהֳרָיִם. הַטּוֹב: כִּי לֹא־כָלוּ רַחֲמֶיךָ, וְהַמְרַחֵם: כִּי־לֹא תַמּוּ חֲסָדֶיךָ, מֵעוֹלָם קִוִּינוּ לָךְ.

We give thanks to You for our lives which are in Your hand, for our souls which are ever in Your keeping, for Your wondrous providence and Your continuous goodness, which You bestow upon us day by day. Truly, Your mercies never fail, and Your love and kindness never cease. Therefore do we forever put our trust in You.

בָּרוּךְ אַתָּה, יְיָ, הַטּוֹב שִׁמְךָ, וּלְךָ נָאֶה לְהוֹדוֹת.

Blessed is the Eternal God, to whom our thanks are due.

◆ ◆

GRANT US PEACE ברכת שלום

שָׁלוֹם רָב עַל־יִשְׂרָאֵל עַמְּךָ וְעַל־כָּל־הָעַמִּים תָּשִׂים לְעוֹלָם, כִּי אַתָּה הוּא מֶלֶךְ אָדוֹן לְכָל־הַשָּׁלוֹם. וְטוֹב בְּעֵינֶיךָ לְבָרֵךְ אֶת־עַמְּךָ יִשְׂרָאֵל וְאֶת־כָּל־הָעַמִּים בְּכָל־עֵת וּבְכָל־שָׁעָה בִּשְׁלוֹמֶךָ. בָּרוּךְ אַתָּה, יְיָ, עוֹשֵׂה הַשָּׁלוֹם.

Grant us peace, Your most precious gift, O Eternal Source of peace, and give us the will to proclaim its message to all the peoples of the earth. Bless our country, that it may always be a stronghold of peace, and its advocate among the nations. May contentment reign within its borders, health and happiness within its homes. Strengthen the bonds of friendship among the inhabitants of all lands. And may the love of Your name hallow every home and every heart. Blessed is the Eternal God, the Source of peace.

◆ ◆

MEDITATION

O God, guard my tongue from evil and my lips from speaking guile. Purify my heart that there be in it no malice, but a prayer for the good of all. Lead me in the ways of righteousness, that I may hurt no one; and help me to bring the blessings of love to others. Open my heart to do Your will. Strengthen my desire to obey Your commandments. May my thoughts and my prayers be acceptable to You, O Lord, my Rock and my Redeemer.

◆ ◆

יִהְיוּ לְרָצוֹן אִמְרֵי־פִי וְהֶגְיוֹן לִבִּי לְפָנֶיךָ, יְיָ, צוּרִי וְגוֹאֲלִי.

May the words of my mouth, and the meditations of my heart, be acceptable to You, O Lord, my Rock and my Redeemer.

or

עֹשֶׂה שָׁלוֹם בִּמְרוֹמָיו, הוּא יַעֲשֶׂה שָׁלוֹם עָלֵינוּ וְעַל כָּל־יִשְׂרָאֵל, וְאִמְרוּ אָמֵן.

May He who causes peace to reign in the high heavens let peace descend on us, on all Israel, and all the world.

◆ ◆

Prayers for Special Occasions are on page 389.

The Rituals for the Reading of Torah begin on page 415.

Concluding Prayers begin on page 613.

ו VI ו

For congregations where the lights are kindled in the synagogue

הדלקת הנרות

In every beginning there is darkness.
The darkness of chaos seems eternal,
yet form emerges: light dawns, and life is born.

"In the beginning the Most High made heaven and earth."

In every beginning there is darkness:
the darkness of ignorance, which smothers human dignity;
the darkness of fear, which chokes the creative will;
the darkness of tyranny, which stifles freedom.

"The Most High said: Let there be light!"

The Sabbath candles celebrate the divine power
that makes for life and light.

◆ ◆

בָּרוּךְ אַתָּה, יְיָ אֱלֹהֵינוּ, מֶלֶךְ הָעוֹלָם,
אֲשֶׁר קִדְּשָׁנוּ בְּמִצְוֹתָיו וְצִוָּנוּ לְהַדְלִיק נֵר שֶׁל שַׁבָּת.

Blessed is the eternal power that inspires our people to kindle the light of Shabbat. Blessed is the source of life and light.

May we be blessed with the light of dignity, creation, and freedom. May we be blessed with a life of joy and love and peace. Amen.

◆ ◆

Welcoming Shabbat קבלת שבת

וַיְכֻלּוּ הַשָּׁמַיִם וְהָאָרֶץ וְכָל־
צְבָאָם. וַיְכַל אֱלֹהִים בַּיּוֹם
הַשְּׁבִיעִי מְלַאכְתּוֹ אֲשֶׁר עָשָׂה;
וַיִּשְׁבֹּת בַּיּוֹם הַשְּׁבִיעִי מִכָּל־
מְלַאכְתּוֹ אֲשֶׁר עָשָׂה. וַיְבָרֶךְ
אֱלֹהִים אֶת־יוֹם הַשְּׁבִיעִי וַיְקַדֵּשׁ
אֹתוֹ, כִּי בוֹ שָׁבַת מִכָּל־מְלַאכְתּוֹ
אֲשֶׁר־בָּרָא אֱלֹהִים לַעֲשׂוֹת.

Now the whole universe – sky, earth, and all their array – was completed. With the seventh day God ended His work of creation; on the seventh day He rested, with all His work completed. Then God blessed the seventh day and called it holy, for with this day He had completed the work of creation.

◆ ◆

MEDITATION

These words from a distant time express the Sabbath's inner meaning. When creation rests and existence is sure, when chaos is ordered and being is securely launched upon its voyage, then is the Sabbath born.

Through the centuries Israel has given itself to the Sabbath, seeing it as the climax of its life even as it was the climax of creation. The Sabbath blessed the people and received in return the grateful responses of their changing lives.

The centuries changed the people, and the people changed the Sabbath. In periods of darkness the Sabbath glowed with the promised Messiah's light. To those in torment the Sabbath brought its healing power of peace. In times of freedom the Sabbath was brilliant with reason and knowledge.

The centuries, the people, the Sabbath continue to change. People belong to their time, the Sabbath belongs to the people.

◆ ◆

Shabbat is a day of freedom and peace, a celebration of life and creation. May it open our eyes to the goodness we have attained, and our hearts to the goodness we may yet achieve.

Let moments of holiness enter the world, uniting matter and spirit in the joy of wholeness, as we welcome Shabbat, the day of days.

◆ ◆

לְכָה דוֹדִי לִקְרַאת כַּלָּה, פְּנֵי שַׁבָּת נְקַבְּלָה.
לְכָה דוֹדִי לִקְרַאת כַּלָּה, פְּנֵי שַׁבָּת נְקַבְּלָה.

Beloved, come to meet the bride;
beloved, come to greet Shabbat.

"שָׁמוֹר" וְ"זָכוֹר", בְּדִבּוּר אֶחָד, הִשְׁמִיעָנוּ אֵל הַמְיֻחָד.
יְיָ אֶחָד וּשְׁמוֹ אֶחָד, לְשֵׁם וּלְתִפְאֶרֶת וְלִתְהִלָּה.
לְכָה . . .

"Keep" and "Remember": a single command the Only God caused us to hear; the Eternal is One, His name is One; His are honor and glory and praise.

Beloved . . .

לִקְרַאת שַׁבָּת לְכוּ וְנֵלְכָה, כִּי הִיא מְקוֹר הַבְּרָכָה,
מֵרֹאשׁ מִקֶּדֶם נְסוּכָה, סוֹף מַעֲשֶׂה, בְּמַחֲשָׁבָה תְּחִלָּה.
לְכָה . . .

Come with me to meet Shabbat, for ever a fountain of blessing. Still it flows, as from the start; the last of days, for which the first was made.

Beloved . . .

הִתְעוֹרְרִי, הִתְעוֹרְרִי, כִּי בָא אוֹרֵךְ! קוּמִי, אוֹרִי,
עוּרִי עוּרִי, שִׁיר דַּבֵּרִי; כְּבוֹד יְיָ עָלַיִךְ נִגְלָה.
לְכָה . . .

Awake, awake, your light has come! Arise, shine, awake and sing: the Eternal's glory dawns upon you.

Beloved . . .

בּוֹאִי בְשָׁלוֹם, עֲטֶרֶת בַּעְלָהּ, גַּם בְּשִׂמְחָה וּבְצָהֳלָה,
תּוֹךְ אֱמוּנֵי עַם סְגֻלָּה. בּוֹאִי, כַלָּה! בּוֹאִי, כַלָּה!
לְכָה . . .

Enter in peace, O crown of your husband; enter in gladness, enter in joy. Come to the people that keeps its faith. Enter, O bride! Enter, O bride!

Beloved . . .

◆ ◆

Now Shabbat is with us. Now we reach out for the divine in ourselves and in the world.

In freedom each of us seeks a Sabbath of the soul.

Here, time and place invite our commitment to the ancient purposes that are our present hopes. Now, time and place are one, bringing promise of triumph over anguish and despair. And when we shall have gone from this place on our separate ways, may our words and promises bring fulfillment and peace.

May our words and promises become deeds, bringing fulfillment and peace.

In this sanctuary we seek to free ourselves from the fears and conflicts that estrange us from one another.

May our words and thoughts give us hope and strength.

We therefore acclaim the eternal power in the universe that helps us to grow in understanding and love, and leads us to freedom.

◆ ◆

READER'S KADDISH — חצי קדיש

יִתְגַּדַּל וְיִתְקַדַּשׁ שְׁמֵהּ רַבָּא בְּעָלְמָא דִּי־בְרָא כִרְעוּתֵהּ,
וְיַמְלִיךְ מַלְכוּתֵהּ בְּחַיֵּיכוֹן וּבְיוֹמֵיכוֹן וּבְחַיֵּי דְכָל־בֵּית
יִשְׂרָאֵל, בַּעֲגָלָא וּבִזְמַן קָרִיב, וְאִמְרוּ: אָמֵן.

יְהֵא שְׁמֵהּ רַבָּא מְבָרַךְ לְעָלַם וּלְעָלְמֵי עָלְמַיָּא.

יִתְבָּרַךְ וְיִשְׁתַּבַּח, וְיִתְפָּאַר וְיִתְרוֹמַם וְיִתְנַשֵּׂא, וְיִתְהַדַּר
וְיִתְעַלֶּה וְיִתְהַלַּל שְׁמֵהּ דְּקוּדְשָׁא, בְּרִיךְ הוּא, לְעֵלָּא מִן
כָּל־בִּרְכָתָא וְשִׁירָתָא, תֻּשְׁבְּחָתָא וְנֶחֱמָתָא דַּאֲמִירָן בְּעָלְמָא,
וְאִמְרוּ: אָמֵן.

◆ ◆

All rise

שמע וברכותיה

בָּרְכוּ אֶת־יְיָ הַמְבֹרָךְ!

בָּרוּךְ יְיָ הַמְבֹרָךְ לְעוֹלָם וָעֶד!

◆ ◆

THE WILL THAT ORDERS THE STARS — מעריב ערבים

בָּרוּךְ אַתָּה, יְיָ אֱלֹהֵינוּ, מֶלֶךְ הָעוֹלָם, אֲשֶׁר בִּדְבָרוֹ מַעֲרִיב
עֲרָבִים. בְּחָכְמָה פּוֹתֵחַ שְׁעָרִים, וּבִתְבוּנָה מְשַׁנֶּה עִתִּים,
וּמַחֲלִיף אֶת־הַזְּמַנִּים, וּמְסַדֵּר אֶת־הַכּוֹכָבִים בְּמִשְׁמְרוֹתֵיהֶם
בָּרָקִיעַ כִּרְצוֹנוֹ.

There was silence; there was chaos; there was a voice. A mind went forth to form worlds: now order reigns where chaos once held sway.

The law makes evening fall; the law brings on the dawn.

בּוֹרֵא יוֹם וָלָיְלָה, גּוֹלֵל אוֹר מִפְּנֵי חֹשֶׁךְ וְחֹשֶׁךְ מִפְּנֵי אוֹר, וּמַעֲבִיר יוֹם וּמֵבִיא לָיְלָה, וּמַבְדִּיל בֵּין יוֹם וּבֵין לָיְלָה, יְיָ צְבָאוֹת שְׁמוֹ.

אֵל חַי וְקַיָּם, תָּמִיד יִמְלוֹךְ עָלֵינוּ, לְעוֹלָם וָעֶד. בָּרוּךְ אַתָּה, יְיָ, הַמַּעֲרִיב עֲרָבִים.

The moon follows accustomed paths, constellations their patterned ways.

Sovereign is the will that orders the stars in their courses in the endless skies: Sovereign is that will!

◆ ◆

HEART STILL TURNED TO LOVE — אהבת עולם

אַהֲבַת עוֹלָם בֵּית יִשְׂרָאֵל עַמְּךָ אָהָבְתָּ: תּוֹרָה וּמִצְוֹת, חֻקִּים וּמִשְׁפָּטִים אוֹתָנוּ לִמַּדְתָּ.

עַל־כֵּן, יְיָ אֱלֹהֵינוּ, בְּשָׁכְבֵנוּ וּבְקוּמֵנוּ נָשִׂיחַ בְּחֻקֶּיךָ, וְנִשְׂמַח בְּדִבְרֵי תוֹרָתְךָ וּבְמִצְוֹתֶיךָ לְעוֹלָם וָעֶד.

כִּי הֵם חַיֵּינוּ וְאֹרֶךְ יָמֵינוּ, וּבָהֶם נֶהְגֶּה יוֹמָם וָלָיְלָה. וְאַהֲבָתְךָ אַל־תָּסִיר מִמֶּנּוּ לְעוֹלָמִים! בָּרוּךְ אַתָּה, יְיָ, אוֹהֵב עַמּוֹ יִשְׂרָאֵל.

And how unyielding is the will of our people Israel! After the long nights, after the days and years when our ashes blackened the sky, Israel endures, heart still turned to love, soul turning still to life.

So day and night, early and late, we will rejoice in the study of Torah, we will walk by the light of Mitzvot: they are our life and the length of our days. Praised be the source of life and love, and Israel our people!

◆ ◆

שְׁמַע יִשְׂרָאֵל: יְיָ אֱלֹהֵינוּ, יְיָ אֶחָד!

בָּרוּךְ שֵׁם כְּבוֹד מַלְכוּתוֹ לְעוֹלָם וָעֶד!

All are seated

וְאָהַבְתָּ אֵת יְיָ אֱלֹהֶיךָ בְּכָל־לְבָבְךָ וּבְכָל־נַפְשְׁךָ וּבְכָל־מְאֹדֶךָ.
וְהָיוּ הַדְּבָרִים הָאֵלֶּה, אֲשֶׁר אָנֹכִי מְצַוְּךָ הַיּוֹם, עַל־לְבָבֶךָ.
וְשִׁנַּנְתָּם לְבָנֶיךָ, וְדִבַּרְתָּ בָּם בְּשִׁבְתְּךָ בְּבֵיתֶךָ, וּבְלֶכְתְּךָ
בַדֶּרֶךְ, וּבְשָׁכְבְּךָ וּבְקוּמֶךָ.

וּקְשַׁרְתָּם לְאוֹת עַל־יָדֶךָ, וְהָיוּ לְטֹטָפֹת בֵּין עֵינֶיךָ, וּכְתַבְתָּם
עַל־מְזֻזוֹת בֵּיתֶךָ, וּבִשְׁעָרֶיךָ.

לְמַעַן תִּזְכְּרוּ וַעֲשִׂיתֶם אֶת־כָּל־מִצְוֹתָי, וִהְיִיתֶם קְדֹשִׁים
לֵאלֹהֵיכֶם. אֲנִי יְיָ אֱלֹהֵיכֶם, אֲשֶׁר הוֹצֵאתִי אֶתְכֶם מֵאֶרֶץ
מִצְרַיִם לִהְיוֹת לָכֶם לֵאלֹהִים. אֲנִי יְיָ אֱלֹהֵיכֶם.

◆ ◆

MEDITATION

THE POWER THAT MAKES FOR FREEDOM — גאולה

We worship the power that unites all the universe into one great harmony. That oneness, however, is not yet. We see imperfection, disorder, and evil all about us. But before our eyes is a vision of perfection, order, and goodness: these too we have known in some measure. There is evil enough to break the heart, good enough to exalt the soul. Our people has experienced untold suffering and wondrous redemptions; we await a redemption more lasting, and more splendid, than any of the past.

◆

When will redemption come?

When we master the violence that fills our world.

When we look upon others as we would have them look upon us.

When we grant to every person the rights we claim for ourselves.

Once we were in bondage, then we were free. In this first liberation our people saw revealed the power of the Most High. They perceived that His presence redeems time and event from the hands of tyrants. We, too, acclaim the power that makes for freedom. We sing the song that celebrates our deliverance from Egypt and all bondage.

מִי־כָמֹכָה בָּאֵלִם, יְיָ? מִי כָּמֹכָה, נֶאְדָּר בַּקֹּדֶשׁ, נוֹרָא תְהִלֹּת, עֹשֵׂה פֶלֶא?

מַלְכוּתְךָ רָאוּ בָנֶיךָ, בּוֹקֵעַ יָם לִפְנֵי מֹשֶׁה; "זֶה אֵלִי!" עָנוּ וְאָמְרוּ: "יְיָ יִמְלֹךְ לְעֹלָם וָעֶד!"

וְנֶאֱמַר: "כִּי־פָדָה יְיָ אֶת־יַעֲקֹב, וּגְאָלוֹ מִיַּד חָזָק מִמֶּנּוּ." בָּרוּךְ אַתָּה, יְיָ, גָּאַל יִשְׂרָאֵל.

◆ ◆

RISE UP TO LIFE RENEWED — השכיבנו

הַשְׁכִּיבֵנוּ, יְיָ אֱלֹהֵינוּ, לְשָׁלוֹם, וְהַעֲמִידֵנוּ, מַלְכֵּנוּ, לְחַיִּים. וּפְרוֹשׂ עָלֵינוּ סֻכַּת שְׁלוֹמֶךָ, וְתַקְּנֵנוּ בְּעֵצָה טוֹבָה מִלְּפָנֶיךָ, וְהוֹשִׁיעֵנוּ לְמַעַן שְׁמֶךָ, וְהָגֵן בַּעֲדֵנוּ. וְהָסֵר מֵעָלֵינוּ אוֹיֵב, דֶּבֶר וְחֶרֶב וְרָעָב וְיָגוֹן; וְהָסֵר שָׂטָן מִלְּפָנֵינוּ וּמֵאַחֲרֵינוּ; וּבְצֵל כְּנָפֶיךָ תַּסְתִּירֵנוּ, כִּי אֵל שׁוֹמְרֵנוּ וּמַצִּילֵנוּ אָתָּה, כִּי אֵל מֶלֶךְ חַנּוּן וְרַחוּם אָתָּה. וּשְׁמוֹר צֵאתֵנוּ וּבוֹאֵנוּ לְחַיִּים וּלְשָׁלוֹם, מֵעַתָּה וְעַד עוֹלָם, וּפְרוֹשׂ עָלֵינוּ סֻכַּת שְׁלוֹמֶךָ. בָּרוּךְ אַתָּה, יְיָ, הַפּוֹרֵשׂ סֻכַּת שָׁלוֹם עָלֵינוּ, וְעַל־כָּל־עַמּוֹ יִשְׂרָאֵל וְעַל יְרוּשָׁלָיִם.

May we lie down this night in peace, and rise up to life renewed. May night spread over us a shelter of peace, of quiet and calm, the blessing of rest.

There will come a time when morning will bring no word of war or famine or anguish; there will come a day of happiness, of contentment and peace.

Praised be the source of joy within us, for the night and its rest, for the promise of peace.

◆ ◆

ושמרו

וְשָׁמְרוּ בְנֵי־יִשְׂרָאֵל אֶת־הַשַּׁבָּת, לַעֲשׂוֹת אֶת־הַשַּׁבָּת לְדֹרֹתָם בְּרִית עוֹלָם. בֵּינִי וּבֵין בְּנֵי יִשְׂרָאֵל אוֹת הִיא לְעֹלָם, כִּי שֵׁשֶׁת יָמִים עָשָׂה יְיָ אֶת־הַשָּׁמַיִם וְאֶת־הָאָרֶץ, וּבַיּוֹם הַשְּׁבִיעִי שָׁבַת וַיִּנָּפַשׁ.

◆ ◆

All rise

תפלה

אֲדֹנָי, שְׂפָתַי תִּפְתָּח, וּפִי יַגִּיד תְּהִלָּתֶךָ.

May our lips and our lives be one in serving eternal truth.

THE DISTANT SHORES OF BLESSING אבות

בָּרוּךְ אַתָּה, יְיָ אֱלֹהֵינוּ וֵאלֹהֵי אֲבוֹתֵינוּ, אֱלֹהֵי אַבְרָהָם, אֱלֹהֵי יִצְחָק, וֵאלֹהֵי יַעֲקֹב: הָאֵל הַגָּדוֹל, הַגִּבּוֹר וְהַנּוֹרָא, אֵל עֶלְיוֹן. גּוֹמֵל חֲסָדִים טוֹבִים, וְקוֹנֵה הַכֹּל, וְזוֹכֵר חַסְדֵי אָבוֹת, וּמֵבִיא גְאֻלָּה לִבְנֵי בְנֵיהֶם, לְמַעַן שְׁמוֹ, בְּאַהֲבָה.

מֶלֶךְ עוֹזֵר וּמוֹשִׁיעַ וּמָגֵן. בָּרוּךְ אַתָּה, יְיָ, מָגֵן אַבְרָהָם.

For two readers or more

Blessed is the power that moved our ancestors and sustained them on their journey.

> Abraham left familiar ways, set forth to an unknown land, and learned to silence terror with a ready heart.

Isaac came to know how parents may risk their children for the sake of a vision; out of his weakness he forged the strength to live and love.

> Jacob dreamed and fought and grew, at last to become the blessing he wrestled for.

So did those who came before us send forth a blessing fashioned out of their own longing to outgrow themselves. And their longing is ours.

Blessed is the power that sustains us on our journeys to the distant shores of blessing.

◆ ◆

IMMORTAL YEARNINGS, UNDYING HOPES — גבורות

אַתָּה גִּבּוֹר לְעוֹלָם, אֲדֹנָי, מְחַיֵּה הַכֹּל אַתָּה, רַב לְהוֹשִׁיעַ.
מְכַלְכֵּל חַיִּים בְּחֶסֶד, מְחַיֵּה הַכֹּל בְּרַחֲמִים רַבִּים. סוֹמֵךְ נוֹפְלִים, וְרוֹפֵא חוֹלִים, וּמַתִּיר אֲסוּרִים, וּמְקַיֵּם אֱמוּנָתוֹ לִישֵׁנֵי עָפָר.
מִי כָמוֹךָ, בַּעַל גְּבוּרוֹת, וּמִי דּוֹמֶה לָּךְ, מֶלֶךְ מֵמִית וּמְחַיֶּה וּמַצְמִיחַ יְשׁוּעָה?
וְנֶאֱמָן אַתָּה לְהַחֲיוֹת הַכֹּל. בָּרוּךְ אַתָּה, יְיָ, מְחַיֵּה הַכֹּל.

For two readers or more

Love is the thread that binds our lives in a lasting fabric which time shall fray,

> Which time shall fray, but only to be rewoven by each generation.

Each generation will lift the fallen to their feet and hold them as they learn to walk.

> And as they learn to walk, the sickness of our time will be healed by those who drink deep from ancient wells of truth.

From ancient wells of truth they will draw strength to keep faith with those who sleep in the dust.

We praise the source of life and power, who has implanted within us immortal yearning, undying hopes.

◆ ◆

קדושת השם

אַתָּה קָדוֹשׁ וְשִׁמְךָ קָדוֹשׁ, וּקְדוֹשִׁים בְּכָל־יוֹם יְהַלְלוּךָ סֶּלָה.
בָּרוּךְ אַתָּה, יְיָ, הָאֵל הַקָּדוֹשׁ.

All are seated

◆ ◆

THE WORLD A SANCTUARY

קדושת היום

אֱלֹהֵינוּ וֵאלֹהֵי אֲבוֹתֵינוּ, רְצֵה בִמְנוּחָתֵנוּ. קַדְּשֵׁנוּ בְּמִצְוֹתֶיךָ וְתֵן חֶלְקֵנוּ בְּתוֹרָתֶךָ. שַׂבְּעֵנוּ מִטּוּבֶךָ, וְשַׂמְּחֵנוּ בִּישׁוּעָתֶךָ, וְטַהֵר לִבֵּנוּ לְעָבְדְּךָ בֶּאֱמֶת. וְהַנְחִילֵנוּ, יְיָ אֱלֹהֵינוּ, בְּאַהֲבָה וּבְרָצוֹן שַׁבַּת קָדְשֶׁךָ, וְיָנוּחוּ בָהּ יִשְׂרָאֵל מְקַדְּשֵׁי שְׁמֶךָ. בָּרוּךְ אַתָּה, יְיָ, מְקַדֵּשׁ הַשַּׁבָּת.

The holiness of this day is not for this day alone. We must make it overflow into all our minutes, to hallow our weekdays from these sacred moments, hour by hour to make the world a sanctuary where every human soul may be at home.

O may the awe we feel at times at the miracle of one another united in prayer, be with us tomorrow: keep tenderness in our words, and our touch, and our look.

Praised be the world and the power within it that makes for holiness.

◆

אַתָּה אֶחָד וְשִׁמְךָ אֶחָד,
וּמִי כְּעַמְּךָ יִשְׂרָאֵל, גּוֹי אֶחָד בָּאָרֶץ?
תִּפְאֶרֶת גְּדֻלָּה וַעֲטֶרֶת יְשׁוּעָה,
יוֹם מְנוּחָה וּקְדֻשָּׁה לְעַמְּךָ נָתָתָּ.

◆ ◆

SILENT PRAYER

ITS OWN ANSWER

עבודה

רְצֵה, יְיָ אֱלֹהֵינוּ, בְּעַמְּךָ יִשְׂרָאֵל, וּתְפִלָּתָם בְּאַהֲבָה תְקַבֵּל, וּתְהִי לְרָצוֹן תָּמִיד עֲבוֹדַת יִשְׂרָאֵל עַמֶּךָ. אֵל קָרוֹב לְכָל-קֹרְאָיו, פְּנֵה אֶל עֲבָדֶיךָ וְחָנֵּנוּ; שְׁפוֹךְ רוּחֲךָ עָלֵינוּ, וְתֶחֱזֶינָה עֵינֵינוּ בְּשׁוּבְךָ לְצִיּוֹן בְּרַחֲמִים.

בָּרוּךְ אַתָּה, יְיָ, הַמַּחֲזִיר שְׁכִינָתוֹ לְצִיּוֹן.

Can I learn to question my doubts even as I have learned to mistrust so much that once seemed clear? I pray that my doubting spirit may learn to entertain hope. And I pray to become free: free to think my thoughts, free to feel, free to love, and free to praise and give thanks for life. May I make of my life an act of reverence — a prayer: the prayer that is its own answer.

◆

VISIONS FULFILLED

We give thanks for the return of our people to Zion. Remembering the pain of her birth, we pray that now and always she may have peace and safety.

We give thanks for freedom in this land, and we pray for the peoples of every continent. May their highest hopes be made real, their noblest visions fulfilled.

Praised be the strength and love that makes every land and people grow toward justice and right!

◆ ◆

A KINGDOM OF JOY AND AWE

O give thanks
that spring will always come
to make the heart leap,
that your winter ear remembers
a summer song,
and autumn colors return
to the jaded eye.

O make song
for lucid air of morning,
bright blood's beating,
life's flow deep and swift,
a kingdom of joy and awe
for us to dwell in.

O be glad
for eye and tongue,
to see and taste
the common of our days.

הודאה

מוֹדִים אֲנַחְנוּ לָךְ
עַל־חַיֵּינוּ הַמְּסוּרִים בְּיָדֶךָ,
וְעַל־נִפְלְאוֹתֶיךָ וְטוֹבוֹתֶיךָ.
הַטּוֹב:
כִּי לֹא־כָלוּ רַחֲמֶיךָ,
וְהַמְרַחֵם:
כִּי לֹא־תַמּוּ חֲסָדֶיךָ.
בָּרוּךְ אַתָּה, יְיָ,
הַטּוֹב שִׁמְךָ,
וּלְךָ נָאֶה לְהוֹדוֹת.

◆ ◆

AND NONE SHALL MAKE THEM AFRAID

ברכת שלום

We live in two worlds: the one that is, and the one that might be. Nothing is ordained for us: neither delight nor defeat, neither peace nor war. Life flows, and we must freely choose. We can, if we will, change the world that is, into the world that may come to be, as we were taught from of old:

Keep your tongue from evil, and your lips from deceitful speech.

Depart from evil, and do good; seek peace and pursue it.

Be of the disciples of Aaron, loving peace and pursuing it;

loving all human beings, and bringing them to the Torah.

The whole Torah exists only to bring peace, as it is written:

Its ways are ways of pleasantness, and all its paths are peace.

Let justice dwell in the wilderness, righteousness in the fruitful field.

for righteousness shall lead to peace; it shall bring quietness and confidence for ever.

Then all shall sit under their vines and under their fig-trees,

and none shall make them afraid.

◆ ◆

MEDITATION

The universe was brought forth by an inexhaustible creative power. It pours out torrents of energy still. Awesome and wondrous and mysterious, it is the source of our being.

Matter was formed out of chaos. Time passed, time beyond imagining; matter crossed a boundary and became life. Time passed, and life gave birth to — us!

Our universe is being formed at every moment. We too are not yet grown to full height. But ours is a special gift, for a special task: to help in our own shaping. For we were made to be free: free to love or to hate, free to destroy or to create.

We are like mountain climbers on a perilous ascent. Often we stumble; sometimes it seems we may dash ourselves on the rocks below. But there is hope, for dimly we have seen a vision, and felt a presence, and faintly heard a voice not ours.

The blazing stars, particles too small to see, the smile of children, the eyes of lovers, melody filling the soul, a flood of joy surprising the heart, mystery at the core of the plainest things — all tell us that we are not alone. They open our eyes to the vision that steadies and sustains us.

◆ ◆

יִהְיוּ לְרָצוֹן אִמְרֵי־פִי וְהֶגְיוֹן לִבִּי לְפָנֶיךָ, יְיָ, צוּרִי וְגוֹאֲלִי.

or

עֹשֶׂה שָׁלוֹם בִּמְרוֹמָיו, הוּא יַעֲשֶׂה שָׁלוֹם עָלֵינוּ וְעַל כָּל-יִשְׂרָאֵל, וְאִמְרוּ אָמֵן.

◆ ◆

Prayers for Special Occasions begin on page 389.

The Rituals for the Reading of Torah begin on page 415.

Concluding Prayers begin on page 613.

ז VII ז

For congregations where the lights are kindled in the synagogue

הדלקת הנרות

Another week of work is ended;
again Shabbat brings welcome peace.

We pause from our labors
to let Shabbat give another dimension to our lives.

These Sabbath candles are symbols
of the holiness we seek.

Their brightness dispels gloom
and lights a path to faith and hope.

Their glow reminds us of the sacred bonds
that link us to our people
over space and time.

Their radiance summons us
to fulfil our people's mission:

To cast the light of freedom, justice, and peace
upon all the world

◆ ◆

בָּרוּךְ אַתָּה, יְיָ אֱלֹהֵינוּ, מֶלֶךְ הָעוֹלָם,
אֲשֶׁר קִדְּשָׁנוּ בְּמִצְוֹתָיו וְצִוָּנוּ לְהַדְלִיק נֵר שֶׁל שַׁבָּת.

Blessed is the Lord our God, Ruler of the universe,
who hallows us with His Mitzvot, and commands us
to kindle the lights of Shabbat.

◆ ◆

Welcoming Shabbat קבלת שבת

"Remember the Sabbath day to keep it holy."

Shabbat cries out to us: Hold sacred all that lives. Reverence and hallow this world, for here you and all life are born and spend your days.

Therefore we welcome Shabbat, day of holiness, day of life.

◆ ◆

יה רבון

יָהּ רִבּוֹן עָלַם וְעָלְמַיָּא, אַנְתְּ הוּא מַלְכָּא, מֶלֶךְ מַלְכַיָּא.
עוֹבַד גְּבוּרְתֵּךְ, וְתִמְהַיָּא, שְׁפַר קֳדָמַי לְהַחֲוָיָה.
יָהּ רִבּוֹן . . .

Lord God of this and all worlds, You are Supreme, the Sovereign God. Your mighty, wondrous work moves my heart to praise You.

שְׁבָחִין אֲסַדֵּר, צַפְרָא וְרַמְשָׁא, לָךְ, אֱלָהָא קַדִּישָׁא דִּי בְרָא
כָּל־נַפְשָׁא. עִירִין קַדִּישִׁין, וּבְנֵי אֱנָשָׁא, חֵיוַת בָּרָא, וְעוֹפֵי
שְׁמַיָּא.
יָהּ רִבּוֹן . . .

Evening and morning I praise You, Holy God who forms all beings: angels and mortals, beasts and birds.

רַבְרְבִין עוֹבְדָיךְ, וְתַקִּיפִין, מָכֵךְ רָמַיָּא וְזָקֵף כְּפִיפִין. לוּ
יְחֵא גְבַר שְׁנִין אַלְפִין, לָא יֵעֹל גְּבוּרְתֵּךְ בְּחֻשְׁבְּנַיָּא.
יָהּ רִבּוֹן . . .

Great are Your works, and mighty; You humble the proud, and lift up those who are bowed down. Were we to live a thousand years, there would not be time enough to tell of Your might!

◆ ◆

God of the beginning, God of the end,
God of all creatures, Lord of all generations:
You created us in Your image, capable of love and justice,
that in creation's long unfolding we might be Your partners.

You stretched out the heavens and ordered the earth, that fruits may grow into sweetness, men and women into goodness. You are our God!

And God saw all that He had made, and found it very good.

The earth is full of God's goodness.

Who among you loves life and longs to enjoy good for many days?
Then guard your tongue from evil, and your lips from deceitful speech;
turn away from evil, and do good; seek peace and pursue it.

Seek good, and not evil, that you may live.

Seek the Eternal One, and you shall live.

For He is the fountain of life; in His light do we see light.

◆ ◆

MEDITATION

The universe whispers that all things are intertwined. Yet at times we hear the loud cry of discord. To which voice shall we listen? Although we long for harmony, we cannot close our ears to the noise of war, the rasp of hate. How dare we speak of concord, when the fact and symbol of our age is Auschwitz?

The intelligent heart does not deny reality. We must not forget the grief of yesterday, nor ignore the pain of today. But yesterday is past. It cannot tell us what tomorrow will bring. If there is goodness at the heart of life, then its power, like the power of evil, is real. Which shall prevail? Moment by moment we choose between them. If we choose rightly, and often enough, the broken fragments of our world will be restored to wholeness.

For this we need strength and help. We turn in hope, therefore, to a Power beyond us. He has many names, but He is One. He creates; He sustains; He loves; He inspires us with the hope that we can make ourselves one as He is One.

◆ ◆

O God, help us to build Your kingdom, one human world united in heart and soul!

READER'S KADDISH — חצי קדיש

יִתְגַּדַּל וְיִתְקַדַּשׁ שְׁמֵהּ רַבָּא בְּעָלְמָא דִּי־בְרָא כִרְעוּתֵהּ,
וְיַמְלִיךְ מַלְכוּתֵהּ בְּחַיֵּיכוֹן וּבְיוֹמֵיכוֹן וּבְחַיֵּי דְכָל־בֵּית
יִשְׂרָאֵל, בַּעֲגָלָא וּבִזְמַן קָרִיב, וְאִמְרוּ: אָמֵן.

יְהֵא שְׁמֵהּ רַבָּא מְבָרַךְ לְעָלַם וּלְעָלְמֵי עָלְמַיָּא.

יִתְבָּרַךְ וְיִשְׁתַּבַּח, וְיִתְפָּאַר וְיִתְרוֹמַם וְיִתְנַשֵּׂא, וְיִתְהַדַּר
וְיִתְעַלֶּה וְיִתְהַלַּל שְׁמֵהּ דְּקוּדְשָׁא, בְּרִיךְ הוּא, לְעֵלָּא מִן
כָּל־בִּרְכָתָא וְשִׁירָתָא, תֻּשְׁבְּחָתָא וְנֶחֱמָתָא דַּאֲמִירָן בְּעָלְמָא,
וְאִמְרוּ: אָמֵן.

Let the glory of God be extolled, let His great name be hallowed in the world whose creation He willed. May His kingdom soon prevail, in our own day, our own lives, and the life of all Israel, and let us say: Amen.

Let His great name be blessed for ever and ever.

Let the name of the Holy One, blessed is He, be glorified, exalted and honored, though He is beyond all the praises, songs, and adorations that we can utter, and let us say: Amen.

◆ ◆

All rise

שמע וברכותיה

בָּרְכוּ אֶת־יְיָ הַמְבֹרָךְ!

Praise the Lord, to whom our praise is due!

בָּרוּךְ יְיָ הַמְבֹרָךְ לְעוֹלָם וָעֶד!

Praised be the Lord, to whom our praise is due,
now and for ever!

◆ ◆

HEAVEN AND EARTH ALIKE — מעריב ערבים

בָּרוּךְ אַתָּה, יְיָ אֱלֹהֵינוּ, מֶלֶךְ הָעוֹלָם, אֲשֶׁר בִּדְבָרוֹ מַעֲרִיב עֲרָבִים. בְּחָכְמָה פּוֹתֵחַ שְׁעָרִים, וּבִתְבוּנָה מְשַׁנֶּה עִתִּים, וּמַחֲלִיף אֶת־הַזְּמַנִּים, וּמְסַדֵּר אֶת־הַכּוֹכָבִים בְּמִשְׁמְרוֹתֵיהֶם בָּרָקִיעַ כִּרְצוֹנוֹ.

בּוֹרֵא יוֹם וָלָיְלָה, גּוֹלֵל אוֹר מִפְּנֵי חֹשֶׁךְ וְחֹשֶׁךְ מִפְּנֵי אוֹר, וּמַעֲבִיר יוֹם וּמֵבִיא לָיְלָה, וּמַבְדִּיל בֵּין יוֹם וּבֵין לָיְלָה, יְיָ צְבָאוֹת שְׁמוֹ.

אֵל חַי וְקַיָּם, תָּמִיד יִמְלוֹךְ עָלֵינוּ, לְעוֹלָם וָעֶד. בָּרוּךְ אַתָּה, יְיָ, הַמַּעֲרִיב עֲרָבִים.

There lives a God:
His presence is the grandeur pervading the world.

There lives a God:
Heaven and earth alike reveal His power and His glory.

Day and night, mountain, meadow, and lake;
Spring and autumn, growth and decay;

Time and eternity, stars in their courses:
All are witness to His creative will.

◆ ◆

UNENDING SEARCH FOR TRUTH — אהבת עולם

אַהֲבַת עוֹלָם בֵּית יִשְׂרָאֵל עַמְּךָ אָהָבְתָּ: תּוֹרָה וּמִצְוֹת, חֻקִּים וּמִשְׁפָּטִים אוֹתָנוּ לִמַּדְתָּ.
עַל־כֵּן, יְיָ אֱלֹהֵינוּ, בְּשָׁכְבֵנוּ וּבְקוּמֵנוּ נָשִׂיחַ בְּחֻקֶּיךָ, וְנִשְׂמַח בְּדִבְרֵי תוֹרָתְךָ וּבְמִצְוֹתֶיךָ לְעוֹלָם וָעֶד.
כִּי הֵם חַיֵּינוּ וְאֹרֶךְ יָמֵינוּ, וּבָהֶם נֶהְגֶּה יוֹמָם וָלָיְלָה. וְאַהֲבָתְךָ אַל־תָּסִיר מִמֶּנּוּ לְעוֹלָמִים! בָּרוּךְ אַתָּה, יְיָ, אוֹהֵב עַמּוֹ יִשְׂרָאֵל.

There lives a God:
His presence is the glow in the human heart.

There lives a God:
We meet Him in the joys of human love.

We see Him in our vision of a better world:
when we choose life and blessing, and turn from death and destruction.

We hear Him in the still, small voice of conscience.
We sense Him in our unending search for truth.

There lives a God, and in love we unite with Him as we call Him One:

שְׁמַע יִשְׂרָאֵל: יְיָ אֱלֹהֵינוּ, יְיָ אֶחָד!

Hear, O Israel: the Lord is our God, the Lord is One!

בָּרוּךְ שֵׁם כְּבוֹד מַלְכוּתוֹ לְעוֹלָם וָעֶד!

Blessed is His glorious kingdom for ever and ever!

All are seated

וְאָהַבְתָּ אֵת יְיָ אֱלֹהֶיךָ בְּכָל־לְבָבְךָ וּבְכָל־נַפְשְׁךָ וּבְכָל־מְאֹדֶךָ.
וְהָיוּ הַדְּבָרִים הָאֵלֶּה, אֲשֶׁר אָנֹכִי מְצַוְּךָ הַיּוֹם, עַל־לְבָבֶךָ.

וְשִׁנַּנְתָּם לְבָנֶיךָ, וְדִבַּרְתָּ בָּם בְּשִׁבְתְּךָ בְּבֵיתֶךָ, וּבְלֶכְתְּךָ בַדֶּרֶךְ, וּבְשָׁכְבְּךָ וּבְקוּמֶךָ.

וּקְשַׁרְתָּם לְאוֹת עַל־יָדֶךָ, וְהָיוּ לְטֹטָפֹת בֵּין עֵינֶיךָ, וּכְתַבְתָּם עַל־מְזֻזוֹת בֵּיתֶךָ, וּבִשְׁעָרֶיךָ.

לְמַעַן תִּזְכְּרוּ וַעֲשִׂיתֶם אֶת־כָּל־מִצְוֹתָי, וִהְיִיתֶם קְדשִׁים לֵאלֹהֵיכֶם. אֲנִי יְיָ אֱלֹהֵיכֶם, אֲשֶׁר הוֹצֵאתִי אֶתְכֶם מֵאֶרֶץ מִצְרַיִם לִהְיוֹת לָכֶם לֵאלֹהִים. אֲנִי יְיָ אֱלֹהֵיכֶם.

For two readers or more

You shall love the Lord your God with all your mind, with all your strength, with all your being.

> The path to the love of God is through the love of others; I do not love God until I love my neighbor as myself.

Set these words, which I command you this day, upon your heart.

> Jewish faith unites mind and heart. Even as my mind seeks to understand life's meaning, so may my life show love for all created things.

Teach them faithfully to your children; speak of them in your home and on your way, when you lie down and when you rise up.

> We do not teach our children by words alone: May I make my life and actions into good teachings, for in my conduct I must exemplify Torah.

Bind them as a sign upon your hand; let them be a symbol before your eyes; inscribe them on the doorposts of your house, and on your gates.

> Let my home glow with the beauty of our heritage. Let my doors be opened wide to wisdom and to righteousness.

Be mindful of all My Mitzvot and do them: so shall you consecrate yourselves to your God.

> Each Mitzvah is a way to holiness. The Mitzvot elevate our humanity. Let me learn to use them to magnify the divine in myself and in the world.

◆ ◆

OUR PEOPLE FOUND HIM גאולה

אֱמֶת וֶאֱמוּנָה כָּל־זֹאת, וְקַיָּם עָלֵינוּ כִּי הוּא יְיָ אֱלֹהֵינוּ וְאֵין זוּלָתוֹ, וַאֲנַחְנוּ יִשְׂרָאֵל עַמּוֹ.

There lives a God:

Our sages beheld Him when they looked up to the heavens.

הַפּוֹדֵנוּ מִיַּד מְלָכִים, מַלְכֵּנוּ הַגּוֹאֲלֵנוּ מִכַּף כָּל־הֶעָרִיצִים.
הָעֹשֶׂה גְדֹלוֹת עַד אֵין חֵקֶר, וְנִפְלָאוֹת עַד־אֵין מִסְפָּר.

There lives a God:

Our poets saw Him when they looked into the soul.

הַשָּׂם נַפְשֵׁנוּ בַּחַיִּים, וְלֹא־נָתַן לַמּוֹט רַגְלֵנוּ.
הָעֹשֶׂה לָנוּ נִסִּים בְּפַרְעֹה, אוֹתוֹת וּמוֹפְתִים בְּאַדְמַת בְּנֵי חָם.
וַיּוֹצֵא אֶת־עַמּוֹ יִשְׂרָאֵל מִתּוֹכָם לְחֵרוּת עוֹלָם.

Our people found Him in their liberation from bondage.

In the wilderness of Sinai they met Him.

וְרָאוּ בָנָיו גְּבוּרָתוֹ; שִׁבְּחוּ וְהוֹדוּ לִשְׁמוֹ.

Through long years of wandering they put their trust in Him.

Through bitter times of oppression they kept their faith in Him.

וּמַלְכוּתוֹ בְּרָצוֹן קִבְּלוּ עֲלֵיהֶם. מֹשֶׁה וּבְנֵי יִשְׂרָאֵל לְךָ עָנוּ שִׁירָה בְּשִׂמְחָה רַבָּה, וְאָמְרוּ כֻלָּם:

There lives a God:

In love He summoned us to bear witness to Him; in love He has preserved us to this day; and in love we declare:

מִי־כָמֹכָה בָּאֵלִם, יְיָ?

Who is like You, Eternal One, among the gods that are worshipped?

מִי כָּמֹכָה, נֶאְדָּר בַּקֹּדֶשׁ,

Who is like You, majestic in holiness,

נוֹרָא תְהִלֹּת, עֹשֵׂה פֶלֶא?

awesome in splendor, doing wonders?

מַלְכוּתְךָ רָאוּ בָנֶיךָ, בּוֹקֵעַ יָם לִפְנֵי מֹשֶׁה; "זֶה אֵלִי!" עָנוּ וְאָמְרוּ: "יְיָ יִמְלֹךְ לְעֹלָם וָעֶד!"

When your children understand the greatness of Your power, they exclaim in awe. "This is my God!" "The Eternal will reign for ever and ever!"

וְנֶאֱמַר: "כִּי־פָדָה יְיָ אֶת־יַעֲקֹב, וּגְאָלוֹ מִיַּד חָזָק מִמֶּנּוּ." בָּרוּךְ אַתָּה, יְיָ, גָּאַל יִשְׂרָאֵל.

You are the Redeemer of Israel and all the oppressed. Blessed is the Eternal God, the God of Israel, the Source of freedom.

◆ ◆

To be read silently or sung

ETERNAL MYSTERIES — השכיבנו

הַשְׁכִּיבֵנוּ, יְיָ אֱלֹהֵינוּ, לְשָׁלוֹם, וְהַעֲמִידֵנוּ, מַלְכֵּנוּ, לְחַיִּים. וּפְרוֹשׂ עָלֵינוּ סֻכַּת שְׁלוֹמֶךָ, וְתַקְּנֵנוּ בְּעֵצָה טוֹבָה מִלְּפָנֶיךָ, וְהוֹשִׁיעֵנוּ לְמַעַן שְׁמֶךָ, וְהָגֵן בַּעֲדֵנוּ. וְהָסֵר מֵעָלֵינוּ אוֹיֵב, דֶּבֶר וְחֶרֶב וְרָעָב וְיָגוֹן; וְהָסֵר שָׂטָן מִלְּפָנֵינוּ וּמֵאַחֲרֵינוּ; וּבְצֵל כְּנָפֶיךָ תַּסְתִּירֵנוּ, כִּי אֵל שׁוֹמְרֵנוּ וּמַצִּילֵנוּ אָתָּה, כִּי אֵל מֶלֶךְ חַנּוּן וְרַחוּם אָתָּה. וּשְׁמוֹר צֵאתֵנוּ וּבוֹאֵנוּ לְחַיִּים

וּלְשָׁלוֹם, מֵעַתָּה וְעַד עוֹלָם, וּפְרוֹשׂ עָלֵינוּ סֻכַּת שְׁלוֹמֶךָ.
בָּרוּךְ אַתָּה, יְיָ, הַפּוֹרֵשׂ סֻכַּת שָׁלוֹם עָלֵינוּ, וְעַל־כָּל־עַמּוֹ
יִשְׂרָאֵל וְעַל יְרוּשָׁלָיִם.

It is evening, and children slowly dream away the storms of day. It is evening, and stars glow gently in the quiet heavens. Can we understand a dream? Find a net to capture the meaning of a glowing star? What bridge spans the vast space we must cross to reach understanding? How small are we who attempt the journey! And yet somehow we learn to find our glory in a brave and endless struggle to comprehend eternal mysteries. We are voyagers in an infinite sea, our destination always beyond the horizon. But we are voyagers.

◆ ◆

THE COVENANT THAT BRINGS LIFE

On the day when our ancestors stood before God in the wilderness, His words came before them and captured their hearts:

"You are standing this day, all of you, before God the Eternal, to enter into His covenant."

It was a covenant of life for them and their descendants. "See, I have set before you this day life and good, death and evil. This day I command you to love the Lord your God, to walk in His ways, to keep His Mitzvot."

It is in God's power to command us, in ours to reject Him.

"But if you do not listen, I tell you this day that you will surely perish. Therefore have I set before you life and death, the blessing and the curse: choose life, then, that you and your children may live."

We will choose life. We will hold fast to the covenant that brings life.

◆

THE COVENANT OF SHABBAT — ושמרו

וְשָׁמְרוּ בְנֵי־יִשְׂרָאֵל אֶת־הַשַּׁבָּת, לַעֲשׂוֹת אֶת־הַשַּׁבָּת לְדֹרֹתָם
בְּרִית עוֹלָם. בֵּינִי וּבֵין בְּנֵי יִשְׂרָאֵל אוֹת הִיא לְעֹלָם, כִּי שֵׁשֶׁת
יָמִים עָשָׂה יְיָ אֶת־הַשָּׁמַיִם וְאֶת־הָאָרֶץ, וּבַיּוֹם הַשְּׁבִיעִי שָׁבַת
וַיִּנָּפַשׁ.

The people of Israel shall keep the Sabbath, observing the Sabbath in every generation as a covenant for all time. It is a sign for ever between Me and the people of Israel, for in six days the Eternal God made heaven and earth, and on the seventh day He rested from His labors.

◆ ◆

An alternative Tefillah begins on page 235.

All rise

תפלה

אֲדֹנָי, שְׂפָתַי תִּפְתָּח, וּפִי יַגִּיד תְּהִלָּתֶךָ.

Eternal God, open my lips, that my mouth may declare Your glory.

A HERITAGE OF FAITH — אבות

בָּרוּךְ אַתָּה, יְיָ אֱלֹהֵינוּ וֵאלֹהֵי אֲבוֹתֵינוּ, אֱלֹהֵי אַבְרָהָם, אֱלֹהֵי
יִצְחָק, וֵאלֹהֵי יַעֲקֹב: הָאֵל הַגָּדוֹל, הַגִּבּוֹר וְהַנּוֹרָא, אֵל עֶלְיוֹן.
גּוֹמֵל חֲסָדִים טוֹבִים, וְקוֹנֵה הַכֹּל, וְזוֹכֵר חַסְדֵי אָבוֹת, וּמֵבִיא
גְאֻלָּה לִבְנֵי בְנֵיהֶם, לְמַעַן שְׁמוֹ, בְּאַהֲבָה.
מֶלֶךְ עוֹזֵר וּמוֹשִׁיעַ וּמָגֵן. בָּרוּךְ אַתָּה, יְיָ, מָגֵן אַבְרָהָם.

Our God and God of our fathers, God of Abraham, Isaac, and Jacob, Amos, Isaiah, and Micah, a heritage has come down to us along all the painful paths our people has travelled.

Our God and God of our mothers, God of Sarah, Rebekah, Leah, and Rachel, Deborah, Hannah, and Ruth, a heritage has come down to us.

When others worshipped gods indifferent to goodness, our mothers and fathers found the One whose law unites all people in justice and love.

A heritage of faith has come down to us out of the life of our people.

When knowledge was the secret lore of princes and priests, our sages opened their doors to all who sought understanding.

A heritage of learning has come down to us out of the life of our people.

◆ ◆

IT IS OUR LIFE גבורות

אַתָּה גִּבּוֹר לְעוֹלָם, אֲדֹנָי, מְחַיֵּה הַכֹּל אַתָּה, רַב לְהוֹשִׁיעַ.
מְכַלְכֵּל חַיִּים בְּחֶסֶד, מְחַיֵּה הַכֹּל בְּרַחֲמִים רַבִּים. סוֹמֵךְ
נוֹפְלִים, וְרוֹפֵא חוֹלִים, וּמַתִּיר אֲסוּרִים, וּמְקַיֵּם אֱמוּנָתוֹ
לִישֵׁנֵי עָפָר.
מִי כָמוֹךָ, בַּעַל גְּבוּרוֹת, וּמִי דּוֹמֶה לָּךְ, מֶלֶךְ מֵמִית וּמְחַיֶּה
וּמַצְמִיחַ יְשׁוּעָה?
וְנֶאֱמָן אַתָּה לְהַחֲיוֹת הַכֹּל. בָּרוּךְ אַתָּה, יְיָ, מְחַיֵּה הַכֹּל.

In a world where the weak were tormented by oppressors, our Torah taught us to love the poor and the stranger.

A heritage of justice has come down to us.

Where the sword was sovereign, we were commanded to seek peace and pursue it.

A heritage of peace has come down to us.

All this now is ours. Ours the teaching, ours the task, to make the heritage live.

For it is our life, and the length of our days!

◆ ◆

קדושת השם

אַתָּה קָדוֹשׁ וְשִׁמְךָ קָדוֹשׁ, וּקְדוֹשִׁים בְּכָל־יוֹם יְהַלְלוּךָ סֶּלָה. בָּרוּךְ אַתָּה, יְיָ, הָאֵל הַקָּדוֹשׁ.

All are seated

◆ ◆

TO SERVE YOU IN TRUTH

קדושת היום

Purify our hearts to serve You in truth.

וְטַהֵר לִבֵּנוּ לְעָבְדְּךָ בֶּאֱמֶת.

or

The world is sustained by three things: by the Torah, by worship, and by loving deeds.

עַל־שְׁלֹשָׁה דְבָרִים הָעוֹלָם עוֹמֵד: עַל הַתּוֹרָה וְעַל הָעֲבוֹדָה וְעַל גְּמִילוּת חֲסָדִים.

◆

PROMISE OF THE KINGDOM

אֱלֹהֵינוּ וֵאלֹהֵי אֲבוֹתֵינוּ, רְצֵה בִמְנוּחָתֵנוּ. קַדְּשֵׁנוּ בְּמִצְוֹתֶיךָ וְתֵן חֶלְקֵנוּ בְּתוֹרָתֶךָ. שַׂבְּעֵנוּ מִטּוּבֶךָ, וְשַׂמְּחֵנוּ בִּישׁוּעָתֶךָ, וְטַהֵר לִבֵּנוּ לְעָבְדְּךָ בֶּאֱמֶת. וְהַנְחִילֵנוּ, יְיָ אֱלֹהֵינוּ, בְּאַהֲבָה וּבְרָצוֹן שַׁבַּת קָדְשֶׁךָ, וְיָנוּחוּ בָהּ יִשְׂרָאֵל מְקַדְּשֵׁי שְׁמֶךָ. בָּרוּךְ אַתָּה, יְיָ, מְקַדֵּשׁ הַשַּׁבָּת.

Great is the gift of life; greater still that we *know* that our life is a gift. Slowly, uncertainly, we have emerged out of the endless, patient work of creation. Great is the gift of life!

And our people came forth: not slowly, but by a leap of the spirit: Israel. Holy is the meeting of a people and its God.

Therefore let Israel give thanks for life and sing the Creator's praise. And let us exult in Shabbat, symbol of creation's joy, reminder and promise of the kingdom we shall slowly build.

◆

MOST PRECIOUS OF DAYS

יִשְׂמְחוּ בְמַלְכוּתְךָ שׁוֹמְרֵי שַׁבָּת וְקוֹרְאֵי עֹנֶג. עַם מְקַדְּשֵׁי שְׁבִיעִי כֻּלָּם יִשְׂבְּעוּ וְיִתְעַנְּגוּ מִטּוּבֶךָ. וְהַשְּׁבִיעִי רָצִיתָ בּוֹ וְקִדַּשְׁתּוֹ. חֶמְדַּת יָמִים אוֹתוֹ קָרָאתָ, זֵכֶר לְמַעֲשֵׂה בְרֵאשִׁית.

Those who keep the Sabbath and call it a delight shall rejoice in Your kingdom. All who hallow the seventh day shall be gladdened by Your goodness. This day is Israel's festival of the spirit, sanctified and blessed by You, the most precious of days, a symbol of the joy of creation.

◆ ◆

BECAUSE I LOVE

עבודה

רְצֵה, יְיָ אֱלֹהֵינוּ, בְּעַמְּךָ יִשְׂרָאֵל, וּתְפִלָּתָם בְּאַהֲבָה תְקַבֵּל, וּתְהִי לְרָצוֹן תָּמִיד עֲבוֹדַת יִשְׂרָאֵל עַמֶּךָ. אֵל קָרוֹב לְכָל-קֹרְאָיו, פְּנֵה אֶל עֲבָדֶיךָ וְחָנֵּנוּ; שְׁפוֹךְ רוּחֲךָ עָלֵינוּ, וְתֶחֱזֶינָה עֵינֵינוּ בְּשׁוּבְךָ לְצִיּוֹן בְּרַחֲמִים.

בָּרוּךְ אַתָּה, יְיָ, הַמַּחֲזִיר שְׁכִינָתוֹ לְצִיּוֹן.

Let me hear You, Lord, when I hear my spirit soaring in prayer. May I sing because I love, not afraid to waste my sweetness upon the void, but reflecting in my soul's flight the universal God who sings through me.

◆ ◆

TO USE OUR LIFE FOR BLESSING

הודאה

מוֹדִים אֲנַחְנוּ לָךְ, שָׁאַתָּה הוּא יְיָ אֱלֹהֵינוּ וֵאלֹהֵי אֲבוֹתֵינוּ, אֱלֹהֵי כָל-בָּשָׂר, יוֹצְרֵנוּ יוֹצֵר בְּרֵאשִׁית.
בְּרָכוֹת וְהוֹדָאוֹת לְשִׁמְךָ הַגָּדוֹל וְהַקָּדוֹשׁ עַל-שֶׁהֶחֱיִיתָנוּ וְקִיַּמְתָּנוּ.

O God of Israel's past, O God of this day, God of all flesh, Creator of all life: We praise You, the Most High, for the gift of life; we give thanks, O Source of good, that life endures.

כֵּן תְּחַיֵּנוּ וּתְקַיְּמֵנוּ, יְיָ אֱלֹהֵינוּ, וּתְאַמְּצֵנוּ לִשְׁמֹר חֻקֶּיךָ, לַעֲשׂוֹת רְצוֹנֶךָ, וּלְעָבְדְךָ בְּלֵבָב שָׁלֵם. בָּרוּךְ אֵל הַהוֹדָאוֹת.

Eternal and Infinite One, help us to use our life for blessing: to live by Your law, to do Your will, to walk in Your way with a whole heart.
We thank You, Eternal God, for the blessing of life.

◆ ◆

LET US NOT BE CONTENT

God of all generations, may the rest and quiet of this hour of worship refresh our inner life, and bring us tranquillity. May we find contentment and peace, our desire for possessions abated, our hope for advantage subdued.

But let us not be content, O God, when others go hungry, or be serene while some lack their daily bread. Teach us to give thanks for what we have by sharing it with those who are in need. Then shall our lives be called good, and our names be remembered for blessing.

◆ ◆

NOT BY MIGHT NOR BY POWER

ברכת שלום

שָׁלוֹם רָב עַל־יִשְׂרָאֵל עַמְּךָ תָּשִׂים לְעוֹלָם, כִּי אַתָּה הוּא מֶלֶךְ אָדוֹן לְכָל הַשָּׁלוֹם. וְטוֹב בְּעֵינֶיךָ לְבָרֵךְ אֶת־עַמְּךָ יִשְׂרָאֵל בְּכָל־עֵת וּבְכָל־שָׁעָה בִּשְׁלוֹמֶךָ.

בָּרוּךְ אַתָּה, יְיָ, הַמְבָרֵךְ אֶת־עַמּוֹ יִשְׂרָאֵל בַּשָּׁלוֹם.

O Lord, may we never become complacent, faltering in our effort to build a world of peace for Your children. Let the nations know and understand that justice and right are better than conquest and dominion; may they come to see that it is not by might nor by power, but by Your spirit, that life prevails.

◆ ◆

SILENT PRAYER

אֱלֹהַי, נְצוֹר לְשׁוֹנִי מֵרָע וּשְׂפָתַי מִדַּבֵּר מִרְמָה. הוֹדִיעֵנִי דֶּרֶךְ־זוּ אֵלֵךְ, כִּי־אֵלֶיךָ נָשָׂאתִי נַפְשִׁי. לֵב טָהוֹר בְּרָא־לִי, אֱלֹהִים, וְרוּחַ נָכוֹן חַדֵּשׁ בְּקִרְבִּי. שְׁגִיאוֹת מִי־יָבִין? מִנִּסְתָּרוֹת נַקֵּנִי! הַדְרִיכֵנִי בַּאֲמִתֶּךָ, וְלַמְּדֵנִי, כִּי־אַתָּה אֱלֹהֵי יִשְׁעִי, אוֹתְךָ קִוִּיתִי כָּל־הַיּוֹם. פְּתַח לִבִּי בְּתוֹרָתֶךָ, וּבְמִצְוֹתֶיךָ תִּרְדּוֹף נַפְשִׁי.

O God, keep my tongue from evil, and my lips from deceitful speech. Let me know the way I should go, for to You do I lift up my soul. Create in me a clean heart, O God, and renew a steadfast spirit within me. But who can see all his own failings? Rid me of faults that are hidden! Lead me in Your truth, and teach me. You are God my Helper, and for You do I wait all the day. Open my heart to Your teaching, and I will make haste to do Your commandments.

◆ ◆

יִהְיוּ לְרָצוֹן אִמְרֵי־פִי וְהֶגְיוֹן לִבִּי לְפָנֶיךָ, יְיָ, צוּרִי וְגוֹאֲלִי.

May the words of my mouth, and the meditations of my heart, be acceptable to You, O Lord, my Rock and my Redeemer.

or

עֹשֶׂה שָׁלוֹם בִּמְרוֹמָיו, הוּא יַעֲשֶׂה שָׁלוֹם עָלֵינוּ וְעַל כָּל־יִשְׂרָאֵל, וְאִמְרוּ אָמֵן.

May He who causes peace to reign in the high heavens let peace descend on us, on all Israel, and all the world.

◆ ◆

Prayers for Special Occasions begin on page 389.

The Rituals for the Reading of Torah begin on page 415.

Concluding Prayers begin on page 613.

Alternative Tefillah

Rabbi Levi said, quoting Rabbi Chanina: It is written: "Let all that breathes praise the Lord." This means: we must praise our Maker for every breath we take.

✦ ✦

Let us rejoice in the light of day, in the glory and warmth of the sun, in the reawakening of life to duty and labor.

We rejoice in the light of day.

In the quiet night, with its rest from toil and its revelation of worlds beyond the dark.

We rejoice in the peace of night.

In the earth with its hills and valleys, its widespread fields of grain, its fruit and hidden treasures.

We rejoice in the beauty of earth.

We rejoice in the strength to win our daily bread, and in homes where we find refuge from the cold and storm.

We rejoice in the shelter of home.

In the love of fathers and mothers who have nurtured our lives, with whose blessing we have gone forth to our own work in the world.

We rejoice in the love of parents.

In the children who bless our homes, whose eager minds and hearts are the promise of tomorrow.

We rejoice in our children.

In friends who share our sorrows and joys, in the fullness of the abundant life, in the serenity of old age, and in the peace that comes at last.

We rejoice, and will rejoice for evermore.

✦ ✦

All rise

אֲדֹנָי, שְׂפָתַי תִּפְתָּח, וּפִי יַגִּיד תְּהִלָּתֶךָ.

Eternal God, open my lips, that my mouth may declare Your glory.

THE VOICE WE HEAR אבות

בָּרוּךְ אַתָּה, יְיָ אֱלֹהֵינוּ וֵאלֹהֵי אֲבוֹתֵינוּ, אֱלֹהֵי אַבְרָהָם, אֱלֹהֵי יִצְחָק, וֵאלֹהֵי יַעֲקֹב: הָאֵל הַגָּדוֹל, הַגִּבּוֹר וְהַנּוֹרָא, אֵל עֶלְיוֹן.

God of the past and future, God of this day, God of Israel and all the world:

גּוֹמֵל חֲסָדִים טוֹבִים, וְקוֹנֵה הַכֹּל, וְזוֹכֵר חַסְדֵי אָבוֹת, וּמֵבִיא גְאֻלָּה לִבְנֵי בְנֵיהֶם, לְמַעַן שְׁמוֹ, בְּאַהֲבָה.

We know Him, yet cannot name Him. With our halting human words we say 'God.' God of Abraham, God of Isaac, God of Jacob. God of freedom and justice and mercy. God of understanding.

מֶלֶךְ עוֹזֵר וּמוֹשִׁיעַ וּמָגֵן. בָּרוּךְ אַתָּה, יְיָ, מָגֵן אַבְרָהָם.

He is the Rule by which we measure ourselves; He is the Voice we hear within us.

◆ ◆

FROM WELLSPRINGS WITHIN גבורות

אַתָּה גִּבּוֹר לְעוֹלָם, אֲדֹנָי, מְחַיֵּה הַכֹּל אַתָּה, רַב לְהוֹשִׁיעַ. מְכַלְכֵּל חַיִּים בְּחֶסֶד, מְחַיֵּה הַכֹּל בְּרַחֲמִים רַבִּים. סוֹמֵךְ נוֹפְלִים, וְרוֹפֵא חוֹלִים, וּמַתִּיר אֲסוּרִים, וּמְקַיֵּם אֱמוּנָתוֹ לִישֵׁנֵי עָפָר.

מִי כָמוֹךָ, בַּעַל גְּבוּרוֹת, וּמִי דּוֹמֶה לָּךְ, מֶלֶךְ מֵמִית וּמְחַיֶּה וּמַצְמִיחַ יְשׁוּעָה?

וְנֶאֱמָן אַתָּה לְהַחֲיוֹת הַכֹּל. בָּרוּךְ אַתָּה, יְיָ, מְחַיֵּה הַכֹּל.

When we call out in empty spaces, we hear echoes of ourselves. Are we, too, echoes of God?

Sometimes a great flow of will surges up from wellsprings within we did not know we had. Are we then echoes of God?

We do not know. We can only grasp the fact of joy, and give thanks to God, who creates through us; who has formed us, like Himself, to be creators.

◆ ◆

קדושת השם

אַתָּה קָדוֹשׁ וְשִׁמְךָ קָדוֹשׁ, וּקְדוֹשִׁים בְּכָל־יוֹם יְהַלְלְוּךָ סֶּלָה.
בָּרוּךְ אַתָּה, יְיָ, הָאֵל הַקָּדוֹשׁ.

THE DREAMS OF PRAYER

The dreams of prayer are made real by those who pray.

The ways of God are deep as love.

And the strength of God is mighty as time, which flows and flows, and has no end.

Part of all, yet separate, is the Eternal God. Separate and apart is God.

He is holy, His name is holy. And this Sabbath day is holy, for it is set apart from other days:

To remember Him, to return to Him, to bring Him back with us into the week.

We praise God as we hallow the seventh day.

All are seated

◆ ◆

MOST PRECIOUS OF DAYS

קדושת היום

Those who keep the Sabbath and call it a delight shall rejoice in Your kingdom. All who hallow the seventh day shall be gladdened by Your goodness. This day is Israel's festival of the spirit, sanctified and blessed by You, the most precious of days, a symbol of the joy of creation.

יִשְׂמְחוּ בְמַלְכוּתְךָ שׁוֹמְרֵי שַׁבָּת וְקוֹרְאֵי עֹנֶג. עַם מְקַדְּשֵׁי שְׁבִיעִי כֻּלָּם יִשְׂבְּעוּ וְיִתְעַנְּגוּ מִטּוּבֶךָ. וְהַשְּׁבִיעִי רָצִיתָ בּוֹ וְקִדַּשְׁתּוֹ. חֶמְדַּת יָמִים אוֹתוֹ קָרָאתָ, זֵכֶר לְמַעֲשֵׂה בְרֵאשִׁית.

◆

LITTLE LESS THAN DIVINE

As the seventh day is set apart from other days, so are we set apart from other creatures, to walk with God. As it has been written:

From Psalm 8

When I consider Your heavens,
the work of Your fingers;
the moon and the stars
that You have established:

כִּי־אֶרְאֶה שָׁמֶיךָ,
מַעֲשֵׂה אֶצְבְּעֹתֶיךָ,
יָרֵחַ וְכוֹכָבִים אֲשֶׁר כּוֹנָנְתָּה:

What are we, that You are mindful of us?
What are we mortals, that You care for us?

מָה־אֱנוֹשׁ כִּי־תִזְכְּרֶנּוּ,
וּבֶן־אָדָם כִּי תִפְקְדֶנּוּ?

Yet You have made us
little less than divine,
and crowned us with glory and honor!

וַתְּחַסְּרֵהוּ מְּעַט מֵאֱלֹהִים,
וְכָבוֹד וְהָדָר תְּעַטְּרֵהוּ!

◆ ◆

MEDITATION

TOWERS OF HOPE

The stars of heaven, awesome in their majesty, are not more wonderful than the one who charts their courses.

The elements, arrayed in perfection, are not marvels greater than the mind that beholds them.

This miracle, matter, begets a wonder: the body thinks, insight comes from flesh; the soul is born of dust to build towers of hope, opening within us doors of lamentation and love.

For You have made us little less than divine, and crowned us with glory and honor!

◆ ◆

YOU ARE THERE

Glory and honor within us: but every age has despised its endowment. And yet, O God, we look with hope beyond the near horizon. Beneath this trampled earth, a seed of goodness will grow, we trust, to be our tree of life. Within and beyond us, O God of life, You are there. You dwell wherever we let You in. When we flee from You, we flee from ourselves. When we seek You, we discover that we are not alone.

◆ ◆

From Psalm 139

Whither can I go from Your spirit?
Whither can I flee from Your presence?
If I ascend to the heavens,
You are there!
If I make my home in the lowest depths,
behold, You are there!
If I take up the wings of the morning,
and dwell on the ocean's farthest shore,
even there Your hand will lead me,
Your right hand will hold me.

אָנָה אֵלֵךְ מֵרוּחֶךָ,
וְאָנָה מִפָּנֶיךָ אֶבְרָח?
אִם־אֶסַּק שָׁמַיִם, שָׁם אָתָּה!
וְאַצִּיעָה שְׁאוֹל, הִנֶּךָּ!
אֶשָּׂא כַנְפֵי־שָׁחַר,
אֶשְׁכְּנָה בְּאַחֲרִית יָם,
גַּם־שָׁם יָדְךָ תַנְחֵנִי,
וְתֹאחֲזֵנִי יְמִינֶךָ.

◆ ◆

MEDITATION

THE GODS WE WORSHIP

Through prayer we struggle to experience the Presence of God. Let us be sure that the One we invoke is the Most High, not a god of battles, of state or status or 'success' — but the Source of peace and mercy and goodness. For, truly: "The gods we worship write their names on our faces, be sure of that. And we will worship something—have no doubt of that either. We may think that our tribute is paid in secret in the dark recesses of the heart — but it will out. That which dominates our imagination and our thoughts will determine our life and character. Therefore it behooves us to be careful what we are worshipping, for what we are worshipping we are becoming."

◆ ◆

LAND OF HOPE AND PROMISE

Eternal God, like all the generations of Israel, we turn to You in hope. We need You as we need air to breathe. Be enthroned in our hearts; let Your law of justice rule the world. O may all Your children be filled with a love of freedom and truth, that tyranny may vanish and the reign of righteousness be established everywhere on earth. Then will the suffering end of all who live in lands of darkness and persecution.

Your spirit pervades the world. Your love encompasses the earth. We pray for the peace of all lands and peoples. And we pray for our brothers and sisters in the land of Israel. In our pilgrimage among the nations, our people have always turned in love to the land where Israel was born, where our prophets taught their imperishable message of justice and peace, and where our poets sang their deathless songs of love for You and of Your love for us and all humanity.

Throughout the ages we have prayed that Zion might be restored: it has been for us the land of hope and promise. May the promise now come true in all its fullness; may we be privileged to bring a new light to shine upon Zion. And may we who live in lands of freedom be imbued with the knowledge that all Jews, wherever they live, are one people, responsible before You to one another. Willingly and joyfully may we share in the work of redemption, that the time may come again when the Law will go forth from the house of Israel, and Your word from the tents of Jacob.

◆ ◆

THESE SHALL YOU DO

אֵלֶּה הַדְּבָרִים אֲשֶׁר תַּעֲשׂוּ: דַּבְּרוּ אֱמֶת אִישׁ אֶת־רֵעֵהוּ, אֱמֶת וּמִשְׁפַּט שָׁלוֹם שִׁפְטוּ בְּשַׁעֲרֵיכֶם, וְאִישׁ אֶת־רָעַת רֵעֵהוּ אַל־תַּחְשְׁבוּ בִּלְבַבְכֶם, וּשְׁבֻעַת שֶׁקֶר אַל־תֶּאֱהָבוּ.

חִדְלוּ הָרֵעַ; לִמְדוּ הֵיטֵב; דִּרְשׁוּ מִשְׁפָּט; אַשְּׁרוּ חָמוֹץ; שִׁפְטוּ יָתוֹם; רִיבוּ אַלְמָנָה.

It is written: These shall you do: speak the truth to one another; render judgments that are true and make for peace; plan no evil against your neighbor; and approve no false oath.

Cease to do evil, learn to do good; seek justice, correct oppression; defend the orphan, plead for the widow.

לֹא־תָלִין פְּעֻלַּת שָׂכִיר אִתְּךָ עַד־בֹּקֶר.

לֹא תְאַמֵּץ אֶת־לְבָבְךָ וְלֹא תִקְפֹּץ אֶת־יָדְךָ מֵאָחִיךָ הָאֶבְיוֹן.

You shall not withhold a laborer's wage beyond the time when it is due.

You shall not harden your heart nor shut your hand against the poor, your kin; you must open your hand to them.

וְגֵר לֹא תִלְחָץ, וְאַתֶּם יְדַעְתֶּם אֶת־נֶפֶשׁ הַגֵּר, כִּי־גֵרִים הֱיִיתֶם בְּאֶרֶץ מִצְרָיִם.

כְּאֶזְרָח מִכֶּם יִהְיֶה לָכֶם הַגֵּר הַגָּר אִתְּכֶם, וְאָהַבְתָּ לוֹ כָּמוֹךָ.

You shall not oppress a stranger, for you know the heart of a stranger, you who were yourselves strangers in Egypt.

The strangers who live among you shall be to you as the native-born, and you shall love them as yourself.

צֶדֶק, צֶדֶק תִּרְדֹּף, לְמַעַן תִּחְיֶה.

וְאָהַבְתָּ לְרֵעֲךָ כָּמוֹךָ, אֲנִי יְיָ.

Justice, justice shall you pursue, that you may live.

You shall love your neighbor as yourself; I am the Lord.

וְהָיָה אַחֲרֵי־כֵן, אֶשְׁפּוֹךְ אֶת־רוּחִי עַל־כָּל־בָּשָׂר; וְנִבְּאוּ בְּנֵיכֶם וּבְנֹתֵיכֶם; זִקְנֵיכֶם חֲלֹמוֹת יַחֲלֹמוּן, בַּחוּרֵיכֶם חֶזְיֹנוֹת יִרְאוּ.

And then it shall come to pass, that a divine spirit will be poured out on all flesh; your sons and daughters shall prophesy; the old shall dream dreams, the young shall see visions: our descendants shall build God's kingdom!

◆ ◆

MEDITATION

When we become aware of Your presence, O God, and when we consider what You mean to us, we discover our life's truth in the knowledge that we can worship You in holiness only as we serve each other in love.

How much we owe to the labors of others! Day by day they endure pain and peril for our sake; time and again brave the terrors of the unknown for truths that shed light on our way. Numberless gifts and blessings have been laid in our cradles as our birthright.

May we then be just and great-hearted in our dealings with one another, sharing the fruits of our common labor, acknowledging that we are but stewards of whatever we possess. Help us, O Eternal One, to be among those who are willing to sacrifice that others may not hunger, who dare to be bearers of light in the dark loneliness of stricken lives, who struggle and even bleed for the triumph of righteousness in the world. So shall we be Your partners in the building of Your kingdom, for that has been our vision and goal through the ages.

◆ ◆

יִהְיוּ לְרָצוֹן אִמְרֵי־פִי וְהֶגְיוֹן לִבִּי לְפָנֶיךָ, יְיָ, צוּרִי וְגוֹאֲלִי.

May the words of my mouth, and the meditations of my heart, be acceptable to You, O Lord, my Rock and my Redeemer.

or

עֹשֶׂה שָׁלוֹם בִּמְרוֹמָיו, הוּא יַעֲשֶׂה שָׁלוֹם עָלֵינוּ וְעַל כָּל־יִשְׂרָאֵל, וְאִמְרוּ אָמֵן.

May He who causes peace to reign in the high heavens let peace descend on us, on all Israel, and all the world.

◆ ◆

Prayers for Special Occasions begin on page 389.

The Rituals for the Reading of Torah begin on page 415.

Concluding Prayers begin on page 613.

ח VIII ח

For congregations where the lights are kindled in the synagogue

הדלקת הנרות

Out of the glaring darkness of life's chaos,
we must struggle for the words
that will bring light,

that nobler life may be.

◆ ◆

בָּרוּךְ אַתָּה, יְיָ אֱלֹהֵינוּ, מֶלֶךְ הָעוֹלָם,
אֲשֶׁר קִדְּשָׁנוּ בְּמִצְוֹתָיו וְצִוָּנוּ לְהַדְלִיק נֵר שֶׁל שַׁבָּת.

Blessed is the Lord our God,
who leads us to holiness through Mitzvot,
who lets us share in the miracle
of our people's life

through light.

◆ ◆

Welcoming Shabbat קַבָּלַת שַׁבָּת

Our noisy day has now descended with the sun beyond our sight.

In the silence of our praying place we close the door upon the hectic joys and fears, the accomplishments and anguish of the week we have left behind.

What was but moments ago the substance of our life has become memory; what we did must now be woven into what we are.

On this day we shall not do, but be.

We are to walk the path of our humanity, no longer ride unseeing through a world we do not touch and only vaguely sense.

No longer can we tear the world apart to make our fire.

On this day heat and warmth and light must come from deep within ourselves.

◆ ◆

This is Israel's day of light and joy, a Sabbath of rest.	יוֹם זֶה לְיִשְׂרָאֵל אוֹרָה וְשִׂמְחָה, שַׁבַּת מְנוּחָה.
When the work of creating the world was done, You chose this day to be holy and blessed, that the heavy-laden might find safety and stillness, a Sabbath of rest.	קִדַּשְׁתָּ בֵּרַכְתָּ אוֹתוֹ מִכָּל־יָמִים, בְּשֵׁשֶׁת כִּלִּיתָ מְלֶאכֶת עוֹלָמִים, בּוֹ מָצְאוּ עֲגוּמִים הַשְׁקֵט וּבִטְחָה, שַׁבַּת מְנוּחָה.
This is Israel's day of light and joy, a Sabbath of rest.	יוֹם זֶה לְיִשְׂרָאֵל אוֹרָה וְשִׂמְחָה, שַׁבַּת מְנוּחָה.

◆ ◆

MEDITATION

For our ancestors, Shabbat was a sign of God's covenant of peace with the universe. They kept it faithfully; when their lives were torn, Shabbat made them whole; when their lives were bitter, it brought them sweetness; when their lives were peaceful, it deepened their joy.

Our ways are not like theirs. We have many idle days, but few Sabbaths; we speak many words, but few prayers; we make the earth yield to our purpose, but are unsure of the ground beneath us. But here, now, we can begin again. Or, having already begun, we can continue our quest for the wholeness we need.

◆ ◆

May the sense of God's presence be with us along our way, helping us to discover the peace and rest some have lost or never known, renewing our covenant of peace with all created things.

And may we become more than we have been, more than we are: reaching for a perfection beyond our grasp, growing and learning one day to make this day's peace a peace for all days, learning one day to do justly, and love mercy, and walk alongside the One who walks with us.

◆ ◆

לְכָה דוֹדִי לִקְרַאת כַּלָּה, פְּנֵי שַׁבָּת נְקַבְּלָה.
לְכָה דוֹדִי לִקְרַאת כַּלָּה, פְּנֵי שַׁבָּת נְקַבְּלָה.

Beloved, come to meet the bride;
beloved, come to greet Shabbat.

"שָׁמוֹר" וְ"זָכוֹר", בְּדִבּוּר אֶחָד, הִשְׁמִיעָנוּ אֵל הַמְיֻחָד.
יְיָ אֶחָד וּשְׁמוֹ אֶחָד, לְשֵׁם וּלְתִפְאֶרֶת וְלִתְהִלָּה.
לְכָה . . .

"Keep" and "Remember": a single command the Only God caused us to hear; the Eternal is One, His name is One; His are honor and glory and praise.

Beloved . . .

לִקְרַאת שַׁבָּת לְכוּ וְנֵלְכָה, כִּי הִיא מְקוֹר הַבְּרָכָה.
מֵרֹאשׁ מִקֶּדֶם נְסוּכָה, סוֹף מַעֲשֶׂה, בְּמַחֲשָׁבָה תְּחִלָּה.
לְכָה . . .

Come with me to meet Shabbat, for ever a fountain of blessing. Still it flows, as from the start: the last of days, for which the first was made.
Beloved . . .

הִתְעוֹרְרִי, הִתְעוֹרְרִי, כִּי בָא אוֹרֵךְ! קוּמִי, אוֹרִי,
עוּרִי עוּרִי, שִׁיר דַּבֵּרִי; כְּבוֹד יְיָ עָלַיִךְ נִגְלָה.
לְכָה . . .

Awake, awake, your light has come! Arise, shine, awake and sing: the Eternal's glory dawns upon you.
Beloved . . .

בּוֹאִי בְשָׁלוֹם, עֲטֶרֶת בַּעְלָהּ, גַּם בְּשִׂמְחָה וּבְצָהֳלָה,
תּוֹךְ אֱמוּנֵי עַם סְגֻלָּה. בּוֹאִי כַלָּה! בּוֹאִי כַלָּה!
לְכָה . . .

Enter in peace, O crown of your husband; enter in gladness, enter in joy. Come to the people that keeps its faith. Enter, O bride! Enter, O bride!
Beloved . . .

◆ ◆

If our prayer were music only, we could surely sing our way into the world we want, into the heaven we desire. Each would put his own words to the melody; from every song would pour a hundred different prayers.

But our past has taught us words, and though we pray the music, we cannot always pray the words.

The words do not always speak for us, nor can we always understand them.

Yet once we understood: to speak the ancient words returns us to that simpler time when as children we felt the world was one, and it was ours.

That understanding is now but a fragile hope. And yet, to speak those ancient words is to say that understanding may return. To speak those words is to give substance to that hope, which has remained alive though we and all our world have changed.

Since that childhood time, many truths and questions have made their home within our minds, but the truth we affirm tonight is the oldest we remember.

The old words lead us all to blessing: for our lives that have emerged from the lights and shadows of the world; for the God who for ever calls forth being from nothingness.

READER'S KADDISH — חצי קדיש

יִתְגַּדַּל וְיִתְקַדַּשׁ שְׁמֵהּ רַבָּא בְּעָלְמָא דִּי־בְרָא כִרְעוּתֵהּ, וְיַמְלִיךְ מַלְכוּתֵהּ בְּחַיֵּיכוֹן וּבְיוֹמֵיכוֹן וּבְחַיֵּי דְכָל־בֵּית יִשְׂרָאֵל, בַּעֲגָלָא וּבִזְמַן קָרִיב, וְאִמְרוּ: אָמֵן.

יְהֵא שְׁמֵהּ רַבָּא מְבָרַךְ לְעָלַם וּלְעָלְמֵי עָלְמַיָּא.

יִתְבָּרַךְ וְיִשְׁתַּבַּח, וְיִתְפָּאַר וְיִתְרוֹמַם וְיִתְנַשֵּׂא, וְיִתְהַדַּר וְיִתְעַלֶּה וְיִתְהַלַּל שְׁמֵהּ דְּקוּדְשָׁא, בְּרִיךְ הוּא, לְעֵלָּא מִן כָּל־בִּרְכָתָא וְשִׁירָתָא, תֻּשְׁבְּחָתָא וְנֶחֱמָתָא דַּאֲמִירָן בְּעָלְמָא, וְאִמְרוּ: אָמֵן.

Let the glory of God be extolled, let His great name be hallowed in the world whose creation He willed. May His kingdom soon prevail, in our own day, our own lives, and the life of all Israel, and let us say: Amen.

Let His great name be blessed for ever and ever.

Let the name of the Holy One, blessed is He, be glorified, exalted and honored, though He is beyond all the praises, songs, and adorations that we can utter, and let us say: Amen.

◆ ◆

All rise

שמע וברכותיה

בָּרְכוּ אֶת־יְיָ הַמְבֹרָךְ!

Praise the Lord, to whom our praise is due!

בָּרוּךְ יְיָ הַמְבֹרָךְ לְעוֹלָם וָעֶד!

Praised be the Lord, to whom our praise is due,
now and for ever!

◆ ◆

THAT CLEAR WAY

מעריב ערבים

בָּרוּךְ אַתָּה, יְיָ אֱלֹהֵינוּ, מֶלֶךְ הָעוֹלָם, אֲשֶׁר בִּדְבָרוֹ מַעֲרִיב עֲרָבִים. בְּחָכְמָה פּוֹתֵחַ שְׁעָרִים, וּבִתְבוּנָה מְשַׁנֶּה עִתִּים, וּמַחֲלִיף אֶת־הַזְּמַנִּים, וּמְסַדֵּר אֶת־הַכּוֹכָבִים בְּמִשְׁמְרוֹתֵיהֶם בָּרָקִיעַ כִּרְצוֹנוֹ.

בּוֹרֵא יוֹם וָלָיְלָה, גּוֹלֵל אוֹר מִפְּנֵי חֹשֶׁךְ וְחֹשֶׁךְ מִפְּנֵי אוֹר, וּמַעֲבִיר יוֹם וּמֵבִיא לָיְלָה, וּמַבְדִּיל בֵּין יוֹם וּבֵין לָיְלָה, יְיָ צְבָאוֹת שְׁמוֹ.

אֵל חַי וְקַיָּם, תָּמִיד יִמְלוֹךְ עָלֵינוּ, לְעוֹלָם וָעֶד. בָּרוּךְ אַתָּה, יְיָ, הַמַּעֲרִיב עֲרָבִים.

Once we learned one truth, and it was cherished or discarded, but it was one.

Now we are told that the world can be perceived by many truths; now, in the reality all of us encounter, some find lessons that others deny.

Once we learned one kind of life, and one reality; it too we either adopted or scorned.

But right was always right, and wrong was always wrong.

Now we are told that there are many rights, that what is wrong may well be wrong for you, but right for me.

Yet we sense that some acts must be wrong for everyone, and that beyond the many half-truths is a single truth all of us may one day grasp.

That clear way, that single truth, is what we seek in coming here, to join our people who saw the eternal One when others saw only the temporal Now.

The call to oneness is an affirmation and a goal; to speak of God as One is to commit ourselves once more to our people's ancient quest.

אהבת עולם

אַהֲבַת עוֹלָם בֵּית יִשְׂרָאֵל עַמְּךָ אָהָבְתָּ: תּוֹרָה וּמִצְוֹת, חֻקִּים וּמִשְׁפָּטִים אוֹתָנוּ לִמַּדְתָּ.
עַל־כֵּן, יְיָ אֱלֹהֵינוּ, בְּשָׁכְבֵנוּ וּבְקוּמֵנוּ נָשִׂיחַ בְּחֻקֶּיךָ, וְנִשְׂמַח בְּדִבְרֵי תוֹרָתְךָ וּבְמִצְוֹתֶיךָ לְעוֹלָם וָעֶד.
כִּי הֵם חַיֵּינוּ וְאֹרֶךְ יָמֵינוּ, וּבָהֶם נֶהְגֶּה יוֹמָם וָלָיְלָה. וְאַהֲבָתְךָ אַל־תָּסִיר מִמֶּנּוּ לְעוֹלָמִים! בָּרוּךְ אַתָּה, יְיָ, אוֹהֵב עַמּוֹ יִשְׂרָאֵל.

◆ ◆

שְׁמַע יִשְׂרָאֵל: יְיָ אֱלֹהֵינוּ, יְיָ אֶחָד!

Hear, O Israel: the Lord is our God, the Lord is One!

בָּרוּךְ שֵׁם כְּבוֹד מַלְכוּתוֹ לְעוֹלָם וָעֶד!

Blessed is His glorious kingdom for ever and ever!

All are seated

וְאָהַבְתָּ אֵת יְיָ אֱלֹהֶיךָ בְּכָל־לְבָבְךָ וּבְכָל־נַפְשְׁךָ וּבְכָל־מְאֹדֶךָ.
וְהָיוּ הַדְּבָרִים הָאֵלֶּה, אֲשֶׁר אָנֹכִי מְצַוְּךָ הַיּוֹם, עַל־לְבָבֶךָ.

וְשִׁנַּנְתָּם לְבָנֶיךָ, וְדִבַּרְתָּ בָּם בְּשִׁבְתְּךָ בְּבֵיתֶךָ, וּבְלֶכְתְּךָ
בַדֶּרֶךְ, וּבְשָׁכְבְּךָ וּבְקוּמֶךָ.
וּקְשַׁרְתָּם לְאוֹת עַל־יָדֶךָ, וְהָיוּ לְטֹטָפֹת בֵּין עֵינֶיךָ, וּכְתַבְתָּם
עַל־מְזֻזוֹת בֵּיתֶךָ, וּבִשְׁעָרֶיךָ.
לְמַעַן תִּזְכְּרוּ וַעֲשִׂיתֶם אֶת־כָּל־מִצְוֹתָי, וִהְיִיתֶם קְדֹשִׁים
לֵאלֹהֵיכֶם. אֲנִי יְיָ אֱלֹהֵיכֶם, אֲשֶׁר הוֹצֵאתִי אֶתְכֶם מֵאֶרֶץ
מִצְרַיִם לִהְיוֹת לָכֶם לֵאלֹהִים. אֲנִי יְיָ אֱלֹהֵיכֶם.

◆

For two readers or more, or responsively

You shall love the Lord your God with all your mind, with all your strength, with all your being.

> In the eyes of the One God, *here* and *there* are the same, *they* and *I* are one. Oceans divide us; God's presence unites us.

Set these words, which I command you this day, upon your heart.

> To pray is to stake our very existence on the truth and on the supreme importance of that which we pray for.

Teach them faithfully to your children; speak of them in your home and on your way, when you lie down and when you rise up.

> The world is not the same since Auschwitz and Hiroshima. The decisions we make, the values we teach must be pondered not only in the halls of learning, but also before the inmates of extermination camps, and in the sight of the mushroom of a nuclear explosion.

Bind them as a sign upon your hand; let them be a symbol before your eyes.

> The groan deepens, the combat burns, the wailing does not abate. In a free society, all are involved in what some are doing.

Inscribe them on the doorposts of your house, and on your gates.

Some are guilty, all are responsible.

Be mindful of all My Mitzvot, and do them: so shall you consecrate yourselves to your God.

Holiness, an essential attribute of God, can become a quality of our own. The human can become holy.

◆ ◆

You shall be holy, for I the Lord your God am holy.

קְדֹשִׁים תִּהְיוּ, כִּי קָדוֹשׁ אֲנִי יְיָ אֱלֹהֵיכֶם.

◆ ◆

TO BE REDEEMED

גאולה

This is our truth: the One God calls forth being from nothingness, and makes all things one.

Blessed is the Holy One of Israel, in whose Oneness we are one.

But we are not yet one in fact: our human race is broken into fragments, and we wait to be redeemed into a lasting unity.

Blessed is the time to come, when all will at last be one.

While hatred rules the earth, redemption will not come.

Let the day be near when love will rule this world.

Until people return from their exile from each other, redemption will not come.

Let all exile be ended: our exile from one another, the exile of God's presence from our lives.

Until we restore the lawless to their true selves and rekindle in them the spark of God, redemption will not come.

Let us also search out the flaws in our own souls, and struggle to remove them.

While we care only for ourselves, redemption will not come.

Let our hearts be moved by the misery of others and dare what must be dared.

וְנֶאֱמַר: "כִּי־פָדָה יְיָ אֶת־יַעֲקֹב, וּגְאָלוֹ מִיַּד חָזָק מִמֶּנּוּ." בָּרוּךְ אַתָּה, יְיָ, גָּאַל יִשְׂרָאֵל.

Blessed is the Lord, who will fulfill the time of redemption for Israel and all the world.

◆

אֱמֶת וֶאֱמוּנָה כָּל־זֹאת, וְקַיָּם עָלֵינוּ כִּי הוּא יְיָ אֱלֹהֵינוּ וְאֵין זוּלָתוֹ, וַאֲנַחְנוּ יִשְׂרָאֵל עַמּוֹ.
הַפּוֹדֵנוּ מִיַּד מְלָכִים, מַלְכֵּנוּ הַגּוֹאֲלֵנוּ מִכַּף כָּל־הֶעָרִיצִים.
הָעֹשֶׂה גְדֹלוֹת עַד אֵין חֵקֶר, וְנִפְלָאוֹת עַד־אֵין מִסְפָּר.
הַשָּׂם נַפְשֵׁנוּ בַּחַיִּים, וְלֹא־נָתַן לַמּוֹט רַגְלֵנוּ.
הָעֹשֶׂה לָנוּ נִסִּים בְּפַרְעֹה, אוֹתוֹת וּמוֹפְתִים בְּאַדְמַת בְּנֵי חָם.
וַיּוֹצֵא אֶת־עַמּוֹ יִשְׂרָאֵל מִתּוֹכָם לְחֵרוּת עוֹלָם.
וְרָאוּ בָנָיו גְּבוּרָתוֹ; שִׁבְּחוּ וְהוֹדוּ לִשְׁמוֹ.
וּמַלְכוּתוֹ בְּרָצוֹן קִבְּלוּ עֲלֵיהֶם. מֹשֶׁה וּבְנֵי יִשְׂרָאֵל לְךָ עָנוּ שִׁירָה בְּשִׂמְחָה רַבָּה, וְאָמְרוּ כֻלָּם:

מִי־כָמֹכָה בָּאֵלִים, יְיָ?
מִי כָּמֹכָה, נֶאְדָּר בַּקֹּדֶשׁ,
נוֹרָא תְהִלֹּת, עֹשֵׂה פֶלֶא?

Who is like You, Eternal One, among the gods that are worshipped?
Who is like You, majestic in holiness,
awesome in splendor, doing wonders?

מַלְכוּתְךָ רָאוּ בָנֶיךָ, בּוֹקֵעַ יָם לִפְנֵי מֹשֶׁה; "זֶה אֵלִי!" עָנוּ וְאָמְרוּ: "יְיָ יִמְלֹךְ לְעֹלָם וָעֶד!"

When Your children understand the greatness of Your power, they exclaim in awe: "This is my God!" "The Eternal will reign for ever and ever!"

◆ ◆

And the covenant with creation shall be fulfilled:

THE COVENANT OF SHABBAT — ושמרו

וְשָׁמְרוּ בְנֵי־יִשְׂרָאֵל אֶת־הַשַּׁבָּת, לַעֲשׂוֹת אֶת־הַשַּׁבָּת לְדֹרֹתָם בְּרִית עוֹלָם. בֵּינִי וּבֵין בְּנֵי יִשְׂרָאֵל אוֹת הִיא לְעֹלָם, כִּי שֵׁשֶׁת יָמִים עָשָׂה יְיָ אֶת־הַשָּׁמַיִם וְאֶת־הָאָרֶץ, וּבַיּוֹם הַשְּׁבִיעִי שָׁבַת וַיִּנָּפַשׁ.

The people of Israel shall keep the Sabbath, observing the Sabbath in every generation as a covenant for all time. It is a sign for ever between Me and the people of Israel, for in six days the Eternal God made heaven and earth, and on the seventh day He rested from His labors.

◆ ◆

For two readers or more

THAT OTHERS MAY FIND BLESSING

Our Fathers prayed, each through his own experience of God, each through his own private vision that his people came to share. And each of our Mothers had her own vision.

> Abraham, who knew the fervor of morning prayer, pleaded the cause of cities. Sarah, who knew the pain of waiting, hoped for new life.

Isaac, meditating in the afternoon, lifted his eyes to find love. Rebekah left home and kin to answer God's call, to share the hope of those who came before her.

> And Jacob, when the sun had set, offered up his night prayer as a ladder reaching into heaven. Rachel and Leah,

sisters, became rivals, then friends. They are the Mothers of this people Israel.

To all their prayers came the response: Your children shall be a blessing. Their striving has come down to us as a command: Act, that others may find blessing through your lives!

God is the Source of blessing. His presence was the Shield of our Fathers, the Help of our Mothers. His promise is our hope.

All rise

תפלה

אבות

בָּרוּךְ אַתָּה, יְיָ אֱלֹהֵינוּ וֵאלֹהֵי אֲבוֹתֵינוּ, אֱלֹהֵי אַבְרָהָם, אֱלֹהֵי
יִצְחָק, וֵאלֹהֵי יַעֲקֹב: הָאֵל הַגָּדוֹל, הַגִּבּוֹר וְהַנּוֹרָא, אֵל עֶלְיוֹן.
גּוֹמֵל חֲסָדִים טוֹבִים, וְקוֹנֵה הַכֹּל, וְזוֹכֵר חַסְדֵי אָבוֹת, וּמֵבִיא
גְאֻלָּה לִבְנֵי בְנֵיהֶם, לְמַעַן שְׁמוֹ, בְּאַהֲבָה.
מֶלֶךְ עוֹזֵר וּמוֹשִׁיעַ וּמָגֵן. בָּרוּךְ אַתָּה, יְיָ, מָגֵן אַבְרָהָם.

◆ ◆

For two readers or more, or responsively

THE POWER WHOSE GIFT IS LIFE — גבורות

אַתָּה גִּבּוֹר לְעוֹלָם, אֲדֹנָי, מְחַיֵּה מֵתִים אַתָּה, רַב לְהוֹשִׁיעַ.

We pray that we might know before whom we stand, the Power whose gift is life, who quickens those who have forgotten how to live.

מַשִּׁיב הָרוּחַ וּמוֹרִיד הַגֶּשֶׁם.

We pray for winds to disperse the choking air of sadness, for cleansing rains to make parched hopes flower, and to give all of us the strength to rise up toward the sun.

מְכַלְכֵּל חַיִּים בְּחֶסֶד, מְחַיֵּה מֵתִים בְּרַחֲמִים רַבִּים.

We pray for love to encompass us for no other reason save that we are human, for love through which we may all blossom into persons who have gained power over our own lives.

סוֹמֵךְ נוֹפְלִים וְרוֹפֵא חוֹלִים וּמַתִּיר אֲסוּרִים, וּמְקַיֵּם אֱמוּנָתוֹ לִישֵׁנֵי עָפָר.

We pray to stand upright, we fallen; to be healed, we sufferers; we pray to break the bonds that keep us from the world of beauty; we pray for opened eyes, we who are blind to our own authentic selves.

מִי כָמוֹךָ, בַּעַל גְּבוּרוֹת, וּמִי דּוֹמֶה לָּךְ, מֶלֶךְ מֵמִית וּמְחַיֶּה וּמַצְמִיחַ יְשׁוּעָה?

We pray that we may walk in the garden of a purposeful life, our own powers in touch with the power of the world.

וְנֶאֱמָן אַתָּה לְהַחֲיוֹת מֵתִים. בָּרוּךְ אַתָּה, יְיָ, מְחַיֵּה הַמֵּתִים.

Praised be the God whose gift is life, whose cleansing rains let parched men and women flower toward the sun.

◆ ◆

IN EVERY HOLY ACT — קדושת השם

אַתָּה קָדוֹשׁ וְשִׁמְךָ קָדוֹשׁ, וּקְדוֹשִׁים בְּכָל־יוֹם יְהַלְלוּךָ סֶּלָה. בָּרוּךְ אַתָּה, יְיָ, הָאֵל הַקָּדוֹשׁ.

Praised be the God whose name speaks out in every holy act, and praised be His Sabbath kingdom, the kingdom of delight:

All are seated

◆ ◆

MOST PRECIOUS OF DAYS — קדושת היום

יִשְׂמְחוּ בְמַלְכוּתְךָ שׁוֹמְרֵי שַׁבָּת וְקוֹרְאֵי עֹנֶג. עַם מְקַדְּשֵׁי שְׁבִיעִי כֻּלָּם יִשְׂבְּעוּ וְיִתְעַנְּגוּ מִטּוּבֶךָ. וְהַשְּׁבִיעִי רָצִיתָ בּוֹ וְקִדַּשְׁתּוֹ. חֶמְדַּת יָמִים אוֹתוֹ קָרָאתָ, זֵכֶר לְמַעֲשֵׂה בְרֵאשִׁית.

Those who keep the Sabbath and call it a delight shall rejoice in Your kingdom. All who hallow the seventh day shall be gladdened by Your goodness. This day is Israel's festival of the spirit, sanctified and blessed by You, the most precious of days, a symbol of the joy of creation.

◆

SILENT PRAYER

HOLINESS OF THIS DAY

אֱלֹהֵינוּ וֵאלֹהֵי אֲבוֹתֵינוּ, רְצֵה בִמְנוּחָתֵנוּ. קַדְּשֵׁנוּ בְּמִצְוֹתֶיךָ
וְתֵן חֶלְקֵנוּ בְּתוֹרָתֶךָ. שַׂבְּעֵנוּ מִטּוּבֶךָ, וְשַׂמְּחֵנוּ בִּישׁוּעָתֶךָ,
וְטַהֵר לִבֵּנוּ לְעָבְדְּךָ בֶּאֱמֶת. וְהַנְחִילֵנוּ, יְיָ אֱלֹהֵינוּ, בְּאַהֲבָה
וּבְרָצוֹן שַׁבַּת קָדְשֶׁךָ, וְיָנוּחוּ בָהּ יִשְׂרָאֵל מְקַדְּשֵׁי שְׁמֶךָ. בָּרוּךְ
אַתָּה, יְיָ, מְקַדֵּשׁ הַשַּׁבָּת.

Our God, God of all generations, may the rest we choose for this Sabbath be pleasing in Your sight. May the Mitzvot we undertake today bring us nearer to holiness. May the portion in Torah that is ours remain with us as a loved one's gift. Let us sense the joy of mastering our own lives, yet know the purity of a heart that reaches out to serve others.

Let us touch the love and holiness of this day, and from its touch find peace. God, You lead us into the holiness of Shabbat, and You are blessed.

◆ ◆

For two readers or more

SEEK PEACE AND PURSUE IT — ברכת שלום

Words there are and prayers, but justice there is not, nor yet peace.

> The prophet said: In the end of days the Lord shall judge between the nations; they shall beat their swords into plowshares and their spears into pruninghooks.

Although we must wait for judgment, we may not wait for peace to fall like rain upon us.

> The teacher said: Those who have made peace in their house, it is as though they have brought peace to all Israel, indeed, to all the world.

Peace will remain a distant vision until we do the work of peace ourselves. If peace is to be brought into the world, we must bring it first to our families and communities.

The Psalmist said: Seek peace and pursue it.

Be not content to make peace in your own household; go forth and work for peace wherever men and women are struggling in its cause.

יְיָ עֹז לְעַמּוֹ יִתֵּן, יְיָ יְבָרֵךְ אֶת־עַמּוֹ בַשָּׁלוֹם!

May God give His people strength, that they may work for peace.

עֹשֶׂה שָׁלוֹם בִּמְרוֹמָיו, הוּא יַעֲשֶׂה שָׁלוֹם עָלֵינוּ וְעַל־כָּל־יִשְׂרָאֵל, וְאִמְרוּ אָמֵן.

May God who makes peace among the stars in heaven enable us to make peace here on earth.

יִשָּׂא יְיָ פָּנָיו אֵלֶיךָ, וְיָשֵׂם לְךָ שָׁלוֹם.

May God, from whom we are so often hid, reveal the brightness of His Presence to us, and place into our outstretched, yearning hands the power of peace.

◆ ◆

MEDITATION

I need strength, humility, courage, patience.

Strength to control my passions, humility to assess my own worth, courage to rise above defeats, patience to cleanse myself of my imperfections.

And the wisdom to learn and to live by the teachings of my heritage.

Let me not be discouraged, O God, by my failings; let me take heart from all that is good and noble in my character. Keep me from falling victim to cynicism. Teach me sincerity and enthusiasm. Endow me with the courage to proclaim Your name, to serve You by helping to bring nearer the day when all humanity will be one family. O God, be my guide and inspiration!

◆ ◆

יִהְיוּ לְרָצוֹן אִמְרֵי־פִי וְהֶגְיוֹן לִבִּי לְפָנֶיךָ, יְיָ, צוּרִי וְגוֹאֲלִי.

May the words of my mouth, and the meditations of my heart, be acceptable to You, O Lord, my Rock and my Redeemer.

or

עֹשֶׂה שָׁלוֹם בִּמְרוֹמָיו, הוּא יַעֲשֶׂה שָׁלוֹם עָלֵינוּ וְעַל כָּל־יִשְׂרָאֵל, וְאִמְרוּ אָמֵן.

May He who causes peace to reign in the high heavens let peace descend on us, on all Israel, and all the world.

◆ ◆

Prayers for Special Occasions begin on page 389.

The Rituals for the Reading of Torah begin on page 415.

Concluding Prayers begin on page 613.

ט IX ט

This service is suggested for occasions when many children are present.

*

For congregations where the lights are kindled in the synagogue

הדלקת הנרות

Come, let us welcome Shabbat and give thanks for its light.

May our homes shine with the lights of Shabbat and our hearts glow with Shabbat joy this week and every week.

We welcome Shabbat and give thanks for its light.

בָּרוּךְ אַתָּה, יְיָ אֱלֹהֵינוּ, מֶלֶךְ הָעוֹלָם,
אֲשֶׁר קִדְּשָׁנוּ בְּמִצְוֹתָיו וְצִוָּנוּ לְהַדְלִיק נֵר שֶׁל שַׁבָּת.

Blessed is the Lord our God, Ruler of the universe,
who gives us Mitzvot that make us holy, and commands us to kindle the lights of Shabbat.

◆ ◆

May God bless us with Shabbat joy.
May God bless us with Shabbat peace.
May God bless us with Shabbat light. Amen.

◆ ◆

When God made the world,
He made it full of light;
the sun to shine by day,
the moon and stars by night.
He made it full of life:
lilies, oaks, and trout,
tigers and bears,
sparrows, hawks, and apes.

And God took clay
from earth's four corners
to give it the breath of life.
And He said: This is very good!

Man, woman, and child.
All are good.
Man, woman, child resemble God.

Like God, we love.
Like God, we think.
Like God, we care.

◆ ◆

Yis · me · chu ha · sha · ma · yim	יִשְׂמְחוּ הַשָּׁמַיִם
ve · ta · geil ha · a · rets.	וְתָגֵל הָאָרֶץ.
Yir · am ha · yam u · me · lo · o.	יִרְעַם הַיָּם וּמְלוֹאוֹ.

Let the heavens be glad and the earth rejoice. Let the sea roar and all that fills it.

◆ ◆

All rise

שמע וברכותיה

בָּרְכוּ אֶת־יְיָ הַמְבֹרָךְ!

Praise the Lord, to whom our praise is due!

בָּרוּךְ יְיָ הַמְבֹרָךְ לְעוֹלָם וָעֶד!

Praised be the Lord, to whom our praise is due,
now and for ever!

◆ ◆

THE MANY GIFTS OF GOD

When woman and man were made,
God left one good thing for last: the day to give thanks for the world and its wonders.
Now the seventh day has come. Now Shabbat begins:

to bring us rest, to bring us joy;
to bring us song, to bring us peace.

How good it is, how filled with beauty!
On this day we remember the goodness of all creation.

On this day we remember the goodness of earth and air,
water and sun, and all that grows.

On this day we remember the many gifts of God.
Let us remember, and let us give thanks.

◆ ◆

שְׁמַע יִשְׂרָאֵל: יְיָ אֱלֹהֵינוּ, יְיָ אֶחָד!

Hear, O Israel: the Lord is our God, the Lord is One!

בָּרוּךְ שֵׁם כְּבוֹד מַלְכוּתוֹ לְעוֹלָם וָעֶד!

Blessed is His glorious kingdom for ever and ever!

All are seated

וְאָהַבְתָּ אֵת יְיָ אֱלֹהֶיךָ בְּכָל־לְבָבְךָ וּבְכָל־נַפְשְׁךָ וּבְכָל־מְאֹדֶךָ. וְהָיוּ הַדְּבָרִים הָאֵלֶּה, אֲשֶׁר אָנֹכִי מְצַוְּךָ הַיּוֹם, עַל־לְבָבֶךָ. וְשִׁנַּנְתָּם לְבָנֶיךָ, וְדִבַּרְתָּ בָּם בְּשִׁבְתְּךָ בְּבֵיתֶךָ, וּבְלֶכְתְּךָ בַדֶּרֶךְ, וּבְשָׁכְבְּךָ וּבְקוּמֶךָ.

You shall love the Lord your God with all your mind, with all your strength, with all your being.
Set these words, which I command you this day, upon your heart. Teach them faithfully to your children; speak of them in your home and on your way, when you lie down and when you rise up.

וּקְשַׁרְתָּם לְאוֹת עַל־יָדֶךָ, וְהָיוּ לְטֹטָפֹת בֵּין עֵינֶיךָ, וּכְתַבְתָּם עַל־מְזֻזוֹת בֵּיתֶךָ, וּבִשְׁעָרֶיךָ.

Bind them as a sign upon your hand; let them be a symbol before your eyes; inscribe them on the doorposts of your house, and on your gates.

לְמַעַן תִּזְכְּרוּ וַעֲשִׂיתֶם אֶת־כָּל־מִצְוֹתָי, וִהְיִיתֶם קְדֹשִׁים לֵאלֹהֵיכֶם. אֲנִי יְיָ אֱלֹהֵיכֶם, אֲשֶׁר הוֹצֵאתִי אֶתְכֶם מֵאֶרֶץ מִצְרַיִם לִהְיוֹת לָכֶם לֵאלֹהִים. אֲנִי יְיָ אֱלֹהֵיכֶם.

Be mindful of all My Mitzvot, and do them: so shall you consecrate yourselves to your God. I, the Lord, am your God who led you out of Egypt to be your God; I, the Lord, am your God.

• •

TO LOVE FREEDOM — גאולה

אֱמֶת וֶאֱמוּנָה כָּל־זֹאת, וְקַיָּם עָלֵינוּ כִּי הוּא יְיָ אֱלֹהֵינוּ וְאֵין זוּלָתוֹ, וַאֲנַחְנוּ יִשְׂרָאֵל עַמּוֹ.
הַפּוֹדֵנוּ מִיַּד מְלָכִים, מַלְכֵּנוּ הַגּוֹאֲלֵנוּ מִכַּף כָּל־הֶעָרִיצִים.
הָעֹשֶׂה גְדֹלוֹת עַד אֵין חֵקֶר, וְנִפְלָאוֹת עַד־אֵין מִסְפָּר.
הַשָּׂם נַפְשֵׁנוּ בַּחַיִּים, וְלֹא־נָתַן לַמּוֹט רַגְלֵנוּ.

הָעֹשֶׂה לָנוּ נִסִּים בְּפַרְעֹה, אוֹתוֹת וּמוֹפְתִים בְּאַדְמַת בְּנֵי חָם.
וַיּוֹצֵא אֶת־עַמּוֹ יִשְׂרָאֵל מִתּוֹכָם לְחֵרוּת עוֹלָם.
וְרָאוּ בָנָיו גְּבוּרָתוֹ; שִׁבְּחוּ וְהוֹדוּ לִשְׁמוֹ. וּמַלְכוּתוֹ בְּרָצוֹן
קִבְּלוּ עֲלֵיהֶם. מֹשֶׁה וּבְנֵי יִשְׂרָאֵל לְךָ עָנוּ שִׁירָה בְּשִׂמְחָה
רַבָּה, וְאָמְרוּ כֻלָּם:

True it is that the Lord is our God; there is none else. His might gives power to the sun. His love brings warmth to the human heart.
The Lord is our God; there is none else.

He is One, our Creator who made us one family on earth. Wherever we fight for freedom, He is with us, as He was with our people when we struggled to break the chains that bound us to Egypt.
The Lord is the God of freedom; there is none else.

God our Creator, teach us to love freedom as we love life. Make us understand that only when all are free can we be free. Let none be masters and none be slaves. Then shall we sing as our people did when they were freed from Pharaoh's grip:

מִי־כָמֹכָה בָּאֵלִם, יְיָ?	Who is like You, Eternal One, among the gods that are worshipped?
מִי כָּמֹכָה, נֶאְדָּר בַּקֹּדֶשׁ,	Who is like You, majestic in holiness,
נוֹרָא תְהִלֹּת, עֹשֵׂה פֶלֶא?	awesome in splendor, doing wonders?

מַלְכוּתְךָ רָאוּ בָנֶיךָ, בּוֹקֵעַ יָם לִפְנֵי מֹשֶׁה; "זֶה אֵלִי!" עָנוּ
וְאָמְרוּ: "יְיָ יִמְלֹךְ לְעֹלָם וָעֶד!"

In their escape from the sea, Your children saw Your sovereign might displayed. "This is my God!" they cried. "The Eternal will reign forever and ever!"

• •

All rise

תפלה

SO MAY YOU TEACH US

אֲדֹנָי, שְׂפָתַי תִּפְתָּח, וּפִי יַגִּיד תְּהִלָּתֶךָ.

Eternal God, open my lips, that my mouth may declare Your glory.

בָּרוּךְ אַתָּה, יְיָ אֱלֹהֵינוּ וֵאלֹהֵי אֲבוֹתֵינוּ, אֱלֹהֵי אַבְרָהָם, אֱלֹהֵי יִצְחָק, וֵאלֹהֵי יַעֲקֹב; הָאֵל הַגָּדוֹל, הַגִּבּוֹר וְהַנּוֹרָא, אֵל עֶלְיוֹן. גּוֹמֵל חֲסָדִים טוֹבִים, וְקוֹנֵה הַכֹּל, וְזוֹכֵר חַסְדֵי אָבוֹת, וּמֵבִיא גְאֻלָּה לִבְנֵי בְנֵיהֶם, לְמַעַן שְׁמוֹ, בְּאַהֲבָה.

מֶלֶךְ עוֹזֵר וּמוֹשִׁיעַ וּמָגֵן. בָּרוּךְ אַתָּה, יְיָ, מָגֵן אַבְרָהָם.

We praise You, Lord our God, God of Abraham, God of Isaac, God of Jacob, God of all generations.

Creator of all things, goodness and kindness are the work of Your hands. You have made us free, and called us to be true to Your teaching:

To uphold the falling, to heal the sick, to free the captive, to comfort all who suffer pain.

As You taught our ancestors through the words of Your Torah, so may Torah teach us to follow the paths of goodness, kindness, and love.

Blessed is the Lord, Shield of Abraham. בָּרוּךְ אַתָּה, יְיָ, מָגֵן אַבְרָהָם.

Blessed is the Lord, Creator of life. בָּרוּךְ אַתָּה, יְיָ, מְחַיֵּה הַכֹּל.

• •

קדושת השם

TO BE HOLY

אַתָּה קָדוֹשׁ וְשִׁמְךָ קָדוֹשׁ, וּקְדוֹשִׁים בְּכָל־יוֹם יְהַלְלוּךָ סֶּלָה.

בָּרוּךְ אַתָּה, יְיָ, הָאֵל הַקָּדוֹשׁ.

We cannot see You, O God, as we see each other, yet through Your goodness we know You. Your holiness calls us to turn to You with all our souls and all our might, and when we turn to You we begin to be holy.

When we honor parents and children, and speak the truth, we begin to be holy.

When we keep the Sabbath for study and prayer, we begin to be holy.

We begin to be holy when our thoughts are kind and our deeds are just.

Blessed is the Lord, the holy God. בָּרוּךְ אַתָּה, יְיָ, הָאֵל הַקָּדוֹשׁ.

All are seated

◆ ◆

DAY OF PEACE AND HOPE קדושת היום

אֱלֹהֵינוּ וֵאלֹהֵי אֲבוֹתֵינוּ, רְצֵה בִמְנוּחָתֵנוּ. קַדְּשֵׁנוּ בְּמִצְוֹתֶיךָ וְתֵן חֶלְקֵנוּ בְּתוֹרָתֶךָ. שַׂבְּעֵנוּ מִטּוּבֶךָ, וְשַׂמְּחֵנוּ בִּישׁוּעָתֶךָ, וְטַהֵר לִבֵּנוּ לְעָבְדְּךָ בֶּאֱמֶת. וְהַנְחִילֵנוּ, יְיָ אֱלֹהֵינוּ, בְּאַהֲבָה וּבְרָצוֹן שַׁבַּת קָדְשֶׁךָ, וְיָנוּחוּ בָהּ יִשְׂרָאֵל מְקַדְּשֵׁי שְׁמֶךָ. בָּרוּךְ אַתָּה, יְיָ, מְקַדֵּשׁ הַשַּׁבָּת.

Our God and God of all ages, may our worship on this Sabbath bring us closer to You.

Make us loyal to Your Torah, and make our hearts pure, that we may truly serve You.

Teach us to keep this day as a day of peace and hope, a day of rest and learning.

We thank You, O Lord, for the holy Sabbath day.

◆ ◆

MEDITATION

Lord our God, we pray for the Jewish people. Help those who are not yet free to find the happiness of freedom. Give strength to those of us who are rebuilding the land of Israel. And teach us all, wherever we live, to grow in knowledge and to love Your Torah. Lord our God, we pray for all peoples. Help the hungry to find bread for their bodies and food for their minds, and teach all Your children to do to others the kindness they would like done to themselves.

◆ ◆

O Lord, my God,	אֵלִי, אֵלִי, Ei·li, Ei·li,
I pray that these things never end:	שֶׁלֹּא יִגָּמֵר לְעוֹלָם she·lo yi·ga·meir le·ol·am
The sand and the sea,	הַחוֹל וְהַיָּם, ha·chol ve·ha·yam,
The rush of the waters,	רִשְׁרוּשׁ שֶׁל הַמַּיִם, rish·rush shel ha·ma·yim,
The crash of the heavens,	בְּרַק הַשָּׁמַיִם, be·rak ha·sha·ma·yim,
The prayer of the heart.	תְּפִלַּת הָאָדָם. te·fi·lat ha·a·dam.
The sand and the sea,	הַחוֹל וְהַיָּם, ha·chol ve·ha·yam,
The rush of the waters,	רִשְׁרוּשׁ שֶׁל הַמַּיִם, rish·rush shel ha·ma·yim,
The crash of the heavens,	בְּרַק הַשָּׁמַיִם, be·rak ha·sha·ma·yim,
The prayer of the heart.	תְּפִלַּת הָאָדָם. te·fi·lat ha·a·dam.

◆ ◆

TO LIVE AT PEACE ברכת שלום

שָׁלוֹם רָב עַל־יִשְׂרָאֵל עַמְּךָ תָּשִׂים לְעוֹלָם, כִּי אַתָּה הוּא מֶלֶךְ אָדוֹן לְכָל הַשָּׁלוֹם. וְטוֹב בְּעֵינֶיךָ לְבָרֵךְ אֶת־עַמְּךָ יִשְׂרָאֵל בְּכָל־עֵת וּבְכָל־שָׁעָה בִּשְׁלוֹמֶךָ.

בָּרוּךְ אַתָּה, יְיָ, הַמְבָרֵךְ אֶת־עַמּוֹ יִשְׂרָאֵל בַּשָּׁלוֹם.

You have given us the power, O God, to bring peace and justice into the world. May we always love peace and pursue it, and love our fellow creatures. Fill Your children with kindness, wisdom, and love. Then shall they learn to live at peace.

Blessed is the Lord, Teacher of peace.

◆ ◆

יִהְיוּ לְרָצוֹן אִמְרֵי־פִי וְהֶגְיוֹן לִבִּי לְפָנֶיךָ, יְיָ, צוּרִי וְגוֹאֲלִי.

May the words of my mouth, and the meditations of my heart, be acceptable to You, O Lord, my Rock and my Redeemer.

or

עֹשֶׂה שָׁלוֹם בִּמְרוֹמָיו, הוּא יַעֲשֶׂה שָׁלוֹם עָלֵינוּ וְעַל כָּל־יִשְׂרָאֵל, וְאִמְרוּ אָמֵן.

May He who causes peace to reign in the high heavens let peace descend on us, on all Israel, and all the world.

◆ ◆

Prayers for Special Occasions begin on page 389.

The Rituals for the Reading of Torah begin on page 415.

Concluding Prayers begin on page 613.

׳ X ׳

This service is suggested for occasions when many children are present.

★

For congregations where the lights are kindled in the synagogue

הדלקת הנרות

As we kindle the lights of Shabbat we remember the words of Torah:

"The Torah is light, the Mitzvah a lamp."

May we observe Shabbat this and every week by learning Torah, by doing Mitzvot, kindling the light of good deeds, and basking in their light.

◆ ◆

בָּרוּךְ אַתָּה, יְיָ אֱלֹהֵינוּ, מֶלֶךְ הָעוֹלָם,
אֲשֶׁר קִדְּשָׁנוּ בְּמִצְוֹתָיו וְצִוָּנוּ לְהַדְלִיק נֵר שֶׁל שַׁבָּת.

Blessed is the Lord our God, Ruler of the universe,
who gives us Mitzvot that make us holy, and commands us
to kindle the lights of Shabbat.

◆ ◆

May we be blessed with Shabbat joy.
May we be blessed with Shabbat peace.
May we be blessed with Shabbat light.

◆ ◆

Welcome, Shabbat, day Jews have always loved! This day let good angels be at our side, together with family and friends. We greet you, Shabbat, with an old song of welcome: Shalom Aleichem: Peace be to you, O angels of peace, messengers of the Most High!

בּוֹאֲכֶם לְשָׁלוֹם, Come to us in peace.
בּוֹאֲכֶם לְשָׁלוֹם, *Come to us in peace.*
בָּרְכוּנִי לְשָׁלוֹם, Bless us with peace.
בָּרְכוּנִי לְשָׁלוֹם, *Bless us with peace.*
צֵאתְכֶם לְשָׁלוֹם, Depart in peace.
צֵאתְכֶם לְשָׁלוֹם, *Depart in peace.*

◆ ◆

שָׁלוֹם עֲלֵיכֶם, מַלְאֲכֵי הַשָּׁרֵת, מַלְאֲכֵי עֶלְיוֹן,
מִמֶּלֶךְ מַלְכֵי הַמְּלָכִים, הַקָּדוֹשׁ בָּרוּךְ הוּא.

Sha·lom a·lei·chem, mal·a·chei ha·sha·reit, mal·a·chei El·yon,
mi·me·lech ma·le·chei ha·me·la·chim, ha·ka·dosh ba·ruch Hu.

בּוֹאֲכֶם לְשָׁלוֹם, מַלְאֲכֵי הַשָּׁלוֹם, מַלְאֲכֵי עֶלְיוֹן,
מִמֶּלֶךְ מַלְכֵי הַמְּלָכִים, הַקָּדוֹשׁ בָּרוּךְ הוּא.

Bo·a·chem le·sha·lom, mal·a·chei ha·sha·lom, mal·a·chei El·yon,
mi·me·lech ma·le·chei ha·me·la·chim, ha·ka·dosh ba·ruch Hu.

בָּרְכוּנִי לְשָׁלוֹם, מַלְאֲכֵי הַשָּׁלוֹם, מַלְאֲכֵי עֶלְיוֹן,
מִמֶּלֶךְ מַלְכֵי הַמְּלָכִים, הַקָּדוֹשׁ בָּרוּךְ הוּא.

Ba·re·chu·ni le·sha·lom, mal·a·chei ha·sha·lom, mal·a·chei El·yon,
mi·me·lech ma·le·chei ha·me·la·chim, ha·ka·dosh ba·ruch Hu.

צֵאתְכֶם לְשָׁלוֹם, מַלְאֲכֵי הַשָּׁלוֹם, מַלְאֲכֵי עֶלְיוֹן,
מִמֶּלֶךְ מַלְכֵי הַמְּלָכִים, הַקָּדוֹשׁ בָּרוּךְ הוּא.

Tsei·te·chem le·sha·lom, mal·a·chei ha·sha·lom, mal·a·chei El·yon,
mi·me·lech ma·le·chei ha·me·la·chim, ha·ka·dosh ba·ruch Hu.

◆ ◆

With 'Shalom' we have begun our service, and with 'Shabbat Shalom' we shall end it. So must our lives begin and end with shalom, for it is our hope, as it is the precious teaching of our faith. May this Shabbat bring peace to us all, and encourage us to bring peace to our homes and our cities, our country and among the nations. As long as there is war, we have not obeyed God's command to seek peace and pursue it.

Grant us peace, Your most precious gift, and help our people Israel to be a messenger of peace to the nations of the world. Bless our country, that it may live in peace, and bring peace and happiness into the world. Blessed is God, the Source of peace.

◆ ◆

SILENT PRAYER

◆ ◆

עֹשֶׂה שָׁלוֹם בִּמְרוֹמָיו, הוּא יַעֲשֶׂה שָׁלוֹם עָלֵינוּ וְעַל כָּל-יִשְׂרָאֵל, וְאִמְרוּ אָמֵן.

May He who causes peace to reign in the high heavens, let peace descend on us, on all Israel, and all the world.

◆ ◆

For the good in us which calls us to a better life, we give thanks;
For the strength to improve the world with our hearts and hands, we give praise;
For the peace in us which leads us to work for peace, we are grateful.
For all these we give thanks to the Creator of life and all nature.

◆ ◆

All rise

שמע וברכותיה

בָּרְכוּ אֶת־יְיָ הַמְבֹרָךְ!

Praise the Lord, to whom our praise is due!

בָּרוּךְ יְיָ הַמְבֹרָךְ לְעוֹלָם וָעֶד!

Praised be the Lord, to whom our praise is due, now and for ever!

CREATOR OF GOODNESS — מעריב ערבים

בָּרוּךְ אַתָּה, יְיָ אֱלֹהֵינוּ, מֶלֶךְ הָעוֹלָם, אֲשֶׁר בִּדְבָרוֹ מַעֲרִיב עֲרָבִים. בְּחָכְמָה פּוֹתֵחַ שְׁעָרִים, וּבִתְבוּנָה מְשַׁנֶּה עִתִּים, וּמַחֲלִיף אֶת־הַזְּמַנִּים, וּמְסַדֵּר אֶת־הַכּוֹכָבִים בְּמִשְׁמְרוֹתֵיהֶם בָּרָקִיעַ כִּרְצוֹנוֹ.

בּוֹרֵא יוֹם וָלָיְלָה, גּוֹלֵל אוֹר מִפְּנֵי חֹשֶׁךְ וְחֹשֶׁךְ מִפְּנֵי אוֹר, וּמַעֲבִיר יוֹם וּמֵבִיא לָיְלָה, וּמַבְדִּיל בֵּין יוֹם וּבֵין לָיְלָה, יְיָ צְבָאוֹת שְׁמוֹ.

אֵל חַי וְקַיָּם, תָּמִיד יִמְלוֹךְ עָלֵינוּ, לְעוֹלָם וָעֶד. בָּרוּךְ אַתָּה, יְיָ, הַמַּעֲרִיב עֲרָבִים.

O Eternal our God, how glorious You are in all the earth!

When we see the heavens, the work of Your fingers, the moon and the stars, the golden sun and the cool grass, the brilliant flowers, and the freshness of flowing streams,

We give thanks to You, Maker of all things, Creator of goodness and beauty.

◆ ◆

ALL THE WORLD SINGS

אהבת עולם

אַהֲבַת עוֹלָם בֵּית יִשְׂרָאֵל עַמְּךָ אָהָבְתָּ: תּוֹרָה וּמִצְוֹת, חֻקִּים וּמִשְׁפָּטִים אוֹתָנוּ לִמַּדְתָּ.

עַל־כֵּן, יְיָ אֱלֹהֵינוּ, בְּשָׁכְבֵנוּ וּבְקוּמֵנוּ נָשִׂיחַ בְּחֻקֶּיךָ, וְנִשְׂמַח בְּדִבְרֵי תוֹרָתְךָ וּבְמִצְוֹתֶיךָ לְעוֹלָם וָעֶד.

כִּי הֵם חַיֵּינוּ וְאֹרֶךְ יָמֵינוּ, וּבָהֶם נֶהְגֶּה יוֹמָם וָלָיְלָה. וְאַהֲבָתְךָ אַל־תָּסִיר מִמֶּנּוּ לְעוֹלָמִים! בָּרוּךְ אַתָּה, יְיָ, אוֹהֵב עַמּוֹ יִשְׂרָאֵל.

All the world sings to You: the song of trees, when wind stirs their leaves; the song of earth, when rain soothes its thirst; the song of the sea, when its waves touch the shore.

And we sing to You, O God, whose goodness makes all things one.

◆ ◆

שְׁמַע יִשְׂרָאֵל: יְיָ אֱלֹהֵינוּ, יְיָ אֶחָד!

Hear, O Israel: the Lord is our God, the Lord is One!

בָּרוּךְ שֵׁם כְּבוֹד מַלְכוּתוֹ לְעוֹלָם וָעֶד!

Blessed is His glorious kingdom for ever and ever!

All are seated

וְאָהַבְתָּ אֵת יְיָ אֱלֹהֶיךָ בְּכָל־לְבָבְךָ וּבְכָל־נַפְשְׁךָ וּבְכָל־מְאֹדֶךָ.
וְהָיוּ הַדְּבָרִים הָאֵלֶּה, אֲשֶׁר אָנֹכִי מְצַוְּךָ הַיּוֹם, עַל־לְבָבֶךָ.
וְשִׁנַּנְתָּם לְבָנֶיךָ, וְדִבַּרְתָּ בָּם בְּשִׁבְתְּךָ בְּבֵיתֶךָ, וּבְלֶכְתְּךָ בַדֶּרֶךְ, וּבְשָׁכְבְּךָ וּבְקוּמֶךָ.

You shall love the Lord your God with all your mind, with all your strength, with all your being.
Set these words, which I command you this day, upon your heart. Teach them faithfully to your children; speak of them in your home and on your way, when you lie down and when you rise up.

וּקְשַׁרְתָּם לְאוֹת עַל־יָדֶךָ, וְהָיוּ לְטֹטָפֹת בֵּין עֵינֶיךָ, וּכְתַבְתָּם עַל־מְזֻזוֹת בֵּיתֶךָ, וּבִשְׁעָרֶיךָ.

Bind them as a sign upon your hand; let them be a symbol before your eyes; inscribe them on the doorposts of your house, and on your gates.

לְמַעַן תִּזְכְּרוּ וַעֲשִׂיתֶם אֶת־כָּל־מִצְוֹתָי, וִהְיִיתֶם קְדֹשִׁים לֵאלֹהֵיכֶם. אֲנִי יְיָ אֱלֹהֵיכֶם, אֲשֶׁר הוֹצֵאתִי אֶתְכֶם מֵאֶרֶץ מִצְרַיִם לִהְיוֹת לָכֶם לֵאלֹהִים. אֲנִי יְיָ אֱלֹהֵיכֶם.

Be mindful of all My Mitzvot, and do them: so shall you consecrate yourselves to your God. I, the Lord, am your God who led you out of Egypt to be your God; I, the Lord, am your God.

◆ ◆

HE IS WITH US

The day has gone, and darkness has fallen. The stars crowd the sky. How great a universe — how little we understand it! And greater still the God who made it. How small we seem to ourselves when we think of the great stars and the greater God. Yet we are small only in size. Our minds can make us very great, when we think of God and try to become like Him.

He is with us and in us, helping our minds to grow.

We cannot see Him, but we can feel Him with our hearts.
He is in our thoughts, and in all the good we do.

He is in gentle and peaceful people.
He is in all who add to the happiness of our world.

All who teach, all who learn.
All who speak truth, all who listen with honest minds.

All who study Torah, all who teach it.
These show us the God we cannot see.

◆ ◆

NONE IS LIKE YOU

Who is like You, O God?
Thus sang Moses long ago, when Israel at last breathed the
air of freedom.
A song of the past, a song of today.

A song for Jews in every age.
A song of the present, a song of tomorrow.

Who, O God, is like You?
*Ein kamocha, none is like You. One God alone created all
things.*

Who is like You, O God?
*Ein kamocha, none is like You. You are spirit, whom we feel
but cannot ever see.*

Are You stone and tree, O God? Are You breeze and sky?
You are God who made them all; the Creator, not the creation.

Who is like God? Who can be compared to Him?
*Neither man nor woman, nor any thing on earth or in the sky.
Only God is God!*

מִי־כָמֹֽכָה בָּאֵלִים, יְיָ? מִי כָּמֹֽכָה, נֶאְדָּר בַּקֹּֽדֶשׁ, נוֹרָא
תְהִלֹּת, עֹֽשֵׂה פֶֽלֶא?

*Who is like You, Eternal One, among the gods that are wor-
shipped? Who is like You, majestic in holiness, awesome in
splendor, doing wonders?*

When Your people see the greatness of Your power, they say:
God will rule for ever and ever!

Who is like You, Eternal One, among the gods that are worshipped?	מִי־כָמֹֽכָה בָּאֵלִם, יְיָ?
Who is like You, majestic in holiness,	מִי כָּמֹֽכָה, נֶאְדָּר בַּקֹּֽדֶשׁ,
awesome in splendor, doing wonders?	נוֹרָא תְהִלֹּת, עֹֽשֵׂה פֶֽלֶא?

מַלְכוּתְךָ רָאוּ בָנֶיךָ, בּוֹקֵעַ יָם לִפְנֵי מֹשֶׁה; "זֶה אֵלִי!" עָנוּ וְאָמְרוּ: "יְיָ יִמְלֹךְ לְעֹלָם וָעֶד!"

In their escape from the sea, Your children saw Your sovereign might displayed. "This is my God!" they cried. "The Eternal will reign for ever and ever!"

◆ ◆

TO FIND OUR HEARTS READY — השכיבנו

הַשְׁכִּיבֵנוּ, אָבִינוּ, לְשָׁלוֹם, וְהַעֲמִידֵנוּ, מַלְכֵּנוּ, לְחַיִּים טוֹבִים וּלְשָׁלוֹם. וּפְרוֹשׂ עָלֵינוּ סֻכַּת שְׁלוֹמֶךָ, וְתַקְּנֵנוּ בְּעֵצָה טוֹבָה מִלְּפָנֶיךָ. וְהוֹשִׁיעֵנוּ מְהֵרָה לְמַעַן שְׁמֶךָ, וְהָגֵן בַּעֲדֵנוּ. וּפְרוֹשׂ עָלֵינוּ סֻכַּת רַחֲמִים וְשָׁלוֹם.

בָּרוּךְ אַתָּה, יְיָ, הַפּוֹרֵשׂ סֻכַּת שָׁלוֹם עָלֵינוּ, וְעַל־עַמּוֹ יִשְׂרָאֵל, וְעַל־יְרוּשָׁלָיִם.

Lord our God, may love and kindness, peace and happiness dwell among us. May we live always among good friends, and be to them faithful companions. May we have hope of goodness in the future, and awaken each morning to find our hearts ready to serve You.

◆ ◆

All rise

תפלה

אֲדֹנָי, שְׂפָתַי תִּפְתָּח, וּפִי יַגִּיד תְּהִלָּתֶךָ.

Eternal God, open my lips, that my mouth may declare Your glory.

אבות

HE WILL LEAD US

בָּרוּךְ אַתָּה, יְיָ אֱלֹהֵינוּ וֵאלֹהֵי אֲבוֹתֵינוּ, אֱלֹהֵי אַבְרָהָם, אֱלֹהֵי יִצְחָק, וֵאלֹהֵי יַעֲקֹב: הָאֵל הַגָּדוֹל, הַגִּבּוֹר וְהַנּוֹרָא, אֵל עֶלְיוֹן.

Blessed is our God: God of Abraham, God of Isaac, God of Jacob, our God, the God of all ages and peoples.

גּוֹמֵל חֲסָדִים טוֹבִים, וְקוֹנֵה הַכֹּל, וְזוֹכֵר חַסְדֵי אָבוֹת, וּמֵבִיא גְאֻלָּה לִבְנֵי בְנֵיהֶם, לְמַעַן שְׁמוֹ, בְּאַהֲבָה.

He led our ancestors from darkness to light, from error to truth, from bondage to freedom. He will lead us to more light, new truth, greater freedom.

מֶלֶךְ עוֹזֵר וּמוֹשִׁיעַ וּמָגֵן. בָּרוּךְ אַתָּה, יְיָ, מָגֵן אַבְרָהָם.

Blessed is the Lord, the Shield of Abraham.

◆ ◆

גבורות

THE POWER HE HAS GIVEN US

אַתָּה גִּבּוֹר לְעוֹלָם, אֲדֹנָי, מְחַיֵּה הַכֹּל אַתָּה, רַב לְהוֹשִׁיעַ.

Great is God's power, and great the power He has given us. His spirit speaks within us, saying:

מְכַלְכֵּל חַיִּים בְּחֶסֶד, מְחַיֵּה הַכֹּל בְּרַחֲמִים רַבִּים. סוֹמֵךְ נוֹפְלִים, וְרוֹפֵא חוֹלִים, וּמַתִּיר אֲסוּרִים, וּמְקַיֵּם אֱמוּנָתוֹ לִישֵׁנֵי עָפָר.

Heal the sick, help the weak, care for the poor, free the captive, be true to your faith.

מִי כָמְוֹךָ, בַּעַל גְּבוּרוֹת, וּמִי דְּוֹמֶה לָּךְ, מֶלֶךְ מֵמִית וּמְחַיֶּה וּמַצְמִיחַ יְשׁוּעָה?

Then we become a holy people, true children of the holy God.

וְנֶאֱמָן אַתָּה לְהַחֲיוֹת הַכֹּל. בָּרוּךְ אַתָּה, יְיָ, מְחַיֵּה הַכֹּל.

Blessed is the Lord, Creator of life, the Holy God.

◆ ◆

THE HOLY GOD — קדושת השם

אַתָּה קָדוֹשׁ וְשִׁמְךָ קָדוֹשׁ, וּקְדוֹשִׁים בְּכָל־יוֹם יְהַלְלְוּךָ סֶּלָה. בָּרוּךְ אַתָּה, יְיָ, הָאֵל הַקָּדוֹשׁ.

You are holy, Your name is holy, and Your worshippers proclaim Your holiness. Blessed is the Eternal One, the holy God.

All are seated

◆ ◆

THE COVENANT OF SHABBAT — קדושת היום

וְשָׁמְרוּ בְנֵי־יִשְׂרָאֵל אֶת־הַשַּׁבָּת, לַעֲשׂוֹת אֶת־הַשַּׁבָּת לְדֹרֹתָם בְּרִית עוֹלָם. בֵּינִי וּבֵין בְּנֵי יִשְׂרָאֵל אוֹת הִיא לְעֹלָם, כִּי שֵׁשֶׁת יָמִים עָשָׂה יְיָ אֶת־הַשָּׁמַיִם וְאֶת־הָאָרֶץ, וּבַיּוֹם הַשְּׁבִיעִי שָׁבַת וַיִּנָּפַשׁ.

The people of Israel shall keep the Sabbath, observing the Sabbath in every generation as a covenant for all time. It is a sign for ever between Me and the people of Israel, for in six days the Eternal God made heaven and earth, and on the seventh day He rested from His labors.

◆

DAY OF PEACE AND HOPE

אֱלֹהֵינוּ וֵאלֹהֵי אֲבוֹתֵינוּ, רְצֵה בִמְנוּחָתֵנוּ. קַדְּשֵׁנוּ בְּמִצְוֹתֶיךָ וְתֵן חֶלְקֵנוּ בְּתוֹרָתֶךָ. שַׂבְּעֵנוּ מִטּוּבֶךָ, וְשַׂמְּחֵנוּ בִּישׁוּעָתֶךָ, וְטַהֵר לִבֵּנוּ לְעָבְדְךָ בֶּאֱמֶת. וְהַנְחִילֵנוּ, יְיָ אֱלֹהֵינוּ, בְּאַהֲבָה

וּבְרָצוֹן שַׁבַּת קָדְשֶׁךָ, וְיָנוּחוּ בָהּ יִשְׂרָאֵל מְקַדְּשֵׁי שְׁמֶךָ. בָּרוּךְ
אַתָּה, יְיָ, מְקַדֵּשׁ הַשַּׁבָּת.

Our God and God of all ages, may our worship on this Sabbath bring us closer to You.

Make us loyal to Your Torah, and make our hearts pure, that we may truly serve You. Teach us to keep this and every Sabbath day as a day of peace and hope, of rest and learning. We thank You, O Lord, for the holy Sabbath day.

◆ ◆

THE THOUGHTS OF OUR HEARTS — עבודה

רְצֵה, יְיָ אֱלֹהֵינוּ, בְּעַמְּךָ יִשְׂרָאֵל, וּתְפִלָּתָם בְּאַהֲבָה תְקַבֵּל,
וּתְהִי לְרָצוֹן תָּמִיד עֲבוֹדַת יִשְׂרָאֵל עַמֶּךָ. אֵל קָרוֹב לְכָל-
קֹרְאָיו, פְּנֵה אֶל עֲבָדֶיךָ וְחָנֵּנוּ; שְׁפוֹךְ רוּחֲךָ עָלֵינוּ, וְתֶחֱזֶינָה
עֵינֵינוּ בְּשׁוּבְךָ לְצִיּוֹן בְּרַחֲמִים.

בָּרוּךְ אַתָּה, יְיָ, הַמַּחֲזִיר שְׁכִינָתוֹ לְצִיּוֹן.

May the words of our mouths with which we come to God be always the same as the thoughts of our hearts. May we hear our own prayers and from them learn the laws of life.

◆ ◆

יִהְיוּ לְרָצוֹן אִמְרֵי־פִי וְהֶגְיוֹן לִבִּי לְפָנֶיךָ, יְיָ, צוּרִי וְגוֹאֲלִי.

May the words of my mouth, and the meditations of my heart, be acceptable to You, O Lord, my Rock and my Redeemer.

◆ ◆

Prayers for Special Occasions begin on page 389

The Rituals for the Reading of Torah begin on page 415.

Concluding Prayers begin on page 613.

תפלות שחרית לשבת

SABBATH MORNING SERVICES

For those who wear the Tallit

Praise the Lord, O my soul!	בָּרְכִי נַפְשִׁי אֶת יְיָ!
O Lord my God, You are very great!	יְיָ אֱלֹהַי, גָּדַלְתָּ מְּאֹד!
Arrayed in glory and majesty,	הוֹד וְהָדָר לָבָשְׁתָּ,
You wrap Yourself in light as with a garment,	עֹטֶה אוֹר כַּשַּׂלְמָה,
You stretch out the heavens like a curtain.	נוֹטֶה שָׁמַיִם כַּיְרִיעָה.

בָּרוּךְ אַתָּה, יְיָ אֱלֹהֵינוּ, מֶלֶךְ הָעוֹלָם,
אֲשֶׁר קִדְּשָׁנוּ בְּמִצְוֹתָיו וְצִוָּנוּ לְהִתְעַטֵּף בַּצִּיצִת.

Blessed is the Lord our God, Ruler of the universe, who hallows us with His Mitzvot, and teaches us to wrap ourselves in the fringed Tallit.

◆ ◆

א I א

The Morning Blessings, pages 283 to 289, might be used for private prayer. In the synagogue, all or a part of them may be read or sung. The 'public' service may begin on page 290 with the reading or chanting of selected פסוקי דזמרה*, Poems of Praise, continuing with Barechu, page 301.*

Morning Blessings ברכות השחר

1. FOR THE BLESSING OF WORSHIP מה טבו

מַה־טֹּבוּ אֹהָלֶיךָ, יַעֲקֹב, מִשְׁכְּנֹתֶיךָ, יִשְׂרָאֵל!

How lovely are your tents, O Jacob, your dwelling-places, O Israel!

וַאֲנִי, בְּרֹב חַסְדְּךָ אָבֹא בֵיתֶךָ,
אֶשְׁתַּחֲוֶה אֶל־הֵיכַל קָדְשְׁךָ בְּיִרְאָתֶךָ.

In Your abundant lovingkindness, O God, let me enter Your house, reverently to worship in Your holy temple.

יְיָ, אָהַבְתִּי מְעוֹן בֵּיתֶךָ, וּמְקוֹם מִשְׁכַּן כְּבוֹדֶךָ.
וַאֲנִי אֶשְׁתַּחֲוֶה וְאֶכְרָעָה, אֶבְרְכָה לִפְנֵי־יְיָ עֹשִׂי.

Lord, I love Your house, the place where Your glory dwells. So I would worship with humility, I would seek blessing in the presence of God, my Maker.

וַאֲנִי תְפִלָּתִי לְךָ, יְיָ, עֵת רָצוֹן.
אֱלֹהִים, בְּרָב־חַסְדֶּךָ, עֲנֵנִי בֶּאֱמֶת יִשְׁעֶךָ.

To You, then, Lord, does my prayer go forth. May this be a time of joy and favor. In Your great love, O God, answer me with Your saving truth.

◆ ◆

2. FOR HEALTH אשר יצר

בָּרוּךְ אַתָּה, יְיָ אֱלֹהֵינוּ, מֶלֶךְ הָעוֹלָם, אֲשֶׁר יָצַר אֶת־הָאָדָם בְּחָכְמָה, וּבָרָא בוֹ נְקָבִים נְקָבִים, חֲלוּלִים חֲלוּלִים. גָּלוּי וְיָדוּעַ לִפְנֵי כִסֵּא כְבוֹדֶךָ, שֶׁאִם יִפָּתֵחַ אֶחָד מֵהֶם, אוֹ יִסָּתֵם אֶחָד מֵהֶם, אִי אֶפְשַׁר לְהִתְקַיֵּם וְלַעֲמוֹד לְפָנֶיךָ. בָּרוּךְ אַתָּה, יְיָ, רוֹפֵא כָל־בָּשָׂר וּמַפְלִיא לַעֲשׂוֹת.

Blessed is our Eternal God, Creator of the universe, who has made our bodies with wisdom, combining veins, arteries, and vital organs into a finely balanced network. Wondrous Fashioner and Sustainer of life, Source of our health and our strength, we give You thanks and praise.

◆ ◆

3. FOR TORAH לעסוק בדברי תורה

בָּרוּךְ אַתָּה, יְיָ אֱלֹהֵינוּ, מֶלֶךְ הָעוֹלָם, אֲשֶׁר קִדְּשָׁנוּ בְּמִצְוֹתָיו וְצִוָּנוּ לַעֲסוֹק בְּדִבְרֵי תוֹרָה.

Blessed is the Eternal, our God, Ruler of the universe, who hallows us with His Mitzvot, and commands us to engage in the study of Torah.

וְהַעֲרֶב־נָא, יְיָ אֱלֹהֵינוּ, אֶת־דִּבְרֵי תוֹרָתְךָ בְּפִינוּ, וּבְפִי עַמְּךָ בֵּית יִשְׂרָאֵל, וְנִהְיֶה אֲנַחְנוּ וְצֶאֱצָאֵינוּ, וְצֶאֱצָאֵי עַמְּךָ בֵּית יִשְׂרָאֵל, כֻּלָּנוּ יוֹדְעֵי שְׁמֶךָ וְלוֹמְדֵי תוֹרָתֶךָ לִשְׁמָהּ. בָּרוּךְ אַתָּה, יְיָ, הַמְלַמֵּד תּוֹרָה לְעַמּוֹ יִשְׂרָאֵל.

Eternal our God, make the words of Your Torah sweet to us, and to the House of Israel, Your people, that we and our children may be lovers of Your name and students of Your Torah.

Blessed is the Eternal, the Teacher of Torah to His people Israel.

◆

אֵלּוּ דְבָרִים שֶׁאֵין לָהֶם שִׁעוּר, שֶׁאָדָם אוֹכֵל פֵּרוֹתֵיהֶם
בָּעוֹלָם הַזֶּה וְהַקֶּרֶן קַיֶּמֶת לוֹ לָעוֹלָם הַבָּא, וְאֵלּוּ הֵן:

These are the obligations without measure, whose reward, too, is without measure:

To honor father and mother;	כִּבּוּד אָב וָאֵם,
to perform acts of love and kindness;	וּגְמִילוּת חֲסָדִים,
to attend the house of study daily;	וְהַשְׁכָּמַת בֵּית הַמִּדְרָשׁ שַׁחֲרִית וְעַרְבִית,
to welcome the stranger;	וְהַכְנָסַת אוֹרְחִים,
to visit the sick;	וּבִקּוּר חוֹלִים,
to rejoice with bride and groom;	וְהַכְנָסַת כַּלָּה,
to console the bereaved;	וּלְוָיַת הַמֵּת,
to pray with sincerity;	וְעִיּוּן תְּפִלָּה,
to make peace when there is strife.	וַהֲבָאַת שָׁלוֹם בֵּין אָדָם לַחֲבֵרוֹ;
And the study of Torah is equal to them all, because it leads to them all.	וְתַלְמוּד תּוֹרָה כְּנֶגֶד כֻּלָּם.

• •

4. FOR THE SOUL — אלהי נשמה

אֱלֹהַי, נְשָׁמָה שֶׁנָּתַתָּ בִּי טְהוֹרָה הִיא! אַתָּה בְרָאתָהּ, אַתָּה
יְצַרְתָּהּ, אַתָּה נְפַחְתָּהּ בִּי, וְאַתָּה מְשַׁמְּרָהּ בְּקִרְבִּי. כָּל־זְמַן
שֶׁהַנְּשָׁמָה בְקִרְבִּי, מוֹדֶה אֲנִי לְפָנֶיךָ, יְיָ אֱלֹהַי וֵאלֹהֵי אֲבוֹתַי,
רִבּוֹן כָּל־הַמַּעֲשִׂים, אֲדוֹן כָּל־הַנְּשָׁמוֹת.

בָּרוּךְ אַתָּה, יְיָ, אֲשֶׁר בְּיָדוֹ נֶפֶשׁ כָּל־חָי, וְרוּחַ כָּל־בְּשַׂר־אִישׁ.

The soul that You have given me, O God, is a pure one! You have created and formed it, breathed it into me, and within me You sustain it. So long as I have breath, therefore, I will give thanks to You, O Lord my God and God of all ages, Master of all creation, Lord of every human spirit.

Blessed is the Lord, in whose hands are the souls of all the living and the spirits of all flesh.

◆ ◆

5. FOR OUR BLESSINGS נסים בכל יום

בָּרוּךְ אַתָּה, יְיָ אֱלֹהֵינוּ, מֶלֶךְ הָעוֹלָם, אֲשֶׁר נָתַן לַשֶּׂכְוִי בִינָה לְהַבְחִין בֵּין יוֹם וּבֵין לָיְלָה.

Blessed is the Eternal our God, Ruler of the universe, who has implanted mind and instinct within every living being.

בָּרוּךְ אַתָּה, יְיָ אֱלֹהֵינוּ, מֶלֶךְ הָעוֹלָם, שֶׁעָשַׂנִי יִשְׂרָאֵל.

Blessed is the Eternal our God, who has made me a Jew.

בָּרוּךְ אַתָּה, יְיָ אֱלֹהֵינוּ, מֶלֶךְ הָעוֹלָם, שֶׁעָשַׂנִי בֶּן חוֹרִין.

Blessed is the Eternal our God, who has made me to be free.

בָּרוּךְ אַתָּה, יְיָ אֱלֹהֵינוּ, מֶלֶךְ הָעוֹלָם, פּוֹקֵחַ עִוְרִים.

Blessed is the Eternal our God, who opens the eyes of the blind.

בָּרוּךְ אַתָּה, יְיָ אֱלֹהֵינוּ, מֶלֶךְ הָעוֹלָם, מַלְבִּישׁ עֲרֻמִּים.

Blessed is the Eternal our God, who provides clothes for the naked.

בָּרוּךְ אַתָּה, יְיָ אֱלֹהֵינוּ, מֶלֶךְ הָעוֹלָם, מַתִּיר אֲסוּרִים.

Blessed is the Eternal our God, who brings freedom to the captive.

בָּרוּךְ אַתָּה, יְיָ אֱלֹהֵינוּ, מֶלֶךְ הָעוֹלָם, זוֹקֵף כְּפוּפִים.

Blessed is the Eternal our God, whose power lifts up the fallen.

בָּרוּךְ אַתָּה, יְיָ אֱלֹהֵינוּ, מֶלֶךְ הָעוֹלָם, הַמֵּכִין מִצְעֲדֵי־גָבֶר.

Blessed is the Eternal our God, who makes firm each person's steps.

בָּרוּךְ אַתָּה, יְיָ אֱלֹהֵינוּ, מֶלֶךְ הָעוֹלָם, אוֹזֵר יִשְׂרָאֵל בִּגְבוּרָה.

Blessed is the Eternal our God, who girds our people Israel with strength.

בָּרוּךְ אַתָּה, יְיָ אֱלֹהֵינוּ, מֶלֶךְ הָעוֹלָם, עוֹטֵר יִשְׂרָאֵל בְּתִפְאָרָה.

Blessed is the Eternal our God, who crowns Israel with glory.

בָּרוּךְ אַתָּה, יְיָ אֱלֹהֵינוּ, מֶלֶךְ הָעוֹלָם, הַנּוֹתֵן לַיָּעֵף כֹּחַ.

Blessed is the Eternal our God, who gives strength to the weary.

בָּרוּךְ אַתָּה, יְיָ אֱלֹהֵינוּ, מֶלֶךְ הָעוֹלָם, הַמַּעֲבִיר שֵׁנָה מֵעֵינַי וּתְנוּמָה מֵעַפְעַפָּי.

Blessed is the Eternal our God, who removes sleep from the eyes, slumber from the eyelids.

• •

6. FOR CONSCIENCE — תורה ומצוות

וִיהִי רָצוֹן מִלְּפָנֶיךָ, יְיָ אֱלֹהֵינוּ וֵאלֹהֵי אֲבוֹתֵינוּ, שֶׁתַּרְגִּילֵנוּ בְּתוֹרָתֶךָ וְדַבְּקֵנוּ בְּמִצְוֹתֶיךָ.

Lord our God and God of all ages, school us in Your Torah and bind us to Your Mitzvot.

וְאַל תְּבִיאֵנוּ לֹא לִידֵי חֵטְא, וְלֹא לִידֵי עֲבֵרָה וְעָוֹן, וְלֹא לִידֵי נִסָּיוֹן, וְלֹא לִידֵי בִזָּיוֹן. וְאַל תַּשְׁלֶט־בָּנוּ יֵצֶר הָרָע, וְהַרְחִיקֵנוּ מֵאָדָם רָע וּמֵחָבֵר רָע.

Help us to keep far from sin, to master temptation, and to avoid falling under its spell. May our darker passions not rule us, nor evil companions lead us astray.

וְדַבְּקֵנוּ בְּיֵצֶר הַטּוֹב וּבְמַעֲשִׂים טוֹבִים; וְכֹף אֶת יִצְרֵנוּ לְהִשְׁתַּעְבֶּד־לָךְ, וּתְנֵנוּ הַיּוֹם וּבְכָל יוֹם לְחֵן וּלְחֶסֶד וּלְרַחֲמִים

בְּעֵינֶיךָ וּבְעֵינֵי כָל־רוֹאֵינוּ, וְתִגְמְלֵנוּ חֲסָדִים טוֹבִים. בָּרוּךְ אַתָּה, יְיָ, גּוֹמֵל חֲסָדִים טוֹבִים לְעַמּוֹ יִשְׂרָאֵל.

Strengthen in us the voice of conscience; prompt us to deeds of goodness; and bend our every impulse to Your service, so that this day and always we may know Your love and the good will of all who behold us. Blessed is the Lord, who bestows love and kindness on His people Israel.

◆ ◆

לְעוֹלָם יְהֵא אָדָם יְרֵא שָׁמַיִם בַּסֵּתֶר וּבַגָּלוּי, וּמוֹדֶה עַל הָאֱמֶת, וְדוֹבֵר אֱמֶת בִּלְבָבוֹ.

At all times let us revere God inwardly as well as outwardly, acknowledge the truth and speak it in our hearts.

◆ ◆

7. OUR SMALLNESS AND OUR GREATNESS — מה אנחנו

רִבּוֹן כָּל־הָעוֹלָמִים, לֹא עַל־צִדְקוֹתֵינוּ אֲנַחְנוּ מַפִּילִים תַּחֲנוּנֵינוּ לְפָנֶיךָ, כִּי עַל רַחֲמֶיךָ הָרַבִּים.

Master of all the worlds, not in reliance upon the righteousness of our deeds do we place our longings before You; we look instead to Your abundant mercy.

מָה אֲנַחְנוּ, מֶה חַיֵּינוּ, מֶה חַסְדֵּנוּ, מַה־צִּדְקֵנוּ, מַה־יְּשׁוּעָתֵנוּ, מַה־כֹּחֵנוּ, מַה־גְּבוּרָתֵנוּ? מַה־נֹּאמַר לְפָנֶיךָ, יְיָ אֱלֹהֵינוּ וֵאלֹהֵי אֲבוֹתֵינוּ?

For what are we? What is our life, and what our faithfulness? What is our goodness, and what our vaunted strength? What can we say in Your presence, O Lord our God and God of all ages?

הֲלֹא כָּל־הַגִּבּוֹרִים כְּאַיִן לְפָנֶיךָ, וְאַנְשֵׁי הַשֵּׁם כְּלֹא הָיוּ, וַחֲכָמִים כִּבְלִי מַדָּע, וּנְבוֹנִים כִּבְלִי הַשְׂכֵּל, כִּי רֹב מַעֲשֵׂיהֶם

תֹּהוּ, וִימֵי חַיֵּיהֶם הֶבֶל לְפָנֶיךָ; וּמוֹתַר הָאָדָם מִן הַבְּהֵמָה אָיִן, כִּי הַכֹּל הָבֶל.

Are not all the conquerors as nothing before You, and those of renown as though they had not been, the learned as if they had no knowledge, and the wise as if without understanding? Many of our works are vain, and our days pass away like a shadow. Since all our achievements are insubstantial as mist, how dare we look upon ourselves as higher than the beasts?

אֲבָל אֲנַחְנוּ עַמְּךָ בְּנֵי בְרִיתֶךָ, וְאוֹתָנוּ קָרָאתָ לַעֲבוֹדָתֶךָ. לְפִיכָךְ אֲנַחְנוּ חַיָּבִים לְהוֹדוֹת לְךָ וּלְשַׁבֵּחֲךָ, וּלְבָרֵךְ וּלְקַדֵּשׁ אֶת־שְׁמֶךָ.

Yet, despite all our frailty, we are Your people, bound to Your covenant, and called to Your service. We therefore thank You and bless You, and proclaim the holiness of Your name.

◆ ◆

How greatly we are blessed!	אַשְׁרֵינוּ!
How good is our portion!	מַה־טּוֹב חֶלְקֵנוּ,
How pleasant our lot!	וּמַה־נָּעִים גּוֹרָלֵנוּ,
How beautiful our heritage!	וּמַה־יָּפָה יְרֻשָּׁתֵנוּ!

◆ ◆

Poems of Praise פסוקי דזמרה

One or more of the following passages may be read or chanted.
Then continue with Barechu, page 301.

FOR LIFE ברוך שאמר

בָּרוּךְ שֶׁאָמַר וְהָיָה הָעוֹלָם, בָּרוּךְ הוּא.
בָּרוּךְ עוֹשֶׂה בְרֵאשִׁית, בָּרוּךְ אוֹמֵר וְעוֹשֶׂה.
בָּרוּךְ גּוֹזֵר וּמְקַיֵּם, בָּרוּךְ מְרַחֵם עַל הָאָרֶץ.
בָּרוּךְ מְרַחֵם עַל הַבְּרִיּוֹת, בָּרוּךְ מְשַׁלֵּם שָׂכָר טוֹב לִירֵאָיו.
בָּרוּךְ חַי לָעַד וְקַיָּם לָנֶצַח, בָּרוּךְ פּוֹדֶה וּמַצִּיל, בָּרוּךְ שְׁמוֹ.
בִּשְׁבָחוֹת וּבִזְמִירוֹת נְגַדֶּלְךָ וּנְשַׁבֵּחֲךָ וּנְפָאֶרְךָ, וְנַזְכִּיר שִׁמְךָ וְנַמְלִיכְךָ, מַלְכֵּנוּ, אֱלֹהֵינוּ. יָחִיד, חֵי הָעוֹלָמִים, מֶלֶךְ, מְשֻׁבָּח וּמְפֹאָר עֲדֵי־עַד שְׁמוֹ הַגָּדוֹל.
בָּרוּךְ אַתָּה, יְיָ, מֶלֶךְ מְהֻלָּל בַּתִּשְׁבָּחוֹת.

Blessed is the One who spoke, and the world came to be.
Blessed is the Source of creation.

Blessed is the One whose word is deed, whose thought is fact.

Blessed is the One whose compassion covers the earth and all its creatures.

Blessed is the living and eternal God, Ruler of the universe, divine Source of deliverance and help.

With songs of praise we extol You and proclaim Your sovereignty, our God and King, for You are the Source of life in the universe.

Blessed is the Eternal King, to whom our praise is due.

◆ ◆

From Psalm 19

הַשָּׁמַיִם מְסַפְּרִים כְּבוֹד־אֵל, וּמַעֲשֵׂה יָדָיו מַגִּיד הָרָקִיעַ.

The heavens declare the glory of God; the arch of sky reveals His handiwork.

יוֹם לְיוֹם יַבִּיעַ אֹמֶר, וְלַיְלָה לְלַיְלָה יְחַוֶּה־דָּעַת.

Day pours out speech to day; one night spreads knowledge to the other.

אֵין־אֹמֶר וְאֵין דְּבָרִים, בְּלִי נִשְׁמָע קוֹלָם –

They have no speech, they use no words, no voice of theirs is heard —

בְּכָל־הָאָרֶץ יָצָא קַוָּם, וּבִקְצֵה תֵבֵל מִלֵּיהֶם!

Yet their call goes out through all the earth, and their words to the edge of the universe!

◆ ◆

From Psalm 33

רַנְּנוּ צַדִּיקִים בַּיְיָ;
לַיְשָׁרִים נָאוָה תְהִלָּה.

Let all who are righteous sing God's song;

the upright do well to acclaim Him.

הוֹדוּ לַייָ בְּכִנּוֹר; בְּנֵבֶל עָשׂוֹר זַמְּרוּ־לוֹ.
שִׁירוּ לוֹ שִׁיר חָדָשׁ; הֵיטִיבוּ נַגֵּן בִּתְרוּעָה.

Thank the Lord on the harp; accompany your chant with strings.

Sing to Him a new song; grace your song with skillful play.

כִּי־יָשָׁר דְּבַר־יְיָ, וְכָל־מַעֲשֵׂהוּ בֶּאֱמוּנָה.
אֹהֵב צְדָקָה וּמִשְׁפָּט; חֶסֶד יְיָ מָלְאָה הָאָרֶץ.

For the word of the Lord holds good; His work commands our trust.

He loves justice and right; His steadfast love fills the earth.

בִּדְבַר יְיָ שָׁמַיִם נַעֲשׂוּ, וּבְרוּחַ פִּיו כָּל־צְבָאָם.
כִּי הוּא אָמַר וַיֶּהִי; הוּא־צִוָּה וַיַּעֲמֹד.

The heavens were made by the word of the Lord; their starry host by the power of His thought.

For He spoke and it was; He commanded and it stood firm.

עֲצַת יְיָ לְעוֹלָם תַּעֲמֹד;
מַחְשְׁבוֹת לִבּוֹ לְדֹר וָדֹר.

The Lord's plan will stand for ever;
His thought will endure for all time.

הַיֹּצֵר יַחַד לִבָּם;
הַמֵּבִין אֶל־כׇּל־מַעֲשֵׂיהֶם.

He fashioned the hearts of us all;
He understands the meaning of our lives.

אֵין הַמֶּלֶךְ נוֹשָׁע בְּרׇב־חָיִל; גִּבּוֹר לֹא־יִנָּצֵל בְּרׇב־כֹּחַ.
שֶׁקֶר הַסּוּס לִתְשׁוּעָה, וּבְרֹב חֵילוֹ לֹא יְמַלֵּט.

No king is saved by the power of his arms, no warrior by reason of his strength.

The war-horse will not help you; for all its strength it cannot save.

נַפְשֵׁנוּ חִכְּתָה לַייָ; עֶזְרֵנוּ וּמָגִנֵּנוּ הוּא.
כִּי־בוֹ יִשְׂמַח לִבֵּנוּ; כִּי בְשֵׁם קׇדְשׁוֹ בָטָחְנוּ.
יְהִי־חַסְדְּךָ יְיָ עָלֵינוּ; כַּאֲשֶׁר יִחַלְנוּ לָךְ.

Therefore we trust in the Lord; He is our Help and our Shield.
In Him will we rejoice; in His holy being will we trust.

Let Your steadfast love rest upon us, O Lord, as we put our trust in You.

◆ ◆

Psalm 92

A SONG FOR THE SABBATH DAY

מִזְמוֹר שִׁיר לְיוֹם הַשַּׁבָּת:
טוֹב לְהֹדוֹת לַייָ, וּלְזַמֵּר לְשִׁמְךָ, עֶלְיוֹן,
לְהַגִּיד בַּבֹּקֶר חַסְדֶּךָ, וֶאֱמוּנָתְךָ בַּלֵּילוֹת,
עֲלֵי־עָשׂוֹר וַעֲלֵי־נָבֶל, עֲלֵי הִגָּיוֹן בְּכִנּוֹר.

It is good to give thanks to the Lord,
to sing hymns to Your name, O Most High!
To tell of Your love in the morning,
to sing at night of Your faithfulness;

to pluck the strings, to sound the lute,
to make the harp vibrate.

כִּי שִׂמַּחְתַּנִי, יְיָ, בְּפָעֳלֶךָ, בְּמַעֲשֵׂי יָדֶיךָ אֲרַנֵּן.
מַה־גָּדְלוּ מַעֲשֶׂיךָ, יְיָ! מְאֹד עָמְקוּ מַחְשְׁבֹתֶיךָ.

Your deeds, O Lord, fill me with gladness,
Your work moves me to song.
How great are Your works, O Lord!
How profound Your design!

אִישׁ־בַּעַר לֹא יֵדָע, וּכְסִיל לֹא־יָבִין אֶת־זֹאת:
בִּפְרֹחַ רְשָׁעִים כְּמוֹ־עֵשֶׂב, וַיָּצִיצוּ כָּל־פֹּעֲלֵי אָוֶן,
לְהִשָּׁמְדָם עֲדֵי־עַד.
וְאַתָּה מָרוֹם לְעֹלָם, יְיָ.

The fool will never learn,
the dullard never grasp this:
the wicked may flourish like grass,
all who do evil may blossom,
yet they are doomed to destruction,
while You, O Lord, are exalted for all time.

כִּי הִנֵּה אֹיְבֶיךָ, יְיָ, כִּי־הִנֵּה אֹיְבֶיךָ יֹאבֵדוּ,
יִתְפָּרְדוּ כָּל־פֹּעֲלֵי אָוֶן.
וַתָּרֶם כִּרְאֵים קַרְנִי, בַּלֹּתִי בְּשֶׁמֶן רַעֲנָן.
וַתַּבֵּט עֵינִי בְּשׁוּרָי, בַּקָּמִים עָלַי מְרֵעִים,
תִּשְׁמַעְנָה אָזְנָי:

See how Your enemies, O Lord,
see how Your enemies shall perish,
how all who do evil shall be scattered.
You lift up my head in pride,
I am bathed in freshening oil.
I shall see the defeat of my foes,
my ears shall hear of their fall.

צַדִּיק כַּתָּמָר יִפְרָח, כְּאֶרֶז בַּלְּבָנוֹן יִשְׂגֶּה.
שְׁתוּלִים בְּבֵית יְיָ, בְּחַצְרוֹת אֱלֹהֵינוּ יַפְרִיחוּ.

עוֹד יְנוּבוּן בְּשֵׂיבָה, דְּשֵׁנִים וְרַעֲנַנִּים יִהְיוּ,
לְהַגִּיד כִּי־יָשָׁר יְיָ, צוּרִי, וְלֹא־עַוְלָֽתָה בּוֹ.

The righteous shall flourish like palms,
grow tall like cedars in Lebanon.
Rooted in the house of the Lord,
they shall be ever fresh and green,
proclaiming that the Lord is just,
my Rock, in whom there is no wrong.

◆ ◆

אשרי

אַשְׁרֵי יוֹשְׁבֵי בֵיתֶךָ; עוֹד יְהַלְלוּךָ סֶּלָה.
אַשְׁרֵי הָעָם שֶׁכָּכָה לּוֹ; אַשְׁרֵי הָעָם שֶׁיְיָ אֱלֹהָיו.

Happy are those who dwell in Your house;
they will sing Your praise for ever.

Happy the people to whom such blessing falls;
happy the people whose God is the Lord.

Psalm 145

תְּהִלָּה לְדָוִד.
אֲרוֹמִמְךָ, אֱלֹהַי הַמֶּלֶךְ, וַאֲבָרְכָה שִׁמְךָ לְעוֹלָם וָעֶד.
בְּכָל־יוֹם אֲבָרְכֶךָּ, וַאֲהַלְלָה שִׁמְךָ לְעוֹלָם וָעֶד.

I will exalt You, my Sovereign God;
I will bless Your name for ever.

Every day will I bless You;
I will extol Your name for ever.

גָּדוֹל יְיָ וּמְהֻלָּל מְאֹד, וְלִגְדֻלָּתוֹ אֵין חֵקֶר.
דּוֹר לְדוֹר יְשַׁבַּח מַעֲשֶׂיךָ, וּגְבוּרֹתֶיךָ יַגִּידוּ.

Great is the Lord and worthy of praise;
His greatness is infinite.

One generation shall acclaim Your work to the next;
they shall tell of Your mighty acts.

הֲדַר כְּבוֹד הוֹדֶךָ,
וְדִבְרֵי נִפְלְאֹתֶיךָ אָשִׂיחָה.

They shall consider Your radiant glory;
they shall reflect on Your wondrous works.

וֶעֱזוּז נוֹרְאוֹתֶיךָ יֹאמֵרוּ, וּגְדֻלָּתְךָ אֲסַפְּרֶנָּה.
זֵכֶר רַב־טוּבְךָ יַבִּיעוּ, וְצִדְקָתְךָ יְרַנֵּנוּ.

They shall speak of Your awesome might,
and make known Your greatness.
They shall tell the world of Your great goodness,
and sing of Your righteousness.

חַנּוּן וְרַחוּם יְיָ, אֶרֶךְ אַפַּיִם וּגְדָל־חָסֶד.
טוֹב־יְיָ לַכֹּל, וְרַחֲמָיו עַל־כָּל־מַעֲשָׂיו.

"The Lord is gracious and compassionate,
endlessly patient, overflowing with love."
"The Lord is good to all; His compassion
shelters all His creatures."

יוֹדוּךָ יְיָ כָּל־מַעֲשֶׂיךָ,
וַחֲסִידֶיךָ יְבָרְכוּכָה.

All Your works, O Lord, shall thank You;
Your faithful shall bless You.

כְּבוֹד מַלְכוּתְךָ יֹאמֵרוּ, וּגְבוּרָתְךָ יְדַבֵּרוּ,
לְהוֹדִיעַ לִבְנֵי הָאָדָם גְּבוּרֹתָיו, וּכְבוֹד הֲדַר מַלְכוּתוֹ.

They shall speak of the glory of Your kingdom,
and tell of Your strength:
to reveal Your power to the world, and
the glorious splendor of Your kingdom.

מַלְכוּתְךָ מַלְכוּת כָּל־עוֹלָמִים,
וּמֶמְשַׁלְתְּךָ בְּכָל־דּוֹר וָדֹר.

Your kingdom is an everlasting kingdom;
Your dominion endures through all generations.

סוֹמֵךְ יְיָ לְכָל־הַנֹּפְלִים, וְזוֹקֵף לְכָל־הַכְּפוּפִים.
עֵינֵי כֹל אֵלֶיךָ יְשַׂבֵּרוּ, וְאַתָּה נוֹתֵן־לָהֶם אֶת־אָכְלָם בְּעִתּוֹ.

Lord, You support the falling;
You raise up all who are bowed down.

The eyes of all are turned to You;
You sustain them in time of need.

פּוֹתֵחַ אֶת־יָדֶךָ, וּמַשְׂבִּיעַ לְכָל־חַי רָצוֹן.
צַדִּיק יְיָ בְּכָל־דְּרָכָיו, וְחָסִיד בְּכָל־מַעֲשָׂיו.

You open Your hand to fulfill the needs of all the living.

Lord, You are just in all Your paths, loving in all Your deeds.

קָרוֹב יְיָ לְכָל־קֹרְאָיו, לְכֹל אֲשֶׁר יִקְרָאֻהוּ בֶאֱמֶת.
רְצוֹן־יְרֵאָיו יַעֲשֶׂה, וְאֶת־שַׁוְעָתָם יִשְׁמַע וְיוֹשִׁיעֵם.

The Lord is near to all who call upon Him,
to all who call upon Him in truth.

He will fulfill the hope of all who revere Him;
He will hear their cry and help them.

שׁוֹמֵר יְיָ אֶת־כָּל־אֹהֲבָיו,
וְאֵת כָּל־הָרְשָׁעִים יַשְׁמִיד.

The Lord preserves those who love Him,

but the lawless He brings to grief.

תְּהִלַּת יְיָ יְדַבֶּר־פִּי
וִיבָרֵךְ כָּל־בָּשָׂר שֵׁם קָדְשׁוֹ לְעוֹלָם וָעֶד.
וַאֲנַחְנוּ נְבָרֵךְ יָהּ מֵעַתָּה וְעַד־עוֹלָם. הַלְלוּיָהּ.

My lips shall declare the glory of the Lord;
let all flesh bless His holy name for ever and ever.

We will bless the Lord now and always. Halleluyah!

◆ ◆

Psalm 150

Halleluyah!	הַלְלוּיָהּ!
Praise God in His sanctuary;	הַלְלוּ־אֵל בְּקָדְשׁוֹ,
Praise Him whose power the heavens proclaim.	הַלְלוּהוּ בִּרְקִיעַ עֻזּוֹ.
Praise Him for His mighty acts;	הַלְלוּהוּ בִגְבוּרֹתָיו,
Praise Him for His surpassing greatness.	הַלְלוּהוּ כְּרֹב גֻּדְלוֹ.
Praise Him with shofar blast;	הַלְלוּהוּ בְּתֵקַע שׁוֹפָר,
Praise Him with harp and lute.	הַלְלוּהוּ בְּנֵבֶל וְכִנּוֹר.
Praise Him with drum and dance;	הַלְלוּהוּ בְּתֹף וּמָחוֹל,
Praise Him with strings and pipe.	הַלְלוּהוּ בְּמִנִּים וְעֻגָב.
Praise Him with cymbals sounding;	הַלְלוּהוּ בְצִלְצְלֵי־שָׁמַע,
Praise Him with cymbals resounding.	הַלְלוּהוּ בְּצִלְצְלֵי תְרוּעָה.
Let every soul praise the Lord.	כֹּל הַנְּשָׁמָה תְּהַלֵּל יָהּ.
Halleluyah!	הַלְלוּיָהּ!

◆ ◆

OUR IMMEASURABLE DEBT TO GOD — נשמת כל־חי

נִשְׁמַת כָּל־חַי תְּבָרֵךְ אֶת־שִׁמְךָ, יְיָ אֱלֹהֵינוּ, וְרוּחַ כָּל־בָּשָׂר תְּפָאֵר וּתְרוֹמֵם זִכְרְךָ, מַלְכֵּנוּ, תָּמִיד. מִן־הָעוֹלָם וְעַד־הָעוֹלָם אַתָּה אֵל; אֵין לָנוּ מֶלֶךְ אֶלָּא אָתָּה.

Let every living soul bless Your name, O Lord our God, and let every human being acclaim Your majesty, for ever and ever. Through all eternity You are God; we have no King but You.

אֱלֹהֵי הָרִאשׁוֹנִים וְהָאַחֲרוֹנִים, אֱלוֹהַּ כָּל־בְּרִיּוֹת, אֲדוֹן כָּל־תּוֹלָדוֹת, הַמְהֻלָּל בְּרֹב הַתִּשְׁבָּחוֹת, הַמְנַהֵג עוֹלָמוֹ בְּחֶסֶד

וּבְרִיּוֹתָיו בְּרַחֲמִים. וַייָ לֹא יָנוּם וְלֹא יִישָׁן; הַמְעוֹרֵר יְשֵׁנִים
וְהַמֵּקִיץ נִרְדָּמִים וְהַמֵּשִׂיחַ אִלְּמִים, וְהַמַּתִּיר אֲסוּרִים
וְהַסּוֹמֵךְ נוֹפְלִים וְהַזּוֹקֵף כְּפוּפִים. לְךָ לְבַדְּךָ אֲנַחְנוּ מוֹדִים.

God of all ages, Ruler of all creatures, Lord of all generations: all praise to You. You guide the world with steadfast love, Your creatures with tender mercy. You neither slumber nor sleep; You awaken the sleeping and arouse the dormant. You give speech to the silent, freedom to the enslaved, and justice to the oppressed. To You alone we give thanks.

אִלּוּ פִינוּ מָלֵא שִׁירָה כַּיָּם, וּלְשׁוֹנֵנוּ רִנָּה כַּהֲמוֹן גַּלָּיו,
וְשִׂפְתוֹתֵינוּ שֶׁבַח כְּמֶרְחֲבֵי רָקִיעַ, וְעֵינֵינוּ מְאִירוֹת כַּשֶּׁמֶשׁ
וְכַיָּרֵחַ, וְיָדֵינוּ פְרוּשׂוֹת כְּנִשְׁרֵי שָׁמָיִם, וְרַגְלֵינוּ קַלּוֹת
כָּאַיָּלוֹת – אֵין אֲנַחְנוּ מַסְפִּיקִים לְהוֹדוֹת לְךָ, יְיָ אֱלֹהֵינוּ
וֵאלֹהֵי אֲבוֹתֵינוּ, וּלְבָרֵךְ אֶת־שְׁמֶךָ עַל־אַחַת מֵאָלֶף, אֶלֶף
אַלְפֵי אֲלָפִים וְרִבֵּי רְבָבוֹת פְּעָמִים הַטּוֹבוֹת שֶׁעָשִׂיתָ עִם־
אֲבֹתֵינוּ וְעִמָּנוּ.

Though our mouths should overflow with song as the sea, our tongues with melody as the roaring waves, our lips with praise as the heavens' wide expanse; and though our eyes were to shine as the sun and the moon, our arms extend like eagles' wings, our feet speed swiftly as deer — still we could not fully thank You, Lord our God and God of all ages, or bless Your name enough, for even one of Your infinite kindnesses to our ancestors and to us.

עַל כֵּן אֵבָרִים שֶׁפִּלַּגְתָּ בָּנוּ, וְרוּחַ וּנְשָׁמָה שֶׁנָּפַחְתָּ בְּאַפֵּינוּ,
וְלָשׁוֹן אֲשֶׁר שַׂמְתָּ בְּפִינוּ, הֵן הֵם יוֹדוּ וִיבָרְכוּ וִישַׁבְּחוּ וִיפָאֲרוּ
אֶת־שִׁמְךָ, מַלְכֵּנוּ. כִּי כָל־פֶּה לְךָ יוֹדֶה, וְכָל־לָשׁוֹן לְךָ
תִשָּׁבַע, וְכָל־בֶּרֶךְ לְךָ תִכְרַע, וְכָל־קוֹמָה לְפָנֶיךָ תִשְׁתַּחֲוֶה,
וְכָל־לְבָבוֹת יִירָאוּךָ, וְכָל־קֶרֶב וּכְלָיוֹת יְזַמְּרוּ לִשְׁמֶךָ.
כַּדָּבָר שֶׁכָּתוּב: כָּל־עַצְמוֹתַי תֹּאמַרְנָה: "יְיָ, מִי כָמוֹךָ?"

כָּאָמוּר, "לְדָוִד בָּרְכִי, נַפְשִׁי, אֶת־יְיָ, וְכָל־קְרָבַי אֶת־שֵׁם קָדְשׁוֹ!"

Therefore, O God, limbs and tongue and heart and mind shall join to praise Your name; every tongue will yet affirm You, and every soul give You allegiance.
As it is written: All my limbs shall say: "Lord, who is like You?" And David sang: "Bless the Lord, O my soul, and let all that is within me bless His holy name!"

• •

הָאֵל בְּתַעֲצֻמוֹת עֻזֶּךָ, הַגָּדוֹל בִּכְבוֹד שְׁמֶךָ, הַגִּבּוֹר לָנֶצַח וְהַנּוֹרָא בְּנוֹרְאוֹתֶיךָ. הַמֶּלֶךְ הַיּוֹשֵׁב עַל כִּסֵּא רָם וְנִשָּׂא.

Tremendous is God in His power, glorious is He in His being, mighty for ever and awesome in His works. He is the King, supreme and exalted.

שׁוֹכֵן עַד, מָרוֹם וְקָדוֹשׁ שְׁמוֹ. וְכָתוּב: רַנְּנוּ צַדִּיקִים בַּייָ; לַיְשָׁרִים נָאוָה תְהִלָּה.

He abides for ever, the High and Holy One. Therefore let all who are righteous sing God's song; the upright do well to acclaim Him.

בְּפִי יְשָׁרִים תִּתְהַלָּל; וּבְדִבְרֵי צַדִּיקִים תִּתְבָּרַךְ; וּבִלְשׁוֹן חֲסִידִים תִּתְרוֹמָם; וּבְקֶרֶב קְדוֹשִׁים תִּתְקַדָּשׁ.

The mouths of the upright acclaim You; the words of the righteous bless You; the tongues of the faithful exalt You; the hearts of all who seek holiness sanctify You.

וּבְמַקְהֲלוֹת רִבְבוֹת עַמְּךָ, בֵּית יִשְׂרָאֵל, בְּרִנָּה יִתְפָּאַר שִׁמְךָ, מַלְכֵּנוּ, בְּכָל־דּוֹר וָדוֹר. יִשְׁתַּבַּח שִׁמְךָ לָעַד, מַלְכֵּנוּ, הָאֵל הַמֶּלֶךְ הַגָּדוֹל וְהַקָּדוֹשׁ בַּשָּׁמַיִם וּבָאָרֶץ.

And the assembled hosts of Your people, the house of Israel, in every generation, O King, glorify Your name in song. O Sovereign God, great and holy King, let Your name be praised for ever in heaven and on earth.

בָּרוּךְ אַתָּה, יְיָ, אֵל מֶלֶךְ, גָּדוֹל בַּתִּשְׁבָּחוֹת, אֵל הַהוֹדָאוֹת, אֲדוֹן הַנִּפְלָאוֹת, הַבּוֹחֵר בְּשִׁירֵי זִמְרָה, מֶלֶךְ אֵל חֵי הָעוֹלָמִים.

Blessed is the Lord, the Sovereign God, the Lord of wonders who delights in song, the Only One, the Life of the universe.

READER'S KADDISH — חצי קדיש

יִתְגַּדַּל וְיִתְקַדַּשׁ שְׁמֵהּ רַבָּא בְּעָלְמָא דִּי־בְרָא כִרְעוּתֵהּ, וְיַמְלִיךְ מַלְכוּתֵהּ בְּחַיֵּיכוֹן וּבְיוֹמֵיכוֹן וּבְחַיֵּי דְכָל־בֵּית יִשְׂרָאֵל, בַּעֲגָלָא וּבִזְמַן קָרִיב, וְאִמְרוּ: אָמֵן.

יְהֵא שְׁמֵהּ רַבָּא מְבָרַךְ לְעָלַם וּלְעָלְמֵי עָלְמַיָּא.

יִתְבָּרַךְ וְיִשְׁתַּבַּח, וְיִתְפָּאַר וְיִתְרוֹמַם וְיִתְנַשֵּׂא, וְיִתְהַדַּר וְיִתְעַלֶּה וְיִתְהַלַּל שְׁמֵהּ דְּקוּדְשָׁא, בְּרִיךְ הוּא, לְעֵלָּא מִן כָּל־בִּרְכָתָא וְשִׁירָתָא, תֻּשְׁבְּחָתָא וְנֶחֱמָתָא דַּאֲמִירָן בְּעָלְמָא, וְאִמְרוּ: אָמֵן.

Let the glory of God be extolled, let His great name be hallowed in the world whose creation He willed. May His kingdom soon prevail, in our own day, our own lives, and the life of all Israel, and let us say: Amen.

Let His great name be blessed for ever and ever.

Let the name of the Holy One, blessed is He, be glorified, exalted and honored, though He is beyond all the praises, songs, and adorations that we can utter, and let us say: Amen.

◆ ◆

All rise

שמע וברכותיה

בָּרְכוּ אֶת־יְיָ הַמְבֹרָךְ!

Praise the Lord, to whom our praise is due!

בָּרוּךְ יְיָ הַמְבֹרָךְ לְעוֹלָם וָעֶד!

Praised be the Lord, to whom our praise is due,
now and for ever!

◆ ◆

CREATION — יוצר

*בָּרוּךְ אַתָּה, יְיָ אֱלֹהֵינוּ, מֶלֶךְ הָעוֹלָם, יוֹצֵר אוֹר וּבוֹרֵא חֹשֶׁךְ, עֹשֶׂה שָׁלוֹם וּבוֹרֵא אֶת־הַכֹּל.

*Praised be the Lord our God, Ruler of the universe, who makes light and creates darkness, who ordains peace and fashions all things.

הַמֵּאִיר לָאָרֶץ וְלַדָּרִים עָלֶיהָ בְּרַחֲמִים, וּבְטוּבוֹ מְחַדֵּשׁ בְּכָל־יוֹם תָּמִיד מַעֲשֵׂה בְרֵאשִׁית.

With compassion He gives light to the earth and all who dwell there; with goodness He renews the work of creation continually, day by day.

מָה רַבּוּ מַעֲשֶׂיךָ, יְיָ! כֻּלָּם בְּחָכְמָה עָשִׂיתָ, מָלְאָה הָאָרֶץ קִנְיָנֶךָ.

How manifold are Your works, O Lord; in wisdom You have made them all; the earth is full of Your creations.

תִּתְבָּרַךְ, יְיָ אֱלֹהֵינוּ, עַל־שֶׁבַח מַעֲשֵׂה יָדֶיךָ, וְעַל־מְאוֹרֵי־אוֹר שֶׁעָשִׂיתָ: יְפָאֲרוּךָ. סֶּלָה. בָּרוּךְ אַתָּה, יְיָ, יוֹצֵר הַמְּאוֹרוֹת.

Let all bless You, O Lord our God, for the excellence of Your handiwork, and for the glowing stars that You have made: let them glorify You for ever. Blessed is the Lord, the Maker of light.

**For a fuller version of Yotser,* *see page 315.*

◆ ◆

REVELATION אהבה רבה

אַהֲבָה רַבָּה אֲהַבְתָּנוּ, יְיָ אֱלֹהֵינוּ, חֶמְלָה גְדוֹלָה וִיתֵרָה חָמַלְתָּ עָלֵינוּ. אָבִינוּ מַלְכֵּנוּ, בַּעֲבוּר אֲבוֹתֵינוּ שֶׁבָּטְחוּ בְךָ וַתְּלַמְּדֵם חֻקֵּי חַיִּים, כֵּן תְּחָנֵּנוּ וּתְלַמְּדֵנוּ.

Deep is Your love for us, O Lord our God, and great is Your compassion. Our Maker and King, our ancestors trusted in You, and You taught them the laws of life: be gracious now to us, and teach us.

אָבִינוּ, הָאָב הָרַחֲמָן, הַמְרַחֵם, רַחֵם עָלֵינוּ וְתֵן בְּלִבֵּנוּ לְהָבִין וּלְהַשְׂכִּיל, לִשְׁמֹעַ לִלְמֹד וּלְלַמֵּד, לִשְׁמֹר וְלַעֲשׂוֹת וּלְקַיֵּם אֶת־כָּל־דִּבְרֵי תַלְמוּד תּוֹרָתֶךָ בְּאַהֲבָה.

Have compassion upon us, O Source of mercy, and guide us to know and understand, learn and teach, observe and uphold with love all the teachings of Your Torah.

וְהָאֵר עֵינֵינוּ בְּתוֹרָתֶךָ, וְדַבֵּק לִבֵּנוּ בְּמִצְוֹתֶיךָ, וְיַחֵד לְבָבֵנוּ לְאַהֲבָה וּלְיִרְאָה אֶת־שְׁמֶךָ. וְלֹא־נֵבוֹשׁ לְעוֹלָם וָעֶד, כִּי בְשֵׁם קָדְשְׁךָ הַגָּדוֹל וְהַנּוֹרָא בָּטָחְנוּ. נָגִילָה וְנִשְׂמְחָה בִּישׁוּעָתֶךָ, כִּי אֵל פּוֹעֵל יְשׁוּעוֹת אָתָּה, וּבָנוּ בָחַרְתָּ וְקֵרַבְתָּנוּ לְשִׁמְךָ הַגָּדוֹל סֶלָה בֶּאֱמֶת, לְהוֹדוֹת לְךָ וּלְיַחֶדְךָ בְּאַהֲבָה.

בָּרוּךְ אַתָּה, יְיָ, הַבּוֹחֵר בְּעַמּוֹ יִשְׂרָאֵל בְּאַהֲבָה.

Enlighten us with Your Teaching, help us to hold fast to Your Mitzvot, and unite our hearts to love and revere Your name.

Then shall we never be shamed, for we shall put our trust in You, the great, holy, and awesome One. We shall rejoice and be glad in Your salvation, for You, O God, are the Author of many deliverances. In love You have chosen us and drawn us near to You to serve You in faithfulness and to proclaim Your unity.

Blessed is the Lord, who in love has chosen His people Israel to serve Him.

◆ ◆

שְׁמַע יִשְׂרָאֵל: יְיָ אֱלֹהֵינוּ, יְיָ אֶחָד!

Hear, O Israel: the Lord is our God, the Lord is One!

בָּרוּךְ שֵׁם כְּבוֹד מַלְכוּתוֹ לְעוֹלָם וָעֶד!

Blessed is His glorious kingdom for ever and ever!

All are seated

וְאָהַבְתָּ אֵת יְיָ אֱלֹהֶיךָ בְּכָל־לְבָבְךָ וּבְכָל־נַפְשְׁךָ וּבְכָל־מְאֹדֶךָ.
וְהָיוּ הַדְּבָרִים הָאֵלֶּה, אֲשֶׁר אָנֹכִי מְצַוְּךָ הַיּוֹם, עַל־לְבָבֶךָ.
וְשִׁנַּנְתָּם לְבָנֶיךָ, וְדִבַּרְתָּ בָּם בְּשִׁבְתְּךָ בְּבֵיתֶךָ, וּבְלֶכְתְּךָ
בַדֶּרֶךְ, וּבְשָׁכְבְּךָ וּבְקוּמֶךָ.

You shall love the Lord your God with all your mind, with all your strength, with all your being.
Set these words, which I command you this day, upon your heart. Teach them faithfully to your children; speak of them in your home and on your way, when you lie down and when you rise up.

וּקְשַׁרְתָּם לְאוֹת עַל־יָדֶךָ, וְהָיוּ לְטֹטָפֹת בֵּין עֵינֶיךָ, וּכְתַבְתָּם
עַל־מְזֻזוֹת בֵּיתֶךָ, וּבִשְׁעָרֶיךָ.

Bind them as a sign upon your hand; let them be a symbol before your eyes; inscribe them on the doorposts of your house, and on your gates.

לְמַעַן תִּזְכְּרוּ וַעֲשִׂיתֶם אֶת־כָּל־מִצְוֹתָי, וִהְיִיתֶם קְדֹשִׁים
לֵאלֹהֵיכֶם. אֲנִי יְיָ אֱלֹהֵיכֶם, אֲשֶׁר הוֹצֵאתִי אֶתְכֶם מֵאֶרֶץ
מִצְרַיִם לִהְיוֹת לָכֶם לֵאלֹהִים. אֲנִי יְיָ אֱלֹהֵיכֶם.

Be mindful of all My mitzvot, and do them: so shall you consecrate yourselves to your God. I, the Lord, am your God who led you out of Egypt to be your God; I, the Lord, am your God.

◆ ◆

REDEMPTION גאולה

אֱמֶת וְיַצִּיב, וְאָהוּב וְחָבִיב, וְנוֹרָא וְאַדִּיר, וְטוֹב וְיָפֶה הַדָּבָר הַזֶּה עָלֵינוּ לְעוֹלָם וָעֶד.
אֱמֶת, אֱלֹהֵי עוֹלָם מַלְכֵּנוּ, צוּר יַעֲקֹב מָגֵן יִשְׁעֵנוּ.

True and enduring, beloved and precious, awesome, good, and beautiful is this eternal teaching.

This truth we hold to be for ever certain: the Eternal God is our King. He is the Rock of Jacob, our protecting Shield.

לְדֹר וָדֹר הוּא קַיָּם, וּשְׁמוֹ קַיָּם, וְכִסְאוֹ נָכוֹן, וּמַלְכוּתוֹ וֶאֱמוּנָתוֹ לָעַד קַיָּמֶת. וּדְבָרָיו חָיִים וְקַיָּמִים, נֶאֱמָנִים וְנֶחֱמָדִים, לָעַד וּלְעוֹלְמֵי עוֹלָמִים.

He abides through all generations; His name is Eternal. His throne stands firm; His sovereignty and faithfulness are everlasting.

His words live and endure, true and precious to all eternity.

מִמִּצְרַיִם גְּאַלְתָּנוּ, יְיָ אֱלֹהֵינוּ, וּמִבֵּית עֲבָדִים פְּדִיתָנוּ.

Lord our God, You redeemed us from Egypt;

You set us free from the house of bondage.

עַל־זֹאת שִׁבְּחוּ אֲהוּבִים וְרוֹמְמוּ אֵל, וְנָתְנוּ יְדִידִים זְמִירוֹת, שִׁירוֹת וְתִשְׁבָּחוֹת, בְּרָכוֹת וְהוֹדָאוֹת לַמֶּלֶךְ, אֵל חַי וְקַיָּם.

For this the people who felt Your love sang songs of praise to You:

The living God, high and exalted, mighty and awesome,

רָם וְנִשָּׂא, גָּדוֹל וְנוֹרָא, מַשְׁפִּיל גֵּאִים וּמַגְבִּיהַּ שְׁפָלִים, מוֹצִיא אֲסִירִים וּפוֹדֶה עֲנָוִים, וְעוֹזֵר דַּלִּים, וְעוֹנֶה לְעַמּוֹ בְּעֵת שַׁוְּעָם אֵלָיו.

Who humbles the proud and raises the lowly, who frees the captive and redeems the oppressed,

who is the Answer to all who cry out to Him.

תְּהִלּוֹת לְאֵל עֶלְיוֹן, בָּרוּךְ הוּא וּמְבֹרָךְ. מֹשֶׁה וּבְנֵי יִשְׂרָאֵל
לְךָ עָנוּ שִׁירָה בְּשִׂמְחָה רַבָּה, וְאָמְרוּ כֻלָּם:

All praise to God Most High, the Source of blessing! Like Moses and Israel, we sing to Him this song of rejoicing:

מִי־כָמֹכָה בָּאֵלִם, יְיָ?
Who is like You, Eternal One, among the gods that are worshipped?

מִי כָּמֹכָה, נֶאְדָּר בַּקֹּדֶשׁ,
Who is like You, majestic in holiness,

נוֹרָא תְהִלֹּת, עֹשֵׂה פֶלֶא?
awesome in splendor, doing wonders?

שִׁירָה חֲדָשָׁה שִׁבְּחוּ גְאוּלִים לְשִׁמְךָ עַל־שְׂפַת הַיָּם; יַחַד כֻּלָּם
הוֹדוּ וְהִמְלִיכוּ וְאָמְרוּ: "יְיָ יִמְלֹךְ לְעוֹלָם וָעֶד!"

A new song the redeemed sang to Your name. At the shore of the Sea, saved from destruction, they proclaimed Your sovereign power: "The Eternal will reign for ever and ever!"

צוּר יִשְׂרָאֵל, קוּמָה בְּעֶזְרַת יִשְׂרָאֵל, וּפְדֵה כִנְאֻמֶךָ יְהוּדָה
וְיִשְׂרָאֵל. גֹּאֲלֵנוּ יְיָ צְבָאוֹת שְׁמוֹ, קְדוֹשׁ יִשְׂרָאֵל.
בָּרוּךְ אַתָּה, יְיָ, גָּאַל יִשְׂרָאֵל.

O Rock of Israel, come to Israel's help. Fulfill Your promise of redemption for Judah and Israel. Our Redeemer is the Lord of Hosts, the Holy One of Israel. Blessed is the Lord, the Redeemer of Israel.

◆ ◆

All rise

תפלה

אֲדֹנָי, שְׂפָתַי תִּפְתָּח, וּפִי יַגִּיד תְּהִלָּתֶךָ.

Eternal God, open my lips, that my mouth may declare Your glory.

GOD OF ALL GENERATIONS — אבות

בָּרוּךְ אַתָּה, יְיָ אֱלֹהֵינוּ וֵאלֹהֵי אֲבוֹתֵינוּ, אֱלֹהֵי אַבְרָהָם, אֱלֹהֵי יִצְחָק, וֵאלֹהֵי יַעֲקֹב: הָאֵל הַגָּדוֹל, הַגִּבּוֹר וְהַנּוֹרָא, אֵל עֶלְיוֹן.

We praise You, Lord our God and God of all generations: God of Abraham, God of Isaac, God of Jacob; great, mighty, and awesome God, God supreme.

גּוֹמֵל חֲסָדִים טוֹבִים, וְקוֹנֵה הַכֹּל, וְזוֹכֵר חַסְדֵי אָבוֹת, וּמֵבִיא גְאֻלָּה לִבְנֵי בְנֵיהֶם, לְמַעַן שְׁמוֹ, בְּאַהֲבָה.*

Master of all the living, Your ways are ways of love. You remember the faithfulness of our ancestors, and in love bring redemption to their children's children for the sake of Your name.*

מֶלֶךְ עוֹזֵר וּמוֹשִׁיעַ וּמָגֵן. בָּרוּךְ אַתָּה, יְיָ, מָגֵן אַבְרָהָם.

You are our King and our Help, our Savior and our Shield. Blessed is the Lord, the Shield of Abraham.

** On Shabbat Shuvah insert:*

זָכְרֵנוּ לְחַיִּים, מֶלֶךְ חָפֵץ בַּחַיִּים.
וְכָתְבֵנוּ בְּסֵפֶר הַחַיִּים, לְמַעַנְךָ אֱלֹהִים חַיִּים.

Remember us unto life, for You are the King who delights in life, and inscribe us in the Book of Life, that Your will may prevail, O God of life.

◆ ◆

GOD'S POWER גבורות

אַתָּה גִּבּוֹר לְעוֹלָם, אֲדֹנָי, מְחַיֵּה הַכֹּל אַתָּה, רַב לְהוֹשִׁיעַ.

Eternal is Your might, O Lord; all life is Your gift; great is Your power to save!

מְכַלְכֵּל חַיִּים בְּחֶסֶד, מְחַיֵּה הַכֹּל בְּרַחֲמִים רַבִּים. סוֹמֵךְ נוֹפְלִים, וְרוֹפֵא חוֹלִים, וּמַתִּיר אֲסוּרִים, וּמְקַיֵּם אֱמוּנָתוֹ לִישֵׁנֵי עָפָר.

With love You sustain the living, with great compassion give life to all. You send help to the falling and healing to the sick; You bring freedom to the captive and keep faith with those who sleep in the dust.

מִי כָמוֹךָ, בַּעַל גְּבוּרוֹת, וּמִי דּוֹמֶה לָּךְ, מֶלֶךְ מֵמִית וּמְחַיֶּה וּמַצְמִיחַ יְשׁוּעָה?*

וְנֶאֱמָן אַתָּה לְהַחֲיוֹת הַכֹּל. בָּרוּךְ אַתָּה, יְיָ, מְחַיֵּה הַכֹּל.

Who is like You, Master of Might? Who is Your equal, O Lord of life and death, Source of salvation? Blessed is the Lord, the Source of life.*

* *On Shabbat Shuvah insert:*

מִי כָמוֹךָ, אַב הָרַחֲמִים, זוֹכֵר יְצוּרָיו לְחַיִּים בְּרַחֲמִים?

Who is like You, Source of mercy, who in compassion sustains the life of His children?

◆ ◆

SANCTIFICATION קדושה

נְקַדֵּשׁ אֶת־שִׁמְךָ בָּעוֹלָם, כְּשֵׁם שֶׁמַּקְדִּישִׁים אוֹתוֹ בִּשְׁמֵי מָרוֹם, כַּכָּתוּב עַל־יַד נְבִיאֶךָ: וְקָרָא זֶה אֶל־זֶה וְאָמַר:

We sanctify Your name on earth, even as all things, to the ends of time and space, proclaim Your holiness; and in the words of the prophet we say:

קָדוֹשׁ, קָדוֹשׁ, קָדוֹשׁ יְיָ צְבָאוֹת, מְלֹא כָל־הָאָֽרֶץ כְּבוֹדוֹ.

Holy, Holy, Holy is the Lord of Hosts; the fullness of the whole earth is His glory!

אַדִּיר אַדִּירֵֽנוּ, יְיָ אֲדֹנֵֽינוּ, מָה־אַדִּיר שִׁמְךָ בְּכָל־הָאָֽרֶץ!

Source of our strength, Sovereign Lord, how majestic is Your presence in all the earth!

בָּרוּךְ כְּבוֹד־יְיָ מִמְּקוֹמוֹ.

Blessed is the glory of God in heaven and earth.

אֶחָד הוּא אֱלֹהֵֽינוּ, הוּא אָבִֽינוּ, הוּא מַלְכֵּֽנוּ, הוּא מוֹשִׁיעֵֽנוּ;
וְהוּא יַשְׁמִיעֵֽנוּ בְּרַחֲמָיו לְעֵינֵי כָּל־חָי:

He alone is our God and our Creator; He is our Ruler and our Helper; and in His mercy He reveals Himself in the sight of all the living:

I AM ADONAI YOUR GOD! "אֲנִי יְיָ אֱלֹהֵיכֶם!"

יִמְלֹךְ יְיָ לְעוֹלָם, אֱלֹהַֽיִךְ צִיּוֹן, לְדֹר וָדֹר. הַלְלוּיָהּ!

The Lord shall reign for ever; your God, O Zion, from generation to generation. Halleluyah!

לְדוֹר וָדוֹר נַגִּיד גָּדְלֶֽךָ, וּלְנֵֽצַח נְצָחִים קְדֻשָּׁתְךָ נַקְדִּישׁ.
וְשִׁבְחֲךָ, אֱלֹהֵֽינוּ, מִפִּֽינוּ לֹא יָמוּשׁ לְעוֹלָם וָעֶד.*
בָּרוּךְ אַתָּה, יְיָ, הָאֵל הַקָּדוֹשׁ.

To all generations we will make known Your greatness, and to all eternity proclaim Your holiness. Your praise, O God, shall never depart from our lips.* Blessed is the Lord, the holy God.

* *On Shabbat Shuvah conclude:*

Blessed is the Lord, the holy King. בָּרוּךְ אַתָּה, יְיָ, הַמֶּֽלֶךְ הַקָּדוֹשׁ.

All are seated

◆ ◆

THE HOLINESS OF SHABBAT

קדושת היום

וְשָׁמְרוּ בְנֵי־יִשְׂרָאֵל אֶת־הַשַּׁבָּת, לַעֲשׂוֹת אֶת־הַשַּׁבָּת לְדֹרֹתָם בְּרִית עוֹלָם. בֵּינִי וּבֵין בְּנֵי יִשְׂרָאֵל אוֹת הִיא לְעֹלָם, כִּי שֵׁשֶׁת יָמִים עָשָׂה יְיָ אֶת־הַשָּׁמַיִם וְאֶת־הָאָרֶץ, וּבַיּוֹם הַשְּׁבִיעִי שָׁבַת וַיִּנָּפַשׁ.

The people of Israel shall keep the Sabbath, observing the Sabbath in every generation as a covenant for all time. It is a sign for ever between Me and the people of Israel, for in six days the Eternal God made heaven and earth, and on the seventh day He rested from His labors.

◆

אֱלֹהֵינוּ וֵאלֹהֵי אֲבוֹתֵינוּ, רְצֵה בִמְנוּחָתֵנוּ. קַדְּשֵׁנוּ בְּמִצְוֹתֶיךָ וְתֵן חֶלְקֵנוּ בְּתוֹרָתֶךָ. שַׂבְּעֵנוּ מִטּוּבֶךָ, וְשַׂמְּחֵנוּ בִּישׁוּעָתֶךָ, וְטַהֵר לִבֵּנוּ לְעָבְדְּךָ בֶּאֱמֶת. וְהַנְחִילֵנוּ, יְיָ אֱלֹהֵינוּ, בְּאַהֲבָה וּבְרָצוֹן שַׁבַּת קָדְשֶׁךָ, וְיָנוּחוּ בָהּ יִשְׂרָאֵל מְקַדְּשֵׁי שְׁמֶךָ. בָּרוּךְ אַתָּה, יְיָ, מְקַדֵּשׁ הַשַּׁבָּת.

Our God and God of ages past, may our rest on this day be pleasing in Your sight. Sanctify us with Your Mitzvot, and let Your Torah be our way of life. Satisfy us with Your goodness, gladden us with Your salvation, and purify our hearts to serve You in truth. In Your gracious love, O Lord our God, let Your holy Sabbath remain our heritage, that all Israel, hallowing Your name, may find rest and peace. Blessed is the Lord, for the Sabbath and its holiness.

◆ ◆

WORSHIP

עבודה

רְצֵה, יְיָ אֱלֹהֵינוּ, בְּעַמְּךָ יִשְׂרָאֵל, וּתְפִלָּתָם בְּאַהֲבָה תְקַבֵּל, וּתְהִי לְרָצוֹן תָּמִיד עֲבוֹדַת יִשְׂרָאֵל עַמֶּךָ. אֵל קָרוֹב לְכָל־

קְרָאָיו, פְּנֵה אֶל עֲבָדֶיךָ וְחָנֵּנוּ; שְׁפוֹךְ רוּחֲךָ עָלֵינוּ, וְתֶחֱזֶינָה עֵינֵינוּ בְּשׁוּבְךָ לְצִיּוֹן בְּרַחֲמִים.

בָּרוּךְ אַתָּה, יְיָ, הַמַּחֲזִיר שְׁכִינָתוֹ לְצִיּוֹן.

Be gracious, O Lord our God, to Your people Israel, and receive our prayers with love. O may our worship always be acceptable to You.

Fill us with the knowledge that You are near to all who seek You in truth. Let our eyes behold Your presence in our midst and in the midst of our people in Zion.

Blessed is the Lord, whose presence gives life to Zion and all Israel.

◆ ◆

ON ROSH CHODESH AND CHOL HAMO-EID

אֱלֹהֵינוּ וֵאלֹהֵי אֲבוֹתֵינוּ, יַעֲלֶה וְיָבֹא וְיִזָּכֵר זִכְרוֹנֵנוּ וְזִכְרוֹן כָּל־עַמְּךָ בֵּית יִשְׂרָאֵל לְפָנֶיךָ, לְטוֹבָה לְחֵן לְחֶסֶד וּלְרַחֲמִים, לְחַיִּים וּלְשָׁלוֹם בְּיוֹם

Our God and God of all ages, be mindful of Your people Israel on this

first day of the new month,	רֹאשׁ הַחֹדֶשׁ הַזֶּה.
day of Pesach,	חַג הַמַּצּוֹת הַזֶּה.
day of Sukkot,	חַג הַסֻּכּוֹת הַזֶּה.

and renew in us love and compassion, goodness, life and peace.

This day remember us for well-being. *Amen.*	זָכְרֵנוּ, יְיָ אֱלֹהֵינוּ, בּוֹ לְטוֹבָה. אָמֵן.
This day bless us with Your nearness. *Amen.*	וּפָקְדֵנוּ בוֹ לִבְרָכָה. אָמֵן.
This day help us to a fuller life. *Amen.*	וְהוֹשִׁיעֵנוּ בוֹ לְחַיִּים. אָמֵן.

◆ ◆

THANKSGIVING הודאה

מוֹדִים אֲנַחְנוּ לָךְ, שָׁאַתָּה הוּא יְיָ אֱלֹהֵינוּ וֵאלֹהֵי אֲבוֹתֵינוּ לְעוֹלָם וָעֶד. צוּר חַיֵּינוּ, מָגֵן יִשְׁעֵנוּ, אַתָּה הוּא לְדוֹר וָדוֹר. נוֹדֶה לְּךָ וּנְסַפֵּר תְּהִלָּתֶךָ, עַל־חַיֵּינוּ הַמְּסוּרִים בְּיָדֶךָ, וְעַל־נִשְׁמוֹתֵינוּ הַפְּקוּדוֹת לָךְ, וְעַל־נִסֶּיךָ שֶׁבְּכָל־יוֹם עִמָּנוּ, וְעַל־נִפְלְאוֹתֶיךָ וְטוֹבוֹתֶיךָ שֶׁבְּכָל־עֵת, עֶרֶב וָבֹקֶר וְצָהֳרָיִם. הַטּוֹב: כִּי לֹא־כָלוּ רַחֲמֶיךָ, וְהַמְרַחֵם: כִּי־לֹא תַמּוּ חֲסָדֶיךָ, מֵעוֹלָם קִוִּינוּ לָךְ.

We gratefully acknowledge that You are the Lord our God and God of our people, the God of all generations. You are the Rock of our life, the Power that shields us in every age. We thank You and sing Your praises: for our lives, which are in Your hands; for our souls, which are in Your keeping; for the signs of Your presence we encounter every day; and for Your wondrous gifts at all times, morning, noon, and night. You are Goodness: Your mercies never end; You are Compassion: Your love will never fail. You have always been our hope.

וְעַל כֻּלָּם יִתְבָּרַךְ וְיִתְרוֹמַם שִׁמְךָ, מַלְכֵּנוּ, תָּמִיד לְעוֹלָם וָעֶד.

For all these things, O Sovereign God, let Your name be for ever exalted and blessed.

On Shabbat Shuvah insert:

וּכְתוֹב לְחַיִּים טוֹבִים כָּל־בְּנֵי בְרִיתֶךָ.

Let life abundant be the heritage of all Your children.

וְכֹל הַחַיִּים יוֹדוּךָ סֶּלָה, וִיהַלְלוּ אֶת שִׁמְךָ בֶּאֱמֶת, הָאֵל יְשׁוּעָתֵנוּ וְעֶזְרָתֵנוּ סֶלָה. בָּרוּךְ אַתָּה, יְיָ, הַטּוֹב שִׁמְךָ וּלְךָ נָאֶה לְהוֹדוֹת.

O God our Redeemer and Helper, let all who live affirm You and praise Your name in truth. Lord, whose nature is Goodness, we give You thanks and praise.

◆ ◆

ON CHANUKAH

עַל הַנִּסִּים וְעַל הַפֻּרְקָן, וְעַל הַגְּבוּרוֹת וְעַל הַתְּשׁוּעוֹת, וְעַל הַמִּלְחָמוֹת, שֶׁעָשִׂיתָ לַאֲבוֹתֵינוּ בַּיָּמִים הָהֵם בַּזְּמַן הַזֶּה.

בִּימֵי מַתִּתְיָהוּ בֶּן־יוֹחָנָן כֹּהֵן גָּדוֹל, חַשְׁמוֹנַי וּבָנָיו, כְּשֶׁעָמְדָה מַלְכוּת יָוָן הָרְשָׁעָה עַל־עַמְּךָ יִשְׂרָאֵל לְהַשְׁכִּיחָם תּוֹרָתֶךָ, וּלְהַעֲבִירָם מֵחֻקֵּי רְצוֹנֶךָ.

וְאַתָּה בְּרַחֲמֶיךָ הָרַבִּים עָמַדְתָּ לָהֶם בְּעֵת צָרָתָם. רַבְתָּ אֶת־רִיבָם, דַּנְתָּ אֶת־דִּינָם, מָסַרְתָּ גִבּוֹרִים בְּיַד חַלָּשִׁים, וְרַבִּים בְּיַד מְעַטִּים, וּטְמֵאִים בְּיַד טְהוֹרִים, וּרְשָׁעִים בְּיַד צַדִּיקִים, וְזֵדִים בְּיַד עוֹסְקֵי תוֹרָתֶךָ.

וּלְךָ עָשִׂיתָ שֵׁם גָּדוֹל וְקָדוֹשׁ בְּעוֹלָמֶךָ, וּלְעַמְּךָ יִשְׂרָאֵל עָשִׂיתָ תְּשׁוּעָה גְדוֹלָה וּפֻרְקָן כְּהַיּוֹם הַזֶּה.

וְאַחַר כֵּן בָּאוּ בָנֶיךָ לִדְבִיר בֵּיתֶךָ, וּפִנּוּ אֶת־הֵיכָלֶךָ, וְטִהֲרוּ אֶת־מִקְדָּשֶׁךָ, וְהִדְלִיקוּ נֵרוֹת בְּחַצְרוֹת קָדְשֶׁךָ, וְקָבְעוּ שְׁמוֹנַת יְמֵי חֲנֻכָּה אֵלּוּ לְהוֹדוֹת וּלְהַלֵּל לְשִׁמְךָ הַגָּדוֹל.

We give thanks for the redeeming wonders and the mighty deeds by which, at this season, our people was saved in days of old.

In the days of the Hasmoneans, a tyrant arose against our ancestors, determined to make them forget Your Torah, and to turn them away from obedience to Your will. But You were at their side in time of trouble. You gave them strength to struggle and to triumph, that they might serve You in freedom.

Through the power of Your spirit the weak defeated the strong, the few prevailed over the many, and the righteous were triumphant. Then Your children returned to Your house, to purify the sanctuary and kindle its lights. And they dedicated these days to give thanks and praise to Your great name.

◆ ◆

PEACE ברכת שלום

שִׂים שָׁלוֹם, טוֹבָה וּבְרָכָה, חֵן וָחֶסֶד וְרַחֲמִים, עָלֵינוּ וְעַל־כָּל־יִשְׂרָאֵל עַמֶּךָ.

Peace, happiness, and blessing; grace and love and mercy: may these descend on us, on all Israel, and all the world.

בָּרְכֵנוּ אָבִינוּ, כֻּלָּנוּ כְּאֶחָד, בְּאוֹר פָּנֶיךָ, כִּי בְאוֹר פָּנֶיךָ נָתַתָּ לָּנוּ, יְיָ אֱלֹהֵינוּ, תּוֹרַת חַיִּים, וְאַהֲבַת חֶסֶד, וּצְדָקָה וּבְרָכָה וְרַחֲמִים, וְחַיִּים וְשָׁלוֹם.

Bless us, our Creator, one and all, with the light of Your presence; for by that light, O God, You have revealed to us the law of life: to love kindness and justice and mercy, to seek blessing, life, and peace.

וְטוֹב בְּעֵינֶיךָ לְבָרֵךְ אֶת־עַמְּךָ יִשְׂרָאֵל בְּכָל־עֵת וּבְכָל־שָׁעָה בִּשְׁלוֹמֶךָ.*

בָּרוּךְ אַתָּה, יְיָ, הַמְבָרֵךְ אֶת־עַמּוֹ יִשְׂרָאֵל בַּשָּׁלוֹם.

O bless Your people Israel and all peoples with enduring peace!*

Praised be the Lord, who blesses His people Israel with peace.

** On Shabbat Shuvah conclude:*

בְּסֵפֶר חַיִּים וּבְרָכָה נִכָּתֵב לְחַיִּים טוֹבִים וּלְשָׁלוֹם.

בָּרוּךְ אַתָּה, יְיָ, עוֹשֵׂה הַשָּׁלוֹם.

Teach us then to find our happiness in the search for righteousness and peace. Blessed is the Lord, the Source of peace.

◆ ◆

SILENT PRAYER

אֱלֹהַי, נְצֹר לְשׁוֹנִי מֵרָע, וּשְׂפָתַי מִדַּבֵּר מִרְמָה, וְלִמְקַלְלַי נַפְשִׁי תִדּוֹם, וְנַפְשִׁי כֶּעָפָר לַכֹּל תִּהְיֶה. פְּתַח לִבִּי בְּתוֹרָתֶךָ, וּבְמִצְוֹתֶיךָ תִּרְדּוֹף נַפְשִׁי, וְכֹל הַחוֹשְׁבִים עָלַי רָעָה, מְהֵרָה

הָפֵר עֲצָתָם וְקַלְקֵל מַחֲשַׁבְתָּם. עֲשֵׂה לְמַעַן שְׁמֶךָ, עֲשֵׂה לְמַעַן יְמִינֶךָ, עֲשֵׂה לְמַעַן קְדֻשָּׁתֶךָ, עֲשֵׂה לְמַעַן תּוֹרָתֶךָ. לְמַעַן יֵחָלְצוּן יְדִידֶיךָ. הוֹשִׁיעָה יְמִינְךָ וַעֲנֵנִי.

O God, keep my tongue from evil and my lips from deceit. Help me to be silent in the face of derision, humble in the presence of all. Open my heart to Your Torah, and I will hasten to do Your Mitzvot. Save me with Your power; in time of trouble be my answer, that those who love You may rejoice.

◆ ◆

יִהְיוּ לְרָצוֹן אִמְרֵי־פִי וְהֶגְיוֹן לִבִּי לְפָנֶיךָ, יְיָ, צוּרִי וְגוֹאֲלִי.

May the words of my mouth, and the meditations of my heart, be acceptable to You, O Lord, my Rock and my Redeemer.

or

עֹשֶׂה שָׁלוֹם בִּמְרוֹמָיו, הוּא יַעֲשֶׂה שָׁלוֹם עָלֵינוּ וְעַל כָּל־יִשְׂרָאֵל, וְאִמְרוּ אָמֵן.

May He who causes peace to reign in the high heavens let peace descend on us, on all Israel, and all the world.

◆ ◆

Prayers for Special Occasions begin on page 389.

On Shabbat during Pesach, Sukkot, and Chanukah, or when Shabbat coincides with Rosh Chodesh or Yom Ha-atsma-ut, a short form of Hallel, page 487, is read.

The Rituals for the Reading of Torah begin on page 415.

Alternative Yotser

בָּרוּךְ אַתָּה, יְיָ אֱלֹהֵינוּ, מֶלֶךְ הָעוֹלָם, יוֹצֵר אוֹר וּבוֹרֵא חֹשֶׁךְ, עֹשֶׂה שָׁלוֹם, וּבוֹרֵא אֶת־הַכֹּל.

Praised be the Lord our God, Ruler of the universe, who makes light and creates darkness, who ordains peace and fashions all things.

One or both of the following might be chanted

I.

הַכֹּל יוֹדוּךָ וְהַכֹּל יְשַׁבְּחוּךָ וְהַכֹּל יֹאמְרוּ: "אֵין קָדוֹשׁ כַּייָ."
הַכֹּל יְרוֹמְמוּךָ סֶּלָה, יוֹצֵר הַכֹּל.

All shall thank You, all shall praise You, and all shall say: "There is none holy as the Lord." All shall extol You for ever, O Creator of all.

הָאֵל הַפּוֹתֵחַ בְּכָל־יוֹם דַּלְתוֹת שַׁעֲרֵי מִזְרָח, וּבוֹקֵעַ חַלּוֹנֵי רָקִיעַ, מוֹצִיא חַמָּה מִמְּקוֹמָהּ וּלְבָנָה מִמְּכוֹן שִׁבְתָּהּ.

He is God. Day by day He unlocks the gates of the east and opens heaven's windows, bringing forth the sun from his place and the moon from her dwelling.

הַמֵּאִיר לָאָרֶץ וְלַדָּרִים עָלֶיהָ בְּרַחֲמִים, וּבְטוּבוֹ מְחַדֵּשׁ בְּכָל־יוֹם תָּמִיד מַעֲשֵׂה בְרֵאשִׁית.

With compassion He gives light to the earth and all who dwell there. With goodness He renews the work of creation, sustaining it day by day.

הַמֶּלֶךְ הַמְּרוֹמָם לְבַדּוֹ מֵאָז, הַמְשֻׁבָּח וְהַמְפֹאָר וְהַמִּתְנַשֵּׂא מִימוֹת עוֹלָם.

He is King, alone exalted from immemorial time, praised and glorified from days of old.

אֱלֹהֵי עוֹלָם, בְּרַחֲמֶיךָ הָרַבִּים רַחֵם עָלֵינוּ: אֲדוֹן עֻזֵּנוּ, צוּר מִשְׂגַּבֵּנוּ, מָגֵן יִשְׁעֵנוּ, מִשְׂגָּב בַּעֲדֵנוּ.

O everlasting God, in Your abundant mercy have mercy upon us, You who are our mighty Lord, our sheltering Rock, our protecting Shield, our only Stronghold.

II.

אֵל אָדוֹן עַל כָּל־הַמַּעֲשִׂים, בָּרוּךְ וּמְבֹרָךְ בְּפִי כָּל־נְשָׁמָה.

God is Lord of all creation: every living being sings His praises.

גָּדְלוֹ וְטוּבוֹ מָלֵא עוֹלָם, דַּעַת וּתְבוּנָה סוֹבְבִים אוֹתוֹ.

His greatness and goodness fill the world; knowledge and insight are round about Him.

זְכוּת וּמִישׁוֹר לִפְנֵי כִסְאוֹ! חֶסֶד וְרַחֲמִים לִפְנֵי כְבוֹדוֹ!

Purity and justice before His throne! Love and mercy His foremost glory!

טוֹבִים מְאוֹרוֹת שֶׁבָּרָא אֱלֹהֵינוּ: יְצָרָם בְּדַעַת, בְּרָאָם בְּהַשְׂכֵּל. כֹּחַ וּגְבוּרָה נָתַן בָּהֶם, לִהְיוֹת מוֹשְׁלִים בְּקֶרֶב תֵּבֵל.

Splendid the stars our God has made: He formed them with knowledge, He made them with wisdom, endowed them with power, imbued them with might. He called them to rule in the midst of His world.

מְלֵאִים זִיו וּמְפִיקִים נֹגַהּ, נָאֶה זִיוָם בְּכָל־הָעוֹלָם.

He filled them with splendor: radiant with brightness, their brilliance is lovely in all the world.

שְׂמֵחִים בְּצֵאתָם וְשָׂשִׂים בְּבוֹאָם, עוֹשִׂים בְּאֵימָה רְצוֹן קוֹנָם.

They rejoice in their rising, and delight in their setting, obeying in awe the will of their Maker.

פְּאֵר וְכָבוֹד נוֹתְנִים לִשְׁמוֹ, צָהֳלָה וְרִנָּה לְזֵכֶר מַלְכָּם.

Glory and honor they give to His name, joyfully singing acclaim to their King.

קָרָא לַשֶּׁמֶשׁ וַיִּזְרַח־אוֹר, רָאָה וְהִתְקִין צוּרַת הַלְּבָנָה. שֶׁבַח נוֹתְנִים־לוֹ כָּל־צְבָא מָרוֹם!

He called to the sun, it blazed forth light; He looked to the moon, it circled the earth. All the hosts of heaven proclaim His praise!

◆

אוֹר חָדָשׁ עַל־צִיּוֹן תָּאִיר, וְנִזְכֶּה כֻלָּנוּ מְהֵרָה לְאוֹרוֹ. בָּרוּךְ אַתָּה, יְיָ, יוֹצֵר הַמְּאוֹרוֹת.

Lord our God, let a new light shine on Zion, and may it be our blessing to see its splendor. Blessed is the Lord, the Maker of light.

◆ ◆

Continue with Ahavah Rabah, page 302.

ב II ב

Psalm 100

Shout joyfully to the Lord, all the earth!	הָרִיעוּ לַייָ כָּל־הָאָרֶץ!
Serve the Lord with gladness!	עִבְדוּ אֶת־יְיָ בְּשִׂמְחָה!
Come into His presence with singing!	בֹּאוּ לְפָנָיו בִּרְנָנָה!
Acknowledge that the Lord is God.	דְּעוּ כִּי־יְיָ הוּא אֱלֹהִים.
He made us and we are His,	הוּא עָשָׂנוּ וְלוֹ אֲנַחְנוּ,
His people, His beloved flock.	עַמּוֹ וְצֹאן מַרְעִיתוֹ.
Enter His gates with thanksgiving,	בֹּאוּ שְׁעָרָיו בְּתוֹדָה,
His courts with praise.	חֲצֵרֹתָיו בִּתְהִלָּה.
Give thanks to Him, bless His name!	הודוּ לוֹ, בָּרְכוּ שְׁמוֹ!
For the Lord is good,	כִּי־טוֹב יְיָ,
His love is everlasting,	לְעוֹלָם חַסְדּוֹ,
His faithfulness for all generations.	וְעַד־דֹּר וָדֹר אֱמוּנָתוֹ.

◆ ◆

Praised be He whose word brought the universe into being. Praised be He who sustains it with His might.

Praised be He who orders the world in wisdom and calls it to righteousness.

Eternal God, You have endowed us with reason to distinguish between right and wrong, and freedom to choose between good and evil. You are near to the hearts of all who seek You and strive to do Your will.

Praised be the Source of freedom; praised be His name.

May the divine in us, O Eternal One, lead us to honor Your name and to bless Israel by our actions. May the goodness within us direct our strength to live by Your word.

Praised be the Source of goodness; praised be His name.

◆ ◆

You are One and Your name is One. May Your truth unite all the world into one holy bond of friendship, and may our love for one another be our crown of glory and armor of strength. Bless us, O God, on this Sabbath day; may it be for us a day of rest and sanctification. May it inspire us to seek truth from the fountain of truth, to become holy as You are holy. In Your love You have set this day apart for us; we consecrate it to You and Your service, as we praise Your great and holy name.

◆ ◆

The heavens shall acknowledge Your wonders; the roar of the waters shall glorify You.

All the peoples shall thank You, and the nations shall praise You.

Our people chose You alone to serve, and no strange God beside You; help us, O God, to choose today to serve You.

You are My witnesses, says the Lord, My chosen servant: know Me and trust Me.

I, the Lord, have called you to righteousness, and taken you by the hand, and kept you. I have made you a covenant people, a light to the nations.

Now, therefore, if you will loyally keep My covenant, you shall be to Me a kingdom of priests, a holy nation.

◆ ◆

READER'S KADDISH חצי קדיש

יִתְגַּדַּל וְיִתְקַדַּשׁ שְׁמֵהּ רַבָּא בְּעָלְמָא דִּי־בְרָא כִרְעוּתֵהּ, וְיַמְלִיךְ מַלְכוּתֵהּ בְּחַיֵּיכוֹן וּבְיוֹמֵיכוֹן וּבְחַיֵּי דְכָל־בֵּית יִשְׂרָאֵל, בַּעֲגָלָא וּבִזְמַן קָרִיב, וְאִמְרוּ: אָמֵן.

יְהֵא שְׁמֵהּ רַבָּא מְבָרַךְ לְעָלַם וּלְעָלְמֵי עָלְמַיָּא.

יִתְבָּרַךְ וְיִשְׁתַּבַּח, וְיִתְפָּאַר וְיִתְרוֹמַם וְיִתְנַשֵּׂא, וְיִתְהַדַּר וְיִתְעַלֶּה וְיִתְהַלַּל שְׁמֵהּ דְּקוּדְשָׁא, בְּרִיךְ הוּא, לְעֵלָּא מִן כָּל־בִּרְכָתָא וְשִׁירָתָא, תֻּשְׁבְּחָתָא וְנֶחֱמָתָא דַּאֲמִירָן בְּעָלְמָא, וְאִמְרוּ: אָמֵן.

Let the glory of God be extolled, let His great name be hallowed in the world whose creation He willed. May His kingdom soon prevail, in our own day, our own lives, and the life of all Israel, and let us say: Amen.

Let His great name be blessed for ever and ever.

Let the name of the Holy One, blessed is He, be glorified, exalted and honored, though He is beyond all the praises, songs, and adorations that we can utter, and let us say: Amen.

◆ ◆

All rise

שמע וברכותיה

בָּרְכוּ אֶת־יְיָ הַמְבֹרָךְ!

Praise the Lord, to whom our praise is due!

בָּרוּךְ יְיָ הַמְבֹרָךְ לְעוֹלָם וָעֶד!

Praised be the Lord, to whom our praise is due, now and for ever!

◆ ◆

FOR MORNING SUN

יוצר

בָּרוּךְ אַתָּה, יְיָ אֱלֹהֵינוּ, מֶלֶךְ הָעוֹלָם, יוֹצֵר אוֹר וּבוֹרֵא חֹשֶׁךְ, עֹשֶׂה שָׁלוֹם וּבוֹרֵא אֶת־הַכֹּל.

הַמֵּאִיר לָאָרֶץ וְלַדָּרִים עָלֶיהָ בְּרַחֲמִים, וּבְטוּבוֹ מְחַדֵּשׁ בְּכָל־יוֹם תָּמִיד מַעֲשֵׂה בְרֵאשִׁית.

We thank You, O God, for this new day, for morning sun and evening star, for flowering tree and flowing tide, for life-giving rains and cooling breezes, for the earth's patient turning, the seasons' alternation, the cycle of growth and decay, of life and death.

מָה רַבּוּ מַעֲשֶׂיךָ, יְיָ! כֻּלָּם בְּחָכְמָה עָשִׂיתָ, מָלְאָה הָאָרֶץ קִנְיָנֶךָ.

תִּתְבָּרַךְ, יְיָ אֱלֹהֵינוּ, עַל־שֶׁבַח מַעֲשֵׂה יָדֶיךָ, וְעַל־מְאוֹרֵי־אוֹר שֶׁעָשִׂיתָ: יְפָאֲרוּךָ. סֶלָה.

בָּרוּךְ אַתָּה, יְיָ, יוֹצֵר הַמְּאוֹרוֹת.

When our eyes behold the world, when we feel its beauty and grandeur, we come to see the wisdom and goodness of its Creator.

We awake, and behold! a new day. Lord, renew us unto life. Teach us to recognize Your presence in creation. Grateful then for Your gifts, we will dedicate all our powers to Your service.

◆ ◆

TO BEAR WITNESS

אהבה רבה

אַהֲבָה רַבָּה אֲהַבְתָּנוּ, יְיָ אֱלֹהֵינוּ, חֶמְלָה גְדוֹלָה וִיתֵרָה חָמַלְתָּ עָלֵינוּ. אָבִינוּ מַלְכֵּנוּ, בַּעֲבוּר אֲבוֹתֵינוּ שֶׁבָּטְחוּ בְךָ וַתְּלַמְּדֵם חֻקֵּי חַיִּים, כֵּן תְּחָנֵּנוּ וּתְלַמְּדֵנוּ.

O God, the guide and inspiration of all humanity, You have spoken in a thousand tongues for all to hear. In every land and age, we, Your children, have heard Your voice and imagined

You in our separate ways. And yet, O God, You are One: though each may see You differently, You are the One God of all humanity.

אָבִינוּ, הָאָב הָרַחֲמָן, הַמְרַחֵם, רַחֵם עָלֵינוּ וְתֵן בְּלִבֵּנוּ לְהָבִין וּלְהַשְׂכִּיל, לִשְׁמֹעַ לִלְמֹד וּלְלַמֵּד, לִשְׁמֹר וְלַעֲשׂוֹת וּלְקַיֵּם אֶת־כָּל־דִּבְרֵי תַלְמוּד תּוֹרָתֶךָ בְּאַהֲבָה.

We give thanks for the sages and teachers of all peoples and faiths, who have brought many to deeper understanding of You and Your will. Gratefully we recall that among them were the lawgivers and prophets, the psalmists and sages of Israel. And joyfully we remember that from the very dawn of Israel's life, Your children have turned to You and found strength.

וְהָאֵר עֵינֵינוּ בְּתוֹרָתֶךָ, וְדַבֵּק לִבֵּנוּ בְּמִצְוֹתֶיךָ, וְיַחֵד לְבָבֵנוּ לְאַהֲבָה וּלְיִרְאָה אֶת־שְׁמֶךָ. וְלֹא־נֵבוֹשׁ לְעוֹלָם וָעֶד, כִּי בְשֵׁם קָדְשְׁךָ הַגָּדוֹל וְהַנּוֹרָא בָּטָחְנוּ. נָגִילָה וְנִשְׂמְחָה בִּישׁוּעָתֶךָ, כִּי אֵל פּוֹעֵל יְשׁוּעוֹת אָתָּה, וּבָנוּ בָחַרְתָּ וְקֵרַבְתָּנוּ לְשִׁמְךָ הַגָּדוֹל סֶלָה בֶּאֱמֶת, לְהוֹדוֹת לְךָ וּלְיַחֶדְךָ בְּאַהֲבָה.

בָּרוּךְ אַתָּה, יְיָ, הַבּוֹחֵר בְּעַמּוֹ יִשְׂרָאֵל בְּאַהֲבָה.

May the teachings of our ancestors live on in our minds, and their passion for righteousness retain its power to move our hearts.

Help us, O God, so to live that our daily conduct may reveal the beauty of our faith, and that the house of Israel may continue to bear witness to Your truth.

◆ ◆

שְׁמַע יִשְׂרָאֵל: יְיָ אֱלֹהֵינוּ, יְיָ אֶחָד!

Hear, O Israel: the Lord is our God, the Lord is One!

בָּרוּךְ שֵׁם כְּבוֹד מַלְכוּתוֹ לְעוֹלָם וָעֶד!

Blessed is His glorious kingdom for ever and ever!

All are seated

וְאָהַבְתָּ אֵת יְיָ אֱלֹהֶיךָ בְּכָל־לְבָבְךָ וּבְכָל־נַפְשְׁךָ וּבְכָל־מְאֹדֶךָ.
וְהָיוּ הַדְּבָרִים הָאֵלֶּה, אֲשֶׁר אָנֹכִי מְצַוְּךָ הַיּוֹם, עַל־לְבָבֶךָ.
וְשִׁנַּנְתָּם לְבָנֶיךָ, וְדִבַּרְתָּ בָּם בְּשִׁבְתְּךָ בְּבֵיתֶךָ, וּבְלֶכְתְּךָ
בַדֶּרֶךְ, וּבְשָׁכְבְּךָ וּבְקוּמֶךָ.

You shall love the Lord your God with all your mind, with all your strength, with all your being.
Set these words, which I command you this day, upon your heart. Teach them faithfully to your children; speak of them in your home and on your way, when you lie down and when you rise up.

וּקְשַׁרְתָּם לְאוֹת עַל־יָדֶךָ, וְהָיוּ לְטֹטָפֹת בֵּין עֵינֶיךָ, וּכְתַבְתָּם
עַל־מְזֻזוֹת בֵּיתֶךָ, וּבִשְׁעָרֶיךָ.

Bind them as a sign upon your hand; let them be a symbol before your eyes; inscribe them on the doorposts of your house, and on your gates.

לְמַעַן תִּזְכְּרוּ וַעֲשִׂיתֶם אֶת־כָּל־מִצְוֹתָי, וִהְיִיתֶם קְדֹשִׁים
לֵאלֹהֵיכֶם. אֲנִי יְיָ אֱלֹהֵיכֶם, אֲשֶׁר הוֹצֵאתִי אֶתְכֶם מֵאֶרֶץ
מִצְרַיִם לִהְיוֹת לָכֶם לֵאלֹהִים. אֲנִי יְיָ אֱלֹהֵיכֶם.

Be mindful of all My Mitzvot, and do them: so shall you consecrate yourselves to your God. I, the Lord, am your God who led you out of Egypt to be your God; I, the Lord, am your God.

◆ ◆

THE VISION OF A WORLD REDEEMED — גאולה

אֱמֶת וְיַצִּיב, וְאָהוּב וְחָבִיב, וְנוֹרָא וְאַדִּיר, וְטוֹב וְיָפֶה הַדָּבָר
הַזֶּה עָלֵינוּ לְעוֹלָם וָעֶד.
אֱמֶת, אֱלֹהֵי עוֹלָם מַלְכֵּנוּ, צוּר יַעֲקֹב מָגֵן יִשְׁעֵנוּ.

לְדֹר וָדֹר הוּא קַיָּם, וּשְׁמוֹ קַיָּם, וְכִסְאוֹ נָכוֹן, וּמַלְכוּתוֹ וֶאֱמוּנָתוֹ לָעַד קַיֶּמֶת.
וּדְבָרָיו חָיִים וְקַיָּמִים, נֶאֱמָנִים וְנֶחֱמָדִים, לָעַד וּלְעוֹלְמֵי עוֹלָמִים.

In a world torn by violence and pain, a world far from wholeness and peace, a world waiting still to be redeemed, give us, Lord, the courage to say: There is One God in heaven and earth.

The high heavens declare His glory; may earth reveal His justice and His love.

מִמִּצְרַיִם גְּאַלְתָּנוּ, יְיָ אֱלֹהֵינוּ, וּמִבֵּית עֲבָדִים פְּדִיתָנוּ.
עַל־זֹאת שִׁבְּחוּ אֲהוּבִים וְרוֹמְמוּ אֵל, וְנָתְנוּ יְדִידִים זְמִירוֹת, שִׁירוֹת וְתִשְׁבָּחוֹת, בְּרָכוֹת וְהוֹדָאוֹת לַמֶּלֶךְ, אֵל חַי וְקַיָּם.

From Egypt, the house of bondage, we were delivered; at Sinai, amid peals of thunder, we bound ourselves to His purpose. Inspired by prophets and instructed by sages, we survived oppression and exile, time and again overcoming the forces that would have destroyed us.

Our failings are many — our faults are great — yet it has been our glory to bear witness to our God, and to keep alive in dark ages the vision of a world redeemed.

רָם וְנִשָּׂא, גָּדוֹל וְנוֹרָא, מַשְׁפִּיל גֵּאִים וּמַגְבִּיהַּ שְׁפָלִים, מוֹצִיא אֲסִירִים וּפוֹדֶה עֲנָוִים, וְעוֹזֵר דַּלִּים, וְעוֹנֶה לְעַמּוֹ בְּעֵת שַׁוְּעָם אֵלָיו.
תְּהִלּוֹת לְאֵל עֶלְיוֹן, בָּרוּךְ הוּא וּמְבֹרָךְ. מֹשֶׁה וּבְנֵי יִשְׂרָאֵל לְךָ עָנוּ שִׁירָה בְּשִׂמְחָה רַבָּה, וְאָמְרוּ כֻלָּם:

May this vision never fade; let us continue to work for the day when the nations will be one and at peace. Then shall we sing with one accord, as Israel sang at the shores of the sea:

Who is like You, Eternal One, among the gods that are worshipped?	מִי־כָמֹכָה בָּאֵלִם, יְיָ?
Who is like You, majestic in holiness,	מִי כָּמֹכָה, נֶאְדָּר בַּקֹּדֶשׁ,
awesome in splendor, doing wonders?	נוֹרָא תְהִלֹּת, עֹשֵׂה פֶלֶא?

שִׁירָה חֲדָשָׁה שִׁבְּחוּ גְאוּלִים לְשִׁמְךָ עַל־שְׂפַת הַיָּם; יַחַד כֻּלָּם הוֹדוּ וְהִמְלִיכוּ וְאָמְרוּ: "יְיָ יִמְלֹךְ לְעוֹלָם וָעֶד!"

A new song the redeemed sang to Your name. At the shore of the sea, saved from destruction, they proclaimed Your sovereign power: "The Eternal will reign for ever and ever!"

צוּר יִשְׂרָאֵל, קוּמָה בְּעֶזְרַת יִשְׂרָאֵל, וּפְדֵה כִנְאֻמֶךָ יְהוּדָה וְיִשְׂרָאֵל. גֹּאֲלֵנוּ יְיָ צְבָאוֹת שְׁמוֹ, קְדוֹשׁ יִשְׂרָאֵל.

בָּרוּךְ אַתָּה, יְיָ, גָּאַל יִשְׂרָאֵל.

O Rock of Israel, come to Israel's help. Fulfill Your promise of redemption for Judah and Israel. Our Redeemer is the Lord of Hosts, the Holy One of Israel.
Blessed is the Lord, the Redeemer of Israel.

◆ ◆

MEDITATION

Prayer invites God to let His presence suffuse our spirits, to let His will prevail in our lives. Prayer cannot bring water to parched fields, or mend a broken bridge, or rebuild a ruined city; but prayer can water an arid soul, mend a broken heart, and rebuild a weakened will.

◆ ◆

All rise

תפלה

אֲדֹנָי, שְׂפָתַי תִּפְתָּח, וּפִי יַגִּיד תְּהִלָּתֶךָ.

Eternal God, open my lips, that my mouth may declare Your glory.

THEIR QUEST IS OURS — אבות

בָּרוּךְ אַתָּה, יְיָ אֱלֹהֵינוּ וֵאלֹהֵי אֲבוֹתֵינוּ, אֱלֹהֵי אַבְרָהָם, אֱלֹהֵי יִצְחָק, וֵאלֹהֵי יַעֲקֹב: הָאֵל הַגָּדוֹל, הַגִּבּוֹר וְהַנּוֹרָא, אֵל עֶלְיוֹן.

גּוֹמֵל חֲסָדִים טוֹבִים, וְקוֹנֵה הַכֹּל, וְזוֹכֵר חַסְדֵי אָבוֹת, וּמֵבִיא
גְאֻלָּה לִבְנֵי בְנֵיהֶם, לְמַעַן שְׁמוֹ, בְּאַהֲבָה.
מֶלֶךְ עוֹזֵר וּמוֹשִׁיעַ וּמָגֵן. בָּרוּךְ אַתָּה, יְיָ, מָגֵן אַבְרָהָם.

Source of all being, we turn to You as did our people in ancient days. They beheld You in the heavens; they felt You in their hearts; they sought You in their lives.

Now their quest is ours. Help us, O God, to see the wonder of being. Give us the courage to search for truth. Teach us the path to a better life. So shall we, by our lives and our labors, bring nearer to realization the great hope inherited from ages past, for a world transformed by liberty, justice, and peace.

◆ ◆

HELP US TO USE OUR STRENGTH גבורות

אַתָּה גִּבּוֹר לְעוֹלָם, אֲדֹנָי, מְחַיֵּה הַכֹּל אַתָּה, רַב לְהוֹשִׁיעַ.
מְכַלְכֵּל חַיִּים בְּחֶסֶד, מְחַיֵּה הַכֹּל בְּרַחֲמִים רַבִּים.
סוֹמֵךְ נוֹפְלִים, וְרוֹפֵא חוֹלִים, וּמַתִּיר אֲסוּרִים, וּמְקַיֵּם אֱמוּנָתוֹ
לִישֵׁנֵי עָפָר.
מִי כָמוֹךָ, בַּעַל גְּבוּרוֹת, וּמִי דּוֹמֶה לָּךְ, מֶלֶךְ מֵמִית וּמְחַיֶּה
וּמַצְמִיחַ יְשׁוּעָה?
וְנֶאֱמָן אַתָּה לְהַחֲיוֹת הַכֹּל. בָּרוּךְ אַתָּה, יְיָ, מְחַיֵּה הַכֹּל.

Your might, O God, is everlasting;

Help us to use our strength for good and not for evil.

You are the Source of life and blessing;

Help us to choose life for ourselves and our children.

You are the support of the falling;

Help us to lift up the fallen.

You are the Author of freedom;

Help us to set free the captive.

You are our hope in death as in life;
Help us to keep faith with those who sleep in the dust.

Your might, O God, is everlasting;
Help us to use our strength for good.

• •

SANCTIFICATION קדושה

נְקַדֵּשׁ אֶת־שִׁמְךָ בָּעוֹלָם, כְּשֵׁם שֶׁמַּקְדִּישִׁים אוֹתוֹ בִּשְׁמֵי מָרוֹם, כַּכָּתוּב עַל־יַד נְבִיאֶךָ: וְקָרָא זֶה אֶל־זֶה וְאָמַר:

We sanctify Your name on earth, even as all things, to the ends of time and space, proclaim Your holiness; and in the words of the prophet we say:

קָדוֹשׁ, קָדוֹשׁ, קָדוֹשׁ יְיָ צְבָאוֹת, מְלֹא כָל־הָאָרֶץ כְּבוֹדוֹ.

Holy, Holy, Holy is the Lord of Hosts; the fullness of the whole earth is His glory!

אַדִּיר אַדִּירֵנוּ, יְיָ אֲדֹנֵינוּ, מָה־אַדִּיר שִׁמְךָ בְּכָל־הָאָרֶץ!

Source of our strength, Sovereign Lord, how majestic is Your presence in all the earth!

בָּרוּךְ כְּבוֹד־יְיָ מִמְּקוֹמוֹ.

Blessed is the glory of God in heaven and earth.

אֶחָד הוּא אֱלֹהֵינוּ, הוּא אָבִינוּ, הוּא מַלְכֵּנוּ, הוּא מוֹשִׁיעֵנוּ; וְהוּא יַשְׁמִיעֵנוּ בְּרַחֲמָיו לְעֵינֵי כָּל־חָי:

He alone is our God and our Creator; He is our Ruler and our Helper; and in His mercy He reveals Himself in the sight of all the living:

"אֲנִי יְיָ אֱלֹהֵיכֶם!"

I AM ADONAI YOUR GOD!

יִמְלֹךְ יְיָ לְעוֹלָם, אֱלֹהַיִךְ צִיּוֹן, לְדֹר וָדֹר. הַלְלוּיָהּ!

The Lord shall reign for ever; your God, O Zion, from generation to generation. Halleluyah!

לְדוֹר וָדוֹר נַגִּיד גָּדְלֶךָ, וּלְנֵצַח נְצָחִים קְדֻשָּׁתְךָ נַקְדִּישׁ. וְשִׁבְחֲךָ, אֱלֹהֵינוּ, מִפִּינוּ לֹא יָמוּשׁ לְעוֹלָם וָעֶד.

בָּרוּךְ אַתָּה, יְיָ, הָאֵל הַקָּדוֹשׁ.

To all generations we will make known Your greatness, and to all eternity proclaim Your holiness. Your praise, O God, shall never depart from our lips. Blessed is the Lord, the holy God.

All are seated

◆ ◆

MOST PRECIOUS OF DAYS — קדושת היום

יִשְׂמְחוּ בְמַלְכוּתְךָ שׁוֹמְרֵי שַׁבָּת וְקוֹרְאֵי עֹנֶג. עַם מְקַדְּשֵׁי שְׁבִיעִי כֻּלָּם יִשְׂבְּעוּ וְיִתְעַנְּגוּ מִטּוּבֶךָ. וְהַשְּׁבִיעִי רָצִיתָ בּוֹ וְקִדַּשְׁתּוֹ. חֶמְדַּת יָמִים אוֹתוֹ קָרָאתָ, זֵכֶר לְמַעֲשֵׂה בְרֵאשִׁית.

Those who keep the Sabbath and call it a delight shall rejoice in Your kingdom. All who hallow the seventh day shall be gladdened by Your goodness. This day is Israel's festival of the spirit, sanctified and blessed by You, the most precious of days, a symbol of the joy of creation.

◆

THE SABBATH AND ITS HOLINESS

אֱלֹהֵינוּ וֵאלֹהֵי אֲבוֹתֵינוּ, רְצֵה בִמְנוּחָתֵנוּ. קַדְּשֵׁנוּ בְּמִצְוֹתֶיךָ וְתֵן חֶלְקֵנוּ בְּתוֹרָתֶךָ. שַׂבְּעֵנוּ מִטּוּבֶךָ, וְשַׂמְּחֵנוּ בִּישׁוּעָתֶךָ, וְטַהֵר לִבֵּנוּ לְעָבְדְּךָ בֶּאֱמֶת. וְהַנְחִילֵנוּ, יְיָ אֱלֹהֵינוּ, בְּאַהֲבָה וּבְרָצוֹן שַׁבַּת קָדְשֶׁךָ, וְיָנוּחוּ בָהּ יִשְׂרָאֵל מְקַדְּשֵׁי שְׁמֶךָ. בָּרוּךְ אַתָּה, יְיָ, מְקַדֵּשׁ הַשַּׁבָּת.

Our God and God of ages past, may our rest on this day be pleasing in Your sight. Sanctify us with Your Mitzvot, and let Your Torah be our way of life. Satisfy us with Your goodness, gladden us with Your salvation, and purify our hearts to serve You in truth. In Your gracious love, O Lord our God, let Your holy Sabbath remain our heritage, that all Israel, hallowing

Your name, may find rest and peace. Blessed is the Lord, for the Sabbath and its holiness.

◆ ◆

MEDITATION

NEW STRENGTH FOR YOUR SERVICE

You are with us in our prayer, in our love and our doubt, in our longing to feel Your presence and do Your will. You are the still, clear voice within us. Therefore, O God, when doubt troubles us, when anxiety makes us tremble, and pain clouds the mind, we look inward for the answer to our prayers. There may we find You, and there find courage, insight, and endurance. And let our worship bring us closer to one another, that all Israel, and all who seek You, may find new strength for Your service.

◆ ◆

IN OUR DEEDS AND OUR PRAYER

עבודה

רְצֵה, יְיָ אֱלֹהֵינוּ, בְּעַמְּךָ יִשְׂרָאֵל, וּתְפִלָּתָם בְּאַהֲבָה תְקַבֵּל,
וּתְהִי לְרָצוֹן תָּמִיד עֲבוֹדַת יִשְׂרָאֵל עַמֶּךָ. שְׁפוֹךְ רוּחֲךָ
עָלֵינוּ, וְתֶחֱזֶינָה עֵינֵינוּ בְּשׁוּבְךָ לְצִיּוֹן בְּרַחֲמִים.

בָּרוּךְ אַתָּה, יְיָ, שֶׁאוֹתְךָ לְבַדְּךָ בְּיִרְאָה נַעֲבוֹד.

O Lord our God, may we, Your people Israel, be worthy in our deeds and our prayer. Wherever we live, wherever we seek You — in this land, in Zion restored, in all lands — You are our God, whom alone we serve in reverence.

◆ ◆

GIFTS AND BLESSINGS

הודאה

מוֹדִים אֲנַחְנוּ לָךְ, שָׁאַתָּה הוּא יְיָ אֱלֹהֵינוּ וֵאלֹהֵי אֲבוֹתֵינוּ
לְעוֹלָם וָעֶד. צוּר חַיֵּינוּ, מָגֵן יִשְׁעֵנוּ, אַתָּה הוּא לְדוֹר וָדוֹר.
נוֹדֶה לְּךָ וּנְסַפֵּר תְּהִלָּתֶךָ, עַל־חַיֵּינוּ הַמְּסוּרִים בְּיָדֶךָ, וְעַל־
נִשְׁמוֹתֵינוּ הַפְּקוּדוֹת לָךְ, וְעַל־נִסֶּיךָ שֶׁבְּכָל־יוֹם עִמָּנוּ, וְעַל־
נִפְלְאוֹתֶיךָ וְטוֹבוֹתֶיךָ שֶׁבְּכָל־עֵת, עֶרֶב וָבֹקֶר וְצָהֳרָיִם. הַטּוֹב:

כִּי לֹא־כָלוּ רַחֲמֶיךָ, וְהַמְרַחֵם: כִּי־לֹא תַמּוּ חֲסָדֶיךָ, מֵעוֹלָם קִוִּינוּ לָךְ.

וְעַל כֻּלָּם יִתְבָּרַךְ וְיִתְרוֹמַם שִׁמְךָ, מַלְכֵּנוּ, תָּמִיד לְעוֹלָם וָעֶד. וְכֹל הַחַיִּים יוֹדוּךָ סֶּלָה, וִיהַלְלוּ אֶת שִׁמְךָ בֶּאֱמֶת, הָאֵל יְשׁוּעָתֵנוּ וְעֶזְרָתֵנוּ סֶלָה. בָּרוּךְ אַתָּה, יְיָ, הַטּוֹב שִׁמְךָ וּלְךָ נָאֶה לְהוֹדוֹת.

Eternal Source of good, we thank You for the numberless gifts and blessings that fill our days: for life itself and its endless variety; for all that sustains body and mind; for love and friendship; for the delights of the senses; and for the excellence of Your Torah, which deepens our life and enriches our days. Help us, O God, to work for a just and compassionate society, where all may share Your gifts in the joy of freedom.

◆ ◆

PEACE AND JUSTICE — ברכת שלום

שִׂים שָׁלוֹם, טוֹבָה וּבְרָכָה, חֵן וָחֶסֶד וְרַחֲמִים, עָלֵינוּ וְעַל־כָּל־יִשְׂרָאֵל וְעַל־כָּל־הָעַמִּים. בָּרְכֵנוּ, אָבִינוּ, כֻּלָּנוּ כְּאֶחָד, בְּאוֹר פָּנֶיךָ, כִּי בְאוֹר פָּנֶיךָ נָתַתָּ לָּנוּ, יְיָ אֱלֹהֵינוּ, תּוֹרַת חַיִּים, וְאַהֲבַת חֶסֶד, וּצְדָקָה וּבְרָכָה וְרַחֲמִים, וְחַיִּים וְשָׁלוֹם.

Grant peace and happiness, blessing and mercy, to all Israel and all the world. Bless us, O God, with the light of Your presence, for by that light we find life, justice, and peace.

וְטוֹב בְּעֵינֶיךָ לְבָרֵךְ אֶת־עַמְּךָ יִשְׂרָאֵל, וְאֶת־כָּל־הָעַמִּים, בְּכָל־עֵת וּבְכָל־שָׁעָה בִּשְׁלוֹמֶךָ.

בָּרוּךְ אַתָּה, יְיָ, עוֹשֵׂה הַשָּׁלוֹם.

May Your children unite to do Your will: to establish peace and justice throughout the world, so that the nations are drawn together by the bond of friendship, and Your law of truth hold sway over our lives.

Blessed is the Lord, the Source of peace.

◆ ◆

SILENT PRAYER

אֱלֹהַי, נְצוֹר לְשׁוֹנִי מֵרָע וּשְׂפָתַי מִדַּבֵּר מִרְמָה.
הוֹדִיעֵנִי דֶּרֶךְ־זוּ אֵלֵךְ, כִּי־אֵלֶיךָ נָשָׂאתִי נַפְשִׁי.
לֵב טָהוֹר בְּרָא־לִי, אֱלֹהִים, וְרוּחַ נָכוֹן חַדֵּשׁ בְּקִרְבִּי.
שְׁגִיאוֹת מִי־יָבִין? מִנִּסְתָּרוֹת נַקֵּנִי!
הַדְרִיכֵנִי בַּאֲמִתֶּךָ, וְלַמְּדֵנִי, כִּי־אַתָּה אֱלֹהֵי יִשְׁעִי, אוֹתְךָ קִוִּיתִי כָּל־הַיּוֹם.
פְּתַח לִבִּי בְּתוֹרָתֶךָ, וּבְמִצְוֹתֶיךָ תִּרְדּוֹף נַפְשִׁי.

O God, keep my tongue from evil, and my lips from deceitful speech. Let me know the way I should go, for to You do I lift up my soul. Create in me a clean heart, O God, and renew a steadfast spirit within me. But who can see all his own failings? Rid me of faults that are hidden! Lead me in Your truth, and teach me. You are God my Helper, and for You do I wait all the day. Open my heart to Your teaching, and I will make haste to do Your commandments.

◆ ◆

יִהְיוּ לְרָצוֹן אִמְרֵי־פִי וְהֶגְיוֹן לִבִּי לְפָנֶיךָ, יְיָ, צוּרִי וְגוֹאֲלִי.

May the words of my mouth, and the meditations of my heart, be acceptable to You, O Lord, my Rock and my Redeemer.

or

עֹשֶׂה שָׁלוֹם בִּמְרוֹמָיו, הוּא יַעֲשֶׂה שָׁלוֹם עָלֵינוּ וְעַל כָּל־יִשְׂרָאֵל, וְאִמְרוּ אָמֵן.

May He who causes peace to reign in the high heavens let peace descend on us, on all Israel, and all the world.

◆ ◆

Prayers for Special Occasions begin on page 389.

On Shabbat during Pesach, Sukkot, and Chanukah, or when Shabbat coincides with Rosh Chodesh or Yom Ha-atsma-ut, a short form of Hallel, page 487, is read.

The Rituals for the Reading of Torah begin on page 415.

ג III ג

שחר אבקשך

Early will I seek You, God my refuge strong; Late prepare to meet You With my evening song.	שַׁחַר אֲבַקֶּשְׁךָ, צוּרִי וּמִשְׂגַּבִּי, אֶעְרוֹךְ לְפָנֶיךָ שַׁחְרִי וְגַם עַרְבִּי.
Though unto Your greatness I with trembling soar, Yet my inmost thinking Lies Your eyes before.	לִפְנֵי גְדֻלָּתְךָ אֶעְמֹד וְאֶבָּהֵל, כִּי עֵינְךָ תִרְאֶה כָּל מַחְשְׁבוֹת לִבִּי.
What this frail heart's dreaming, And my tongue's poor speech, Can they even distant To Your greatness reach?	מַה־זֶּה אֲשֶׁר יוּכַל הַלֵּב וְהַלָּשׁוֹן לַעֲשׂוֹת, וּמַה כֹּחַ רוּחִי בְּתוֹךְ קִרְבִּי?
Being great in mercy, You will not despise Praises which till death's hour From my soul will rise.	הִנֵּה לְךָ תִיטַב זִמְרַת אֱנוֹשׁ; עַל כֵּן אוֹדְךָ בְּעוֹד תִּהְיֶה נִשְׁמַת אֱלוֹהַּ בִּי.

◆ ◆

The synagogue is the sanctuary of Israel. Born out of our longing for the living God, it has been to Israel, throughout our wanderings, a visible token of the presence of God in His people's midst. Its beauty is the beauty of holiness; steadfast it has stood as the champion of justice, mercy, and peace.

Its truths are true for all people. Its love is a love for all people. Its God is the God of all people, as it has been said: "My house shall be called a house of prayer for all peoples."

Let all the family of Israel, all who hunger for righteousness, all who seek the Eternal find Him here — and here find life!

◆ ◆

MEDITATION

Each of us enters this sanctuary with a different need.

Some hearts are full of gratitude and joy:
They are overflowing with the happiness of love and the joy of life; they are eager to confront the day, to make the world more fair; they are recovering from illness or have escaped misfortune.
And we rejoice with them.

Some hearts ache with sorrow:
Disappointments weigh heavily upon them, and they have tasted despair; families have been broken; loved ones lie on a bed of pain; death has taken those whom they cherished.
May our presence and sympathy bring them comfort.

Some hearts are embittered:
They have sought answers in vain; ideals are mocked and betrayed; life has lost its meaning and value.
May the knowledge that we too are searching, restore their hope and give them courage to believe that not all is emptiness.

Some spirits hunger:
They long for friendship; they crave understanding; they yearn for warmth.
May we in our common need and striving gain strength from one another, as we share our joys, lighten each other's burdens, and pray for the welfare of our community.

◆ ◆

Lord our God, You are our unfailing help. Darkness does not conceal You from the eye of faith, nor do the forces of destruction obscure Your presence. Above the fury of human evil and the blows of chance You abide, the Eternal God. When pain and sorrow try our souls, grant us courage to meet them undismayed and with faith that does not waver. Let not the tears that must come to every eye blind us to Your goodness. Amen.

◆ ◆

READER'S KADDISH — חצי קדיש

יִתְגַּדַּל וְיִתְקַדַּשׁ שְׁמֵהּ רַבָּא בְּעָלְמָא דִּי־בְרָא כִרְעוּתֵהּ, וְיַמְלִיךְ מַלְכוּתֵהּ בְּחַיֵּיכוֹן וּבְיוֹמֵיכוֹן וּבְחַיֵּי דְכָל־בֵּית יִשְׂרָאֵל, בַּעֲגָלָא וּבִזְמַן קָרִיב, וְאִמְרוּ: אָמֵן.

יְהֵא שְׁמֵהּ רַבָּא מְבָרַךְ לְעָלַם וּלְעָלְמֵי עָלְמַיָּא.

יִתְבָּרַךְ וְיִשְׁתַּבַּח, וְיִתְפָּאַר וְיִתְרוֹמַם וְיִתְנַשֵּׂא, וְיִתְהַדַּר וְיִתְעַלֶּה וְיִתְהַלַּל שְׁמֵהּ דְּקוּדְשָׁא, בְּרִיךְ הוּא, לְעֵלָּא מִן כָּל־בִּרְכָתָא וְשִׁירָתָא, תֻּשְׁבְּחָתָא וְנֶחֱמָתָא דַּאֲמִירָן בְּעָלְמָא, וְאִמְרוּ: אָמֵן.

Let the glory of God be extolled, let His great name be hallowed in the world whose creation He willed. May His kingdom soon prevail, in our own day, our own lives, and the life of all Israel, and let us say: Amen.

Let His great name be blessed for ever and ever.

Let the name of the Holy One, blessed is He, be glorified, exalted and honored, though He is beyond all the praises, songs, and adorations that we can utter, and let us say: Amen.

◆ ◆

All rise

שמע וברכותיה

בָּרְכוּ אֶת־יְיָ הַמְבֹרָךְ!

Praise the Lord, to whom our praise is due!

בָּרוּךְ יְיָ הַמְבֹרָךְ לְעוֹלָם וָעֶד!

Praised be the Lord, to whom our praise is due, now and for ever!

◆ ◆

THE HEAVENS DECLARE YOUR GLORY

יוצר

בָּרוּךְ אַתָּה, יְיָ אֱלֹהֵינוּ, מֶלֶךְ הָעוֹלָם, יוֹצֵר אוֹר וּבוֹרֵא חֹשֶׁךְ, עֹשֶׂה שָׁלוֹם וּבוֹרֵא אֶת־הַכֹּל. הַמֵּאִיר לָאָרֶץ וְלַדָּרִים עָלֶיהָ בְּרַחֲמִים, וּבְטוּבוֹ מְחַדֵּשׁ בְּכָל־יוֹם תָּמִיד מַעֲשֵׂה בְרֵאשִׁית.

Praised be the Lord our God, Ruler of the universe. In His mercy He makes light to shine over the earth and all its inhabitants, and in His goodness He renews day by day the work of creation.

מָה רַבּוּ מַעֲשֶׂיךָ, יְיָ! כֻּלָּם בְּחָכְמָה עָשִׂיתָ, מָלְאָה הָאָרֶץ קִנְיָנֶךָ. תִּתְבָּרַךְ, יְיָ אֱלֹהֵינוּ, עַל־שֶׁבַח מַעֲשֵׂה יָדֶיךָ, וְעַל־מְאוֹרֵי־אוֹר שֶׁעָשִׂיתָ: יְפָאֲרוּךָ. סֶּלָה.

בָּרוּךְ אַתָּה, יְיָ, יוֹצֵר הַמְּאוֹרוֹת.

How manifold are Your works, O Lord! In wisdom You have made them all. The heavens declare Your glory. The earth reveals Your creative power. You form light and darkness, bring harmony into nature and peace to the human heart.

Blessed is the Lord, Creator of light.

• •

YOU HAVE TAUGHT US

אהבה רבה

אַהֲבָה רַבָּה אֲהַבְתָּנוּ, יְיָ אֱלֹהֵינוּ, חֶמְלָה גְדוֹלָה וִיתֵרָה חָמַלְתָּ עָלֵינוּ. אָבִינוּ מַלְכֵּנוּ, בַּעֲבוּר אֲבוֹתֵינוּ שֶׁבָּטְחוּ בְךָ וַתְּלַמְּדֵם חֻקֵּי חַיִּים, כֵּן תְּחָנֵּנוּ וּתְלַמְּדֵנוּ.

אָבִינוּ, הָאָב הָרַחֲמָן, הַמְרַחֵם, רַחֵם עָלֵינוּ וְתֵן בְּלִבֵּנוּ לְהָבִין וּלְהַשְׂכִּיל, לִשְׁמֹעַ לִלְמֹד וּלְלַמֵּד, לִשְׁמֹר וְלַעֲשׂוֹת וּלְקַיֵּם אֶת־כָּל־דִּבְרֵי תַלְמוּד תּוֹרָתֶךָ בְּאַהֲבָה.

Deep is Your love for us, abiding Your compassion. From of old we have put our trust in You, and You have taught us the laws of life. Be gracious now to us, that we may understand and fulfill the teachings of Your word.

וְהָאֵר עֵינֵינוּ בְּתוֹרָתֶךָ, וְדַבֵּק לִבֵּנוּ בְּמִצְוֹתֶיךָ, וְיַחֵד לְבָבֵנוּ לְאַהֲבָה וּלְיִרְאָה אֶת־שְׁמֶךָ. וְלֹא־נֵבוֹשׁ לְעוֹלָם וָעֶד, כִּי בְשֵׁם קָדְשְׁךָ הַגָּדוֹל וְהַנּוֹרָא בָּטָחְנוּ. נָגִילָה וְנִשְׂמְחָה בִּישׁוּעָתֶךָ, כִּי אֵל פּוֹעֵל יְשׁוּעוֹת אָתָּה, וּבָנוּ בָחַרְתָּ וְקֵרַבְתָּנוּ לְשִׁמְךָ הַגָּדוֹל סֶלָה בֶּאֱמֶת, לְהוֹדוֹת לְךָ וּלְיַחֶדְךָ בְּאַהֲבָה.

בָּרוּךְ אַתָּה, יְיָ, הַבּוֹחֵר בְּעַמּוֹ יִשְׂרָאֵל בְּאַהֲבָה.

Enlighten our eyes in Your Torah, that we may cling to Your Mitzvot. Unite our hearts to love and revere Your name.

We trust in You and rejoice in Your saving power, for You are the Source of our help. You have called us and drawn us near to You to serve You in faithfulness.

Joyfully we lift up our voices and proclaim Your unity, O God who has chosen us in love!

◆ ◆

שְׁמַע יִשְׂרָאֵל: יְיָ אֱלֹהֵינוּ, יְיָ אֶחָד!

Hear, O Israel: the Lord is our God, the Lord is One!

בָּרוּךְ שֵׁם כְּבוֹד מַלְכוּתוֹ לְעוֹלָם וָעֶד!

Blessed is His glorious kingdom for ever and ever!

All are seated

וְאָהַבְתָּ אֵת יְיָ אֱלֹהֶיךָ בְּכָל־לְבָבְךָ וּבְכָל־נַפְשְׁךָ וּבְכָל־מְאֹדֶךָ. וְהָיוּ הַדְּבָרִים הָאֵלֶּה, אֲשֶׁר אָנֹכִי מְצַוְּךָ הַיּוֹם, עַל־לְבָבֶךָ. וְשִׁנַּנְתָּם לְבָנֶיךָ, וְדִבַּרְתָּ בָּם בְּשִׁבְתְּךָ בְּבֵיתֶךָ, וּבְלֶכְתְּךָ בַדֶּרֶךְ, וּבְשָׁכְבְּךָ וּבְקוּמֶךָ.

You shall love the Lord your God with all your mind, with all your strength, with all your being.

Set these words, which I command you this day, upon your heart. Teach them faithfully to your children; speak of them in your home and on your way, when you lie down and when you rise up.

וּקְשַׁרְתָּם לְאוֹת עַל־יָדֶךָ, וְהָיוּ לְטֹטָפֹת בֵּין עֵינֶיךָ, וּכְתַבְתָּם עַל־מְזֻזוֹת בֵּיתֶךָ, וּבִשְׁעָרֶיךָ.

Bind them as a sign upon your hand; let them be a symbol before your eyes; inscribe them on the doorposts of your house, and on your gates.

לְמַעַן תִּזְכְּרוּ וַעֲשִׂיתֶם אֶת־כָּל־מִצְוֹתָי, וִהְיִיתֶם קְדֹשִׁים לֵאלֹהֵיכֶם. אֲנִי יְיָ אֱלֹהֵיכֶם, אֲשֶׁר הוֹצֵאתִי אֶתְכֶם מֵאֶרֶץ מִצְרַיִם לִהְיוֹת לָכֶם לֵאלֹהִים. אֲנִי יְיָ אֱלֹהֵיכֶם.

Be mindful of all My Mitzvot, and do them: so shall you consecrate yourselves to your God. I, the Lord, am your God who led you out of Egypt to be your God; I, the Lord, am your God.

◆ ◆

THE HELP OF OUR PEOPLE — גאולה

אֱמֶת וְיַצִּיב, וְאָהוּב וְחָבִיב, וְנוֹרָא וְאַדִּיר, וְטוֹב וְיָפֶה הַדָּבָר הַזֶּה עָלֵינוּ לְעוֹלָם וָעֶד.

אֱמֶת, אֱלֹהֵי עוֹלָם מַלְכֵּנוּ, צוּר יַעֲקֹב מָגֵן יִשְׁעֵנוּ.

לְדֹר וָדֹר הוּא קַיָּם, וּשְׁמוֹ קַיָּם, וְכִסְאוֹ נָכוֹן, וּמַלְכוּתוֹ וֶאֱמוּנָתוֹ לָעַד קַיֶּמֶת.

וּדְבָרָיו חָיִים וְקַיָּמִים, נֶאֱמָנִים וְנֶחֱמָדִים, לָעַד וּלְעוֹלְמֵי עוֹלָמִים.

מִמִּצְרַיִם גְּאַלְתָּנוּ, יְיָ אֱלֹהֵינוּ, וּמִבֵּית עֲבָדִים פְּדִיתָנוּ.

עַל־זֹאת שִׁבְּחוּ אֲהוּבִים וְרוֹמְמוּ אֵל, וְנָתְנוּ יְדִידִים זְמִירוֹת, שִׁירוֹת וְתִשְׁבָּחוֹת, בְּרָכוֹת וְהוֹדָאוֹת לַמֶּלֶךְ, אֵל חַי וְקַיָּם.

רָם וְנִשָּׂא, גָּדוֹל וְנוֹרָא, מַשְׁפִּיל גֵּאִים וּמַגְבִּיהַּ שְׁפָלִים, מוֹצִיא אֲסִירִים וּפוֹדֶה עֲנָוִים, וְעוֹזֵר דַּלִּים, וְעוֹנֶה לְעַמּוֹ בְּעֵת שַׁוְּעָם אֵלָיו.

True and enduring are the words spoken by our prophets.
You are the living God; Your word brings life and light to the soul.

You are the First and the Last:
besides You there is no redeemer or savior.

You are the strength of our life, the Power that saves us.
Your kingdom and Your truth abide for ever.

You have been the help of our people in time of trouble;
You are our refuge in all generations.

Your power was manifest when we went free out of Egypt;
in every liberation from bondage we see it.

May Your law of freedom rule the hearts of all Your children,
and Your law of justice unite them in friendship.

May the righteous of all nations rejoice in Your love and triumph by Your power.
O God, our refuge and our hope, we glorify Your name now as did our people in ancient days:

תְּהִלּוֹת לְאֵל עֶלְיוֹן, בָּרוּךְ הוּא וּמְבֹרָךְ. מֹשֶׁה וּבְנֵי יִשְׂרָאֵל לְךָ עָנוּ שִׁירָה בְּשִׂמְחָה רַבָּה, וְאָמְרוּ כֻלָּם:

Who is like You, Eternal One, among the gods that are worshipped? — מִי־כָמֹכָה בָּאֵלִם, יְיָ?

Who is like You, majestic in holiness, — מִי כָּמֹכָה, נֶאְדָּר בַּקֹּדֶשׁ,

awesome in splendor, doing wonders? — נוֹרָא תְהִלֹּת, עֹשֵׂה פֶלֶא?

שִׁירָה חֲדָשָׁה שִׁבְּחוּ גְאוּלִים לְשִׁמְךָ עַל־שְׂפַת הַיָּם; יַחַד כֻּלָּם הוֹדוּ וְהִמְלִיכוּ וְאָמְרוּ: "יְיָ יִמְלֹךְ לְעוֹלָם וָעֶד!"

A new song the redeemed sang to Your name. At the shore of the sea, saved from destruction, they proclaimed Your sovereign power: "The Eternal will reign for ever and ever!"

צוּר יִשְׂרָאֵל, קוּמָה בְּעֶזְרַת יִשְׂרָאֵל, וּפְדֵה כִנְאֻמֶךָ יְהוּדָה וְיִשְׂרָאֵל. גֹּאֲלֵנוּ יְיָ צְבָאוֹת שְׁמוֹ, קְדוֹשׁ יִשְׂרָאֵל.

בָּרוּךְ אַתָּה, יְיָ, גָּאַל יִשְׂרָאֵל.

O Rock of Israel, come to Israel's help. Fulfill Your promise of redemption for Judah and Israel. Our Redeemer is the Lord of Hosts, the Holy One of Israel. Blessed is the Lord, the Redeemer of Israel.

◆ ◆

All rise

תפלה

אֲדֹנָי, שְׂפָתַי תִּפְתָּח, וּפִי יַגִּיד תְּהִלָּתֶךָ.

Eternal God, open my lips, that my mouth may declare Your glory.

THE SHIELD OF ABRAHAM — אבות

בָּרוּךְ אַתָּה, יְיָ אֱלֹהֵינוּ וֵאלֹהֵי אֲבוֹתֵינוּ, אֱלֹהֵי אַבְרָהָם, אֱלֹהֵי יִצְחָק, וֵאלֹהֵי יַעֲקֹב: הָאֵל הַגָּדוֹל, הַגִּבּוֹר וְהַנּוֹרָא, אֵל עֶלְיוֹן.

Blessed is the Lord our God and God of all generations, God of Abraham, God of Isaac, and God of Jacob, great, mighty, and exalted.

גּוֹמֵל חֲסָדִים טוֹבִים, וְקוֹנֵה הַכֹּל, וְזוֹכֵר חַסְדֵי אָבוֹת, וּמֵבִיא גְאֻלָּה לִבְנֵי בְנֵיהֶם, לְמַעַן שְׁמוֹ, בְּאַהֲבָה.

He bestows love and kindness on all His children. He remembers the devotion of ages past. In His love, He brings redemption to their descendants for the sake of His name.

מֶלֶךְ עוֹזֵר וּמוֹשִׁיעַ וּמָגֵן. בָּרוּךְ אַתָּה, יְיָ, מָגֵן אַבְרָהָם.

He is our Ruler and Helper, our Savior and Protector. Blessed is the Eternal God, the Shield of Abraham.

◆ ◆

THE SOURCE OF LIFE — גבורות

אַתָּה גִּבּוֹר לְעוֹלָם, אֲדֹנָי, מְחַיֵּה הַכֹּל אַתָּה, רַב לְהוֹשִׁיעַ. מְכַלְכֵּל חַיִּים בְּחֶסֶד, מְחַיֵּה הַכֹּל בְּרַחֲמִים רַבִּים. סוֹמֵךְ נוֹפְלִים, וְרוֹפֵא חוֹלִים, וּמַתִּיר אֲסוּרִים, וּמְקַיֵּם אֱמוּנָתוֹ לִישֵׁנֵי עָפָר.

Eternal is Your might, O Lord, and great is Your saving power. In love You sustain the living; in Your great mercy, You sustain us all. You uphold the falling and heal the sick; free the captives and keep faith with Your children in death as in life.

מִי כָמוֹךָ, בַּעַל גְּבוּרוֹת, וּמִי דוֹמֶה לָּךְ, מֶלֶךְ מֵמִית וּמְחַיֶּה וּמַצְמִיחַ יְשׁוּעָה?

וְנֶאֱמָן אַתָּה לְהַחֲיוֹת הַכֹּל. בָּרוּךְ אַתָּה, יְיָ, מְחַיֵּה הַכֹּל.

Who is like You, Almighty God, Author of life and death, Source of salvation?

Blessed is the Eternal God, the Source of life.

◆ ◆

SANCTIFICATION — קדושה

נְקַדֵּשׁ אֶת־שִׁמְךָ בָּעוֹלָם, כְּשֵׁם שֶׁמַּקְדִּישִׁים אוֹתוֹ בִּשְׁמֵי מָרוֹם, כַּכָּתוּב עַל־יַד נְבִיאֶךָ: וְקָרָא זֶה אֶל־זֶה וְאָמַר:

We sanctify Your name on earth, even as all things, to the ends of time and space, proclaim Your holiness; and in the words of the prophet we say:

קָדוֹשׁ, קָדוֹשׁ, קָדוֹשׁ יְיָ צְבָאוֹת, מְלֹא כָל־הָאָרֶץ כְּבוֹדוֹ.

Holy, Holy, Holy is the Lord of Hosts; the fullness of the whole earth is His glory!

אַדִּיר אַדִּירֵנוּ, יְיָ אֲדֹנֵינוּ, מָה־אַדִּיר שִׁמְךָ בְּכָל־הָאָרֶץ!

Source of our strength, Sovereign Lord, how majestic is Your presence in all the earth!

בָּרוּךְ כְּבוֹד־יְיָ מִמְּקוֹמוֹ.

Blessed is the glory of God in heaven and earth.

אֶחָד הוּא אֱלֹהֵינוּ, הוּא אָבִינוּ, הוּא מַלְכֵּנוּ, הוּא מוֹשִׁיעֵנוּ;
וְהוּא יַשְׁמִיעֵנוּ בְּרַחֲמָיו לְעֵינֵי כָּל־חָי:

He alone is our God and our Creator; He is our Ruler and our Helper; and in His mercy He reveals Himself in the sight of all the living:

I AM ADONAI YOUR GOD! "אֲנִי יְיָ אֱלֹהֵיכֶם!"

יִמְלֹךְ יְיָ לְעוֹלָם, אֱלֹהַיִךְ צִיּוֹן, לְדֹר וָדֹר. הַלְלוּיָהּ!

The Lord shall reign for ever; your God, O Zion, from generation to generation. Halleluyah!

לְדוֹר וָדוֹר נַגִּיד גָּדְלֶךָ, וּלְנֵצַח נְצָחִים קְדֻשָּׁתְךָ נַקְדִּישׁ.
וְשִׁבְחֲךָ, אֱלֹהֵינוּ, מִפִּינוּ לֹא יָמוּשׁ לְעוֹלָם וָעֶד.
בָּרוּךְ אַתָּה, יְיָ, הָאֵל הַקָּדוֹשׁ.

To all generations we will make known Your greatness, and to all eternity proclaim Your holiness. Your praise, O God, shall never depart from our lips. Blessed is the Lord, the holy God.

All are seated

◆ ◆

THE COVENANT OF SHABBAT קדושת היום

וְשָׁמְרוּ בְנֵי־יִשְׂרָאֵל אֶת־הַשַּׁבָּת, לַעֲשׂוֹת אֶת־הַשַּׁבָּת לְדֹרֹתָם
בְּרִית עוֹלָם. בֵּינִי וּבֵין בְּנֵי יִשְׂרָאֵל אוֹת הִיא לְעֹלָם, כִּי שֵׁשֶׁת
יָמִים עָשָׂה יְיָ אֶת־הַשָּׁמַיִם וְאֶת־הָאָרֶץ, וּבַיּוֹם הַשְּׁבִיעִי שָׁבַת
וַיִּנָּפַשׁ.

The people of Israel shall keep the Sabbath, observing the Sabbath in every generation as a covenant for all time. It is a sign for ever between Me and the people of Israel, for in six days the Eternal God made heaven and earth, and on the seventh day He rested from His labors.

◆

THE SABBATH AND ITS HOLINESS

אֱלֹהֵֽינוּ וֵאלֹהֵי אֲבוֹתֵֽינוּ, רְצֵה בִמְנוּחָתֵֽנוּ. קַדְּשֵֽׁנוּ בְּמִצְוֹתֶֽיךָ וְתֵן חֶלְקֵֽנוּ בְּתוֹרָתֶֽךָ. שַׂבְּעֵֽנוּ מִטּוּבֶֽךָ, וְשַׂמְּחֵֽנוּ בִּישׁוּעָתֶֽךָ, וְטַהֵר לִבֵּֽנוּ לְעָבְדְּךָ בֶּאֱמֶת. וְהַנְחִילֵֽנוּ, יְיָ אֱלֹהֵֽינוּ, בְּאַהֲבָה וּבְרָצוֹן שַׁבַּת קָדְשֶֽׁךָ, וְיָנֽוּחוּ בָהּ יִשְׂרָאֵל מְקַדְּשֵׁי שְׁמֶֽךָ. בָּרוּךְ אַתָּה, יְיָ, מְקַדֵּשׁ הַשַּׁבָּת.

Our God and God of all Israel, grant that our worship on this Sabbath be acceptable in Your sight. Sanctify us with Your Mitzvot that we may share in the blessings of Your word. Teach us to be satisfied with the gifts of Your goodness and gratefully to rejoice in all Your mercies. Purify our hearts that we may serve You in truth. O help us to preserve the Sabbath from generation to generation, that it may bring rest and joy, peace and comfort to the dwellings of our people, and through it Your name be hallowed in all the earth. We thank You, O God, for the Sabbath and its holiness.

◆

AND BLESS US

O God our Creator, establish this sanctuary, dedicated to Your holy name, so that the worship offered within its walls may be worthy of Your greatness and Your love. May every heart which seeks Your presence here find it, as did our people in the Temple on Zion, that this house may be a house of prayer for all peoples.

O God our Creator, hear our prayer and bless us.

Have compassion upon all the House of Israel. Preserve us from sickness, from war, from strife. Keep us from hatred and uncharitableness toward our neighbors. And grant that, dwelling in safety and walking in uprightness, we may enjoy the fruit of our labor in peace.

O God our Creator, hear our prayer and bless us.

Be with all men and women who spend themselves for the good of humanity and bear the burdens of others, who give bread to the hungry, clothe the naked, and provide shelter for the homeless. Establish, O God, the work of their hands, and grant them an abundant harvest of the good seed they are sowing.

O God our Creator, hear our prayer and bless us.

Bless our children, O God, and help us so to fashion their souls by precept and example that they may ever love the good and turn from evil, revere Your Teaching and bring honor to their people. May they guard for future ages the truths revealed to our ancestors.

O God our Creator, hear our prayer and bless us.

◆

MOST PRECIOUS OF DAYS

יִשְׂמְחוּ בְמַלְכוּתְךָ שׁוֹמְרֵי שַׁבָּת וְקוֹרְאֵי עֹנֶג. עַם מְקַדְּשֵׁי שְׁבִיעִי כֻּלָּם יִשְׂבְּעוּ וְיִתְעַנְּגוּ מִטּוּבֶךָ. וְהַשְּׁבִיעִי רָצִיתָ בּוֹ וְקִדַּשְׁתּוֹ. חֶמְדַּת יָמִים אוֹתוֹ קָרָאתָ, זֵכֶר לְמַעֲשֵׂה בְרֵאשִׁית.

Those who keep the Sabbath and call it a delight shall rejoice in Your kingdom. All who hallow the seventh day shall be gladdened by Your goodness. This day is Israel's festival of the spirit, sanctified and blessed by You, the most precious of days, a symbol of the joy of creation.

◆ ◆

WHOM ALONE WE SERVE IN REVERENCE עבודה

רְצֵה, יְיָ אֱלֹהֵינוּ, בְּעַמְּךָ יִשְׂרָאֵל, וּתְפִלָּתָם בְּאַהֲבָה תְקַבֵּל, וּתְהִי לְרָצוֹן תָּמִיד עֲבוֹדַת יִשְׂרָאֵל עַמֶּךָ.

בָּרוּךְ אַתָּה, יְיָ, שֶׁאוֹתְךָ לְבַדְּךָ בְּיִרְאָה נַעֲבוֹד.

Look with favor, O Lord, upon us, and may our service be acceptable to You. Blessed is the Eternal God, whom alone we serve with reverence.

◆ ◆

MEDITATION

Lord, we give thanks for the freedom that is ours, and we pray for those in other lands who are persecuted and oppressed. Help them to bear their burdens and keep alive in them the love of freedom and the hope of deliverance. Uphold also the hands of our brothers and sisters in the land of Israel. Cause a new light to shine upon Zion and upon us all, that the time may come again when Your Torah will go forth from the house of Israel, Your word from the tents of Jacob. Blessed is our God, whose presence gives life to His people Israel.

◆ ◆

TO WHOM OUR THANKS ARE DUE — הודאה

מוֹדִים אֲנַחְנוּ לָךְ, שָׁאַתָּה הוּא יְיָ אֱלֹהֵינוּ וֵאלֹהֵי אֲבוֹתֵינוּ לְעוֹלָם וָעֶד. צוּר חַיֵּינוּ, מָגֵן יִשְׁעֵנוּ, אַתָּה הוּא לְדוֹר וָדוֹר. נוֹדֶה לְּךָ וּנְסַפֵּר תְּהִלָּתֶךָ, עַל־חַיֵּינוּ הַמְּסוּרִים בְּיָדֶךָ, וְעַל־נִשְׁמוֹתֵינוּ הַפְּקוּדוֹת לָךְ, וְעַל־נִסֶּיךָ שֶׁבְּכָל־יוֹם עִמָּנוּ, וְעַל־נִפְלְאוֹתֶיךָ וְטוֹבוֹתֶיךָ שֶׁבְּכָל־עֵת, עֶרֶב וָבֹקֶר וְצָהֳרָיִם. הַטּוֹב: כִּי לֹא־כָלוּ רַחֲמֶיךָ, וְהַמְרַחֵם: כִּי־לֹא תַמּוּ חֲסָדֶיךָ, מֵעוֹלָם קִוִּינוּ לָךְ.

וְעַל כֻּלָּם יִתְבָּרַךְ וְיִתְרוֹמַם שִׁמְךָ, מַלְכֵּנוּ, תָּמִיד לְעוֹלָם וָעֶד. וְכֹל הַחַיִּים יוֹדוּךָ סֶּלָה, וִיהַלְלוּ אֶת שִׁמְךָ בֶּאֱמֶת, הָאֵל יְשׁוּעָתֵנוּ וְעֶזְרָתֵנוּ סֶלָה. בָּרוּךְ אַתָּה, יְיָ, הַטּוֹב שִׁמְךָ וּלְךָ נָאֶה לְהוֹדוֹת.

We gratefully acknowledge, O Lord our God, that You are our Creator and Preserver, the Rock of our life and our protecting Shield. We give thanks to You for our lives which are in Your hand, for our souls which are ever in Your keeping, for Your wondrous providence and Your continuous goodness, which You bestow upon us day by day. Truly, Your mercies never fail, and Your love and kindness never cease. Therefore do we for ever put our trust in You. Blessed is the Eternal God, to whom our thanks are due.

• •

GRANT US PEACE / ברכת שלום

שִׂים שָׁלוֹם, טוֹבָה וּבְרָכָה, חֵן וָחֶסֶד וְרַחֲמִים, עָלֵינוּ וְעַל־כָּל־יִשְׂרָאֵל וְעַל־כָּל־הָעַמִּים. בָּרְכֵנוּ, אָבִינוּ, כֻּלָּנוּ כְּאֶחָד, בְּאוֹר פָּנֶיךָ, כִּי בְאוֹר פָּנֶיךָ נָתַתָּ לָּנוּ, יְיָ אֱלֹהֵינוּ, תּוֹרַת חַיִּים, וְאַהֲבַת חֶסֶד, וּצְדָקָה וּבְרָכָה וְרַחֲמִים, וְחַיִּים וְשָׁלוֹם. וְטוֹב בְּעֵינֶיךָ לְבָרֵךְ אֶת־עַמְּךָ יִשְׂרָאֵל, וְאֶת־כָּל־הָעַמִּים, בְּכָל־עֵת וּבְכָל־שָׁעָה בִּשְׁלוֹמֶךָ.

בָּרוּךְ אַתָּה, יְיָ, עוֹשֵׂה הַשָּׁלוֹם.

Grant us peace, Your most precious gift, O Eternal Source of peace, and give us the will to proclaim its message to all the peoples of the earth. Bless our country, that it may always be a stronghold of peace, and its advocate among the nations. May contentment reign within its borders, health and happiness within its homes. Strengthen the bonds of friendship among the inhabitants of all lands. And may the love of Your name hallow every home and every heart.

Blessed is the Eternal God, the Source of peace.

• •

MEDITATION

In this moment of silence a still, small voice speaks in the depths of my spirit. It speaks to me of all that I must do to come closer to God and grow in His likeness. I must work with untiring faithfulness, even when no one's eye is upon me. I must come to the end of each day with a feeling that I used its gifts wisely and faced its trials courageously. I must try to judge others less harshly and love them more freely. I must be loyal to my people and heritage, seeking greater knowledge of our tradition and putting its teachings to work in my life. May I become ever more conscious of my dignity as a child of God, and may I learn to see the divinity in every person I meet. Then indeed shall I come closer to God and grow in His likeness.

◆ ◆

Psalm 15

יְיָ, מִי־יָגוּר בְּאָהֳלֶךָ, מִי־יִשְׁכֹּן בְּהַר קָדְשֶׁךָ?
הוֹלֵךְ תָּמִים וּפֹעֵל צֶדֶק וְדֹבֵר אֱמֶת בִּלְבָבוֹ.

Lord, who may abide in Your house? Who may dwell in Your holy mountain?

Those who are upright; who do justly; who speak the truth within their hearts.

לֹא־רָגַל עַל־לְשֹׁנוֹ, לֹא־עָשָׂה לְרֵעֵהוּ רָעָה, וְחֶרְפָּה לֹא־נָשָׂא עַל־קְרֹבוֹ.
נִבְזֶה בְּעֵינָיו נִמְאָס, וְאֶת־יִרְאֵי יְיָ יְכַבֵּד.

Who do not slander others, or wrong them, or bring shame upon them.

Who scorn the lawless, but honor those who revere the Lord.

נִשְׁבַּע לְהָרַע וְלֹא יָמִיר.
כַּסְפּוֹ לֹא־נָתַן בְּנֶשֶׁךְ וְשֹׁחַד עַל־נָקִי לֹא לָקָח.

Who give their word, and, come what may, do not retract.

Who do not exploit others, who never take bribes.

עֹשֵׂה אֵלֶּה לֹא יִמּוֹט לְעוֹלָם.

Those who live in this way shall never be shaken.

◆ ◆

יִהְיוּ לְרָצוֹן אִמְרֵי־פִי וְהֶגְיוֹן לִבִּי לְפָנֶיךָ, יְיָ, צוּרִי וְגוֹאֲלִי.

May the words of my mouth, and the meditations of my heart, be acceptable to You, O Lord, my Rock and my Redeemer.

or

עֹשֶׂה שָׁלוֹם בִּמְרוֹמָיו, הוּא יַעֲשֶׂה שָׁלוֹם עָלֵינוּ וְעַל כָּל־יִשְׂרָאֵל, וְאִמְרוּ אָמֵן.

May He who causes peace to reign in the high heavens let peace descend on us, on all Israel, and all the world.

◆ ◆

Prayers for Special Occasions begin on page 389.

On Shabbat during Pesach, Sukkot, and Chanukah, or when Shabbat coincides with Rosh Chodesh or Yom Ha-atsma-ut, a short form of Hallel, page 487, is read.

The Rituals for the Reading of Torah begin on page 415.

ד IV ד

FOR THE BLESSING OF WORSHIP מה טבו

מַה־טֹּבוּ אֹהָלֶיךָ, יַעֲקֹב, מִשְׁכְּנֹתֶיךָ, יִשְׂרָאֵל!

How lovely are Your tents, O Jacob, your dwelling-places, O Israel!

וַאֲנִי, בְּרֹב חַסְדְּךָ אָבֹא בֵיתֶךָ,
אֶשְׁתַּחֲוֶה אֶל־הֵיכַל קָדְשְׁךָ בְּיִרְאָתֶךָ.

In Your abundant lovingkindness, O God, let me enter Your house, reverently to worship in Your holy temple.

יְיָ, אָהַבְתִּי מְעוֹן בֵּיתֶךָ, וּמְקוֹם מִשְׁכַּן כְּבוֹדֶךָ.
וַאֲנִי אֶשְׁתַּחֲוֶה וְאֶכְרָעָה, אֶבְרְכָה לִפְנֵי־יְיָ עֹשִׂי.

Lord, I love Your house, the place where Your glory dwells. So I would worship with humility, I would seek blessing in the presence of God, my Maker.

וַאֲנִי תְפִלָּתִי לְךָ, יְיָ, עֵת רָצוֹן.
אֱלֹהִים, בְּרָב־חַסְדֶּךָ, עֲנֵנִי בֶּאֱמֶת יִשְׁעֶךָ.

To You, then, Lord, does my prayer go forth. May this be a time of joy and favor. In Your great love, O God, answer me with Your saving truth.

◆ ◆

MEDITATION

During the past week, I took much for granted: the body's health, the mind's resilience, my strength of heart and will. These are among the countless gifts and blessings that are my daily portion. I pray that I may learn to give thanks for them, and never to take them for granted.

During the past week, I was sometimes thoughtful, sometimes self-centered. I pray that I may better meet the days to come, with growing consideration for those I love.

During the past week I thought little, or not at all, of the deep harmony I seek within myself and with others. I pray that here and now I may come to recognize that harmony as the Way of God.

The Way of God! How I would rejoice to be free of doubts and perplexities, to know in my inmost being that I stand in the presence of the Most High all my days and nights. And yet I know how unclear is my vision of God, how uncertain are my words of praise when they are directed to the Highest. I pray therefore that I may learn to worship, even as I hope to find a path to the nameless One, to the Power at the heart of life.

O Eternal One, send forth Your light, that I may see the way of Your Mitzvot. Let them guide me through days of labor and Sabbaths of rest. Let them lead me through the practice of kindness and justice to know You, that my words and my life may be one.

◆ ◆

Often our world is dark and our way confused. We search within for a light to illumine life's path. We grope for a clearer, more certain truth. The days pass, and still we yearn for the road to be revealed. O God, we remember that once our people saw a way, as it is written: "You show me the path of life." Therefore, as we awaken to Shabbat, may understanding, too, awaken within us. May the light of Torah shine within us, to dispel our darkness, to reveal Your path.

◆ ◆

MEDITATION

Rabbi Chayim of Tsanz used to tell this parable: A man, wandering lost in the forest for several days, finally encountered another. He called out: Brother, show me the way out of this forest! The man replied: Brother, I too am lost. I can only tell you this: the ways I have tried lead nowhere; they have only led me astray. Take my hand, and let us search for the way together. Rabbi Chayim would add: So it is with us. When we go our separate ways, we may go astray; let us join hands and look for the way together.

◆ ◆

From Psalm 119

אַשְׁרֵי תְמִימֵי־דָרֶךְ, הַהֹלְכִים בְּתוֹרַת יְיָ.
אַשְׁרֵי נֹצְרֵי עֵדֹתָיו, בְּכָל־לֵב יִדְרְשׁוּהוּ.

Happy are those whose way is blameless, who walk in the light of the Eternal.

Happy are those who follow His teaching, who seek Him with a whole heart.

נֵר־לְרַגְלִי דְבָרֶךָ, וְאוֹר לִנְתִיבָתִי.
פֵּתַח דְּבָרֶיךָ יָאִיר, מֵבִין פְּתָיִים.

His word is a lamp for our feet, a light for our path.

His words unfold to give us light; they bring understanding even to the simple.

עַל־כֵּן אָהַבְתִּי מִצְוֺתֶיךָ מִזָּהָב וּמִפָּז.
שָׁלוֹם רָב לְאֹהֲבֵי תוֹרָתֶךָ, וְאֵין־לָמוֹ מִכְשׁוֹל.

Therefore we love His commandments above gold, above all wealth.

Great peace have those who love His Torah; nothing can make them stumble.

◆ ◆

READER'S KADDISH | חצי קדיש

יִתְגַּדַּל וְיִתְקַדַּשׁ שְׁמֵהּ רַבָּא בְּעָלְמָא דִּי־בְרָא כִרְעוּתֵהּ, וְיַמְלִיךְ מַלְכוּתֵהּ בְּחַיֵּיכוֹן וּבְיוֹמֵיכוֹן וּבְחַיֵּי דְכָל־בֵּית יִשְׂרָאֵל, בַּעֲגָלָא וּבִזְמַן קָרִיב, וְאִמְרוּ: אָמֵן.

יְהֵא שְׁמֵהּ רַבָּא מְבָרַךְ לְעָלַם וּלְעָלְמֵי עָלְמַיָּא.

יִתְבָּרַךְ וְיִשְׁתַּבַּח, וְיִתְפָּאַר וְיִתְרוֹמַם וְיִתְנַשֵּׂא, וְיִתְהַדַּר וְיִתְעַלֶּה וְיִתְהַלַּל שְׁמֵהּ דְּקוּדְשָׁא, בְּרִיךְ הוּא, לְעֵלָּא מִן כָּל־בִּרְכָתָא וְשִׁירָתָא, תֻּשְׁבְּחָתָא וְנֶחֱמָתָא דַּאֲמִירָן בְּעָלְמָא, וְאִמְרוּ: אָמֵן.

Let the glory of God be extolled, let His great name be hallowed in the world whose creation He willed. May His kingdom soon prevail, in our own day, our own lives, and the life of all Israel, and let us say: Amen.

Let His great name be blessed for ever and ever.

Let the name of the Holy One, blessed is He, be glorified, exalted and honored, though He is beyond all the praises, songs, and adorations that we can utter, and let us say: Amen.

◆ ◆

All rise

שמע וברכותיה

בָּרְכוּ אֶת־יְיָ הַמְבֹרָךְ!

Praise the Lord, to whom our praise is due!

בָּרוּךְ יְיָ הַמְבֹרָךְ לְעוֹלָם וָעֶד!

Praised be the Lord, to whom our praise is due,
now and for ever!

◆ ◆

GOD OF TIMES AND SEASONS — יוצר

בָּרוּךְ אַתָּה, יְיָ אֱלֹהֵינוּ, מֶלֶךְ הָעוֹלָם, יוֹצֵר אוֹר וּבוֹרֵא חֹשֶׁךְ, עֹשֶׂה שָׁלוֹם וּבוֹרֵא אֶת־הַכֹּל.

Lord God of night and dawn, be with us on this Sabbath day.

God of times and seasons, be with us this day.

הַמֵּאִיר לָאָרֶץ וְלַדָּרִים עָלֶיהָ בְּרַחֲמִים, וּבְטוּבוֹ מְחַדֵּשׁ בְּכָל־יוֹם תָּמִיד מַעֲשֵׂה בְרֵאשִׁית.

Lord God of hope and joy, be with us this day.

God of the loving heart, be with us this day.

מָה רַבּוּ מַעֲשֶׂיךָ, יְיָ! כֻּלָּם בְּחָכְמָה עָשִׂיתָ, מָלְאָה הָאָרֶץ קִנְיָנֶךָ.
תִּתְבָּרַךְ, יְיָ אֱלֹהֵינוּ, עַל־שֶׁבַח מַעֲשֵׂה יָדֶיךָ, וְעַל־מְאוֹרֵי־אוֹר שֶׁעָשִׂיתָ: יְפָאֲרוּךָ. סֶּלָה.

בָּרוּךְ אַתָּה, יְיָ, יוֹצֵר הַמְּאוֹרוֹת.

Be with us as we look for strength to be free: strength to defeat those who worship power, and strength to resist all who would oppress us.

God of freedom and right, be with us this day.

◆ ◆

IN EVERY ACT OF GOODNESS — אהבה רבה

אַהֲבָה רַבָּה אֲהַבְתָּנוּ, יְיָ אֱלֹהֵינוּ, חֶמְלָה גְדוֹלָה וִיתֵרָה חָמַלְתָּ עָלֵינוּ. אָבִינוּ מַלְכֵּנוּ, בַּעֲבוּר אֲבוֹתֵינוּ שֶׁבָּטְחוּ בְךָ וַתְּלַמְּדֵם חֻקֵּי חַיִּים, כֵּן תְּחָנֵּנוּ וּתְלַמְּדֵנוּ.
אָבִינוּ, הָאָב הָרַחֲמָן, הַמְרַחֵם, רַחֵם עָלֵינוּ וְתֵן בְּלִבֵּנוּ לְהָבִין וּלְהַשְׂכִּיל, לִשְׁמֹעַ לִלְמֹד וּלְלַמֵּד, לִשְׁמֹר וְלַעֲשׂוֹת וּלְקַיֵּם אֶת־כָּל־דִּבְרֵי תַלְמוּד תּוֹרָתֶךָ בְּאַהֲבָה.

You are manifest in the heavens, the work of Your hands. In our own life, too, in every act of goodness, we feel Your spirit within us.

You are present in the life of Your people Israel, Your messenger and witness from Sinai until now.

וְהָאֵר עֵינֵינוּ בְּתוֹרָתֶךָ, וְדַבֵּק לִבֵּנוּ בְּמִצְוֹתֶיךָ, וְיַחֵד לְבָבֵנוּ לְאַהֲבָה וּלְיִרְאָה אֶת־שְׁמֶךָ. וְלֹא־נֵבוֹשׁ לְעוֹלָם וָעֶד, כִּי בְשֵׁם קָדְשְׁךָ הַגָּדוֹל וְהַנּוֹרָא בָּטָחְנוּ. נָגִילָה וְנִשְׂמְחָה בִּישׁוּעָתֶךָ, כִּי אֵל פּוֹעֵל יְשׁוּעוֹת אָתָּה, וּבָנוּ בָחַרְתָּ וְקֵרַבְתָּנוּ לְשִׁמְךָ הַגָּדוֹל סֶלָה בֶּאֱמֶת, לְהוֹדוֹת לְךָ וּלְיַחֶדְךָ בְּאַהֲבָה.

בָּרוּךְ אַתָּה, יְיָ, הַבּוֹחֵר בְּעַמּוֹ יִשְׂרָאֵל בְּאַהֲבָה.

Help us, O God, to hold fast to the truths our ancestors taught, and to welcome the truths that are yet to unfold today and tomorrow.

O God of Israel, help us to bear witness to Your presence in the world, in hearts that invite You to enter.

◆ ◆

שְׁמַע יִשְׂרָאֵל: יְיָ אֱלֹהֵינוּ, יְיָ אֶחָד!

Hear, O Israel: the Lord is our God, the Lord is One!

בָּרוּךְ שֵׁם כְּבוֹד מַלְכוּתוֹ לְעוֹלָם וָעֶד!

Blessed is His glorious kingdom for ever and ever!

All are seated

וְאָהַבְתָּ אֵת יְיָ אֱלֹהֶיךָ בְּכָל־לְבָבְךָ וּבְכָל־נַפְשְׁךָ וּבְכָל־מְאֹדֶךָ. וְהָיוּ הַדְּבָרִים הָאֵלֶּה, אֲשֶׁר אָנֹכִי מְצַוְּךָ הַיּוֹם, עַל־לְבָבֶךָ. וְשִׁנַּנְתָּם לְבָנֶיךָ, וְדִבַּרְתָּ בָּם בְּשִׁבְתְּךָ בְּבֵיתֶךָ, וּבְלֶכְתְּךָ בַדֶּרֶךְ, וּבְשָׁכְבְּךָ וּבְקוּמֶךָ.

You shall love the Lord your God with all your mind, with all your strength, with all your being.
Set these words, which I command you this day, upon your heart. Teach them faithfully to your children; speak of them in your home and on your way, when you lie down and when you rise up.

וּקְשַׁרְתָּם לְאוֹת עַל־יָדֶךָ, וְהָיוּ לְטֹטָפֹת בֵּין עֵינֶיךָ, וּכְתַבְתָּם עַל־מְזֻזוֹת בֵּיתֶךָ, וּבִשְׁעָרֶיךָ.

Bind them as a sign upon your hand; let them be a symbol before your eyes; inscribe them on the doorposts of your house, and on your gates.

לְמַעַן תִּזְכְּרוּ וַעֲשִׂיתֶם אֶת־כָּל־מִצְוֹתָי, וִהְיִיתֶם קְדֹשִׁים לֵאלֹהֵיכֶם. אֲנִי יְיָ אֱלֹהֵיכֶם, אֲשֶׁר הוֹצֵאתִי אֶתְכֶם מֵאֶרֶץ מִצְרַיִם לִהְיוֹת לָכֶם לֵאלֹהִים. אֲנִי יְיָ אֱלֹהֵיכֶם.

Be mindful of all My mitzvot, and do them: so shall you consecrate yourselves to your God. I, the Lord, am your God who led you out of Egypt to be your God; I, the Lord, am your God.

◆ ◆

WE SHALL NOT FEAR — גאולה

אֱמֶת וְיַצִּיב, וְאָהוּב וְחָבִיב, וְנוֹרָא וְאַדִּיר, וְטוֹב וְיָפֶה הַדָּבָר הַזֶּה עָלֵינוּ לְעוֹלָם וָעֶד.
אֱמֶת, אֱלֹהֵי עוֹלָם מַלְכֵּנוּ, צוּר יַעֲקֹב מָגֵן יִשְׁעֵנוּ.
לְדֹר וָדֹר הוּא קַיָּם, וּשְׁמוֹ קַיָּם, וְכִסְאוֹ נָכוֹן, וּמַלְכוּתוֹ וֶאֱמוּנָתוֹ לָעַד קַיֶּמֶת.
וּדְבָרָיו חָיִים וְקַיָּמִים, נֶאֱמָנִים וְנֶחֱמָדִים, לָעַד וּלְעוֹלְמֵי עוֹלָמִים.

Infinite God, Creator and Redeemer of all being, You are Most High, Most Near. In all generations we have cried out to You;

we have put our trust in You; we have borne witness to Your truth before the nations! O now let Your light and truth appear to us and lead us; let them bring us to Your holy mountain.

מִמִּצְרַיִם גְּאַלְתָּנוּ, יְיָ אֱלֹהֵינוּ, וּמִבֵּית עֲבָדִים פְּדִיתָנוּ. עַל־זֹאת שִׁבְּחוּ אֲהוּבִים וְרוֹמְמוּ אֵל, וְנָתְנוּ יְדִידִים זְמִירוֹת, שִׁירוֹת וְתִשְׁבָּחוֹת, בְּרָכוֹת וְהוֹדָאוֹת לַמֶּלֶךְ, אֵל חַי וְקַיָּם.

We shall not fear, then, though earth itself should shake, though the mountains fall into the heart of the sea, though its waters thunder and rage, though the winds lift its waves to the very vault of heaven.

רָם וְנִשָּׂא, גָּדוֹל וְנוֹרָא, מַשְׁפִּיל גֵּאִים וּמַגְבִּיהַּ שְׁפָלִים, מוֹצִיא אֲסִירִים וּפוֹדֶה עֲנָוִים, וְעוֹזֵר דַּלִּים, וְעוֹנֶה לְעַמּוֹ בְּעֵת שַׁוְּעָם אֵלָיו.

תְּהִלּוֹת לְאֵל עֶלְיוֹן, בָּרוּךְ הוּא וּמְבֹרָךְ. מֹשֶׁה וּבְנֵי יִשְׂרָאֵל לְךָ עָנוּ שִׁירָה בְּשִׂמְחָה רַבָּה, וְאָמְרוּ כֻלָּם:

We shall not fear, for You are with us; we shall rejoice in Your deliverance. Then shall we know You, our Redeemer and our God, and in the shadow of Your wings we shall sing with joy:

Who is like You, Eternal One, among the gods that are worshipped?	מִי־כָמֹכָה בָּאֵלִם, יְיָ?
Who is like You, majestic in holiness,	מִי כָּמֹכָה, נֶאְדָּר בַּקֹּדֶשׁ,
awesome in splendor, doing wonders?	נוֹרָא תְהִלֹּת, עֹשֵׂה פֶלֶא?

שִׁירָה חֲדָשָׁה שִׁבְּחוּ גְאוּלִים לְשִׁמְךָ עַל־שְׂפַת הַיָּם; יַחַד כֻּלָּם הוֹדוּ וְהִמְלִיכוּ וְאָמְרוּ: "יְיָ יִמְלֹךְ לְעוֹלָם וָעֶד!"

May the day dawn when all shall sit under their vines and their fig-trees, with none to make them afraid.

With great joy the redeemed shall accept You as their King, and all will say with one accord: "The Eternal will reign for ever and ever!"

◆ ◆

All rise

תפלה

אֲדֹנָי, שְׂפָתַי תִּפְתָּח, וּפִי יַגִּיד תְּהִלָּתֶךָ.

Eternal God, open my lips, that my mouth may declare Your glory.

WE ARE THEIR FUTURE — אבות

בָּרוּךְ אַתָּה, יְיָ אֱלֹהֵינוּ וֵאלֹהֵי אֲבוֹתֵינוּ, אֱלֹהֵי אַבְרָהָם, אֱלֹהֵי יִצְחָק, וֵאלֹהֵי יַעֲקֹב: הָאֵל הַגָּדוֹל, הַגִּבּוֹר וְהַנּוֹרָא, אֵל עֶלְיוֹן.

Lord, You are our God, even as You were the God of Abraham and Sarah, the God of our fathers and mothers, the God of all the ages of Israel.

They are our past as we are their future.

גּוֹמֵל חֲסָדִים טוֹבִים, וְקוֹנֵה הַכֹּל, וְזוֹכֵר חַסְדֵי אָבוֹת, וּמֵבִיא גְאֻלָּה לִבְנֵי בְנֵיהֶם, לְמַעַן שְׁמוֹ, בְּאַהֲבָה.
מֶלֶךְ עוֹזֵר וּמוֹשִׁיעַ וּמָגֵן. בָּרוּךְ אַתָּה, יְיָ, מָגֵן אַבְרָהָם.

We recall their vision and pray for the strength to keep it alive: Help us, O God and Shield, to keep their faith.

O God, Shield of Abraham, Sarah's Help, in all generations be our Help, our Shield, our God!

◆ ◆

FILLED WITH YOUR STRENGTH — גבורות

אַתָּה גִּבּוֹר לְעוֹלָם, אֲדֹנָי, מְחַיֵּה הַכֹּל אַתָּה, רַב לְהוֹשִׁיעַ.

Eternal God, the power of Your spirit pervades all creation. When we open our hearts to You, we are filled with Your strength: the strength to bear our afflictions, the strength to refuse them victory, the strength to overcome them.

מְכַלְכֵּל חַיִּים בְּחֶסֶד, מְחַיֵּה הַכֹּל בְּרַחֲמִים רַבִּים. סוֹמֵךְ נוֹפְלִים, וְרוֹפֵא חוֹלִים, וּמַתִּיר אֲסוּרִים, וּמְקַיֵּם אֱמוּנָתוֹ לִישֵׁנֵי עָפָר.

And then our will is renewed: to lift up the fallen, to set free the captive, to heal the sick, to bring light to all who dwell in darkness.

מִי כָמוֹךָ, בַּעַל גְּבוּרוֹת, וּמִי דּוֹמֶה לָּךְ, מֶלֶךְ מֵמִית וּמְחַיֶּה וּמַצְמִיחַ יְשׁוּעָה?

וְנֶאֱמָן אַתָּה לְהַחֲיוֹת הַכֹּל. בָּרוּךְ אַתָּה, יְיָ, מְחַיֵּה הַכֹּל.

Add Your strength to ours, O God, so that when death casts its shadow, we shall yet be able to say: O Source of blessing, You are with us in death as in life!

◆ ◆

SANCTIFICATION קדושה

נְקַדֵּשׁ אֶת־שִׁמְךָ בָּעוֹלָם, כְּשֵׁם שֶׁמַּקְדִּישִׁים אוֹתוֹ בִּשְׁמֵי מָרוֹם, כַּכָּתוּב עַל־יַד נְבִיאֶךָ: וְקָרָא זֶה אֶל־זֶה וְאָמַר:

We sanctify Your name on earth, even as all things, to the ends of time and space, proclaim Your holiness; and in the words of the prophet we say:

קָדוֹשׁ, קָדוֹשׁ, קָדוֹשׁ יְיָ צְבָאוֹת, מְלֹא כָל־הָאָרֶץ כְּבוֹדוֹ.

Holy, Holy, Holy is the Lord of Hosts; the fullness of the whole earth is His glory!

אַדִּיר אַדִּירֵנוּ, יְיָ אֲדֹנֵינוּ, מָה־אַדִּיר שִׁמְךָ בְּכָל־הָאָרֶץ!

Source of our strength, Sovereign Lord, how majestic is Your presence in all the earth!

בָּרוּךְ כְּבוֹד־יְיָ מִמְּקוֹמוֹ.

Blessed is the glory of God in heaven and earth.

אֶחָד הוּא אֱלֹהֵינוּ, הוּא אָבִינוּ, הוּא מַלְכֵּנוּ, הוּא מוֹשִׁיעֵנוּ;
וְהוּא יַשְׁמִיעֵנוּ בְּרַחֲמָיו לְעֵינֵי כָּל־חָי:

He alone is our God and our Creator; He is our Ruler and our Helper; and in His mercy He reveals Himself in the sight of all the living:

I AM ADONAI YOUR GOD! "אֲנִי יְיָ אֱלֹהֵיכֶם!"

יִמְלֹךְ יְיָ לְעוֹלָם, אֱלֹהַיִךְ צִיּוֹן, לְדֹר וָדֹר. הַלְלוּיָהּ!

The Lord shall reign for ever; your God, O Zion, from generation to generation. Halleluyah!

לְדוֹר וָדוֹר נַגִּיד גָּדְלֶךָ, וּלְנֵצַח נְצָחִים קְדֻשָּׁתְךָ נַקְדִּישׁ.
וְשִׁבְחֲךָ, אֱלֹהֵינוּ, מִפִּינוּ לֹא יָמוּשׁ לְעוֹלָם וָעֶד.

בָּרוּךְ אַתָּה, יְיָ, הָאֵל הַקָּדוֹשׁ.

To all generations we will make known Your greatness, and to all eternity proclaim Your holiness. Your praise, O God, shall never depart from our lips. Blessed is the Lord, the holy God.

All are seated

◆ ◆

THE DREAMS OF PRAYER

The dreams of prayer are made real by those who pray.

The ways of God are deep as love.

And the strength of God is mighty as time, which flows and flows, and has no end.

Part of all, yet separate, is the Eternal God. Separate and apart is God.

He is holy, His name is holy. And this Sabbath day is holy, for it is set apart from other days:

To remember Him, to return to Him, to bring Him back with us into the week.

We praise God as we hallow the seventh day.

◆ ◆

MOST PRECIOUS OF DAYS

קדושת היום

יִשְׂמְחוּ בְמַלְכוּתְךָ שׁוֹמְרֵי שַׁבָּת וְקוֹרְאֵי עֹנֶג. עַם מְקַדְּשֵׁי שְׁבִיעִי כֻּלָּם יִשְׂבְּעוּ וְיִתְעַנְּגוּ מִטּוּבֶךָ. וְהַשְּׁבִיעִי רָצִיתָ בּוֹ וְקִדַּשְׁתּוֹ. חֶמְדַּת יָמִים אוֹתוֹ קָרָאתָ, זֵכֶר לְמַעֲשֵׂה בְרֵאשִׁית.

Those who keep the Sabbath and call it a delight shall rejoice in Your kingdom. All who hallow the seventh day shall be gladdened by Your goodness. This day is Israel's festival of the spirit, sanctified and blessed by You, the most precious of days, a symbol of the joy of creation.

✦

MEDITATION

The universe whispers that all things are intertwined. Yet at times we hear the loud cry of discord. To which voice shall we listen? Although we long for harmony, we cannot close our ears to the noise of war, the rasp of hate. How dare we speak of concord, when the fact and symbol of our age is Auschwitz?

The intelligent heart does not deny reality. We must not forget the grief of yesterday, nor ignore the pain of today. But yesterday is past. It cannot tell us what tomorrow will bring. If there is goodness at the heart of life, then its power, like the power of evil, is real. Which shall prevail? Moment by moment we choose between them. If we choose rightly, and often enough, the broken fragments of our world will be restored to wholeness.

For this we need strength and help. We turn in hope, therefore, to a Power beyond us. He has many names, but He is One. He creates; He sustains; He loves; He inspires us with the hope that we can make ourselves one as He is One.

✦

O God, help us to build Your kingdom, one human world united in heart and soul!

✦

A GARLAND OF GLORY

אַתָּה אֶחָד וְשִׁמְךָ אֶחָד, וּמִי כְּעַמְּךָ יִשְׂרָאֵל, גּוֹי אֶחָד בָּאָרֶץ?

You are One, Your name is One, and there is none like Your people Israel, a people unique on the earth.

תִּפְאֶרֶת גְּדֻלָּה וַעֲטֶרֶת יְשׁוּעָה, יוֹם מְנוּחָה וּקְדֻשָּׁה לְעַמְּךָ נָתָתָּ: אַבְרָהָם יָגֵל, יִצְחָק יְרַנֵּן, יַעֲקֹב וּבָנָיו יָנוּחוּ בוֹ.

A garland of glory have You given us, a crown of salvation: a day of rest and holiness. Abraham rejoiced in it, Isaac sang, Jacob and his children were refreshed by its rest.

מְנוּחַת אַהֲבָה וּנְדָבָה, מְנוּחַת אֱמֶת וֶאֱמוּנָה, מְנוּחַת שָׁלוֹם וְשַׁלְוָה וְהַשְׁקֵט וָבֶטַח. מְנוּחָה שְׁלֵמָה שֶׁאַתָּה רוֹצֶה בָּהּ.

In this rest are love and sharing, truth and faithfulness and peace, quiet and safety. It is the perfect rest that You have willed.

יַכִּירוּ בָנֶיךָ וְיֵדְעוּ כִּי מֵאִתְּךָ הִיא מְנוּחָתָם, וְעַל־מְנוּחָתָם יַקְדִּישׁוּ אֶת־שְׁמֶךָ.

May Your children come to understand that this Sabbath rest links them to You, that by it they may hallow Your name.

◆ ◆

A LAND REMEMBERED AND WAITING — עבודה

רְצֵה, יְיָ אֱלֹהֵינוּ, בְּעַמְּךָ יִשְׂרָאֵל, וּתְפִלָּתָם בְּאַהֲבָה תְקַבֵּל, וּתְהִי לְרָצוֹן תָּמִיד עֲבוֹדַת יִשְׂרָאֵל עַמֶּךָ. אֵל קָרוֹב לְכָל־קֹרְאָיו, פְּנֵה אֶל עֲבָדֶיךָ וְחָנֵּנוּ; שְׁפוֹךְ רוּחֲךָ עָלֵינוּ, וְתֶחֱזֶינָה עֵינֵינוּ בְּשׁוּבְךָ לְצִיּוֹן בְּרַחֲמִים.

בָּרוּךְ אַתָּה, יְיָ, הַמַּחֲזִיר שְׁכִינָתוֹ לְצִיּוֹן.

Let us rejoice and give thanks to God whose name is blessed. He has sustained us to witness the ingathering of the exiles of our people. From all the corners of the world came a people without a land to a land remembered and waiting.

They rebuilt the neglected country, and were healed from their sufferings. They made the soil fruitful, and they were blessed.

Their children now grow in a land of their own. They brought life to the land, renewed vigor to our people.

We rejoice and give thanks to God. Their peace is our hope; their freedom is our joy; their creation is our pride. Together may we become a light to the nations.

◆ ◆

TO SEE THE WORLD ANEW — הודאה

מוֹדִים אֲנַחְנוּ לָךְ, שָׁאַתָּה הוּא יְיָ אֱלֹהֵינוּ וֵאלֹהֵי אֲבוֹתֵינוּ, אֱלֹהֵי כָל־בָּשָׂר, יוֹצְרֵנוּ יוֹצֵר בְּרֵאשִׁית.

Were the sun to rise but once a year, we would all cry out: How great are Your works, O God, and how glorious! Our hymns would rise up, our thanks would ascend. O God, Your wonders are endless, yet we do not see!

Give us new eyes, O God; restore our childhood sense of wonder.

בְּרָכוֹת וְהוֹדָאוֹת לְשִׁמְךָ הַגָּדוֹל וְהַקָּדוֹשׁ עַל־שֶׁהֶחֱיִיתָנוּ וְקִיַּמְתָּנוּ.

Then we shall explore the richness of our being: we shall taste ecstasy and sorrow, know mystery and revelation.

Give us, O God, vision to see the world anew.

כֵּן תְּחַיֵּנוּ וּתְקַיְּמֵנוּ, יְיָ אֱלֹהֵינוּ, וּתְאַמְּצֵנוּ לִשְׁמֹר חֻקֶּיךָ, לַעֲשׂוֹת רְצוֹנֶךָ, וּלְעָבְדְךָ בְּלֵבָב שָׁלֵם.

בָּרוּךְ אֵל הַהוֹדָאוֹת.

And we will give thanks; as we have been blessed, so shall we give blessing.

Give us understanding, O God; help us to know we are blessed.

◆ ◆

AN AGE OF BLESSING

We pray for the peace of Israel and all the nations. Our prophets envisioned an age of blessing. Still we yearn for it, and work for it. As we have learned:

Let justice dwell in the wilderness, righteousness in the fruitful field.

For righteousness shall lead to peace; it shall bring quietness and confidence for ever.

Then all shall sit under their vines and under their fig-trees, and none shall make them afraid.

◆ ◆

MEDITATION

God of the beginning, God of the end, God of all creatures, Lord of all generations: with love You guide the world, with love You walk hand in hand with all the living.

You created us in Your image, capable of love and justice, that in creation's long unfolding we might be Your partners. You endowed people with freedom; we must not enslave them; You gave them judgment; we must not dictate their course.

You set before us many paths to tread, that we might search and find the way that is true for us. We thank You for Your gift of choice. Without it, where would our greatness lie? Where our triumphs and where our failures? We will then consider our lives as persons and as a people who are called upon to choose.

Let our reflections help us to bring into our lives the harmony we seek and the love we would share.

◆ ◆

יִהְיוּ לְרָצוֹן אִמְרֵי־פִי וְהֶגְיוֹן לִבִּי לְפָנֶיךָ, יְיָ, צוּרִי וְגוֹאֲלִי.

May the words of my mouth, and the meditations of my heart, be acceptable to You, O Lord, my Rock and my Redeemer.

or

עֹשֶׂה שָׁלוֹם בִּמְרוֹמָיו, הוּא יַעֲשֶׂה שָׁלוֹם עָלֵינוּ וְעַל־כָּל־יִשְׂרָאֵל, וְאִמְרוּ אָמֵן.

May He who causes peace to reign in the high heavens let peace descend on us, on all Israel, and all the world.

◆ ◆

Prayers for Special Occasions begin on page 389.

On Shabbat during Pesach, Sukkot, and Chanukah, or when Shabbat coincides with Rosh Chodesh or Yom Ha-atsma-ut, a short form of Hallel, page 487, is read.

The Rituals for the Reading of Torah begin on page 415.

ה V ה

God of the morning, noon, and evening of my life: when the day is fierce with heat, may I find the comfort of Your shade. When the day dims, let the light I have kindled abide.

God of light and sun, we thank You for the morning and the day to come.

May each new morning find me renewed, moving with the day toward fullness, reaching for the heavens with each breath.

Eternal God, we thank You for the day and its light, for a measure of time in which to live.

◆ ◆

Sweet hymns and songs will I recite
To sing of You, by day and night.
Of You, who are my soul's delight.

אַנְעִים זְמִירוֹת וְשִׁירִים אֶאֱרוֹג,
כִּי אֵלֶיךָ נַפְשִׁי תַעֲרוֹג.

How does my soul within me yearn
Beneath Your shadow to return,
Your secret mysteries to learn.

נַפְשִׁי חָמְדָה בְּצֵל יָדֶךָ,
לָדַעַת כָּל־רָז סוֹדֶךָ.

And e'en while yet Your glory fires
My words, and hymns of praise inspires,
Your love it is my heart desires.

מִדֵּי דַבְּרִי בִּכְבוֹדֶךָ,
הוֹמֶה לִבִּי אֶל־דּוֹדֶיךָ.

My meditation day and night,
May it be pleasant in Your sight,
For You are all my soul's delight.

יֶעֱרַב־נָא שִׂיחִי עָלֶיךָ,
כִּי נַפְשִׁי תַעֲרוֹג אֵלֶיךָ.

◆ ◆

נִשְׁמַת כָּל־חַי תְּבָרֵךְ אֶת־שִׁמְךָ, יְיָ אֱלֹהֵינוּ, וְרוּחַ כָּל־בָּשָׂר תְּפָאֵר וּתְרוֹמֵם זִכְרְךָ, מַלְכֵּנוּ, תָּמִיד.

Let every living soul bless Your name, O Lord our God, and let every human being acclaim Your majesty for ever and ever.

◆

FOR OUR BLESSINGS

נסים בכל יום

בָּרוּךְ אַתָּה, יְיָ אֱלֹהֵינוּ, מֶלֶךְ הָעוֹלָם, אֲשֶׁר נָתַן לַשֶּׂכְוִי בִינָה לְהַבְחִין בֵּין יוֹם וּבֵין לָיְלָה.

Blessed is the Eternal our God, Ruler of the universe, who has implanted mind and instinct within every living being.

בָּרוּךְ אַתָּה, יְיָ אֱלֹהֵינוּ, מֶלֶךְ הָעוֹלָם, שֶׁעָשַׂנִי יִשְׂרָאֵל.

Blessed is the Eternal our God, who has made me a Jew.

בָּרוּךְ אַתָּה, יְיָ אֱלֹהֵינוּ, מֶלֶךְ הָעוֹלָם, שֶׁעָשַׂנִי בֶּן־חוֹרִין.

Blessed is the Eternal our God, who has made me to be free.

בָּרוּךְ אַתָּה, יְיָ אֱלֹהֵינוּ, מֶלֶךְ הָעוֹלָם, פּוֹקֵחַ עִוְרִים.

Blessed is the Eternal our God, who opens the eyes of the blind.

בָּרוּךְ אַתָּה, יְיָ אֱלֹהֵינוּ, מֶלֶךְ הָעוֹלָם, מַלְבִּישׁ עֲרֻמִּים.

Blessed is the Eternal our God, who provides clothes for the naked.

בָּרוּךְ אַתָּה, יְיָ אֱלֹהֵינוּ, מֶלֶךְ הָעוֹלָם, מַתִּיר אֲסוּרִים.

Blessed is the Eternal our God, who brings freedom to the captive.

בָּרוּךְ אַתָּה, יְיָ אֱלֹהֵינוּ, מֶלֶךְ הָעוֹלָם, זוֹקֵף כְּפוּפִים.

Blessed is the Eternal our God, whose power lifts up the fallen.

בָּרוּךְ אַתָּה, יְיָ אֱלֹהֵינוּ, מֶלֶךְ הָעוֹלָם, הַמֵּכִין מִצְעֲדֵי־גָבֶר.

Blessed is the Eternal our God, who makes firm each person's steps.

בָּרוּךְ אַתָּה, יְיָ אֱלֹהֵינוּ, מֶלֶךְ הָעוֹלָם, אוֹזֵר יִשְׂרָאֵל בִּגְבוּרָה.

Blessed is the Eternal our God, who girds our people Israel with strength.

בָּרוּךְ אַתָּה, יְיָ אֱלֹהֵינוּ, מֶלֶךְ הָעוֹלָם, עוֹטֵר יִשְׂרָאֵל בְּתִפְאָרָה.

Blessed is the Eternal our God, who crowns Israel with glory.

◆

לְפִיכָךְ אֲנַחְנוּ חַיָּבִים לְהוֹדוֹת לְךָ וּלְשַׁבֵּחֲךָ, וּלְבָרֵךְ וּלְקַדֵּשׁ אֶת־שְׁמֶךָ.

אַשְׁרֵינוּ! מַה־טּוֹב חֶלְקֵנוּ, וּמַה־נָּעִים גּוֹרָלֵנוּ, וּמַה־יָּפָה יְרֻשָּׁתֵנוּ!

How greatly we are blessed! How good is our portion! How pleasant our lot! How beautiful our heritage! We therefore thank and bless You, and proclaim the holiness of Your name.

READER'S KADDISH — חצי קדיש

יִתְגַּדַּל וְיִתְקַדַּשׁ שְׁמֵהּ רַבָּא בְּעָלְמָא דִּי־בְרָא כִרְעוּתֵהּ, וְיַמְלִיךְ מַלְכוּתֵהּ בְּחַיֵּיכוֹן וּבְיוֹמֵיכוֹן וּבְחַיֵּי דְכָל־בֵּית יִשְׂרָאֵל, בַּעֲגָלָא וּבִזְמַן קָרִיב, וְאִמְרוּ: אָמֵן.

יְהֵא שְׁמֵהּ רַבָּא מְבָרַךְ לְעָלַם וּלְעָלְמֵי עָלְמַיָּא.

יִתְבָּרַךְ וְיִשְׁתַּבַּח, וְיִתְפָּאַר וְיִתְרוֹמַם וְיִתְנַשֵּׂא, וְיִתְהַדַּר וְיִתְעַלֶּה וְיִתְהַלַּל שְׁמֵהּ דְּקוּדְשָׁא, בְּרִיךְ הוּא, לְעֵלָּא מִן כָּל־בִּרְכָתָא וְשִׁירָתָא, תֻּשְׁבְּחָתָא וְנֶחֱמָתָא דַּאֲמִירָן בְּעָלְמָא, וְאִמְרוּ: אָמֵן.

Let the glory of God be extolled, let His great name be hallowed in the world whose creation He willed. May His kingdom soon prevail, in our own day, our own lives, and the life of all Israel, and let us say: Amen.

Let His great name be blessed for ever and ever.

Let the name of the Holy One, blessed is He, be glorified, exalted and honored, though He is beyond all the praises, songs, and adorations that we can utter, and let us say: Amen.

◆ ◆

All rise

שמע וברכותיה

בָּרְכוּ אֶת־יְיָ הַמְבֹרָךְ!

Praise the Lord, to whom our praise is due!

בָּרוּךְ יְיָ הַמְבֹרָךְ לְעוֹלָם וָעֶד!

Praised be the Lord, to whom our praise is due,
now and for ever!

• •

THE WORK OF YOUR HANDS

יוצר

בָּרוּךְ אַתָּה, יְיָ אֱלֹהֵינוּ, מֶלֶךְ הָעוֹלָם, יוֹצֵר אוֹר וּבוֹרֵא חֹשֶׁךְ, עֹשֶׂה שָׁלוֹם וּבוֹרֵא אֶת־הַכֹּל.

הַמֵּאִיר לָאָרֶץ וְלַדָּרִים עָלֶיהָ בְּרַחֲמִים, וּבְטוּבוֹ מְחַדֵּשׁ בְּכָל־יוֹם תָּמִיד מַעֲשֵׂה בְרֵאשִׁית.

Heaven and earth, O Lord, are the work of Your hands. The roaring seas and the life within them issue forth from Your creative will. The universe is one vast wonder proclaiming Your wisdom and singing Your greatness.

מָה רַבּוּ מַעֲשֶׂיךָ, יְיָ! כֻּלָּם בְּחָכְמָה עָשִׂיתָ, מָלְאָה הָאָרֶץ קִנְיָנֶךָ.

תִּתְבָּרַךְ, יְיָ אֱלֹהֵינוּ, עַל־שֶׁבַח מַעֲשֵׂה יָדֶיךָ, וְעַל־מְאוֹרֵי־אוֹר שֶׁעָשִׂיתָ: יְפָאֲרוּךָ. סֶּלָה.

בָּרוּךְ אַתָּה, יְיָ, יוֹצֵר הַמְּאוֹרוֹת.

The mysteries of life and death, of growth and decay, alike display the miracle of Your creative power.

O God, the whole universe is Your dwelling-place, all being a hymn to Your glory!

• •

YOUR POWER AND YOUR LOVE אהבה רבה

אַהֲבָה רַבָּה אֲהַבְתָּנוּ, יְיָ אֱלֹהֵינוּ, חֶמְלָה גְדוֹלָה וִיתֵרָה חָמַלְתָּ עָלֵינוּ. אָבִינוּ מַלְכֵּנוּ, בַּעֲבוּר אֲבוֹתֵינוּ שֶׁבָּטְחוּ בְךָ וַתְּלַמְּדֵם חֻקֵּי חַיִּים, כֵּן תְּחָנֵּנוּ וּתְלַמְּדֵנוּ.

אָבִינוּ, הָאָב הָרַחֲמָן, הַמְרַחֵם, רַחֵם עָלֵינוּ וְתֵן בְּלִבֵּנוּ לְהָבִין וּלְהַשְׂכִּיל, לִשְׁמֹעַ לִלְמֹד וּלְלַמֵּד, לִשְׁמֹר וְלַעֲשׂוֹת וּלְקַיֵּם אֶת־כָּל־דִּבְרֵי תַלְמוּד תּוֹרָתֶךָ בְּאַהֲבָה.

O One and Only God, You have made each of us unique, and formed us to be united in one family of life. Be with us, Eternal One, as we seek to unite our lives with Your power and Your love.

וְהָאֵר עֵינֵינוּ בְּתוֹרָתֶךָ, וְדַבֵּק לִבֵּנוּ בְּמִצְוֹתֶיךָ, וְיַחֵד לְבָבֵנוּ לְאַהֲבָה וּלְיִרְאָה אֶת־שְׁמֶךָ. וְלֹא־נֵבוֹשׁ לְעוֹלָם וָעֶד, כִּי בְשֵׁם קָדְשְׁךָ הַגָּדוֹל וְהַנּוֹרָא בָּטָחְנוּ. נָגִילָה וְנִשְׂמְחָה בִּישׁוּעָתֶךָ, כִּי אֵל פּוֹעֵל יְשׁוּעוֹת אָתָּה, וּבָנוּ בָחַרְתָּ וְקֵרַבְתָּנוּ לְשִׁמְךָ הַגָּדוֹל סֶלָה בֶּאֱמֶת, לְהוֹדוֹת לְךָ וּלְיַחֶדְךָ בְּאַהֲבָה.

בָּרוּךְ אַתָּה, יְיָ, הַבּוֹחֵר בְּעַמּוֹ יִשְׂרָאֵל בְּאַהֲבָה.

We proclaim now Your Oneness and our own hope for unity; we acclaim Your creative power in the universe and in ourselves, the Law that binds world to world and heart to heart:

שְׁמַע יִשְׂרָאֵל: יְיָ אֱלֹהֵינוּ, יְיָ אֶחָד!

Hear, O Israel: the Lord is our God, the Lord is One!

בָּרוּךְ שֵׁם כְּבוֹד מַלְכוּתוֹ לְעוֹלָם וָעֶד!

Blessed is His glorious kingdom for ever and ever!

All are seated

וְאָהַבְתָּ אֵת יְיָ אֱלֹהֶיךָ בְּכָל־לְבָבְךָ וּבְכָל־נַפְשְׁךָ וּבְכָל־מְאֹדֶךָ.
וְהָיוּ הַדְּבָרִים הָאֵלֶּה, אֲשֶׁר אָנֹכִי מְצַוְּךָ הַיּוֹם, עַל־לְבָבֶךָ.

וְשִׁנַּנְתָּם לְבָנֶיךָ, וְדִבַּרְתָּ בָּם בְּשִׁבְתְּךָ בְּבֵיתֶךָ, וּבְלֶכְתְּךָ
בַדֶּרֶךְ, וּבְשָׁכְבְּךָ וּבְקוּמֶךָ.

You shall love the Lord your God with all your mind, with all your strength, with all your being.
Set these words, which I command you this day, upon your heart. Teach them faithfully to your children; speak of them in your home and on your way, when you lie down and when you rise up.

וּקְשַׁרְתָּם לְאוֹת עַל־יָדֶךָ, וְהָיוּ לְטֹטָפֹת בֵּין עֵינֶיךָ, וּכְתַבְתָּם
עַל־מְזֻזוֹת בֵּיתֶךָ, וּבִשְׁעָרֶיךָ.

Bind them as a sign upon your hand; let them be a symbol before your eyes; inscribe them on the doorposts of your house, and on your gates.

לְמַעַן תִּזְכְּרוּ וַעֲשִׂיתֶם אֶת־כָּל־מִצְוֹתָי, וִהְיִיתֶם קְדֹשִׁים
לֵאלֹהֵיכֶם. אֲנִי יְיָ אֱלֹהֵיכֶם, אֲשֶׁר הוֹצֵאתִי אֶתְכֶם מֵאֶרֶץ
מִצְרַיִם לִהְיוֹת לָכֶם לֵאלֹהִים. אֲנִי יְיָ אֱלֹהֵיכֶם.

Be mindful of all My Mitzvot, and do them: so shall you consecrate yourselves to your God. I, the Lord, am your God who led you out of Egypt to be your God; I, the Lord, am your God.

◆ ◆

THE GOD OF FREEDOM

גאולה

אֲנִי, יְיָ, קְרָאתִיךָ בְצֶדֶק וְאַחְזֵק
בְּיָדֶךָ, וְאֶצָּרְךָ; וְאֶתֶּנְךָ לִבְרִית
עָם, לְאוֹר גּוֹיִם.

I, the Eternal, have called you to righteousness, and taken you by the hand, and kept you; I have made you a covenant people, a light to the nations.

We are Israel: witness to the covenant between God and His children.

כִּי זֹאת הַבְּרִית אֲשֶׁר אֶכְרֹת אֶת־בֵּית יִשְׂרָאֵל: נָתַתִּי אֶת־תּוֹרָתִי בְּקִרְבָּם, וְעַל־לִבָּם אֶכְתֲּבֶנָּה. וְהָיִיתִי לָהֶם לֵאלֹהִים, וְהֵמָּה יִהְיוּ־לִי לְעָם.

This is the covenant I make with Israel: I will place My Torah in your midst, and write it upon your hearts. I will be your God, and you will be My people.

We are Israel: our Torah forbids the worship of race or nation, possessions or power.

הַמִּתְפַּלְלִים אֶל־אֵל לֹא־יוֹשִׁיעַ, שִׁמְעוּ דְּבַר־יְיָ: "הֲלֹא אֲנִי יְיָ, וְאֵין־עוֹד אֱלֹהִים מִבַּלְעָדַי!"

You who worship gods that cannot save you, hear the words of the Eternal: "I am God, there is none else!"

We are Israel: our prophets proclaimed an exalted vision for the world.

שִׂנְאוּ־רָע, וְאֶהֱבוּ טוֹב. וְיִגַּל כַּמַּיִם מִשְׁפָּט וּצְדָקָה כְּנַחַל אֵיתָן.

Hate evil and love what is good. Let justice well up as waters and righteousness as a mighty stream.

We are Israel, schooled in the suffering of the oppressed.

לֹא־תַעֲשֹׁק אֶת־רֵעֲךָ וְלֹא תִגְזֹל. לֹא תַעֲמֹד עַל־דַּם רֵעֶךָ.

You shall not oppress your neighbors nor rob them. You shall not stand idle while your neighbor bleeds.

We are Israel, taught to beat swords into plowshares, commanded to pursue peace.

לֹא־יִשָּׁמַע עוֹד חָמָס בְּאַרְצֵךְ, שֹׁד וָשֶׁבֶר בִּגְבוּלָיִךְ. וְכָל־בָּנַיִךְ לִמּוּדֵי יְיָ, וְרַב שְׁלוֹם בָּנָיִךְ.

Violence shall no longer be heard in your land, desolation and destruction within your borders. All your children shall be taught of the Lord, and great shall be the peace of your children.

We are Israel, O God, when we are witnesses to Your will and messengers of Your truth.

אַתֶּם עֵדַי, נְאֻם יְיָ, וְעַבְדִּי אֲשֶׁר בָּחָרְתִּי; לְמַעַן תֵּדְעוּ וְתַאֲמִינוּ לִי.

You are My witnesses, says the Eternal, and My servant whom I have chosen; know Me, therefore, and put your trust in Me.

We are Israel, O Lord, when we proclaim You the God of freedom, as did our ancestors on the shores of the sea:

מִי־כָמֹכָה בָּאֵלִם, יְיָ?
מִי כָּמֹכָה, נֶאְדָּר בַּקֹּדֶשׁ,
נוֹרָא תְהִלֹּת, עֹשֵׂה פֶלֶא?

Who is like You, Eternal One, among the gods that are worshipped?
Who is like You, majestic in holiness,
awesome in splendor, doing wonders?

שִׁירָה חֲדָשָׁה שִׁבְּחוּ גְאוּלִים לְשִׁמְךָ עַל־שְׂפַת הַיָּם; יַחַד כֻּלָּם הוֹדוּ וְהִמְלִיכוּ וְאָמְרוּ: "יְיָ יִמְלֹךְ לְעֹלָם וָעֶד!"

A new song the redeemed sang to Your name. At the shore of the sea, saved from destruction, they proclaimed Your sovereign power: "The Eternal will reign for ever and ever!"

צוּר יִשְׂרָאֵל, קוּמָה בְּעֶזְרַת יִשְׂרָאֵל, וּפְדֵה כִנְאֻמֶךָ יְהוּדָה וְיִשְׂרָאֵל. גֹּאֲלֵנוּ יְיָ צְבָאוֹת שְׁמוֹ, קְדוֹשׁ יִשְׂרָאֵל. בָּרוּךְ אַתָּה, יְיָ, גָּאַל יִשְׂרָאֵל.

O Rock of Israel, come to Israel's help. Fulfill Your promise of redemption for Judah and Israel. Our Redeemer is the Lord of Hosts, the Holy One of Israel. Blessed is the Lord, the Redeemer of Israel.

◆ ◆

All rise

תפלה

אֲדֹנָי, שְׂפָתַי תִּפְתָּח, וּפִי יַגִּיד תְּהִלָּתֶךָ.

Eternal God, open my lips, that my mouth may declare Your glory.

אבות

A COVENANT PEOPLE, ETERNAL . . .

בָּרוּךְ אַתָּה, יְיָ אֱלֹהֵינוּ וֵאלֹהֵי אֲבוֹתֵינוּ, אֱלֹהֵי אַבְרָהָם, אֱלֹהֵי יִצְחָק, וֵאלֹהֵי יַעֲקֹב: הָאֵל הַגָּדוֹל, הַגִּבּוֹר וְהַנּוֹרָא, אֵל עֶלְיוֹן.

גּוֹמֵל חֲסָדִים טוֹבִים, וְקוֹנֵה הַכֹּל, וְזוֹכֵר חַסְדֵי אָבוֹת, וּמֵבִיא גְאֻלָּה לִבְנֵי בְנֵיהֶם, לְמַעַן שְׁמוֹ, בְּאַהֲבָה.
מֶלֶךְ עוֹזֵר וּמוֹשִׁיעַ וּמָגֵן. בָּרוּךְ אַתָּה, יְיָ, מָגֵן אַבְרָהָם.

Lord, You are the God of all generations: the ones that are past, and those yet unborn. You are our God.

You are the First; You are the Last; You are the Only One.

You made the earth and brought us forth to dwell in it.

You called Abraham to righteousness, his children to bear witness to Your glory.

You formed us to be a covenant people, eternal as the hosts of heaven.

O God, You are the Shield of our people, our everlasting light.

• •

TO PLANT SEEDS OF LOVE גבורות

אַתָּה גִּבּוֹר לְעוֹלָם, אֲדֹנָי, מְחַיֵּה הַכֹּל אַתָּה, רַב לְהוֹשִׁיעַ.
מְכַלְכֵּל חַיִּים בְּחֶסֶד, מְחַיֵּה הַכֹּל בְּרַחֲמִים רַבִּים. סוֹמֵךְ נוֹפְלִים, וְרוֹפֵא חוֹלִים, וּמַתִּיר אֲסוּרִים, וּמְקַיֵּם אֱמוּנָתוֹ לִישֵׁנֵי עָפָר.
מִי כָמְוֹךָ, בַּעַל גְּבוּרוֹת, וּמִי דּוֹמֶה לָּךְ, מֶלֶךְ מֵמִית וּמְחַיֶּה וּמַצְמִיחַ יְשׁוּעָה?
וְנֶאֱמָן אַתָּה לְהַחֲיוֹת הַכֹּל. בָּרוּךְ אַתָּה, יְיָ, מְחַיֵּה הַכֹּל.

Great is the power of Your love. You have made us in Your image and raised us high above all others. You have exalted us to struggle against evil, to strive for holiness, to plant seeds of love in all our dwellings. And You, the Eternal One, help us to face death with the trust that what is good and lovely shall not perish.

Lord and Creator, joyfully we embrace Your call to life. Help us to live with courage, that we may hallow our lives as we sanctify Your name.

◆ ◆

SANCTIFICATION קדושה

Days pass and the years vanish, and we walk sightless among miracles. Lord, fill our eyes with seeing and our minds with knowing; let there be moments when the lightning of Your Presence illumines the darkness in which we walk.

Help us to see, wherever we gaze, that the bush burns unconsumed.

And we, clay touched by God, will reach out for holiness, and exclaim in wonder:

How filled with awe is this place, and we did not know it! Blessed is the Eternal One, the holy God!

נְקַדֵּשׁ אֶת־שִׁמְךָ בָּעוֹלָם, כְּשֵׁם שֶׁמַּקְדִּישִׁים אוֹתוֹ בִּשְׁמֵי מָרוֹם, כַּכָּתוּב עַל־יַד נְבִיאֶךָ: וְקָרָא זֶה אֶל־זֶה וְאָמַר:

קָדוֹשׁ, קָדוֹשׁ, קָדוֹשׁ יְיָ צְבָאוֹת, מְלֹא כָל־הָאָרֶץ כְּבוֹדוֹ.

אַדִּיר אַדִּירֵנוּ, יְיָ אֲדֹנֵינוּ, מָה־אַדִּיר שִׁמְךָ בְּכָל־הָאָרֶץ!

בָּרוּךְ כְּבוֹד־יְיָ מִמְּקוֹמוֹ.

אֶחָד הוּא אֱלֹהֵינוּ, הוּא אָבִינוּ, הוּא מַלְכֵּנוּ, הוּא מוֹשִׁיעֵנוּ;
וְהוּא יַשְׁמִיעֵנוּ בְּרַחֲמָיו לְעֵינֵי כָּל־חָי:
"אֲנִי יְיָ אֱלֹהֵיכֶם!"

יִמְלֹךְ יְיָ לְעוֹלָם, אֱלֹהַיִךְ צִיּוֹן, לְדֹר וָדֹר. הַלְלוּיָהּ!

לְדוֹר וָדוֹר נַגִּיד גָּדְלֶךָ, וּלְנֵצַח נְצָחִים קְדֻשָּׁתְךָ נַקְדִּישׁ.
וְשִׁבְחֲךָ, אֱלֹהֵינוּ, מִפִּינוּ לֹא יָמוּשׁ לְעוֹלָם וָעֶד.

בָּרוּךְ אַתָּה, יְיָ, הָאֵל הַקָּדוֹשׁ.

To all generations we will make known Your greatness, and to all eternity proclaim Your holiness. Your praise, O God, shall never depart from our lips. Blessed is the Eternal One, the holy God.

All are seated

◆ ◆

THE HOLINESS OF SHABBAT קדושת היום

וְשָׁמְרוּ בְנֵי־יִשְׂרָאֵל אֶת־הַשַּׁבָּת, לַעֲשׂוֹת אֶת־הַשַּׁבָּת לְדֹרֹתָם בְּרִית עוֹלָם. בֵּינִי וּבֵין בְּנֵי יִשְׂרָאֵל אוֹת הִיא לְעֹלָם, כִּי שֵׁשֶׁת יָמִים עָשָׂה יְיָ אֶת־הַשָּׁמַיִם וְאֶת־הָאָרֶץ, וּבַיּוֹם הַשְּׁבִיעִי שָׁבַת וַיִּנָּפַשׁ.

The people of Israel shall keep the Sabbath, observing the Sabbath in every generation as a covenant for all time. It is a sign for ever between Me and the people of Israel, for in six days the Eternal God made heaven and earth, and on the seventh day He rested from His labors.

◆

READY TO SERVE YOU

אֱלֹהֵינוּ וֵאלֹהֵי אֲבוֹתֵינוּ, רְצֵה בִמְנוּחָתֵנוּ. קַדְּשֵׁנוּ בְּמִצְוֹתֶיךָ, וְתֵן חֶלְקֵנוּ בְּתוֹרָתֶךָ; וְשַׂמְּחֵנוּ בִּישׁוּעָתֶךָ, וְטַהֵר לִבֵּנוּ לְעָבְדְּךָ בֶּאֱמֶת. בָּרוּךְ אַתָּה, יְיָ, מְקַדֵּשׁ הַשַּׁבָּת.

God of all ages, enable us through Sabbath rest to learn, impart, and uphold the commandments of Your Torah. Let us rejoice to strive for the triumph of Your will. Make our hearts ready to serve You. We thank You, O Lord, for the Sabbath and its holiness.

◆

MOST PRECIOUS OF DAYS

יִשְׂמְחוּ בְמַלְכוּתְךָ שׁוֹמְרֵי שַׁבָּת וְקוֹרְאֵי עֹנֶג. עַם מְקַדְּשֵׁי שְׁבִיעִי כֻּלָּם יִשְׂבְּעוּ וְיִתְעַנְּגוּ מִטּוּבֶךָ. וְהַשְּׁבִיעִי רָצִיתָ בּוֹ וְקִדַּשְׁתּוֹ. חֶמְדַּת יָמִים אוֹתוֹ קָרָאתָ, זֵכֶר לְמַעֲשֵׂה בְרֵאשִׁית.

Those who keep the Sabbath and call it a delight shall rejoice in Your kingdom. All who hallow the seventh day shall be gladdened by Your goodness. This day is Israel's festival of the spirit, sanctified and blessed by You, the most precious of days, a symbol of the joy of creation.

◆ ◆

IN OUR DEEDS AND OUR PRAYER עבודה

רְצֵה, יְיָ אֱלֹהֵינוּ, בְּעַמְּךָ יִשְׂרָאֵל, וּתְפִלָּתָם בְּאַהֲבָה תְקַבֵּל, וּתְהִי לְרָצוֹן תָּמִיד עֲבוֹדַת יִשְׂרָאֵל עַמֶּךָ. שְׁפוֹךְ רוּחֲךָ עָלֵינוּ, וְתֶחֱזֶינָה עֵינֵינוּ בְּשׁוּבְךָ לְצִיּוֹן בְּרַחֲמִים.

בָּרוּךְ אַתָּה, יְיָ, שֶׁאוֹתְךָ לְבַדְּךָ בְּיִרְאָה נַעֲבוֹד.

O Lord our God, may we, Your people Israel, be worthy in our deeds and our prayer. Wherever we live, wherever we seek You — in this land, in Zion restored, in all lands — You are our God, whom alone we serve in reverence.

◆ ◆

TEACH US TO GIVE THANKS

God of all generations, may the rest and quiet of this hour of worship refresh our inner life, and bring us tranquillity. May we find contentment and peace, our desire for possessions abated, our hope for advantage subdued.

But let us not be content, O God, when others go hungry, or be serene while some lack their daily bread. Teach us to give thanks for what we have by sharing it with those who are in need. Then shall our lives be called good, and our names be remembered for blessing.

◆ ◆

ONE HUMAN FAMILY ברכת שלום

שִׂים שָׁלוֹם, טוֹבָה, וּבְרָכָה, חֵן וָחֶסֶד וְרַחֲמִים עַל־כָּל־יִשְׂרָאֵל וְעַל־כָּל־יִרְאֵי שְׁמֶךָ. יְהִי רָצוֹן מִלְּפָנֶיךָ, שֶׁתְּבַטֵּל מִלְחָמוֹת וּשְׁפִיכוּת דָּמִים מִן הָעוֹלָם. וְיֵעָשׂוּ כֻלָּם אֲגוּדָה אַחַת, לַעֲשׂוֹת רְצוֹנְךָ בְּלֵבָב שָׁלֵם. יְיָ שָׁלוֹם, בָּרְכֵנוּ בְשָׁלוֹם!

Grant peace to our world, goodness and blessing, mercy and compassion, life and love. Inspire us to banish for ever hatred, war, and bloodshed. Help us to establish for ever one human family doing Your will in love and peace. O God of peace, bless us with peace.

◆ ◆

MEDITATION

Pray as if everything depended on God, and act as if everything depended on you.

Master of the universe, grant me the ability to be alone:

> may it be my custom to go outdoors each day,
> among the trees and grasses, among all growing things,
> there to be alone and enter into prayer.
>
> There may I express all that is in my heart,
> talking with Him to whom I belong.
>
> And may all grasses, trees, and plants
> awake at my coming.
>
> Send the power of their life into my prayer,
> making whole my heart and my speech
> through the life and spirit of growing things,
> made whole by their transcendent Source.

O that they would enter into my prayer!
Then would I fully open my heart
in prayer, supplication, and holy speech;
then, O God, would I pour out the words
of my heart before Your presence.

◆ ◆

יִהְיוּ לְרָצוֹן אִמְרֵי־פִי וְהֶגְיוֹן לִבִּי לְפָנֶיךָ, יְיָ, צוּרִי וְגוֹאֲלִי.

May the words of my mouth, and the meditations of my heart, be acceptable to You, O Lord, my Rock and my Redeemer.

or

עֹשֶׂה שָׁלוֹם בִּמְרוֹמָיו, הוּא יַעֲשֶׂה שָׁלוֹם עָלֵינוּ וְעַל כָּל־ יִשְׂרָאֵל, וְאִמְרוּ אָמֵן.

May He who causes peace to reign in the high heavens let peace descend on us, on all Israel, and all the world.

◆ ◆

Prayers for Special Occasions begin on page 389.

On Shabbat during Pesach, Sukkot, and Chanukah, or when Shabbat coincides with Rosh Chodesh or Yom Ha-atsma-ut, a short form of Hallel, page 487, is read.

The Rituals for the Reading of Torah begin on page 415.

ו VI ו

This service is suggested for those occasions when many children are present

מַה־טֹּבוּ אֹהָלֶיךָ, יַעֲקֹב, מִשְׁכְּנֹתֶיךָ, יִשְׂרָאֵל! וַאֲנִי, בְּרֹב
חַסְדְּךָ אָבוֹא בֵיתֶךָ, אֶשְׁתַּחֲוֶה אֶל־הֵיכַל קָדְשְׁךָ בְּיִרְאָתֶךָ.

How lovely are your tents, O Jacob, your dwelling-places, O Israel! In Your great love, O God, let me enter Your house, humbly to worship in Your holy temple.

◆ ◆

For cities and towns, factories and farms, flowers and trees, sea and sky —

Lord, we praise You for the world and its beauty.

For family and friends, neighbors and cousins —

Lord, we thank You for friendship and love.

For kind hearts, smiling faces, and helping hands —

Lord, we praise You for those who care for others.

For commandments that teach us how to live —

Lord, we thank You for those who help us to understand Your laws.

And for making us one family on earth, the children of One God —

Lord, we praise You, who made all people different, yet alike.

◆ ◆

הַלְלוּהוּ בְּצִלְצְלֵי־שָׁמַע,

Ha·le·lu·hu, ha·le·lu·hu,
be·tsil·tse·lei sha·ma.

Praise Him, praise, with trumpet and drum, with strings and winds and voice;

הַלְלוּהוּ בְּצִלְצְלֵי תְרוּעָה.

Ha·le·lu·hu, ha·le·lu·hu,
be·tsil·tse·lei te·ru·a.

Praise Him, praise, with song and with prayer, with joy, with dance, and with love.

כֹּל הַנְּשָׁמָה תְּהַלֵּל יָהּ, הַלְלוּיָהּ!

Kol ha·ne·sha·ma te·ha·leil yah,
ha·le·lu·yah, ha·le·lu·yah!

Let all who breathe sing praise to the Lord, Halleluyah, Halleluyah!

כֹּל הַנְּשָׁמָה תְּהַלֵּל יָהּ, הַלְלוּיָהּ!

Kol ha·ne·sha·ma te·ha·leil yah,
ha·le·lu·yah, ha·le·lu·yah!

Let all who breathe sing praise to the Lord, Halleluyah, Halleluyah!

◆ ◆

All rise

שמע וברכותיה

בָּרְכוּ אֶת־יְיָ הַמְבֹרָךְ!

Praise the Lord, to whom our praise is due!

בָּרוּךְ יְיָ הַמְבֹרָךְ לְעוֹלָם וָעֶד!

Praised be the Lord, to whom our praise is due,
now and for ever!

◆ ◆

CREATOR OF LIGHT — יוצר

בָּרוּךְ אַתָּה, יְיָ אֱלֹהֵינוּ, מֶלֶךְ הָעוֹלָם, יוֹצֵר אוֹר וּבוֹרֵא חֹשֶׁךְ, עֹשֶׂה שָׁלוֹם וּבוֹרֵא אֶת־הַכֹּל.

הַמֵּאִיר לָאָרֶץ וְלַדָּרִים עָלֶיהָ בְּרַחֲמִים, וּבְטוּבוֹ מְחַדֵּשׁ בְּכָל־יוֹם תָּמִיד מַעֲשֵׂה בְרֵאשִׁית. בָּרוּךְ אַתָּה, יְיָ, יוֹצֵר הַמְּאוֹרוֹת.

We praise You, Lord our God, Eternal King, Maker of light and Creator of darkness, Giver of peace and Creator of all things.
In Your mercy You give light to the earth and to all the living, and in Your goodness You renew the work of creation again and again, day by day. Blessed is the Lord, Creator of light.

◆ ◆

GREAT IS YOUR LOVE — אהבה רבה

אַהֲבָה רַבָּה אֲהַבְתָּנוּ, יְיָ אֱלֹהֵינוּ, חֶמְלָה גְדוֹלָה וִיתֵרָה
חָמַלְתָּ עָלֵינוּ.

Great is Your love, O Lord our God, and endless Your mercy.

אָבִינוּ, הָאָב הָרַחֲמָן, הַמְרַחֵם, רַחֵם עָלֵינוּ וְתֵן בְּלִבֵּנוּ
לְהָבִין וּלְהַשְׂכִּיל, לִשְׁמֹעַ לִלְמֹד וּלְלַמֵּד, לִשְׁמֹר וְלַעֲשׂוֹת
וּלְקַיֵּם אֶת־כָּל־דִּבְרֵי תַלְמוּד תּוֹרָתֶךָ בְּאַהֲבָה.

Our people have trusted in You, and You have taught us the laws of life. We too will trust in You: help us to learn and love Your Torah.

וְהָאֵר עֵינֵינוּ בְּתוֹרָתֶךָ, וְדַבֵּק לִבֵּנוּ בְּמִצְוֹתֶיךָ, וְיַחֵד לְבָבֵנוּ
לְאַהֲבָה וּלְיִרְאָה אֶת־שְׁמֶךָ.

בָּרוּךְ אַתָּה, יְיָ, הַבּוֹחֵר בְּעַמּוֹ יִשְׂרָאֵל בְּאַהֲבָה.

Make our eyes shine with joy when we study Your Torah. May we learn to obey Your Mitzvot and to love You with united hearts. Blessed is the Lord, who in love has chosen His people Israel to serve Him.

◆ ◆

שְׁמַע יִשְׂרָאֵל: יְיָ אֱלֹהֵינוּ, יְיָ אֶחָד!

Hear, O Israel: the Lord is our God, the Lord is One!

בָּרוּךְ שֵׁם כְּבוֹד מַלְכוּתוֹ לְעוֹלָם וָעֶד!

Blessed is His glorious kingdom for ever and ever!

All are seated

וְאָהַבְתָּ אֵת יְיָ אֱלֹהֶיךָ בְּכָל־לְבָבְךָ וּבְכָל־נַפְשְׁךָ וּבְכָל־מְאֹדֶךָ. וְהָיוּ הַדְּבָרִים הָאֵלֶּה, אֲשֶׁר אָנֹכִי מְצַוְּךָ הַיּוֹם, עַל־לְבָבֶךָ. וְשִׁנַּנְתָּם לְבָנֶיךָ, וְדִבַּרְתָּ בָּם בְּשִׁבְתְּךָ בְּבֵיתֶךָ, וּבְלֶכְתְּךָ בַדֶּרֶךְ, וּבְשָׁכְבְּךָ וּבְקוּמֶךָ.

You shall love the Lord your God with all your mind, with all your strength, with all your being.
Set these words, which I command you this day, upon your heart. Teach them faithfully to your children; speak of them in your home and on your way, when you lie down and when you rise up.

וּקְשַׁרְתָּם לְאוֹת עַל־יָדֶךָ, וְהָיוּ לְטֹטָפֹת בֵּין עֵינֶיךָ, וּכְתַבְתָּם עַל־מְזֻזוֹת בֵּיתֶךָ, וּבִשְׁעָרֶיךָ.

Bind them as a sign upon your hand; let them be a symbol before your eyes; inscribe them on the doorposts of your house, and on your gates.

לְמַעַן תִּזְכְּרוּ וַעֲשִׂיתֶם אֶת־כָּל־מִצְוֹתָי, וִהְיִיתֶם קְדֹשִׁים לֵאלֹהֵיכֶם. אֲנִי יְיָ אֱלֹהֵיכֶם, אֲשֶׁר הוֹצֵאתִי אֶתְכֶם מֵאֶרֶץ מִצְרַיִם לִהְיוֹת לָכֶם לֵאלֹהִים. אֲנִי יְיָ אֱלֹהֵיכֶם.

Be mindful of all My Mitzvot, and do them: so shall you consecrate yourselves to your God. I, the Lord, am your God who led you out of Egypt to be your God; I, the Lord, am your God.

◆ ◆

FOR THE FREEDOM OF ALL גאולה

אֱמֶת וְיַצִּיב, וְאָהוּב וְחָבִיב, וְנוֹרָא וְאַדִּיר, וְטוֹב וְיָפֶה הַדָּבָר הַזֶּה עָלֵינוּ לְעוֹלָם וָעֶד.

מִמִּצְרַיִם גְּאַלְתָּנוּ, יְיָ אֱלֹהֵינוּ, וּמִבֵּית עֲבָדִים פְּדִיתָנוּ.

Lord, You are One, the Creator of all. And it is Your will that all Your children worship You in freedom.

עַל־זֹאת שִׁבְּחוּ אֲהוּבִים וְרוֹמְמוּ אֵל, וְנָתְנוּ יְדִידִים זְמִירוֹת, שִׁירוֹת וְתִשְׁבָּחוֹת, בְּרָכוֹת וְהוֹדָאוֹת לַמֶּלֶךְ, אֵל חַי וְקַיָּם. תְּהִלּוֹת לְאֵל עֶלְיוֹן, בָּרוּךְ הוּא וּמְבֹרָךְ. מֹשֶׁה וּבְנֵי יִשְׂרָאֵל לְךָ עָנוּ שִׁירָה בְּשִׂמְחָה רַבָּה, וְאָמְרוּ כֻלָּם:

Therefore we must work for the freedom of all, that all may be glad as were our ancestors when they were freed from Egyptian bondage. They gave thanks to You and sang with joy:

Who is like You, Eternal One, among the gods that are worshipped?	מִי־כָמֹכָה בָּאֵלִם, יְיָ?
Who is like You, majestic in holiness,	מִי כָּמֹכָה, נֶאְדָּר בַּקֹּדֶשׁ,
awesome in splendor, doing wonders?	נוֹרָא תְהִלֹּת, עֹשֵׂה פֶלֶא?

שִׁירָה חֲדָשָׁה שִׁבְּחוּ גְאוּלִים לְשִׁמְךָ עַל־שְׂפַת הַיָּם; יַחַד כֻּלָּם הוֹדוּ וְהִמְלִיכוּ וְאָמְרוּ: "יְיָ יִמְלֹךְ לְעוֹלָם וָעֶד!"

A new song the redeemed sang to Your name. At the shore of the sea, saved from destruction, they proclaimed Your sovereign power: "The Eternal will reign for ever and ever!"

◆ ◆

All rise

תפלה

אֲדֹנָי, שְׂפָתַי תִּפְתָּח, וּפִי יַגִּיד תְּהִלָּתֶךָ.

Eternal God, open my lips, that my mouth may declare Your glory.

SHIELD OF ABRAHAM אבות

בָּרוּךְ אַתָּה, יְיָ אֱלֹהֵינוּ וֵאלֹהֵי אֲבוֹתֵינוּ, אֱלֹהֵי אַבְרָהָם, אֱלֹהֵי יִצְחָק, וֵאלֹהֵי יַעֲקֹב: הָאֵל הַגָּדוֹל, הַגִּבּוֹר וְהַנּוֹרָא, אֵל עֶלְיוֹן.

We praise You, Lord our God, God of Abraham, God of Isaac, God of Jacob, God of all generations.

גּוֹמֵל חֲסָדִים טוֹבִים, וְקוֹנֵה הַכֹּל, וְזוֹכֵר חַסְדֵי אָבוֹת, וּמֵבִיא גְאֻלָּה לִבְנֵי בְנֵיהֶם, לְמַעַן שְׁמוֹ, בְּאַהֲבָה.

Creator of all things, goodness and kindness are the works of Your hands. You have made us free, and called us to be true to Your teaching.

מֶלֶךְ עוֹזֵר וּמוֹשִׁיעַ וּמָגֵן. בָּרוּךְ אַתָּה, יְיָ, מָגֵן אַבְרָהָם.

As You taught our ancestors through the words of Your Torah, so may Torah teach us to follow the paths of goodness, kindness, and love. Blessed is the Lord, Shield of Abraham.

◆ ◆

CREATOR OF LIFE גבורות

אַתָּה גִּבּוֹר לְעוֹלָם, אֲדֹנָי, מְחַיֵּה הַכֹּל אַתָּה, רַב לְהוֹשִׁיעַ.

Great is Your power, O Lord, and endless Your love. The evening stars tell of Your might, and growing things are a song of Your love.

מְכַלְכֵּל חַיִּים בְּחֶסֶד, מְחַיֵּה הַכֹּל בְּרַחֲמִים רַבִּים. סוֹמֵךְ נוֹפְלִים, וְרוֹפֵא חוֹלִים, וּמַתִּיר אֲסוּרִים, וּמְקַיֵּם אֱמוּנָתוֹ לִישֵׁנֵי עָפָר.

You have taught us to uphold the falling, to heal the sick, to free the captive, to comfort all who suffer pain.

מִי כָמוֹךָ, בַּעַל גְּבוּרוֹת, וּמִי דוֹמֶה לָּךְ, מֶלֶךְ מֵמִית וּמְחַיֶּה וּמַצְמִיחַ יְשׁוּעָה?

וְנֶאֱמָן אַתָּה לְהַחֲיוֹת הַכֹּל. בָּרוּךְ אַתָּה, יְיָ, מְחַיֵּה הַכֹּל.

In sickness and in health, in life and in death, You are with us. Blessed is the Lord, Creator of life.

◆ ◆

THE HOLY GOD — קדושה

You are the holy God. Wherever we look, we feel Your greatness: in the sun rising from the dark night, in the ocean waves beating against the rocky shore, or in the mountains proudly raising their heads to the sky. In all the wonders of life we find You, their Maker. O God, when we look to the heavens above and at the earth around us, we cry out as did Isaiah:

קָדוֹשׁ קָדוֹשׁ קָדוֹשׁ, יְיָ צְבָאוֹת, מְלֹא כָל־הָאָרֶץ כְּבוֹדוֹ.

Holy, Holy, Holy is the Lord of Hosts; the fullness of the whole earth is His glory.

אַדִּיר אַדִּירֵנוּ, יְיָ אֲדוֹנֵינוּ, מָה אַדִּיר שִׁמְךָ בְּכָל־הָאָרֶץ!

Source of our strength, Sovereign Lord, how majestic is Your presence in all the earth!

בָּרוּךְ כְּבוֹד יְיָ מִמְּקוֹמוֹ.

Blessed is the glory of God in heaven and earth.

אֶחָד הוּא אֱלֹהֵינוּ, הוּא אָבִינוּ, הוּא מַלְכֵּנוּ, הוּא מוֹשִׁיעֵנוּ;
וְהוּא יַשְׁמִיעֵנוּ בְּרַחֲמָיו לְעֵינֵי כָּל־חָי:

He alone is our God and our Creator; He is our Ruler and our Helper; and in His mercy He reveals Himself in the sight of all the living:

I AM ADONAI YOUR GOD! — "אֲנִי יְיָ אֱלֹהֵיכֶם!"

יִמְלֹךְ יְיָ לְעוֹלָם, אֱלֹהַיִךְ צִיּוֹן, לְדֹר וָדֹר. הַלְלוּיָהּ!

The Lord shall reign for ever; your God, O Zion, from generation to generation. Praise the Lord!

בָּרוּךְ אַתָּה, יְיָ, הָאֵל הַקָּדוֹשׁ.

We praise You, O Lord, the holy God.

All are seated

◆ ◆

THE HOLINESS OF SHABBAT קדושת היום

אֱלֹהֵינוּ וֵאלֹהֵי אֲבוֹתֵינוּ, רְצֵה בִמְנוּחָתֵנוּ. קַדְּשֵׁנוּ בְּמִצְוֹתֶיךָ וְתֵן חֶלְקֵנוּ בְּתוֹרָתֶךָ. שַׂבְּעֵנוּ מִטּוּבֶךָ, וְשַׂמְּחֵנוּ בִּישׁוּעָתֶךָ, וְטַהֵר לִבֵּנוּ לְעָבְדְּךָ בֶּאֱמֶת. וְהַנְחִילֵנוּ, יְיָ אֱלֹהֵינוּ, בְּאַהֲבָה וּבְרָצוֹן שַׁבַּת קָדְשֶׁךָ, וְיָנוּחוּ בָהּ יִשְׂרָאֵל מְקַדְּשֵׁי שְׁמֶךָ. בָּרוּךְ אַתָּה, יְיָ, מְקַדֵּשׁ הַשַּׁבָּת.

Our God and God of all ages, may our worship on this Sabbath bring us closer to You.

Make us loyal to Your Torah, and make our hearts pure, that we may truly serve You.

Teach us to keep this day as a day of peace and hope, a day of rest and learning.

We thank You, O Lord, for the holy Sabbath day.

◆

MOST PRECIOUS OF DAYS

יִשְׂמְחוּ בְמַלְכוּתְךָ שׁוֹמְרֵי שַׁבָּת וְקוֹרְאֵי עֹנֶג. עַם מְקַדְּשֵׁי שְׁבִיעִי כֻּלָּם יִשְׂבְּעוּ וְיִתְעַנְּגוּ מִטּוּבֶךָ. וְהַשְּׁבִיעִי רָצִיתָ בּוֹ וְקִדַּשְׁתּוֹ. חֶמְדַּת יָמִים אוֹתוֹ קָרָאתָ, זֵכֶר לְמַעֲשֵׂה בְרֵאשִׁית.

Those who keep the Sabbath and call it a delight shall rejoice in Your kingdom. All who hallow the seventh day shall be gladdened by Your goodness. This day is Israel's festival of the spirit, sanctified and blessed by You, the most precious of days, a symbol of the joy of creation.

◆ ◆

MEDITATION

Lord our God, we pray for the Jewish people. Help those who are not yet free to find the happiness of freedom. Give strength to those of us who are rebuilding the land of Israel. And teach us all, wherever we live, to grow in knowledge and to love Your Torah. Lord our God, we pray for all peoples. Help the hungry to find bread for their bodies and food for their minds, and teach all Your children to do to others the kindness they would like done to themselves.

◆ ◆

WE GIVE THANKS הודאה

מוֹדִים אֲנַחְנוּ לָךְ, שָׁאַתָּה הוּא יְיָ אֱלֹהֵינוּ וֵאלֹהֵי אֲבוֹתֵינוּ,
אֱלֹהֵי כָל־בָּשָׂר, יוֹצְרֵנוּ יוֹצֵר בְּרֵאשִׁית.

O God, we give thanks for many things, but there is much to do before we can be content with our world. We give thanks for Your creation:

For sun and moon, for sea and sky, for bird and beast, for snow and mist, for city streets, for country lanes, for all that lives, for all that makes Your children happy.

בְּרָכוֹת וְהוֹדָאוֹת לְשִׁמְךָ הַגָּדוֹל וְהַקָּדוֹשׁ עַל־שֶׁהֶחֱיִיתָנוּ
וְקִיַּמְתָּנוּ.

But we remember that there is much to do, before we can be content:

The lost and hungry to be found and fed, the sick and the sad to be healed and cheered, a peaceful world to be built and kept, wrongs to be set right, and people to be taught.

כֵּן תְּחַיֵּנוּ וּתְקַיְּמֵנוּ, יְיָ אֱלֹהֵינוּ, וּתְאַמְּצֵנוּ לִשְׁמֹר חֻקֶּיךָ,
לַעֲשׂוֹת רְצוֹנֶךָ, וּלְעָבְדְּךָ בְּלֵבָב שָׁלֵם.
בָּרוּךְ אֵל הַהוֹדָאוֹת.

May we learn, O God, to make this beautiful world a place of goodness and happiness for all Your children.

◆ ◆

BLESSING AND PEACE ברכת שלום

שֶׁהַשָּׁלוֹם שֶׁלּוֹ יָשִׂים עָלֵינוּ בְּרָכָה וְשָׁלוֹם. מִשְּׂמֹאל וּמִיָּמִין, עַל יִשְׂרָאֵל שָׁלוֹם. הָרַחֲמָן הוּא יְבָרֵךְ אֶת עַמּוֹ בַשָּׁלוֹם.

May the God of peace help us find blessing and peace for all, far and near. May He in mercy bless His people with peace.

וְיִזְכּוּ לִרְאוֹת בָּנִים וּבְנֵי בָנִים עוֹסְקִים בַּתּוֹרָה וּבְמִצְוֹת, עַל יִשְׂרָאֵל שָׁלוֹם. פֶּלֶא יוֹעֵץ, אֵל גִּבּוֹר, אֲבִי עַד, שַׂר שָׁלוֹם.

Then we will live to see our children and their children busy with Torah and Mitzvot, and all Israel at peace. Blessed is the mighty God, the eternal Creator, the Author of peace.

◆ ◆

SILENT PRAYER

◆ ◆

יִהְיוּ לְרָצוֹן אִמְרֵי־פִי וְהֶגְיוֹן לִבִּי לְפָנֶיךָ, יְיָ, צוּרִי וְגוֹאֲלִי.

May the words of my mouth, and the meditations of my heart, be acceptable to You, O Lord, my Rock and my Redeemer.

or

עֹשֶׂה שָׁלוֹם בִּמְרוֹמָיו, הוּא יַעֲשֶׂה שָׁלוֹם עָלֵינוּ וְעַל כָּל־יִשְׂרָאֵל, וְאִמְרוּ אָמֵן.

May He who causes peace to reign in the high heavens let peace descend on us, on all Israel, and all the world.

◆ ◆

Prayers for Special Occasions begin on page 389.

On Shabbat during Pesach, Sukkot, and Chanukah, or when Shabbat coincides with Rosh Chodesh or Yom Ha-atsma-ut, a short form of Hallel, page 487, is read.

The Rituals for the Reading of Torah begin on page 415.

PRAYERS AND READINGS FOR SPECIAL OCCASIONS

Sabbath of Repentance שבת שובה

For an Evening Service

Holy and awesome God, we stand in Your presence filled with regret for our many sins and failings. Though there is greatness in us, and a deep longing for goodness, we have often denied our better selves and refused to hear Your voice within us calling us to rise to the full height of our humanity.

For there is weakness in us, as well as strength. At times we choose to walk in darkness, our vision obscured. We do not care to look within, and we are unwilling to look beyond at those who need our help.

O God, we are too weak to walk unaided. Be with us as a strong and wise Friend, and teach us to walk by the light of Your truth.

◆ ◆

וִיהִי רָצוֹן מִלְּפָנֶיךָ, יְיָ אֱלֹהֵינוּ וֵאלֹהֵי אֲבוֹתֵינוּ, שֶׁתִּשְׁבֹּר וְתַשְׁבִּית עֻלּוֹ שֶׁל־יֵצֶר הָרָע מִלִּבֵּנוּ, שֶׁכָּךְ בְּרָאתָנוּ לַעֲשׂוֹת רְצוֹנֶךָ, וַאֲנוּ חַיָּבִים לַעֲשׂוֹת רְצוֹנֶךָ. אַתְּ חָפֵץ וַאֲנוּ חֲפֵצִים, וּמִי מְעַכֵּב? שְׂאוֹר שֶׁבָּעִסָּה. גָּלוּי וְיָדוּעַ לְפָנֶיךָ שֶׁאֵין בָּנוּ כֹּחַ לַעֲמוֹד בּוֹ, אֶלָּא יְהִי רָצוֹן מִלְּפָנֶיךָ, יְיָ אֱלֹהֵינוּ וֵאלֹהֵי אֲבוֹתֵינוּ, שֶׁתַּשְׁבִּיתֵהוּ מֵעָלֵינוּ וְתַכְנִיעֵהוּ, וְנַעֲשֶׂה רְצוֹנְךָ כִּרְצוֹנֵנוּ בְּלֵבָב שָׁלֵם.

Lord our God and God of all generations, help us to break the hold that the impulse to do evil has upon our hearts. For You have created us able to do Your will. But in our nature there is a wayward spirit that hinders us and keeps us from doing what we should. O Lord our God, help us to subdue it, so that we may, with a whole heart, make Your will our own.

◆ ◆

When heavy burdens oppress us, and our spirits grow faint, and the gloom of failure settles upon us, help us to see through the darkness to the light beyond.

To You, O Lord, we turn for light; turn to us and help us.

When we come to doubt the value of life because suffering blinds us to life's goodness, give us the understanding to bear pain without despair.

To You, O God, we turn for understanding; turn to us and help us.

When we are tempted to suppress the voice of conscience, to call evil good and good evil, turn our hearts to the rights of others, and make us more responsive to their needs.

To You, O Lord, we turn for guidance; turn to us and help us.

And when we become immersed in material cares and worldly pleasures, forgetting You, may we find that all things bear witness to You, O God, and let them lead us back into Your presence.

To You, O God, we turn for meaning; turn to us and help us.

◆ ◆

יְיָ, יְיָ אֵל רַחוּם וְחַנּוּן, אֶרֶךְ
אַפַּיִם וְרַב־חֶסֶד וֶאֱמֶת, נוֹצֵר
חֶסֶד לָאֲלָפִים, נֹשֵׂא עָוֹן וָפֶשַׁע
וְחַטָּאָה וְנַקֵּה.

The Lord, the Lord God is merciful and gracious, endlessly patient, loving, and true, showing mercy to thousands, forgiving iniquity, transgression, and sin, and granting pardon.

◆ ◆

Better one hour of repentance and good deeds in this world than the whole life of the world-to-come.

Where a penitent sinner stands, even the wholly righteous may not stand.

If we say: "I will sin and repent, and sin again and repent," our repentance will not avail.

If we say: "I will sin, and the Day of Atonement will atone for me," the Day of Atonement will not atone.

Only for our transgression against God does the Day of Atonement atone.

But for our transgression against another human being, it does not atone unless we have obtained that person's pardon.

◆ ◆

אָבִינוּ מַלְכֵּנוּ, חָנֵּנוּ וַעֲנֵנוּ, כִּי אֵין בָּנוּ מַעֲשִׂים. עֲשֵׂה עִמָּנוּ צְדָקָה וָחֶסֶד וְהוֹשִׁיעֵנוּ.

Avinu Malkeinu, be gracious to us and answer us, for there is little merit in us. Treat us generously and with kindness, and be our help.

◆ ◆

For a Morning Service

זוֹכֵר חַסְדֵי אָבוֹת, וְעוֹנֶה לְבָנִים בְּעֵת צָרָתָם, לְמַעַן שְׁמוֹ אֲשֶׁר נִקְרָא עֲלֵיהֶם, וּלְמַעַן זְכוּת אֲבוֹתֵיהֶם, כַּאֲשֶׁר עָשָׂה מִימֵי קֶדֶם, פְּעַל זוּ פָּעַל לָהֶם, כַּכָּתוּב: "וַיָּחָן יְיָ אֹתָם וַיְרַחֲמֵם וַיִּפֶן עֲלֵיהֶם." עַל כֵּן נְבַקְשָׁה מִמְּךָ, יְיָ אֱלֹהֵינוּ, שָׁלֹשׁ הַמִּדּוֹת הָאֵלּוּ: לְחָנֵּנוּ, וּלְרַחֲמֵנוּ, וְלִפְנוֹת אֵלֵינוּ.

O God, You remember the faithfulness of our ancestors; You respond to their children in time of need. God, whose name is bound up in our people's name, You have done great deeds for our people, as it is written: "The Lord was gracious to them, showed them compassion, and turned to them."

Therefore, Lord our God, be gracious to us, show compassion to us, and turn to us.

אָנָּא, יְיָ, חָנֵּנוּ בִּשְׁמִיעַת תְּפִלָּתֵנוּ בְּרָצוֹן, כַּכָּתוּב: "הִנֵּה כְעֵינֵי עֲבָדִים אֶל־יַד אֲדוֹנֵיהֶם . . . כֵּן עֵינֵינוּ אֶל־יְיָ אֱלֹהֵינוּ עַד

שֶׁיְּחָנֵּנוּ." אָנָּא, יְיָ, חָנֵּנוּ בְּקַבּוּל תְּשׁוּבָתֵנוּ בְּכַפָּרָה, כַּכָּתוּב: "לָכֵן כֹּה אָמַר יְיָ יֶהוִֹה עַתָּה אָשִׁיב אֶת־שְׁבוּת יַעֲקֹב וְרִחַמְתִּי כָּל־בֵּית יִשְׂרָאֵל."

Be gracious to us and accept our prayers, as it is written: "We look to You for compassion, as servants to their master."

With compassion accept our return to You in penitence, as it is written: "Therefore, says the Eternal God, I will turn Jacob back to prosperity, and show compassion to the whole House of Israel."

אָנָּא, יְיָ, פְּנֵה אֵלֵינוּ בְּמַלֹּאת שְׁאֵלָתֵנוּ לְחַיִּים, כַּכָּתוּב: "וּפָנִיתִי אֲלֵיכֶם וְהִפְרֵיתִי אֶתְכֶם." כִּי בְּרִיתְךָ נֶאֱמֶנֶת לָעַד, וֶאֱמוּנָתְךָ כִּימֵי שָׁמַיִם, וְצִדְקָתְךָ לָעַד תִּהְיֶה, וִישׁוּעָתְךָ לְדוֹר דּוֹרִים.

And turn to us, that our aspirations may be fulfilled by abundant life, as it is written: "I will turn to you and make you fruitful."

For Your covenant is sure, Your faithfulness enduring as the heavens. Your righteousness is everlasting, Your deliverance for all generations.

◆ ◆

אָבִינוּ מַלְכֵּנוּ, חָנֵּנוּ וַעֲנֵנוּ, כִּי אֵין בָּנוּ מַעֲשִׂים. עֲשֵׂה עִמָּנוּ צְדָקָה וָחֶסֶד וְהוֹשִׁיעֵנוּ.

Avinu Malkeinu, be gracious to us and answer us, for there is little merit in us. Treat us generously and with kindness, and be our help.

שבת חול המועד סכות

For the Sabbath in Sukkot

For an Evening Service

The Lord has brought you into a good land, a land with streams and springs and lakes issuing from plain and hill, a land where you may eat food without scarcity, where you will lack nothing.

Take care lest you forget the Lord your God and fail to keep His commandments. When you have eaten and are satisfied, and have built fine houses to live in, and your herds and flocks have multiplied, and your silver and gold have increased, and everything you own has prospered, beware lest your hearts grow haughty and you forget the Lord your God, and you say to yourselves: My own power and the might of my hand have won all this for me. Remember that it is the Lord your God who gives you the power to prosper.

And now, O Israel, what is it that the Lord your God demands of you? It is to revere the Lord your God, to walk always in His paths, to love Him and to serve the Lord your God with all your heart and soul, keeping His laws and commandments. . . . He upholds the cause of the orphan and the widow, and loves the strangers, providing them with food and clothing. You too must love the stranger, for you were strangers in the land of Egypt.

May our observance of this festival of Sukkot inspire us with gratitude for the wondrous gifts that are ours, and fill us with the resolve to share them with all who are in need. Let us hold precious one another, and the world which provides us with sustenance and beauty. And let a song of thanksgiving be on our lips to the Creator and Sustainer of life.

◆ ◆

For a Morning Service

The glorious promise of spring, the mystery of summer growth, and the fulfillment of autumn's harvest reveal the greatness and goodness of God.

In ancient times, when the fruits of the field were gathered in, our people made pilgrimage to Jerusalem to give thanks for life and its blessings. We too have come as pilgrims to our sanctuary, to rejoice in the goodness of life.

O God, make us more conscious of Your gifts to us, and help us to see that no work truly prospers until it brings blessings to others. May our observance of this festival teach us not to withhold from others a share in the bounty that is ours, nor to dispossess them of what they have gleaned by their own efforts.

Help us, O Lord, so to live that when we have gathered our final harvest, many shall rise up and call us blessed.

For the Sabbath in Chanukah שבת חנוכה

With grateful hearts we remember Your protection, when tyrants sought to destroy Your people and to uproot the religion of Israel. We take pride in the valor of the Maccabees, their faith in You, their devotion to Your law which inspired them to deeds of heroism. We commemorate the rededication of Your sanctuary, the consecration of its altar to Your worship, and celebrate the rekindling of the eternal light, whose rays shone forth out of the encircling darkness as the symbol of Your presence and the beacon light of Your truth for all the world.

Be with us now — with us and our children. Make us strong to do Your will. Help us to understand and proclaim the truth, that not by might and not by power, but by Your spirit alone can we prevail. Grant to each person and every nation the blessings of liberty, justice, and peace. Let injustice and oppression cease, and hatred, cruelty, and wrong pass away, so that all human beings may unite to worship You in love and devotion.

Bless, O God, the Chanukah lights, that they may shed their radiance into our homes and our lives. May they kindle within us the flame of faith and zeal, that, like the Maccabees of old, we battle bravely for Your cause. Then shall we be worthy of Your love and Your blessing, O God, our Shield and our Protector. Amen.

From I Maccabees

On the twenty-fifth day of the month of Kislev, the messengers of King Antiochus set up an idol on the altar of God, and had incense burnt in its honor.

They decreed that the people of Judea should forsake the Law and the covenant, profane the Sabbath and pollute the sanctuary.

But many stood firm and chose to die rather than forsake the holy covenant.

Then the king's officers came to the city of Modin, and said to Mattathias, the son of John: You are a leader, honored and great in this city, and supported by sons and brothers. Now be the first to come and do what the king commands. Then you and your sons will be numbered among the friends of the king, and rewarded.

But Mattathias answered and said in a loud voice: Though all the nations that live under the king's rule obey him, and depart from their ancestral faith, yet we will live by the covenant of our ancestors.

We will not obey the king's words by turning aside from our religion to the right hand or the left.

Then Mattathias cried out in the city in a loud voice, saying: Let everyone who is whole-hearted for the Law and supports the covenant come out with me!

And he and his sons fled into the mountains. They went about pulling down pagan altars, and they rescued the Law out of the hands of the Gentiles.

Now the days drew near for Mattathias to die, and he said to his sons: Show zeal for the Law, and give your lives for the covenant of our ancestors.

Remember the deeds they did in their own times. Did not Abraham prove faithful when tested? It was reckoned to him as righteousness. David, for being merciful, inherited the throne of the kingdom for ever.

Throughout the ages, none who put their trust in God lacked strength.

My children, be courageous and grow strong in the Law, for by it you will gain honor.

Then Judah, called Maccabee, took command in his place. His brothers and all who had joined his father helped him; they gladly fought for Israel.

He battled like a lion; the lawless shrank back for fear of him. He made Jacob glad by his deeds, and his memory is blessed for ever.

When the people feared and trembled at the sight of the great number of the enemy, and said: How can we, few as we are, fight against so great and strong a multitude? Judah replied: In the sight of Heaven there is no difference between saving by many or by a few. We fight for our lives and our laws. All the people shall know that there is One who redeems and saves Israel. Judah then led them into battle and crushed the enemy; many fell, and the rest fled.

Then Israel sang hymns and praises to God, for He is good, for His mercy is everlasting.

Then, on the twenty-fifth day of Kislev, the very day on which, three years before, the altar of God had been profaned, the sanctuary of God was rededicated with songs and music, and the people praised the Eternal One, who had given them a great victory.

They celebrated the Dedication of the Altar for eight days; there was very great gladness among the people.

And Judah and his brothers and the whole community of Israel determined that every year at this season the days of the Dedication of the Altar should be observed with gladness and joy for eight days.

The blessings for kindling the Chanukah lights are on page 643.

Shabbat Zachor

שַׁבָּת זָכוֹר

How often our people has had to defy prejudice and slander, hatred and oppression! In many lands and ages Amalek and his cruel descendants have risen up against us, and untold suffering has been our lot. For our loyalty to God and to our ancestral heritage we have paid dearly.

But the same heritage has given us strength to bear our suffering with dignity and fortitude, and to remain unshaken in our conviction that in the end good must triumph over evil, truth over falsehood, and love over hate.

We have survived all those who vowed to destroy us. We lament those who perished at their hands. We give thanks for our many deliverances and for the steadfast faith of those who endured, whose love of life did not falter. They have left us an example of courage never to be forgotten.

◆ ◆

From Psalm 124

לוּלֵי יְיָ שֶׁהָיָה לָֽנוּ
בְּקוּם עָלֵֽינוּ אָדָם,
אֲזַי חַיִּים בְּלָעֽוּנוּ.

If the Eternal had not been at our side when they assailed us, they would have swallowed us alive.

אֲזַי הַמַּֽיִם שְׁטָפֽוּנוּ,
נַֽחְלָה עָבַר עַל־נַפְשֵֽׁנוּ;
אֲזַי עָבַר עַל־נַפְשֵֽׁנוּ
הַמַּֽיִם הַזֵּידוֹנִים.

The waters would have carried us away and the torrent swept over us; we would have been overwhelmed by the seething waters.

נַפְשֵֽׁנוּ כְּצִפּוֹר נִמְלְטָה
מִפַּח יוֹקְשִׁים; הַפַּח נִשְׁבָּר,
וַאֲנַֽחְנוּ נִמְלָֽטְנוּ.

We have escaped like a bird from the fowler's trap; the trap broke, and we escaped.

עֶזְרֵנוּ בְּשֵׁם יְיָ,
עֹשֵׂה שָׁמַיִם וָאָרֶץ.

For the Eternal Himself is our help,
the Maker of heaven and earth.

◆ ◆

הַבֹּטְחִים בַּייָ כְּהַר־צִיּוֹן, לֹא יִמּוֹט, לְעוֹלָם יֵשֵׁב. יְרוּשָׁלַםִ
הָרִים סָבִיב לָהּ, וַייָ סָבִיב לְעַמּוֹ, מֵעַתָּה וְעַד־עוֹלָם.

Those who trust in the Lord are like Mount Zion, which cannot be shaken but stands fast for ever. As the mountains surround Jerusalem, so the Lord is round about His people, now and always.

◆ ◆

יְיָ, מָה־רַבּוּ צָרָי, רַבִּים קָמִים עָלָי!
רַבִּים אֹמְרִים לְנַפְשִׁי: "אֵין יְשׁוּעָתָה לּוֹ בֵאלֹהִים."

Lord, how many are my foes, how many those who rise up against me!

Many say to me: "There is no help for you in God."

טָמְנוּ גֵאִים פַּח־לִי, וַחֲבָלִים; פָּרְשׂוּ רֶשֶׁת לְיַד־מַעְגָּל.
מֹקְשִׁים שָׁתוּ־לִי. וְדִבְרֵי שִׂנְאָה סְבָבוּנִי.

The arrogant lay snares for me, and chains; They have spread a net along the road.

They have set traps for me. On all sides they beset me.

וְאַתָּה, יְיָ, מָגֵן בַּעֲדִי; כְּבוֹדִי וּמֵרִים רֹאשִׁי.
וְאַתָּה אַל־תִּירָא, עַבְדִּי יַעֲקֹב. וְאַל־תֵּחַת, יִשְׂרָאֵל.

But You, O Lord, are a shield to me; You are my glory who lifts my head up high.

As it has been said: Have no fear, Jacob My servant, says the Lord. Do not be afraid, O Israel.

כִּי הִנְנִי מוֹשִׁיעֲךָ מֵרָחוֹק, וְאֶת־זַרְעֲךָ מֵאֶרֶץ שִׁבְיָם.
וְשָׁב יַעֲקֹב וְשָׁקַט וְשַׁאֲנַן, וְאֵין מַחֲרִיד.

For I will save you from afar, and your descendants from their land of exile.

And Jacob shall again be tranquil and serene, with none to make them afraid.

◆ ◆

O God, inspire us anew this day with loyalty to You, to our faith and our people. Help us to be strong against adversity, and let the heritage that has been entrusted to us be secure in our keeping. Amen.

We come before You, O God, with words of praise and thanksgiving for the care and guidance under which Your people Israel has ever lived, and for the manifold blessings You have showered upon us and all humanity.

This day brings to mind the darkness and gloom we have experienced in many generations. Painful trials and bitter struggles, torment of body and agony of mind have been our portion too many times. But sustained by the undying hope that in the end right will triumph over wrong, good over evil, and love over hate, we have held aloft the banner of Your truth.

Loyal to the memory of our heroic ancestors, we have come to affirm the living hope born in the prophetic soul of Israel, our people. Before the mighty onrush of Your light and love, we shall yet see the forces of darkness, cruel Amalek and vindictive Haman, succumb and vanish. And although many a bitter experience may await us before prejudice and hate shall have vanished, still we trust that in the end all humanity will unite in love.

Grant us, Lord, the vision to see and the courage to do Your will. Imbue our hearts with the fidelity of Mordecai and the devotion of Esther, that we may never swerve from the path of duty and loyalty to our heritage. Endow us with patience and strength, with purity of heart and unity of purpose, that we may continue to proclaim Your law of love and truth to the peoples of the earth, until all have learned that they are one, the children of the Eternal God. Amen.

◆ ◆

The Scroll of Esther is read, in whole or in part, at Purim evening and morning services. It is preceded by these blessings:

בָּרוּךְ אַתָּה, יְיָ אֱלֹהֵינוּ, מֶלֶךְ הָעוֹלָם,
אֲשֶׁר קִדְּשָׁנוּ בְּמִצְוֹתָיו וְצִוָּנוּ עַל־מִקְרָא מְגִלָּה.

Blessed is the Lord our God, Ruler of the universe,
who hallows us with His Mitzvot, and calls us to read the Megillah.

בָּרוּךְ אַתָּה, יְיָ אֱלֹהֵינוּ, מֶלֶךְ הָעוֹלָם,
שֶׁעָשָׂה נִסִּים לַאֲבוֹתֵינוּ בַּיָּמִים הָהֵם בַּזְּמַן הַזֶּה.

Blessed is the Lord our God, Ruler of the universe,
who performed wondrous deeds for our ancestors
in days of old, at this season.

בָּרוּךְ אַתָּה, יְיָ אֱלֹהֵינוּ, מֶלֶךְ הָעוֹלָם,
שֶׁהֶחֱיָנוּ וְקִיְּמָנוּ וְהִגִּיעָנוּ לַזְּמַן הַזֶּה.

Blessed is the Lord our God, Ruler of the universe,
for giving us life, for sustaining us, and for enabling
us to celebrate this festive day.

שבת חול המועד פסח

For the Sabbath in Pesach

For an Evening Service

Let every living soul bless Your name, O Lord our God, and let every human spirit acclaim Your majesty, for ever and ever.

Through all eternity You are God; we have no King but You.

God of all ages, Ruler of all creatures, Lord of all the living, all praise to You. You guide the world with steadfast love, Your creatures with tender mercy. You neither slumber nor sleep; You awaken the sleeping and arouse the dormant. You give speech to the silent, freedom to the enslaved, and justice to the oppressed.

In every generation You have redeemed our people from the house of bondage.

Our God and God of our people, You have been our help in all ages; Your mercy and kindness are with us still. May the House of Israel show its love for You by laboring for the day when freedom shall be the heritage of all Your children.

◆ ◆

For a Morning Service

Great was our people's joy,
after generations of bondage,
to be free!

Now we, their children,
triumph in our heritage of freedom.

Exultant and awed,
they sang and wept:
the people in chains were free!

Now we, their children,
hear their song
resounding in the heart.

O God, blessed Source of freedom,
let the time come speedily
when all the oppressed shall find deliverance.

Let the yoke of bondage be dissolved,
and all people serve You in freedom.

May this Passover feast
bring us new understanding
of the holiness of freedom.

Then we will rejoice before You,
with festive gladness, O God.

◆

זֶה הַיּוֹם עָשָׂה יְיָ;
נָגִילָה וְנִשְׂמְחָה בוֹ!

This is the day the Lord has made;
let us rejoice and be glad in it.

In Remembrance of Jewish Suffering

All peoples have suffered cruelty, and our hearts go out to them. But this day we think especially of the pain suffered by the House of Israel. Exile and oppression, expulsion and ghettos, pogroms and death camps: the agony of our people numbs the mind and turns the heart to stone. When we consider this, we are tempted to say, with one of our poets: "To me the whole world is one gallows."

We can only wonder at the fortitude of our fathers and mothers who said, not once but many times: "Though You slay me, yet will I trust in You." And we can only pray to be blessed with a measure of the faith that enabled them to remain true to God and His Torah, even when He seemed remote from them and life itself might have lost all meaning.

◆ ◆

קוֹל בְּרָמָה נִשְׁמָע, נְהִי בְּכִי תַמְרוּרִים!
רָחֵל מְבַכָּה עַל־בָּנֶיהָ, מֵאֲנָה לְהִנָּחֵם עַל־בָּנֶיהָ, כִּי אֵינֶנּוּ.

A voice is heard in Ramah, lamentation and bitter weeping!

Rachel is weeping for her children, refusing to be comforted for them, for they are no more.

לֹא אֲלֵיכֶם, כָּל־עֹבְרֵי דֶרֶךְ?
הַבִּיטוּ וּרְאוּ: אִם־יֵשׁ מַכְאוֹב כְּמַכְאֹבִי אֲשֶׁר עוֹלַל לִי?

Is it nothing to you, all you who pass along the road?

Look and see: is there any pain like that which has befallen me?

מָה אַשְׁוֶה־לָּךְ וַאֲנַחֲמֵךְ, בְּתוּלַת בַּת־צִיּוֹן? כִּי־גָדוֹל כַּיָּם
שִׁבְרֵךְ, מִי יִרְפָּא־לָךְ?
עַד־אָנָה יְיָ? תִּשְׁכָּחֵנִי נֶצַח? עַד־אָנָה תַּסְתִּיר אֶת־פָּנֶיךָ מִמֶּנִּי?

To what shall I liken you, how comfort you, O innocent daughter of Zion? Truly, your ruin is vast as the sea! Who can heal you?

How long, O Lord? Will we be forgotten for ever? How long will Your face be hidden from us?

כָּל־זֹאת בָּאַתְנוּ וְלֹא שְׁכַחֲנוּךָ, וְלֹא־שִׁקַּרְנוּ בִּבְרִיתֶךָ.
כִּי־עָלֶיךָ הֹרַגְנוּ כָל־הַיּוֹם, נֶחְשַׁבְנוּ כְּצֹאן טִבְחָה.

All this has befallen us, yet we have not forgotten You, nor been false to Your covenant.

It is for Your sake that we have been slain all the day long, and accounted as sheep for the slaughter.

◆ ◆

And there was silence! How many stood aside, mute and unconcerned, forgetting the divine command: "You shall not stand idle while your neighbor bleeds."

For the sin of silence,
For the sin of indifference,
For the secret complicity of the neutral.
For the closing of borders,
For the washing of hands,
For the crime of indifference.
For the sin of silence,
For the closing of borders —

Let there be no forgetfulness before the Throne of Glory, and let memory startle us on sunny afternoons, in sudden silences when we are with friends, when we lie down and when we rise up. For we remember the harsh words of the prophet to Edom, early and cruel oppressor of our people:

בְּיוֹם עֲמָדְךָ מִנֶּגֶד,
בְּיוֹם שְׁבוֹת זָרִים חֵילוֹ,
וְנָכְרִים בָּאוּ שְׁעָרָיו וְעַל־יְרוּשָׁלַםִ יַדּוּ גוֹרָל,
גַּם־אַתָּה כְּאַחַד מֵהֶם.

On the day when you stood aloof,
on the day when barbarians carried off their wealth,
and strangers entered their gates to cast lots for Jerusalem,
you too were like one of them.

וְאַל־תֵּרֶא בְיוֹם־אָחִיךָ בְּיוֹם־נָכְרוֹ!
וְאַל־תִּשְׂמַח לִבְנֵי־יְהוּדָה בְּיוֹם אָבְדָם!

You should not have gloated over your kin in the days of their misfortune!

You should not have rejoiced over the people of Judah in the days of their ruin!

וְאַל־תַּגְדֵּל פִּיךָ בְּיוֹם צָרָה!
אַל־תָּבוֹא בְשַׁעַר־עַמִּי בְּיוֹם אֵידָם!

You should not have widened your mouth on the day of distress!

You should not have entered My people's gate on the day of their calamity!

וְאַל־תַּעֲמֹד עַל־הַפֶּרֶק לְהַכְרִית אֶת־פְּלִיטָיו!
וְאַל־תַּסְגֵּר שְׂרִידָיו בְּיוֹם צָרָה!

You should not have stood at the crossroads to cut off their fugitives!

You should not have betrayed their survivors on the day of distress!

◆

Lord, You see it; You see that none comes to help, none to intervene. In the high places there is astonishment and anger. And down below, the winds carry dust to earth's four corners, the dust of Jews.

◆ ◆

MEDITATION

"וְשַׂמְתִּי אֶת־זַרְעֲךָ כַּעֲפַר הָאָרֶץ."

מָה עֲפַר הָאָרֶץ מִסּוֹף הָעוֹלָם וְעַד סוֹפוֹ, כָּךְ בָּנֶיךָ יִהְיוּ מְפֻזָּרִים מִסּוֹף הָעוֹלָם וְעַד סוֹפוֹ.

"And I will make your seed as the dust of the earth."

As the dust of the earth extends from one end of the earth to the other, so will your children be scattered from one end of the earth to the other.

וּמָה עֲפַר הָאָרֶץ אֵינוֹ מִתְבָּרֵךְ אֶלָּא בַּמַּיִם, אַף יִשְׂרָאֵל אֵינָן מִתְבָּרְכִים אֶלָּא בִּזְכוּת הַתּוֹרָה, שֶׁנִּמְשְׁלָה לְמָיִם.

And as the dust of the earth can be blessed only through water, so Israel too can be blessed only through the Torah, which is to the thirsty soul what water is to the body.

וּמָה עָפָר עָשׂוּי דַּיִשׁ, אַף בָּנֶיךָ עֲשׂוּיִין דַּיִשׁ לַמַּלְכֻיּוֹת.

And as dust is made to be trampled on, so too will your children be made for kingdoms to trample upon.

וּמָה עָפָר מְבַלֶּה אֶת כְּלֵי מַתָּכוֹת וְהוּא קַיָּם לְעוֹלָם, כָּךְ יִשְׂרָאֵל: כָּל עוֹבְדֵי כוֹכָבִים בְּטֵלִים, וְהֵם קַיָּמִים.

And as dust wears vessels of metal away, but itself endures for ever, so with Israel: all your enemies will be nought, but you shall endure.

◆ ◆

We have been dust, yet have endured. We look back, knowing that the past cannot be undone; but it can be redeemed, today and tomorrow.

We look ahead. Is not hope better than despair? Out of all our losses must come the spirit's triumph: to cling to life, to live for justice, to walk with integrity, until the day when all will dwell in a happier world. As it has been said:

"נַחֲמוּ נַחֲמוּ עַמִּי," יֹאמַר אֱלֹהֵיכֶם.
זֹאת אָשִׁיב אֶל־לִבִּי, עַל־כֵּן אוֹחִיל:

"Take comfort, take comfort, My people," says your God.

This I call to mind, and therefore have I hope:

בִּלַּע הַמָּוֶת לָנֶצַח, וּמָחָה אֲדֹנָי אֱלֹהִים דִּמְעָה מֵעַל כָּל־פָּנִים.
וְחֶרְפַּת עַמּוֹ יָסִיר מֵעַל כָּל־הָאָרֶץ, כִּי יְיָ דִּבֵּר.

He will swallow up death for ever; the Lord God will wipe the tears from every face.

He will remove from all the earth the reproach that lies upon His people.

כֹּה אָמַר יְיָ: "מִנְעִי קוֹלֵךְ מִבֶּכִי, וְעֵינַיִךְ מִדִּמְעָה! כִּי יֵשׁ שָׂכָר לִפְעֻלָּתֵךְ."
"וְיֵשׁ־תִּקְוָה לְאַחֲרִיתֵךְ," נְאֻם־יְיָ.

Thus says the Lord: "Hold back your voice from weeping, your eyes from tears! For your labor shall have its reward."

"There is hope for your future," says the Lord.

• •

אֲנִי מַאֲמִין בֶּאֱמוּנָה שְׁלֵמָה בְּבִיאַת הַמָּשִׁיחַ. וְאַף עַל פִּי שֶׁיִּתְמַהְמֵהַּ, עִם כָּל־זֶה אֲנִי מַאֲמִין, עִם כָּל־זֶה אֲחַכֶּה־לּוֹ בְּכָל־יוֹם שֶׁיָּבוֹא.

I believe with perfect faith in the Messiah's coming.
And even if he be delayed, I will await him.

On the Sabbath before Yom Ha-atsma-ut

As we stood at the edge of the crag,
a great wind began to blow,
and all fell back dismayed.
But I took hold of the sledgehammer
preserved here from ages past,
and began to strike the rock.
And the wind answered: Amen, Amen.

◆ ◆

Today we turn our thoughts to the land of Israel. It is the cradle of our faith, a land hallowed by memories of kings and prophets, of poets and sages. In all the ages of our history, and in all the lands of our dispersion, we have remembered it with love and longing, saying with the Psalmist:

If I forget you, O Jerusalem,
let my right hand wither.
Let my tongue cleave
to the roof of my mouth
if I do not remember you,
if I do not set Jerusalem
above my highest joy.

אִם־אֶשְׁכָּחֵךְ יְרוּשָׁלָֽםִ,
תִּשְׁכַּח יְמִינִי.
תִּדְבַּק לְשׁוֹנִי לְחִכִּי
אִם־לֹא אֶזְכְּרֵֽכִי,
אִם־לֹא אַעֲלֶה אֶת־יְרוּשָׁלַםִ
עַל רֹאשׁ שִׂמְחָתִי.

◆ ◆

Blessed are the eyes that behold Israel reborn in its ancient land of promise! Blessed the age that has seen our people outlive death's kingdom! With gratitude we recall the devotion of Israel's builders and the valor of its defenders. We give thanks for this example of courage, this expression of our creative will.

For every anguished yesterday let there be a joyful tomorrow. Let the Jewish spirit flower on its reclaimed soil. Rise up, all creation, and sing!

רָנּוּ, שָׁמַיִם; וְגִילִי אָרֶץ; וּפִצְחוּ הָרִים רִנָּה! כִּי־נִחַם יְיָ עַמּוֹ, וַעֲנִיָּו יְרַחֵם.

Sing, O heavens; be joyful, O earth; break out in song, O mountains! For the Lord has comforted Zion, and shown compassion for His afflicted.

וַיָּשֶׂם מִדְבָּרָהּ כְּעֵדֶן, וְעַרְבָתָהּ כְּגַן־יְיָ, שָׂשׂוֹן וְשִׂמְחָה יִמָּצֵא בָהּ, תּוֹדָה וְקוֹל זִמְרָה.

He has made her wilderness like Eden, her desert like a garden. Joy and gladness shall be found there, thanksgiving and jubilant song.

◆ ◆

אַשְׁרֵי הַגַּפְרוּר שֶׁנִּשְׂרַף וְהִצִּית לְהָבוֹת.
אַשְׁרֵי הַלֶּהָבָה שֶׁבָּעֲרָה בְּסִתְרֵי לְבָבוֹת.

Blessed is the match consumed in kindling flame.

Blessed is the flame that burns in the heart's secret places.

אַשְׁרֵי הַלְּבָבוֹת שֶׁיָּדְעוּ לַחֲדוֹל בְּכָבוֹד.
אַשְׁרֵי הַגַּפְרוּר שֶׁנִּשְׂרַף וְהִצִּית לְהָבוֹת.

Blessed is the heart with strength to stop its beating for honor's sake.

Blessed is the match consumed in kindling flame.

◆ ◆

Israel, born in pain, has lived in peril. We pray for the welfare of her people and their land. May they dwell in safety and live in peace and friendship with their neighbors.

שַׁאֲלוּ שְׁלוֹם יְרוּשָׁלָֽםִ:
יִשְׁלָֽיוּ אֹהֲבָֽיִךְ!
יְהִי־שָׁלוֹם בְּחֵילֵךְ,
שַׁלְוָה בְּאַרְמְנוֹתָֽיִךְ.
לְמַֽעַן אַחַי וְרֵעָי
אֲדַבְּרָה־נָּא שָׁלוֹם בָּךְ.
לְמַֽעַן בֵּית־יְיָ אֱלֹהֵֽינוּ
אֲבַקְשָׁה טוֹב לָךְ.

Pray for the peace of Jerusalem:
may those who love you prosper!
Let there be peace in your homes,
safety within your borders.
For the sake of my people, my friends, I pray you find peace.
For the sake of the house of the Lord our God, I will seek your good.

◆ ◆

Guardian of Israel and Redeemer of all the world, grant that Zion may become a light to the nations. Give its people strength to build a land in which the vision of justice and mercy shall be fulfilled for the good of all the world. Then shall the brightness of truth, compassion, and peace shine forth from Zion, as it is written:

כִּי מִצִּיּוֹן תֵּצֵא תוֹרָה וּדְבַר־יְיָ מִירוּשָׁלָֽיִם.

Out of Zion shall go forth Torah, and the word of the Lord from Jerusalem.

סדר קריאת התורה

FOR THE READING OF THE TORAH

א I א

אֵין כָּמְוֹךָ בָאֱלֹהִים, יְיָ, וְאֵין כְּמַעֲשֶׂיךָ. מַלְכוּתְךָ מַלְכוּת כָּל־עֹלָמִים וּמֶמְשַׁלְתְּךָ בְּכָל־דּוֹר וָדֹר.

There is none like You, O Lord, among the gods that are worshipped, and there are no deeds like Yours. Your kingdom is an everlasting kingdom, and Your dominion endures through all generations.

יְיָ מֶלֶךְ, יְיָ מָלָךְ, יְיָ יִמְלֹךְ לְעוֹלָם וָעֶד. יְיָ עֹז לְעַמּוֹ יִתֵּן, יְיָ יְבָרֵךְ אֶת־עַמּוֹ בַשָּׁלוֹם.

The Lord rules; the Lord will reign for ever and ever. May the Lord give strength to His people; may the Lord bless His people with peace.

◆ ◆

All rise

אַב הָרַחֲמִים, הֵיטִיבָה בִרְצוֹנְךָ אֶת־צִיּוֹן; תִּבְנֶה חוֹמוֹת יְרוּשָׁלָיִם.

כִּי בְךָ לְבַד בָּטָחְנוּ, מֶלֶךְ אֵל רָם וְנִשָּׂא, אֲדוֹן עוֹלָמִים.

Source of mercy, let Your goodness be a blessing to Zion; let Jerusalem be rebuilt.

In You alone do we trust, O Sovereign God, high and exalted, Lord of all the worlds.

◆ ◆

The Ark is opened

הָבוּ גֹדֶל לֵאלֹהֵינוּ וּתְנוּ כָבוֹד לַתּוֹרָה.

Let us declare the greatness of our God and give honor to the Torah.

◆ ◆

The Torah is taken from the Ark

כִּי מִצִּיּוֹן תֵּצֵא תוֹרָה, וּדְבַר־יְיָ מִירוּשָׁלָיִם.

For out of Zion shall go forth Torah, and the word of the Lord from Jerusalem.

בָּרוּךְ שֶׁנָּתַן תּוֹרָה לְעַמּוֹ יִשְׂרָאֵל בִּקְדֻשָּׁתוֹ.

Praised be the One who in His holiness has given the Torah to His people Israel.

◆ ◆

שְׁמַע יִשְׂרָאֵל: יְיָ אֱלֹהֵינוּ, יְיָ אֶחָד!

Hear, O Israel: the Lord is our God, the Lord is One!

אֶחָד אֱלֹהֵינוּ, גָּדוֹל אֲדוֹנֵינוּ, קָדוֹשׁ שְׁמוֹ.

Our God is One; our Lord is great; holy is His name.

◆ ◆

גַּדְּלוּ לַייָ אִתִּי וּנְרוֹמְמָה שְׁמוֹ יַחְדָּו.

O magnify the Lord with me, and together let us exalt His name.

◆ ◆

לְךָ, יְיָ, הַגְּדֻלָּה וְהַגְּבוּרָה וְהַתִּפְאֶרֶת וְהַנֵּצַח וְהַהוֹד, כִּי כֹל בַּשָּׁמַיִם וּבָאָרֶץ, לְךָ יְיָ הַמַּמְלָכָה וְהַמִּתְנַשֵּׂא לְכֹל לְרֹאשׁ.

Yours, Lord, is the greatness, the power, the glory, the victory, and the majesty; for all that is in heaven and earth is Yours. Yours is the kingdom, O Lord; You are supreme over all.

All are seated

◆ ◆

Reading of the Torah

For transliteration, see page 772.

Before the Reading

בָּרְכוּ אֶת־יְיָ הַמְבֹרָךְ!

בָּרוּךְ יְיָ הַמְבֹרָךְ לְעוֹלָם וָעֶד!

בָּרוּךְ אַתָּה, יְיָ אֱלֹהֵינוּ, מֶלֶךְ הָעוֹלָם, אֲשֶׁר בָּחַר־בָּנוּ מִכָּל־הָעַמִּים וְנָתַן־לָנוּ אֶת־תּוֹרָתוֹ. בָּרוּךְ אַתָּה, יְיָ, נוֹתֵן הַתּוֹרָה.

Praise the Lord, to whom our praise is due!

Praised be the Lord, to whom our praise is due,
now and for ever!

Blessed is the Lord our God, Ruler of the universe, who has chosen us from all peoples by giving us His Torah. Blessed is the Lord, Giver of the Torah.

◆ ◆

After the Reading

בָּרוּךְ אַתָּה, יְיָ אֱלֹהֵינוּ, מֶלֶךְ הָעוֹלָם, אֲשֶׁר נָתַן לָנוּ תּוֹרַת אֱמֶת וְחַיֵּי עוֹלָם נָטַע בְּתוֹכֵנוּ. בָּרוּךְ אַתָּה, יְיָ, נוֹתֵן הַתּוֹרָה.

Blessed is the Lord our God, Ruler of the universe, who has given us a Torah of truth, implanting within us eternal life. Blessed is the Lord, Giver of the Torah.

◆ ◆

As the reading is completed, the Torah might be held high while this is said:

וְזֹאת הַתּוֹרָה אֲשֶׁר־שָׂם מֹשֶׁה לִפְנֵי בְּנֵי יִשְׂרָאֵל, עַל־פִּי יְיָ בְּיַד־מֹשֶׁה.

This is the Torah that Moses placed before the people of Israel to fulfill the word of God.

◆ ◆

Reading of the Haftarah

For transliteration, see page 773.

Before the Reading

בָּרוּךְ אַתָּה, יְיָ אֱלֹהֵינוּ, מֶלֶךְ הָעוֹלָם, אֲשֶׁר בָּחַר בִּנְבִיאִים טוֹבִים וְרָצָה בְדִבְרֵיהֶם הַנֶּאֱמָרִים בֶּאֱמֶת. בָּרוּךְ אַתָּה, יְיָ, הַבּוֹחֵר בַּתּוֹרָה וּבְמֹשֶׁה עַבְדּוֹ וּבְיִשְׂרָאֵל עַמּוֹ וּבִנְבִיאֵי הָאֱמֶת וָצֶדֶק.

Blessed is the Lord our God, Ruler of the universe, who has chosen faithful prophets to speak words of truth. Blessed is the Lord, for the revelation of Torah, for Moses His servant and Israel His people, and for the prophets of truth and righteousness.

◆ ◆

After the Reading

An alternative version of this Benediction follows below

בָּרוּךְ אַתָּה, יְיָ אֱלֹהֵינוּ, מֶלֶךְ הָעוֹלָם, צוּר כָּל־הָעוֹלָמִים, צַדִּיק בְּכָל־הַדּוֹרוֹת, הָאֵל הַנֶּאֱמָן, הָאוֹמֵר וְעוֹשֶׂה, הַמְדַבֵּר וּמְקַיֵּם, שֶׁכָּל־דְּבָרָיו אֱמֶת וָצֶדֶק.

Blessed is the Lord our God, Ruler of the universe, Rock of all creation, Righteous One of all generations, the faithful God whose word is deed, whose every command is just and true.

עַל־הַתּוֹרָה וְעַל־הָעֲבוֹדָה וְעַל־הַנְּבִיאִים וְעַל־יוֹם הַשַּׁבָּת הַזֶּה, שֶׁנָּתַתָּ־לָּנוּ, יְיָ אֱלֹהֵינוּ, לִקְדֻשָּׁה וְלִמְנוּחָה, לְכָבוֹד וּלְתִפְאָרֶת, עַל־הַכֹּל, יְיָ אֱלֹהֵינוּ, אֲנַחְנוּ מוֹדִים לָךְ, וּמְבָרְכִים אוֹתָךְ. יִתְבָּרַךְ שִׁמְךָ בְּפִי כָּל־חַי תָּמִיד לְעוֹלָם וָעֶד.

בָּרוּךְ אַתָּה, יְיָ, מְקַדֵּשׁ הַשַּׁבָּת.

For the Torah, for the privilege of worship, for the prophets, and for this Shabbat that You, O Lord our God, have given us for holiness and rest, for honor and glory, we thank and bless You. May Your name be blessed for ever by every living being. Blessed is the Lord, for the Sabbath and its holiness.

◆ ◆

Alternative Version

בָּרוּךְ אַתָּה, יְיָ אֱלֹהֵינוּ, מֶלֶךְ הָעוֹלָם, צוּר כָּל־הָעוֹלָמִים, צַדִּיק בְּכָל־הַדּוֹרוֹת, הָאֵל הַנֶּאֱמָן, הָאוֹמֵר וְעוֹשֶׂה, הַמְדַבֵּר וּמְקַיֵּם, שֶׁכָּל־דְּבָרָיו אֱמֶת וָצֶדֶק.

Blessed is the Lord our God, Ruler of the universe, Rock of all creation, Righteous One of all generations, the faithful God whose word is deed, whose every command is just and true.

נֶאֱמָן אַתָּה הוּא יְיָ אֱלֹהֵינוּ, וְנֶאֱמָנִים דְּבָרֶיךָ, וְדָבָר אֶחָד מִדְּבָרֶיךָ אָחוֹר לֹא־יָשׁוּב רֵיקָם, כִּי אֵל מֶלֶךְ נֶאֱמָן וְרַחֲמָן אָתָּה. בָּרוּךְ אַתָּה, יְיָ, הָאֵל הַנֶּאֱמָן בְּכָל־דְּבָרָיו.

You are the Faithful One, O Lord our God, and faithful is Your word. Not one word of Yours goes forth without accomplishing its task, O faithful and compassionate God and King. Blessed is the Lord, the faithful God.

רַחֵם עַל־צִיּוֹן כִּי הִיא בֵּית חַיֵּינוּ, וְלַעֲלוּבַת נֶפֶשׁ תּוֹשִׁיעַ בִּמְהֵרָה בְיָמֵינוּ. בָּרוּךְ אַתָּה, יְיָ, מְשַׂמֵּחַ צִיּוֹן בְּבָנֶיהָ.

Show compassion for Zion, our House of Life, and banish all sadness speedily, in our own day. Blessed is the Lord, who brings joy to Zion's children.

שַׂמְּחֵנוּ, יְיָ אֱלֹהֵינוּ, בְּאֵלִיָּהוּ הַנָּבִיא עַבְדֶּךָ, וּבְמַלְכוּת בֵּית דָּוִד מְשִׁיחֶךָ, בִּמְהֵרָה יָבֹא וְיָגֵל לִבֵּנוּ. עַל־כִּסְאוֹ לֹא־יֵשֵׁב זָר וְלֹא־יִנְחֲלוּ עוֹד אֲחֵרִים אֶת־כְּבוֹדוֹ. כִּי בְשֵׁם קָדְשְׁךָ נִשְׁבַּעְתָּ לוֹ שֶׁלֹּא־יִכְבֶּה נֵרוֹ לְעוֹלָם וָעֶד. בָּרוּךְ אַתָּה, יְיָ, מָגֵן דָּוִד.

Lord our God, bring us the joy of Your kingdom: let our dream of Elijah and David bear fruit. Speedily let redemption come to gladden our hearts. Let Your solemn promise be fulfilled: David's light shall not for ever be extinguished! Blessed is the Lord, the Shield of David.

עַל־הַתּוֹרָה וְעַל־הָעֲבוֹדָה וְעַל־הַנְּבִיאִים וְעַל־יוֹם הַשַּׁבָּת הַזֶּה, שֶׁנָּתַתָּ־לָּנוּ, יְיָ אֱלֹהֵינוּ, לִקְדֻשָּׁה וְלִמְנוּחָה, לְכָבוֹד וּלְתִפְאָרֶת, עַל־הַכֹּל, יְיָ אֱלֹהֵינוּ, אֲנַחְנוּ מוֹדִים לָךְ, וּמְבָרְכִים אוֹתָךְ. יִתְבָּרַךְ שִׁמְךָ בְּפִי כָּל־חַי תָּמִיד לְעוֹלָם וָעֶד.

בָּרוּךְ אַתָּה, יְיָ, מְקַדֵּשׁ הַשַּׁבָּת.

For the Torah, for the privilege of worship, for the prophets, and for this Shabbat that You, O Lord our God, have given us for holiness and rest, for honor and glory, we thank and bless You. May Your name be blessed for ever by every living being. Blessed is the Lord, for the Sabbath and its holiness.

◆ ◆

Special prayers begin on page 449.

◆ ◆

Returning the Torah to the Ark

All rise

יְהַלְלוּ אֶת־שֵׁם יְיָ, כִּי נִשְׂגָּב שְׁמוֹ לְבַדּוֹ.

Let us praise the name of the Lord, for His name alone is exalted.

◆ ◆

הוֹדוֹ עַל אֶרֶץ וְשָׁמָיִם, וַיָּרֶם קֶרֶן לְעַמּוֹ, תְּהִלָּה לְכָל-
חֲסִידָיו, לִבְנֵי יִשְׂרָאֵל עַם קְרוֹבוֹ. הַלְלוּיָהּ.

God's splendor covers heaven and earth; He is the strength of His people, making glorious His faithful ones, Israel, a people close to Him. Halleluyah!

◆ ◆

Some congregations continue with Psalm 29

מִזְמוֹר לְדָוִד. הָבוּ לַייָ, בְּנֵי אֵלִים, הָבוּ לַייָ כָּבוֹד וָעֹז!
הָבוּ לַייָ כְּבוֹד שְׁמוֹ, הִשְׁתַּחֲווּ לַייָ בְּהַדְרַת־קֹדֶשׁ.

A Song of David.
Praise the Lord, all celestial beings, praise the Lord for His glory and strength! Praise the Lord, whose name is great; worship the Lord in the beauty of holiness.

קוֹל יְיָ עַל־הַמָּיִם! אֵל־הַכָּבוֹד הִרְעִים! יְיָ עַל־מַיִם רַבִּים!
קוֹל יְיָ בַּכֹּחַ, קוֹל יְיָ בֶּהָדָר, קוֹל יְיָ שֹׁבֵר אֲרָזִים, וַיְשַׁבֵּר
יְיָ אֶת־אַרְזֵי הַלְּבָנוֹן. וַיַּרְקִידֵם כְּמוֹ־עֵגֶל לְבָנוֹן וְשִׂרְיוֹן כְּמוֹ
בֶן־רְאֵמִים.

The Eternal's voice above the waters! The God of glory thunders! The Eternal's voice, with power—the Eternal's voice, majestic—the Eternal's voice breaks cedars, He shatters Lebanon's cedars: till Lebanon skips like a calf, Sirion like a wild young ox.

קוֹל־יְיָ חֹצֵב לַהֲבוֹת אֵשׁ; קוֹל יְיָ יָחִיל מִדְבָּר; יָחִיל יְיָ
מִדְבַּר קָדֵשׁ; קוֹל יְיָ יְחוֹלֵל אַיָּלוֹת, וַיֶּחֱשֹׂף יְעָרוֹת, וּבְהֵיכָלוֹ
כֻּלּוֹ אֹמֵר: "כָּבוֹד!"

The Lord: His voice sparks fiery flames; the Lord: His voice makes the desert spin; the Lord: His voice shakes the Kadesh desert: the Lord: His voice uproots the oaks, and strips the forests bare, while in His temple all cry: "Glory!"

יְיָ לַמַּבּוּל יָשָׁב, וַיֵּשֶׁב יְיָ מֶלֶךְ לְעוֹלָם. יְיָ עֹז לְעַמּוֹ יִתֵּן, יְיָ
יְבָרֵךְ אֶת־עַמּוֹ בַשָּׁלוֹם.

The Lord, enthroned above the flood, the Lord will reign for ever. The Lord will give strength to His people, the Lord will bless His people with peace.

◆ ◆

תּוֹרַת יְיָ תְּמִימָה, מְשִׁיבַת נָפֶשׁ;
עֵדוּת יְיָ נֶאֱמָנָה, מַחְכִּימַת פֶּתִי;

The Torah of the Lord is perfect, reviving the soul;
The teaching of the Lord is sure, making wise the simple;

פִּקּוּדֵי יְיָ יְשָׁרִים, מְשַׂמְּחֵי־לֵב;
מִצְוַת יְיָ בָּרָה, מְאִירַת עֵינָיִם;

The precepts of the Lord are right, delighting the mind;
The Mitzvah of the Lord is clear, giving light to the eyes;

יִרְאַת יְיָ טְהוֹרָה, עוֹמֶדֶת לָעַד;
מִשְׁפְּטֵי יְיָ אֱמֶת, צָדְקוּ יַחְדָּו.

The word of the Lord is pure, enduring for ever;
The judgments of the Lord are true, and altogether just.

◆ ◆

כִּי לֶקַח טוֹב נָתַתִּי לָכֶם, תּוֹרָתִי אַל־תַּעֲזֹבוּ.
עֵץ־חַיִּים הִיא לַמַּחֲזִיקִים בָּהּ, וְתֹמְכֶיהָ מְאֻשָּׁר.
דְּרָכֶיהָ דַרְכֵי־נֹעַם, וְכָל־נְתִיבוֹתֶיהָ שָׁלוֹם.

Behold, a good doctrine has been given you, My Torah; do not forsake it. It is a tree of life to those who hold it fast, and all who cling to it find happiness. Its ways are ways of pleasantness, and all its paths are peace.

הֲשִׁיבֵנוּ יְיָ אֵלֶיךָ, וְנָשׁוּבָה. חַדֵּשׁ יָמֵינוּ כְּקֶדֶם.

Help us to return to You, O Lord; then truly shall we return. Renew our days as in the past.

The Ark is closed

All are seated

ב II ב

הַקְהֵל אֶת־הָעָם – הָאֲנָשִׁים וְהַנָּשִׁים וְהַטַּף וְגֵרְךָ אֲשֶׁר בִּשְׁעָרֶיךָ – לְמַעַן יִשְׁמְעוּ וּלְמַעַן יִלְמְדוּ וְיָרְאוּ אֶת־יְיָ אֱלֹהֵיכֶם, וְשָׁמְרוּ לַעֲשׂוֹת אֶת־כָּל־דִּבְרֵי הַתּוֹרָה הַזֹּאת. וּבְנֵיהֶם אֲשֶׁר לֹא־יָדְעוּ יִשְׁמְעוּ וְלָמְדוּ לְיִרְאָה אֶת־יְיָ אֱלֹהֵיכֶם.

Assemble the people — men, women, and children, and the strangers in your cities — to hear, to learn to revere the Lord your God, to observe faithfully the words of this Torah. And let their children who do not yet know it hear, that they too may learn to revere the Lord your God.

◆ ◆

All rise

וַאֲנִי זֹאת בְּרִיתִי אוֹתָם, אָמַר יְיָ: רוּחִי אֲשֶׁר עָלֶיךָ, וּדְבָרַי אֲשֶׁר־שַׂמְתִּי בְּפִיךָ, לֹא־יָמוּשׁוּ מִפִּיךָ וּמִפִּי זַרְעֲךָ וּמִפִּי זֶרַע זַרְעֲךָ, אָמַר יְיָ, מֵעַתָּה וְעַד־עוֹלָם.

As for Me, this is My covenant with them, says the Lord: Let not My spirit, and the words that I have put in your mouth, depart from you, nor from your children or their children, from this time forth and for ever.

◆ ◆

The Ark is opened

The Torah is taken from the Ark

בֵּית יַעֲקֹב: לְכוּ, וְנֵלְכָה בְּאוֹר יְיָ.

O House of Jacob: come, let us walk by the light of the Lord.

◆ ◆

שְׁמַע יִשְׂרָאֵל: יְיָ אֱלֹהֵינוּ, יְיָ אֶחָד!

Hear, O Israel: the Lord is our God, the Lord is One!

אֶחָד אֱלֹהֵינוּ, גָּדוֹל אֲדוֹנֵינוּ, קָדוֹשׁ שְׁמוֹ.

Our God is One; our Lord is great; holy is His name.

◆ ◆

לְךָ, יְיָ, הַגְּדֻלָּה וְהַגְּבוּרָה וְהַתִּפְאֶרֶת וְהַנֵּצַח וְהַהוֹד, כִּי כֹל בַּשָּׁמַיִם וּבָאָרֶץ, לְךָ יְיָ הַמַּמְלָכָה וְהַמִּתְנַשֵּׂא לְכֹל לְרֹאשׁ.

Yours, Lord, is the greatness, the power, the glory, the victory, and the majesty; for all that is in heaven and earth is Yours. Yours is the kingdom, O Lord; You are supreme over all.

All are seated

◆ ◆

Reading of the Torah

For transliteration, see page 772.

Before the Reading

בָּרְכוּ אֶת־יְיָ הַמְבֹרָךְ!

בָּרוּךְ יְיָ הַמְבֹרָךְ לְעוֹלָם וָעֶד!

בָּרוּךְ אַתָּה, יְיָ אֱלֹהֵינוּ, מֶלֶךְ הָעוֹלָם, אֲשֶׁר בָּחַר־בָּנוּ מִכָּל־הָעַמִּים וְנָתַן־לָנוּ אֶת־תּוֹרָתוֹ. בָּרוּךְ אַתָּה, יְיָ, נוֹתֵן הַתּוֹרָה.

Praise the Lord, to whom our praise is due!

Praised be the Lord, to whom our praise is due,
now and for ever!

Blessed is the Lord our God, Ruler of the universe, who has chosen us from all peoples by giving us His Torah. Blessed is the Lord, Giver of the Torah.

◆ ◆

After the Reading

בָּרוּךְ אַתָּה, יְיָ אֱלֹהֵינוּ, מֶלֶךְ הָעוֹלָם, אֲשֶׁר נָתַן לָנוּ תּוֹרַת אֱמֶת וְחַיֵּי עוֹלָם נָטַע בְּתוֹכֵנוּ. בָּרוּךְ אַתָּה, יְיָ, נוֹתֵן הַתּוֹרָה.

Blessed is the Lord our God, Ruler of the universe, who has given us a Torah of truth, implanting within us eternal life. Blessed is the Lord, Giver of the Torah.

◆ ◆

As the reading is completed, the Torah might be held high while this is said:

וְזֹאת הַתּוֹרָה אֲשֶׁר־שָׂם מֹשֶׁה לִפְנֵי בְּנֵי יִשְׂרָאֵל, עַל־פִּי יְיָ בְּיַד־מֹשֶׁה.

This is the Torah that Moses placed before the people of Israel to fulfill the word of God.

◆ ◆

Reading of the Haftarah

For transliteration, see page 773.

Before the Reading

בָּרוּךְ אַתָּה, יְיָ אֱלֹהֵינוּ, מֶלֶךְ הָעוֹלָם, אֲשֶׁר בָּחַר בִּנְבִיאִים טוֹבִים וְרָצָה בְדִבְרֵיהֶם הַנֶּאֱמָרִים בֶּאֱמֶת. בָּרוּךְ אַתָּה, יְיָ, הַבּוֹחֵר בַּתּוֹרָה וּבְמֹשֶׁה עַבְדּוֹ וּבְיִשְׂרָאֵל עַמּוֹ וּבִנְבִיאֵי הָאֱמֶת וָצֶדֶק.

Blessed is the Lord our God, Ruler of the universe, who has chosen faithful prophets to speak words of truth. Blessed is the Lord, for the revelation of Torah, for Moses His servant and Israel His people, and for the prophets of truth and righteousness.

◆ ◆

After the Reading

בָּרוּךְ אַתָּה, יְיָ אֱלֹהֵינוּ, מֶלֶךְ הָעוֹלָם, צוּר כָּל־הָעוֹלָמִים, צַדִּיק בְּכָל־הַדּוֹרוֹת, הָאֵל הַנֶּאֱמָן, הָאוֹמֵר וְעוֹשֶׂה, הַמְדַבֵּר וּמְקַיֵּם, שֶׁכָּל־דְּבָרָיו אֱמֶת וָצֶדֶק.

Blessed is the Lord our God, Ruler of the universe, Rock of all creation, Righteous One of all generations, the faithful God whose word is deed, whose every command is just and true.

עַל־הַתּוֹרָה וְעַל־הָעֲבוֹדָה וְעַל־הַנְּבִיאִים וְעַל־יוֹם הַשַּׁבָּת הַזֶּה, שֶׁנָּתַתָּ־לָּנוּ, יְיָ אֱלֹהֵינוּ, לִקְדֻשָּׁה וְלִמְנוּחָה, לְכָבוֹד וּלְתִפְאָרֶת, עַל־הַכֹּל, יְיָ אֱלֹהֵינוּ, אֲנַחְנוּ מוֹדִים לָךְ, וּמְבָרְכִים אוֹתָךְ. יִתְבָּרַךְ שִׁמְךָ בְּפִי כָּל־חַי תָּמִיד לְעוֹלָם וָעֶד.

בָּרוּךְ אַתָּה, יְיָ, מְקַדֵּשׁ הַשַּׁבָּת.

For the Torah, for the privilege of worship, for the prophets, and for this Shabbat that You, O Lord our God, have given us for holiness and rest, for honor and glory, we thank and bless You. May Your name be blessed for ever by every living being.

Blessed is the Lord, for the Sabbath and its holiness.

◆ ◆

Special prayers begin on page 449.

Returning the Torah to the Ark

All rise

תּוֹרָה צִוָּה־לָֽנוּ יְיָ בְּיַד מֹשֶׁה וְהַנְּבִיאִים מוֹרָשָׁה קְהִלַּת יַעֲקֹב.

The Torah commanded us by God through Moses and the prophets is the heritage of the House of Jacob.

◆ ◆

הוֹדוֹ עַל אֶֽרֶץ וְשָׁמָֽיִם, וַיָּֽרֶם קֶֽרֶן לְעַמּוֹ, תְּהִלָּה לְכָל־חֲסִידָיו, לִבְנֵי יִשְׂרָאֵל עַם קְרוֹבוֹ. הַלְלוּיָהּ!

God's splendor covers heaven and earth; He is the strength of His people, making glorious His faithful ones, Israel, a people close to Him. Halleluyah!

◆ ◆

כִּי זֹאת הַבְּרִית אֲשֶׁר אֶכְרֹת אֶת־בֵּית יִשְׂרָאֵל אַחֲרֵי הַיָּמִים הָהֵם, נְאֻם־יְיָ: נָתַֽתִּי אֶת־תּוֹרָתִי בְּקִרְבָּם וְעַל־לִבָּם אֶכְתֲּבֶֽנָּה, וְהָיִֽיתִי לָהֶם לֵאלֹהִים וְהֵֽמָּה יִהְיוּ־לִי לְעָם.

This is the covenant I will make with the House of Israel in days to come: I will put My Torah within them, and engrave it on their hearts; I will be their God, and they shall be My people.

וְלֹא יְלַמְּדוּ עוֹד אִישׁ אֶת־רֵעֵֽהוּ וְאִישׁ אֶת־אָחִיו לֵאמֹר, "דְּעוּ אֶת־יְיָ," כִּי כוּלָּם יֵדְעוּ אוֹתִי, לְמִקְּטַנָּם וְעַד־גְּדוֹלָם, נְאֻם־יְיָ.

No longer shall anyone need to teach a neighbor to know the Lord, for they shall all know Me, young and old!

◆ ◆

כִּי לֶקַח טוֹב נָתַתִּי לָכֶם, תּוֹרָתִי אַל־תַּעֲזֹבוּ.
עֵץ־חַיִּים הִיא לַמַּחֲזִיקִים בָּהּ, וְתֹמְכֶיהָ מְאֻשָּׁר.
דְּרָכֶיהָ דַרְכֵי־נֹעַם, וְכָל־נְתִיבוֹתֶיהָ שָׁלוֹם.

Behold, I have given you a good doctrine; do not forsake it. It is a tree of life to those who hold it fast, and all who cling to it find happiness. Its ways are ways of pleasantness, and all its paths are peace.

הֲשִׁיבֵנוּ יְיָ אֵלֶיךָ, וְנָשׁוּבָה. חַדֵּשׁ יָמֵינוּ כְּקֶדֶם.

Help us to return to You, O Lord; then truly shall we return. Renew our days as in the past.

The Ark is closed

All are seated

ג III ג

Our light is Torah; Mitzvot are our lamp.

Pleasing are the ways of Torah, and all her paths are peace.

Dark and twisting is the road to peace; happy the generation whose light will guide them to its end.

The students of Torah add peace to the world, as it is said:

When all your children are taught of the Lord, great shall be the peace of your children.

◆ ◆

All rise

לֹא־יָרֵעוּ וְלֹא יַשְׁחִיתוּ בְּכָל־הַר קָדְשִׁי, כִּי־מָלְאָה הָאָרֶץ
דֵּעָה אֶת־יְיָ כַּמַּיִם לַיָּם מְכַסִּים. וְיָשְׁבוּ אִישׁ תַּחַת גַּפְנוֹ וְתַחַת
תְּאֵנָתוֹ, וְאֵין מַחֲרִיד.

They shall not hurt or destroy in all My holy mountain, for the earth shall be filled with the knowledge of the Lord as the sea-bed is covered by water. And all shall sit under their vines and their fig-trees, and none shall make them afraid.

◆ ◆

The Ark is opened

This is the covenant that binds Israel to the One and Eternal God.

This is the Torah, a light for our eyes, a lamp for our way.

It has been told you what is good, and what the Lord demands of you:

To do justly, to love mercy, to walk humbly in His presence.

◆ ◆

The Torah is taken from the Ark

בֵּית יַעֲקֹב: לְכוּ, וְנֵלְכָה בְּאוֹר יְיָ.

O House of Jacob: come, let us walk by the light of the Lord.

◆ ◆

שְׁמַע יִשְׂרָאֵל: יְיָ אֱלֹהֵינוּ, יְיָ אֶחָד!

Hear, O Israel: the Lord is our God, the Lord is One!

אֶחָד אֱלֹהֵינוּ, גָּדוֹל אֲדוֹנֵינוּ, קָדוֹשׁ שְׁמוֹ.

Our God is One; our Lord is great; holy is His name.

◆ ◆

לְךָ, יְיָ, הַגְּדֻלָּה וְהַגְּבוּרָה וְהַתִּפְאֶרֶת וְהַנֵּצַח וְהַהוֹד, כִּי כֹל בַּשָּׁמַיִם וּבָאָרֶץ, לְךָ יְיָ הַמַּמְלָכָה וְהַמִּתְנַשֵּׂא לְכֹל לְרֹאשׁ.

Yours, Lord, is the greatness, the power, the glory, the victory, and the majesty; for all that is in heaven and earth is Yours. Yours is the kingdom, O Lord; You are supreme over all.

All are seated

◆ ◆

Reading of the Torah

For transliteration, see page 772.

Before the Reading

בָּרְכוּ אֶת־יְיָ הַמְבֹרָךְ!

בָּרוּךְ יְיָ הַמְבֹרָךְ לְעוֹלָם וָעֶד!

בָּרוּךְ אַתָּה, יְיָ אֱלֹהֵינוּ, מֶלֶךְ הָעוֹלָם, אֲשֶׁר בָּחַר־בָּנוּ מִכָּל־הָעַמִּים וְנָתַן־לָנוּ אֶת־תּוֹרָתוֹ. בָּרוּךְ אַתָּה, יְיָ, נוֹתֵן הַתּוֹרָה.

Praise the Lord, to whom our praise is due!

Praised be the Lord, to whom our praise is due,
now and for ever!

Blessed is the Lord our God, Ruler of the universe, who has chosen us from all peoples by giving us His Torah. Blessed is the Lord, Giver of the Torah.

◆ ◆

After the Reading

בָּרוּךְ אַתָּה, יְיָ אֱלֹהֵינוּ, מֶלֶךְ הָעוֹלָם, אֲשֶׁר נָתַן לָנוּ תּוֹרַת אֱמֶת וְחַיֵּי עוֹלָם נָטַע בְּתוֹכֵנוּ. בָּרוּךְ אַתָּה, יְיָ, נוֹתֵן הַתּוֹרָה.

Blessed is the Lord our God, Ruler of the universe, who has given us a Torah of truth, implanting within us eternal life. Blessed is the Lord, Giver of the Torah.

◆ ◆

As the reading is completed, the Torah might be held high while this is said:

וְזֹאת הַתּוֹרָה אֲשֶׁר־שָׂם מֹשֶׁה לִפְנֵי בְּנֵי יִשְׂרָאֵל, עַל־פִּי יְיָ בְּיַד־מֹשֶׁה.

This is the Torah that Moses placed before the people of Israel to fulfill the word of God.

◆ ◆

Reading of the Haftarah

For transliteration, see page 773.

Before the Reading

בָּרוּךְ אַתָּה, יְיָ אֱלֹהֵינוּ, מֶלֶךְ הָעוֹלָם, אֲשֶׁר בָּחַר בִּנְבִיאִים טוֹבִים וְרָצָה בְדִבְרֵיהֶם הַנֶּאֱמָרִים בֶּאֱמֶת. בָּרוּךְ אַתָּה, יְיָ, הַבּוֹחֵר בַּתּוֹרָה וּבְמֹשֶׁה עַבְדּוֹ וּבְיִשְׂרָאֵל עַמּוֹ וּבִנְבִיאֵי הָאֱמֶת וָצֶדֶק.

Blessed is the Lord our God, Ruler of the universe, who has chosen faithful prophets to speak words of truth. Blessed is the Lord, for the revelation of Torah, for Moses His servant and Israel His people, and for the prophets of truth and righteousness.

◆ ◆

After the Reading

בָּרוּךְ אַתָּה, יְיָ אֱלֹהֵינוּ, מֶלֶךְ הָעוֹלָם, צוּר כָּל־הָעוֹלָמִים, צַדִּיק בְּכָל־הַדּוֹרוֹת, הָאֵל הַנֶּאֱמָן, הָאוֹמֵר וְעוֹשֶׂה, הַמְדַבֵּר וּמְקַיֵּם, שֶׁכָּל־דְּבָרָיו אֱמֶת וָצֶדֶק.

Blessed is the Lord our God, Ruler of the universe, Rock of all creation, Righteous One of all generations, the faithful God whose word is deed, whose every command is just and true.

עַל־הַתּוֹרָה וְעַל־הָעֲבוֹדָה וְעַל־הַנְּבִיאִים וְעַל־יוֹם הַשַּׁבָּת הַזֶּה, שֶׁנָּתַתָּ־לָּנוּ, יְיָ אֱלֹהֵינוּ, לִקְדֻשָּׁה וְלִמְנוּחָה, לְכָבוֹד וּלְתִפְאָרֶת, עַל־הַכֹּל, יְיָ אֱלֹהֵינוּ, אֲנַחְנוּ מוֹדִים לָךְ, וּמְבָרְכִים אוֹתָךְ. יִתְבָּרַךְ שִׁמְךָ בְּפִי כָּל־חַי תָּמִיד לְעוֹלָם וָעֶד.

בָּרוּךְ אַתָּה, יְיָ, מְקַדֵּשׁ הַשַּׁבָּת.

For the Torah, for the privilege of worship, for the prophets, and for this Shabbat that You, O Lord our God, have given us for holiness and rest, for honor and glory, we thank and bless You. May Your name be blessed for ever by every living being.

Blessed is the Lord, for the Sabbath and its holiness.

◆ ◆

Special prayers begin on page 449.

◆ ◆

Returning the Torah to the Ark

All rise

שְׁכֹן, יְיָ, בְּתוֹךְ עַמֶּךָ, וְתָנוּחַ רוּחֲךָ בְּבֵית תְּפִלָּתֶךָ.

Dwell, O Lord, among Your people; let Your spirit abide within Your house.

כִּי כָל־פֶּה וְכָל־לָשׁוֹן יִתְּנוּ הוֹד וְהָדָר לְמַלְכוּתֶךָ:

Let every human being acknowledge the splendor of Your kingdom, and its glory.

Lord our God, unite our hearts in the love of Your name; bring us together as one people with hearts turned by Torah to a life of peace and joy. May we look to You and Your Teaching, to speed the day for which we hope, when violence will be heard no more in our land, nor devastation within our world.

וְכִתְּתוּ חַרְבוֹתָם לְאִתִּים
וַחֲנִיתוֹתֵיהֶם לְמַזְמֵרוֹת;
לֹא־יִשָּׂא גוֹי אֶל־גּוֹי חֶרֶב
וְלֹא־יִלְמְדוּ עוֹד מִלְחָמָה.

They shall beat their swords into plowshares and their spears into pruninghooks; nation shall not lift up sword against nation, nor ever again shall they train for war.

◆ ◆

תּוֹרַת יְיָ תְּמִימָה, מְשִׁיבַת נָפֶשׁ;
עֵדוּת יְיָ נֶאֱמָנָה, מַחְכִּימַת פֶּתִי;

The Torah of the Lord is perfect, reviving the soul;
The teaching of the Lord is sure, making wise the simple;

פִּקּוּדֵי יְיָ יְשָׁרִים, מְשַׂמְּחֵי־לֵב;
מִצְוַת יְיָ בָּרָה, מְאִירַת עֵינָיִם;

The precepts of the Lord are right, delighting the mind;
The Mitzvah of the Lord is clear, giving light to the eyes;

יִרְאַת יְיָ טְהוֹרָה, עוֹמֶדֶת לָעַד;
מִשְׁפְּטֵי יְיָ אֱמֶת, צָדְקוּ יַחְדָּו.

The word of the Lord is pure, enduring for ever;
The judgments of the Lord are true, and altogether just.

◆ ◆

כִּי לֶקַח טוֹב נָתַתִּי לָכֶם, תּוֹרָתִי אַל־תַּעֲזֹבוּ.
עֵץ־חַיִּים הִיא לַמַּחֲזִיקִים בָּהּ, וְתֹמְכֶיהָ מְאֻשָּׁר.
דְּרָכֶיהָ דַרְכֵי־נֹעַם, וְכָל־נְתִיבוֹתֶיהָ שָׁלוֹם.

Behold, a good doctrine has been given you, do not forsake it. It is a tree of life to those who hold it fast, and all who cling to it find happiness. Its ways are ways of pleasantness, and all its paths are peace.

הֲשִׁיבֵנוּ יְיָ אֵלֶיךָ, וְנָשׁוּבָה. חַדֵּשׁ יָמֵינוּ כְּקֶדֶם.

Help us to return to You, O Lord; then truly shall we return. Renew our days as in the past.

The Ark is closed

All are seated

ד IV ד

Happy is the one who finds wisdom,	אַשְׁרֵי אָדָם מָצָא חָכְמָה,
the one who gains understanding;	וְאָדָם יָפִיק תְּבוּנָה,
For its fruits are better than silver,	כִּי טוֹב סַחְרָהּ מִסְּחַר־כָּסֶף,
its yield than fine gold.	וּמֵחָרוּץ תְּבוּאָתָהּ.
It is more precious than rubies;	יְקָרָה הִיא מִפְּנִינִים,
No treasure can match it.	וְכָל־חֲפָצֶיךָ לֹא יִשְׁווּ־בָהּ.

◆ ◆

All rise

עַל־שְׁלֹשָׁה דְבָרִים הָעוֹלָם עוֹמֵד: עַל הַתּוֹרָה וְעַל הָעֲבוֹדָה וְעַל גְּמִילוּת חֲסָדִים.

The world is sustained by three things: by Torah, by worship, by loving deeds.

◆ ◆

The Ark is opened

The Torah is taken from the Ark

In this scroll is the secret of our people's life from Sinai until now. Its teaching is love and justice, goodness and hope. Freedom is its gift to all who treasure it.

◆ ◆

שְׁמַע יִשְׂרָאֵל: יְיָ אֱלֹהֵינוּ, יְיָ אֶחָד!

Hear, O Israel: the Lord is our God, the Lord is One!

אֶחָד אֱלֹהֵינוּ, גָּדוֹל אֲדֹנֵינוּ, קָדוֹשׁ שְׁמוֹ.

Our God is One; our Lord is great; holy is His name.

◆ ◆

לְךָ, יְיָ, הַגְּדֻלָּה וְהַגְּבוּרָה וְהַתִּפְאֶרֶת וְהַנֵּצַח וְהַהוֹד, כִּי כֹל בַּשָּׁמַיִם וּבָאָרֶץ, לְךָ יְיָ הַמַּמְלָכָה וְהַמִּתְנַשֵּׂא לְכֹל לְרֹאשׁ.

Yours, Lord, is the greatness, the power, the glory, the victory, and the majesty; for all that is in heaven and earth is Yours. Yours is the kingdom, O Lord; You are supreme over all.

All are seated

◆ ◆

Reading of the Torah

For transliteration, see page 772.

Before the Reading

בָּרְכוּ אֶת־יְיָ הַמְבֹרָךְ!

בָּרוּךְ יְיָ הַמְבֹרָךְ לְעוֹלָם וָעֶד!

בָּרוּךְ אַתָּה, יְיָ אֱלֹהֵינוּ, מֶלֶךְ הָעוֹלָם, אֲשֶׁר בָּחַר־בָּנוּ מִכָּל־הָעַמִּים וְנָתַן־לָנוּ אֶת־תּוֹרָתוֹ. בָּרוּךְ אַתָּה, יְיָ, נוֹתֵן הַתּוֹרָה.

Praise the Lord, to whom our praise is due!

Praised be the Lord, to whom our praise is due,
now and for ever!

Blessed is the Lord our God, Ruler of the universe, who has chosen us from all peoples by giving us His Torah. Blessed is the Lord, Giver of the Torah.

◆ ◆

After the Reading

בָּרוּךְ אַתָּה, יְיָ אֱלֹהֵינוּ, מֶלֶךְ הָעוֹלָם, אֲשֶׁר נָתַן לָנוּ תּוֹרַת אֱמֶת וְחַיֵּי עוֹלָם נָטַע בְּתוֹכֵנוּ. בָּרוּךְ אַתָּה, יְיָ, נוֹתֵן הַתּוֹרָה.

Blessed is the Lord our God, Ruler of the universe, who has given us a Torah of truth, implanting within us eternal life. Blessed is the Lord, Giver of the Torah.

◆ ◆

As the reading is completed, the Torah might be held high while this is said:

וְזֹאת הַתּוֹרָה אֲשֶׁר־שָׂם מֹשֶׁה לִפְנֵי בְּנֵי יִשְׂרָאֵל, עַל־פִּי יְיָ בְּיַד־מֹשֶׁה.

This is the Torah that Moses placed before the people of Israel to fulfill the word of God.

◆ ◆

Reading of the Haftarah

For transliteration, see page 773.

Before the Reading

בָּרוּךְ אַתָּה, יְיָ אֱלֹהֵינוּ, מֶלֶךְ הָעוֹלָם, אֲשֶׁר בָּחַר בִּנְבִיאִים טוֹבִים וְרָצָה בְדִבְרֵיהֶם הַנֶּאֱמָרִים בֶּאֱמֶת. בָּרוּךְ אַתָּה, יְיָ, הַבּוֹחֵר בַּתּוֹרָה וּבְמֹשֶׁה עַבְדּוֹ וּבְיִשְׂרָאֵל עַמּוֹ וּבִנְבִיאֵי הָאֱמֶת וָצֶדֶק.

Blessed is the Lord our God, Ruler of the universe, who has chosen faithful prophets to speak words of truth. Blessed is the Lord, for the revelation of Torah, for Moses His servant and Israel His people, and for the prophets of truth and righteousness.

◆ ◆

After the Reading

בָּרוּךְ אַתָּה, יְיָ אֱלֹהֵינוּ, מֶלֶךְ הָעוֹלָם, צוּר כָּל־הָעוֹלָמִים, צַדִּיק בְּכָל־הַדּוֹרוֹת, הָאֵל הַנֶּאֱמָן, הָאוֹמֵר וְעוֹשֶׂה, הַמְדַבֵּר וּמְקַיֵּם, שֶׁכָּל־דְּבָרָיו אֱמֶת וָצֶדֶק.

Blessed is the Lord our God, Ruler of the universe, Rock of all creation, Righteous One of all generations, the faithful God whose word is deed, whose every command is just and true.

עַל־הַתּוֹרָה וְעַל־הָעֲבוֹדָה וְעַל־הַנְּבִיאִים וְעַל־יוֹם הַשַּׁבָּת הַזֶּה, שֶׁנָּתַתָּ־לָּנוּ, יְיָ אֱלֹהֵינוּ, לִקְדֻשָּׁה וְלִמְנוּחָה, לְכָבוֹד

וּלְתִפְאָרֶת, עַל־הַכֹּל, יְיָ אֱלֹהֵינוּ, אֲנַחְנוּ מוֹדִים לָךְ, וּמְבָרְכִים אוֹתָךְ. יִתְבָּרַךְ שִׁמְךָ בְּפִי כָּל־חַי תָּמִיד לְעוֹלָם וָעֶד.

בָּרוּךְ אַתָּה, יְיָ, מְקַדֵּשׁ הַשַּׁבָּת.

For the Torah, for the privilege of worship, for the prophets, and for this Shabbat that You, O Lord our God, have given us for holiness and rest, for honor and glory, we thank and bless You. May Your name be blessed for ever by every living being.

Blessed is the Lord, for the Sabbath and its holiness.

◆ ◆

Special prayers begin on page 449.

◆ ◆

Returning the Torah to the Ark

All rise

עַל־שְׁלֹשָׁה דְבָרִים הָעוֹלָם קַיָּם: עַל־הָאֱמֶת וְעַל־הַדִּין וְעַל־הַשָּׁלוֹם.

The world is sustained by three things: by truth, by justice, and by peace.

◆ ◆

יְהֵא רַעֲוָא קֳדָמָךְ דְּתִפְתַּח לִבִּי בְּאוֹרַיְתָא, וְתַשְׁלִים מִשְׁאֲלִין דְּלִבִּי, וְלִבָּא דְכָל־עַמָּךְ יִשְׂרָאֵל, לְטַב וּלְחַיִּין וְלִשְׁלָם.

May it be God's will to open our hearts to His Teaching, fulfilling the wishes of our hearts and the hearts of all His people Israel for good, for life, and for peace.

◆ ◆

When Torah entered the world, freedom entered it.
The whole Torah exists only to establish peace.

Its highest teaching is love and kindness.
What is hateful to you, do not do to any person.

That is the whole Torah. All the rest is commentary. Go and learn it.
Those who study Torah are the true guardians of civilization.

Honoring one another, doing acts of kindness, and making peace: these are our highest duties.
But the study of Torah is equal to them all, because it leads to them all.

Let us learn in order to teach;
Let us learn in order to do!

◆ ◆

עֵץ־חַיִּים הִיא לַמַּחֲזִיקִים בָּהּ, וְתֹמְכֶיהָ מְאֻשָּׁר.
דְּרָכֶיהָ דַרְכֵי־נֹעַם, וְכָל־נְתִיבוֹתֶיהָ שָׁלוֹם.

It is a tree of life to those who hold it fast, and all who cling to it find happiness. Its ways are ways of pleasantness, and all its paths are peace.

הֲשִׁיבֵנוּ יְיָ אֵלֶיךָ, וְנָשׁוּבָה. חַדֵּשׁ יָמֵינוּ כְּקֶדֶם.

Help us to return to You, O Lord; then truly shall we return. Renew our days as in the past.

The Ark is closed

All are seated

ה V ה

From Psalm 24

לַייָ הָאָרֶץ וּמְלוֹאָהּ, תֵּבֵל וְיֹשְׁבֵי בָהּ. כִּי־הוּא עַל־יַמִּים יְסָדָהּ, וְעַל־נְהָרוֹת יְכוֹנְנֶהָ. מִי־יַעֲלֶה בְהַר־יְיָ, וּמִי־יָקוּם בִּמְקוֹם קָדְשׁוֹ?

The earth is the Lord's, and all its fullness, the world and all who dwell there. For He has laid its foundations in the sea, and established it upon the currents. Who may ascend the mountain of the Lord? Who may stand in His holy place?

נְקִי כַפַּיִם וּבַר־לֵבָב, אֲשֶׁר לֹא־נָשָׂא לַשָּׁוְא נַפְשׁוֹ וְלֹא נִשְׁבַּע לְמִרְמָה. יִשָּׂא בְרָכָה מֵאֵת יְיָ וּצְדָקָה מֵאֱלֹהֵי יִשְׁעוֹ.

Those with clean hands and pure hearts, who never speak with malice, who never swear deceitfully. They shall receive blessings from the Lord, justice from God, their Helper.

זֶה דּוֹר דֹּרְשָׁו, מְבַקְשֵׁי פָנֶיךָ, יַעֲקֹב. סֶלָה.

Such are the people who turn to Him, who seek Your presence, O God of Jacob.

◆ ◆

Lift up your heads, O gates!	שְׂאוּ שְׁעָרִים רָאשֵׁיכֶם,
Lift yourselves up, O ancient doors!	וְהִנָּשְׂאוּ פִּתְחֵי עוֹלָם,
Let the King of Glory enter.	וְיָבוֹא מֶלֶךְ הַכָּבוֹד!
Who is this King of Glory?	מִי הוּא זֶה מֶלֶךְ הַכָּבוֹד?
The Lord of Hosts –	יְיָ צְבָאוֹת –
He is the King of Glory!	הוּא מֶלֶךְ הַכָּבוֹד! סֶלָה.

◆ ◆

The Ark is opened

The Torah is taken from the Ark

רוֹמְמוּ יְיָ אֱלֹהֵינוּ, וְהִשְׁתַּחֲווּ לְהַר קָדְשׁוֹ, כִּי קָדוֹשׁ יְיָ אֱלֹהֵינוּ.

Let us exalt the Lord our God, and worship at His holy mountain, for the Lord our God is holy.

◆ ◆

שְׁמַע יִשְׂרָאֵל: יְיָ אֱלֹהֵינוּ, יְיָ אֶחָד!

Hear, O Israel: the Lord is our God, the Lord is One!

אֶחָד אֱלֹהֵינוּ, גָּדוֹל אֲדוֹנֵינוּ, קָדוֹשׁ שְׁמוֹ.

Our God is One; our Lord is great; holy is His name.

◆ ◆

לְךָ, יְיָ, הַגְּדֻלָּה וְהַגְּבוּרָה וְהַתִּפְאֶרֶת וְהַנֵּצַח וְהַהוֹד, כִּי כֹל בַּשָּׁמַיִם וּבָאָרֶץ, לְךָ יְיָ הַמַּמְלָכָה וְהַמִּתְנַשֵּׂא לְכֹל לְרֹאשׁ.

Yours, Lord, is the greatness, the power, the glory, the victory, and the majesty; for all that is in heaven and earth is Yours. Yours is the kingdom, O Lord; You are supreme over all.

All are seated

◆ ◆

Reading of the Torah

For transliteration, see page 772.

Before the Reading

בָּרְכוּ אֶת־יְיָ הַמְבֹרָךְ!

בָּרוּךְ יְיָ הַמְבֹרָךְ לְעוֹלָם וָעֶד!

בָּרוּךְ אַתָּה, יְיָ אֱלֹהֵינוּ, מֶלֶךְ הָעוֹלָם, אֲשֶׁר בָּחַר־בָּנוּ מִכָּל־הָעַמִּים וְנָתַן־לָנוּ אֶת־תּוֹרָתוֹ. בָּרוּךְ אַתָּה, יְיָ, נוֹתֵן הַתּוֹרָה.

Praise the Lord, to whom our praise is due!

Praised be the Lord, to whom our praise is due,
now and for ever!

Blessed is the Lord our God, Ruler of the universe, who has chosen us from all peoples by giving us His Torah. Blessed is the Lord, Giver of the Torah.

◆ ◆

After the Reading

בָּרוּךְ אַתָּה, יְיָ אֱלֹהֵינוּ, מֶלֶךְ הָעוֹלָם, אֲשֶׁר נָתַן לָנוּ תּוֹרַת
אֱמֶת וְחַיֵּי עוֹלָם נָטַע בְּתוֹכֵנוּ. בָּרוּךְ אַתָּה, יְיָ, נוֹתֵן הַתּוֹרָה.

Blessed is the Lord our God, Ruler of the universe, who has given us a Torah of truth, implanting within us eternal life. Blessed is the Lord, Giver of the Torah.

◆ ◆

As the reading is completed, the Toraḥ might be held high while this is said:

וְזֹאת הַתּוֹרָה אֲשֶׁר־שָׂם מֹשֶׁה לִפְנֵי בְּנֵי יִשְׂרָאֵל, עַל־פִּי יְיָ
בְּיַד־מֹשֶׁה.

This is the Torah that Moses placed before the people of Israel to fulfill the word of God.

◆ ◆

Reading of the Haftarah

For transliteration, see page 773.

◆ ◆

Before the Reading

בָּרוּךְ אַתָּה, יְיָ אֱלֹהֵינוּ, מֶלֶךְ הָעוֹלָם, אֲשֶׁר בָּחַר בִּנְבִיאִים
טוֹבִים וְרָצָה בְדִבְרֵיהֶם הַנֶּאֱמָרִים בֶּאֱמֶת. בָּרוּךְ אַתָּה, יְיָ,

הַבּוֹחֵר בַּתּוֹרָה וּבְמֹשֶׁה עַבְדּוֹ וּבְיִשְׂרָאֵל עַמּוֹ וּבִנְבִיאֵי הָאֱמֶת וָצֶדֶק.

Blessed is the Lord our God, Ruler of the universe, who has chosen faithful prophets to speak words of truth. Blessed is the Lord, for the revelation of Torah, for Moses His servant and Israel His people, and for the prophets of truth and righteousness.

◆ ◆

After the Reading

בָּרוּךְ אַתָּה, יְיָ אֱלֹהֵינוּ, מֶלֶךְ הָעוֹלָם, צוּר כָּל־הָעוֹלָמִים, צַדִּיק בְּכָל־הַדּוֹרוֹת, הָאֵל הַנֶּאֱמָן, הָאוֹמֵר וְעוֹשֶׂה, הַמְדַבֵּר וּמְקַיֵּם, שֶׁכָּל־דְּבָרָיו אֱמֶת וָצֶדֶק.

Blessed is the Lord our God, Ruler of the universe, Rock of all creation, Righteous One of all generations, the faithful God whose word is deed, whose every command is just and true.

עַל־הַתּוֹרָה וְעַל־הָעֲבוֹדָה וְעַל־הַנְּבִיאִים וְעַל־יוֹם הַשַּׁבָּת הַזֶּה, שֶׁנָּתַתָּ־לָּנוּ, יְיָ אֱלֹהֵינוּ, לִקְדֻשָּׁה וְלִמְנוּחָה, לְכָבוֹד וּלְתִפְאָרֶת, עַל־הַכֹּל, יְיָ אֱלֹהֵינוּ, אֲנַחְנוּ מוֹדִים לָךְ, וּמְבָרְכִים אוֹתָךְ. יִתְבָּרַךְ שִׁמְךָ בְּפִי כָּל־חַי תָּמִיד לְעוֹלָם וָעֶד.

בָּרוּךְ אַתָּה, יְיָ, מְקַדֵּשׁ הַשַּׁבָּת.

For the Torah, for the privilege of worship, for the prophets, and for this Shabbat that You, O Lord our God, have given us for holiness and rest, for honor and glory, we thank and bless You. May Your name be blessed for ever by every living being.

Blessed is the Lord, for the Sabbath and its holiness.

◆ ◆

Special prayers begin on page 449.

◆ ◆

Returning the Torah to the Ark

הָבוּ גֹדֶל לֵאלֹהֵינוּ וּתְנוּ כָבוֹד לַתּוֹרָה.

Let us declare the greatness of our God and give honor to the Torah.

בָּרוּךְ שֶׁנָּתַן תּוֹרָה לְעַמּוֹ יִשְׂרָאֵל בִּקְדֻשָּׁתוֹ.

Praised be the One who in His holiness has given the Torah to His people Israel.

◆ ◆

הוֹדוֹ עַל אֶרֶץ וְשָׁמָיִם, וַיָּרֶם קֶרֶן לְעַמּוֹ, תְּהִלָּה לְכָל־
חֲסִידָיו, לִבְנֵי יִשְׂרָאֵל עַם קְרוֹבוֹ. הַלְלוּיָהּ!

God's splendor covers heaven and earth; He is the strength of His people, making glorious His faithful ones, Israel, a people close to Him. Halleluyah!

◆ ◆

תּוֹרַת יְיָ תְּמִימָה, מְשִׁיבַת נָפֶשׁ;
עֵדוּת יְיָ נֶאֱמָנָה, מַחְכִּימַת פֶּתִי;

The Torah of the Lord is perfect, reviving the soul;
The teaching of the Lord is sure, making wise the simple;

פִּקּוּדֵי יְיָ יְשָׁרִים, מְשַׂמְּחֵי־לֵב;
מִצְוַת יְיָ בָּרָה, מְאִירַת עֵינָיִם;

The precepts of the Lord are right, delighting the mind;
The Mitzvah of the Lord is clear, giving light to the eyes;

יִרְאַת יְיָ טְהוֹרָה, עוֹמֶדֶת לָעַד;
מִשְׁפְּטֵי יְיָ אֱמֶת, צָדְקוּ יַחְדָּו.

The word of the Lord is pure, enduring for ever;
The judgments of the Lord are true, and altogether just.

◆ ◆

כִּי לֶקַח טוֹב נָתַתִּי לָכֶם, תּוֹרָתִי אַל־תַּעֲזֹבוּ.
עֵץ־חַיִּים הִיא לַמַּחֲזִיקִים בָּהּ, וְתֹמְכֶיהָ מְאֻשָּׁר.
דְּרָכֶיהָ דַרְכֵי־נֹעַם, וְכָל־נְתִיבוֹתֶיהָ שָׁלוֹם.

Behold, I have given you a good doctrine, My Torah: do not forsake it. It is a tree of life to those who hold it fast, and all who cling to it find happiness. Its ways are ways of pleasantness, and all its paths are peace.

הֲשִׁיבֵנוּ יְיָ אֵלֶיךָ, וְנָשׁוּבָה. חַדֵּשׁ יָמֵינוּ כְּקֶדֶם.

Help us to return to You, O Lord; then truly shall we return. Renew our days as in the past.

The Ark is closed

All are seated

SPECIAL PRAYERS

For a Bar or Bat Mitzvah

The following might be said by a parent

Into our hands, O God, You have placed Your Torah, to be held high by parents and children, and taught by one generation to the next.

Whatever has befallen us, our people have remained steadfast in loyalty to the Torah. It was carried into exile in the arms of parents that their children might not be deprived of their birthright.

And now I pray that you, my child, will always be worthy of this inheritance. Take its teaching into your heart, and in turn pass it on to your children and those who come after you. May you be a faithful Jew, searching for wisdom and truth, working for justice and peace. Thus will you be among those who labor to bring nearer the day when the Lord shall be One and His name shall be One.

◆ ◆

The following might be said after the Reading of the Torah

May the God of our people, the God of the universe, bless you. May the One who has always been our guide inspire you to bring honor to our family and to our people Israel.

בָּרוּךְ אַתָּה, יְיָ אֱלֹהֵינוּ, מֶלֶךְ הָעוֹלָם, שֶׁהֶחֱיָנוּ וְקִיְּמָנוּ וְהִגִּיעָנוּ לַזְּמַן הַזֶּה.

We give thanks to You, O Lord our God, Ruler of the universe, for giving us life, for sustaining us, and for enabling us to reach this day of joy. Amen.

For Our People and Our Nation

Bless, O God, this congregation, those who lead and serve it, those who contribute to its strength. Bless all who enter this House, that the worship offered within its walls may be worthy of Your greatness and Your love, and that all who seek Your presence here may find it. For the joy of community, the gift of diversity, and the vision of harmony, we offer our grateful thanks.

Bless our land and all its inhabitants. Prosper us in all our undertakings. Be with those whom we have chosen to lead us, that they may strive to establish justice and opportunity for all, and labor to bring peace to the family of nations.

Bless the household of Israel wherever they dwell. Be with us here, where we worship You in freedom. And may those who live under oppressive rule find release and liberty speedily, in our own day.

May Your favor rest upon Israel, her land, her people. Protect her against hatred and war. Grant that the promise of her beginning may ripen into fulfillment, bringing comfort to those who seek refuge, light to those who dwell in darkness, new hope to all humanity. And let us say: Amen.

◆ ◆

This prayer might be added on Yom Tov

May He who saved Israel from Egyptian bondage,
who brought them near to Him in an enduring covenant,
and sustained them in their many wanderings,
be with the whole House of Israel,
now and for evermore.

As we cherish the freedom that is ours,
so do we pray that those of our brothers and sisters
who live in lands of oppression,
may find liberation speedily, in our own day.
And may all — women, men, and children —
find freedom, prosperity, and contentment,
their heritage as children of God. Amen.

For the New Month ברכת החדש

According to our calendar, the month of . . . begins on . . .

יְהִי רָצוֹן מִלְּפָנֶיךָ, יְיָ אֱלֹהֵינוּ וֵאלֹהֵי אֲבוֹתֵינוּ, שֶׁתְּחַדֵּשׁ עָלֵינוּ אֶת הַחֹדֶשׁ הַזֶּה לְטוֹבָה וְלִבְרָכָה. וְתִתֶּן־לָנוּ חַיִּים אֲרֻכִּים, חַיִּים שֶׁל־שָׁלוֹם, חַיִּים שֶׁל־טוֹבָה, חַיִּים שֶׁל־בְּרָכָה, חַיִּים שֶׁתְּהִי בָנוּ אַהֲבַת תּוֹרָה וְיִרְאַת שָׁמַיִם, חַיִּים שֶׁיִּמָּלְאוּ מִשְׁאֲלוֹת לִבֵּנוּ לְטוֹבָה.

O Lord our God, let the coming month bring us renewed good and blessing.

May we have long life, a life of peace, prosperity, and health, a life full of blessing, a life exalted by love of Your Torah and devotion to Your service, a life in which our heart's desires are fulfilled for good.

מִי שֶׁעָשָׂה נִסִּים לַאֲבוֹתֵינוּ וְגָאַל אוֹתָם מֵעַבְדוּת לְחֵרוּת, הוּא יִגְאַל אוֹתָנוּ בְּקָרוֹב, חֲבֵרִים כָּל־יִשְׂרָאֵל, וְנֹאמַר: אָמֵן.

O wondrous God who in ancient days led our people from bondage to freedom, redeem us now out of our exile from one another, making all Israel one united people.

רֹאשׁ חֹדֶשׁ . . . יִהְיֶה בְּיוֹם . . . הַבָּא עָלֵינוּ וְעַל־כָּל־יִשְׂרָאֵל לְטוֹבָה.

יְחַדְּשֵׁהוּ הַקָּדוֹשׁ בָּרוּךְ הוּא עָלֵינוּ וְעַל־כָּל־עַמּוֹ בֵּית יִשְׂרָאֵל לְחַיִּים וּלְשָׁלוֹם, לְשָׂשׂוֹן וּלְשִׂמְחָה, לִישׁוּעָה וּלְנֶחָמָה, וְנֹאמַר: אָמֵן.

God of holiness, let the new month bring for us, and for the whole House of Israel, life and peace, joy and happiness, deliverance and comfort, and let us say: Amen.

תפלת ערבית ליום טוב

FESTIVAL EVENING SERVICE

הדלקת הנרות

For congregations where the lights are kindled in the synagogue

It has been said:
"You shall keep
the flame burning
on the altar
continually;
it shall not go out."

In this spirit
would we
keep alive within us
the flame of faith.

And in this spirit
we kindle
the Yom Tov lights.

◆ ◆

בָּרוּךְ אַתָּה, יְיָ אֱלֹהֵינוּ, מֶלֶךְ הָעוֹלָם, אֲשֶׁר קִדְּשָׁנוּ בְּמִצְוֹתָיו
וְצִוָּנוּ לְהַדְלִיק נֵר שֶׁל (שַׁבָּת וְשֶׁל) יוֹם טוֹב.

Blessed is the Lord our God, Ruler of the universe, who hallows us with His Mitzvot, and commands us to kindle the lights of (Shabbat and) Yom Tov.

◆ ◆

May we be blessed with joy.
May we be blessed with light.
May we be blessed with peace.

◆ ◆

Evening Service

עַרְבִית לְיוֹם טוֹב

FOR ALL FESTIVALS

It is written: "Three times a year shall you hold a festival before God: the feast of Matzot, in the month of Spring, the time when you came out of Egypt; the feast of the harvest of the first fruit of your labor in the field; and the feast of ingathering the harvest at summer's end."

The Festivals are times to celebrate our joys and give thanks for them. We are blessed with food enough to sustain life, with beauty that delights the eye, with freedom to be ourselves, and with knowledge of the law that forms our moral being.

In all that works for our blessing we behold divine love. In the laws of growth, by which seed entrusted to earth ripens into flower and fruit, we see God's creative will. And the history of our people speaks of His redemptive will.

We give thanks for vineyard and field, and for all who tend them; for nature's unfailing order, which brings ripeness to the earth and joy to the heart; and for the law in human life, which brings happiness to all who follow it. Praised be our God, for life, for sustenance, and for this festive day.

בָּרוּךְ אַתָּה, יְיָ אֱלֹהֵינוּ, מֶלֶךְ הָעוֹלָם, שֶׁהֶחֱיָנוּ וְקִיְּמָנוּ וְהִגִּיעָנוּ לַזְּמַן הַזֶּה.

⋄ ⋄

ON SHABBAT

Psalm 92

A SONG FOR THE SABBATH DAY

מִזְמוֹר שִׁיר לְיוֹם הַשַּׁבָּת.

טוֹב לְהֹדוֹת לַיְיָ, וּלְזַמֵּר לְשִׁמְךָ, עֶלְיוֹן,

לְהַגִּיד בַּבֹּקֶר חַסְדֶּךָ, וֶאֱמוּנָתְךָ בַּלֵּילוֹת,

עֲלֵי־עָשׂוֹר וַעֲלֵי־נָבֶל, עֲלֵי הִגָּיוֹן בְּכִנּוֹר.

It is good to give thanks to the Lord,
to sing hymns to Your name, O Most High!
To tell of Your love in the morning,
to sing at night of Your faithfulness;
to pluck the strings, to sound the lute,
to make the harp vibrate.

כִּי שִׂמַּחְתַּנִי, יְיָ, בְּפָעֳלֶךָ, בְּמַעֲשֵׂי יָדֶיךָ אֲרַנֵּן.
מַה־גָּדְלוּ מַעֲשֶׂיךָ, יְיָ! מְאֹד עָמְקוּ מַחְשְׁבֹתֶיךָ.

Your deeds, O Lord, fill me with gladness,
Your work moves me to song.
How great are Your works, O Lord!
How profound Your design!

אִישׁ־בַּעַר לֹא יֵדָע, וּכְסִיל לֹא־יָבִין אֶת־זֹאת:
בִּפְרֹחַ רְשָׁעִים כְּמוֹ־עֵשֶׂב, וַיָּצִיצוּ כָּל־פֹּעֲלֵי אָוֶן,
לְהִשָּׁמְדָם עֲדֵי־עַד.
וְאַתָּה מָרוֹם לְעֹלָם, יְיָ.

The fool will never learn,
the dullard never grasp this:
the wicked may flourish like grass,
all who do evil may blossom,
yet they are doomed to destruction,
while You, O Lord, are exalted for all time.

כִּי הִנֵּה אֹיְבֶיךָ, יְיָ, כִּי־הִנֵּה אֹיְבֶיךָ יֹאבֵדוּ,
יִתְפָּרְדוּ כָּל־פֹּעֲלֵי אָוֶן.
וַתָּרֶם כִּרְאֵים קַרְנִי, בַּלֹּתִי בְּשֶׁמֶן רַעֲנָן.
וַתַּבֵּט עֵינִי בְּשׁוּרָי, בַּקָּמִים עָלַי מְרֵעִים,
תִּשְׁמַעְנָה אָזְנָי:

See how Your enemies, O Lord,
see how Your enemies shall perish,
how all who do evil shall be scattered.
You lift up my head in pride,
I am bathed in freshening oil.
I shall see the defeat of my foes,
my ears shall hear of their fall.

צַדִּיק כַּתָּמָר יִפְרָח, כְּאֶרֶז בַּלְּבָנוֹן יִשְׂגֶּה.
שְׁתוּלִים בְּבֵית יְיָ, בְּחַצְרוֹת אֱלֹהֵינוּ יַפְרִיחוּ.
עוֹד יְנוּבוּן בְּשֵׂיבָה, דְּשֵׁנִים וְרַעֲנַנִּים יִהְיוּ,
לְהַגִּיד כִּי־יָשָׁר יְיָ, צוּרִי, וְלֹא־עַוְלָתָה בּוֹ.

The righteous shall flourish like palms,
grow tall like cedars in Lebanon.
Rooted in the house of the Lord,
they shall be ever fresh and green,
proclaiming that the Lord is just,
my Rock, in whom there is no wrong.

◆

Psalm 93

יְיָ מָלָךְ, גֵּאוּת לָבֵשׁ;
לָבֵשׁ יְיָ, עֹז הִתְאַזָּר;
אַף־תִּכּוֹן תֵּבֵל, בַּל־תִּמּוֹט.
נָכוֹן כִּסְאֲךָ מֵאָז,
מֵעוֹלָם אָתָּה.

The Eternal is enthroned,
He is robed in grandeur;
the Eternal is robed,
He is girded with strength.
And He founded the solid earth
to be unmoving.
Ageless is Your throne,
endless Your being.

נָשְׂאוּ נְהָרוֹת, יְיָ,
נָשְׂאוּ נְהָרוֹת קוֹלָם,
יִשְׂאוּ נְהָרוֹת דָּכְיָם;
מִקֹּלוֹת מַיִם רַבִּים,
אַדִּירִים מִשְׁבְּרֵי־יָם,
אַדִּיר בַּמָּרוֹם יְיָ.

The oceans cry out, O Eternal God,
the oceans cry out their thunder,
the oceans rage in their fury;
but greater than the thunder of the torrents,
mightier than the breakers of the sea,
is the Lord's majesty on high!

עֵדֹתֶיךָ נֶאֶמְנוּ מְאֹד;
לְבֵיתְךָ נַאֲוָה־קֹדֶשׁ,
יְיָ, לְאֹרֶךְ יָמִים.

Your law stands firm;
and in Your temple, O Eternal God,
holiness reigns to the end of time!

◆ ◆

ליל ראשון של פסח

For the First Eve of Pesach

One of the following

1

With joyful hearts
we greet the festival of our freedom.

Through the power of the spirit
Israel went forth
from bondage to freedom,
from degradation to dignity.

We give thanks
for the many liberations
we have experienced in days gone by.

And we pray that those
who suffer still
may go forth from bondage
into a new day of freedom.

Lord, may all who hunger
come to rejoice in a new Passover.

Let all the human family
sit at Your table,
eat the bread of freedom,
drink the wine of deliverance.

Continue on page 475

2

Great was our people's joy,
after generations of bondage,
to be free!

Now we, their children,
triumph in our heritage of freedom.

Exultant and awed,
they sang and wept:
the people in chains were free!

Now we, their children,
hear their song
resounding in the heart.

O God, blessed Source of freedom,
let the time come speedily
when all the oppressed shall find deliverance.

Let the yoke of bondage be dissolved.
and all people serve You in freedom.

May this Passover feast
bring us new understanding
of the holiness of freedom.

Then we will rejoice before You,
with festive gladness, O God.

◆

This is the day the Lord has made;	זֶה הַיּוֹם עָשָׂה יְיָ;
Let us rejoice and be glad in it!	נָגִילָה וְנִשְׂמְחָה בוֹ!

Continue on page 475

3

אַשְׁרֵי שֹׁמְרֵי מִשְׁפָּט, עֹשֵׂה צְדָקָה.
צֶדֶק, צֶדֶק תִּרְדֹּף.

Blessed are those who do justly and act righteously.

Justice, justice shall you pursue.

וְכִי־יָמוּךְ אָחִיךָ וּמָטָה יָדוֹ עִמָּךְ, וְהֶחֱזַקְתָּ בּוֹ. גֵּר וְתוֹשָׁב, וָחַי עִמָּךְ.

צֶדֶק, צֶדֶק תִּרְדֹּף.

If your kin grow poor and begin to fall, you must uphold them. They shall live with you as do strangers and settlers.

Justice, justice shall you pursue.

כִּי־עֲבָדַי הֵם אֲשֶׁר־הוֹצֵאתִי אֹתָם מֵאֶרֶץ מִצְרָיִם; לֹא יִמָּכְרוּ מִמְכֶּרֶת עָבֶד.

וְזָכַרְתָּ כִּי־עֶבֶד הָיִיתָ בְּמִצְרָיִם.

For they are My servants whom I led out of Egypt; they shall not be sold as slaves.

Remember that you were slaves in Egypt.

וְגֵר לֹא תִלְחָץ, וְאַתֶּם יְדַעְתֶּם אֶת־נֶפֶשׁ הַגֵּר, כִּי־גֵרִים הֱיִיתֶם בְּאֶרֶץ מִצְרָיִם.

וְזָכַרְתָּ כִּי־עֶבֶד הָיִיתָ בְּמִצְרָיִם.

You shall not oppress the stranger, for you know the heart of a stranger, for you yourselves were strangers in Egypt.

Remember that you were slaves in Egypt.

אֲנִי יְיָ מְקַדִּשְׁכֶם, הַמּוֹצִיא אֶתְכֶם מֵאֶרֶץ מִצְרַיִם לִהְיוֹת לָכֶם לֵאלֹהִים.

צֶדֶק, צֶדֶק תִּרְדֹּף. וְזָכַרְתָּ כִּי־עֶבֶד הָיִיתָ בְּמִצְרָיִם.

I am the Lord who hallows you, who led you out of Egypt to be your God.

Justice, justice shall you pursue. Remember that you were slaves in Egypt.

Continue on page 475

ליל שביעי של פסח

For the Last Eve of Pesach

One of the following

1

Not without suffering
did we win our way through the deadly waters
to the shore of refuge and new life.
The oppressor's fury grows as his grip begins to weaken.
In his rage he pursues us even to his own destruction.

In his drowning
part of us is lost as well.
The remnant sings songs,
yet a sadness remains.

So many must die,
slave and master alike,
before a few can sing.

O God, teach us to rejoice in freedom,
but not in its cost
for us and our enemies.
Let there come a day
when hate and greed shall be no more,
and we will be free
to rejoice without sadness,
to sing without tears.

Continue on page 475

2

From Psalm 105

הוֹדוּ לַייָ, קִרְאוּ בִשְׁמוֹ.
הוֹדִיעוּ בָעַמִּים עֲלִילוֹתָיו!

O give thanks to the Lord, call upon His name.
Make known His deeds among the peoples!

שִׁירוּ־לוֹ, זַמְּרוּ לוֹ;
שִׂיחוּ בְּכָל־נִפְלְאוֹתָיו!

Sing to Him, sing praises to Him;
tell of all His wonders!

הִתְהַלְלוּ בְּשֵׁם קָדְשׁוֹ;
יִשְׂמַח לֵב מְבַקְשֵׁי יְיָ!

Glory in His holy name;
let the hearts of those who seek the Lord rejoice!

דִּרְשׁוּ יְיָ וְעֻזּוֹ; בַּקְּשׁוּ פָנָיו תָּמִיד.
הוּא יְיָ אֱלֹהֵינוּ; בְּכָל־הָאָרֶץ מִשְׁפָּטָיו.

Seek the Lord and His strength; seek His presence continually.
He is the Lord our God; His judgments fill the earth.

זָכַר לְעוֹלָם בְּרִיתוֹ, דָּבָר צִוָּה לְאֶלֶף דּוֹר:
אֲשֶׁר כָּרַת אֶת־אַבְרָהָם, וּשְׁבוּעָתוֹ לְיִשְׂחָק,

He is for ever mindful of His covenant, the word He commanded for a thousand generations:

The covenant He made with Abraham, His sworn promise to Isaac,

וַיַּעֲמִידֶהָ לְיַעֲקֹב לְחֹק, לְיִשְׂרָאֵל בְּרִית עוֹלָם.
וַיָּבֹא יִשְׂרָאֵל מִצְרָיִם, וְיַעֲקֹב גָּר בְּאֶרֶץ־חָם.

The commitment He made to Jacob, His everlasting covenant with Israel.

Israel went down to Egypt, Jacob dwelt in the land of the Nile.

כִּי־זָכַר אֶת־דְּבַר קָדְשׁוֹ, אֶת־אַבְרָהָם עַבְדּוֹ,
וַיּוֹצִא עַמּוֹ בְשָׂשׂוֹן, בְּרִנָּה אֶת־בְּחִירָיו.

Then He remembered His sacred promise, and Abraham His servant,

and He led forth His people with joy, His chosen ones with singing.

Continue on page 475

3

Psalm 114

בְּצֵאת יִשְׂרָאֵל מִמִּצְרָיִם, בֵּית יַעֲקֹב מֵעַם לֹעֵז,
הָיְתָה יְהוּדָה לְקָדְשׁוֹ, יִשְׂרָאֵל מַמְשְׁלוֹתָיו.
הַיָּם רָאָה וַיָּנֹס, הַיַּרְדֵּן יִסֹּב לְאָחוֹר.
הֶהָרִים רָקְדוּ כְאֵילִים, גְּבָעוֹת כִּבְנֵי־צֹאן.

When Israel went forth from Egypt, the House of Jacob from an alien people, Judah became His sanctuary, Israel His dominion.

The sea saw it and fled, the Jordan turned back.
The mountains skipped like rams, the hills like young lambs.

מַה־לְּךָ הַיָּם כִּי תָנוּס? הַיַּרְדֵּן תִּסֹּב לְאָחוֹר?
הֶהָרִים תִּרְקְדוּ כְאֵילִים? גְּבָעוֹת כִּבְנֵי־צֹאן?
מִלִּפְנֵי אָדוֹן חוּלִי אָרֶץ, מִלִּפְנֵי אֱלוֹהַּ יַעֲקֹב,
הַהֹפְכִי הַצּוּר אֲגַם־מָיִם, חַלָּמִישׁ לְמַעְיְנוֹ־מָיִם.

What ails you, O sea, that you turn away? Why, O Jordan, do you turn back? O mountains, why do you skip like rams? Why, O hills, like young lambs?

Dance, O earth, before the Lord; at the presence of the God of Jacob, who turns the rock into a pool of water, the flint into a flowing spring.

Continue on page 475

For the Eve of Shavuot ליל שבועות

One of the following

1

MEDITATION

Now summer's prospect,
the world ripening and growing softer,
the promise of harvest fulfilled,
the warming sun, lies before us.

Now the vision of Torah,
the world at peace and growing gentler,
the promise of goodness fulfilled,
the loving heart, lies open to the mind.

In every generation our people has sought You;
hallowed is their seeking.

We too seek You
with trust that Your light is not hidden
from those who seek You with a whole heart.

◆

Endless are Your revelations, O Eternal One, to every age and to all the peoples.

For Your revelations to the House of Israel, those of our first days, and those of later ages, and for the discoveries we make for ourselves, we give thanks.

Deliver us from the darkness of ignorance, that we may see Your law with unclouded vision: help us to take these teachings into our lives.

Teach us Your Torah and enable us to hallow our lives with Your Mitzvot. O Source of truth and law, You are blessed for ever. Amen.

Continue on page 475

2

It has been said:

"Arise, shine, for your light has come:
the glory of the Lord dawns upon you.

קוּמִי, אוֹרִי, כִּי בָא אוֹרֵךְ:
וּכְבוֹד יְיָ עָלַיִךְ זָרָח.

Though darkness covers the earth,
and deep darkness the peoples,

כִּי־הִנֵּה הַחֹשֶׁךְ יְכַסֶּה־אֶרֶץ,
וַעֲרָפֶל לְאֻמִּים,

the Lord shall rise over you as a sun,
and His glory will be revealed to you.

וְעָלַיִךְ יִזְרַח יְיָ,
וּכְבוֹדוֹ עָלַיִךְ יֵרָאֶה.

Then the nations shall come to your light,
and kings to the brightness of your rising."

וְהָלְכוּ גוֹיִם לְאוֹרֵךְ,
וּמְלָכִים לְנֹגַהּ זַרְחֵךְ.

Continue on page 475

3

O God, Your light shines continually upon the path of all who sincerely seek to know You and to do Your will. Help us always to search for You, always to listen for Your voice.

For the impulse within us to seek righteousness, and for the measure of truth that we have found, we praise Your holy name. May the observance of this Festival of Revelation inspire us to walk in Your ways, as it is written: "You shall be holy, for I the Lord your God am holy."

וְאַתֶּם תִּהְיוּ־לִי מַמְלֶכֶת כֹּהֲנִים וְגוֹי קָדוֹשׁ.

You shall be to me a kingdom of priests, a holy people.

כִּי הַמִּצְוָה הַזֹּאת אֲשֶׁר אָנֹכִי מְצַוְּךָ הַיּוֹם לֹא־נִפְלֵאת הִוא מִמְּךָ, וְלֹא־רְחֹקָה הִוא.
כִּי־קָרוֹב אֵלֶיךָ הַדָּבָר מְאֹד, בְּפִיךָ וּבִלְבָבְךָ, לַעֲשֹׂתוֹ.

For this commandment which I command you this day is not too difficult for you, nor too remote.

No, the word is very near to you, in your mouth and in your heart, that you may do it.

הִנֵּה יָמִים בָּאִים, נְאֻם־יְיָ, וְכָרַתִּי אֶת־בֵּית יִשְׂרָאֵל וְאֶת־בֵּית יְהוּדָה בְּרִית חֲדָשָׁה.
נָתַתִּי אֶת־תּוֹרָתִי בְּקִרְבָּם, וְעַל־לִבָּם אֶכְתֲּבֶנָּה.

The days are coming, says the Lord, when I will make a new covenant with the House of Israel and the House of Judah.

I will put My Torah within them, and engrave it on their hearts.

וְהָיִיתִי לָהֶם לֵאלֹהִים; וְהֵמָּה יִהְיוּ־לִי לְעָם.
וְהָיָה אַחֲרֵי־כֵן, אֶשְׁפּוֹךְ אֶת־רוּחִי עַל־כָּל בָּשָׂר.

I will be their God; they shall be My people.

And then it shall come to pass, that I will pour out My spirit upon all flesh.

Continue on page 475

For the Eve of Sukkot

ליל סכות

One of the following

1

On this day we give thanks for the creative power that pours forth its bounty in grass and grain. The earth and its fullness is Yours, O God: You are the seed within the seed, giving it life, and sustaining all Your creatures. Spring and summer and autumn Your radiant power makes the earth yield its fruit.

For this we give praise, and pledge that more than words shall show our thankfulness.

We shall cherish the good earth You have placed in our keeping.

We shall share with others the food we have gathered.

We shall help them to harvest the crop they have planted.

And we shall labor to make this a world where only good is sown, that our harvest may be contentment and peace.

Continue on page 475

2

The glorious promise of spring, the mystery of summer growth, and the fulfillment of autumn's harvest reveal the greatness and goodness of God.

In ancient times, when the fruits of the field were gathered in, our people made pilgrimage to Jerusalem to give thanks for life and its blessings. We too have come as pilgrims to our sanctuary, to rejoice in the goodness of life.

O God, make us more conscious of Your gifts to us, and help us to see that no work truly prospers until it brings blessings to others. May our observance of this festival teach us not to withhold from others a share in the bounty that is ours, nor to dispossess them of what they have gleaned by their own efforts.

Help us, O Lord, so to live that when we have gathered our final harvest, many shall rise up and call us blessed.

הוֹשִׁיעָה אֶת־עַמֶּךָ, וּבָרֵךְ אֶת־נַחֲלָתֶךָ, וּרְעֵם וְנַשְּׂאֵם עַד־הָעוֹלָם.

Help Your people; bless Your loved ones; guide and be with them for ever.

◆

וְיִהְיוּ דְבָרַי אֵלֶּה אֲשֶׁר הִתְחַנַּנְתִּי לִפְנֵי יְיָ קְרֹבִים אֶל־יְיָ אֱלֹהֵינוּ יוֹמָם וָלָיְלָה, לַעֲשׂוֹת מִשְׁפַּט עַבְדּוֹ וּמִשְׁפַּט עַמּוֹ יִשְׂרָאֵל, דְּבַר־יוֹם בְּיוֹמוֹ.

Let the words that we pour out to the Eternal be acceptable to Him always, that He may uphold from day to day the cause of His servant, the cause of His people Israel.

לְמַעַן דַּעַת כָּל־עַמֵּי הָאָרֶץ כִּי יְיָ הוּא הָאֱלֹהִים; אֵין עוֹד.

Then shall all the peoples of the earth know that the Lord is God; there is none else.

Continue on page 475

3

Earth and sky, rain and sun, flower and fruit speak to us of God's creative power. Like generations before us, we give thanks for His goodness.

Into this sanctuary we have brought the symbols of Sukkot: The lulav, the palm that resembles the human spine, to remind us that we can stand straight with courage and integrity.

May we serve God by standing up for justice, truth, and peace.

The myrtle, whose leaves are shaped like eyes that can behold the grandeur and beauty of the universe.

May we serve God by looking with kindness at every living being.

The willow of the brook, whose leaves are shaped like human lips.

May these lips sing God's praise and bless His children.

The etrog, shaped like the human heart. May we remember that love is the doorway through which we pass from selfishness to service, and from loneliness to kinship with all the world.

O God of Israel and all the world, with palm and myrtle, willow and etrog, with spine and eyes, with lips and heart, we praise You.

Continue on page 475

ליל עצרת-שמחת תורה

For the Eve of Atzeret–Simchat Torah

One of the following

1

We have heard the sound of the Shofar
calling us to reawakening.

We have fasted and prayed,
and considered our lives and our deeds.

We have given thanks for harvest,
and peered heavenward
through the Sukkah's spaces.

Now our cycle ends
and begins again,
with song and dance,
as to our hearts we clasp
our tree of life.

Eternal Torah!
The more we hold you close,
the more you lift us up.
We will be glad,
we will rejoice.

Continue on page 475

2

Our sages likened the Torah to water, wine, milk, and honey.
They said:

מַה הַמַּיִם חַיִּים לָעוֹלָם,
כָּךְ תּוֹרָה חַיִּים לָעוֹלָם.

As water gives life to the world,

So the Torah gives life to the world.

מַה הַמַּיִם מְשִׁיבִים נַפְשׁוֹ שֶׁל אָדָם,
כָּךְ תּוֹרָה מְשִׁיבָה נַפְשׁוֹ שֶׁל אָדָם.

As water revives our life,
So the Torah revives the spirit.

מַה הַמַּיִם מְטַהֲרִים אֶת־הָאָדָם,
כָּךְ תּוֹרָה מְטַהֶרֶת אֶת־הָאָדָם.

As water cleanses the body,
So the Torah cleanses the soul.

מַה הַמַּיִם יוֹרְדִים טִפִּין־טִפִּין וְנַעֲשִׂים נְחָלִים־נְחָלִים,
כָּךְ תּוֹרָה אָדָם לוֹמֵד קִמְעָא־קִמְעָא עַד שֶׁנַּעֲשֶׂה כְּנַחַל נוֹבֵעַ.

As water, gathering drop by drop, becomes a rushing stream,
So the Torah, learned little by little, becomes a stream of wisdom.

מַה הַמַּיִם מַנִּיחִים מָקוֹם גָּבֹהַּ וְהוֹלְכִים בְּמָקוֹם נָמוּךְ,
כָּךְ תּוֹרָה מַנַּחַת מִי שֶׁדַּעְתּוֹ גְבוֹהָה עָלָיו וּמִדַּבֶּקֶת בְּמִי שֶׁדַּעְתּוֹ נְמוּכָה עָלָיו.

As water seeks its level, descending from high places,
So does the Torah elude the arrogant and find the modest spirit.

מַה הַמַּיִם מְגַדְּלִים אֶת־הַצְּמָחִים,
כָּךְ דִּבְרֵי תוֹרָה מְגַדְּלִין כָּל־מִי שֶׁעָמֵל בָּהֶם.

As water helps plants to grow,
So the Torah helps us to grow in spirit.

מַה הַיַּיִן כָּל־זְמַן שֶׁהוּא מִתְיַשֵּׁן מִשְׁתַּבֵּחַ,
כָּךְ דִּבְרֵי תוֹרָה כָּל־זְמַן שֶׁמִּתְיַשְּׁנִים בָּאָדָם מִשְׁתַּבְּחִים.

As wine improves with age,
So with advancing years does understanding of the Torah improve.

מַה הַיַּיִן מְשַׂמֵּחַ אֶת־הַלֵּב,
כָּךְ דִּבְרֵי תוֹרָה מְשַׂמְּחִים אֶת־הַלֵּב.

As wine gladdens the heart,
So do the words of Torah gladden the heart.

מַה דְּבַשׁ וְחָלָב מְתוּקִים,
כָּךְ דִּבְרֵי תוֹרָה מְתוּקִים.

As milk and honey are sweet to the taste,
So are the words of the Torah sweet to the mind.

עֵץ־חַיִּים הִיא לַמַּחֲזִיקִים בָּהּ, וְתֹמְכֶיהָ מְאֻשָּׁר.
דְּרָכֶיהָ דַרְכֵי־נֹעַם, וְכָל־נְתִיבוֹתֶיהָ שָׁלוֹם.

It is a tree of life to all who hold it fast, and all who cling to it find happiness.

Its ways are ways of pleasantness, and all its paths are peace.

Continue on page 475

3

This day we complete the reading of the Torah and begin it anew. For our eternal and inexhaustible Teaching, whose gift is new life to all who turn to it, we give thanks.

Grant that this sanctuary may always be a place of joy, O Eternal God, and that our love and reverence of Torah never fade. And may our worship within these walls fill us with fervor and gladness all the days of our lives. Amen.

◆ ◆

READER'S KADDISH — חצי קדיש

יִתְגַּדַּל וְיִתְקַדַּשׁ שְׁמֵהּ רַבָּא בְּעָלְמָא דִּי־בְרָא כִרְעוּתֵהּ,
וְיַמְלִיךְ מַלְכוּתֵהּ בְּחַיֵּיכוֹן וּבְיוֹמֵיכוֹן וּבְחַיֵּי דְכָל־בֵּית
יִשְׂרָאֵל, בַּעֲגָלָא וּבִזְמַן קָרִיב, וְאִמְרוּ: אָמֵן.

יְהֵא שְׁמֵהּ רַבָּא מְבָרַךְ לְעָלַם וּלְעָלְמֵי עָלְמַיָּא.

יִתְבָּרַךְ וְיִשְׁתַּבַּח, וְיִתְפָּאַר וְיִתְרוֹמַם וְיִתְנַשֵּׂא, וְיִתְהַדַּר
וְיִתְעַלֶּה וְיִתְהַלַּל שְׁמֵהּ דְּקוּדְשָׁא, בְּרִיךְ הוּא, לְעֵלָּא מִן
כָּל־בִּרְכָתָא וְשִׁירָתָא, תֻּשְׁבְּחָתָא וְנֶחֱמָתָא דַּאֲמִירָן בְּעָלְמָא,
וְאִמְרוּ: אָמֵן.

Let the glory of God be extolled, let His great name be hallowed in the world whose creation He willed. May His kingdom soon prevail, in our own day, our own lives, and the life of all Israel, and let us say: Amen.

Let His great name be blessed for ever and ever.

Let the name of the Holy One, blessed is He, be glorified, exalted and honored, though He is beyond all the praises, songs, and adorations that we can utter, and let us say: Amen.

◆ ◆

All rise

שמע וברכותיה

בָּרְכוּ אֶת־יְיָ הַמְבֹרָךְ!

Praise the Lord, to whom our praise is due!

בָּרוּךְ יְיָ הַמְבֹרָךְ לְעוֹלָם וָעֶד!

Praised be the Lord, to whom our praise is due,
now and for ever!

◆ ◆

CREATION | מעריב ערבים

בָּרוּךְ אַתָּה, יְיָ אֱלֹהֵינוּ, מֶלֶךְ הָעוֹלָם, אֲשֶׁר בִּדְבָרוֹ מַעֲרִיב עֲרָבִים. בְּחָכְמָה פּוֹתֵחַ שְׁעָרִים, וּבִתְבוּנָה מְשַׁנֶּה עִתִּים, וּמַחֲלִיף אֶת־הַזְּמַנִּים, וּמְסַדֵּר אֶת־הַכּוֹכָבִים בְּמִשְׁמְרוֹתֵיהֶם בָּרָקִיעַ כִּרְצוֹנוֹ.

Praised be the Lord our God, Ruler of the universe, whose word brings on the evening. His wisdom opens heaven's gates; His understanding makes the ages pass and the seasons alternate; and His will controls the stars as they travel through the skies.

בּוֹרֵא יוֹם וָלָיְלָה, גּוֹלֵל אוֹר מִפְּנֵי חֹשֶׁךְ וְחֹשֶׁךְ מִפְּנֵי אוֹר, וּמַעֲבִיר יוֹם וּמֵבִיא לָיְלָה, וּמַבְדִּיל בֵּין יוֹם וּבֵין לָיְלָה, יְיָ צְבָאוֹת שְׁמוֹ.

He is Creator of day and night, rolling light away from darkness, and darkness from light; He causes day to pass and brings on the night; He sets day and night apart: He is the Lord of Hosts.

אֵל חַי וְקַיָּם, תָּמִיד יִמְלוֹךְ עָלֵינוּ, לְעוֹלָם וָעֶד. בָּרוּךְ אַתָּה, יְיָ, הַמַּעֲרִיב עֲרָבִים.

May the living and eternal God rule us always, to the end of time! Blessed is the Lord, whose word makes evening fall.

◆ ◆

REVELATION | אהבת עולם

אַהֲבַת עוֹלָם בֵּית יִשְׂרָאֵל עַמְּךָ אָהָבְתָּ: תּוֹרָה וּמִצְוֹת, חֻקִּים וּמִשְׁפָּטִים אוֹתָנוּ לִמַּדְתָּ.

Unending is Your love for Your people, the House of Israel: Torah and Mitzvot, laws and precepts have You taught us.

עַל־כֵּן, יְיָ אֱלֹהֵינוּ, בְּשָׁכְבֵנוּ וּבְקוּמֵנוּ נָשִׂיחַ בְּחֻקֶּיךָ, וְנִשְׂמַח בְּדִבְרֵי תוֹרָתְךָ וּבְמִצְוֹתֶיךָ לְעוֹלָם וָעֶד.

Therefore, O Lord our God, when we lie down and when we rise up, we will meditate on Your laws and rejoice in Your Torah and Mitzvot for ever.

כִּי הֵם חַיֵּינוּ וְאֹרֶךְ יָמֵינוּ, וּבָהֶם נֶהְגֶּה יוֹמָם וָלָיְלָה. וְאַהֲבָתְךָ אַל־תָּסִיר מִמֶּנּוּ לְעוֹלָמִים! בָּרוּךְ אַתָּה, יְיָ, אוֹהֵב עַמּוֹ יִשְׂרָאֵל.

Day and night we will reflect on them, for they are our life and the length of our days. Then Your love shall never depart from our hearts! Blessed is the Lord, who loves His people Israel.

◆ ◆

שְׁמַע יִשְׂרָאֵל: יְיָ אֱלֹהֵינוּ, יְיָ אֶחָד!

Hear, O Israel: the Lord is our God, the Lord is One!

בָּרוּךְ שֵׁם כְּבוֹד מַלְכוּתוֹ לְעוֹלָם וָעֶד!

Blessed is His glorious kingdom for ever and ever!

All are seated

וְאָהַבְתָּ אֵת יְיָ אֱלֹהֶיךָ בְּכָל־לְבָבְךָ וּבְכָל־נַפְשְׁךָ וּבְכָל־מְאֹדֶךָ.
וְהָיוּ הַדְּבָרִים הָאֵלֶּה, אֲשֶׁר אָנֹכִי מְצַוְּךָ הַיּוֹם, עַל־לְבָבֶךָ.
וְשִׁנַּנְתָּם לְבָנֶיךָ, וְדִבַּרְתָּ בָּם בְּשִׁבְתְּךָ בְּבֵיתֶךָ, וּבְלֶכְתְּךָ בַדֶּרֶךְ, וּבְשָׁכְבְּךָ וּבְקוּמֶךָ.

You shall love the Lord your God with all your mind, with all your strength, with all your being.
Set these words, which I command you this day, upon your heart. Teach them faithfully to your children; speak of them in your home and on your way, when you lie down and when you rise up.

וּקְשַׁרְתָּם לְאוֹת עַל־יָדֶךָ, וְהָיוּ לְטֹטָפֹת בֵּין עֵינֶיךָ, וּכְתַבְתָּם עַל־מְזֻזוֹת בֵּיתֶךָ, וּבִשְׁעָרֶיךָ.

Bind them as a sign upon your hand; let them be a symbol before your eyes; inscribe them on the doorposts of your house, and on your gates.

לְמַעַן תִּזְכְּרוּ וַעֲשִׂיתֶם אֶת־כָּל־מִצְוֹתָי, וִהְיִיתֶם קְדֹשִׁים לֵאלֹהֵיכֶם. אֲנִי יְיָ אֱלֹהֵיכֶם, אֲשֶׁר הוֹצֵאתִי אֶתְכֶם מֵאֶרֶץ מִצְרַיִם לִהְיוֹת לָכֶם לֵאלֹהִים. אֲנִי יְיָ אֱלֹהֵיכֶם.

Be mindful of all My Mitzvot, and do them: so shall you consecrate yourselves to your God. I, the Lord, am your God who led you out of Egypt to be your God; I, the Lord, am your God.

◆ ◆

REDEMPTION — גאולה

אֱמֶת וֶאֱמוּנָה כָּל־זֹאת, וְקַיָּם עָלֵינוּ כִּי הוּא יְיָ אֱלֹהֵינוּ וְאֵין זוּלָתוֹ, וַאֲנַחְנוּ יִשְׂרָאֵל עַמּוֹ.
הַפּוֹדֵנוּ מִיַּד מְלָכִים, מַלְכֵּנוּ הַגּוֹאֲלֵנוּ מִכַּף כָּל־הֶעָרִיצִים.

All this we hold to be true and sure: He alone is our God: there is none else, and we are Israel His people.

He is our King: He delivers us from the hand of oppressors, and saves us from the fist of tyrants.

הָעֹשֶׂה גְדֹלוֹת עַד אֵין חֵקֶר, וְנִפְלָאוֹת עַד־אֵין מִסְפָּר.
הַשָּׂם נַפְשֵׁנוּ בַּחַיִּים, וְלֹא־נָתַן לַמּוֹט רַגְלֵנוּ.

He does wonders without number, marvels that pass our understanding.

He gives us our life; by His help we survive all who seek our destruction.

הָעֹשֶׂה לָּנוּ נִסִּים בְּפַרְעֹה, אוֹתוֹת וּמוֹפְתִים בְּאַדְמַת בְּנֵי חָם.
וַיּוֹצֵא אֶת־עַמּוֹ יִשְׂרָאֵל מִתּוֹכָם לְחֵרוּת עוֹלָם.

He did wonders for us in the land of Egypt, miracles and marvels in the land of Pharaoh.
He led His people Israel out, for ever to serve Him in freedom.

וְרָאוּ בָנָיו גְּבוּרָתוֹ; שִׁבְּחוּ וְהוֹדוּ לִשְׁמוֹ. וּמַלְכוּתוֹ בְּרָצוֹן קִבְּלוּ עֲלֵיהֶם. מֹשֶׁה וּבְנֵי יִשְׂרָאֵל לְךָ עָנוּ שִׁירָה בְּשִׂמְחָה רַבָּה, וְאָמְרוּ כֻלָּם:

When His children witnessed His power they extolled Him and gave Him thanks; freely they acclaimed Him King; and full of joy, Moses and all Israel sang this song:

מִי־כָמֹכָה בָּאֵלִם, יְיָ?
מִי כָּמֹכָה, נֶאְדָּר בַּקֹּדֶשׁ,
נוֹרָא תְהִלֹּת, עֹשֵׂה פֶלֶא?

Who is like You, Eternal One, among
the gods that are worshipped?
Who is like You, majestic in holiness,
awesome in splendor, doing wonders?

מַלְכוּתְךָ רָאוּ בָנֶיךָ, בּוֹקֵעַ יָם לִפְנֵי מֹשֶׁה; "זֶה אֵלִי!" עָנוּ וְאָמְרוּ: "יְיָ יִמְלֹךְ לְעֹלָם וָעֶד!"

In their escape from the sea, Your children saw Your sovereign might displayed. "This is my God!" they cried. "The Eternal will reign for ever and ever!"

וְנֶאֱמַר: "כִּי־פָדָה יְיָ אֶת־יַעֲקֹב, וּגְאָלוֹ מִיַּד חָזָק מִמֶּנּוּ." בָּרוּךְ אַתָּה, יְיָ, גָּאַל יִשְׂרָאֵל.

And it has been said: "The Eternal delivered Jacob, and redeemed him from the hand of one stronger than himself." Blessed is the Lord, the Redeemer of Israel.

◆ ◆

DIVINE PROVIDENCE

השכיבנו

הַשְׁכִּיבֵנוּ, יְיָ אֱלֹהֵינוּ, לְשָׁלוֹם, וְהַעֲמִידֵנוּ, מַלְכֵּנוּ, לְחַיִּים. וּפְרוֹשׂ עָלֵינוּ סֻכַּת שְׁלוֹמֶךָ, וְתַקְּנֵנוּ בְּעֵצָה טוֹבָה מִלְּפָנֶיךָ, וְהוֹשִׁיעֵנוּ לְמַעַן שְׁמֶךָ, וְהָגֵן בַּעֲדֵנוּ. וְהָסֵר מֵעָלֵינוּ אוֹיֵב, דֶּבֶר וְחֶרֶב וְרָעָב וְיָגוֹן; וְהָסֵר שָׂטָן מִלְּפָנֵינוּ וּמֵאַחֲרֵינוּ;

וּבְצֵל כְּנָפֶיךָ תַּסְתִּירֵנוּ, כִּי אֵל שׁוֹמְרֵנוּ וּמַצִּילֵנוּ אָתָּה, כִּי אֵל מֶלֶךְ חַנּוּן וְרַחוּם אָתָּה. וּשְׁמוֹר צֵאתֵנוּ וּבוֹאֵנוּ לְחַיִּים וּלְשָׁלוֹם, מֵעַתָּה וְעַד עוֹלָם, וּפְרוֹשׂ עָלֵינוּ סֻכַּת שְׁלוֹמֶךָ. בָּרוּךְ אַתָּה, יְיָ, הַפּוֹרֵשׂ סֻכַּת שָׁלוֹם עָלֵינוּ, וְעַל־כָּל־עַמּוֹ יִשְׂרָאֵל וְעַל יְרוּשָׁלָיִם.

Grant, O Eternal God, that we may lie down in peace, and raise us up, O Sovereign, to life renewed. Spread over us the shelter of Your peace; guide us with Your good counsel; and for Your name's sake, be our Help.

Shield us from hatred and plague; keep us from war and famine and anguish; subdue our inclination to evil. O God our Guardian and Helper, our gracious and merciful Ruler, give us refuge in the shadow of Your wings. O guard our coming and our going, that now and always we have life and peace.

Blessed is the Lord, whose shelter of peace is spread over us, over all His people Israel, and over Jerusalem.

◆ ◆

ON SHABBAT:

COVENANT — ושמרו

וְשָׁמְרוּ בְנֵי־יִשְׂרָאֵל אֶת־הַשַּׁבָּת, לַעֲשׂוֹת אֶת־הַשַּׁבָּת לְדֹרֹתָם בְּרִית עוֹלָם. בֵּינִי וּבֵין בְּנֵי יִשְׂרָאֵל אוֹת הִיא לְעֹלָם, כִּי שֵׁשֶׁת יָמִים עָשָׂה יְיָ אֶת־הַשָּׁמַיִם וְאֶת־הָאָרֶץ, וּבַיּוֹם הַשְּׁבִיעִי שָׁבַת וַיִּנָּפַשׁ.

The people of Israel shall keep the Sabbath, observing the Sabbath in every generation as a covenant for all time. It is a sign for ever between Me and the people of Israel, for in six days the Eternal God made heaven and earth, and on the seventh day He rested from His labors.

◆ ◆

וַיְדַבֵּר מֹשֶׁה אֶת־מֹעֲדֵי יְיָ אֶל־בְּנֵי יִשְׂרָאֵל.

And Moses declared the appointed seasons of the Lord to the people of Israel.

◆ ◆

All rise

תפלה

אֲדֹנָי, שְׂפָתַי תִּפְתָּח, וּפִי יַגִּיד תְּהִלָּתֶךָ.

Eternal God, open my lips, that my mouth may declare Your glory.

GOD OF ALL GENERATIONS
אבות

בָּרוּךְ אַתָּה, יְיָ אֱלֹהֵינוּ וֵאלֹהֵי אֲבוֹתֵינוּ, אֱלֹהֵי אַבְרָהָם, אֱלֹהֵי יִצְחָק, וֵאלֹהֵי יַעֲקֹב; הָאֵל הַגָּדוֹל, הַגִּבּוֹר וְהַנּוֹרָא, אֵל עֶלְיוֹן.

We praise You, Lord our God and God of all generations: God of Abraham, God of Isaac, God of Jacob; great, mighty, and awesome God, God supreme.

גּוֹמֵל חֲסָדִים טוֹבִים, וְקוֹנֵה הַכֹּל, וְזוֹכֵר חַסְדֵי אָבוֹת, וּמֵבִיא גְאֻלָּה לִבְנֵי בְנֵיהֶם, לְמַעַן שְׁמוֹ, בְּאַהֲבָה.

Master of all the living, Your ways are ways of love. You remember the faithfulness of our ancestors, and in love bring redemption to their children's children for the sake of Your name.

מֶלֶךְ עוֹזֵר וּמוֹשִׁיעַ וּמָגֵן. בָּרוּךְ אַתָּה, יְיָ, מָגֵן אַבְרָהָם.

You are our King and our Help, our Savior and our Shield. Blessed is the Lord, the Shield of Abraham.

◆ ◆

GOD'S POWER
גבורות

אַתָּה גִּבּוֹר לְעוֹלָם, אֲדֹנָי, מְחַיֵּה הַכֹּל אַתָּה, רַב לְהוֹשִׁיעַ.

Eternal is Your might, O Lord; all life is Your gift; great is Your power to save!

מְכַלְכֵּל חַיִּים בְּחֶסֶד, מְחַיֵּה הַכֹּל בְּרַחֲמִים רַבִּים. סוֹמֵךְ נוֹפְלִים, וְרוֹפֵא חוֹלִים, וּמַתִּיר אֲסוּרִים, וּמְקַיֵּם אֱמוּנָתוֹ לִישֵׁנֵי עָפָר.

With love You sustain the living, with great compassion give life to all. You send help to the falling and healing to the sick; You bring freedom to the captive and keep faith with those who sleep in the dust.

מִי כָמְוֹךָ, בַּעַל גְּבוּרוֹת, וּמִי דְוֹמֶה לָּךְ, מֶלֶךְ מֵמִית וּמְחַיֶּה וּמַצְמִיחַ יְשׁוּעָה?

וְנֶאֱמָן אַתָּה לְהַחֲיוֹת הַכֹּל. בָּרוּךְ אַתָּה, יְיָ, מְחַיֵּה הַכֹּל.

Who is like You, Master of Might? Who is Your equal, O Lord of life and death, Source of salvation? Blessed is the Lord, the Source of life.

◆ ◆

GOD'S HOLINESS — קדושת השם

אַתָּה קָדוֹשׁ וְשִׁמְךָ קָדוֹשׁ, וּקְדוֹשִׁים בְּכָל־יוֹם יְהַלְלְוּךָ סֶּלָה. בָּרוּךְ אַתָּה, יְיָ, הָאֵל הַקָּדוֹשׁ.

You are holy, Your name is holy, and those who strive to be holy declare Your glory day by day. Blessed is the Lord, the holy God.

All are seated

◆ ◆

THE HOLINESS OF YOM TOV — קדושת היום

אַתָּה בְחַרְתָּנוּ מִכָּל־הָעַמִּים, אָהַבְתָּ אוֹתָנוּ, וְרָצִיתָ בָּנוּ, וְרוֹמַמְתָּנוּ מִכָּל־הַלְּשׁוֹנוֹת, וְקִדַּשְׁתָּנוּ בְּמִצְוֹתֶיךָ. וְקֵרַבְתָּנוּ, מַלְכֵּנוּ, לַעֲבוֹדָתֶךָ, וְשִׁמְךָ הַגָּדוֹל וְהַקָּדוֹשׁ עָלֵינוּ קָרָאתָ.

In love and favor, O God, You have chosen us from all the peoples, exalting us by hallowing us with Your Mitzvot. Our Sovereign, You have summoned us to Your service, that through us Your great and holy name may become known in all the earth.

וַתִּתֶּן לָנוּ, יְיָ אֱלֹהֵינוּ, בְּאַהֲבָה [שַׁבָּתוֹת לִמְנוּחָה וּ] מוֹעֲדִים לְשִׂמְחָה, חַגִּים וּזְמַנִּים לְשָׂשׂוֹן: אֶת־יוֹם [הַשַּׁבָּת הַזֶּה וְאֶת־יוֹם]

In Your love, O Lord our God, You have given us [Sabbaths of rest,] feasts of gladness and seasons of joy: this [Sabbath day and this] festival of

Pesach — season of our freedom, — חַג הַמַּצּוֹת הַזֶּה – זְמַן חֵרוּתֵנוּ,

Shavuot — season of revelation, — חַג הַשָּׁבֻעוֹת הַזֶּה – זְמַן מַתַּן תּוֹרָתֵנוּ,

Sukkot — season of thanksgiving, חַג הַסֻּכּוֹת הַזֶּה – זְמַן שִׂמְחָתֵנוּ,

Atzeret–Simchat Torah — season of our gladness, הַשְּׁמִינִי חַג הָעֲצֶרֶת הַזֶּה – זְמַן שִׂמְחָתֵנוּ,

מִקְרָא קֹדֶשׁ, זֵכֶר לִיצִיאַת מִצְרָיִם.

to unite in worship and recall the Exodus from Egypt.

◆

אֱלֹהֵינוּ וֵאלֹהֵי אֲבוֹתֵינוּ, יַעֲלֶה וְיָבֹא וְיִזָּכֵר זִכְרוֹנֵנוּ וְזִכְרוֹן כָּל־עַמְּךָ בֵּית יִשְׂרָאֵל לְפָנֶיךָ, לְטוֹבָה לְחֵן לְחֶסֶד וּלְרַחֲמִים לְחַיִּים וּלְשָׁלוֹם בְּיוֹם

Our God and God of all ages, be mindful of Your people Israel on this

Feast of Pesach, חַג הַמַּצּוֹת הַזֶּה.

Feast of Shavuot, חַג הַשָּׁבֻעוֹת הַזֶּה.

Feast of Sukkot, חַג הַסֻּכּוֹת הַזֶּה.

Feast of Atzeret–Simchat Torah, הַשְּׁמִינִי חַג הָעֲצֶרֶת הַזֶּה.

and renew in us love and compassion, goodness, life, and peace.

זָכְרֵנוּ, יְיָ אֱלֹהֵינוּ, בּוֹ לְטוֹבָה. אָמֵן.

This day remember us for well-being. Amen.

וּפָקְדֵנוּ בוֹ לִבְרָכָה. אָמֵן.

This day bless us with Your nearness. Amen.

וְהוֹשִׁיעֵנוּ בוֹ לְחַיִּים. אָמֵן.

This day help us to a fuller life. Amen.

וְהַשִּׂיאֵנוּ, יְיָ אֱלֹהֵינוּ, אֶת־בִּרְכַּת מוֹעֲדֶיךָ לְחַיִּים וּלְשָׁלוֹם, לְשִׂמְחָה וּלְשָׂשׂוֹן, כַּאֲשֶׁר רָצִיתָ, וְאָמַרְתָּ לְבָרְכֵנוּ. אֱלֹהֵינוּ וֵאלֹהֵי אֲבוֹתֵינוּ, [רְצֵה בִמְנוּחָתֵנוּ,] קַדְּשֵׁנוּ בְּמִצְוֹתֶיךָ, וְתֵן חֶלְקֵנוּ בְּתוֹרָתֶךָ. שַׂבְּעֵנוּ מִטּוּבֶךָ, וְשַׂמְּחֵנוּ בִּישׁוּעָתֶךָ, וְטַהֵר לִבֵּנוּ לְעָבְדְּךָ בֶּאֱמֶת. וְהַנְחִילֵנוּ, יְיָ אֱלֹהֵינוּ, [בְּאַהֲבָה וּבְרָצוֹן,]

בְּשִׂמְחָה וּבְשָׂשׂוֹן [שַׁבַּת וּ]מוֹעֲדֵי קָדְשֶׁךָ, וְיִשְׂמְחוּ בְךָ יִשְׂרָאֵל, מְקַדְּשֵׁי שְׁמֶךָ. בָּרוּךְ אַתָּה, יְיָ, מְקַדֵּשׁ [הַשַּׁבָּת וְ] יִשְׂרָאֵל וְהַזְּמַנִּים.

Bestow upon us the blessing of Your holy Festivals, and may we so celebrate them as to be worthy of Your favor.

Our God and God of ages past, sanctify us with Your Mitzvot, and let Your Torah be our way of life. [*May our rest on this day be pleasing in Your sight.*] *Satisfy us with Your goodness, gladden us with Your salvation, and purify our hearts to serve You in truth.* [*In Your gracious love let Your holy Sabbath remain our heritage.*] *Let us celebrate Your holy Festivals with joy and gladness, that all Israel, hallowing Your name, may have cause to rejoice. Blessed is the Lord, who hallows* [*the Sabbath,*] *the House of Israel and the Festivals.*

◆ ◆

WORSHIP — עבודה

רְצֵה, יְיָ אֱלֹהֵינוּ, בְּעַמְּךָ יִשְׂרָאֵל, וּתְפִלָּתָם בְּאַהֲבָה תְקַבֵּל, וּתְהִי לְרָצוֹן תָּמִיד עֲבוֹדַת יִשְׂרָאֵל עַמֶּךָ.

Be gracious, O Lord our God, to Your people Israel, and receive our prayers with love. O may our worship always be acceptable to You.

אֵל קָרוֹב לְכָל־קֹרְאָיו, פְּנֵה אֶל עֲבָדֶיךָ וְחָנֵּנוּ; שְׁפוֹךְ רוּחֲךָ עָלֵינוּ, וְתֶחֱזֶינָה עֵינֵינוּ בְּשׁוּבְךָ לְצִיּוֹן בְּרַחֲמִים.

בָּרוּךְ אַתָּה, יְיָ, הַמַּחֲזִיר שְׁכִינָתוֹ לְצִיּוֹן.

Fill us with the knowledge that You are near to all who seek You in truth. Let our eyes behold Your presence in our midst and in the midst of our people in Zion.

Blessed is the Lord, whose presence gives life to Zion and all Israel.

◆ ◆

THANKSGIVING

הודאה

מוֹדִים אֲנַחְנוּ לָךְ, שָׁאַתָּה הוּא יְיָ אֱלֹהֵינוּ וֵאלֹהֵי אֲבוֹתֵינוּ לְעוֹלָם וָעֶד. צוּר חַיֵּינוּ, מָגֵן יִשְׁעֵנוּ, אַתָּה הוּא לְדוֹר וָדוֹר. נוֹדֶה לְךָ וּנְסַפֵּר תְּהִלָּתֶךָ, עַל־חַיֵּינוּ הַמְּסוּרִים בְּיָדֶךָ, וְעַל־נִשְׁמוֹתֵינוּ הַפְּקוּדוֹת לָךְ, וְעַל־נִסֶּיךָ שֶׁבְּכָל־יוֹם עִמָּנוּ, וְעַל־נִפְלְאוֹתֶיךָ וְטוֹבוֹתֶיךָ שֶׁבְּכָל־עֵת, עֶרֶב וָבֹקֶר וְצָהֳרָיִם. הַטּוֹב: כִּי לֹא־כָלוּ רַחֲמֶיךָ, וְהַמְרַחֵם: כִּי־לֹא תַמּוּ חֲסָדֶיךָ, מֵעוֹלָם קִוִּינוּ לָךְ.

We gratefully acknowledge that You are the Lord our God and God of our people, the God of all generations. You are the Rock of our life, the Power that shields us in every age. We thank You and sing Your praises: for our lives, which are in Your hand; for our souls, which are in Your keeping; for the signs of Your presence we encounter every day; and for Your wondrous gifts at all times, morning, noon, and night. You are Goodness: Your mercies never end; You are Compassion: Your love will never fail. You have always been our hope.

וְעַל כֻּלָּם יִתְבָּרַךְ וְיִתְרוֹמַם שִׁמְךָ, מַלְכֵּנוּ, תָּמִיד לְעוֹלָם וָעֶד. וְכֹל הַחַיִּים יוֹדוּךָ סֶּלָה, וִיהַלְלוּ אֶת שִׁמְךָ בֶּאֱמֶת, הָאֵל יְשׁוּעָתֵנוּ וְעֶזְרָתֵנוּ סֶלָה. בָּרוּךְ אַתָּה, יְיָ, הַטּוֹב שִׁמְךָ וּלְךָ נָאֶה לְהוֹדוֹת.

For all these things, O Sovereign God, let Your name be for ever exalted and blessed. O God our Redeemer and Helper, let all who live affirm You and praise Your name in truth. Lord, whose nature is Goodness, we give You thanks and praise.

◆ ◆

PEACE

ברכת שלום

שָׁלוֹם רָב עַל־יִשְׂרָאֵל עַמְּךָ תָּשִׂים לְעוֹלָם, כִּי אַתָּה הוּא מֶלֶךְ אָדוֹן לְכָל הַשָּׁלוֹם. וְטוֹב בְּעֵינֶיךָ לְבָרֵךְ אֶת־עַמְּךָ יִשְׂרָאֵל בְּכָל־עֵת וּבְכָל־שָׁעָה בִּשְׁלוֹמֶךָ.

בָּרוּךְ אַתָּה, יְיָ, הַמְבָרֵךְ אֶת־עַמּוֹ יִשְׂרָאֵל בַּשָּׁלוֹם.

Grant us peace, Your most precious gift, O Eternal Source of peace, and give us the will to proclaim its message to all the peoples of the earth. Bless our country, that it may always be a stronghold of peace, and its advocate among the nations. May contentment reign within its borders, health and happiness within its homes. Strengthen the bonds of friendship among the inhabitants of all lands. And may the love of Your name hallow every home and every heart. Blessed is the Eternal God, the Source of peace.

◆ ◆

MEDITATION

O God, guard my tongue from evil and my lips from speaking guile! Let there be in me no malice, but a prayer for the good of all. Show me the way of righteousness, that I may hurt no one; and help me to bring the blessings of love to others. Open my heart to do Your will; strengthen my desire to obey Your commandments. May my thoughts and my prayers be acceptable to You, O Lord, my Rock and my Redeemer.

◆ ◆

יִהְיוּ לְרָצוֹן אִמְרֵי־פִי וְהֶגְיוֹן לִבִּי לְפָנֶיךָ, יְיָ, צוּרִי וְגוֹאֲלִי.

May the words of my mouth, and the meditations of my heart, be acceptable to You, O Lord, my Rock and my Redeemer.

or

עֹשֶׂה שָׁלוֹם בִּמְרוֹמָיו, הוּא יַעֲשֶׂה שָׁלוֹם עָלֵינוּ וְעַל כָּל־יִשְׂרָאֵל, וְאִמְרוּ אָמֵן.

May He who causes peace to reign in the high heavens let peace descend on us, on all Israel, and all the world.

◆ ◆

Short Form of Hallel

This Hallel might be used at an evening service

Psalm 117

Praise the Lord, all you nations!
Extol Him, all you peoples!
For great is His love for us,
everlasting His faithfulness.
Halleluyah!

הַלְלוּ אֶת־יְיָ כָּל־גּוֹיִם!
שַׁבְּחוּהוּ כָּל־הָאֻמִּים!
כִּי גָבַר עָלֵינוּ חַסְדּוֹ,
וֶאֱמֶת־יְיָ לְעוֹלָם.
הַלְלוּיָהּ!

From Psalm 118

O give thanks to the Lord, for He is good;
For His love is everlasting.

הוֹדוּ לַייָ כִּי־טוֹב,
כִּי לְעוֹלָם חַסְדּוֹ.

Let Israel now say:
His love is everlasting.

יֹאמַר־נָא יִשְׂרָאֵל:
כִּי לְעוֹלָם חַסְדּוֹ.

Let the House of Aaron now say:
His love is everlasting.

יֹאמְרוּ־נָא בֵית־אַהֲרֹן:
כִּי לְעוֹלָם חַסְדּוֹ.

Let all who revere the Lord now say:
His love is everlasting.

יֹאמְרוּ־נָא יִרְאֵי יְיָ:
כִּי לְעוֹלָם חַסְדּוֹ.

Blessed is the one who comes to
seek the Lord; we bless you from
the house of the Lord.

בָּרוּךְ הַבָּא בְּשֵׁם יְיָ,
בֵּרַכְנוּכֶם מִבֵּית יְיָ.

You are my God, and I will thank You;
You are my God, I will exalt You.

אֵלִי אַתָּה וְאוֹדֶךָּ,
אֱלֹהַי אֲרוֹמְמֶךָּ.

O give thanks to the Lord, for He is good;
For His love is everlasting.

הוֹדוּ לַייָ כִּי־טוֹב,
כִּי לְעוֹלָם חַסְדּוֹ.

◆ ◆

The Ritual for the Reading of Torah begins on page 531.

The Ritual for the Reading of Torah on Atzeret—Simchat Torah begins on page 538.

Concluding Prayers begin on page 613.

תפלת שחרית ליום טוב

FESTIVAL MORNING SERVICE

For All Festivals

Those who wear the Tallit may find the ritual on page 282

At the great festivals of the year our people made pilgrimage to Jerusalem, the city of peace and of prayer. There they sang songs of celebration. This we now remember, and we remember Jerusalem, the capital city of our souls.

From Psalm 122

שָׂמַחְתִּי בְּאֹמְרִים לִי: בֵּית יְיָ נֵלֵךְ.
עֹמְדוֹת הָיוּ רַגְלֵינוּ בִּשְׁעָרַיִךְ, יְרוּשָׁלָםִ!

I rejoiced when they said to me: Let us go up to the House of the Lord.
Now we stand within your gates, O Jerusalem!

יְרוּשָׁלַםִ הַבְּנוּיָה! כְּעִיר שֶׁחֻבְּרָה־לָּהּ יַחְדָּו!
יְרוּשָׁלַםִ, הַבְּנוּיָה כְּעִיר שֶׁחֻבְּרָה־לָּהּ יַחְדָּו.

Jerusalem restored! The city united and whole!
Jerusalem, built to be a city where people come together as one.

שַׁאֲלוּ שְׁלוֹם יְרוּשָׁלָםִ: יִשְׁלָיוּ אֹהֲבָיִךְ!
יְהִי־שָׁלוֹם בְּחֵילֵךְ, שַׁלְוָה בְּאַרְמְנוֹתָיִךְ.

Pray for the peace of Jerusalem: may those who love you prosper!
Let there be peace in your homes, safety within your borders.

לְמַעַן אַחַי וְרֵעָי אֲדַבְּרָה־נָּא שָׁלוֹם בָּךְ.
לְמַעַן בֵּית יְיָ אֱלֹהֵינוּ, אֲבַקְשָׁה טוֹב לָךְ.

For the sake of my people, my friends, I pray you find peace.
For the sake of the house of the Lord our God, I will seek your good.

◆ ◆

Selections from the Morning Blessings, pages 283 to 289, may be read here

יום ראשון של פסח

For the First Morning of Pesach

One of the following

1

We rejoice now in the memory of our deliverance from bondage, and we celebrate the goodness we have known through the ages. For the strength our people have shown in the face of oppressors, we are grateful.

We give thanks for the courage that sustained them in times of suffering.

Not once but many times have we been delivered. Time and again we went from bondage to freedom, from darkness to light, from sorrow to joy.

In this season of liberation we celebrate the freedom to live without fear, the freedom to earn one's daily bread, the freedom to speak one's mind.

And we celebrate the season that brings new life to the growing world: we rejoice in the first harvest of Zion's soil, the promise of life in every land, the flower and tree reborn.

For now the winter is past, and flowers appear on the earth. The time of singing has come:

The Lord is our strength and our song!

Praised be God, Giver of freedom, Source of life.

Continue on page 507

2

"Let My people go, that they may serve Me!"

On this Passover morning we rejoice in Israel's deliverance from the bondage of Egypt. And because freedom is hard to gain and easily lost, we preserve the memory of our deliverance as though it had happened not only to our ancestors, but to ourselves. We hope through our observance to experience in our own spirits the drama of redemption, to strengthen our devotion to freedom and to the Eternal God who makes all freedom possible.

O God of freedom, let the memory of past enslavements make us more careful to hold fast to the liberty we enjoy today, and more sensitive to the rights of others. And may we never cease to labor for the day when oppression will be no more, and the whole human race will live in freedom. Amen.

Continue on page 507

3

"For now the winter is past,
the rains are over and gone.
The flowers appear on the earth,
the time of singing has come.
The song of the dove
will be heard in our land."

"כִּי־הִנֵּה הַסְּתָו עָבָר,
הַגֶּשֶׁם חָלַף הָלַךְ לוֹ.
הַנִּצָּנִים נִרְאוּ בָאָרֶץ,
עֵת הַזָּמִיר הִגִּיעַ.
וְקוֹל הַתּוֹר
נִשְׁמַע בְּאַרְצֵנוּ."

Let standing corn grow ripe,
As dew-drops bring their blessing:
Food for the hungry,
Healing for the sick.
Let bare vines be draped with grape blossoms,
As the heavens yield their dew.

רְאֵה קָמָה לְמַלֹּאת
בִּרְסִיסֵי בְּרָכָה:
לֶחֶם לָאוֹכֵל,
וּמַרְפֵּא וַאֲרוּכָה.
לְמַלְבִּישׁ סוּת סְמָדָר
עֲרוּמֵי שׂוֹרֵקָה;
וְהַשָּׁמַיִם יִתְּנוּ טַלָּם.

Let oases drip with plenty
And hills be wrapped in gladness:

יִרְעֲפוּ נְאוֹת מִדְבָּר
וְגַם תַּחְגֹּרְנָה גְבָעוֹת גִּיל:

וּבִפְטוּרֵי צִצִּים
תְּאֶזְרְנָה פְּתִיגִיל,
יָרֹנּוּ יַחְדָּו רֹב חֲסָדֶיךָ בְּמִלָּם,
וְהַשָּׁמַיִם יִתְּנוּ טַלָּם.

Dressed with flowers
In the colors of spring,
Singing Your endless goodness,
As the heavens yield their dew.

יִשְׂבְּעוּ עֲצֵי יְיָ
בַּשְּׁפֵלָה וּבָהָר,
וּמָלְאוּ הַגְּרָנוֹת בָּר,
וְהַיְקָבִים תִּירוֹשׁ וְיִצְהָר.
תְּרַנֵּנָּה פְּרָזוֹת,
עוֹמְדוֹת עַל־תִּלָּם
וְהַשָּׁמַיִם יִתְּנוּ טַלָּם.

Let the trees God made
Be fed on valley and hill,
The granaries filled with grain,
The vats with wine and oil.
Let every village be safe from war,
And sing for joy
As the heavens yield their dew.

הֱיוֹת הוֹגֵי דָת נְסוּכָה
כְּכֹכָבִים בְּהִלָּם.
וּמַשְׂבִּיעַ בְּטוּבוֹ
נֶפֶשׁ שׁוֹקֵקָה
וּרְעֵבָה וְרֵקָה
בְּמַעֲדַנָּיו מְמַלְאָם
וְהַשָּׁמַיִם יִתְּנוּ טַלָּם.

Let those who spend themselves
For Torah's sake
Shine bright as stars.
O God of goodness,
You feed the hungry soul,
The dry and empty heart,
filling it with delight
As the heavens yield their dew.

שְׁלַח רוּחֲךָ הַטּוֹב
לְהַחֲיוֹת גְּוִיֵּינוּ!
לְקַדְמוּתָהּ תָּשִׁיב
נַחֲלַת צִבְיֵנוּ.
מִמְּךָ טוֹב לַכֹּל יִמָּצֵא פִּדְיֵנוּ,
הֲלֹא אַתָּה תָּשׁוּב תְּחַיֵּנוּ.

Breathe new life into us,
O Lord of life!
Restore to its ancient glory
The land of Your heritage.
Let redemption appear at last,
O Source of life and its renewal.

אֱלֹהֵינוּ וֵאלֹהֵי אֲבוֹתֵינוּ,

בְּטַלְלֵי אוֹרָה תָּאִיר אֲדָמָה,
בְּטַלְלֵי בְרָכָה תְּבָרֵךְ אֲדָמָה,
בְּטַלְלֵי גִּילָה תָּגִיל אֲדָמָה,
בְּטַלְלֵי דִיצָה תְּדַשֵּׁן אֲדָמָה,
בְּטַלְלֵי זִמְרָה תְּזַמֵּר אֲדָמָה,
בְּטַלְלֵי חַיִּים תְּחַיֶּה אֲדָמָה,
בְּטַלְלֵי טוֹבָה תֵּטִיב אֲדָמָה,
בְּטַלְלֵי יְשׁוּעָה תּוֹשִׁיעַ אֲדָמָה,
בְּטַלְלֵי כַלְכָּלָה תְּכַלְכֵּל אֲדָמָה.

Our God and God of our ancestors,

let sunlight and blessing
come to earth
with the coming of spring.
Let there descend with the dew
joy and gladness.
And with the dew
let harvest and song descend,
goodness and life,
sustenance and help. Amen.

Continue on page 507

יום שביעי של פסח

For the Last Morning of Pesach

One of the following

1

This seventh day of Pesach is the anniversary of Israel's deliverance from the tyrant's wrath. This day Israel sang a song of praise to the God of freedom at the shores of the sea. Many times since has Israel known oppression and bondage; each time we have remembered the message of Passover and taken heart. Never have we forgotten the bitterness of slavery; never have we despaired of liberation. May we have such a heart as this always.

O God of freedom, cleanse the hearts of all men and women. Free them of the passions of hate and strife, of greed and the lust for power, and fill them with good will and the love of justice. Hasten the Passover of the future, when sword and spear shall be broken, and freedom and peace shall reign for ever. On that day all shall come to know their kinship, and gladly proclaim You their God and Redeemer.

Continue on page 507

2

אֱלֹהִים, בַּקֹּדֶשׁ דַּרְכֶּךָ. מִי־אֵל גָּדוֹל כֵּאלֹהִים?
אַתָּה הָאֵל עֹשֵׂה פֶלֶא. הוֹדַעְתָּ בָעַמִּים עֻזֶּךָ.

Your way, O God, is holiness. What god is so great as God?

You are the One who does wonders. You have shown the nations Your power.

גָּאַֽלְתָּ בִּזְרֽוֹעַ עַמֶּֽךָ, בְּנֵי־יַעֲקֹב וְיוֹסֵף. סֶֽלָה.

בַּיָּם דַּרְכֶּֽךָ, וּשְׁבִילְךָ בְּמַֽיִם רַבִּים, וְעִקְּבוֹתֶֽיךָ לֹא נוֹדָֽעוּ.

You redeemed Your people with strength, the children of
Jacob and Joseph.

*Your path was through the sea, Your way through raging
waters, yet Your steps were unseen.*

נָחִֽיתָ כַצֹּאן עַמֶּֽךָ,

בְּיַד־מֹשֶׁה וְאַהֲרֹן.

You led Your people like a flock,
by the hand of Moses and Aaron.

Continue on page 507

3

From Psalm 57

My heart is ready, O God,
my heart is ready!
I will sing, I will sing praises!
Awake, O my soul!
Awake, O harp and lyre!
I will arouse the dawn!
I will give thanks to You, O Lord,
among the peoples,
and sing Your praises
among the nations.
For Your love is high
as the heavens.
Your faithfulness reaches
to the clouds.
Be exalted, O God,
above the heavens;
let Your glory extend
over all the earth!

נָכוֹן לִבִּי, אֱלֹהִים,

נָכוֹן לִבִּי!

אָשִֽׁירָה וַאֲזַמֵּֽרָה!

עֽוּרָה, כְבוֹדִי!

עֽוּרָה, הַנֵּֽבֶל וְכִנּוֹר!

אָעִֽירָה שָּֽׁחַר!

אוֹדְךָ בָעַמִּים,

אֲדֹנָי,

אֲזַמֶּרְךָ בַּלְאֻמִּים.

כִּי־גָדֹל עַד־שָׁמַֽיִם חַסְדֶּֽךָ,

וְעַד־שְׁחָקִים אֲמִתֶּֽךָ.

רֽוּמָה עַל־שָׁמַֽיִם, אֱלֹהִים,

עַל כָּל־הָאָֽרֶץ כְּבוֹדֶֽךָ!

Continue on page 507

For the Morning of Shavuot שבועות

One of the following

1

On this Chag Habikkurim,
Festival of the First Fruits,
we give thanks for
the first fruits of Israel's spirit.

Assembled at a mountain,
our people,
still bent from oppression,
found You,
found Your Torah,
found Your truth,
and embraced the destiny
that has shaped worlds.

Give us strength
to offer to You
the first fruits of our hearts
and the work of our hands!

Help us still to shape the world
according to Your will,
that this world
may reveal itself to You
as You have revealed Yourself to our people:
in love.

Continue on page 507

2

"I, the Lord, am your God who led you out of Egypt, the house of bondage."

Our deliverance from bondage was not an end but a beginning. And now we celebrate its climax: the day when our ancestors, assembled at Sinai, entered into a covenant with their God. They became a kingdom of priests, a holy people pledged to obey the divine law, a witness to God's goodness before the world.

We are witness and messenger, bearers of the knowledge of God for all time. Every generation of Israel is called to affirm its loyalty to the God of Israel and His law of life.

O God of Israel, may the vision of Sinai remain with us to strengthen our faithfulness to Your covenant. And may our children and their children learn the joy of the Mitzvot, that they may love and revere Your holy name, and hold fast to Your purpose for ever.

Continue on page 507

3

From Psalm 111

אוֹדֶה יְיָ בְּכָל־לֵבָב, בְּסוֹד יְשָׁרִים וְעֵדָה.
תְּהִלָּתוֹ עֹמֶדֶת לָעַד!

I will give thanks to the Lord with all my heart, where the upright meet and the people assemble.
Let Him be praised for ever!

גְּדֹלִים מַעֲשֵׂי יְיָ; דְּרוּשִׁים לְכָל־חֶפְצֵיהֶם.
תְּהִלָּתוֹ עֹמֶדֶת לָעַד!

The works of the Lord are sublime; let all who delight in them meditate upon them.
Let Him be praised for ever!

הוֹד וְהָדָר פָּעֳלוֹ; וְצִדְקָתוֹ עֹמֶדֶת לָעַד.
תְּהִלָּתוֹ עֹמֶדֶת לָעַד!

Majestic and glorious are His acts; His righteousness stands fast for ever.
Let Him be praised for ever!

מַעֲשֵׂי יָדָיו אֱמֶת וּמִשְׁפָּט, נֶאֱמָנִים כָּל־פִּקּוּדָיו.
תְּהִלָּתוֹ עֹמֶדֶת לָעַד!

Truth and justice are the work of His hands, and His precepts are firmly based.

Let Him be praised for ever!

סְמוּכִים לָעַד לְעוֹלָם, עֲשׂוּיִם בֶּאֱמֶת וְיָשָׁר.
תְּהִלָּתוֹ עֹמֶדֶת לָעַד!

They are established for ever and ever, they are done in goodness and in truth.

Let Him be praised for ever!

פְּדוּת שָׁלַח לְעַמּוֹ; צִוָּה לְעוֹלָם בְּרִיתוֹ.
תְּהִלָּתוֹ עֹמֶדֶת לָעַד!

He sends redemption to His people; He has ordained His covenant for all time.

Let Him be praised for ever!

רֵאשִׁית חָכְמָה יִרְאַת יְיָ; שֵׂכֶל טוֹב לְכָל־עֹשֵׂיהֶם.
תְּהִלָּתוֹ עֹמֶדֶת לָעַד!

The beginning of wisdom is awe of God; those who live by it grow in understanding.

Let Him be praised for ever!

Continue on page 507

For the Morning of Sukkot

סכות

One of the following

1

יְיָ, מִי־יָגוּר בְּאָהֳלֶךָ, מִי־יִשְׁכֹּן בְּהַר קָדְשֶׁךָ?

Lord, who may abide in Your tabernacle? Who may dwell in Your holy mountain?

הוֹלֵךְ תָּמִים וּפֹעֵל צֶדֶק וְדֹבֵר אֱמֶת בִּלְבָבוֹ.

Those who are upright; who act justly, who speak the truth within their hearts.

לֹא־רָגַל עַל־לְשֹׁנוֹ, לֹא־עָשָׂה לְרֵעֵהוּ רָעָה, וְחֶרְפָּה לֹא־נָשָׂא עַל־קְרֹבוֹ.

Who do not slander others, or wrong them, or bring shame upon them.

נִבְזֶה בְּעֵינָיו נִמְאָס, וְאֶת־יִרְאֵי יְיָ יְכַבֵּד.

Who scorn the lawless, but honor those who revere the Lord.

נִשְׁבַּע לְהָרַע וְלֹא יָמִר. כַּסְפּוֹ לֹא־נָתַן בְּנֶשֶׁךְ וְשֹׁחַד עַל־נָקִי לֹא לָקָח.

Who give their word, and, come what may, do not retract. Who do not exploit others, who never take bribes.

דֹּבֵר שְׁקָרִים לֹא־יִכּוֹן לְנֶגֶד עֵינָי.

The one who tells lies has no standing in My sight.

עֵינַי בְּנֶאֶמְנֵי־אֶרֶץ לָשֶׁבֶת עִמָּדִי. הֹלֵךְ בְּדֶרֶךְ תָּמִים, הוּא יְשָׁרְתֵנִי. קָרוֹב יְיָ לְכָל־קֹרְאָיו, לְכֹל אֲשֶׁר יִקְרָאֻהוּ בֶאֱמֶת.

My eyes are upon the faithful; they may dwell with Me. Only those who walk with integrity shall minister to Me. The Lord is near to all who call upon Him, to all who call upon Him in truth.

שְׁלַח־אוֹרְךָ וַאֲמִתְּךָ, הֵמָּה יַנְחוּנִי; יְבִיאוּנִי אֶל־הַר־קָדְשְׁךָ וְאֶל־מִשְׁכְּנוֹתֶיךָ.

Send forth Your light and Your truth to lead me; let them bring me to Your holy mountain and to Your dwelling-place.

Continue on page 507

2

In ancient times, after the year's final harvest, our people made the hard journey to Jerusalem to offer thanks for the blessing of fruit and grain, and to share the harvest with the poor and needy, as they had been commanded.

We too are commanded: the rich must give to the poor, the strong help the weak, and all live together in peace. And we have learned: not charity, but justice, is demanded of us. We must so order society that all people may earn their daily bread with dignity.

Help us, O God, to understand the needs of others, and give us the will to help them. Put within us that spirit of sympathy and friendship which is a reflection of Your love. May this holy day renew our will to build a world in which the plea of the prophets will be fulfilled:

"Let justice roll down like waters, and righteousness like an everlasting stream. Then with joy shall we draw water from the wells of our salvation."

Continue on page 507

3

From Psalm 85

אֶשְׁמְעָה מַה־יְדַבֵּר הָאֵל יְיָ, כִּי יְדַבֵּר שָׁלוֹם אֶל־עַמּוֹ, וְאֶל־חֲסִידָיו, וְאַל־יָשׁוּבוּ לְכִסְלָה.

אַךְ קָרוֹב לִירֵאָיו יִשְׁעוֹ, לִשְׁכֹּן כָּבוֹד בְּאַרְצֵנוּ.

Let us listen to the words of God the Eternal, for they are words of peace to His people, to His faithful ones, to those who turn their hearts to Him.

Help is near to those who revere Him, that glory may abide in our land.

חֶסֶד־וֶאֱמֶת נִפְגָּשׁוּ, צֶדֶק וְשָׁלוֹם נָשָׁקוּ.

אֱמֶת מֵאֶרֶץ תִּצְמָח, וְצֶדֶק מִשָּׁמַיִם נִשְׁקָף.

Love and truth shall meet, justice and peace shall embrace.

Truth shall spring up from the earth, and justice look down from the sky.

גַּם־יְיָ יִתֵּן הַטּוֹב, וְאַרְצֵנוּ תִּתֵּן יְבוּלָהּ.

צֶדֶק לְפָנָיו יְהַלֵּךְ, וְיָשֵׂם לְדֶרֶךְ פְּעָמָיו.

The Lord shall give of His goodness, the earth shall yield its harvest.

Justice shall go before Him, paving the way for our steps.

Continue on page 507

שמיני עצרת-שמחת תורה

For the Morning of Atzeret–Simchat Torah

One of the following

1

Today we celebrate the eternal creative power
that gives meaning to life.
And we rejoice that in an immeasurable
and unfathomable universe,
we have found light
to dispel the darkness:
The light that is Torah.

There our struggle for awareness
finds high expression.
There the divine flame within us
burns most brightly.
Hope and faith and love
are its enduring foundation.
Now and for ever
we give thanks
for the heritage
that gives life
to us and to our people.

Continue on page 507

2

God is in the faith
by which we overcome
the fear of loneliness, of helplessness,
of failure and of death.

God is in the hope
which, like a shaft of light,
cleaves the dark abyss
of sin, suffering, and despair.

God is in the love
which creates, protects, forgives.
His is the spirit
which broods over the chaos we have wrought,
disturbing its static wrongs,
and stirring into life the formless beginnings
of the new and better world.

You are my portion, my cup,
O Eternal; my life is Yours.
You show me the path of life.
Your presence brings fullness of joy.
Enduring happiness is Your gift.

Continue on page 507

3

From Psalms 67 and 68

God be gracious to us and bless us,
and smile upon us.
Let Your ways be known upon earth,
Your deliverance among all nations.
Let the peoples praise You, O God,
let all the peoples praise You.
Let the nations shout for joy,
for You rule the world with justice.
You judge the peoples with equity,
and guide the nations of the earth.

אֱלֹהִים יְחָנֵּנוּ וִיבָרְכֵנוּ,
יָאֵר פָּנָיו אִתָּנוּ, סֶלָה.
לָדַעַת בָּאָרֶץ דַּרְכֶּךָ,
בְּכָל־גּוֹיִם יְשׁוּעָתֶךָ.
יוֹדוּךָ עַמִּים, אֱלֹהִים,
יוֹדוּךָ עַמִּים כֻּלָּם.
יִשְׂמְחוּ וִירַנְּנוּ לְאֻמִּים,
כִּי־תִשְׁפֹּט עַמִּים מִישׁוֹר,
וּלְאֻמִּים בָּאָרֶץ תַּנְחֵם, סֶלָה.

Let the peoples praise You, O God,
let all the peoples praise You!
The earth has yielded her harvest;

יוֹדוּךָ עַמִּים, אֱלֹהִים,
יוֹדוּךָ עַמִּים כֻּלָּם!
אֶרֶץ נָתְנָה יְבוּלָהּ;

God, our God, has blessed us. יְבָרְכֵנוּ אֱלֹהִים אֱלֹהֵינוּ.
God has blessed us: יְבָרְכֵנוּ אֱלֹהִים:
let the ends of earth revere Him! וְיִירְאוּ אוֹתוֹ כָּל־אַפְסֵי־אָרֶץ!

Your procession, O God, comes into view, רָאוּ הֲלִיכוֹתֶיךָ, אֱלֹהִים,
the procession of my God and King הֲלִיכוֹת אֵלִי מַלְכִּי
into the sanctuary: בַקֹּדֶשׁ:

Singers at its head, musicians behind, קִדְּמוּ שָׁרִים, אַחַר נֹגְנִים,
girls playing tambourines among them. בְּתוֹךְ, עֲלָמוֹת תּוֹפֵפוֹת.

Praise God in your choirs, בְּמַקְהֵלוֹת בָּרְכוּ אֱלֹהִים,
Praise the Lord,
O offspring of Israel! אֲדוֹנָי, מִמְּקוֹר יִשְׂרָאֵל!

ON A WEEKDAY

Psalm 100

הָרִיעוּ לַייָ כָּל־הָאָרֶץ!
עִבְדוּ אֶת־יְיָ בְּשִׂמְחָה!
בֹּאוּ לְפָנָיו בִּרְנָנָה!
דְּעוּ כִּי־יְיָ הוּא אֱלֹהִים.
הוּא עָשָׂנוּ וְלוֹ אֲנַחְנוּ,
עַמּוֹ וְצֹאן מַרְעִיתוֹ.
בֹּאוּ שְׁעָרָיו בְּתוֹדָה,
חֲצֵרֹתָיו בִּתְהִלָּה;
הוֹדוּ לוֹ, בָּרְכוּ שְׁמוֹ!
כִּי־טוֹב יְיָ,
לְעוֹלָם חַסְדּוֹ,
וְעַד־דֹּר וָדֹר אֱמוּנָתוֹ.

Shout joyfully to the Lord, all the earth!
Serve the Lord with gladness!
Come into His presence with singing!
Acknowledge that the Lord is God.
He made us and we are His,
His people, His beloved flock.
Enter His gates with thanksgiving,
His courts with praise;
give thanks to Him, bless His name!
For the Lord is good,
His love is everlasting,
His faithfulness for all generations.

ON SHABBAT

Psalm 92

מִזְמוֹר שִׁיר לְיוֹם הַשַּׁבָּת.

A SONG FOR THE SABBATH DAY

טוֹב לְהֹדוֹת לַייָ, וּלְזַמֵּר לְשִׁמְךָ, עֶלְיוֹן,
לְהַגִּיד בַּבֹּקֶר חַסְדֶּךָ, וֶאֱמוּנָתְךָ בַּלֵּילוֹת,
עֲלֵי־עָשׂוֹר וַעֲלֵי־נָבֶל, עֲלֵי הִגָּיוֹן בְּכִנּוֹר.

It is good to give thanks to the Lord,
to sing hymns to Your name, O Most High!
To tell of Your love in the morning,
to sing at night of Your faithfulness;
to pluck the strings, to sound the lute,
to make the harp vibrate.

כִּי שִׂמַּחְתַּנִי, יְיָ, בְּפָעֳלֶךָ, בְּמַעֲשֵׂי יָדֶיךָ אֲרַנֵּן.
מַה־גָּדְלוּ מַעֲשֶׂיךָ, יְיָ! מְאֹד עָמְקוּ מַחְשְׁבֹתֶיךָ.

Your deeds, O Lord, fill me with gladness,
Your work moves me to song.
How great are Your works, O Lord!
How profound Your design!

אִישׁ־בַּעַר לֹא יֵדָע, וּכְסִיל לֹא־יָבִין אֶת־זֹאת:
בִּפְרֹחַ רְשָׁעִים כְּמוֹ־עֵשֶׂב, וַיָּצִיצוּ כָּל־פֹּעֲלֵי אָוֶן,
לְהִשָּׁמְדָם עֲדֵי־עַד.
וְאַתָּה מָרוֹם לְעֹלָם, יְיָ.

The fool will never learn,
the dullard never grasp this:
the wicked may flourish like grass,
all who do evil may blossom,
yet they are doomed to destruction,
while You, O Lord, are exalted for all time.

כִּי הִנֵּה אֹיְבֶיךָ, יְיָ, כִּי־הִנֵּה אֹיְבֶיךָ יֹאבֵדוּ,
יִתְפָּרְדוּ כָּל־פֹּעֲלֵי אָוֶן.
וַתָּרֶם כִּרְאֵים קַרְנִי, בַּלֹּתִי בְּשֶׁמֶן רַעֲנָן.
וַתַּבֵּט עֵינִי בְּשׁוּרָי, בַּקָּמִים עָלַי מְרֵעִים,
תִּשְׁמַעְנָה אָזְנָי:

See how Your enemies, O Lord,
see how Your enemies shall perish,
how all who do evil shall be scattered.
You lift up my head in pride,
I am bathed in freshening oil.
I shall see the defeat of my foes,
my ears shall hear of their fall.

צַדִּיק כַּתָּמָר יִפְרָח, כְּאֶרֶז בַּלְּבָנוֹן יִשְׂגֶּה.
שְׁתוּלִים בְּבֵית יְיָ, בְּחַצְרוֹת אֱלֹהֵינוּ יַפְרִיחוּ.
עוֹד יְנוּבוּן בְּשֵׂיבָה, דְּשֵׁנִים וְרַעֲנַנִּים יִהְיוּ,
לְהַגִּיד כִּי־יָשָׁר יְיָ, צוּרִי, וְלֹא־עַוְלָתָה בּוֹ.

The righteous shall flourish like palms,
grow tall like cedars in Lebanon.
Rooted in the house of the Lord,
they shall be ever fresh and green,
proclaiming that the Lord is just,
my Rock, in whom there is no wrong.

For All Festivals

Lord our God, Source of life and blessing,
we give thanks for the festivals and their meaning:
for the freedom that gives dignity to our being,
for the Torah that gives direction to our life,
and for the harvest that sustains our bodies.

As our ancestors made pilgrimage to Jerusalem,
there to give thanks to You and to praise Your name,
so are we now voyagers toward You,
as heart and spirit rise to praise You.

READER'S KADDISH

חצי קדיש

יִתְגַּדַּל וְיִתְקַדַּשׁ שְׁמֵהּ רַבָּא בְּעָלְמָא דִּי־בְרָא כִרְעוּתֵהּ,
וְיַמְלִיךְ מַלְכוּתֵהּ בְּחַיֵּיכוֹן וּבְיוֹמֵיכוֹן וּבְחַיֵּי דְכָל־בֵּית
יִשְׂרָאֵל, בַּעֲגָלָא וּבִזְמַן קָרִיב, וְאִמְרוּ: אָמֵן.

יְהֵא שְׁמֵהּ רַבָּא מְבָרַךְ לְעָלַם וּלְעָלְמֵי עָלְמַיָּא.

יִתְבָּרַךְ וְיִשְׁתַּבַּח, וְיִתְפָּאַר וְיִתְרוֹמַם וְיִתְנַשֵּׂא, וְיִתְהַדַּר
וְיִתְעַלֶּה וְיִתְהַלַּל שְׁמֵהּ דְּקוּדְשָׁא, בְּרִיךְ הוּא, לְעֵלָּא מִן
כָּל־בִּרְכָתָא וְשִׁירָתָא, תֻּשְׁבְּחָתָא וְנֶחֱמָתָא דַּאֲמִירָן בְּעָלְמָא,
וְאִמְרוּ: אָמֵן.

Let the glory of God be extolled, let His great name be hallowed in the world whose creation He willed. May His kingdom soon prevail, in our own day, our own lives, and the life of all Israel, and let us say: Amen.

Let His great name be blessed for ever and ever.

Let the name of the Holy One, blessed is He, be glorified, exalted and honored, though He is beyond all the praises, songs, and adorations that we can utter, and let us say: Amen.

◆ ◆

All rise

שמע וברכותיה

בָּרְכוּ אֶת־יְיָ הַמְבֹרָךְ!

Praise the Lord, to whom our praise is due!

בָּרוּךְ יְיָ הַמְבֹרָךְ לְעוֹלָם וָעֶד!

Praised be the Lord, to whom our praise is due, now and for ever!

◆ ◆

CREATION | יוצר

בָּרוּךְ אַתָּה, יְיָ אֱלֹהֵינוּ, מֶלֶךְ הָעוֹלָם, יוֹצֵר אוֹר וּבוֹרֵא חֹשֶׁךְ, עֹשֶׂה שָׁלוֹם וּבוֹרֵא אֶת־הַכֹּל.

Praised be the Lord our God, Ruler of the universe, who makes light and creates darkness, who ordains peace and fashions all things.

הַמֵּאִיר לָאָרֶץ וְלַדָּרִים עָלֶיהָ בְּרַחֲמִים, וּבְטוּבוֹ מְחַדֵּשׁ בְּכָל־יוֹם תָּמִיד מַעֲשֵׂה בְרֵאשִׁית.

With compassion He gives light to the earth and all who dwell there; with goodness He renews the work of creation continually, day by day.

מָה רַבּוּ מַעֲשֶׂיךָ, יְיָ! כֻּלָּם בְּחָכְמָה עָשִׂיתָ, מָלְאָה הָאָרֶץ קִנְיָנֶךָ.

How manifold are Your works, O Lord; in wisdom You have made them all; the earth is full of Your creations.

תִּתְבָּרַךְ, יְיָ אֱלֹהֵינוּ, עַל־שֶׁבַח מַעֲשֵׂה יָדֶיךָ, וְעַל־מְאוֹרֵי־אוֹר שֶׁעָשִׂיתָ: יְפָאֲרוּךָ. סֶּלָה.

בָּרוּךְ אַתָּה, יְיָ, יוֹצֵר הַמְּאוֹרוֹת.

Let all bless You, O Lord our God, for the excellence of Your handiwork, and for the glowing stars that You have made: let them glorify You for ever. Blessed is the Lord, the Maker of light.

◆ ◆

REVELATION

אהבה רבה

אַהֲבָה רַבָּה אֲהַבְתָּנוּ, יְיָ אֱלֹהֵינוּ, חֶמְלָה גְדוֹלָה וִיתֵרָה חָמַלְתָּ עָלֵינוּ. אָבִינוּ מַלְכֵּנוּ, בַּעֲבוּר אֲבוֹתֵינוּ שֶׁבָּטְחוּ בְךָ וַתְּלַמְּדֵם חֻקֵּי חַיִּים, כֵּן תְּחָנֵּנוּ וּתְלַמְּדֵנוּ.

Deep is Your love for us, O Lord our God, and great is Your compassion. Our Maker and King, our ancestors trusted in You, and You taught them the laws of life: be gracious now to us, and teach us.

אָבִינוּ, הָאָב הָרַחֲמָן, הַמְרַחֵם, רַחֵם עָלֵינוּ וְתֵן בְּלִבֵּנוּ לְהָבִין וּלְהַשְׂכִּיל, לִשְׁמֹעַ לִלְמֹד וּלְלַמֵּד, לִשְׁמֹר וְלַעֲשׂוֹת וּלְקַיֵּם אֶת־כָּל־דִּבְרֵי תַלְמוּד תּוֹרָתֶךָ בְּאַהֲבָה.

Have compassion upon us, O Source of mercy, and guide us to know and understand, learn and teach, observe and uphold with love all the teachings of Your Torah.

וְהָאֵר עֵינֵינוּ בְּתוֹרָתֶךָ, וְדַבֵּק לִבֵּנוּ בְּמִצְוֹתֶיךָ, וְיַחֵד לְבָבֵנוּ לְאַהֲבָה וּלְיִרְאָה אֶת־שְׁמֶךָ. וְלֹא־נֵבוֹשׁ לְעוֹלָם וָעֶד, כִּי בְשֵׁם קָדְשְׁךָ הַגָּדוֹל וְהַנּוֹרָא בָּטָחְנוּ. נָגִילָה וְנִשְׂמְחָה בִּישׁוּעָתֶךָ, כִּי אֵל פּוֹעֵל יְשׁוּעוֹת אָתָּה, וּבָנוּ בָחַרְתָּ וְקֵרַבְתָּנוּ לְשִׁמְךָ הַגָּדוֹל סֶלָה בֶּאֱמֶת, לְהוֹדוֹת לְךָ וּלְיַחֶדְךָ בְּאַהֲבָה.

בָּרוּךְ אַתָּה, יְיָ, הַבּוֹחֵר בְּעַמּוֹ יִשְׂרָאֵל בְּאַהֲבָה.

Enlighten us with Your Teaching, help us to hold fast to Your Mitzvot, and unite our hearts to love and revere Your name.

Then shall we never be shamed, for we shall put our trust in You, the great, holy, and awesome One. We shall rejoice and be glad in Your salvation; for You, O God, are the Author of many deliverances. In love You have chosen us and drawn us near to You to serve You in faithfulness and to proclaim Your unity.

Blessed is the Lord, who in love has chosen His people Israel to serve Him.

◆ ◆

שְׁמַע יִשְׂרָאֵל: יְיָ אֱלֹהֵינוּ, יְיָ אֶחָד!

Hear, O Israel: the Lord is our God, the Lord is One!

בָּרוּךְ שֵׁם כְּבוֹד מַלְכוּתוֹ לְעוֹלָם וָעֶד!

Blessed is His glorious kingdom for ever and ever!

All are seated

וְאָהַבְתָּ אֵת יְיָ אֱלֹהֶיךָ בְּכָל־לְבָבְךָ וּבְכָל־נַפְשְׁךָ וּבְכָל־מְאֹדֶךָ. וְהָיוּ הַדְּבָרִים הָאֵלֶּה, אֲשֶׁר אָנֹכִי מְצַוְּךָ הַיּוֹם, עַל־לְבָבֶךָ. וְשִׁנַּנְתָּם לְבָנֶיךָ, וְדִבַּרְתָּ בָּם בְּשִׁבְתְּךָ בְּבֵיתֶךָ, וּבְלֶכְתְּךָ בַדֶּרֶךְ, וּבְשָׁכְבְּךָ וּבְקוּמֶךָ.

You shall love the Lord your God with all your mind, with all your strength, with all your being.
Set these words, which I command you this day, upon your heart. Teach them faithfully to your children; speak of them in your home and on your way, when you lie down and when you rise up.

וּקְשַׁרְתָּם לְאוֹת עַל־יָדֶךָ, וְהָיוּ לְטֹטָפֹת בֵּין עֵינֶיךָ, וּכְתַבְתָּם עַל־מְזֻזוֹת בֵּיתֶךָ, וּבִשְׁעָרֶיךָ.

Bind them as a sign upon your hand; let them be a symbol before your eyes; inscribe them on the doorposts of your house, and on your gates.

לְמַעַן תִּזְכְּרוּ וַעֲשִׂיתֶם אֶת־כָּל־מִצְוֹתָי, וִהְיִיתֶם קְדֹשִׁים לֵאלֹהֵיכֶם. אֲנִי יְיָ אֱלֹהֵיכֶם, אֲשֶׁר הוֹצֵאתִי אֶתְכֶם מֵאֶרֶץ מִצְרַיִם לִהְיוֹת לָכֶם לֵאלֹהִים. אֲנִי יְיָ אֱלֹהֵיכֶם.

Be mindful of all My Mitzvot, and do them: so shall you consecrate yourselves to your God. I, the Lord, am your God who led you out of Egypt to be your God; I, the Lord, am your God.

◆ ◆

REDEMPTION

גאולה

אֱמֶת וְיַצִּיב, וְאָהוּב וְחָבִיב, וְנוֹרָא וְאַדִּיר, וְטוֹב וְיָפֶה הַדָּבָר הַזֶּה עָלֵינוּ לְעוֹלָם וָעֶד.

אֱמֶת, אֱלֹהֵי עוֹלָם מַלְכֵּנוּ, צוּר יַעֲקֹב מָגֵן יִשְׁעֵנוּ.

True and enduring, beloved and precious, awesome, good, and beautiful is this eternal teaching.

This truth we hold to be for ever certain: the Eternal God is our King. He is the Rock of Jacob, our protecting Shield.

לְדֹר וָדֹר הוּא קַיָּם, וּשְׁמוֹ קַיָּם, וְכִסְאוֹ נָכוֹן, וּמַלְכוּתוֹ וֶאֱמוּנָתוֹ לָעַד קַיָּמֶת.

וּדְבָרָיו חָיִים וְקַיָּמִים, נֶאֱמָנִים וְנֶחֱמָדִים, לָעַד וּלְעוֹלְמֵי עוֹלָמִים.

He abides through all generations; His name is Eternal. His throne stands firm; His sovereignty and faithfulness are everlasting.

His words live and endure, true and precious to all eternity.

מִמִּצְרַיִם גְּאַלְתָּנוּ, יְיָ אֱלֹהֵינוּ, וּמִבֵּית עֲבָדִים פְּדִיתָנוּ.

Lord our God, You redeemed us from Egypt;

You set us free from the house of bondage.

עַל־זֹאת שִׁבְּחוּ אֲהוּבִים וְרוֹמְמוּ אֵל, וְנָתְנוּ יְדִידִים זְמִירוֹת, שִׁירוֹת וְתִשְׁבָּחוֹת, בְּרָכוֹת וְהוֹדָאוֹת לַמֶּלֶךְ, אֵל חַי וְקַיָּם.

For this the people who felt Your love sang songs of praise to You:

The living God, high and exalted, mighty and awesome,

רָם וְנִשָּׂא, גָּדוֹל וְנוֹרָא, מַשְׁפִּיל גֵּאִים וּמַגְבִּיהַּ שְׁפָלִים, מוֹצִיא אֲסִירִים וּפוֹדֶה עֲנָוִים, וְעוֹזֵר דַּלִּים, וְעוֹנֶה לְעַמּוֹ בְּעֵת שַׁוְּעָם אֵלָיו.

Who humbles the proud and raises the lowly, who frees the captive and redeems the oppressed,

who is the Answer to all who cry out to Him.

תְּהִלּוֹת לְאֵל עֶלְיוֹן, בָּרוּךְ הוּא וּמְבֹרָךְ. מֹשֶׁה וּבְנֵי יִשְׂרָאֵל
לְךָ עָנוּ שִׁירָה בְּשִׂמְחָה רַבָּה, וְאָמְרוּ כֻלָּם:

All praise to God Most High, the Source of blessing! Like Moses and Israel, we sing to Him this song of rejoicing:

מִי־כָמֹכָה בָּאֵלִם, יְיָ?
מִי כָּמֹכָה, נֶאְדָּר בַּקֹּדֶשׁ,
נוֹרָא תְהִלֹּת, עֹשֵׂה פֶלֶא?

Who is like You, Eternal One, among the gods that are worshipped?
Who is like You, majestic in holiness,
awesome in splendor, doing wonders?

שִׁירָה חֲדָשָׁה שִׁבְּחוּ גְאוּלִים לְשִׁמְךָ עַל־שְׂפַת הַיָּם; יַחַד כֻּלָּם
הוֹדוּ וְהִמְלִיכוּ וְאָמְרוּ: "יְיָ יִמְלֹךְ לְעוֹלָם וָעֶד!"

A new song the redeemed sang to Your name. At the shore of the sea, saved from destruction, they proclaimed Your sovereign power: "The Eternal will reign for ever and ever!"

צוּר יִשְׂרָאֵל, קוּמָה בְּעֶזְרַת יִשְׂרָאֵל, וּפְדֵה כִנְאֻמֶךָ יְהוּדָה
וְיִשְׂרָאֵל. גֹּאֲלֵנוּ יְיָ צְבָאוֹת שְׁמוֹ, קְדוֹשׁ יִשְׂרָאֵל.
בָּרוּךְ אַתָּה, יְיָ, גָּאַל יִשְׂרָאֵל.

O Rock of Israel, come to Israel's help. Fulfill Your promise of redemption for Judah and Israel. Our Redeemer is the Lord of Hosts, the Holy One of Israel. Blessed is the Lord, the Redeemer of Israel.

◆ ◆

All rise

תפלה

אֲדֹנָי, שְׂפָתַי תִּפְתָּח, וּפִי יַגִּיד תְּהִלָּתֶךָ.

Eternal God, open my lips, that my mouth may declare Your glory.

GOD OF ALL GENERATIONS — אבות

בָּרוּךְ אַתָּה, יְיָ אֱלֹהֵינוּ וֵאלֹהֵי אֲבוֹתֵינוּ, אֱלֹהֵי אַבְרָהָם, אֱלֹהֵי יִצְחָק, וֵאלֹהֵי יַעֲקֹב: הָאֵל הַגָּדוֹל, הַגִּבּוֹר וְהַנּוֹרָא, אֵל עֶלְיוֹן.

We praise You, Lord our God and God of all generations: God of Abraham, God of Isaac, God of Jacob; great, mighty, and awesome God, God supreme.

גּוֹמֵל חֲסָדִים טוֹבִים, וְקוֹנֵה הַכֹּל, וְזוֹכֵר חַסְדֵי אָבוֹת, וּמֵבִיא גְאֻלָּה לִבְנֵי בְנֵיהֶם, לְמַעַן שְׁמוֹ, בְּאַהֲבָה.

Master of all the living, Your ways are ways of love. You remember the faithfulness of our ancestors, and in love bring redemption to their children's children for the sake of Your name.

מֶלֶךְ עוֹזֵר וּמוֹשִׁיעַ וּמָגֵן. בָּרוּךְ אַתָּה, יְיָ, מָגֵן אַבְרָהָם.

You are our King and our Help, our Savior and our Shield. Blessed is the Lord, the Shield of Abraham.

◆ ◆

GOD'S POWER — גבורות

אַתָּה גִּבּוֹר לְעוֹלָם, אֲדֹנָי, מְחַיֵּה הַכֹּל אַתָּה, רַב לְהוֹשִׁיעַ.

Eternal is Your might, O Lord; all life is Your gift; great is Your power to save!

מְכַלְכֵּל חַיִּים בְּחֶסֶד, מְחַיֵּה הַכֹּל בְּרַחֲמִים רַבִּים. סוֹמֵךְ נוֹפְלִים, וְרוֹפֵא חוֹלִים, וּמַתִּיר אֲסוּרִים, וּמְקַיֵּם אֱמוּנָתוֹ לִישֵׁנֵי עָפָר.

With love You sustain the living, with great compassion give life to all. You send help to the falling and healing to the sick; You bring freedom to the captive and keep faith with those who sleep in the dust.

מִי כָמוֹךָ, בַּעַל גְּבוּרוֹת, וּמִי דּוֹמֶה לָּךְ, מֶלֶךְ מֵמִית וּמְחַיֶּה וּמַצְמִיחַ יְשׁוּעָה?

וְנֶאֱמָן אַתָּה לְהַחֲיוֹת הַכֹּל. בָּרוּךְ אַתָּה, יְיָ, מְחַיֵּה הַכֹּל.

Who is like You, Master of Might? Who is Your equal, O Lord of life and death, Source of salvation? Blessed is the Lord, the Source of life.

◆

FOR THE FIRST MORNING OF PESACH AND FOR ATZERET—SIMCHAT TORAH

A WORLD OF LIFE

O Source of life and blessing, at this season, from of old, our people in the land of Israel have prayed for rain and dew, for sustenance and health. We, too, now call upon You: Grant that all Your children may enjoy the fruits of the earth in abundance, and that none may ever suffer hunger. May rain and dew descend in season.

O Fountain of light and truth, Your teaching is like rain that falls on the parched soil; Your word is like dew settling upon the flower; Your Torah bears fruits of righteousness.

So it has been said: "I will pour water upon the thirsty land and streams upon the dry ground; I will pour My spirit upon your children and My blessing on your descendants."

לִבְרָכָה וְלֹא לִקְלָלָה, אָמֵן.

Let blessings abound and hurts be healed. Amen.

לְשׂוֹבַע וְלֹא לְרָזוֹן, אָמֵן.

Let us know plenty and escape famine. Amen.

לְחַיִּים וְלֹא לְמָוֶת, אָמֵן.

Let there be life and not destruction. Amen.

• •

קדושה

SANCTIFICATION

נְקַדֵּשׁ אֶת־שִׁמְךָ בָּעוֹלָם, כְּשֵׁם שֶׁמַּקְדִּישִׁים אוֹתוֹ בִּשְׁמֵי מָרוֹם, כַּכָּתוּב עַל־יַד נְבִיאֶךָ: וְקָרָא זֶה אֶל־זֶה וְאָמַר:

We sanctify Your name on earth, even as all things, to the ends of time and space, proclaim Your holiness; and in the words of the prophet we say:

קָדוֹשׁ, קָדוֹשׁ, קָדוֹשׁ יְיָ צְבָאוֹת, מְלֹא כָל־הָאָרֶץ כְּבוֹדוֹ.

Holy, Holy, Holy is the Lord of Hosts; the fullness of the whole earth is His glory!

אַדִּיר אַדִּירֵנוּ, יְיָ אֲדוֹנֵנוּ, מָה־אַדִּיר שִׁמְךָ בְּכָל־הָאָרֶץ!

Source of our strength, Sovereign Lord, how majestic is Your presence in all the earth!

בָּרוּךְ כְּבוֹד יְיָ מִמְּקוֹמוֹ.

Blessed is the glory of God in heaven and earth.

אֶחָד הוּא אֱלֹהֵינוּ, הוּא אָבִינוּ, הוּא מַלְכֵּנוּ, הוּא מוֹשִׁיעֵנוּ, וְהוּא יַשְׁמִיעֵנוּ בְּרַחֲמָיו לְעֵינֵי כָּל־חָי:

He alone is our God and our Creator; He is our Ruler and our Helper; and in His mercy He reveals Himself in the sight of all the living:

I AM ADONAI YOUR GOD! "אֲנִי יְיָ אֱלֹהֵיכֶם!"

יִמְלֹךְ יְיָ לְעוֹלָם, אֱלֹהַיִךְ צִיּוֹן, לְדֹר וָדֹר. הַלְלוּיָהּ!

The Lord shall reign for ever; your God, O Zion, from generation to generation. Halleluyah!

לְדוֹר וָדוֹר נַגִּיד גָּדְלֶךָ, וּלְנֵצַח נְצָחִים קְדֻשָּׁתְךָ נַקְדִּישׁ.
וְשִׁבְחֲךָ, אֱלֹהֵינוּ, מִפִּינוּ לֹא יָמוּשׁ לְעוֹלָם וָעֶד.
בָּרוּךְ אַתָּה, יְיָ, הָאֵל הַקָּדוֹשׁ.

To all generations we will make known Your greatness, and to all eternity proclaim Your holiness. Your praise, O God, shall never depart from our lips. Blessed is the Lord, the holy God.

All are seated

◆ ◆

THE HOLINESS OF YOM TOV קדושת היום

אַתָּה בְחַרְתָּנוּ מִכָּל־הָעַמִּים, אָהַבְתָּ אוֹתָנוּ, וְרָצִיתָ בָּנוּ, וְרוֹמַמְתָּנוּ מִכָּל־הַלְּשׁוֹנוֹת, וְקִדַּשְׁתָּנוּ בְּמִצְוֹתֶיךָ. וְקֵרַבְתָּנוּ, מַלְכֵּנוּ, לַעֲבוֹדָתֶךָ, וְשִׁמְךָ הַגָּדוֹל וְהַקָּדוֹשׁ עָלֵינוּ קָרָאתָ.

In love and favor, O God, You have chosen us from all the peoples, exalting us by hallowing us with Your Mitzvot. Our Sovereign, You have summoned us to Your service, that through us Your great and holy name may become known in all the earth.

וַתִּתֶּן לָנוּ, יְיָ אֱלֹהֵינוּ, בְּאַהֲבָה [שַׁבָּתוֹת לִמְנוּחָה וּ] מוֹעֲדִים לְשִׂמְחָה, חַגִּים וּזְמַנִּים לְשָׂשׂוֹן: אֶת־יוֹם [הַשַּׁבָּת הַזֶּה וְאֶת־יוֹם]

In Your love, O Lord our God, You have given us [Sabbaths of rest,] feasts of gladness and seasons of joy: this [Sabbath day and this] festival of

Pesach — season of our freedom,	חַג הַמַּצּוֹת הַזֶּה – זְמַן חֵרוּתֵנוּ,
Shavuot — season of revelation,	חַג הַשָּׁבֻעוֹת הַזֶּה – זְמַן מַתַּן תּוֹרָתֵנוּ,
Sukkot — season of thanksgiving,	חַג הַסֻּכּוֹת הַזֶּה – זְמַן שִׂמְחָתֵנוּ,
Atzeret–Simchat Torah — season of our gladness,	הַשְּׁמִינִי חַג הָעֲצֶרֶת הַזֶּה – זְמַן שִׂמְחָתֵנוּ,

מִקְרָא קֹדֶשׁ, זֵכֶר לִיצִיאַת מִצְרָיִם.

to unite in worship and recall the Exodus from Egypt.

◆

אֱלֹהֵינוּ וֵאלֹהֵי אֲבוֹתֵינוּ, יַעֲלֶה וְיָבֹא וְיִזָּכֵר זִכְרוֹנֵנוּ וְזִכְרוֹן כָּל־עַמְּךָ בֵּית יִשְׂרָאֵל לְפָנֶיךָ, לְטוֹבָה לְחֵן לְחֶסֶד וּלְרַחֲמִים לְחַיִּים וּלְשָׁלוֹם בְּיוֹם

Our God and God of all ages, be mindful of Your people Israel on this

Feast of Pesach,	חַג הַמַּצּוֹת הַזֶּה.
Feast of Shavuot,	חַג הַשָּׁבֻעוֹת הַזֶּה.
Feast of Sukkot,	חַג הַסֻּכּוֹת הַזֶּה.
Feast of Atzeret–Simchat Torah,	הַשְּׁמִינִי חַג הָעֲצֶרֶת הַזֶּה.

and renew in us love and compassion, goodness, life, and peace.

זָכְרֵנוּ, יְיָ אֱלֹהֵינוּ, בּוֹ לְטוֹבָה. אָמֵן.

This day remember us for well-being. Amen.

וּפָקְדֵנוּ בוֹ לִבְרָכָה. אָמֵן.

This day bless us with Your nearness. Amen.

וְהוֹשִׁיעֵנוּ בוֹ לְחַיִּים. אָמֵן.

This day help us to a fuller life. Amen.

וְהַשִּׂיאֵנוּ, יְיָ אֱלֹהֵינוּ, אֶת־בִּרְכַּת מוֹעֲדֶיךָ לְחַיִּים וּלְשָׁלוֹם, לְשִׂמְחָה וּלְשָׂשׂוֹן, כַּאֲשֶׁר רָצִיתָ, וְאָמַרְתָּ לְבָרְכֵנוּ. אֱלֹהֵינוּ וֵאלֹהֵי אֲבוֹתֵינוּ, [רְצֵה בִמְנוּחָתֵנוּ] קַדְּשֵׁנוּ בְּמִצְוֹתֶיךָ, וְתֵן חֶלְקֵנוּ בְּתוֹרָתֶךָ. שַׂבְּעֵנוּ מִטּוּבֶךָ, וְשַׂמְּחֵנוּ בִּישׁוּעָתֶךָ, וְטַהֵר לִבֵּנוּ לְעָבְדְּךָ בֶּאֱמֶת. וְהַנְחִילֵנוּ, יְיָ אֱלֹהֵינוּ, [בְּאַהֲבָה וּבְרָצוֹן,] בְּשִׂמְחָה וּבְשָׂשׂוֹן [שַׁבַּת וּ] מוֹעֲדֵי קָדְשֶׁךָ, וְיִשְׂמְחוּ בְךָ יִשְׂרָאֵל, מְקַדְּשֵׁי שְׁמֶךָ. בָּרוּךְ אַתָּה, יְיָ, מְקַדֵּשׁ [הַשַּׁבָּת וְ] יִשְׂרָאֵל וְהַזְּמַנִּים.

Bestow upon us the blessing of Your holy Festivals, and may we so celebrate them as to be worthy of Your favor.

Our God and God of ages past, sanctify us with Your Mitzvot, and let Your Torah be our way of life. [May our rest on this day be pleasing in Your sight.] Satisfy us with Your goodness, gladden us with Your salvation, and purify our hearts to serve You in truth. [In Your gracious love let Your holy Sabbath remain our heritage.] Let us celebrate Your holy Festivals with joy and gladness, that all Israel, hallowing Your name, may have cause to rejoice. Blessed is the Lord, who hallows [the Sabbath,] the House of Israel and the Festivals.

◆ ◆

WORSHIP — עבודה

רְצֵה, יְיָ אֱלֹהֵינוּ, בְּעַמְּךָ יִשְׂרָאֵל, וּתְפִלָּתָם בְּאַהֲבָה תְקַבֵּל, וּתְהִי לְרָצוֹן תָּמִיד עֲבוֹדַת יִשְׂרָאֵל עַמֶּךָ.

בָּרוּךְ אַתָּה, יְיָ, שֶׁאוֹתְךָ לְבַדְּךָ בְּיִרְאָה נַעֲבוֹד.

Look with favor, O Lord, upon us, and may our service be acceptable to You.

Blessed is the Eternal God, whom alone we serve with reverence.

◆ ◆

MEDITATION

Hear my prayer, O God: I pray as my fathers prayed, I hope as my mothers hoped, when on the great festivals they turned their hearts to You.

These festivals once saw them go to Jerusalem with sacrifice and song. Then the land was laid waste, her cities ruined, her people driven far from their homes. Now my people have returned to Zion. They have rebuilt her cities, restored her soil. Keep them safe from anguish and war; prosper their work; inspire their hearts to love and serve You. And let there be peace in the four corners of the earth: as You show compassion for Zion, so let the homeless of every land and race find a home. Then shall all the world hold festival, and songs of praise shall ascend to the heavens. Blessed are You, O God, whose presence gives life to Israel and all the world.

◆ ◆

THANKSGIVING

הודאה

מוֹדִים אֲנַֽחְנוּ לָךְ, שָׁאַתָּה הוּא יְיָ אֱלֹהֵֽינוּ וֵאלֹהֵי אֲבוֹתֵֽינוּ לְעוֹלָם וָעֶד. צוּר חַיֵּֽינוּ, מָגֵן יִשְׁעֵֽנוּ, אַתָּה הוּא לְדוֹר וָדוֹר. נוֹדֶה לְּךָ וּנְסַפֵּר תְּהִלָּתֶֽךָ, עַל־חַיֵּֽינוּ הַמְּסוּרִים בְּיָדֶֽךָ, וְעַל־נִשְׁמוֹתֵֽינוּ הַפְּקוּדוֹת לָךְ, וְעַל־נִסֶּֽיךָ שֶׁבְּכָל־יוֹם עִמָּֽנוּ, וְעַל־נִפְלְאוֹתֶֽיךָ וְטוֹבוֹתֶֽיךָ שֶׁבְּכָל־עֵת, עֶֽרֶב וָבֹֽקֶר וְצָהֳרָֽיִם. הַטּוֹב: כִּי לֹא־כָלוּ רַחֲמֶֽיךָ, וְהַמְרַחֵם: כִּי־לֹא תַֽמּוּ חֲסָדֶֽיךָ, מֵעוֹלָם קִוִּֽינוּ לָךְ.

We gratefully acknowledge that You are the Lord our God and God of our people, the God of all generations. You are the Rock of our life, the Power that shields us in every age. We thank You and sing Your praises: for our lives, which are in Your hand; for our souls, which are in Your keeping; for the signs of Your presence we encounter every day; and for Your wondrous gifts at all times, morning, noon, and night. You are Goodness: Your mercies never end; You are Compassion: Your love will never fail. You have always been our hope.

וְעַל כֻּלָּם יִתְבָּרַךְ וְיִתְרוֹמַם שִׁמְךָ, מַלְכֵּנוּ, תָּמִיד לְעוֹלָם וָעֶד. וְכל הַחַיִּים יוֹדוּךָ סֶּלָה, וִיהַלְלוּ אֶת שִׁמְךָ בֶּאֱמֶת, הָאֵל יְשׁוּעָתֵנוּ וְעֶזְרָתֵנוּ סֶלָה. בָּרוּךְ אַתָּה, יְיָ, הַטּוֹב שִׁמְךָ וּלְךָ נָאֶה לְהוֹדוֹת.

For all these things, O Sovereign God, let Your name be for ever exalted and blessed. O God our Redeemer and Helper, let all who live affirm You and praise Your name in truth. Lord, whose nature is Goodness, we give You thanks and praise.

• •

PEACE ברכת שלום

אֱלֹהֵינוּ וֵאלֹהֵי אֲבוֹתֵינוּ, בָּרְכֵנוּ בַּבְּרָכָה הַמְשֻׁלֶּשֶׁת הַכְּתוּבָה בַּתּוֹרָה:

Our God and God of all ages, bless us with the threefold benediction of the Torah:

יְבָרֶכְךָ יְיָ וְיִשְׁמְרֶךָ. כֵּן יְהִי רָצוֹן!

The Lord bless you and keep you.
Be this His will!

יָאֵר יְיָ פָּנָיו אֵלֶיךָ וִיחֻנֶּךָּ. כֵּן יְהִי רָצוֹן!

The Lord look kindly upon you and be gracious to you.
Be this His will!

יִשָּׂא יְיָ פָּנָיו אֵלֶיךָ וְיָשֵׂם לְךָ שָׁלוֹם. כֵּן יְהִי רָצוֹן!

The Lord bestow His favor upon you and give you peace.
Be this His will!

שִׂים שָׁלוֹם, טוֹבָה וּבְרָכָה, חֵן וָחֶסֶד וְרַחֲמִים, עָלֵינוּ וְעַל־כָּל־יִשְׂרָאֵל וְעַל־כָּל־הָעַמִּים. בָּרְכֵנוּ, אָבִינוּ, כֻּלָּנוּ כְּאֶחָד, בְּאוֹר פָּנֶיךָ, כִּי בְאוֹר פָּנֶיךָ נָתַתָּ לָּנוּ, יְיָ אֱלֹהֵינוּ, תּוֹרַת

חַיִּים, וְאַהֲבַת חֶסֶד, וּצְדָקָה וּבְרָכָה וְרַחֲמִים, וְחַיִּים וְשָׁלוֹם. וְטוֹב בְּעֵינֶיךָ לְבָרֵךְ אֶת־עַמְּךָ יִשְׂרָאֵל, וְאֶת־כָּל־הָעַמִּים, בְּכָל־עֵת וּבְכָל־שָׁעָה בִּשְׁלוֹמֶךָ. בָּרוּךְ אַתָּה, יְיָ, עוֹשֵׂה הַשָּׁלוֹם.

Grant peace and happiness, blessing and mercy, to all Israel and all the world. Bless us, O God, with the light of Your presence, for by that light we find life, justice, and peace. May Your children unite to do Your will: to establish peace and justice throughout the world, so that the nations are drawn together by the bond of friendship, and Your law of truth hold sway over our lives. Blessed is the Lord, the Source of peace.

◆ ◆

SILENT PRAYER

אֱלֹהַי, נְצוֹר לְשׁוֹנִי מֵרָע וּשְׂפָתַי מִדַּבֵּר מִרְמָה.
הוֹדִיעֵנִי דֶּרֶךְ־זוּ אֵלֵךְ, כִּי־אֵלֶיךָ נָשָׂאתִי נַפְשִׁי.
לֵב טָהוֹר בְּרָא־לִי, אֱלֹהִים, וְרוּחַ נָכוֹן חַדֵּשׁ בְּקִרְבִּי.
שְׁגִיאוֹת מִי־יָבִין? מִנִּסְתָּרוֹת נַקֵּנִי!
הַדְרִיכֵנִי בַּאֲמִתֶּךָ, וְלַמְּדֵנִי, כִּי־אַתָּה אֱלֹהֵי יִשְׁעִי, אוֹתְךָ קִוִּיתִי כָּל־הַיּוֹם.
פְּתַח לִבִּי בְּתוֹרָתֶךָ, וּבְמִצְוֹתֶיךָ תִּרְדּוֹף נַפְשִׁי.

O God, keep my tongue from evil, and my lips from deceitful speech. Let me know the way I should go, for to You do I lift up my soul. Create in me a clean heart, O God, and renew a steadfast spirit within me. But who can see all his own failings? Rid me of faults that are hidden! Lead me in Your truth, and teach me. You are God my Helper, and for You do I wait all the day. Open my heart to Your teaching, and I will make haste to do Your commandments.

◆ ◆

יִהְיוּ לְרָצוֹן אִמְרֵי־פִי וְהֶגְיוֹן לִבִּי לְפָנֶיךָ, יְיָ, צוּרִי וְגוֹאֲלִי.

May the words of my mouth, and the meditations of my heart, be acceptable to You, O Lord, my Rock and my Redeemer.

or

עֹשֶׂה שָׁלוֹם בִּמְרוֹמָיו, הוּא יַעֲשֶׂה שָׁלוֹם עָלֵינוּ וְעַל כָּל־
יִשְׂרָאֵל, וְאִמְרוּ אָמֵן.

May He who causes peace to reign in the high heavens let peace descend on us, on all Israel, and all the world.

✦ ✦

ON SUKKOT, HOLDING THE LULAV AND ETROG

בָּרוּךְ אַתָּה, יְיָ אֱלֹהֵינוּ, מֶלֶךְ הָעוֹלָם,
אֲשֶׁר קִדְּשָׁנוּ בְּמִצְוֹתָיו וְצִוָּנוּ עַל־נְטִילַת לוּלָב.

Blessed is the Lord our God, Ruler of the universe, who hallows us with His Mitzvot, and gives us the Mitzvah of the Lulav.

✦ ✦

Hallel

הלל

בָּרוּךְ אַתָּה, יְיָ אֱלֹהֵינוּ, מֶלֶךְ הָעוֹלָם,
אֲשֶׁר קִדְּשָׁנוּ בְּמִצְוֹתָיו וְצִוָּנוּ לִקְרֹא אֶת־הַהַלֵּל.

Blessed is the Lord our God, Ruler of the universe, who hallows us with His Mitzvot, and inspires us to sing Hymns of Praise.

◆ ◆

From Psalm 113

הַלְלוּיָהּ!
הַלְלוּ, עַבְדֵי יְיָ, הַלְלוּ אֶת־שֵׁם יְיָ!
יְהִי שֵׁם יְיָ מְבֹרָךְ, מֵעַתָּה וְעַד־עוֹלָם.

Halleluyah! Sing praises, you servants of the Lord, praise His name!

Blessed be the name of the Eternal, now and for ever.

מִמִּזְרַח־שֶׁמֶשׁ עַד־מְבוֹאוֹ, מְהֻלָּל שֵׁם יְיָ.
רָם עַל־כָּל־גּוֹיִם יְיָ, עַל הַשָּׁמַיִם כְּבוֹדוֹ.

Let the Lord's name be praised from sunrise to sunset.

The Eternal is supreme above the nations, His glory higher than the heavens.

מִי כַּייָ אֱלֹהֵינוּ, הַמַּגְבִּיהִי לָשָׁבֶת,
הַמַּשְׁפִּילִי לִרְאוֹת בַּשָּׁמַיִם וּבָאָרֶץ?

Who is like our eternal God in heaven and earth?

Who so exalted, and yet so near?

מְקִימִי מֵעָפָר דָּל, מֵאַשְׁפֹּת יָרִים אֶבְיוֹן,
לְהוֹשִׁיבִי עִם־נְדִיבִים, עִם נְדִיבֵי עַמּוֹ.
הַלְלוּיָהּ!

He raises the poor from the dust, He lifts the wretched from the dirt,

so that they sit with princes, with the princes of His people. Halleluyah!

◆ ◆

Psalm 114

בְּצֵאת יִשְׂרָאֵל מִמִּצְרָיִם, בֵּית יַעֲקֹב מֵעַם לֹעֵז,
הָיְתָה יְהוּדָה לְקָדְשׁוֹ, יִשְׂרָאֵל מַמְשְׁלוֹתָיו.
הַיָּם רָאָה וַיָּנֹס, הַיַּרְדֵּן יִסֹּב לְאָחוֹר.
הֶהָרִים רָקְדוּ כְאֵילִים, גְּבָעוֹת כִּבְנֵי־צֹאן.

When Israel went forth from Egypt, the House of Jacob from an alien people, Judah became His sanctuary, Israel His dominion.

The sea saw it and fled, the Jordan turned back.
The mountains skipped like rams, the hills like young rams.

מַה־לְּךָ הַיָּם כִּי תָנוּס? הַיַּרְדֵּן, תִּסֹּב לְאָחוֹר?
הֶהָרִים, תִּרְקְדוּ כְאֵילִים? גְּבָעוֹת, כִּבְנֵי־צֹאן?
מִלִּפְנֵי אָדוֹן חוּלִי אָרֶץ, מִלִּפְנֵי אֱלוֹהַּ יַעֲקֹב,
הַהֹפְכִי הַצּוּר אֲגַם־מָיִם, חַלָּמִישׁ לְמַעְיְנוֹ־מָיִם.

What ails you, O sea, that you run away? Why, O Jordan, do you turn back? O mountains, why do you skip like rams? Why, O hills, like young lambs?

Dance, O earth, before the Lord; at the presence of the God of Jacob, who turns the rock into a pool of water, the flint into a flowing spring.

◆ ◆

From Psalm 115

יִשְׂרָאֵל, בְּטַח בַּייָ; עֶזְרָם וּמָגִנָּם הוּא.
יְיָ זְכָרָנוּ, יְבָרֵךְ, יְבָרֵךְ אֶת־בֵּית יִשְׂרָאֵל, יְבָרֵךְ אֶת־בֵּית אַהֲרֹן. יְבָרֵךְ יִרְאֵי יְיָ, הַקְּטַנִּים עִם־הַגְּדֹלִים.

Trust in the Lord, O Israel, for He is your Help and your Shield. The Lord is mindful of us, He will bless us.

He will bless the House of Israel, He will bless all who revere Him, the small and the great.

בְּרוּכִים אַתֶּם לַיָי, עֹשֵׂה שָׁמַיִם וָאָרֶץ.
הַשָּׁמַיִם שָׁמַיִם לַיָי, וְהָאָרֶץ נָתַן לִבְנֵי־אָדָם.

You will be blessed by the Lord, the Maker of heaven and earth.

The heavens belong to the Lord, but the earth is given to mortals.

לֹא־הַמֵּתִים יְהַלְלוּ־יָהּ, וְלֹא כָּל־יֹרְדֵי דוּמָה.
וַאֲנַחְנוּ נְבָרֵךְ יָהּ מֵעַתָּה וְעַד־עוֹלָם. הַלְלוּיָהּ!

It is not the dead who praise the Lord, it is not those who go down to silence.

But we shall bless the Lord now and for ever. Halleluyah!

◆ ◆

From Psalm 116

מָה־אָשִׁיב לַיָי כָּל־תַּגְמוּלוֹהִי עָלָי?
כּוֹס־יְשׁוּעוֹת אֶשָּׂא, וּבְשֵׁם יְיָ אֶקְרָא.
לְךָ־אֶזְבַּח זֶבַח תּוֹדָה, וּבְשֵׁם יְיָ אֶקְרָא!

How can I repay the Lord for all His gifts to me? I will lift up the cup of deliverance and glorify the name of the Lord. I will offer You the tribute of thanksgiving, and glorify Your name, O Lord!

◆ ◆

Psalm 117

הַלְלוּ אֶת־יְיָ כָּל־גּוֹיִם!
שַׁבְּחוּהוּ כָּל־הָאֻמִּים!
כִּי גָבַר עָלֵינוּ חַסְדּוֹ,
וֶאֱמֶת־יְיָ לְעוֹלָם.
הַלְלוּיָהּ!

Praise the Lord, all you nations!
extol Him, all you peoples!
For great is His love for us,
everlasting His faithfulness.
Halleluyah!

◆ ◆

From Psalm 118

הודו לַייָ כִּי־טוֹב,
כִּי לְעוֹלָם חַסְדּוֹ.

O give thanks to the Lord, for He is good;
For His love is everlasting.

יֹאמַר־נָא יִשְׂרָאֵל:
כִּי לְעוֹלָם חַסְדּוֹ.

Let Israel now say:
His love is everlasting.

יֹאמְרוּ־נָא בֵית־אַהֲרֹן:
כִּי לְעוֹלָם חַסְדּוֹ.

Let the House of Aaron now say:
His love is everlasting.

יֹאמְרוּ־נָא יִרְאֵי יְיָ:
כִּי לְעוֹלָם חַסְדּוֹ.

Let all who revere the Lord now say:
His love is everlasting.

מִן־הַמֵּצַר קָרָאתִי יָּהּ, עָנָנִי בַמֶּרְחָב יָהּ.
יְיָ לִי, לֹא אִירָא; מַה־יַּעֲשֶׂה לִי אָדָם?

In distress I called upon the Lord; He answered me by setting me free.

With the Lord at my side, I am not afraid: what can mere mortals do to me?

טוֹב לַחֲסוֹת בַּייָ מִבְּטֹחַ בָּאָדָם.
טוֹב לַחֲסוֹת בַּייָ מִבְּטֹחַ בִּנְדִיבִים.

It is better to trust in the Lord than to rely on mortals.

It is better to trust in the Lord than to rely on princes.

כָּל־גּוֹיִם סְבָבוּנִי, בְּשֵׁם יְיָ כִּי אֲמִילַם! סַבּוּנִי גַם־סְבָבוּנִי,
בְּשֵׁם יְיָ כִּי אֲמִילַם!
סַבּוּנִי כִדְבוֹרִים, דֹּעֲכוּ כְּאֵשׁ קוֹצִים, בְּשֵׁם יְיָ כִּי אֲמִילַם!

Though all the nations surround me, in God's name I will overcome them! Though they surround me and blockade me, in God's name I will overcome them!

Though they swarm about me like bees, and blaze like a fire among thorns, in the name of God I will overcome them!

עָזִּי וְזִמְרָת יָהּ, וַיְהִי־לִי לִישׁוּעָה. קוֹל רִנָּה וִישׁוּעָה בְּאָהֳלֵי צַדִּיקִים: יְמִין יְיָ עֹשָׂה חָיִל! יְמִין יְיָ רוֹמֵמָה, יְמִין יְיָ עֹשָׂה חָיִל!

The Lord is my strength and my shield; He has become my help. Hear! Glad songs of triumph in the tents of the just:

The power of the Lord is triumphant!

The power of the Lord is supreme!

The power of the Lord is triumphant!

לֹא־אָמוּת כִּי־אֶחְיֶה, וַאֲסַפֵּר מַעֲשֵׂי יָהּ.
פִּתְחוּ־לִי שַׁעֲרֵי־צֶדֶק; אָבֹא־בָם, אוֹדֶה יָהּ.

I shall not die but live
and tell the deeds of the Lord.

Open for me the gates of righteousness;
let me enter and give thanks to the Lord.

זֶה־הַשַּׁעַר לַייָ, צַדִּיקִים יָבֹאוּ בוֹ.
אוֹדְךָ כִּי עֲנִיתָנִי, וַתְּהִי־לִי לִישׁוּעָה.

This is the gateway to the Lord;
the righteous shall enter it.

I thank You, for You have answered me,
and have become my help.

אֶבֶן מָאֲסוּ הַבּוֹנִים, הָיְתָה לְרֹאשׁ פִּנָּה.
מֵאֵת יְיָ הָיְתָה זֹּאת; הִיא נִפְלָאת בְּעֵינֵינוּ.

The stone the builders rejected
has become the chief cornerstone.

This is the Lord's doing;
it is wonderful in our eyes.

זֶה־הַיּוֹם עָשָׂה יְיָ, נָגִילָה וְנִשְׂמְחָה בוֹ.

This is the day the Lord has made;
let us rejoice and be glad in it.

Eternal God, be our help! אָנָּא יְיָ, הוֹשִׁיעָה נָּא!

Eternal God, be our help! אָנָּא יְיָ, הוֹשִׁיעָה נָּא!

Eternal God, sustain us!	!אָנָּא יְיָ, הַצְלִיחָה נָּא
Eternal God, sustain us!	!אָנָּא יְיָ, הַצְלִיחָה נָּא
Blessed is the one who comes to seek the Lord;	בָּרוּךְ הַבָּא בְּשֵׁם יְיָ,
we bless you from the house of the Lord.	בֵּרַכְנוּכֶם מִבֵּית יְיָ.
You are my God, and I will thank You;	אֵלִי אַתָּה וְאוֹדֶךָּ,
You are my God, I will exalt You.	אֱלֹהַי אֲרוֹמְמֶךָּ.
O give thanks to the Lord, for He is good;	הוֹדוּ לַיְיָ כִּי־טוֹב,
For His love is everlasting.	כִּי לְעוֹלָם חַסְדּוֹ.

◆ ◆

The Ritual for the Reading of Torah begins on the next page.

On Atzeret–Simchat Torah, continue on page 538.

סדר קריאת התורה ליום טוב

For the Reading of the Torah

אֵין כָּמוֹךָ בָאֱלֹהִים, יְיָ, וְאֵין כְּמַעֲשֶׂיךָ. מַלְכוּתְךָ מַלְכוּת כָּל־עוֹלָמִים וּמֶמְשַׁלְתְּךָ בְּכָל־דּוֹר וָדֹר.

There is none like You, O Lord, among the gods that are worshipped, and there are no deeds like Yours. Your kingdom is an everlasting kingdom, and Your dominion endures through all generations.

יְיָ מֶלֶךְ, יְיָ מָלָךְ, יְיָ יִמְלֹךְ לְעוֹלָם וָעֶד. יְיָ עֹז לְעַמּוֹ יִתֵּן, יְיָ יְבָרֵךְ אֶת־עַמּוֹ בַשָּׁלוֹם.

The Lord rules; the Lord will reign for ever and ever. May the Lord give strength to His people; may the Lord bless His people with peace.

◆ ◆

All rise

אַב הָרַחֲמִים, הֵיטִיבָה בִרְצוֹנְךָ אֶת־צִיּוֹן; תִּבְנֶה חוֹמוֹת יְרוּשָׁלָיִם.

כִּי בְךָ לְבַד בָּטָחְנוּ, מֶלֶךְ אֵל רָם וְנִשָּׂא, אֲדוֹן עוֹלָמִים.

Source of mercy, let Your goodness be a blessing to Zion; let Jerusalem be rebuilt.
In You alone do we trust, O Sovereign God, high and exalted, Lord of all the worlds.

◆ ◆

The Ark is opened

יְיָ, יְיָ אֵל רַחוּם וְחַנּוּן, אֶרֶךְ אַפַּיִם וְרַב־חֶסֶד וֶאֱמֶת, נֹצֵר חֶסֶד לָאֲלָפִים, נֹשֵׂא עָוֹן וָפֶשַׁע וְחַטָּאָה וְנַקֵּה.

The Lord, the Lord God is merciful and gracious, endlessly patient, loving, and true, showing mercy to thousands, forgiving iniquity, transgression, and sin, and granting pardon.

◆ ◆

הָבוּ גֹדֶל לֵאלֹהֵינוּ וּתְנוּ כָבוֹד לַתּוֹרָה.

Let us declare the greatness of our God and give honor to the Torah.

◆ ◆

The Torah is taken from the Ark

כִּי מִצִּיּוֹן תֵּצֵא תוֹרָה, וּדְבַר־יְיָ מִירוּשָׁלָיִם.

For out of Zion shall go forth Torah, and the word of the Lord from Jerusalem.

בָּרוּךְ שֶׁנָּתַן תּוֹרָה לְעַמּוֹ יִשְׂרָאֵל בִּקְדֻשָּׁתוֹ.

Praised be the One who in His holiness has given the Torah to His people Israel.

◆ ◆

שְׁמַע יִשְׂרָאֵל: יְיָ אֱלֹהֵינוּ, יְיָ אֶחָד!

Hear, O Israel: the Lord is our God, the Lord is One!

אֶחָד אֱלֹהֵינוּ, גָּדוֹל אֲדוֹנֵינוּ, קָדוֹשׁ שְׁמוֹ.

Our God is One; our Lord is great; holy is His name.

◆ ◆

גַּדְּלוּ לַייָ אִתִּי וּנְרוֹמְמָה שְׁמוֹ יַחְדָּו.

O magnify the Lord with me, and together let us exalt His name.

◆ ◆

לְךָ, יְיָ, הַגְּדֻלָּה וְהַגְּבוּרָה וְהַתִּפְאֶרֶת וְהַנֵּצַח וְהַהוֹד, כִּי כֹל בַּשָּׁמַיִם וּבָאָרֶץ, לְךָ יְיָ הַמַּמְלָכָה וְהַמִּתְנַשֵּׂא לְכֹל לְרֹאשׁ.

Yours, Lord, is the greatness, the power, the glory, the victory, and the majesty; for all that is in heaven and earth is Yours. Yours is the kingdom, O Lord; You are supreme over all.

All are seated

◆ ◆

Reading of the Torah

For transliteration, see page 772.

Before the Reading

בָּרְכוּ אֶת־יְיָ הַמְבֹרָךְ!

בָּרוּךְ יְיָ הַמְבֹרָךְ לְעוֹלָם וָעֶד!

בָּרוּךְ אַתָּה, יְיָ אֱלֹהֵינוּ, מֶלֶךְ הָעוֹלָם, אֲשֶׁר בָּחַר־בָּנוּ מִכָּל־הָעַמִּים וְנָתַן־לָנוּ אֶת־תּוֹרָתוֹ. בָּרוּךְ אַתָּה, יְיָ, נוֹתֵן הַתּוֹרָה.

Praise the Lord, to whom our praise is due!

Praised be the Lord, to whom our praise is due,
now and for ever!

Blessed is the Lord our God, Ruler of the universe, who has chosen us from all peoples by giving us His Torah. Blessed is the Lord, Giver of the Torah.

◆ ◆

After the Reading

בָּרוּךְ אַתָּה, יְיָ אֱלֹהֵינוּ, מֶלֶךְ הָעוֹלָם, אֲשֶׁר נָתַן לָנוּ תּוֹרַת אֱמֶת וְחַיֵּי עוֹלָם נָטַע בְּתוֹכֵנוּ. בָּרוּךְ אַתָּה, יְיָ, נוֹתֵן הַתּוֹרָה.

Blessed is the Lord our God, Ruler of the universe, who has given us a Torah of truth, implanting within us eternal life. Blessed is the Lord, Giver of the Torah.

◆ ◆

As the reading is completed, the Torah might be held high while this is said:

וְזֹאת הַתּוֹרָה אֲשֶׁר־שָׂם מֹשֶׁה לִפְנֵי בְּנֵי יִשְׂרָאֵל, עַל־פִּי יְיָ בְּיַד־מֹשֶׁה.

This is the Torah that Moses placed before the people of Israel
to fulfill the word of God.

◆ ◆

Reading of the Haftarah

Before the Reading

בָּרוּךְ אַתָּה, יְיָ אֱלֹהֵינוּ, מֶלֶךְ הָעוֹלָם, אֲשֶׁר בָּחַר בִּנְבִיאִים טוֹבִים וְרָצָה בְדִבְרֵיהֶם הַנֶּאֱמָרִים בֶּאֱמֶת. בָּרוּךְ אַתָּה, יְיָ, הַבּוֹחֵר בַּתּוֹרָה וּבְמֹשֶׁה עַבְדּוֹ וּבְיִשְׂרָאֵל עַמּוֹ וּבִנְבִיאֵי הָאֱמֶת וָצֶדֶק.

Blessed is the Lord our God, Ruler of the universe, who has chosen faithful prophets to speak words of truth. Blessed is the Lord, for the revelation of Torah, for Moses His servant and Israel His people, and for the prophets of truth and righteousness.

After the Reading

בָּרוּךְ אַתָּה, יְיָ אֱלֹהֵינוּ, מֶלֶךְ הָעוֹלָם, צוּר כָּל־הָעוֹלָמִים, צַדִּיק בְּכָל־הַדּוֹרוֹת, הָאֵל הַנֶּאֱמָן, הָאוֹמֵר וְעוֹשֶׂה, הַמְדַבֵּר וּמְקַיֵּם, שֶׁכָּל־דְּבָרָיו אֱמֶת וָצֶדֶק.

Blessed is the Lord our God, Ruler of the universe, Rock of all creation, Righteous One of all generations, the faithful God whose word is deed, whose every command is just and true.

FOR YOM TOV

עַל־הַתּוֹרָה וְעַל־הָעֲבוֹדָה וְעַל־הַנְּבִיאִים וְעַל־יוֹם [הַשַּׁבָּת הַזֶּה, וְעַל־יוֹם]

For the Torah, for the privilege of worship, for the prophets, [for this Shabbat,] and for this feast of

Pesach	חַג הַמַּצּוֹת הַזֶּה
Shavuot	חַג הַשָּׁבֻעוֹת הַזֶּה
Sukkot	חַג הַסֻּכּוֹת הַזֶּה

שֶׁנָּתַתָּ־לָּנוּ, יְיָ אֱלֹהֵינוּ, [לִקְדֻשָּׁה וְלִמְנוּחָה] לְשָׂשׂוֹן וּלְשִׂמְחָה, לְכָבוֹד וּלְתִפְאָרֶת, עַל־הַכֹּל, יְיָ אֱלֹהֵינוּ, אֲנַחְנוּ מוֹדִים לָךְ, וּמְבָרְכִים אוֹתָךְ. יִתְבָּרַךְ שִׁמְךָ בְּפִי כָּל־חַי תָּמִיד לְעוֹלָם וָעֶד.

בָּרוּךְ אַתָּה, יְיָ, מְקַדֵּשׁ [הַשַּׁבָּת וְ] יִשְׂרָאֵל וְהַזְּמַנִּים.

that You, O Lord our God, have given us [for holiness and rest,] for joy and gladness, for honor and glory, we thank and bless You. May Your name be blessed for ever by every living being. Blessed is the Lord, who hallows [the Sabbath,] the House of Israel and the Festivals.

◆ ◆

FOR YOM HA-ATSMA-UT

עַל־הַתּוֹרָה וְעַל־הָעֲבוֹדָה וְעַל־הַנְּבִיאִים וְעַל־יוֹם [הַשַּׁבָּת הַזֶּה, וְעַל־יוֹם] הָעַצְמָאוּת הַזֶּה, אֲנַחְנוּ מוֹדִים לָךְ, וּמְבָרְכִים אוֹתָךְ.

בָּרוּךְ אַתָּה, יְיָ, מְשַׂמֵּחַ צִיּוֹן בְּבָנֶיהָ.

For the Torah, for the privilege of worship, for the prophets, [for this Shabbat,] and for this Day of Independence, we thank You and bless You.

Blessed is the Lord, who brings joy to Zion's children.

On the seventh day of Pesach, and, if desired, on Shavuot and Atzeret-Simchat Torah, the Memorial Service, on page 546, might be read here.

Special prayers begin on page 449.

◆ ◆

Returning the Torah to the Ark

All rise

יְהַלְלוּ אֶת־שֵׁם יְיָ, כִּי נִשְׂגָּב שְׁמוֹ לְבַדּוֹ.

Let us praise the name of the Lord, for His name alone is exalted.

◆ ◆

הוֹדוֹ עַל אֶרֶץ וְשָׁמָיִם, וַיָּרֶם קֶרֶן לְעַמּוֹ, תְּהִלָּה לְכָל־
חֲסִידָיו, לִבְנֵי יִשְׂרָאֵל עַם קְרוֹבוֹ. הַלְלוּיָהּ.

God's splendor covers heaven and earth; He is the strength of His people, making glorious His faithful ones, Israel, a people close to Him. Halleluyah!

◆ ◆

תּוֹרַת יְיָ תְּמִימָה, מְשִׁיבַת נָפֶשׁ;
עֵדוּת יְיָ נֶאֱמָנָה, מַחְכִּימַת פֶּתִי;

The Torah of the Lord is perfect, reviving the soul;
The teaching of the Lord is sure, making wise the simple;

פִּקּוּדֵי יְיָ יְשָׁרִים, מְשַׂמְּחֵי־לֵב;
מִצְוַת יְיָ בָּרָה, מְאִירַת עֵינָיִם;

The precepts of the Lord are right, delighting the mind;
The Mitzvah of the Lord is clear, giving light to the eyes;

יִרְאַת יְיָ טְהוֹרָה, עוֹמֶדֶת לָעַד;
מִשְׁפְּטֵי יְיָ אֱמֶת, צָדְקוּ יַחְדָּו.

The word of the Lord is pure, enduring for ever;
The judgments of the Lord are true, and altogether just.

◆ ◆

כִּי לֶקַח טוֹב נָתַתִּי לָכֶם, תּוֹרָתִי אַל־תַּעֲזֹבוּ.
עֵץ חַיִּים הִיא לַמַּחֲזִיקִים בָּהּ, וְתֹמְכֶיהָ מְאֻשָּׁר.
דְּרָכֶיהָ דַרְכֵי־נֹעַם, וְכָל־נְתִיבוֹתֶיהָ שָׁלוֹם.

Behold, a good doctrine has been given you, My Torah; do not forsake it. It is a tree of life to those who hold it fast, and all who cling to it find happiness. Its ways are ways of pleasantness, and all its paths are peace.

הֲשִׁיבֵנוּ יְיָ אֵלֶיךָ, וְנָשׁוּבָה. חַדֵּשׁ יָמֵינוּ כְּקֶדֶם.

Help us to return to You, O Lord; then truly shall we return. Renew our days as in the past.

The Ark is closed

All are seated

סדר קריאת התורה לעצרת-שמחת תורה

For the Reading of Torah on Atzeret–Simchat Torah

כֹּהֲנֶיךָ יִלְבְּשׁוּ־צֶדֶק, וַחֲסִידֶיךָ יְרַנֵּנוּ. וְאָמַר בַּיּוֹם הַהוּא: "הִנֵּה אֱלֹהֵינוּ זֶה, קִוִּינוּ לוֹ וְיוֹשִׁיעֵנוּ, זֶה יְיָ קִוִּינוּ לוֹ; נָגִילָה וְנִשְׂמְחָה בִּישׁוּעָתוֹ!"

Those who serve You shall be adorned in justice, and Your faithful ones will sing for joy. And it shall be said on that day: "Behold our God! We have kept faith with Him, and He will help us. This is the Eternal! We have kept faith with Him; let us rejoice and be glad in His deliverance."

◆ ◆

The Ark is opened

אַתָּה הָרְאֵתָ לָדַעַת, כִּי יְיָ הוּא הָאֱלֹהִים, אֵין עוֹד מִלְּבַדּוֹ. לְעֹשֵׂה נִפְלָאוֹת גְּדֹלוֹת לְבַדּוֹ, כִּי לְעוֹלָם חַסְדּוֹ.

You have been shown, that you may know, that the Eternal alone is our God; there is none beside Him. He Himself does great wonders, for His love is everlasting.

אֵין כָּמוֹךָ בָאֱלֹהִים, יְיָ, וְאֵין כְּמַעֲשֶׂיךָ. יְהִי כְבוֹד יְיָ לְעוֹלָם, יִשְׂמַח יְיָ בְּמַעֲשָׂיו. יְהִי שֵׁם יְיָ מְבֹרָךְ, מֵעַתָּה וְעַד עוֹלָם.

There is none like You, O Eternal One, among the gods that are worshipped, and there are no deeds like Yours. Let the Eternal be honored for ever, and He will rejoice in His works. Let the name of the Eternal be blessed, now and for ever.

יְהִי יְיָ אֱלֹהֵינוּ עִמָּנוּ, כַּאֲשֶׁר הָיָה עִם אֲבֹתֵינוּ, אַל יַעַזְבֵנוּ וְאַל יִטְּשֵׁנוּ. וְאִמְרוּ: "הוֹשִׁיעֵנוּ אֱלֹהֵי יִשְׁעֵנוּ, לְהוֹדוֹת לְשֵׁם קָדְשֶׁךָ, לְהִשְׁתַּבֵּחַ בִּתְהִלָּתֶךָ."

The Eternal God be with us, as He was with our ancestors; may He not leave us or forsake us. Say now: "Deliver us, O God our Help, that we may give thanks to Your holy name, and triumph in Your praise."

יְיָ מֶלֶךְ, יְיָ מָלָךְ, יְיָ יִמְלֹךְ לְעוֹלָם וָעֶד. יְיָ עֹז לְעַמּוֹ יִתֵּן, יְיָ יְבָרֵךְ אֶת־עַמּוֹ בַשָּׁלוֹם.

The Eternal is King, the Eternal will reign for ever and ever. The Eternal will give strength to His people; the Eternal will bless His people with peace.

The Sifrei Torah are taken from the Ark

הָבוּ גֹדֶל לֵאלֹהֵינוּ וּתְנוּ כָבוֹד לַתּוֹרָה.

Let us declare the greatness of our God and give honor to the Torah.

כִּי מִצִּיּוֹן תֵּצֵא תוֹרָה, וּדְבַר־יְיָ מִירוּשָׁלָיִם.

For out of Zion shall go forth Torah, and the word of the Lord from Jerusalem.

בָּרוּךְ שֶׁנָּתַן תּוֹרָה לְעַמּוֹ יִשְׂרָאֵל בִּקְדֻשָּׁתוֹ.

Praised be the One who in His holiness has given the Torah to His people Israel.

◆ ◆

שְׁמַע יִשְׂרָאֵל: יְיָ אֱלֹהֵינוּ, יְיָ אֶחָד!

Hear, O Israel: the Lord is our God, the Lord is One!

אֶחָד אֱלֹהֵינוּ, גָּדוֹל אֲדוֹנֵינוּ, קָדוֹשׁ שְׁמוֹ.

Our God is One; our Lord is great; holy is His name.

◆ ◆

אַשְׁרֵיכֶם יִשְׂרָאֵל, אַשְׁרֵיכֶם יִשְׂרָאֵל, אַשְׁרֵיכֶם יִשְׂרָאֵל, אֲשֶׁר בָּחַר בָּכֶם אֵל, וְהִנְחִילְכֶם הַתּוֹרָה.

How blessed you are, O Israel, how fortunate and privileged — you whom God has singled out, by making the Torah your heritage.

◆ ◆

CONSECRATION

It is the custom in some congregations to consecrate the children who are beginning their formal Jewish education. The children ascend the Bima in procession. They recite the Shema. The Rabbi may offer this prayer:

O God, our Creator and our Teacher, bless these children who have come into Your sanctuary with eager minds and warm hearts. This day may they be consecrated to the study of Torah, to lives of loyalty and goodness. Thus will they bring joy to all who love them and honor to the household of Israel. Strengthen them and guide them in all their ways. Blessed is the Lord, the Teacher of Torah to His people Israel.

The Priestly Blessing may be recited. The children join in the Hakafot. They may be called to the reading of Genesis.

◆ ◆

While the following is sung, the Scrolls are carried in procession in a series of Hakafot (circuits)

Eternal God, be our Help; Eternal God, sustain us; Eternal God, be our Answer when we call upon You.	אָנָּא יְיָ, הוֹשִׁיעָה נָּא, אָנָּא יְיָ ,הַצְלִיחָה נָא, אָנָּא יְיָ, עֲנֵנוּ בְּיוֹם קָרְאֵנוּ.
God of all being, be our Help; Searcher of hearts, sustain us; Mighty Redeemer, be our Answer when we call upon You.	אֱלֹהֵי הָרוּחוֹת, הוֹשִׁיעָה נָּא. בּוֹחֵן לְבָבוֹת, הַצְלִיחָה נָא. גּוֹאֵל חָזָק, עֲנֵנוּ בְּיוֹם קָרְאֵנוּ.
Proclaimer of justice, be our Help; God surrounded by glory, sustain us; Steadfast and loving One, be our Answer when we call upon You.	דּוֹבֵר צְדָקוֹת, הוֹשִׁיעָה נָּא. הָדוּר בִּלְבוּשׁוֹ, הַצְלִיחָה נָא. וָתִיק וְחָסִיד, עֲנֵנוּ בְּיוֹם קָרְאֵנוּ.
Pure and upright One, be our Help; Friend of the poor, sustain us; Inspiration to goodness, be our Answer when we call upon You.	זַךְ וְיָשָׁר, הוֹשִׁיעָה נָּא. חוֹמֵל דַּלִּים, הַצְלִיחָה נָא. טוֹב וּמֵטִיב, עֲנֵנוּ בְּיוֹם קָרְאֵנוּ.

יוֹדֵעַ מַחֲשָׁבוֹת, הוֹשִׁיעָה נָּא.
כַּבִּיר וְנָאוֹר, הַצְלִיחָה נָא.
לוֹבֵשׁ צְדָקוֹת, עֲנֵנוּ בְּיוֹם קָרְאֵנוּ.

Mind of the universe, be our Help;
God of power and splendor, sustain us;
Lord arrayed in justice, be our
Answer when we call upon You.

מֶלֶךְ עוֹלָמִים, הוֹשִׁיעָה נָּא.
נָאוֹר וְאַדִּיר, הַצְלִיחָה נָא.
סוֹמֵךְ נוֹפְלִים, עֲנֵנוּ בְּיוֹם קָרְאֵנוּ.

Eternal Ruler, be our Help;
Radiant and glorious God, sustain us;
Upholder of the falling, be our
Answer when we call upon You.

עוֹזֵר דַּלִּים, הוֹשִׁיעָה נָּא.
פּוֹדֶה וּמַצִּיל, הַצְלִיחָה נָא.
צוּר עוֹלָמִים, עֲנֵנוּ בְּיוֹם קָרְאֵנוּ.

Helper of the weak, be our Help;
Redeemer and Deliverer, sustain us;
Eternal Rock, be our Answer
when we call upon You.

קָדוֹשׁ וְנוֹרָא, הוֹשִׁיעָה נָּא.
רַחוּם וְחַנּוּן, הַצְלִיחָה נָא.
שׁוֹמֵר הַבְּרִית, עֲנֵנוּ בְּיוֹם קָרְאֵנוּ.

Holy and awesome One, be our Help;
Merciful and gracious God, sustain us;
Keeper of the Covenant, be our
Answer when we call upon You.

תּוֹמֵךְ תְּמִימִים, הוֹשִׁיעָה נָּא.
תַּקִּיף לָעַד, הַצְלִיחָה נָא.
תָּמִים בְּמַעֲשָׂיו, עֲנֵנוּ בְּיוֹם קָרְאֵנוּ

Support of the innocent, be our Help;
Mighty for ever, sustain us;
Pure in Your ways, be our Answer
when we call upon You.

◆ ◆

Upon the conclusion of the Hakafot, two Scrolls are prepared for reading while the following is sung

שִׂישׂוּ וְשִׂמְחוּ בְּשִׂמְחַת תּוֹרָה, וּתְנוּ כָבוֹד לַתּוֹרָה.
כִּי טוֹב סַחֲרָהּ מִכָּל־סְחוֹרָה, מִפָּז וּמִפְּנִינִים יְקָרָה.

Rejoice and be glad on Simchat Torah, and give honor to the Torah.
For nothing is its equal in value; it is more precious than gold and gems.

נָגִיל וְנָשִׂישׂ בְּזֹאת הַתּוֹרָה, כִּי הִיא לָנוּ עֹז וְאוֹרָה.
תּוֹרָה הִיא עֵץ חַיִּים, לְכֻלָּם חַיִּים, כִּי עִמְּךָ מְקוֹר חַיִּים.

We will exult and rejoice in our Torah, for it is our strength and our light.
The Torah is a tree of life, life for all. And You, O God, are the fountain of life.

אֲהַלֵּל אֱלֹהַי וְאֶשְׂמְחָה בוֹ, וְאָשִׂימָה תִקְוָתִי בּוֹ.
אֲהוֹדֶנּוּ בְּסוֹד עַם קְרוֹבוֹ, אֱלוֹהַּ צוּרִי אֶחֱסֶה בּוֹ.

I will praise my God and rejoice in Him; in Him will I put my faith.
I will thank Him in the council of the people who seek His presence;
in Him, my God and my Rock, will I trust.

◆ ◆

Reading of the Torah

For transliteration, see page 772.

Before the Reading

בָּרְכוּ אֶת־יְיָ הַמְבֹרָךְ!

בָּרוּךְ יְיָ הַמְבֹרָךְ לְעוֹלָם וָעֶד!

בָּרוּךְ אַתָּה, יְיָ אֱלֹהֵינוּ, מֶלֶךְ הָעוֹלָם, אֲשֶׁר בָּחַר־בָּנוּ מִכָּל־
הָעַמִּים וְנָתַן־לָנוּ אֶת־תּוֹרָתוֹ. בָּרוּךְ אַתָּה, יְיָ, נוֹתֵן הַתּוֹרָה.

Praise the Lord, to whom our praise is due!

Praised be the Lord, to whom our praise is due,
now and for ever!

Blessed is the Lord our God, Ruler of the universe, who has chosen us from all peoples by giving us His Torah. Blessed is the Lord, Giver of the Torah.

◆ ◆

After the Reading

בָּרוּךְ אַתָּה, יְיָ אֱלֹהֵינוּ, מֶלֶךְ הָעוֹלָם, אֲשֶׁר נָתַן לָנוּ תּוֹרַת
אֱמֶת וְחַיֵּי עוֹלָם נָטַע בְּתוֹכֵנוּ. בָּרוּךְ אַתָּה, יְיָ, נוֹתֵן הַתּוֹרָה.

Blessed is the Lord our God, Ruler of the universe, who has given us a Torah of truth, implanting within us eternal life. Blessed is the Lord, Giver of the Torah.

After the first scroll

חֲזַק חֲזַק וְנִתְחַזֵּק.

Let us be strong, and give each other strength.

After the second scroll

רוֹמְמוּ יְיָ אֱלֹהֵינוּ, וְהִשְׁתַּחֲווּ לְהַר קָדְשׁוֹ, כִּי קָדוֹשׁ יְיָ אֱלֹהֵינוּ.

Let us exalt the Lord our God, and worship at His holy mountain, for the Lord our God is holy.

◆ ◆

As the reading is completed, each Torah in turn might be held high while this is said:

וְזֹאת הַתּוֹרָה אֲשֶׁר־שָׂם מֹשֶׁה לִפְנֵי בְּנֵי יִשְׂרָאֵל, עַל־פִּי יְיָ בְּיַד־מֹשֶׁה.

This is the Torah that Moses placed before the people of Israel to fulfill the word of God.

Reading of the Haftarah

Before the Reading

בָּרוּךְ אַתָּה, יְיָ אֱלֹהֵינוּ, מֶלֶךְ הָעוֹלָם, אֲשֶׁר בָּחַר בִּנְבִיאִים טוֹבִים וְרָצָה בְדִבְרֵיהֶם הַנֶּאֱמָרִים בֶּאֱמֶת. בָּרוּךְ אַתָּה, יְיָ, הַבּוֹחֵר בַּתּוֹרָה וּבְמֹשֶׁה עַבְדּוֹ וּבְיִשְׂרָאֵל עַמּוֹ וּבִנְבִיאֵי הָאֱמֶת וָצֶדֶק.

Blessed is the Lord our God, Ruler of the universe, who has chosen faithful prophets to speak words of truth. Blessed is the Lord, for the revelation of Torah, for Moses His servant and Israel His people, and for the prophets of truth and righteousness.

◆ ◆

After the Reading

בָּרוּךְ אַתָּה, יְיָ אֱלֹהֵינוּ, מֶלֶךְ הָעוֹלָם, צוּר כָּל־הָעוֹלָמִים, צַדִּיק בְּכָל־הַדּוֹרוֹת, הָאֵל הַנֶּאֱמָן, הָאוֹמֵר וְעוֹשֶׂה, הַמְדַבֵּר וּמְקַיֵּם, שֶׁכָּל־דְּבָרָיו אֱמֶת וָצֶדֶק.

Blessed is the Lord our God, Ruler of the universe, Rock of all creation, Righteous One of all generations, the faithful God whose word is deed, whose every command is just and true.

עַל־הַתּוֹרָה וְעַל־הָעֲבוֹדָה וְעַל־הַנְּבִיאִים וְעַל־יוֹם [הַשַּׁבָּת הַזֶּה, וְעַל־יוֹם] הַשְּׁמִינִי חַג הָעֲצֶרֶת הַזֶּה, שֶׁנָּתַתָּ־לָּנוּ, יְיָ אֱלֹהֵינוּ, [לִקְדֻשָּׁה וְלִמְנוּחָה,] לְשָׂשׂוֹן וּלְשִׂמְחָה, לְכָבוֹד וּלְתִפְאָרֶת, עַל־הַכֹּל, יְיָ אֱלֹהֵינוּ, אֲנַחְנוּ מוֹדִים לָךְ, וּמְבָרְכִים אוֹתָךְ. יִתְבָּרַךְ שִׁמְךָ בְּפִי כָּל־חַי תָּמִיד לְעוֹלָם וָעֶד. בָּרוּךְ אַתָּה, יְיָ, מְקַדֵּשׁ [הַשַּׁבָּת וְ] יִשְׂרָאֵל וְהַזְּמַנִּים.

For the Torah, for the privilege of worship, for the prophets, [for this Shabbat,] and for this feast of Atzeret-Simchat Torah that You, O Lord our God, have given us [for holiness and rest,] for joy and gladness, for honor and glory, we thank and bless You. May Your name be blessed for ever by every living being. Blessed is the Lord, who hallows [the Sabbath,] the House of Israel and the Festivals.

The Memorial Service, on page 546, might be read here.

Special Prayers begin on page 449.

Returning the Torah to the Ark

All rise

תּוֹרָה צִוָּה־לָנוּ יְיָ בְּיַד מֹשֶׁה וְהַנְּבִיאִים מוֹרָשָׁה קְהִלַּת יַעֲקֹב.

The Torah commanded us by God through Moses and the prophets is the heritage of the House of Jacob.

• •

הודו עַל אֶרֶץ וְשָׁמָיִם, וַיָּרֶם קֶרֶן לְעַמּוֹ, תְּהִלָּה לְכָל-
חֲסִידָיו, לִבְנֵי יִשְׂרָאֵל עַם קְרוֹבוֹ. הַלְלוּיָהּ.

God's splendor covers heaven and earth. He is the strength of His people, making glorious His faithful ones, Israel, a people close to Him. Halleluyah!

◆ ◆

כִּי לֶקַח טוֹב נָתַתִּי לָכֶם, תּוֹרָתִי אַל-תַּעֲזֹבוּ. עֵץ-חַיִּים הִיא
לַמַּחֲזִיקִים בָּהּ, וְתֹמְכֶיהָ מְאֻשָּׁר. דְּרָכֶיהָ דַרְכֵי-נֹעַם, וְכָל-
נְתִיבֹתֶיהָ שָׁלוֹם.

Behold, a good doctrine has been given you, My Torah: do not forsake it. It is a tree of life to those who hold it fast, and all who cling to it find happiness. Its ways are ways of pleasantness, and all its paths are peace.

הֲשִׁיבֵנוּ יְיָ אֵלֶיךָ, וְנָשׁוּבָה. חַדֵּשׁ יָמֵינוּ כְּקֶדֶם.

Help us to return to You, O Lord; then truly shall we return. Renew our days as in the past.

The Ark is closed

All are seated

Memorial Service הזכרת נשמות

For the seventh day of Pesach, and, if desired, for Shavuot and Atzeret–Simchat Torah.

Psalm 23

מִזְמוֹר לְדָוִד.
יְיָ רֹעִי, לֹא אֶחְסָר.
בִּנְאוֹת דֶּשֶׁא יַרְבִּיצֵנִי, עַל־מֵי מְנֻחוֹת יְנַהֲלֵנִי.
נַפְשִׁי יְשׁוֹבֵב, יַנְחֵנִי בְמַעְגְּלֵי־צֶדֶק לְמַעַן שְׁמוֹ.
גַּם כִּי אֵלֵךְ בְּגֵיא צַלְמָוֶת לֹא אִירָא רָע, כִּי אַתָּה עִמָּדִי.
שִׁבְטְךָ וּמִשְׁעַנְתֶּךָ, הֵמָּה יְנַחֲמֻנִי.
תַּעֲרֹךְ לְפָנַי שֻׁלְחָן נֶגֶד צֹרְרָי.
דִּשַּׁנְתָּ בַשֶּׁמֶן רֹאשִׁי, כּוֹסִי רְוָיָה.
אַךְ טוֹב וָחֶסֶד יִרְדְּפוּנִי כָּל־יְמֵי חַיָּי,
וְשַׁבְתִּי בְּבֵית־יְיָ לְאֹרֶךְ יָמִים.

The Lord is my shepherd, I shall not want.
He makes me lie down in green pastures,
He leads me beside still waters. He restores my soul.
He leads me in right paths for the sake of His name.
Even when I walk in the valley of the shadow of death,
I shall fear no evil, for You are with me;
With rod and staff You comfort me.
You have set a table before me in the presence of my enemies;
You have anointed my head with oil, my cup overflows.
Surely goodness and mercy shall follow me all the days of my life, and I shall dwell in the house of the Lord for ever.

◆ ◆

Psalm 121

אֶשָּׂא עֵינַי אֶל־הֶהָרִים, מֵאַיִן יָבוֹא עֶזְרִי?
עֶזְרִי מֵעִם יְיָ, עֹשֵׂה שָׁמַיִם וָאָרֶץ.

אַל־יִתֵּן לַמּוֹט רַגְלֶךָ, אַל־יָנוּם שֹׁמְרֶךָ.
הִנֵּה לֹא־יָנוּם וְלֹא יִישָׁן שׁוֹמֵר יִשְׂרָאֵל.
יְיָ שֹׁמְרֶךָ, יְיָ צִלְּךָ עַל־יַד יְמִינֶךָ.
יוֹמָם הַשֶּׁמֶשׁ לֹא־יַכֶּכָּה, וְיָרֵחַ בַּלָּיְלָה.
יְיָ יִשְׁמָרְךָ מִכָּל־רָע, יִשְׁמֹר אֶת־נַפְשֶׁךָ.
יְיָ יִשְׁמָר־צֵאתְךָ וּבוֹאֶךָ, מֵעַתָּה וְעַד־עוֹלָם.

I lift up my eyes to the mountains:
what is the source of my help?
My help will come from the Lord,
Maker of heaven and earth.
He will not allow your foot to slip;
your Guardian will not slumber.
Behold, the Guardian of Israel neither slumbers nor sleeps.
The Eternal is your Keeper,
the Lord is your shade at your right hand.
The sun shall not harm you by day, nor the moon by night.
The Lord will guard you from all evil,
He will protect your being.
The Lord will guard you, coming and going,
from this time forth, and for ever.

◆ ◆

MEDITATION

O God of life, amid the ceaseless tides of change which sweep away the generations, Your living spirit remains to comfort us and give us hope. Around us is life and death, decay and renewal; the flowing rhythm that all things obey.

Our life is a dance to a song we cannot hear. Its melody courses through us for a little while, then seems to cease. Whence the melody, and whither does it go? In darkness as in light, we turn to You, Lord, the Source of life, the Answer to all its mysteries.

Can it be that we, Your children, are given over to destruction, when our few days on earth are done? Or do we live in ways we cannot know?

Only this have we been taught, and in this we put our trust: from You comes the spirit, and to You it must return. You are our dwelling-place in life and in death.

More we cannot say, for all else is hidden from our sight by an impenetrable veil. We thank You, then, for the life we have, and for the gifts that daily are our portion:

For health and healing, for labor and repose, for the ever-renewed beauty of earth and sky, for thoughts of truth and justice that move us to acts of goodness, and for the contemplation of Your eternal Presence, which fills us with the hope that what is good and lovely will not perish.

Lord, what are we? A breath, a passing shadow. Yet You have made us little less than divine.

◆ ◆

יְיָ, מָה־אָדָם וַתֵּדָעֵהוּ?
בֶּן־אֱנוֹשׁ וַתְּחַשְּׁבֵהוּ?
אָדָם לַהֶבֶל דָּמָה;
יָמָיו כְּצֵל עוֹבֵר.
בַּבֹּקֶר יָצִיץ וְחָלָף,
לָעֶרֶב יְמוֹלֵל וְיָבֵשׁ.
תָּשֵׁב אֱנוֹשׁ עַד־דַּכָּא,
וַתֹּאמֶר: "שׁוּבוּ, בְנֵי־אָדָם!"

Lord, what are we, that You have regard for us? What are we, that You are mindful of us? We are like a breath; our days are as a passing shadow; we come and go like grass which in the morning shoots up, renewed, and in the evening fades and withers. You cause us to revert to dust, saying: "Return, O mortal creatures!"

◆ ◆

From Psalm 90

אֲדֹנָי, מָעוֹן אַתָּה הָיִיתָ לָּנוּ בְּדֹר וָדֹר.
בְּטֶרֶם הָרִים יֻלָּדוּ, וַתְּחוֹלֵל אֶרֶץ וְתֵבֵל, וּמֵעוֹלָם עַד־עוֹלָם אַתָּה אֵל.

Lord, You have been our refuge in all generations.

Before the mountains were born, or earth and universe brought forth, from eternity to eternity You are God.

כִּי אֶלֶף שָׁנִים בְּעֵינֶיךָ כְּיוֹם אֶתְמוֹל כִּי יַעֲבֹר, וְאַשְׁמוּרָה בַלָּיְלָה.

זְרַמְתָּם; שֵׁנָה יִהְיוּ; בַּבֹּקֶר כֶּחָצִיר יַחֲלֹף: בַּבֹּקֶר יָצִיץ וְחָלָף, לָעֶרֶב יְמוֹלֵל וְיָבֵשׁ.

For a thousand years in Your sight are but as yesterday when it is past, or as a watch in the night.

You sweep us away; we are like a dream at daybreak; we come and go like grass which in the morning shoots up, renewed, and in the evening fades and withers.

יְמֵי־שְׁנוֹתֵינוּ בָהֶם שִׁבְעִים שָׁנָה, וְאִם בִּגְבוּרֹת, שְׁמוֹנִים שָׁנָה; וְרָהְבָּם עָמָל וָאָוֶן, כִּי־גָז חִישׁ, וַנָּעֻפָה. לִמְנוֹת יָמֵינוּ כֵּן הוֹדַע, וְנָבִא לְבַב חָכְמָה.

יֵרָאֶה אֶל־עֲבָדֶיךָ פָעֳלֶךָ, וַהֲדָרְךָ עַל־בְּנֵיהֶם.

The number of our years may be many or few; yet vain toil fills their span, for it is soon ended, and we fly away. So teach us to number our days that we may grow wise in heart.

Let Your servants understand Your ways, and Your children see Your glory.

וִיהִי נֹעַם אֲדֹנָי אֱלֹהֵינוּ עָלֵינוּ, וּמַעֲשֵׂה יָדֵינוּ כּוֹנְנָה עָלֵינוּ. וּמַעֲשֵׂה יָדֵינוּ כּוֹנְנֵהוּ!

Let the beauty of our Eternal God be with us, and may our work have lasting value.

O let the work of our hands be enduring!

◆ ◆

שִׁוִּיתִי יְיָ לְנֶגְדִּי תָמִיד;
כִּי מִימִינִי בַּל־אֶמּוֹט.
לָכֵן שָׂמַח לִבִּי וַיָּגֶל כְּבוֹדִי;

I have set the Eternal always before me; He is at my side, I shall not be moved. Therefore does my heart exult and my soul rejoice;

אַף־בְּשָׂרִי יִשְׁכֹּן לָבֶטַח.
כִּי לֹא־תַעֲזֹב נַפְשִׁי לִשְׁאוֹל,
לֹא־תִתֵּן חֲסִידְךָ לִרְאוֹת שָׁחַת.
תּוֹדִיעֵנִי אֹרַח חַיִּים;
שֹׂבַע שְׂמָחוֹת אֶת־פָּנֶיךָ;
נְעִמוֹת בִּימִינְךָ נֶצַח.

my being is secure. For You will not abandon me to death nor let Your faithful ones see destruction. You show me the path of life; Your presence brings fullness of joy; enduring happiness is Your gift.

◆ ◆

O God, this hour revives in us memories of loved ones who are no more. What happiness we shared when they walked among us! What joy, when, loving and loved, we lived our lives together!
Their memory is a blessing for ever.

Months or years may have passed, yet we feel near to them. Our hearts yearn for them. Though the bitter grief has softened, a duller pain abides, for the place where once they stood is empty now for ever. The links of life are broken. But the links of love and longing cannot break.
Their souls are bound up in ours for ever.

We see them now with the eye of memory, their faults forgiven, their virtues grown larger. So does goodness live, and weakness fade from sight. We remember them with gratitude and bless their names.
Their memory is a blessing for ever.

And we remember as well the men and women who but yesterday were part of our congregation and community. To all who cared for us and labored for the well-being of our people and of humanity, we pay tribute. May we prove worthy of carrying on the tradition of our people and our faith, for now the task is ours.
Their souls are bound up in ours for ever.

We think, too, of the whole household of Israel and its martyrs. The tragedy of our own age is still a fresh wound within us.

And we recall how often in ages past our people walked through the flames of the furnace. Merciful God, let the memory never fade of the faithful and upright of our people who have given their lives to hallow Your name. Even in death they continue to speak to us of faith and courage. They rest in nameless graves, but their deeds endure, and their sacrifices will not be forgotten. Their souls are bound up in the bond of eternal life. No evil shall touch them: they are at peace.

We will remember, and never forget them.

In gratitude for all the blessings our loved ones, friends, teachers, and the martyrs of our people have brought to us, to our people, and to humanity, we dedicate ourselves anew to the sacred faith for which they lived and died, and to the tasks they have bequeathed to us. Let them be remembered for blessing, O God, together with the righteous of all peoples, and let us say: Amen.

◆ ◆

SILENT REMEMBRANCE — יזכור

יִזְכּוֹר אֱלֹהִים נִשְׁמוֹת יַקִּירַי .... שֶׁהָלְכוּ לְעוֹלָמָם. אָנָּא תִּהְיֶינָה נַפְשׁוֹתֵיהֶם צְרוּרוֹת בִּצְרוֹר הַחַיִּים וּתְהִי מְנוּחָתָם כָּבוֹד. שֹׂבַע שְׂמָחוֹת אֶת־פָּנֶיךָ, נְעִימוֹת בִּימִינְךָ נֶצַח. אָמֵן.

May God remember for ever my dear ones .... who have gone to their eternal rest. May they be at one with the One who is life eternal. May the beauty of their lives shine for evermore, and may my life always bring honor to their memory.

יִזְכּוֹר אֱלֹהִים נִשְׁמוֹת כָּל־אַחֵינוּ בְּנֵי יִשְׂרָאֵל שֶׁמָּסְרוּ אֶת־נַפְשׁוֹתֵיהֶם עַל קִדּוּשׁ הַשֵּׁם. אָנָּא תִּהְיֶינָה נַפְשׁוֹתֵיהֶם צְרוּרוֹת בִּצְרוֹר הַחַיִּים וּתְהִי מְנוּחָתָם כָּבוֹד. שֹׂבַע שְׂמָחוֹת אֶת־פָּנֶיךָ, נְעִימוֹת בִּימִינְךָ נֶצַח. אָמֵן.

May God remember for ever our brothers and sisters of the House of Israel who gave their lives for the Sanctification of the Divine Name. May they be at one with the One who is life eternal. May the beauty of their lives shine for evermore, and may my life always bring honor to their memory.

◆ ◆

In the rising of the sun and in its going down, we remember them.

In the blowing of the wind and in the chill of winter, we remember them.

In the opening of buds and in the rebirth of spring, we remember them.

In the blueness of the sky and in the warmth of summer, we remember them.

In the rustling of leaves and in the beauty of autumn, we remember them.

In the beginning of the year and when it ends, we remember them.

When we are weary and in need of strength, we remember them.

When we are lost and sick at heart, we remember them.

When we have joys we yearn to share, we remember them.

So long as we live, they too shall live, for they are now a part of us, as we remember them.

◆ ◆

All rise

אֵל מָלֵא רַחֲמִים, שׁוֹכֵן בַּמְּרוֹמִים, הַמְצֵא מְנוּחָה נְכוֹנָה
תַּחַת כַּנְפֵי הַשְּׁכִינָה עִם קְדוֹשִׁים וּטְהוֹרִים כְּזֹהַר הָרָקִיעַ
מַזְהִירִים לְנִשְׁמוֹת יַקִּירֵינוּ שֶׁהָלְכוּ לְעוֹלָמָם. בַּעַל הָרַחֲמִים

יַסְתִּירֵם בְּסֵתֶר כְּנָפָיו לְעוֹלָמִים, וְיִצְרוֹר בִּצְרוֹר הַחַיִּים
אֶת־נִשְׁמָתָם. יְיָ הוּא נַחֲלָתָם. וְיָנוּחוּ בְּשָׁלוֹם עַל מִשְׁכָּבָם,
וְנֹאמַר: אָמֵן.

O God full of compassion, Eternal Spirit of the universe, grant perfect rest under the wings of Your Presence to our loved ones who have entered eternity. Master of Mercy, let them find refuge for ever in the shadow of Your wings, and let their souls be bound up in the bond of eternal life. The Eternal God is their inheritance. May they rest in peace, and let us say: Amen.

◆ ◆

Special Prayers begin on page 449.

The Ritual for returning the Torah to the Ark begins on page 536 or page 544.

מנחה לשבת וליום טוב

Afternoon Service for Shabbat and Yom Tov

אשרי

אַשְׁרֵי יוֹשְׁבֵי בֵיתֶךָ; עוֹד יְהַלְלוּךָ סֶּלָה.
אַשְׁרֵי הָעָם שֶׁכָּכָה לּוֹ; אַשְׁרֵי הָעָם שֶׁיְיָ אֱלֹהָיו.

Happy are those who dwell in Your house;
they will sing Your praise for ever.

Happy the people to whom such blessing falls;
happy the people whose God is the Lord.

Psalm 145

תְּהִלָּה לְדָוִד
אֲרוֹמִמְךָ, אֱלֹהַי הַמֶּלֶךְ, וַאֲבָרְכָה שִׁמְךָ לְעוֹלָם וָעֶד.
בְּכָל־יוֹם אֲבָרְכֶךָּ, וַאֲהַלְלָה שִׁמְךָ לְעוֹלָם וָעֶד.

I will exalt You, my Sovereign God;
I will bless Your name for ever.

Every day will I bless You;
I will extol Your name for ever.

גָּדוֹל יְיָ וּמְהֻלָּל מְאֹד, וְלִגְדֻלָּתוֹ אֵין חֵקֶר.
דּוֹר לְדוֹר יְשַׁבַּח מַעֲשֶׂיךָ, וּגְבוּרֹתֶיךָ יַגִּידוּ.

Great is the Lord and worthy of praise;
His greatness is infinite.

One generation shall acclaim Your work to the next;
they shall tell of Your mighty acts.

הֲדַר כְּבוֹד הוֹדֶךָ,
וְדִבְרֵי נִפְלְאֹתֶיךָ אָשִׂיחָה.

They shall consider Your radiant glory;

they shall reflect on Your wondrous works.

וֶעֱזוּז נוֹרְאוֹתֶיךָ יֹאמֵרוּ, וּגְדֻלָּתְךָ אֲסַפְּרֶנָּה.
זֵכֶר רַב־טוּבְךָ יַבִּיעוּ, וְצִדְקָתְךָ יְרַנֵּנוּ.

They shall speak of Your awesome might,
and make known Your greatness.

*They shall tell the world of Your great goodness,
and sing of Your righteousness.*

חַנּוּן וְרַחוּם יְיָ, אֶרֶךְ אַפַּיִם וּגְדָל־חָסֶד.
טוֹב־יְיָ לַכֹּל, וְרַחֲמָיו עַל־כָּל־מַעֲשָׂיו.

"The Lord is gracious and compassionate,
endlessly patient, overflowing with love."

*"The Lord is good to all; His compassion
shelters all His creatures."*

יוֹדוּךָ יְיָ כָּל־מַעֲשֶׂיךָ,
וַחֲסִידֶיךָ יְבָרְכוּכָה.

All Your works, O Lord, shall thank You;

Your faithful shall bless You.

כְּבוֹד מַלְכוּתְךָ יֹאמֵרוּ, וּגְבוּרָתְךָ יְדַבֵּרוּ,
לְהוֹדִיעַ לִבְנֵי הָאָדָם גְּבוּרֹתָיו, וּכְבוֹד הֲדַר מַלְכוּתוֹ.

They shall speak of the glory of Your kingdom,
and tell of Your strength:

*to reveal Your power to the world, and
the glorious splendor of Your kingdom.*

מַלְכוּתְךָ מַלְכוּת כָּל־עֹלָמִים,
וּמֶמְשַׁלְתְּךָ בְּכָל־דּוֹר וָדֹר.

Your kingdom is an everlasting kingdom;

Your dominion endures through all generations.

סוֹמֵךְ יְיָ לְכָל־הַנֹּפְלִים, וְזוֹקֵף לְכָל־הַכְּפוּפִים.
עֵינֵי כֹל אֵלֶיךָ יְשַׂבֵּרוּ, וְאַתָּה נוֹתֵן־לָהֶם אֶת־אָכְלָם בְּעִתּוֹ.

Lord, You support the falling;
You raise up all who are bowed down.

The eyes of all are turned to You;
You sustain them in time of need.

פּוֹתֵחַ אֶת־יָדֶךָ וּמַשְׂבִּיעַ לְכָל־חַי רָצוֹן.
צַדִּיק יְיָ בְּכָל־דְּרָכָיו, וְחָסִיד בְּכָל־מַעֲשָׂיו.

You open Your hand to fulfill the needs of all the living.

Lord, You are just in all Your paths, loving in all Your deeds.

קָרוֹב יְיָ לְכָל־קֹרְאָיו, לְכֹל אֲשֶׁר יִקְרָאֻהוּ בֶאֱמֶת.
רְצוֹן־יְרֵאָיו יַעֲשֶׂה, וְאֶת־שַׁוְעָתָם יִשְׁמַע וְיוֹשִׁיעֵם.

The Lord is near to all who call upon Him,
to all who call upon Him in truth.

He will fulfill the hope of all who revere Him;
He will hear their cry and help them.

שׁוֹמֵר יְיָ אֶת־כָּל־אֹהֲבָיו,
וְאֵת כָּל־הָרְשָׁעִים יַשְׁמִיד.

The Lord preserves those who love Him,

but the lawless He brings to grief.

תְּהִלַּת יְיָ יְדַבֶּר־פִּי
וִיבָרֵךְ כָּל־בָּשָׂר שֵׁם קָדְשׁוֹ לְעוֹלָם וָעֶד.
וַאֲנַחְנוּ נְבָרֵךְ יָהּ מֵעַתָּה וְעַד־עוֹלָם. הַלְלוּיָהּ.

My lips shall declare the glory of the Lord;
let all flesh bless His holy name for ever and ever.

We will bless the Lord now and always. Halleluyah!

◆ ◆

On a Festival, continue on page 558 or 559

ON SHABBAT

צִדְקָתְךָ צֶדֶק לְעוֹלָם, וְתוֹרָתְךָ אֱמֶת.
יְיָ צְבָאוֹת, אַשְׁרֵי אָדָם בֹּטֵחַ בָּךְ.
בָּרוּךְ הַגֶּבֶר אֲשֶׁר יִבְטַח בַּייָ, וְהָיָה יְיָ מִבְטַחוֹ.

Your righteousness is everlasting and Your Torah is truth.
O Lord of Hosts, happy is the one who trusts in You.

Blessed are those who trust in God, who make the Lord their refuge.

בָּרוּךְ אֱלֹהֵינוּ שֶׁבְּרָאָנוּ לִכְבוֹדוֹ, וּקְרָאָנוּ לַעֲבוֹדָתוֹ, וְנָתַן לָנוּ תּוֹרַת אֱמֶת, וְחַיֵּי עוֹלָם נָטַע בְּתוֹכֵנוּ. הוּא יִפְתַּח לִבֵּנוּ בְּתוֹרָתוֹ, וְיָשֵׂם בְּלִבֵּנוּ אַהֲבָתוֹ וְיִרְאָתוֹ, לַעֲשׂוֹת רְצוֹנוֹ וּלְעָבְדוֹ בְּלֵבָב שָׁלֵם.

תִּתֵּן אֱמֶת לְיַעֲקֹב, חֶסֶד לְאַבְרָהָם, אֲשֶׁר־נִשְׁבַּעְתָּ לַאֲבֹתֵינוּ מִימֵי קֶדֶם.

Let us praise God, who has touched us with His glory and called us to serve Him; who has given us a Torah of truth, placing eternity into our lives. May He open our hearts to His Torah, and fill us with love and reverence, that we may learn to do His will, and serve Him with a whole heart.

You will show Your truth to Jacob, Your unfailing love to Abraham, as You promised our people long ago.

וּבָא לְצִיּוֹן גּוֹאֵל, וּלְשָׁבֵי פֶשַׁע בְּיַעֲקֹב, נְאֻם יְיָ.

בָּרוּךְ יְיָ, יוֹם יוֹם יַעֲמָס לָנוּ; הָאֵל יְשׁוּעָתֵנוּ, סֶלָה.

To Zion redemption will come, to those in Jacob who turn to God. Blessed is the Lord who daily bears our burden; He is God, our Deliverer.

יְהִי רָצוֹן מִלְּפָנֶיךָ, יְיָ אֱלֹהֵינוּ וֵאלֹהֵי אֲבוֹתֵינוּ, שֶׁנִּשְׁמוֹר חֻקֶּיךָ בָּעוֹלָם הַזֶּה, וְנִזְכֶּה וְנִחְיֶה וְנִרְאֶה, וְנִירַשׁ טוֹבָה וּבְרָכָה, לִשְׁנֵי יְמוֹת הַמָּשִׁיחַ וּלְחַיֵּי הָעוֹלָם הַבָּא.

May it be Your will, O Lord our God, that we obey Your precepts this and every day of our lives, that we may merit the blessed happiness of the messianic time and the life of the world to come.

◆ ◆

וַאֲנִי זֹאת בְּרִיתִי אוֹתָם, אָמַר יְיָ: רוּחִי אֲשֶׁר עָלֶיךָ, וּדְבָרַי אֲשֶׁר־שַׂמְתִּי בְּפִיךָ, לֹא־יָמוּשׁוּ מִפִּיךָ וּמִפִּי זַרְעֲךָ וּמִפִּי זֶרַע זַרְעֲךָ, אָמַר יְיָ, מֵעַתָּה וְעַד־עוֹלָם.

As for Me, this is My covenant with them, says the Lord: Let not My spirit, and the words that I have put in your mouth, depart from you, nor from your children or their children, from this time forth and for ever.

◆ ◆

The Reader's Kaddish is on page 561

The Tefillah is on page 562

ON PESACH AND SUKKOT

From Psalm 136

Give thanks to the Lord, for He is good; *His love is everlasting!*	הוֹדוּ לַייָ, כִּי־טוֹב; כִּי לְעוֹלָם חַסְדּוֹ!
Give thanks to God supreme; *His love is everlasting!*	הוֹדוּ לֵאלֹהֵי הָאֱלֹהִים; כִּי לְעוֹלָם חַסְדּוֹ!
Give thanks to the Lord supreme; *His love is everlasting!*	הוֹדוּ לַאֲדֹנֵי הָאֲדֹנִים; כִּי לְעוֹלָם חַסְדּוֹ!
He made the heavens with wisdom; *His love is everlasting!*	לְעֹשֵׂה הַשָּׁמַיִם בִּתְבוּנָה; כִּי לְעוֹלָם חַסְדּוֹ!
The sun to rule by day; *His love is everlasting!*	אֶת־הַשֶּׁמֶשׁ לְמֶמְשֶׁלֶת בַּיּוֹם; כִּי לְעוֹלָם חַסְדּוֹ!
The moon and stars to hold sway by night; *His love is everlasting!*	אֶת־הַיָּרֵחַ וְכוֹכָבִים לְמֶמְשְׁלוֹת בַּלָּיְלָה; כִּי לְעוֹלָם חַסְדּוֹ!
He led Israel forth from Egypt; *His love is everlasting!*	וַיּוֹצֵא יִשְׂרָאֵל מִמִּצְרָיִם; כִּי לְעוֹלָם חַסְדּוֹ!

בְּיָד חֲזָקָה וּבִזְרוֹעַ נְטוּיָה;
כִּי לְעוֹלָם חַסְדּוֹ!

With a mighty hand and an outstretched arm;
His love is everlasting!

לְמוֹלִיךְ עַמּוֹ בַּמִּדְבָּר;
כִּי לְעוֹלָם חַסְדּוֹ!

He was with His people in the wilderness;
His love is everlasting!

וְנָתַן אַרְצָם לְנַחֲלָה;
כִּי לְעוֹלָם חַסְדּוֹ!

He gave them a land to dwell in;
His love is everlasting!

שֶׁבְּשִׁפְלֵנוּ זָכַר לָנוּ;
כִּי לְעוֹלָם חַסְדּוֹ!

When we were cast down He remembered us;
His love is everlasting!

וַיִּפְרְקֵנוּ מִצָּרֵינוּ;
כִּי לְעוֹלָם חַסְדּוֹ!

He released us from our foes;
His love is everlasting!

נֹתֵן לֶחֶם לְכָל־בָּשָׂר;
כִּי לְעוֹלָם חַסְדּוֹ!

He sustains every living being;
His love is everlasting!

הוֹדוּ לְאֵל הַשָּׁמָיִם;
כִּי לְעוֹלָם חַסְדּוֹ!

Give thanks to the God of the universe;
His love is everlasting!

◆ ◆

The Reader's Kaddish is on page 561

The Tefillah is on page 562

ON SHAVUOT AND ATZERET—SIMCHAT TORAH

Psalm 1

אַשְׁרֵי הָאִישׁ אֲשֶׁר לֹא הָלַךְ בַּעֲצַת רְשָׁעִים, וּבְדֶרֶךְ חַטָּאִים
לֹא עָמָד, וּבְמוֹשַׁב לֵצִים לֹא יָשָׁב.
כִּי אִם בְּתוֹרַת יְיָ חֶפְצוֹ, וּבְתוֹרָתוֹ יֶהְגֶּה יוֹמָם וָלָיְלָה.

Happy are those who do not follow the schemes of the wicked, who do not stand on the path of the sinner, who do not dwell in the circle of the cynic.

Happy are those whose desire is for the Torah of God, who meditate on it day and night.

וְהָיָה כְּעֵץ שָׁתוּל עַל־פַּלְגֵי מָיִם אֲשֶׁר פִּרְיוֹ יִתֵּן בְּעִתּוֹ, וְעָלֵהוּ לֹא־יִבּוֹל, וְכֹל אֲשֶׁר יַעֲשֶׂה יַצְלִיחַ.
לֹא־כֵן הָרְשָׁעִים; כִּי אִם־כַּמֹּץ אֲשֶׁר־תִּדְּפֶנּוּ רוּחַ. עַל־כֵּן לֹא־יָקֻמוּ רְשָׁעִים בַּמִּשְׁפָּט; וְחַטָּאִים בַּעֲדַת צַדִּיקִים.

Then they are like trees rooted near running streams: they bear fruit in due season; their leaf does not wither, and their fruit is sound.

The wicked are not like that; they are like chaff before the wind. They cannot withstand judgment; sinners stand outside the circle of the just.

כִּי־יוֹדֵעַ יְיָ דֶּרֶךְ צַדִּיקִים, וְדֶרֶךְ רְשָׁעִים תֹּאבֵד.

The Lord is with the righteous on their way, and the way of the wicked shall be lost.

◆

זִרְעוּ לָכֶם לִצְדָקָה; קִצְרוּ לְפִי־חֶסֶד. נִירוּ לָכֶם נִיר, וְעֵת לִדְרוֹשׁ אֶת־יְיָ, עַד־יָבוֹא וְיֹרֶה צֶדֶק לָכֶם.

Sow for yourselves righteousness; reap the fruit of steadfast love. Break up your fallow ground, for it is time to seek the Lord, until He comes to rain righteousness upon you.

וְכָרַתִּי לָהֶם בְּרִית בַּיּוֹם הַהוּא, עִם־חַיַּת הַשָּׂדֶה, וְעִם־עוֹף הַשָּׁמַיִם, וְרֶמֶשׂ הָאֲדָמָה; וְקֶשֶׁת וְחֶרֶב וּמִלְחָמָה אֶשְׁבּוֹר מִן־הָאָרֶץ, וְהִשְׁכַּבְתִּים לָבֶטַח.

On that day, says the Lord, I will make for you a covenant with the beasts of the field, the birds of the air, and the insects of the ground; I will abolish the bow, the sword, and war from the earth, and you shall live in peace.

וְאֵרַשְׂתִּיךְ לִי לְעוֹלָם; וְאֵרַשְׂתִּיךְ לִי בְּצֶדֶק וּבְמִשְׁפָּט, וּבְחֶסֶד וּבְרַחֲמִים; וְאֵרַשְׂתִּיךְ לִי בֶּאֱמוּנָה, וְיָדַעַתְּ אֶת־יְיָ.

I will betroth you to Me for ever; I will betroth you to Me in righteousness and justice, in love and compassion; I will betroth you to Me in faithfulness, and you shall know the Lord.

◆ ◆

READER'S KADDISH

חצי קדיש

יִתְגַּדַּל וְיִתְקַדַּשׁ שְׁמֵהּ רַבָּא בְּעָלְמָא דִּי־בְרָא כִרְעוּתֵהּ, וְיַמְלִיךְ מַלְכוּתֵהּ בְּחַיֵּיכוֹן וּבְיוֹמֵיכוֹן וּבְחַיֵּי דְכָל־בֵּית יִשְׂרָאֵל, בַּעֲגָלָא וּבִזְמַן קָרִיב, וְאִמְרוּ: אָמֵן.

יְהֵא שְׁמֵהּ רַבָּא מְבָרַךְ לְעָלַם וּלְעָלְמֵי עָלְמַיָּא.

יִתְבָּרַךְ וְיִשְׁתַּבַּח, וְיִתְפָּאַר וְיִתְרוֹמַם וְיִתְנַשֵּׂא, וְיִתְהַדַּר וְיִתְעַלֶּה וְיִתְהַלַּל שְׁמֵהּ דְּקוּדְשָׁא, בְּרִיךְ הוּא, לְעֵלָּא מִן כָּל־בִּרְכָתָא וְשִׁירָתָא, תֻּשְׁבְּחָתָא וְנֶחֱמָתָא דַּאֲמִירָן בְּעָלְמָא, וְאִמְרוּ: אָמֵן.

Let the glory of God be extolled, let His great name be hallowed in the world whose creation He willed. May His kingdom soon prevail, in our own day, our own lives, and the life of all Israel, and let us say: Amen.

Let His great name be blessed for ever and ever.

Let the name of the Holy One, blessed is He, be glorified, exalted and honored, though He is beyond all the praises, songs, and adorations that we can utter, and let us say: Amen.

◆ ◆

All rise

תפלה

אֲדֹנָי, שְׂפָתַי תִּפְתָּח, וּפִי יַגִּיד תְּהִלָּתֶךָ.

Eternal God, open my lips, that my mouth may declare Your glory.

◆ ◆

GOD OF ALL GENERATIONS אבות

בָּרוּךְ אַתָּה, יְיָ אֱלֹהֵינוּ וֵאלֹהֵי אֲבוֹתֵינוּ, אֱלֹהֵי אַבְרָהָם, אֱלֹהֵי יִצְחָק וֵאלֹהֵי יַעֲקֹב: הָאֵל הַגָּדוֹל, הַגִּבּוֹר וְהַנּוֹרָא, אֵל עֶלְיוֹן.

We praise You, Lord our God and God of all generations: God of Abraham, God of Isaac, God of Jacob; great, mighty, and awesome God, God supreme.

גּוֹמֵל חֲסָדִים טוֹבִים, וְקוֹנֵה הַכֹּל, וְזוֹכֵר חַסְדֵי אָבוֹת, וּמֵבִיא גְאֻלָּה לִבְנֵי בְנֵיהֶם, לְמַעַן שְׁמוֹ, בְּאַהֲבָה.*

Master of all the living, Your ways are ways of love. You remember the faithfulness of our ancestors, and in love bring redemption to their children's children for the sake of Your name.*

מֶלֶךְ עוֹזֵר וּמוֹשִׁיעַ וּמָגֵן. בָּרוּךְ אַתָּה, יְיָ, מָגֵן אַבְרָהָם.

You are our King and our Help, our Savior and our Shield. Blessed is the Lord, the Shield of Abraham.

** On Shabbat Shuvah insert:*

זָכְרֵנוּ לְחַיִּים, מֶלֶךְ חָפֵץ בַּחַיִּים,
וְכָתְבֵנוּ בְּסֵפֶר הַחַיִּים, לְמַעַנְךָ אֱלֹהִים חַיִּים.

Remember us unto life, for You are the King who delights in life, and inscribe us in the Book of Life, that Your will may prevail, O God of life.

◆ ◆

GOD'S POWER גבורות

אַתָּה גִּבּוֹר לְעוֹלָם, אֲדֹנָי, מְחַיֵּה הַכֹּל אַתָּה, רַב לְהוֹשִׁיעַ.

Eternal is Your might, O Lord; all life is Your gift; great is Your power to save!

מְכַלְכֵּל חַיִּים בְּחֶסֶד, מְחַיֵּה הַכֹּל בְּרַחֲמִים רַבִּים. סוֹמֵךְ נוֹפְלִים, וְרוֹפֵא חוֹלִים, וּמַתִּיר אֲסוּרִים, וּמְקַיֵּם אֱמוּנָתוֹ לִישֵׁנֵי עָפָר.

With love You sustain the living, with great compassion give life to all. You send help to the falling and bring healing to the sick; You bring freedom to the captive and keep faith with those who sleep in the dust.

מִי כָמוֹךָ, בַּעַל גְּבוּרוֹת, וּמִי דּוֹמֶה לָּךְ, מֶלֶךְ מֵמִית וּמְחַיֶּה וּמַצְמִיחַ יְשׁוּעָה?*

וְנֶאֱמָן אַתָּה לְהַחֲיוֹת הַכֹּל. בָּרוּךְ אַתָּה, יְיָ, מְחַיֵּה הַכֹּל.

Who is like You, Master of Might? Who is Your equal, O Lord of life and death, Source of salvation? Blessed is the Lord, the Source of life.*

** On Shabbat Shuvah insert:*

מִי כָמוֹךָ, אַב הָרַחֲמִים, זוֹכֵר יְצוּרָיו לְחַיִּים בְּרַחֲמִים?

Who is like You, Source of mercy, who in compassion sustains the life of His children?

◆ ◆

SANCTIFICATION קדושה

נְקַדֵּשׁ אֶת־שִׁמְךָ בָּעוֹלָם כְּשֵׁם שֶׁמַּקְדִּישִׁים אוֹתוֹ בִּשְׁמֵי מָרוֹם, כַּכָּתוּב עַל־יַד נְבִיאֶךָ: וְקָרָא זֶה אֶל־זֶה וְאָמַר:

We sanctify Your name on earth, even as all things, to the ends of time and space, proclaim Your holiness; and in the words of the prophet we say:

קָדוֹשׁ, קָדוֹשׁ, קָדוֹשׁ יְיָ צְבָאוֹת, מְלֹא כָל־הָאָרֶץ כְּבוֹדוֹ.

Holy, Holy, Holy is the Lord of Hosts; the fullness of the whole earth is His glory!

לְעֻמָּתָם בָּרוּךְ יֹאמֵרוּ:

They respond to Your glory with blessing:

בָּרוּךְ כְּבוֹד יְיָ מִמְּקוֹמוֹ.

Blessed is the glory of God in heaven and earth.

וּבְדִבְרֵי קָדְשְׁךָ כָּתוּב לֵאמֹר:

And this is Your sacred word:

יִמְלֹךְ יְיָ לְעוֹלָם, אֱלֹהַיִךְ צִיּוֹן לְדֹר וָדֹר, הַלְלוּיָהּ.

The Lord shall reign for ever; your God, O Zion, from generation to generation. Halleluyah!

לְדוֹר וָדוֹר נַגִּיד גָּדְלֶךָ, וּלְנֵצַח נְצָחִים קְדֻשָּׁתְךָ נַקְדִּישׁ.
וְשִׁבְחֲךָ, אֱלֹהֵינוּ, מִפִּינוּ לֹא יָמוּשׁ לְעוֹלָם וָעֶד.*
בָּרוּךְ אַתָּה, יְיָ, הָאֵל הַקָּדוֹשׁ.

To all generations we will make known Your greatness, and to all eternity proclaim Your holiness. Your praise, O God, shall never depart from our lips.*
Blessed is the Lord, the holy God.

** On Shabbat Shuvah conclude:*

Blessed is the Lord, the holy King. בָּרוּךְ אַתָּה, יְיָ, הַמֶּלֶךְ הַקָּדוֹשׁ.

All are seated

◆ ◆

On Yom Tov, continue on page 566.

ON SHABBAT

THE HOLINESS OF SHABBAT

קדושת היום

אַתָּה אֶחָד וְשִׁמְךָ אֶחָד, וּמִי כְּעַמְּךָ יִשְׂרָאֵל, גּוֹי אֶחָד בָּאָרֶץ? תִּפְאֶרֶת גְּדֻלָּה וַעֲטֶרֶת יְשׁוּעָה, יוֹם מְנוּחָה וּקְדֻשָּׁה לְעַמְּךָ נָתָתָּ:

You are One, Your name is One, and there is none like Your people Israel, a people unique on the earth. A garland of glory have You given us, a crown of salvation: a day of rest and holiness.

אַבְרָהָם יָגֵל, יִצְחָק יְרַנֵּן, יַעֲקֹב וּבָנָיו יָנוּחוּ בוֹ. מְנוּחַת אַהֲבָה וּנְדָבָה, מְנוּחַת אֱמֶת וֶאֱמוּנָה, מְנוּחַת שָׁלוֹם וְשַׁלְוָה וְהַשְׁקֵט וָבֶטַח. מְנוּחָה שְׁלֵמָה שֶׁאַתָּה רוֹצֶה בָּהּ.

Abraham rejoiced in it, Isaac sang, Jacob and his children were refreshed by its rest. In this rest are love and sharing, truth and faithfulness and peace, quiet and safety. It is the perfect rest that You have willed.

יַכִּירוּ בָנֶיךָ וְיֵדְעוּ כִּי מֵאִתְּךָ הִיא מְנוּחָתָם, וְעַל־מְנוּחָתָם יַקְדִּישׁוּ אֶת־שְׁמֶךָ.

May Your children come to understand that this Sabbath rest links them to You, that by it they may hallow Your name.

◆

אֱלֹהֵינוּ וֵאלֹהֵי אֲבוֹתֵינוּ, רְצֵה בִמְנוּחָתֵנוּ. קַדְּשֵׁנוּ בְּמִצְוֹתֶיךָ, וְתֵן חֶלְקֵנוּ בְּתוֹרָתֶךָ. שַׂבְּעֵנוּ מִטּוּבֶךָ, וְשַׂמְּחֵנוּ בִּישׁוּעָתֶךָ, וְטַהֵר לִבֵּנוּ לְעָבְדְּךָ בֶּאֱמֶת. וְהַנְחִילֵנוּ, יְיָ אֱלֹהֵינוּ, בְּאַהֲבָה וּבְרָצוֹן שַׁבַּת קָדְשֶׁךָ, וְיָנוּחוּ בָהּ יִשְׂרָאֵל מְקַדְּשֵׁי שְׁמֶךָ. בָּרוּךְ אַתָּה, יְיָ, מְקַדֵּשׁ הַשַּׁבָּת.

Our God and God of ages past, may our rest on this day be pleasing in Your sight. Sanctify us with Your Mitzvot, and let

Your Torah be our way of life. Satisfy us with Your goodness, gladden us with Your salvation, and purify our hearts to serve You in truth. In Your gracious love, O Lord our God, let Your holy Sabbath remain our heritage, that all Israel, hallowing Your name, may find rest and peace. Blessed is the Lord, for the Sabbath and its holiness.

◆ ◆

Continue with Retsei, on page 568.

ON YOM TOV

THE HOLINESS OF YOM TOV — קדושת היום

אַתָּה בְחַרְתָּנוּ מִכָּל־הָעַמִּים, אָהַבְתָּ אוֹתָנוּ, וְרָצִיתָ בָּנוּ, וְרוֹמַמְתָּנוּ מִכָּל־הַלְּשׁוֹנוֹת, וְקִדַּשְׁתָּנוּ בְּמִצְוֹתֶיךָ. וְקֵרַבְתָּנוּ, מַלְכֵּנוּ, לַעֲבוֹדָתֶךָ, וְשִׁמְךָ הַגָּדוֹל וְהַקָּדוֹשׁ עָלֵינוּ קָרָאתָ.

In love and favor, O God, You have chosen us from all the peoples, exalting us by hallowing us with Your Mitzvot. Our Sovereign, You have summoned us to Your service, that through us Your great and holy name may become known in all the earth.

וַתִּתֶּן לָנוּ, יְיָ אֱלֹהֵינוּ, בְּאַהֲבָה [שַׁבָּתוֹת לִמְנוּחָה וּ] מוֹעֲדִים לְשִׂמְחָה, חַגִּים וּזְמַנִּים לְשָׂשׂוֹן: אֶת־יוֹם [הַשַּׁבָּת הַזֶּה וְאֶת־יוֹם]

In Your love, O Lord our God, You have given us [Sabbaths of rest,] feasts of gladness and seasons of joy: this [Sabbath day and this] festival of

Pesach – season of our freedom,	חַג הַמַּצּוֹת הַזֶּה – זְמַן חֵרוּתֵנוּ,
Shavuot – season of revelation,	חַג הַשָּׁבֻעוֹת הַזֶּה – זְמַן מַתַּן תּוֹרָתֵנוּ,
Sukkot – season of thanksgiving,	חַג הַסֻּכּוֹת הַזֶּה – זְמַן שִׂמְחָתֵנוּ,
Atzeret-Simchat Torah – season of our gladness,	הַשְּׁמִינִי חַג הָעֲצֶרֶת הַזֶּה – זְמַן שִׂמְחָתֵנוּ,

מִקְרָא קֹדֶשׁ, זֵכֶר לִיצִיאַת מִצְרָיִם.

to unite in worship and recall the Exodus from Egypt.

◆

אֱלֹהֵינוּ וֵאלֹהֵי אֲבוֹתֵינוּ, יַעֲלֶה וְיָבֹא וְיִזָּכֵר זִכְרוֹנֵנוּ וְזִכְרוֹן כָּל־עַמְּךָ בֵּית יִשְׂרָאֵל לְפָנֶיךָ, לְטוֹבָה לְחֵן לְחֶסֶד וּלְרַחֲמִים לְחַיִּים וּלְשָׁלוֹם בְּיוֹם

Our God and God of all ages, be mindful of Your people Israel on this

Feast of Pesach,	חַג הַמַּצּוֹת הַזֶּה.
Feast of Shavuot,	חַג הַשָּׁבֻעוֹת הַזֶּה.
Feast of Sukkot,	חַג הַסֻּכּוֹת הַזֶּה.
Feast of Atzeret–Simchat Torah,	הַשְּׁמִינִי חַג הָעֲצֶרֶת הַזֶּה.

and renew in us love and compassion, goodness, life, and peace.

זָכְרֵנוּ, יְיָ אֱלֹהֵינוּ, בּוֹ לְטוֹבָה. אָמֵן.

This day remember us for well-being. Amen.

וּפָקְדֵנוּ בוֹ לִבְרָכָה. אָמֵן.

This day bless us with Your nearness. Amen.

וְהוֹשִׁיעֵנוּ בוֹ לְחַיִּים. אָמֵן.

This day help us to a fuller life. Amen.

◆

וְהַשִּׂיאֵנוּ, יְיָ אֱלֹהֵינוּ, אֶת־בִּרְכַּת מוֹעֲדֶיךָ לְחַיִּים וּלְשָׁלוֹם, לְשִׂמְחָה וּלְשָׂשׂוֹן, כַּאֲשֶׁר רָצִיתָ, וְאָמַרְתָּ לְבָרְכֵנוּ. אֱלֹהֵינוּ וֵאלֹהֵי אֲבוֹתֵינוּ, [רְצֵה בִמְנוּחָתֵנוּ,] קַדְּשֵׁנוּ בְּמִצְוֹתֶיךָ, וְתֵן חֶלְקֵנוּ בְּתוֹרָתֶךָ. שַׂבְּעֵנוּ מִטּוּבֶךָ, וְשַׂמְּחֵנוּ בִּישׁוּעָתֶךָ, וְטַהֵר לִבֵּנוּ לְעָבְדְּךָ בֶּאֱמֶת. וְהַנְחִילֵנוּ, יְיָ אֱלֹהֵינוּ, [בְּאַהֲבָה וּבְרָצוֹן,] בְּשִׂמְחָה וּבְשָׂשׂוֹן [שַׁבַּת וּ] מוֹעֲדֵי קָדְשֶׁךָ, וְיִשְׂמְחוּ בְךָ יִשְׂרָאֵל, מְקַדְּשֵׁי שְׁמֶךָ. בָּרוּךְ אַתָּה, יְיָ, מְקַדֵּשׁ [הַשַּׁבָּת וְ] יִשְׂרָאֵל וְהַזְּמַנִּים.

Bestow upon us the blessing of Your holy Festivals, and may we so celebrate them as to be worthy of Your favor.

Our God and God of ages past, sanctify us with Your Mitzvot, and let Your Torah be our way of life. [May our rest on this day be pleasing in Your sight.] Satisfy us with Your goodness, gladden us with Your salvation, and purify our hearts to serve You in truth. [In Your gracious love let Your holy Sabbath remain our heritage.] Let us celebrate Your holy Festivals with joy and gladness, that all Israel, hallowing Your name, may have cause to rejoice. Blessed is the Lord, who hallows [the Sabbath,] the House of Israel and the Festivals.

◆ ◆

WORSHIP עבודה

רְצֵה, יְיָ אֱלֹהֵינוּ, בְּעַמְּךָ יִשְׂרָאֵל, וּתְפִלָּתָם בְּאַהֲבָה תְקַבֵּל,
וּתְהִי לְרָצוֹן תָּמִיד עֲבוֹדַת יִשְׂרָאֵל עַמֶּךָ.

Be gracious, O Lord our God, to Your people Israel, and receive our prayers with love. O may our worship always be acceptable to You.

אֵל קָרוֹב לְכָל־קֹרְאָיו, פְּנֵה אֶל עֲבָדֶיךָ וְחָנֵּנוּ; שְׁפוֹךְ רוּחֲךָ
עָלֵינוּ, וְתֶחֱזֶינָה עֵינֵינוּ בְּשׁוּבְךָ לְצִיּוֹן בְּרַחֲמִים.
בָּרוּךְ אַתָּה, יְיָ, הַמַּחֲזִיר שְׁכִינָתוֹ לְצִיּוֹן.

Fill us with the knowledge that You are near to all who seek You in truth. Let our eyes behold Your presence in our midst and in the midst of our people in Zion. Blessed is the Lord, whose presence gives life to Zion and all Israel.

◆ ◆

ON ROSH CHODESH AND CHOL HAMO-EID

אֱלֹהֵינוּ וֵאלֹהֵי אֲבוֹתֵינוּ, יַעֲלֶה וְיָבֹא וְיִזָּכֵר זִכְרוֹנֵנוּ וְזִכְרוֹן כָּל־עַמְּךָ בֵּית יִשְׂרָאֵל לְפָנֶיךָ, לְטוֹבָה לְחֵן לְחֶסֶד וּלְרַחֲמִים, לְחַיִּים וּלְשָׁלוֹם בְּיוֹם

Our God and God of all ages, be mindful of Your people Israel on this

first day of the new month,	רֹאשׁ הַחֹדֶשׁ הַזֶּה.
day of Pesach,	חַג הַמַּצּוֹת הַזֶּה.
day of Sukkot,	חַג הַסֻּכּוֹת הַזֶּה.

and renew in us love and compassion, goodness, life and peace.

זָכְרֵנוּ, יְיָ אֱלֹהֵינוּ, בּוֹ לְטוֹבָה. אָמֵן.

This day remember us for well-being. Amen.

וּפָקְדֵנוּ בוֹ לִבְרָכָה. אָמֵן.

This day bless us with Your nearness. Amen.

וְהוֹשִׁיעֵנוּ בוֹ לְחַיִּים. אָמֵן.

This day help us to a fuller life. Amen.

◆ ◆

THANKSGIVING — הודאה

מוֹדִים אֲנַחְנוּ לָךְ, שָׁאַתָּה הוּא יְיָ אֱלֹהֵינוּ וֵאלֹהֵי אֲבוֹתֵינוּ לְעוֹלָם וָעֶד. צוּר חַיֵּינוּ, מָגֵן יִשְׁעֵנוּ, אַתָּה הוּא לְדוֹר וָדוֹר. נוֹדֶה לְּךָ וּנְסַפֵּר תְּהִלָּתֶךָ, עַל־חַיֵּינוּ הַמְּסוּרִים בְּיָדֶךָ, וְעַל־נִשְׁמוֹתֵינוּ הַפְּקוּדוֹת לָךְ, וְעַל־נִסֶּיךָ שֶׁבְּכָל־יוֹם עִמָּנוּ, וְעַל־נִפְלְאוֹתֶיךָ וְטוֹבוֹתֶיךָ שֶׁבְּכָל־עֵת, עֶרֶב וָבֹקֶר וְצָהֳרָיִם. הַטּוֹב: כִּי לֹא־כָלוּ רַחֲמֶיךָ, וְהַמְרַחֵם: כִּי־לֹא תַמּוּ חֲסָדֶיךָ, מֵעוֹלָם קִוִּינוּ לָךְ.

We gratefully acknowledge that You are the Lord our God and God of our people, the God of all generations. You are the Rock of our life, the Power that shields us in every age. We thank You and sing Your praises: for our lives, which are in Your hand; for our souls, which are in Your keeping; for the signs of Your presence we encounter every day; and for Your wondrous gifts at all times, morning, noon, and night. You are Goodness: Your mercies never end; You are Compassion: Your love will never fail. You have always been our hope.

וְעַל כֻּלָּם יִתְבָּרַךְ וְיִתְרוֹמַם שִׁמְךָ, מַלְכֵּנוּ, תָּמִיד לְעוֹלָם וָעֶד.

For all these things, O Sovereign God, let Your name be for ever exalted and blessed.

On Shabbat Shuvah insert:

וּכְתוֹב לְחַיִּים טוֹבִים כָּל־בְּנֵי בְרִיתֶךָ.

Let life abundant be the heritage of all Your children.

וְכֹל הַחַיִּים יוֹדְוּךָ סֶּלָה, וִיהַלְלוּ אֶת שִׁמְךָ בֶּאֱמֶת, הָאֵל יְשׁוּעָתֵנוּ וְעֶזְרָתֵנוּ סֶלָה. בָּרוּךְ אַתָּה, יְיָ, הַטּוֹב שִׁמְךָ וּלְךָ נָאֶה לְהוֹדוֹת.

O God our Redeemer and Helper, let all who live affirm You and praise Your name in truth. Lord, whose nature is Goodness, we give You thanks and praise.

◆ ◆

ON CHANUKAH

עַל הַנִּסִּים וְעַל הַפֻּרְקָן, וְעַל הַגְּבוּרוֹת וְעַל הַתְּשׁוּעוֹת, וְעַל הַמִּלְחָמוֹת, שֶׁעָשִׂיתָ לַאֲבוֹתֵינוּ בַּיָּמִים הָהֵם בַּזְּמַן הַזֶּה.

בִּימֵי מַתִּתְיָהוּ בֶּן־יוֹחָנָן כֹּהֵן גָּדוֹל, חַשְׁמוֹנַי וּבָנָיו, כְּשֶׁעָמְדָה מַלְכוּת יָוָן הָרְשָׁעָה עַל־עַמְּךָ יִשְׂרָאֵל לְהַשְׁכִּיחָם תּוֹרָתֶךָ, וּלְהַעֲבִירָם מֵחֻקֵּי רְצוֹנֶךָ.

וְאַתָּה בְּרַחֲמֶיךָ הָרַבִּים עָמַדְתָּ לָהֶם בְּעֵת צָרָתָם. רַבְתָּ אֶת־רִיבָם, דַּנְתָּ אֶת־דִּינָם, מָסַרְתָּ גִבּוֹרִים בְּיַד חַלָּשִׁים, וְרַבִּים בְּיַד מְעַטִּים, וּטְמֵאִים בְּיַד טְהוֹרִים, וּרְשָׁעִים בְּיַד צַדִּיקִים, וְזֵדִים בְּיַד עוֹסְקֵי תוֹרָתֶךָ.

וּלְךָ עָשִׂיתָ שֵׁם גָּדוֹל וְקָדוֹשׁ בְּעוֹלָמֶךָ, וּלְעַמְּךָ יִשְׂרָאֵל עָשִׂיתָ תְּשׁוּעָה גְדוֹלָה וּפֻרְקָן כְּהַיּוֹם הַזֶּה.

וְאַחַר כֵּן בָּאוּ בָנֶיךָ לִדְבִיר בֵּיתֶךָ, וּפִנּוּ אֶת־הֵיכָלֶךָ, וְטִהֲרוּ אֶת־מִקְדָּשֶׁךָ, וְהִדְלִיקוּ נֵרוֹת בְּחַצְרוֹת קָדְשֶׁךָ, וְקָבְעוּ שְׁמוֹנַת יְמֵי חֲנֻכָּה אֵלּוּ לְהוֹדוֹת וּלְהַלֵּל לְשִׁמְךָ הַגָּדוֹל.

We give thanks for the redeeming wonders and the mighty deeds by which, at this season, our people was saved in days of old.

In the days of the Hasmoneans, a tyrant arose against our ancestors, determined to make them forget Your Torah, and to turn them away from obedience to Your will. But You were at their side in time of trouble. You gave them strength to struggle and to triumph, that they might serve You in freedom.

Through the power of Your spirit the weak defeated the strong, the few prevailed over the many, and the righteous were triumphant. Then Your children returned to Your house, to purify the sanctuary and kindle its lights. And they dedicated these days to give thanks and praise to Your great name.

◆ ◆

PEACE — ברכת שלום

שָׁלוֹם רָב עַל־יִשְׂרָאֵל עַמְּךָ תָּשִׂים לְעוֹלָם, כִּי אַתָּה הוּא מֶלֶךְ אָדוֹן לְכָל הַשָּׁלוֹם. וְטוֹב בְּעֵינֶיךָ לְבָרֵךְ אֶת־עַמְּךָ יִשְׂרָאֵל בְּכָל־עֵת וּבְכָל־שָׁעָה בִּשְׁלוֹמֶךָ.*

בָּרוּךְ אַתָּה, יְיָ, הַמְבָרֵךְ אֶת־עַמּוֹ יִשְׂרָאֵל בַּשָּׁלוֹם.

*O Sovereign Lord of peace, let Israel Your people know enduring peace, for it is good in Your sight continually to bless Israel with Your peace.**

Praised be the Lord, who blesses His people Israel with peace.

** On Shabbat Shuvah conclude:*

בְּסֵפֶר חַיִּים וּבְרָכָה נִכָּתֵב לְחַיִּים טוֹבִים וּלְשָׁלוֹם.

בָּרוּךְ אַתָּה, יְיָ, עוֹשֵׂה הַשָּׁלוֹם.

Teach us then to find our happiness in the search for righteousness and peace.
Blessed is the Lord, the Source of peace.

◆ ◆

SILENT PRAYER

אֱלֹהַי, נְצוֹר לְשׁוֹנִי מֵרָע, וּשְׂפָתַי מִדַּבֵּר מִרְמָה, וְלִמְקַלְלַי נַפְשִׁי תִדּוֹם, וְנַפְשִׁי כֶּעָפָר לַכֹּל תִּהְיֶה. פְּתַח לִבִּי בְּתוֹרָתֶךָ, וּבְמִצְוֹתֶיךָ תִּרְדּוֹף נַפְשִׁי, וְכֹל הַחוֹשְׁבִים עָלַי רָעָה, מְהֵרָה הָפֵר עֲצָתָם וְקַלְקֵל מַחֲשַׁבְתָּם. עֲשֵׂה לְמַעַן שְׁמֶךָ, עֲשֵׂה לְמַעַן יְמִינֶךָ, עֲשֵׂה לְמַעַן קְדֻשָּׁתֶךָ, עֲשֵׂה לְמַעַן תּוֹרָתֶךָ. לְמַעַן יֵחָלְצוּן יְדִידֶיךָ, הוֹשִׁיעָה יְמִינְךָ וַעֲנֵנִי.

O God, keep my tongue from evil and my lips from deceit. Help me to be silent in the face of derision, humble in the presence of all. Open my heart to Your Torah, and I will hasten to do Your Mitzvot. Save me with Your power; in time of trouble be my answer, that those who love You may rejoice.

◆ ◆

יִהְיוּ לְרָצוֹן אִמְרֵי־פִי וְהֶגְיוֹן לִבִּי לְפָנֶיךָ, יְיָ, צוּרִי וְגוֹאֲלִי.

May the words of my mouth, and the meditations of my heart, be acceptable to You, O Lord, my Rock and my Redeemer.

or

עֹשֶׂה שָׁלוֹם בִּמְרוֹמָיו, הוּא יַעֲשֶׂה שָׁלוֹם עָלֵינוּ וְעַל כָּל־יִשְׂרָאֵל, וְאִמְרוּ אָמֵן.

May He who causes peace to reign in the high heavens let peace descend on us, on all Israel, and all the world.

◆ ◆

The Rituals for the Reading of Torah on Shabbat begin on page 415.

Concluding Prayers begin on page 613.

תפלות לתשעה באב וליום השואה

Service for Tish'a be-Av and Yom Hasho-ah

In the presence of eyes
which witnessed the slaughter,
which saw the oppression
the heart could not bear,
and as witness the heart
that once taught compassion
until the days came to pass
that crushed human feeling,
I have taken an oath: To remember it all,
to remember, not once to forget!
Forget not one thing to the last generation
when degradation shall cease,
to the last, to its ending,
when the rod of instruction
shall have come to conclusion.
An oath: Not in vain passed over
the night of the terror.
An oath: No morning shall see me at
    flesh-pots again.
An oath: Lest from this we learned
    nothing.

◆ ◆

Ear of mankind
overgrown with nettles,
would you hear?

If the voices of the prophets blew
on flutes made of murdered children's bones
and exhaled airs burnt with
martyrs' cries —
if they built a bridge of old men's dying groans —

Ear of mankind
occupied with small sounds,
would you hear?

◆ ◆

זאָג ניט קיינמאָל אַז דו גייסט דעם לעצטן וועג,
ווען הימלען בלײַענע פֿאַרשטעלן בלויע טעג.
ווײַל קומען וועט נאָך אונדזער אויסגעבענקטע שעה,
ס'וועט אַ פּויק טאָן אונדזער טראָט: מיר זײַנען דאָ!

You must not say that you now walk the final way,
Because the darkened heavens hide the blue of day.
The time we've longed for will at last draw near,
And our steps, as drums, will sound that we are here.

פֿון גרינעם פּאַלמען-לאַנד ביז ווײַסן לאַנד פֿון שניי,
מיר זײַנען דאָ, מיט אונדזער פּײַן, מיט אונדזער וויי.
און וווּ געפֿאַלן ס'איז אַ שפּריץ פֿון אונדזער בלוט,
וועט אַ שפּראָץ טאָן אונדזער גבֿורה, אונדזער מוט.

From land all green with palms to lands all white with snow
We now arrive with all our pain and all our woe.
Where our blood sprayed out and came to touch the land,
There our courage and our faith will rise and stand.

◆ ◆

MEDITATION

The universe whispers that all things are intertwined. Yet at times we hear the loud cry of discord. To which voice shall we listen? Although we long for harmony, we cannot close our ears to the noise of war, the rasp of hate. How dare we speak of concord, when the fact and symbol of our age is Auschwitz?

The intelligent heart does not deny reality. We must not forget the grief of yesterday, nor ignore the pain of today. But yesterday is past. It cannot tell us what tomorrow will bring. If there is goodness at the heart of life, then its power, like the power of evil, is real. Which shall prevail? Moment by moment we choose between them. If we choose rightly, and often enough, the broken fragments of our world will be restored to wholeness.

For this we need strength and help. We turn in hope, therefore, to a Power beyond us. He has many names, but He is One. He creates; He sustains; He loves; He inspires us with the hope that we can make ourselves one as He is One.

◆ ◆

O God, help us to build Your kingdom, one human world united in heart and soul!

◆ ◆

אֲנִי מַאֲמִין בֶּאֱמוּנָה שְׁלֵמָה בְּבִיאַת הַמָּשִׁיחַ. וְאַף עַל פִּי שֶׁיִּתְמַהְמֵהַּ, עִם כָּל־זֶה אֲנִי מַאֲמִין, עִם כָּל־זֶה אֲחַכֶּה־לוֹ בְּכָל־יוֹם שֶׁיָּבוֹא.

I believe with perfect faith in the Messiah's coming.
And even if he be delayed, I will await him.

◆ ◆

READER'S KADDISH — חצי קדיש

יִתְגַּדַּל וְיִתְקַדַּשׁ שְׁמֵהּ רַבָּא בְּעָלְמָא דִּי־בְרָא כִרְעוּתֵהּ,
וְיַמְלִיךְ מַלְכוּתֵהּ בְּחַיֵּיכוֹן וּבְיוֹמֵיכוֹן וּבְחַיֵּי דְכָל־בֵּית
יִשְׂרָאֵל, בַּעֲגָלָא וּבִזְמַן קָרִיב, וְאִמְרוּ: אָמֵן.

יְהֵא שְׁמֵהּ רַבָּא מְבָרַךְ לְעָלַם וּלְעָלְמֵי עָלְמַיָּא.

יִתְבָּרַךְ וְיִשְׁתַּבַּח, וְיִתְפָּאַר וְיִתְרוֹמַם וְיִתְנַשֵּׂא, וְיִתְהַדַּר
וְיִתְעַלֶּה וְיִתְהַלַּל שְׁמֵהּ דְּקוּדְשָׁא, בְּרִיךְ הוּא, לְעֵלָּא מִן
כָּל־בִּרְכָתָא וְשִׁירָתָא, תֻּשְׁבְּחָתָא וְנֶחֱמָתָא דַּאֲמִירָן בְּעָלְמָא,
וְאִמְרוּ: אָמֵן.

Let the glory of God be extolled, let His great name be hallowed in the world whose creation He willed. May His kingdom soon prevail, in our own day, our own lives, and the life of all Israel, and let us say. Amen.

Let His great name be blessed for ever and ever.

Let the name of the Holy One, blessed is He, be glorified, exalted and honored, though He is beyond all the praises, songs, and adorations that we can utter, and let us say: Amen.

◆ ◆

שמע וברכותיה

All rise

בָּרְכוּ אֶת־יְיָ הַמְבֹרָךְ!

Praise the Lord, to whom our praise is due!

בָּרוּךְ יְיָ הַמְבֹרָךְ לְעוֹלָם וָעֶד!

Praised be the Lord, to whom our praise is due,
now and for ever!

◆ ◆

Morning

בָּרוּךְ אַתָּה, יְיָ אֱלֹהֵינוּ, מֶלֶךְ הָעוֹלָם, יוֹצֵר אוֹר וּבוֹרֵא חֹשֶׁךְ, עֹשֶׂה שָׁלוֹם וּבוֹרֵא אֶת־הַכֹּל. הַמֵּאִיר לָאָרֶץ וְלַדָּרִים עָלֶיהָ בְּרַחֲמִים, וּבְטוּבוֹ מְחַדֵּשׁ בְּכָל־יוֹם תָּמִיד מַעֲשֵׂה בְרֵאשִׁית. מָה רַבּוּ מַעֲשֶׂיךָ, יְיָ! כֻּלָּם בְּחָכְמָה עָשִׂיתָ, מָלְאָה הָאָרֶץ קִנְיָנֶךָ.

תִּתְבָּרַךְ, יְיָ אֱלֹהֵינוּ, עַל־שֶׁבַח מַעֲשֵׂה יָדֶיךָ, וְעַל־מְאוֹרֵי־אוֹר שֶׁעָשִׂיתָ; יְפָאֲרוּךָ. סֶּלָה.

בָּרוּךְ אַתָּה, יְיָ, יוֹצֵר הַמְּאוֹרוֹת.

Evening

בָּרוּךְ אַתָּה, יְיָ אֱלֹהֵינוּ, מֶלֶךְ הָעוֹלָם, אֲשֶׁר בִּדְבָרוֹ מַעֲרִיב עֲרָבִים. בְּחָכְמָה פּוֹתֵחַ שְׁעָרִים, וּבִתְבוּנָה מְשַׁנֶּה עִתִּים, וּמַחֲלִיף אֶת־הַזְּמַנִּים, וּמְסַדֵּר אֶת־הַכּוֹכָבִים בְּמִשְׁמְרוֹתֵיהֶם בָּרָקִיעַ כִּרְצוֹנוֹ. בּוֹרֵא יוֹם וָלָיְלָה, גּוֹלֵל אוֹר מִפְּנֵי חֹשֶׁךְ וְחֹשֶׁךְ מִפְּנֵי אוֹר, וּמַעֲבִיר יוֹם וּמֵבִיא לָיְלָה, וּמַבְדִּיל בֵּין יוֹם וּבֵין לָיְלָה, יְיָ צְבָאוֹת שְׁמוֹ. אֵל חַי וְקַיָּם, תָּמִיד יִמְלוֹךְ עָלֵינוּ, לְעוֹלָם וָעֶד. בָּרוּךְ אַתָּה, יְיָ, הַמַּעֲרִיב עֲרָבִים.

Blessed is the Lord our God, Ruler of the universe, by whose law the shadows of evening fall and the gates of morn are opened. In wisdom You have established the changes of times and seasons and ordered the ways of the stars in their heavenly courses. Creator of heaven and earth, O ever-living God, rule over us for ever. Blessed is the Lord, for the day and its work and for the night and its rest.

◆ ◆

Morning

אַהֲבָה רַבָּה אֲהַבְתָּנוּ, יְיָ אֱלֹהֵינוּ, חֶמְלָה גְדוֹלָה וִיתֵרָה חָמַלְתָּ עָלֵינוּ. אָבִינוּ מַלְכֵּנוּ, בַּעֲבוּר אֲבוֹתֵינוּ שֶׁבָּטְחוּ בְךָ וַתְּלַמְּדֵם חֻקֵּי חַיִּים, כֵּן תְּחָנֵּנוּ

Evening

אַהֲבַת עוֹלָם בֵּית יִשְׂרָאֵל עַמְּךָ אָהָבְתָּ: תּוֹרָה וּמִצְוֹת, חֻקִּים וּמִשְׁפָּטִים אוֹתָנוּ לִמַּדְתָּ.

עַל־כֵּן, יְיָ אֱלֹהֵינוּ, בְּשָׁכְבֵנוּ וּבְקוּמֵנוּ נָשִׂיחַ בְּחֻקֶּיךָ, וְנִשְׂמַח

Evening

בְּדִבְרֵי תוֹרָתֶךָ וּבְמִצְוֹתֶיךָ לְעוֹלָם וָעֶד. כִּי הֵם חַיֵּינוּ וְאֹרֶךְ יָמֵינוּ, וּבָהֶם נֶהְגֶּה יוֹמָם וָלָיְלָה. וְאַהֲבָתְךָ אַל־תָּסִיר מִמֶּנּוּ לְעוֹלָמִים! בָּרוּךְ אַתָּה, יְיָ, אוֹהֵב עַמּוֹ יִשְׂרָאֵל.

Morning

וּתְלַמְּדֵנוּ. אָבִינוּ, הָאָב הָרַחֲמָן, הַמְרַחֵם, רַחֵם עָלֵינוּ וְתֵן בְּלִבֵּנוּ לְהָבִין וּלְהַשְׂכִּיל, לִשְׁמֹעַ לִלְמֹד וּלְלַמֵּד, לִשְׁמֹר וְלַעֲשׂוֹת וּלְקַיֵּם אֶת־כָּל־דִּבְרֵי תַלְמוּד תּוֹרָתֶךָ בְּאַהֲבָה. וְהָאֵר עֵינֵינוּ בְּתוֹרָתֶךָ, וְדַבֵּק לִבֵּנוּ בְּמִצְוֹתֶיךָ, וְיַחֵד לְבָבֵנוּ לְאַהֲבָה וּלְיִרְאָה אֶת־שְׁמֶךָ. וְלֹא־נֵבוֹשׁ לְעוֹלָם וָעֶד, כִּי בְשֵׁם קָדְשְׁךָ הַגָּדוֹל וְהַנּוֹרָא בָּטָחְנוּ. נָגִילָה וְנִשְׂמְחָה בִּישׁוּעָתֶךָ, כִּי אֵל פּוֹעֵל יְשׁוּעוֹת אָתָּה, וּבָנוּ בָחַרְתָּ וְקֵרַבְתָּנוּ לְשִׁמְךָ הַגָּדוֹל סֶלָה בֶּאֱמֶת, לְהוֹדוֹת לְךָ וּלְיַחֶדְךָ בְּאַהֲבָה. בָּרוּךְ אַתָּה, יְיָ, הַבּוֹחֵר בְּעַמּוֹ יִשְׂרָאֵל בְּאַהֲבָה.

We now proclaim the supreme truth of our faith. In every crisis of our life, in the very presence of death, we Jews have affirmed our faith in the One and Only God. This was our armor against the fury and suffering of the centuries, and by this have we risen to a sublime ministry of service. So do we take up the ancient witness of our ancestors which binds generation to generation in everlasting covenant:

שְׁמַע יִשְׂרָאֵל: יְיָ אֱלֹהֵינוּ, יְיָ אֶחָד!

Hear, O Israel: the Lord is our God, the Lord is One!

בָּרוּךְ שֵׁם כְּבוֹד מַלְכוּתוֹ לְעוֹלָם וָעֶד!

Blessed is His glorious kingdom for ever and ever!

All are seated

וְאָהַבְתָּ אֵת יְיָ אֱלֹהֶיךָ בְּכָל־לְבָבְךָ וּבְכָל־נַפְשְׁךָ וּבְכָל־מְאֹדֶךָ. וְהָיוּ הַדְּבָרִים הָאֵלֶּה, אֲשֶׁר אָנֹכִי מְצַוְּךָ הַיּוֹם, עַל־לְבָבֶךָ. וְשִׁנַּנְתָּם לְבָנֶיךָ, וְדִבַּרְתָּ בָּם בְּשִׁבְתְּךָ בְּבֵיתֶךָ, וּבְלֶכְתְּךָ בַדֶּרֶךְ, וּבְשָׁכְבְּךָ וּבְקוּמֶךָ.

וּקְשַׁרְתָּם לְאוֹת עַל־יָדֶךָ, וְהָיוּ לְטֹטָפֹת בֵּין עֵינֶיךָ, וּכְתַבְתָּם עַל־מְזֻזוֹת בֵּיתֶךָ, וּבִשְׁעָרֶיךָ.

לְמַעַן תִּזְכְּרוּ וַעֲשִׂיתֶם אֶת־כׇּל־מִצְוֺתָי, וִהְיִיתֶם קְדֹשִׁים לֵאלֹהֵיכֶם. אֲנִי יְיָ אֱלֹהֵיכֶם, אֲשֶׁר הוֹצֵאתִי אֶתְכֶם מֵאֶרֶץ מִצְרַיִם לִהְיוֹת לָכֶם לֵאלֹהִים. אֲנִי יְיָ אֱלֹהֵיכֶם.

◆

For two readers or more, or responsively

You shall love the Lord your God with all your mind, with all your strength, with all your being.

> In the eyes of the One God, *here* and *there* are the same, *they* and *I* are one. Oceans divide us; God's presence unites us.

Set these words, which I command you this day, upon your heart.

> To pray is to stake our very existence on the truth and on the supreme importance of that which we pray for.

Teach them faithfully to your children; speak of them in your home and on your way, when you lie down and when you rise up.

> The world is not the same since Auschwitz and Hiroshima. The decisions we make, the values we teach must be pondered not only in the halls of learning, but also before the inmates of extermination camps, and in the sight of the mushroom of a nuclear explosion.

Bind them as a sign upon your hand; let them be a symbol before your eyes.

> The groan deepens, the combat burns, the wailing does not abate. In a free society, all are involved in what some are doing.

Inscribe them on the doorposts of your house, and on your gates.

Some are guilty, all are responsible.

Be mindful of all My Mitzvot, and do them: so shall you consecrate yourselves to your God.

Holiness, an essential attribute of God, can become a quality of our own. The human can become holy.

◆ ◆

קְדֹשִׁים תִּהְיוּ, כִּי קָדוֹשׁ אֲנִי יְיָ אֱלֹהֵיכֶם.

You shall be holy, for I the Lord your God am holy.

◆ ◆

Morning

עַל־הָרִאשׁוֹנִים וְעַל־הָאַחֲרוֹנִים דָּבָר טוֹב וְקַיָּם לְעוֹלָם וָעֶד. אֱמֶת וֶאֱמוּנָה, חֹק וְלֹא יַעֲבוֹר. אֱמֶת שָׁאַתָּה הוּא יְיָ אֱלֹהֵינוּ וֵאלֹהֵי אֲבוֹתֵינוּ, מַלְכֵּנוּ מֶלֶךְ אֲבוֹתֵינוּ, גּוֹאֲלֵנוּ גּוֹאֵל אֲבוֹתֵינוּ, יוֹצְרֵנוּ, צוּר יְשׁוּעָתֵנוּ. פּוֹדֵנוּ וּמַצִּילֵנוּ מֵעוֹלָם הוּא שְׁמֶךָ, אֵין אֱלֹהִים זוּלָתֶךָ.

עֶזְרַת אֲבוֹתֵינוּ אַתָּה הוּא מֵעוֹלָם, מָגֵן וּמוֹשִׁיעַ לִבְנֵיהֶם אַחֲרֵיהֶם בְּכָל־דּוֹר וָדוֹר. בְּרוּם עוֹלָם מוֹשָׁבֶךָ וּמִשְׁפָּטֶיךָ וְצִדְקָתְךָ עַד אַפְסֵי־אָרֶץ.

אַשְׁרֵי אִישׁ שֶׁיִּשְׁמַע לְמִצְוֹתֶיךָ, וְתוֹרָתְךָ וּדְבָרְךָ יָשִׂים עַל־לִבּוֹ.

Evening

אֱמֶת וֶאֱמוּנָה כָּל־זֹאת, וְקַיָּם עָלֵינוּ כִּי הוּא יְיָ אֱלֹהֵינוּ וְאֵין זוּלָתוֹ, וַאֲנַחְנוּ יִשְׂרָאֵל עַמּוֹ.

הַפּוֹדֵנוּ מִיַּד מְלָכִים, מַלְכֵּנוּ הַגּוֹאֲלֵנוּ מִכַּף כָּל־הֶעָרִיצִים.

הָעֹשֶׂה גְדֹלוֹת עַד אֵין חֵקֶר, וְנִפְלָאוֹת עַד־אֵין מִסְפָּר.

הָעֹשֶׂה לָּנוּ נִסִּים בְּפַרְעֹה, אוֹתוֹת וּמוֹפְתִים בְּאַדְמַת בְּנֵי חָם.

וַיּוֹצֵא אֶת־עַמּוֹ יִשְׂרָאֵל מִתּוֹכָם לְחֵרוּת עוֹלָם. וְרָאוּ בָנָיו גְּבוּרָתוֹ; שִׁבְּחוּ וְהוֹדוּ לִשְׁמוֹ.

וּמַלְכוּתוֹ בְּרָצוֹן קִבְּלוּ עֲלֵיהֶם. מֹשֶׁה וּבְנֵי יִשְׂרָאֵל לְךָ עָנוּ שִׁירָה בְּשִׂמְחָה רַבָּה, וְאָמְרוּ כֻלָּם:

And now this is the word of the Lord, the word of your Creator, O Jacob, of Him who formed you, O Israel:

Have no fear, for I am redeeming you; I have called you by name and you are Mine.

When you pass through the waters, I am with you; when you pass through torrents, they will not overwhelm you.

When you walk through fire, you will not be scorched; the flames will not consume you.

Have no fear, for I am with you; I will bring your offspring from the east, and gather you from the west; to the north I will say: 'Yield!' and to the south: 'Do not withhold; bring My sons from afar and My daughters from the ends of the earth, all those who bear My name, whom I have touched with My glory, whom I formed and made.'

Who is like You, Eternal One, among the gods that are worshipped?	מִי־כָמֹכָה בָּאֵלִם, יְיָ?
Who is like You, majestic in holiness,	מִי כָּמֹכָה, נֶאְדָּר בַּקֹּדֶשׁ,
awesome in splendor, doing wonders?	נוֹרָא תְהִלֹּת, עֹשֵׂה פֶלֶא?

Morning

שִׁירָה חֲדָשָׁה שִׁבְּחוּ גְאוּלִים לְשִׁמְךָ עַל־שְׂפַת הַיָּם; יַחַד כֻּלָּם הוֹדוּ וְהִמְלִיכוּ וְאָמְרוּ:

"יְיָ יִמְלֹךְ לְעוֹלָם וָעֶד!"

צוּר יִשְׂרָאֵל, קוּמָה בְּעֶזְרַת יִשְׂרָאֵל, וּפְדֵה כִנְאֻמֶךָ יְהוּדָה וְיִשְׂרָאֵל. גֹּאֲלֵנוּ יְיָ צְבָאוֹת שְׁמוֹ, קְדוֹשׁ יִשְׂרָאֵל.

בָּרוּךְ אַתָּה, יְיָ, גָּאַל יִשְׂרָאֵל.

Evening

מַלְכוּתְךָ רָאוּ בָנֶיךָ, בּוֹקֵעַ יָם לִפְנֵי מֹשֶׁה; "זֶה אֵלִי!" עָנוּ וְאָמְרוּ:

"יְיָ יִמְלֹךְ לְעֹלָם וָעֶד!"

וְנֶאֱמַר: "כִּי־פָדָה יְיָ אֶת־יַעֲקֹב, וּגְאָלוֹ מִיַּד חָזָק מִמֶּנּוּ."

בָּרוּךְ אַתָּה, יְיָ, גָּאַל יִשְׂרָאֵל.

You are the Redeemer of Israel and all the oppressed. Blessed is the Eternal One, the God of Israel, the Source of freedom.

◆ ◆

All rise

תפלה

BE PRAISED

אבות

בָּרוּךְ אַתָּה, יְיָ אֱלֹהֵינוּ וֵאלֹהֵי אֲבוֹתֵינוּ, אֱלֹהֵי אַבְרָהָם, אֱלֹהֵי יִצְחָק, וֵאלֹהֵי יַעֲקֹב: הָאֵל הַגָּדוֹל, הַגִּבּוֹר וְהַנּוֹרָא, אֵל עֶלְיוֹן, קוֹנֵה שָׁמַיִם וָאָרֶץ.

Be praised, O Lord, God of all generations, of Abraham, of Isaac and Jacob; our God. Your wondrous creative power fills heaven and earth.

◆ ◆

GOD OF ETERNAL MIGHT

גבורות

אַתָּה גִבּוֹר לְעוֹלָם, יְיָ, סוֹמֵךְ נוֹפְלִים וְרוֹפֵא חוֹלִים וּמַתִּיר אֲסוּרִים, וּמְקַיֵּם אֱמוּנָתוֹ לִישֵׁנֵי עָפָר. בָּרוּךְ אַתָּה, יְיָ, מְחַיֵּה הַכֹּל.

God of eternal might, through us send help to the falling, healing to the sick, freedom to the captive. Confirm Your faithfulness to those who sleep in the dust. We praise You, the Source of life.

◆ ◆

For an Evening Service

BE HOLY

קדושת השם

אַתָּה קָדוֹשׁ וְשִׁמְךָ קָדוֹשׁ, וּקְדוֹשִׁים בְּכָל־יוֹם יְהַלְלוּךָ סֶּלָה. בָּרוּךְ אַתָּה, יְיָ, הָאֵל הַקָּדוֹשׁ.

You are holy, Your name is holy, and those who strive to be holy declare Your glory day by day. Blessed is the Lord, the holy God.

All are seated

◆ ◆

For a Morning Service

SANCTIFICATION קדושה

נְקַדֵּשׁ אֶת־שִׁמְךָ בָּעוֹלָם, כְּשֵׁם שֶׁמַּקְדִּישִׁים אוֹתוֹ בִּשְׁמֵי מָרוֹם, כַּכָּתוּב עַל־יַד נְבִיאֶךָ: וְקָרָא זֶה אֶל־זֶה וְאָמַר:

We sanctify Your name on earth, even as all things, to the ends of time and space, proclaim Your holiness; and in the words of the prophet we say:

קָדוֹשׁ, קָדוֹשׁ, קָדוֹשׁ יְיָ צְבָאוֹת, מְלֹא כָל־הָאָרֶץ כְּבוֹדוֹ.

Holy, Holy, Holy is the Lord of Hosts; the fullness of the whole earth is His glory!

לְעֻמָּתָם בָּרוּךְ יֹאמֵרוּ:

They respond to Your glory with blessing:

בָּרוּךְ כְּבוֹד יְיָ מִמְּקוֹמוֹ.

Blessed is the glory of God in heaven and earth.

וּבְדִבְרֵי קָדְשְׁךָ כָּתוּב לֵאמֹר:

And this is Your sacred word:

יִמְלֹךְ יְיָ לְעוֹלָם, אֱלֹהַיִךְ צִיּוֹן, לְדֹר וָדֹר, הַלְלוּיָהּ.

The Lord shall reign for ever; your God, O Zion, from generation to generation. Halleluyah!

לְדוֹר וָדוֹר נַגִּיד גָּדְלֶךָ, וּלְנֵצַח נְצָחִים קְדֻשָּׁתְךָ נַקְדִּישׁ.
וְשִׁבְחֲךָ, אֱלֹהֵינוּ, מִפִּינוּ לֹא יָמוּשׁ לְעוֹלָם וָעֶד.
בָּרוּךְ אַתָּה, יְיָ, הָאֵל הַקָּדוֹשׁ.

To all generations we will make known Your greatness, and to all eternity proclaim Your holiness. Your praise, O God, shall never depart from our lips.

Blessed is the Lord, the holy God.

All are seated

◆ ◆

GIVE US INSIGHT הבינגו

הֲבִינֵנוּ, יְיָ אֱלֹהֵינוּ, לָדַעַת דְּרָכֶיךָ; וּמוֹל אֶת לְבָבֵנוּ לְיִרְאָתֶךָ. וְתִסְלַח לָנוּ לִהְיוֹת גְּאוּלִים; וְרַחֲקֵנוּ מִמַּכְאוֹב. וְדַשְּׁנֵנוּ בִּנְאוֹת אַרְצֶךָ, וּנְפוּצוֹתֵינוּ מֵאַרְבַּע כַּנְפוֹת הָאָרֶץ תְּקַבֵּץ. וְהַתּוֹעִים עַל דַּעְתְּךָ יִשָּׁפֵטוּ; וְעַל הָרְשָׁעִים תָּנִיף יָדֶךָ. וְיִשְׂמְחוּ צַדִּיקִים בְּבִנְיַן עִירֶךָ, וּבִצְמִיחַת קֶרֶן יְשׁוּעָתֶךָ. טֶרֶם נִקְרָא אַתָּה תַעֲנֶה. בָּרוּךְ אַתָּה, יְיָ, שׁוֹמֵעַ תְּפִלָּה.

Give us insight, Lord our God, to understand Your ways, and consecrate our hearts to revere You.

From our sins redeem us with forgiveness; from pain and sorrow keep us far.

Bestow upon us Your earth's abundance, and gather our exiles from earth's four corners.

To those who stray, bring correction; upon the lawless, place Your hand.

Let the righteous rejoice in the building of Your city and the flowering of Your redemption.

Blessed is the Lord, who hearkens to prayer.

◆ ◆

ANSWER US עננו

עֲנֵנוּ, יְיָ, עֲנֵנוּ בְּיוֹם זִכְרוֹן יְגוֹנֵנוּ,
כִּי פְעָמִים רַבּוֹת בָּאָה צָרָה עָלֵינוּ.
אַל־תֵּפֶן אֶל־רִשְׁעֵנוּ, וְאַל־תַּסְתֵּר פָּנֶיךָ מִמֶּנּוּ,
וְאַל־תִּתְעַלַּם מִתְּחִנָּתֵנוּ.

Answer us, O Lord, answer us as we remember our affliction,
The grievous trouble that so often overtook us.

Consider not our wrongdoings; turn not away from us;
Be mindful of our plea, and heed our supplication.

הֱיֵה נָא קָרוֹב לְשַׁוְעָתֵנוּ, יְהִי נָא חַסְדְּךָ לְנַחֲמֵנוּ,
טֶרֶם נִקְרָא אֵלֶיךָ עֲנֵנוּ, כַּדָּבָר שֶׁנֶּאֱמַר:
"וְהָיָה טֶרֶם יִקְרָאוּ, וַאֲנִי אֶעֱנֶה,
עוֹד הֵם מְדַבְּרִים, וַאֲנִי אֶשְׁמָע."

Your love is our comfort; answer before we call.
This is the promise spoken by Your prophet:

"I shall answer before they have spoken;
I shall heed their call before it is uttered."

כִּי אַתָּה, יְיָ, הָעוֹנֶה בְּעֵת צָרָה,
פּוֹדֶה וּמַצִּיל בְּכָל־עֵת צָרָה וְצוּקָה.
בָּרוּךְ אַתָּה, יְיָ, הָעוֹנֶה בְּעֵת צָרָה.

You, O Lord, answer us in time of trouble;
You rescue and redeem in time of distress.

Blessed is the Lord, who answers the afflicted.

◆ ◆

COMFORTER OF ZION
מנחם ציון

נַחֵם, יְיָ אֱלֹהֵינוּ, אֶת־אֲבֵלֵי צִיּוֹן, וְאֶת־אֲבֵלֵי יְרוּשָׁלַיִם, וְאֶת־הָעִיר הָאֲבֵלָה, וְהַחֲרֵבָה, וְהַבְּזוּיָה וְהַשּׁוֹמֵמָה:

Lord our God, You are the comforter of Zion's mourners, the mourners of Jerusalem. How long has the city mourned, despised and crushed, desolate.

הָאֲבֵלָה מִבְּלִי בָנֶיהָ, וְהַחֲרֵבָה מִמְּעוֹנוֹתֶיהָ, וְהַבְּזוּיָה מִכְּבוֹדָהּ, וְהַשּׁוֹמֵמָה מֵאֵין יוֹשֵׁב.

How long were her children exiled, her homes ruined, her glory mocked, her people gone.

וְהִיא יוֹשֶׁבֶת וְרֹאשָׁהּ חָפוּי, כְּאִשָּׁה עֲקָרָה שֶׁלֹּא יָלָדָה.
וַיְבַלְּעוּהָ לִגְיוֹנוֹת, וַיִּירָשׁוּהָ עוֹבְדֵי פְסִילִים.

There she sat with head bowed like a woman bereft. Legions overran her, strangers dispossessed her.

וַיָּטִילוּ אֶת־עַמְּךָ יִשְׂרָאֵל לֶחָרֶב, וַיַּהַרְגוּ בְזָדוֹן חֲסִידֵי עֶלְיוֹן.

They put Your people Israel to the sword; the arrogant slaughtered Your faithful ones.

עַל־כֵּן צִיּוֹן בְּמַר תִּבְכֶּה, וִירוּשָׁלַיִם תִּתֵּן קוֹלָהּ.
לִבִּי לִבִּי עַל חַלְלֵיהֶם, מֵעַי מֵעַי עַל חַלְלֵיהֶם.

Therefore did Zion weep bitterly, therefore Jerusalem cried aloud. My heart, my heart goes out to the slain! My bowels are knotted for the slain!

כִּי אַתָּה, יְיָ, בָּאֵשׁ הִצַּתָּהּ, וּבָאֵשׁ אַתָּה עָתִיד לִבְנוֹתָהּ, כָּאָמוּר: וַאֲנִי אֶהְיֶה־לָּהּ, נְאֻם־יְיָ, חוֹמַת אֵשׁ סָבִיב, וּלְכָבוֹד אֶהְיֶה בְתוֹכָהּ.

Lord, You saw her consumed with fire, and with fire do You see her rebuilt. As it is said: As for Me, says the Lord, I will be a fiery wall about her, and a glory in her midst.

בָּרוּךְ אַתָּה, יְיָ, מְנַחֵם צִיּוֹן וּבוֹנֵה יְרוּשָׁלָיִם.

Blessed is the Lord, Comforter of Zion and Rebuilder of Jerusalem.

◆ ◆

WORSHIP עבודה

רְצֵה, יְיָ אֱלֹהֵינוּ, בְּעַמְּךָ יִשְׂרָאֵל, וּתְפִלָּתָם בְּאַהֲבָה תְקַבֵּל,
וּתְהִי לְרָצוֹן תָּמִיד עֲבוֹדַת יִשְׂרָאֵל עַמֶּךָ.
בָּרוּךְ אַתָּה, יְיָ, שֶׁאוֹתְךָ לְבַדְּךָ בְּיִרְאָה נַעֲבוֹד.

Be gracious, O Lord our God, to Your people Israel, and receive our prayers with love. O may our worship always be acceptable to You.
Blessed is the Lord, whom alone we serve with reverence.

◆ ◆

Eternal God, may Your love rest on Zion. Grant that the promise of her beginning may grow into a redemption for all Israel and all the world. Blessed is the Lord, whose presence gives life to His people Israel.

◆ ◆

THANKSGIVING הודאה

מוֹדִים אֲנַחְנוּ לָךְ, שָׁאַתָּה הוּא יְיָ אֱלֹהֵינוּ וֵאלֹהֵי אֲבוֹתֵינוּ,
אֱלֹהֵי כָל־בָּשָׂר, יוֹצְרֵנוּ יוֹצֵר בְּרֵאשִׁית.
בְּרָכוֹת וְהוֹדָאוֹת לְשִׁמְךָ הַגָּדוֹל וְהַקָּדוֹשׁ עַל־שֶׁהֶחֱיִיתָנוּ
וְקִיַּמְתָּנוּ.

O God of Israel's past, O God of this day, God of all flesh, Creator of all life: We praise You, the Most High, for the gift of life; we give thanks, O Source of good, that life endures.

כֵּן תְּחַיֵּנוּ וּתְקַיְּמֵנוּ, יְיָ אֱלֹהֵינוּ, וּתְאַמְּצֵנוּ לִשְׁמֹר חֻקֶּיךָ,
לַעֲשׂוֹת רְצוֹנֶךָ, וּלְעָבְדְךָ בְּלֵבָב שָׁלֵם. בָּרוּךְ אֵל הַהוֹדָאוֹת.

Eternal and Infinite One, help us to use our life for blessing: to live by Your law, to do Your will, to walk in Your way with a whole heart.
We thank You, Eternal God, for the blessing of life.

◆ ◆

MEDITATION

How can we give thanks when we remember Treblinka? Only silence speaks loudly enough for our millions who were marched into the abyss.

We have been where we did not find You, O Hidden One! Yet even there, even there, our people sang: I believe in redemption. *Ani Maamin.* And they sang again:

זאָג ניט קיינמאָל אַז דו גייסט דעם לעצטן וועג.

Never say you walk the final road!

And even then this deathless people was renewing itself, its life.

Whose faith is equal to this people's? Whose will to live? The storm ends. In the sky, a rainbow signals hope and new life. Again, and yet again, there is a song to sing.

◆ ◆

PEACE — ברכת שלום

Morning

שִׂים שָׁלוֹם, טוֹבָה וּבְרָכָה, חֵן וָחֶסֶד וְרַחֲמִים, עָלֵינוּ וְעַל־כָּל יִשְׂרָאֵל עַמֶּךָ.
בָּרְכֵנוּ אָבִינוּ, כֻּלָּנוּ כְּאֶחָד, בְּאוֹר פָּנֶיךָ, כִּי בְאוֹר פָּנֶיךָ נָתַתָּ לָּנוּ, יְיָ אֱלֹהֵינוּ, תּוֹרַת חַיִּים, וְאַהֲבַת חֶסֶד, וּצְדָקָה וּבְרָכָה וְרַחֲמִים, וְחַיִּים וְשָׁלוֹם.

Evening

שָׁלוֹם רָב עַל־יִשְׂרָאֵל עַמְּךָ תָּשִׂים לְעוֹלָם, כִּי אַתָּה הוּא מֶלֶךְ אָדוֹן לְכָל הַשָּׁלוֹם. וְטוֹב בְּעֵינֶיךָ לְבָרֵךְ אֶת־עַמְּךָ יִשְׂרָאֵל בְּכָל־עֵת וּבְכָל־שָׁעָה בִּשְׁלוֹמֶךָ. בָּרוּךְ אַתָּה, יְיָ, הַמְבָרֵךְ אֶת־עַמּוֹ יִשְׂרָאֵל בַּשָּׁלוֹם.

וְטוֹב בְּעֵינֶיךָ לְבָרֵךְ אֶת־עַמְּךָ יִשְׂרָאֵל בְּכָל־עֵת וּבְכָל־שָׁעָה בִּשְׁלוֹמֶךָ. בָּרוּךְ אַתָּה, יְיָ, הַמְבָרֵךְ אֶת־עַמּוֹ יִשְׂרָאֵל בַּשָּׁלוֹם.

Let the day come when we turn to the Lord of peace, when all are a single family doing His will with a perfect heart.

O Source of peace, lead us to peace, a peace profound and true; lead us to a healing, to mastery of all that drives us to war within ourselves and with others.

O Lord of peace, bless us with peace.

◆ ◆

MEDITATION

Our mission involves other peoples. Jews do not live alone. As a result of what the world has done to us, it may find a way to save itself. By now it must admit that we do have in our possession the key to survival. We have not survived centuries of atrocities for nothing.

This is what I think we are trying to prove to ourselves, desperately, because it is desperately needed: in a world of absurdity, we must invent reason; we must create beauty out of nothingness. And because there is murder in this world — and we are the first ones to know it — and we know how hopeless our battle may appear, we have to fight murder and absurdity, and give meaning to the battle, if not to our hope.

This is not a lesson; this is not an answer. It is only a question.

◆ ◆

יִהְיוּ לְרָצוֹן אִמְרֵי־פִי וְהֶגְיוֹן לִבִּי לְפָנֶיךָ, יְיָ, צוּרִי וְגוֹאֲלִי.

May the words of my mouth, and the meditations of my heart, be acceptable to You, O Lord, my Rock and my Redeemer.

or

עֹשֶׂה שָׁלוֹם בִּמְרוֹמָיו, הוּא יַעֲשֶׂה שָׁלוֹם עָלֵינוּ וְעַל כָּל־יִשְׂרָאֵל, וְאִמְרוּ אָמֵן.

May He who causes peace to reign in the high heavens let peace descend on us, on all Israel, and all the world.

◆ ◆

Deuteronomy 4.30–40 might be read here.

The Rituals for the Reading of Torah begin on page 415.

תפלות ליום העצמאות

Service for Yom Ha-atsma-ut

For a morning service, when Yom Ha-atsma-ut falls on a weekday, the following is suggested: Morning Service (page 49 to 71), followed by Hallel (page 487), supplementary reading (page 605), the Reading of the Torah (page 531), and Concluding Prayers.

For a morning service, when Yom Ha-atsama-ut falls on Shabbat, the following is suggested: Morning Service, page 282 to 314, followed by Hallel (page 487), supplementary reading (page 605), the Reading of the Torah (page 531), and Concluding Prayers.

הדלקת הנרות

אַשְׁרֵי הַגַּפְרוּר שֶׁנִּשְׂרַף וְהִצִּית לְהָבוֹת.
אַשְׁרֵי הַלֶּהָבָה שֶׁבָּעֲרָה בְּסִתְרֵי לְבָבוֹת.
אַשְׁרֵי הַלְּבָבוֹת שֶׁיָּדְעוּ לַחֲדוֹל בְּכָבוֹד.
אַשְׁרֵי הַגַּפְרוּר שֶׁנִּשְׂרַף וְהִצִּית לְהָבוֹת.

Blessed is the match consumed in kindling flame.
Blessed is the flame that burns in the heart's secret places.
Blessed is the heart with strength to stop its beating for honor's sake.
Blessed is the match consumed in kindling flame.

◆ ◆

ON SHABBAT

בָּרוּךְ אַתָּה, יְיָ אֱלֹהֵינוּ, מֶלֶךְ הָעוֹלָם,
אֲשֶׁר קִדְּשָׁנוּ בְּמִצְוֹתָיו וְצִוָּנוּ לְהַדְלִיק נֵר שֶׁל שַׁבָּת.

Blessed is the Lord our God, Ruler of the universe,
who hallows us with His Mitzvot, and commands us to kindle the lights of Shabbat.

◆ ◆

לְמַעַן צִיּוֹן לֹא אֶחֱשֶׁה, וּלְמַעַן יְרוּשָׁלַיִם לֹא אֶשְׁקוֹט, עַד־יֵצֵא כַנֹּגַהּ צִדְקָהּ, וִישׁוּעָתָהּ כְּלַפִּיד יִבְעָר.

יְשֻׂשׂוּם מִדְבָּר וְצִיָּה, וְתָגֵל עֲרָבָה וְתִפְרַח כַּחֲבַצָּלֶת.

For Zion's sake I will not keep silence; for Jerusalem's sake I will speak out, until her right shines forth like the sunrise, her deliverance like a blazing torch.

Let the wilderness and the thirsty land be glad, let the desert rejoice and burst into flower.

הָעָם הַהֹלְכִים בַּחֹשֶׁךְ רָאוּ אוֹר גָּדוֹל.

יֹשְׁבֵי בְּאֶרֶץ צַלְמָוֶת, אוֹר נָגַהּ עֲלֵיהֶם.

The people who walked in darkness have seen a great light.

On those who dwelt in a land dark as death, a light has dawned.

◆ ◆

בָּרוּךְ אַתָּה, יְיָ אֱלֹהֵינוּ, מֶלֶךְ הָעוֹלָם, שֶׁהֶחֱיָנוּ, וְקִיְּמָנוּ, וְהִגִּיעָנוּ לַזְּמַן הַזֶּה.

Blessed is the Lord our God, Ruler of the universe, for giving us life, for sustaining us, and for enabling us to reach this joyous day.

◆ ◆

From Psalm 107

הוֹדוּ לַיְיָ, כִּי־טוֹב,
כִּי לְעוֹלָם חַסְדּוֹ!

Give thanks to the Lord, for He is good;
For His love is everlasting!

יֹאמְרוּ גְּאוּלֵי יְיָ, אֲשֶׁר גְּאָלָם מִיַּד־צָר:
כִּי לְעוֹלָם חַסְדּוֹ!

So let them say whom the Lord has redeemed, whom He has redeemed from the oppressor's hand:
For His love is everlasting!

וּמֵאֲרָצוֹת קִבְּצָם, מִמִּזְרָח וּמִמַּעֲרָב, מִצָּפוֹן וּמִיָּם:
כִּי לְעוֹלָם חַסְדּוֹ!

He gathered them out of every land, from east and west, from north and south:

For His love is everlasting!

תָּעוּ בַמִּדְבָּר בִּישִׁימוֹן; רְעֵבִים גַּם־צְמֵאִים, נַפְשָׁם בָּהֶם תִּתְעַטָּף. וַיִּצְעֲקוּ אֶל־יְיָ בַּצַּר לָהֶם, מִמְּצוּקוֹתֵיהֶם יַצִּילֵם:
כִּי לְעוֹלָם חַסְדּוֹ!

Some were lost in desert wastes; hungry and thirsty, their spirit sank within them. So they cried to the Lord in their trouble, and He rescued them from their distress:

For His love is everlasting!

יוֹצִיאֵם מֵחֹשֶׁךְ וְצַלְמָוֶת, וּמוֹסְרוֹתֵיהֶם יְנַתֵּק:
כִּי לְעוֹלָם חַסְדּוֹ!

He brought them out of darkness, dark as death, and broke their chains:

For His love is everlasting!

יָשֵׂם מִדְבָּר לַאֲגַם־מַיִם, וְאֶרֶץ צִיָּה לְמֹצָאֵי מָיִם. וַיּוֹשֶׁב שָׁם רְעֵבִים, וַיְכוֹנְנוּ עִיר מוֹשָׁב. וַיִּזְרְעוּ שָׂדוֹת וַיִּטְּעוּ כְרָמִים וַיַּעֲשׂוּ פְּרִי תְבוּאָה.
הוֹדוּ לַייָ, כִּי־טוֹב, כִּי לְעוֹלָם חַסְדּוֹ!

He turns wilderness into flowing streams, parched lands into springs of water. There He gives the hungry a home, where they build cities to live in. They sow fields and plant vineyards and reap a fruitful harvest.

Give thanks to the Lord, for He is good; For His love is everlasting!

◆ ◆

ירושלים

מֵעַל פִּסְגַּת הַר הַצּוֹפִים, שָׁלוֹם לָךְ יְרוּשָׁלַיִם.

Mei·al pis·gat har ha·tso·fim, sha·lom lach Ye·ru·sha·la·yim.

מֵעַל פִּסְגַּת הַר הַצּוֹפִים, אֶשְׁתַּחֲוֶה לָךְ אַפַּיִם.

Mei·al pis·gat har ha·tso·fim, esh·ta·cha·veh lach a·pa·yim.

מֵאָה דוֹרוֹת חָלַמְתִּי עָלַיִךְ, לִזְכּוֹת לִרְאוֹת בְּאוֹר פָּנַיִךְ.

Mei·a do·rot cha·lam·ti a·la·yich, liz·kot lir·ot be·or pa·na·yich.

יְרוּשָׁלַיִם, יְרוּשָׁלַיִם! הָאִירִי פָּנַיִךְ לִבְנֵךְ!

Ye·ru·sha·la·yim, Ye·ru·sha·la·yim! ha·i·ri fa·na·yich li·ve·neich!

יְרוּשָׁלַיִם, יְרוּשָׁלַיִם! מֵחָרְבוֹתַיִךְ אֶבְנֵךְ!

Ye·ru·sha·la·yim, Ye·ru·sha·la·yim! mei·cho·re·vo·ta·yich ev·neich!

From the peak of Mt. Scopus, shalom, Jerusalem! From the peak of Mt. Scopus, I greet you, Jerusalem. A hundred generations I have dreamed of you, once more to be privileged to see you rebuilt. Jerusalem, O Jerusalem! Smile on your children once more! Jerusalem, O Jerusalem! Out of your ruins will I rebuild you!

READER'S KADDISH — חצי קדיש

יִתְגַּדַּל וְיִתְקַדַּשׁ שְׁמֵהּ רַבָּא בְּעָלְמָא דִּי־בְרָא כִרְעוּתֵהּ, וְיַמְלִיךְ מַלְכוּתֵהּ בְּחַיֵּיכוֹן וּבְיוֹמֵיכוֹן וּבְחַיֵּי דְכָל־בֵּית יִשְׂרָאֵל, בַּעֲגָלָא וּבִזְמַן קָרִיב, וְאִמְרוּ: אָמֵן.

יְהֵא שְׁמֵהּ רַבָּא מְבָרַךְ לְעָלַם וּלְעָלְמֵי עָלְמַיָּא.

יִתְבָּרַךְ וְיִשְׁתַּבַּח, וְיִתְפָּאַר וְיִתְרוֹמַם וְיִתְנַשֵּׂא, וְיִתְהַדַּר וְיִתְעַלֶּה וְיִתְהַלַּל שְׁמֵהּ דְּקוּדְשָׁא, בְּרִיךְ הוּא, לְעֵלָּא מִן כָּל־בִּרְכָתָא וְשִׁירָתָא, תֻּשְׁבְּחָתָא וְנֶחֱמָתָא דַּאֲמִירָן בְּעָלְמָא, וְאִמְרוּ: אָמֵן.

Let the glory of God be extolled, let His great name be hallowed in the world whose creation He willed. May His kingdom soon prevail, in our own day, our own lives, and the life of all Israel, and let us say: Amen.

Let His great name be blessed for ever and ever.

Let the name of the Holy One, blessed is He, be glorified, exalted and honored, though He is beyond all the praises, songs, and adorations that we can utter, and let us say: Amen.

◆ ◆

All rise

שמע וברכותיה

בָּרְכוּ אֶת־יְיָ הַמְבֹרָךְ!

Praise the Lord, to whom our praise is due!

בָּרוּךְ יְיָ הַמְבֹרָךְ לְעוֹלָם וָעֶד!

Praised be the Lord, to whom our praise is due,
now and for ever!

◆ ◆

GOD OF TIMES AND SEASONS — מעריב ערבים

בָּרוּךְ אַתָּה, יְיָ אֱלֹהֵינוּ, מֶלֶךְ הָעוֹלָם, אֲשֶׁר בִּדְבָרוֹ מַעֲרִיב עֲרָבִים. בְּחָכְמָה פּוֹתֵחַ שְׁעָרִים, וּבִתְבוּנָה מְשַׁנֶּה עִתִּים, וּמַחֲלִיף אֶת־הַזְּמַנִּים, וּמְסַדֵּר אֶת־הַכּוֹכָבִים בְּמִשְׁמְרוֹתֵיהֶם בָּרָקִיעַ כִּרְצוֹנוֹ.

בּוֹרֵא יוֹם וָלָיְלָה, גּוֹלֵל אוֹר מִפְּנֵי חֹשֶׁךְ וְחֹשֶׁךְ מִפְּנֵי אוֹר, וּמַעֲבִיר יוֹם וּמֵבִיא לָיְלָה, וּמַבְדִּיל בֵּין יוֹם וּבֵין לָיְלָה, יְיָ צְבָאוֹת שְׁמוֹ.

אֵל חַי וְקַיָּם, תָּמִיד יִמְלוֹךְ עָלֵינוּ, לְעוֹלָם וָעֶד. בָּרוּךְ אַתָּה, יְיָ, הַמַּעֲרִיב עֲרָבִים.

Lord God of night and dawn, be with us this day.

God of times and seasons, be with us this day.

Lord God of hope and joy, be with us this day.

God of the loving heart, be with us this day.

Be with us as we look for strength to be free: strength to defeat those who worship power, and strength to resist all who would oppress us.

God of freedom and right, be with us this day.

◆ ◆

IN EVERY ACT OF GOODNESS

אהבת עולם

אַהֲבַת עוֹלָם בֵּית יִשְׂרָאֵל עַמְּךָ אָהָבְתָּ: תּוֹרָה וּמִצְוֹת, חֻקִּים וּמִשְׁפָּטִים אוֹתָנוּ לִמַּדְתָּ.

עַל־כֵּן, יְיָ אֱלֹהֵינוּ, בְּשָׁכְבֵנוּ וּבְקוּמֵנוּ נָשִׂיחַ בְּחֻקֶּיךָ, וְנִשְׂמַח בְּדִבְרֵי תוֹרָתְךָ וּבְמִצְוֹתֶיךָ לְעוֹלָם וָעֶד.

כִּי הֵם חַיֵּינוּ וְאֹרֶךְ יָמֵינוּ, וּבָהֶם נֶהְגֶּה יוֹמָם וָלָיְלָה. וְאַהֲבָתְךָ אַל־תָּסִיר מִמֶּנּוּ לְעוֹלָמִים! בָּרוּךְ אַתָּה, יְיָ, אוֹהֵב עַמּוֹ יִשְׂרָאֵל.

You are manifest in the heavens, the work of Your hands. In our own life, too, in our every act of goodness, we feel Your presence.

You are present in the life of Your people, Your messenger and witness from Sinai until now.

Help us, O God, to hold fast to the truths our ancestors taught, and to welcome the truths that are yet to unfold today and tomorrow.

O God of Israel, help us to bear witness to Your presence in the world, in hearts that invite You to enter.

◆

לְמַעַן אַהֲבַת עֲמוּסִים
נָטַעְתָּ עֵץ חַיִּים.
(שַׁבַּת קָדַשְׁתָּ מִיָּמִים
וְאוֹתָהּ הִנְחַלְתָּ לִתְמִימִים.)
וְאַהֲבָתְךָ לֹא תָסוּר מִמֶּנּוּ,
כִּי הִיא עֲטֶרֶת רֹאשֵׁנוּ
נֵצַח נְצָחִים!
וְשִׁמְךָ אֲנַחְנוּ מְיַחֲדִים:

With love for all whom You have
borne,
You planted a tree of life for us.
In love have You given us Torah.
[In love have You made Shabbat
the heritage of all who seek You.]
O Your love is our crowning glory:
may it never depart from our lives!
And in love returned
we will proclaim You One:

שְׁמַע יִשְׂרָאֵל: יְיָ אֱלֹהֵינוּ, יְיָ אֶחָד!

Hear, O Israel: the Lord is our God, the Lord is One!

בָּרוּךְ שֵׁם כְּבוֹד מַלְכוּתוֹ לְעוֹלָם וָעֶד!

Blessed is His glorious kingdom for ever and ever!

All are seated

וְאָהַבְתָּ אֵת יְיָ אֱלֹהֶיךָ בְּכָל־לְבָבְךָ וּבְכָל־נַפְשְׁךָ וּבְכָל־מְאֹדֶךָ. וְהָיוּ הַדְּבָרִים הָאֵלֶּה, אֲשֶׁר אָנֹכִי מְצַוְּךָ הַיּוֹם, עַל־לְבָבֶךָ. וְשִׁנַּנְתָּם לְבָנֶיךָ, וְדִבַּרְתָּ בָּם בְּשִׁבְתְּךָ בְּבֵיתֶךָ, וּבְלֶכְתְּךָ בַדֶּרֶךְ, וּבְשָׁכְבְּךָ וּבְקוּמֶךָ.

You shall love the Lord your God with all your mind, with all your strength, with all your being.
Set these words, which I command you this day, upon your heart. Teach them faithfully to your children; speak of them in your home and on your way, when you lie down and when you rise up.

וּקְשַׁרְתָּם לְאוֹת עַל־יָדֶךָ, וְהָיוּ לְטֹטָפֹת בֵּין עֵינֶיךָ, וּכְתַבְתָּם עַל־מְזֻזוֹת בֵּיתֶךָ, וּבִשְׁעָרֶיךָ.

Bind them as a sign upon your hand; let them be a symbol before your eyes; inscribe them on the doorposts of your house, and on your gates.

לְמַעַן תִּזְכְּרוּ וַעֲשִׂיתֶם אֶת־כָּל־מִצְוֹתָי, וִהְיִיתֶם קְדֹשִׁים לֵאלֹהֵיכֶם. אֲנִי יְיָ אֱלֹהֵיכֶם, אֲשֶׁר הוֹצֵאתִי אֶתְכֶם מֵאֶרֶץ מִצְרַיִם לִהְיוֹת לָכֶם לֵאלֹהִים. אֲנִי יְיָ אֱלֹהֵיכֶם.

Be mindful of all My Mitzvot, and do them: so shall you consecrate yourselves to your God. I, the Lord, am your God who led you out of Egypt to be your God; I, the Lord, am your God.

◆ ◆

CAN THESE BONES LIVE

גאולה

אֱמֶת וֶאֱמוּנָה כָּל־זֹאת, וְקַיָּם עָלֵינוּ כִּי הוּא יְיָ אֱלֹהֵינוּ וְאֵין זוּלָתוֹ, וַאֲנַחְנוּ יִשְׂרָאֵל עַמּוֹ.
הַפּוֹדֵנוּ מִיַּד מְלָכִים, מַלְכֵּנוּ הַגּוֹאֲלֵנוּ מִכַּף כָּל־הֶעָרִיצִים.
הָעֹשֶׂה גְדֹלוֹת עַד אֵין חֵקֶר, וְנִפְלָאוֹת עַד־אֵין מִסְפָּר.
הַשָּׂם נַפְשֵׁנוּ בַּחַיִּים, וְלֹא־נָתַן לַמּוֹט רַגְלֵנוּ.
הָעֹשֶׂה לָּנוּ נִסִּים בְּפַרְעֹה, אוֹתוֹת וּמוֹפְתִים בְּאַדְמַת בְּנֵי חָם.
וַיּוֹצֵא אֶת־עַמּוֹ יִשְׂרָאֵל מִתּוֹכָם לְחֵרוּת עוֹלָם.
וְרָאוּ בָנָיו גְּבוּרָתוֹ; שִׁבְּחוּ וְהוֹדוּ לִשְׁמוֹ.
וּמַלְכוּתוֹ בְּרָצוֹן קִבְּלוּ עֲלֵיהֶם. מֹשֶׁה וּבְנֵי יִשְׂרָאֵל לְךָ עָנוּ שִׁירָה בְּשִׂמְחָה רַבָּה, וְאָמְרוּ כֻלָּם:

The hand of the Lord was upon me, and He set me down in the midst of a valley. It was full of bones, and they were very dry. He said to me: Son of man, can these bones live? I answered: O Lord God, You alone know. Then He said to me: Prophesy to these bones, and say to them, O dry bones, hear the word of the Lord:

Behold, I will cause breath to enter you, that you may live. I will lay sinews upon you, and cause flesh to come upon you, and cover you with skin, and put breath in you, that you may live. Then you shall know that I am the Lord.

So I prophesied as He commanded me, and the breath came into them, and they lived. They stood on their feet, a very great host. Then He said to me:

These bones are the whole house of Israel. Behold, they say, Our bones are dried up, our hope is lost, and we are cut off.

Therefore prophesy and say to them: Thus says the Lord God. Behold, I will open your graves, O My people; and I will bring you home to the land of Israel.

I will put My spirit within you, and you shall live. I will place you in your own land; then you shall know that I, the Lord, have spoken and acted.

מִי־כָמֹכָה בָּאֵלִם, יְיָ?
Who is like You, Eternal One, among the gods that are worshipped?

מִי כָּמֹכָה, נֶאְדָּר בַּקֹּדֶשׁ,
Who is like You, majestic in holiness,

נוֹרָא תְהִלֹּת, עֹשֵׂה פֶלֶא?
awesome in splendor, doing wonders?

מַלְכוּתְךָ רָאוּ בָנֶיךָ, בּוֹקֵעַ יָם לִפְנֵי מֹשֶׁה; "זֶה אֵלִי!" עָנוּ וְאָמְרוּ: "יְיָ יִמְלֹךְ לְעֹלָם וָעֶד!"

In their escape from the sea, Your children saw Your sovereign might displayed. "This is my God!" they cried. "The Eternal will reign for ever and ever!"

וְנֶאֱמַר: "כִּי־פָדָה יְיָ אֶת־יַעֲקֹב, וּגְאָלוֹ מִיַּד חָזָק מִמֶּנּוּ." בָּרוּךְ אַתָּה, יְיָ, גָּאַל יִשְׂרָאֵל.

And it has been said: "The Eternal delivered Jacob, and redeemed him from the hand of one stronger than himself." Blessed is the Lord, the Redeemer of Israel.

◆ ◆

THE SHELTER OF YOUR PEACE — השכיבנו

הַשְׁכִּיבֵנוּ, אָבִינוּ, לְשָׁלוֹם, וְהַעֲמִידֵנוּ, מַלְכֵּנוּ, לְחַיִּים טוֹבִים וּלְשָׁלוֹם. וּפְרוֹשׂ עָלֵינוּ סֻכַּת שְׁלוֹמֶךָ, וְתַקְּנֵנוּ בְּעֵצָה טוֹבָה מִלְּפָנֶיךָ. וְהוֹשִׁיעֵנוּ מְהֵרָה לְמַעַן שְׁמֶךָ, וְהָגֵן בַּעֲדֵנוּ. וּפְרוֹשׂ עָלֵינוּ סֻכַּת רַחֲמִים וְשָׁלוֹם. בָּרוּךְ אַתָּה, יְיָ, הַפּוֹרֵשׂ סֻכַּת שָׁלוֹם עָלֵינוּ, וְעַל־עַמּוֹ יִשְׂרָאֵל, וְעַל־יְרוּשָׁלָיִם.

Cause us, our Creator, to lie down in peace, and raise us up, O Sovereign God, to renewed life and peace. Spread over us the shelter of Your peace; guide us with Your good counsel; and be our shield of mercy and of peace. Blessed is the Lord, whose shelter of peace is spread over us, over all His people Israel, and over Jerusalem.

◆ ◆

All rise

תפלה

אֲדֹנָי, שְׂפָתַי תִּפְתָּח, וּפִי יַגִּיד תְּהִלָּתֶךָ.

Eternal God, open my lips, that my mouth may declare Your glory.

אבות
OUR SHIELD

בָּרוּךְ אַתָּה, יְיָ אֱלֹהֵינוּ וֵאלֹהֵי אֲבוֹתֵינוּ, אֱלֹהֵי אַבְרָהָם, אֱלֹהֵי יִצְחָק, וֵאלֹהֵי יַעֲקֹב: הָאֵל הַגָּדוֹל, הַגִּבּוֹר וְהַנּוֹרָא, אֵל עֶלְיוֹן, קוֹנֵה שָׁמַיִם וָאָרֶץ.

Blessed is the Lord our God and God of all generations: God of Abraham, God of Isaac, God of Jacob; great, mighty, and awesome God, God supreme, Maker of heaven and earth.

מָגִנֵּנוּ וּמָגֵן אֲבוֹתֵינוּ, מִבְטָחֵנוּ בְּכָל־דּוֹר וָדוֹר. בָּרוּךְ אַתָּה, יְיָ, מָגֵן אַבְרָהָם.

He is our Shield, the Shield of Abraham, our stronghold in every age. Blessed is the Lord, the Shield of Abraham.

◆ ◆

גבורות
BY YOUR MIGHT

אַתָּה גִּבּוֹר, מַשְׁפִּיל גֵּאִים; חָזָק וּמֵדִין עָרִיצִים; חֵי עוֹלָמִים. מְקַיֵּם מֵתִים, מַשִּׁיב הָרוּחַ וּמוֹרִיד הַטָּל, מְכַלְכֵּל חַיִּים, מְחַיֵּה הַמֵּתִים. כְּהֶרֶף עַיִן יְשׁוּעָה לָנוּ תַצְמִיחַ. בָּרוּךְ אַתָּה, יְיָ, מְחַיֵּה הַמֵּתִים.

Life of the universe, Your greatness humbles the proud, Your power brings judgment upon tyrants. By Your might the dead live, the winds blow, the dew descends. You sustain the living and give life to the dead; You are the Source of our deliverance. Blessed is the Lord, who gives life to the dead.

◆ ◆

AWE AND REVERENCE קדושת השם

קָדוֹשׁ אַתָּה וְנוֹרָא שְׁמֶךָ, וְאֵין אֱלוֹהַּ מִבַּלְעָדֶיךָ.
בָּרוּךְ אַתָּה, יְיָ, הָאֵל הַקָּדוֹשׁ.

You are holy, inspiring awe and reverence; we have no God but You.

Blessed is the Lord, the holy God.

All are seated

◆ ◆

ON SHABBAT

THE HOLINESS OF SHABBAT קדושת היום

אַתָּה אֶחָד וְשִׁמְךָ אֶחָד, וּמִי כְּעַמְּךָ יִשְׂרָאֵל, גּוֹי אֶחָד בָּאָרֶץ? תִּפְאֶרֶת גְּדֻלָּה וַעֲטֶרֶת יְשׁוּעָה, יוֹם מְנוּחָה וּקְדֻשָּׁה לְעַמְּךָ נָתָתָּ.

You are One, Your name is One, and there is none like Your people Israel, a people unique on the earth. A garland of glory have You given us, a crown of salvation: a day of rest and holiness.

אֱלֹהֵינוּ וֵאלֹהֵי אֲבוֹתֵינוּ, רְצֵה בִמְנוּחָתֵנוּ. קַדְּשֵׁנוּ בְּמִצְוֹתֶיךָ, וְתֵן חֶלְקֵנוּ בְּתוֹרָתֶךָ. שַׂבְּעֵנוּ מִטּוּבֶךָ, וְשַׂמְּחֵנוּ בִּישׁוּעָתֶךָ, וְטַהֵר לִבֵּנוּ לְעָבְדְּךָ בֶּאֱמֶת. וְהַנְחִילֵנוּ, יְיָ אֱלֹהֵינוּ, בְּאַהֲבָה וּבְרָצוֹן שַׁבַּת קָדְשֶׁךָ, וְיָנוּחוּ בָהּ יִשְׂרָאֵל מְקַדְּשֵׁי שְׁמֶךָ. בָּרוּךְ אַתָּה, יְיָ, מְקַדֵּשׁ הַשַּׁבָּת.

Our God and God of ages past, may our rest on this day be pleasing in Your sight. Sanctify us with Your Mitzvot, and let Your Torah be our way of life. Satisfy us with Your goodness, gladden us with Your salvation, and purify our hearts to serve You in truth. In Your gracious love, O Lord our God, let Your holy Sabbath remain our heritage, that all Israel, hallowing Your name, may find rest and peace. Blessed is the Lord, for the Sabbath and its holiness.

◆ ◆

וְלִירוּשָׁלַיִם עִירְךָ בְּרַחֲמִים תִּפְנֶה. וּמְלוֹךְ בְּכָל־הָאָרֶץ כַּאֲשֶׁר דִּבַּרְתָּ, וְקַיֵּם מַלְכוּתְךָ בְּקָרוֹב בְּיָמֵינוּ מַלְכוּת עוֹלָמִים.

Lord our God, turn in compassion to Jerusalem, Your city, and rule all the earth, as You have promised. O let Your kingdom be established soon, in our own day, as an everlasting kingdom!

אֶת־צֶמַח צְדָקָה מְהֵרָה תַצְמִיחַ, וְקֶרֶן יְשׁוּעָה תָּרוּם כִּנְאֻמֶךָ, כִּי לִישׁוּעָתְךָ קִוִּינוּ כָּל־הַיּוֹם.

Cause the plant of justice to spring up soon, and let the light of deliverance shine forth, according to Your word, for we await Your deliverance all the day.

◆ ◆

אֱלֹהֵינוּ וֵאלֹהֵי אֲבוֹתֵינוּ, יַעֲלֶה וְיָבֹא וְיִזָּכֵר זִכְרוֹנֵנוּ וְזִכְרוֹן כָּל־עַמְּךָ בֵּית יִשְׂרָאֵל לְפָנֶיךָ, לְטוֹבָה לְחֵן לְחֶסֶד וּלְרַחֲמִים לְחַיִּים וּלְשָׁלוֹם בְּיוֹם הָעַצְמָאוּת הַזֶּה.

Our God and God of ages past, be mindful of Your people Israel on this day of Independence, and renew in us love and compassion, goodness, life, and peace.

זָכְרֵנוּ, יְיָ אֱלֹהֵינוּ, בּוֹ לְטוֹבָה. אָמֵן.

This day remember us for well-being. Amen.

וּפָקְדֵנוּ בוֹ לִבְרָכָה. אָמֵן.

This day bless us with Your nearness. Amen.

וְהוֹשִׁיעֵנוּ בוֹ לְחַיִּים. אָמֵן.

This day help us to a fuller life. Amen.

◆ ◆

IN OUR DEEDS AND OUR PRAYER — עבודה

רְצֵה, יְיָ אֱלֹהֵינוּ, וּשְׁכוֹן בְּצִיּוֹן, וְיַעַבְדוּךָ עֲבָדֶיךָ בִּירוּשָׁלָיִם.
בָּרוּךְ אַתָּה, יְיָ, שֶׁאוֹתְךָ לְבַדְּךָ בְּיִרְאָה נַעֲבוֹד.

O Lord our God, may we, Your people Israel, be worthy in our deeds and our prayer. Wherever we live, wherever we seek You — in this land, in Zion restored, in all lands — You are our God, whom alone we serve in reverence.

◆ ◆

FOR THE GLORY OF LIFE — הודאה

מוֹדִים אֲנַחְנוּ לָךְ עַל־חַיֵּינוּ הַמְּסוּרִים בְּיָדֶךָ, וְעַל־נִפְלְאוֹתֶיךָ וְטוֹבוֹתֶיךָ. הַטּוֹב: כִּי לֹא־כָלוּ רַחֲמֶיךָ, וְהַמְרַחֵם: כִּי לֹא־תַמּוּ חֲסָדֶיךָ.
בָּרוּךְ אַתָּה, יְיָ, הַטּוֹב שִׁמְךָ, וּלְךָ נָאֶה לְהוֹדוֹת.

For the glory of life, O Lord, and for its wonder, we give thanks. You are Goodness, You are Compassion. We give thanks to You for ever.

◆ ◆

KNOW PEACE FOR EVER — ברכת שלום

שָׁלוֹם רָב עַל־יִשְׂרָאֵל עַמְּךָ, וְעַל־כָּל־הָעַמִּים, תָּשִׂים לְעוֹלָם.

Let Israel Your people, and all peoples, know peace for ever.

Let the great shofar of freedom be sounded for us and all peoples.

Let peace and freedom reign in all the world.

Let every wanderer come home from the bitterness of exile.

And may our eyes behold Your return to Zion in mercy.

Then will Jerusalem, the city of David, be the city of peace, the joy of all the world.

The land of Israel and its people will see peace and freedom.

בָּרוּךְ אַתָּה, יְיָ, עוֹשֵׂה הַשָּׁלוֹם.

Blessed is the Lord, the Source of peace.

◆ ◆

MEDITATION

אָמַר רַבִּי יְהוֹשֻׁעַ בֶּן לֵוִי: "יְרוּשָׁלַיִם הַבְּנוּיָה כְּעִיר שֶׁחֻבְּרָה־לָּהּ יַחְדָּו" – עִיר שֶׁהִיא עוֹשָׂה כָּל־יִשְׂרָאֵל חֲבֵרִים.

Rabbi Joshua ben Levi said: The verse "Jerusalem, meant to be a city where people come together as one" means the city which makes all Israel comrades — one united people.

אָמַר הַקָּדוֹשׁ בָּרוּךְ הוּא לְמשֶׁה: הָאָרֶץ חֲבִיבָה עָלַי, וְיִשְׂרָאֵל חֲבִיבִים עָלַי; אַכְנִיס אֶת־יִשְׂרָאֵל, שֶׁהֵם חֲבִיבִים עָלַי, לָאָרֶץ שֶׁחֲבִיבָה עָלַי.

The Holy One said to Moses: The Land is beloved to Me, and Israel is beloved to Me; therefore will I bring Israel, My beloved people, into the beloved Land.

אֵין מְדִינָה נִתְּנָה עַל מַגָּשׁ שֶׁל כֶּסֶף.

No state is handed to a people on a silver platter.

אִם תִּרְצוּ, אֵין זוֹ אַגָּדָה.

If you will it, it is no fable.

◆

O God, we are a people who walked in darkness; grant that we may stand in Your light. We have seen desolation and destruction; help us now to share in the renewal and rebirth of our people in the land of Israel, and in all our habitations.

We dream of a new day; may we labor for its fulfillment.

How beautiful upon the mountains are the feet of the herald, the one who proclaims peace, who brings tidings of good and proclaims deliverance, who says to Zion: 'Your God reigns.' O ruins of Jerusalem, hear your sentries raise their voices and shout together in triumph; for with their own eyes they shall see the Lord returning to Zion. And all the world shall see the salvation of our God.

◆ ◆

יִהְיוּ לְרָצוֹן אִמְרֵי־פִי וְהֶגְיוֹן לִבִּי לְפָנֶיךָ, יְיָ, צוּרִי וְגוֹאֲלִי.

May the words of my mouth, and the meditations of my heart, be acceptable to You, O Lord, my Rock and my Redeemer.

or

עֹשֶׂה שָׁלוֹם בִּמְרוֹמָיו, הוּא יַעֲשֶׂה שָׁלוֹם עָלֵינוּ וְעַל כָּל־יִשְׂרָאֵל, וְאִמְרוּ אָמֵן.

May He who causes peace to reign in the high heavens let peace descend on us, on all Israel, and all the world.

◆ ◆

Hallel, page 487, may be read here.

The Ritual for the Reading of Torah is on page 531.

Concluding Prayers begin on page 613.

נִפְלָאִים מַעֲשֶׂיךָ וְנַפְשִׁי יֹדַעַת מְאֹד!
מִי יְמַלֵּל גְּבוּרוֹתֶיךָ, מִי יְחַוֶּה גְדֻלּוֹתֶיךָ?
מִי יַזְכִּיר תְּהִלּוֹתֶיךָ, מִי יְסַפֵּר צִדְקוֹתֶיךָ?
מִי יַבִּיעַ נוֹרְאוֹתֶיךָ, מִי יֵדַע הֲלִיכוֹתֶיךָ?

Wonderful are Your works; how well my soul knows it! Who can speak of Your power, or express Your greatness? Who can describe Your glory, or tell of Your justice? Who can expound Your awesome deeds, and who can explore Your paths?

Who can explain Your ways?
Who can fathom Your design?

יְיָ, מִי יַחְקוֹר תַּעֲלֻמוֹתֶיךָ? יְיָ, מִי יַעֲמִיק לְמַחְשְׁבוֹתֶיךָ?
מִי יַעֲמִיק לְמַחְשְׁבוֹתֶיךָ וְלַדֶּרֶךְ בָּהּ הוֹלַכְתָּ אֶת־עַמֶּךָ?
אָז לִפְנֵי דוֹר דּוֹרוֹת גָּלָה יְקָרֵנוּ
וְנוּטַל כָּבוֹד מִבֵּית חַיֵּינוּ,
עֲטֶרֶת תִּפְאַרְתֵּנוּ הֵסַרְתָּ, וְקֶרֶן יִשְׂרָאֵל לֶעָפָר הִשְׁפַּלְתָּ.
יְיָ, מִי יַחְקוֹר תַּעֲלֻמוֹתֶיךָ? יְיָ, מִי יַעֲמִיק לְמַחְשְׁבוֹתֶיךָ?

Who can fathom Your design, and the path Your people has travelled? Exile almost endless, our House of Life defiled, our glory debased, Israel's greatness thrown to the dust: who can understand it?

Who can explain Your ways?
Who can fathom Your design?

אֲבוֹתֵינוּ גָּלוּ מֵאַרְצָם וְנִתְרַחֲקוּ מֵעַל אַדְמָתָם.
וּמֵאָז וְעַד יָמֵינוּ מִגָּלוּת לְגָלוּת עָבַרְנוּ, וְרַגְלֵנוּ לֹא מָצְאָה מָנוֹחַ.
נַחֲלָתֵנוּ נֶהֶפְכָה לְזָרִים, בָּתֵּינוּ לְנָכְרִים!
יְיָ, מִי יַחְקוֹר תַּעֲלֻמוֹתֶיךָ? יְיָ, מִי יַעֲמִיק לְמַחְשְׁבוֹתֶיךָ?

Why Israel's exile from its land, kept far from its native soil? Why did we pass from one exile to the next, allowed no place to rest, our heritage the spoil of strangers, our House in alien hands?

Who can explain Your ways?
Who can fathom Your design?

אָכֵן אַתָּה אֵל מִסְתַּתֵּר, אֱלֹהֵי יִשְׂרָאֵל מוֹשִׁיעַ.
זֵרִיתָנוּ בָּאֲרָצוֹת, הָיִינוּ חֶרְפָּה לִשְׁכֵנֵינוּ וָקֶלֶס לִסְבִיבוֹתֵינוּ.
עַל צַוָּארֵנוּ נִרְדָּפְנוּ, יָגַעְנוּ וְלֹא הוּנַח לָנוּ.

יְיָ, מִי יַחְקוֹר תַּעֲלֻמוֹתֶיךָ? יְיָ, מִי יַעֲמִיק לְמַחְשְׁבוֹתֶיךָ?

A redeeming God! A hidden God! Why were we so long strangers in lands not ours, crushed by enemies, heads bowed, toiling without rest or reward?

Who can explain Your ways?
Who can fathom Your design?

אֵיכָה יָעִיב בְּאַפּוֹ אֲדֹנָי אֶת־בַּת־צִיּוֹן, הִשְׁלִיךְ מִשָּׁמַיִם אֶרֶץ
תִּפְאֶרֶת יִשְׂרָאֵל, וְלֹא־זָכַר הֲדֹם־רַגְלָיו בְּיוֹם אַפּוֹ; בִּלַּע
אֲדֹנָי וְלֹא חָמַל: אֵת כָּל־נְאוֹת יַעֲקֹב הָרַס בְּעֶבְרָתוֹ, מִבְצְרֵי
בַת־יְהוּדָה הִגִּיעַ לָאָרֶץ, חִלֵּל מַמְלָכָה וְשָׂרֶיהָ. הָיָה אֲדֹנָי
כְּאוֹיֵב: בִּלַּע יִשְׂרָאֵל, בִּלַּע כָּל־אַרְמְנוֹתֶיהָ, שִׁחֵת מִבְצָרָיו,
וַיֶּרֶב בְּבַת־יְהוּדָה תַּאֲנִיָּה וַאֲנִיָּה.

Dark is the life of the daughter of Zion; the precious land of Israel is cast down, the faithful people forgotten. Where is God, amid the broken ramparts, the shattered cities? Where is God?

◆

From Psalm 137

עַל נַהֲרוֹת בָּבֶל, שָׁם יָשַׁבְנוּ, גַּם־בָּכִינוּ בְּזָכְרֵנוּ אֶת־צִיּוֹן. עַל־
עֲרָבִים בְּתוֹכָהּ תָּלִינוּ כִּנֹּרוֹתֵינוּ. כִּי שָׁם שְׁאֵלוּנוּ שׁוֹבֵינוּ
דִּבְרֵי־שִׁיר וְתוֹלָלֵינוּ שִׂמְחָה: 'שִׁירוּ לָנוּ מִשִּׁיר צִיּוֹן.' אֵיךְ
נָשִׁיר אֶת־שִׁיר יְיָ עַל אַדְמַת נֵכָר? אִם־אֶשְׁכָּחֵךְ, יְרוּשָׁלָםִ,

תִּשְׁכַּח יְמִינִי, תִּדְבַּק לְשׁוֹנִי לְחִכִּי, אִם־לֹא אֶזְכְּרֵכִי, אִם־לֹא אַעֲלֶה אֶת־יְרוּשָׁלַיִם עַל רֹאשׁ שִׂמְחָתִי!

By the waters of Babylon, we sat down and wept, as we remembered Zion. There, by the willows, we put aside our harps. For there our captors demanded of us song; our tormentors called for mirth: 'Sing us some songs of Zion.' How can we sing the Lord's song in a land of exile? If I forget you, O Jerusalem, let my right hand wither; let my tongue cleave to the roof of my mouth, if I do not remember you, if I do not set Jerusalem above my highest joy!

✦

יְיָ, מִי יַחְקוֹר תַּעֲלֻמוֹתֶיךָ? יְיָ, מִי יַעֲמִיק לְמַחְשְׁבוֹתֶיךָ?

O God, who can explain Your ways?

Who can fathom Your design, O God?
Who can explain Your ways?

✦

אַב הָרַחֲמִים, הֵיטִיבָה בִרְצוֹנְךָ אֶת־צִיּוֹן, תִּבְנֶה חוֹמוֹת יְרוּשָׁלָיִם.

Source of mercy, let Your goodness be a blessing to Zion; let Jerusalem be rebuilt.

✦

נַחֲמוּ, נַחֲמוּ עַמִּי, יֹאמַר אֱלֹהֵיכֶם. דַּבְּרוּ עַל־לֵב יְרוּשָׁלַיִם וְקִרְאוּ אֵלֶיהָ כִּי מָלְאָה צְבָאָהּ כִּי נִרְצָה עֲוֹנָהּ כִּי לָקְחָה מִיַּד יְיָ כִּפְלַיִם בְּכָל־חַטֹּאתֶיהָ. מַה־נָּאווּ עַל־הֶהָרִים רַגְלֵי מְבַשֵּׂר, מַשְׁמִיעַ שָׁלוֹם, מְבַשֵּׂר טוֹב, מַשְׁמִיעַ יְשׁוּעָה, אֹמֵר לְצִיּוֹן: 'מָלַךְ אֱלֹהָיִךְ.' קוֹל צֹפַיִךְ נָשְׂאוּ קוֹל יַחְדָּו יְרַנֵּנוּ, כִּי עַיִן בְּעַיִן יִרְאוּ בְּשׁוּב יְיָ צִיּוֹן. פִּצְחוּ, רַנְּנוּ יַחְדָּו חָרְבוֹת יְרוּשָׁלָיִם, כִּי־נִחַם יְיָ עַמּוֹ, גָּאַל יְרוּשָׁלָיִם.

יְיָ, מִי יַחְקוֹר תַּעֲלֻמוֹתֶיךָ? יְיָ, מִי יַעֲמִיק לְמַחְשְׁבוֹתֶיךָ?

Take comfort, take comfort, My people, says the Lord. How beautiful upon the mountains are the feet of the herald, the one who proclaims peace, who brings tidings of good and proclaims deliverance, who says to Zion: 'Your God reigns.' O ruins of Jerusalem, hear your sentries raise their voices and shout together in triumph, for clearly they see the return of the Lord to Zion. For the Lord has comforted His people and redeemed Jerusalem!

O God, who can explain Your ways?
Who can fathom Your design?

◆

Psalm 126

A SONG OF ASCENTS שִׁיר הַמַּעֲלוֹת

בְּשׁוּב יְיָ אֶת־שִׁיבַת צִיּוֹן, הָיִינוּ כְּחֹלְמִים. אָז יִמָּלֵא שְׂחוֹק פִּינוּ, וּלְשׁוֹנֵנוּ רִנָּה. אָז יֹאמְרוּ בַגּוֹיִם: 'הִגְדִּיל יְיָ לַעֲשׂוֹת עִם־אֵלֶּה.'

When the Lord restores the exiles to Zion, it will seem like a dream. Then our mouths will fill with laughter, our tongues with joyful song. Then they will say among the nations: 'The Lord has done great things for them.'

הִגְדִּיל יְיָ לַעֲשׂוֹת עִמָּנוּ, הָיִינוּ שְׂמֵחִים! שׁוּבָה יְיָ אֶת־שְׁבִיתֵנוּ כַּאֲפִיקִים בַּנֶּגֶב. הַזֹּרְעִים בְּדִמְעָה, בְּרִנָּה יִקְצֹרוּ. הָלוֹךְ יֵלֵךְ וּבָכֹה, נֹשֵׂא מֶשֶׁךְ־הַזָּרַע, בֹּא־יָבֹא בְרִנָּה, נֹשֵׂא אֲלֻמֹּתָיו.

It is for us that the Lord is doing great things: we will rejoice. Lord, restore our fortunes, as streams revive the desert. Then those who sow in tears shall reap in joy. Those who go forth weeping, bearing sacks of seeds, shall come home with shouts of joy, bearing their sheaves.

◆

מִי דוֹר כְּדוֹרֵנוּ אֲשֶׁר רָאָה אֶת־שֶׁבֶר בַּת עַמֵּנוּ? וּמִי דוֹר כְּדוֹרֵנוּ אֲשֶׁר זָכָה בְּנֶחָמַת צִיּוֹן וּבְבִנְיַן יְרוּשָׁלַיִם? מַה מַּכְאוֹב כְּמַכְאוֹבֵנוּ, וְאֵיזוֹ שִׂמְחָה כְּשִׂמְחָתֵנוּ?

אַךְ לֹא בָאנוּ עַד עַתָּה אֶל הַמְּנוּחָה וְאֶל הַנַּחֲלָה: עוֹד נִמְשֶׁכֶת הַגָּלוּת – גָּלוּת עַמֵּנוּ, גָּלוּת הָאָדָם, וְגָלוּת שְׁכִינָתֶךָ.

עוֹד אוֹמְרִים שׂוֹנְאֵינוּ, עָרוּ עָרוּ עַד הַיְסוֹד בָּהּ. עוֹד כּוֹתְתִים אִתִּים לַחֲרָבוֹת וּמַזְמֵרוֹת לִרְמָחִים. עוֹד שׁוֹאֶפֶת הָאָרֶץ וּמְלוֹאָהּ לַגְּאוּלָּה הַשְּׁלֵמָה.

You are the hidden God; You are Israel's God; You are the God who redeems. Our people crushed, Zion restored, in a single generation! None has felt such pain as ours, none has known such joy!

And yet, even now, Exile persists, no less real than before: for still our enemies plot to destroy us, still they hack at our roots. Still nations beat plowshares into swords and pruning-hooks into spears. Still earth awaits its true redemption.

וַאֲנַחְנוּ הִנֵּה בָּאנוּ בֵּיתֶךָ לִסְפּוֹד וְלִבְכּוֹת אֶת־חֲלָלֵינוּ. לְהוֹדוֹת וּלְהַלֵּל עַל הַגְּבוּרוֹת וְעַל הַתְּשׁוּעוֹת, לְהָבִין וּלְהַשְׂכִּיל אֶת־הַדֶּרֶךְ בָּהּ הוֹלַכְתָּנוּ, וְאֶת־הֶעָתִיד אֲשֶׁר אֵלָיו אַתָּה מַגִּיעֵנוּ.

And so we pray, and rage, and weep over our dead; and still, even now, we search for strength to praise and celebrate God's wonder. And still we ponder His ways, the paths we have travelled, the destiny that is ours.

הַשְׁקִיפָה מִמְּעוֹן קָדְשֶׁךָ, וּבָרֵךְ אֶת־עַמְּךָ יִשְׂרָאֵל בְּכָל־מְקוֹמוֹת מוֹשְׁבוֹתֵיהֶם. בָּרֵךְ אֶת־מְדִינַת־יִשְׂרָאֵל, וְהָגֵן עָלֶיהָ בְּאֶבְרַת חַסְדֶּךָ. חַזֵּק אֶת־יְדֵי מָגִנֵּי הַמְּדִינָה, וְתֵן שָׁלוֹם בָּאָרֶץ וְשִׂמְחַת עוֹלָם לְיוֹשְׁבֶיהָ. וְהוֹפַע בַּהֲדַר גְּאוֹן עֻזֶּךָ עַל כָּל־יוֹשְׁבֵי תֵבֵל אַרְצֶךָ. וְיֹאמַר כֹּל אֲשֶׁר נְשָׁמָה בְאַפּוֹ, יְיָ אֱלֹהֵי יִשְׂרָאֵל מֶלֶךְ וּמַלְכוּתוֹ בַּכֹּל מָשָׁלָה. אָז תִּשְׁפּוֹךְ אֶת־רוּחֲךָ עַל־כָּל־בָּשָׂר, וְנִבְּאוּ בָּנֵינוּ וּבְנוֹתֵינוּ; זְקֵנֵינוּ חֲלוֹמוֹת יַחֲלוֹמוּן, וּבַחוּרֵינוּ חֶזְיוֹנוֹת יִרְאוּ.

We ask blessing for Israel's land and its people, a brand plucked from the burning; blessing for ourselves, a branch of that people refusing to die; blessing for the world, that world so silent. Let all who breathe enthrone You in their hearts, their words, their hands. Let the vision become reality:

לֹא־יָרֵעוּ וְלֹא יַשְׁחִיתוּ בְּכָל־הַר קָדְשִׁי, כִּי־מָלְאָה הָאָרֶץ דֵּעָה אֶת־יְיָ כַּמַּיִם לַיָּם מְכַסִּים. כִּי מִצִּיּוֹן תֵּצֵא תוֹרָה, וּדְבַר־יְיָ מִירוּשָׁלָיִם.

They shall not hurt or destroy in all My holy mountain; for the earth shall be filled with the knowledge of the Lord as the sea-bed is covered by water. For out of Zion shall go forth Torah, and the word of the Lord from Jerusalem.

✦

אֲרֻכָּה הַדֶּרֶךְ וּמַכְאִיבָה מֵחוּרְבַּן יְרוּשָׁלַיִם וְעַד בִּנְיָנָהּ, וּמִבִּנְיַן יְרוּשָׁלַיִם וְעַד תִּקּוּן כָּל־הָעוֹלָם בְּמַלְכוּתֶךָ. בִּקְרוֹבֶיךָ תִּקָּדֵשׁ, יְיָ, וְעַל קְדוּשַּׁת שִׁמְךָ רְבָבוֹת מִבְּנֵי עַמֵּנוּ מָסְרוּ נַפְשָׁם. בְּזָכְרֵנוּ אֶת־קְדוֹשֵׁינוּ וְאֶת־גִּבּוֹרֵינוּ שֶׁצִּפּוּ לִגְאוּלָּה וְנִלְחֲמוּ בַּעֲדָהּ, נְהַלֵּל אֶת־מְקוֹר הַחַיִּים שֶׁמִּמֶּנּוּ בָּאוּ וְשֶׁאֵלָיו שָׁבוּ.

A long road, full of torment, from the fall of Jerusalem to its rebuilding. A long road from Jerusalem rebuilt, to the building of God's kingdom. We cannot be silent over our loss. We cannot pretend to understand. And yet, O Lord, we cannot give You up; we will not give the tyrant the final victory. We stand before You in pain and need, remembering our martyrs and heroes, praising the Source of life, from whom we come, to whom we return.

✦

עַם יִשְׂרָאֵל חַי!

Am Yisraeil chai!

✦

מֵעַל־פִּסְגַּת הַר הַצּוֹפִים, שָׁלוֹם לָךְ יְרוּשָׁלַיִם.

Mei·al pis·gat har ha·tso·fim, sha·lom lach Ye·ru·sha·la·yim.

אַלְפֵי גוֹלִים מִקְצוֹת כָּל־תֵּבֵל, נוֹשְׂאִים אֵלַיִךְ עֵינַיִם.

A·le·fei go·lim mi·ke·tsot kol tei·veil, no·se·im ei·la·yich ei·na·yim.

בְּאַלְפֵי בְרָכוֹת הֲיִי בְרוּכָה, מִקְדַּשׁ מֶלֶךְ עִיר מְלוּכָה.

Be·a·le·fei ve·ra·chot ha·yi ve·ru·cha, mik·dash me·lech ir me·lu·cha:

יְרוּשָׁלַיִם, יְרוּשָׁלַיִם! אֲנִי לֹא אָזוּז מִפֹּה!

Ye·ru·sha·la·yim, Ye·ru·sha·la·yim! A·ni lo a·zuz mi·po.

יְרוּשָׁלַיִם, יְרוּשָׁלַיִם! יָבֹא הַמָּשִׁיחַ, יָבֹא!

Ye·ru·sha·la·yim, Ye·ru·sha·la·yim! Ya·vo ha·ma·shi·ach, ya·vo!

From the peak of Mt. Scopus, shalom, Jerusalem. A thousand exiles from all the ends of earth lift up their eyes to you. Be blessed with a thousand blessings, O royal shrine, city of kings. Jerusalem, O Jerusalem! I will not budge from this place! Jerusalem! O Jerusalem! Let the redemption come, let it come!

The Ritual for the Reading of Torah is on page 531.

Concluding Prayers begin on page 613.

CONCLUDING PRAYERS

א I א

עלינו

All rise

עָלֵינוּ לְשַׁבֵּחַ לַאֲדוֹן הַכֹּל, לָתֵת גְּדֻלָּה לְיוֹצֵר בְּרֵאשִׁית,
שֶׁלֹּא עָשָׂנוּ כְּגוֹיֵי הָאֲרָצוֹת, וְלֹא שָׂמָנוּ כְּמִשְׁפְּחוֹת הָאֲדָמָה;
שֶׁלֹּא שָׂם חֶלְקֵנוּ כָּהֶם, וְגֹרָלֵנוּ כְּכָל־הֲמוֹנָם.

We must praise the Lord of all, the Maker of heaven and earth, who has set us apart from the other families of earth, giving us a destiny unique among the nations.

וַאֲנַחְנוּ כּוֹרְעִים וּמִשְׁתַּחֲוִים וּמוֹדִים לִפְנֵי מֶלֶךְ מַלְכֵי הַמְּלָכִים, הַקָּדוֹשׁ בָּרוּךְ הוּא,

We therefore bow in awe and thanksgiving before the One who is Sovereign over all, the Holy One, blessed be He.

All are seated

שֶׁהוּא נוֹטֶה שָׁמַיִם וְיוֹסֵד אָרֶץ, וּמוֹשַׁב יְקָרוֹ בַּשָּׁמַיִם מִמַּעַל, וּשְׁכִינַת עֻזּוֹ בְּגָבְהֵי מְרוֹמִים. הוּא אֱלֹהֵינוּ, אֵין עוֹד; אֱמֶת מַלְכֵּנוּ, אֶפֶס זוּלָתוֹ, כַּכָּתוּב בְּתוֹרָתוֹ: "וְיָדַעְתָּ הַיּוֹם וַהֲשֵׁבֹתָ אֶל־לְבָבֶךָ, כִּי יְיָ הוּא הָאֱלֹהִים בַּשָּׁמַיִם מִמַּעַל וְעַל־הָאָרֶץ מִתָּחַת, אֵין עוֹד."

He spread out the heavens and established the earth; He is our God; there is none else. In truth He alone is our King, as it is written: "Know then this day and take it to heart: the Lord is God in the heavens above and on the earth below; there is none else."

עַל־כֵּן נְקַוֶּה לְךָ, יְיָ אֱלֹהֵינוּ, לִרְאוֹת מְהֵרָה בְּתִפְאֶרֶת עֻזֶּךָ, לְהַעֲבִיר גִּלּוּלִים מִן־הָאָרֶץ, וְהָאֱלִילִים כָּרוֹת יִכָּרֵתוּן,

לְתַקֵּן עוֹלָם בְּמַלְכוּת שַׁדַּי. וְכָל־בְּנֵי בָשָׂר יִקְרְאוּ בִשְׁמֶךָ, לְהַפְנוֹת אֵלֶיךָ כָּל־רִשְׁעֵי אָרֶץ.

We therefore hope, O Lord our God, soon to behold the glory of Your might. Then will false gods vanish from our hearts, and the world will be perfected under Your unchallenged rule. And then will all acclaim You as their God, and, forsaking evil, turn to You alone.

יַכִּירוּ וְיֵדְעוּ כָּל־יוֹשְׁבֵי תֵבֵל כִּי לְךָ תִּכְרַע כָּל־בֶּרֶךְ, תִּשָּׁבַע כָּל־לָשׁוֹן. לְפָנֶיךָ, יְיָ אֱלֹהֵינוּ, יִכְרְעוּ וְיִפֹּלוּ, וְלִכְבוֹד שִׁמְךָ יְקָר יִתֵּנוּ, וִיקַבְּלוּ כֻלָּם אֶת־עֹל מַלְכוּתֶךָ, וְתִמְלוֹךְ עֲלֵיהֶם מְהֵרָה לְעוֹלָם וָעֶד.

Let all who dwell on earth acknowledge that unto You every knee must bend and every tongue swear loyalty. Before You, O Lord our God, let them humble themselves. To Your glorious name let them give honor. Let all accept the yoke of Your kingdom, that You may rule over them soon and for ever.

כִּי הַמַּלְכוּת שֶׁלְּךָ הִיא, וּלְעוֹלְמֵי עַד תִּמְלוֹךְ בְּכָבוֹד, כַּכָּתוּב בְּתוֹרָתֶךָ: "יְיָ יִמְלֹךְ לְעֹלָם וָעֶד."

For the kingdom is Yours, and to all eternity You will reign in glory, as it is written: "The Lord will reign for ever and ever."

וְנֶאֱמַר: "וְהָיָה יְיָ לְמֶלֶךְ עַל־כָּל־הָאָרֶץ; בַּיּוֹם הַהוּא יִהְיֶה יְיָ אֶחָד וּשְׁמוֹ אֶחָד."

And it has been said: "The Lord shall reign over all the earth; on that day the Lord shall be One and His name shall be One."

Continue on page 622.

ב II ב

עלינו

All rise

עָלֵינוּ לְשַׁבֵּחַ לַאֲדוֹן הַכֹּל,
לָתֵת גְּדֻלָּה לְיוֹצֵר בְּרֵאשִׁית,
שֶׁהוּא נוֹטֶה שָׁמַיִם וְיוֹסֵד אָרֶץ,
וּמוֹשַׁב יְקָרוֹ בַּשָּׁמַיִם מִמַּעַל,
וּשְׁכִינַת עֻזּוֹ בְּגָבְהֵי מְרוֹמִים.
הוּא אֱלֹהֵינוּ, אֵין עוֹד.

Let us adore
the ever-living God,
and render praise
unto Him
who spread out the heavens
and established the earth,
whose glory
is revealed in the heavens above,
and whose greatness
is manifest throughout the world.
He is our God; there is none else.

וַאֲנַחְנוּ כּוֹרְעִים וּמִשְׁתַּחֲוִים וּמוֹדִים
לִפְנֵי מֶלֶךְ מַלְכֵי הַמְּלָכִים הַקָּדוֹשׁ בָּרוּךְ הוּא.

We therefore bow in awe and thanksgiving before the One who is Sovereign over all, the Holy One, blessed be He.

All are seated

May the time not be distant, O God, when Your name shall be worshipped in all the earth, when unbelief shall disappear and error be no more. Fervently we pray that the day may come when all shall turn to You in love, when corruption and evil shall give way to integrity and goodness, when superstition shall no longer enslave the mind, nor idolatry blind the eye, when all who dwell on earth shall know that You alone are God. O may all, created in Your image, become one in spirit and one in friendship, for ever united in Your service. Then shall Your kingdom be established on earth, and the word of Your prophet fulfilled: "The Lord will reign for ever and ever."

בַּיּוֹם הַהוּא יִהְיֶה יְיָ אֶחָד וּשְׁמוֹ אֶחָד.

On that day the Lord shall be One and His name shall be One.

Continue on page 622.

ג III ג

עלינו

All rise

עָלֵינוּ לְשַׁבֵּחַ לַאֲדוֹן הַכֹּל,
לָתֵת גְּדֻלָּה לְיוֹצֵר בְּרֵאשִׁית,
שֶׁהוּא נוֹטֶה שָׁמַיִם וְיוֹסֵד אָרֶץ,
וּמוֹשַׁב יְקָרוֹ בַּשָּׁמַיִם מִמַּעַל,
וּשְׁכִינַת עֻזּוֹ בְּגָבְהֵי מְרוֹמִים.
הוּא אֱלֹהֵינוּ, אֵין עוֹד.

Let us revere the God of life, and sing the praise of Nature's Lord, who spread out the heavens and established the earth, whose glory is proclaimed by the starry skies, and whose wonders are revealed in the human heart. He is our God; there is none else. With love and awe we acclaim the Eternal God, the Holy One, blessed be He.

וַאֲנַחְנוּ כּוֹרְעִים וּמִשְׁתַּחֲוִים וּמוֹדִים לִפְנֵי מֶלֶךְ מַלְכֵי הַמְּלָכִים הַקָּדוֹשׁ בָּרוּךְ הוּא.

All are seated

The day will come when all shall turn with trust to God, hearkening to His voice, bearing witness to His truth.

We pray with all our hearts: let violence be gone; let the day come soon when evil shall give way to goodness, when war shall be forgotten, hunger be no more, and all at last shall live in freedom.

O Source of life: may we, created in Your image, embrace one another in friendship and in joy. Then shall we be one family, and then shall Your kingdom be established on earth, and the word of Your prophet fulfilled: "The Lord will reign for ever and ever."

בַּיּוֹם הַהוּא יִהְיֶה יְיָ אֶחָד וּשְׁמוֹ אֶחָד.

On that day the Lord shall be One and His name shall be One.

יְהִי שֵׁם יְיָ מְבֹרָךְ מֵעַתָּה וְעַד־עוֹלָם, וְיִמָּלֵא כְבוֹדוֹ אֶת־כָּל־הָאָרֶץ. אָמֵן וְאָמֵן.

Blessed be the name of the Lord for ever; and let the whole world be filled with His glory. Amen and Amen.

Continue on page 622.

ד IV ד

עלינו

All rise

עָלֵינוּ לְשַׁבֵּחַ לַאֲדוֹן הַכֹּל, לָתֵת גְּדֻלָּה לְיוֹצֵר בְּרֵאשִׁית, שֶׁהוּא שָׂם חֶלְקֵנוּ לְיַחֵד אֶת־שְׁמוֹ, וְגוֹרָלֵנוּ לְהַמְלִיךְ מַלְכוּתוֹ.

We praise Him who gave us life. In our rejoicing He is God; He is God in our grief. In anguish and deliverance alike, we praise; in darkness and light we affirm our faith. Therefore we bow our heads in reverence, before the Eternal God of life, the Holy One, blessed be He.

וַאֲנַחְנוּ כֹּרְעִים וּמִשְׁתַּחֲוִים וּמוֹדִים לִפְנֵי מֶלֶךְ מַלְכֵי הַמְּלָכִים, הַקָּדוֹשׁ בָּרוּךְ הוּא.

All are seated

עַל־כֵּן נְקַוֶּה לְךָ, יְיָ אֱלֹהֵינוּ, לִרְאוֹת מְהֵרָה בְּתִפְאֶרֶת עֻזֶּךָ, לְהַעֲבִיר גִּלּוּלִים מִן הָאָרֶץ, וְהָאֱלִילִים כָּרוֹת יִכָּרֵתוּן, לְתַקֵּן עוֹלָם בְּמַלְכוּת שַׁדַּי. וְכָל־בְּנֵי בָשָׂר יִקְרְאוּ בִשְׁמֶךָ, לְהַפְנוֹת אֵלֶיךָ כָּל־רִשְׁעֵי אָרֶץ.

Eternal God, we face the morrow with hope made stronger by the vision of Your kingdom, a world where poverty and war are banished, where injustice and hate are gone.

יַכִּירוּ וְיֵדְעוּ כָּל־יוֹשְׁבֵי תֵבֵל כִּי לְךָ תִּכְרַע כָּל־בֶּרֶךְ, תִּשָּׁבַע כָּל־לָשׁוֹן. לְפָנֶיךָ, יְיָ אֱלֹהֵינוּ, יִכְרְעוּ וְיִפֹּלוּ, וְלִכְבוֹד שִׁמְךָ יְקָר יִתֵּנוּ, וִיקַבְּלוּ כֻלָּם אֶת־עֹל מַלְכוּתֶךָ, וְתִמְלוֹךְ עֲלֵיהֶם מְהֵרָה לְעוֹלָם וָעֶד.

Teach us more and more to share the pain of others, to heed Your call for justice, to pursue the blessing of peace. Help us, O God, to gain victory over evil, to bring nearer the day when all the world shall be one.

כִּי הַמַּלְכוּת שֶׁלְּךָ הִיא, וּלְעוֹלְמֵי עַד תִּמְלֹךְ בְּכָבוֹד,
כַּכָּתוּב בְּתוֹרָתֶךָ: "יְיָ יִמְלֹךְ לְעוֹלָם וָעֶד."
וְנֶאֱמַר: "וְהָיָה יְיָ לְמֶלֶךְ עַל־כָּל־הָאָרֶץ; בַּיּוֹם הַהוּא יִהְיֶה
יְיָ אֶחָד וּשְׁמוֹ אֶחָד."

On that day the age-old hope shall come true. On that day, O God, You shall be One and Your name shall be One.

Before The Kaddish

Our thoughts turn to those who have departed this earth: our own loved ones, those whom our friends and neighbors have lost, the martyrs of our people whose graves are unmarked, and those of every race and nation whose lives have been a blessing to humanity. As we remember them, let us meditate on the meaning of love and loss, of life and death.

◆ ◆

Meditations

1. The Tradition of the Kaddish

The origins of the Kaddish are mysterious; angels are said to have brought it down from heaven. . . .

It possesses wonderful power. Truly, if there is any bond strong enough to chain heaven to earth, it is this prayer. It keeps the living together, and forms a bridge to the mysterious realm of the dead. One might almost say that this prayer is the . . . guardian of the people by whom alone it is uttered; therein lies the warrant of its continuance. Can a people disappear and be annihilated so long as a child remembers its parents?

Because this prayer does not acknowledge death, because it permits the blossom, which has fallen from the tree of humankind, to flower and develop again in the human heart, therefore it possesses sanctifying power.

2. Facing Death

The contemplation of death should plant within the soul elevation and peace. Above all, it should make us see things in their true light. For all things which seem foolish in the light of death are really foolish in themselves. To be annoyed because So-and-so has slighted us or has been somewhat more successful in social distinctions, pulled himself somehow one rung higher up the ladder than ourselves — how ridiculous all this seems when we couple it with the thought of death!

To pass each day simply and solely in the eager pursuit of money or fame, this also seems like living with shadows when one might take one's part with realities. Surely when death is at hand we should desire to say, 'I have contributed my grain to the great store of the eternal. I have borne my part in the struggle for goodness.' And let no man or woman suppose that the smallest social act of goodness is wasted for society at large. All our help, petty though it be, is needed; and though we know not the manner, the fruit of every faithful service is gathered in. Let the true and noble words of a great teacher ring in conclusion upon our ears: 'The growing good of the world is partly dependent on unhistoric acts; and that things are not so ill with you and me as they might have been, is half owing to the number who lived faithfully a hidden life and rest in unvisited tombs.'

3. In Recent Grief

When cherished ties are broken, and the chain of love is shattered, only trust and the strength of faith can lighten the heaviness of the heart. At times, the pain of separation seems more than we can bear, but if we dwell too long on our loss we embitter our hearts and harm ourselves and those about us.

The Psalmist said that in his affliction he learned the law of God. And in truth, grief is a great teacher, when it sends us back to serve and bless the living. We learn how to counsel and comfort those who, like ourselves, are bowed with sorrow. We learn when to keep silence in their presence, and when a word will assure them of our love and concern.

Thus, even when they are gone, the departed are with us, moving us to live as, in their higher moments, they themselves wished to live. We remember them now; they live in our hearts; they are an abiding blessing.

4. After a Tragic Loss

O God, help me to live with my grief!

Death has taken my beloved, and I feel that I cannot go on. My faith is shaken; my mind keeps asking: Why? Why does joy end in sorrow? Why does love exact its price in tears? Why?

O God, help me to live with my grief!

Help me to accept the mystery of life. Help me to see that even if my questions were answered, even if I did know why, the pain would be no less, the loneliness would remain bitter beyond words. Still my heart would ache.

O God, help me to triumph over my grief!

Help me to endure this night of anguish. Help me to walk through the darkness with faith in tomorrow. Give me comfort; give me courage; turn me to deeds that bless the living.

O God, help me to triumph over my grief.

5. How Can We Understand Death?

What can we know of death, we who cannot understand life?

We study the seed and the cell, but the power deep within them will always elude us.

Though we cannot understand, we accept life as the gift of God. Yet death, life's twin, we face with fear.

But why be afraid? Death is a haven to the weary, a relief for the sorely afflicted. We are safe in death as in life.

There is no pain in death. There is only the pain of the living as they recall shared loves, and as they themselves fear to die.

Calm us, O Lord, when we cry out in our fear and our grief. Turn us anew toward life and the world. Awaken us to the warmth of human love that speaks to us of You.

We shall fear no evil as we affirm Your kingdom of life.

6. A Philosophy of Life and Death

Judaism teaches us to understand death as part of the Divine pattern of the universe. Actually, we could not have our sensitivity without fragility. Mortality is the tax that we pay for the privilege of love, thought, creative work — the toll on the bridge of being from which clods of earth and snow-peaked mountain summits are exempt. Just because we are human, we are prisoners of the years. Yet that very prison is the room of discipline in which we, driven by the urgency of time, create.

7. The Blessing of Memory

It is hard to sing of oneness when our world is not complete, when those who once brought wholeness to our life have gone, and naught but memory can fill the emptiness their passing leaves behind.

But memory can tell us only what we were, in company with those we loved; it cannot help us find what each of us, alone, must now become. Yet no one is really alone; those who live no more, echo still within our thoughts and words, and what they did is part of what we have become.

We do best homage to our dead when we live our lives most fully, even in the shadow of our loss. For each of our lives is worth the life of the whole world; in each one is the breath of the Ultimate One. In affirming the One, we affirm the worth of each one whose life, now ended, brought us closer to the Source of life, in whose unity no one is alone and every life finds purpose.

8. In Praise of Lives Now Gone

יִתְגַּדַּל וְיִתְקַדַּשׁ שְׁמֵהּ רַבָּא

This the profound praise of the living,
Praise for the generous gift of life.

Praise for the presence of loved ones,
the bonds of friendship,
the link of memory.

Praise for the toil and searching,
the dedication and vision,
the ennobling aspirations.

Praise for the precious moorings of faith,
for courageous souls,
for prophets, psalmists, and sages.

Praise for those who walked before us,
the sufferers in the valley of shadows,
the steadfast in the furnace of hate.

יִתְגַּדַּל וְיִתְקַדַּשׁ שְׁמֵהּ רַבָּא

Praise for the God of our people,
the Source of all growth and goodness.
the Promise on which we build tomorrow.

9. We Live In Our Work

Eternal God, the generations come and go before You. Brief is their time. Passing, they leave many of their tasks unfinished, their plans unfulfilled, their dreams unrealized. It would be more than we could bear, but for the faith that our little day finds its permanence in Your eternity, and our work its completion in the unfolding of Your purpose for humanity.

At this sacred moment we turn our thoughts to those we love who have gone from life. We recall the joy of their companionship. We feel a pang, the echo of that intenser grief when first their death lay before our stricken eyes. Now we know that they will never vanish, so long as heart and thought remain within us. By love are they remembered, and in memory they live.

O God, grant that their memory may bring strength and blessing. May the nobility in their lives and the high ideals they cherished endure in our thoughts and live on in our deeds. May we, carrying on their work, help to redeem Your promise that life shall prevail.

10. The Life of Eternity

The light of life is a finite flame. Like the Sabbath candles, life is kindled, it burns, it glows, it is radiant with warmth and beauty. But soon it fades; its substance is consumed, and it is no more.

In light we see; in light we are seen. The flames dance and our lives are full. But as night follows day, the candle of our life burns down and gutters. There is an end to the flames. We see no more and are no more seen. Yet we do not despair, for we are more than a memory slowly fading into the darkness. With our lives we give life. Something of us can never die: we move in the eternal cycle of darkness and death, of light and life.

11. The Spirit Lives On

"The Lord gives; the Lord takes away; blessed be the name of the Lord."

Early or late, all must answer the summons to return to the Reservoir of Being. For we loose our hold on life when our time has come, as the leaf falls from the bough when its day is done. The deeds of the righteous enrich the world, as the fallen leaf enriches the soil beneath. The dust returns to the earth, the spirit lives on with God.

Like the stars by day, our beloved dead are not seen by mortal eyes. Yet they shine on for ever; theirs is eternal peace.

Let us be thankful for the companionship that continues in a love stronger than death. Sanctifying the name of God, we do honor to their memory.

12. Strength for Those Who Mourn

In nature's ebb and flow, God's eternal law abides. He who is our support in the struggles of life is also our hope in death. In His care are the souls of all the living and the spirits of all flesh. His power gives us strength; His love comforts us. O Life of our life, Soul of our soul, cause Your light to shine into our hearts. Fill us with trust in You, and turn us again to the tasks of life. And may the memory of our loved ones inspire us to continue their work for the coming of Your kingdom.

13. Our Martyrs

We have lived in numberless towns and villages; and in too many of them we have endured cruel suffering. Some we have forgotten; others are sealed into our memory, a wound that does not heal. A hundred generations of victims and martyrs; still their blood cries out from the earth. And so many, so many at Dachau, at Buchenwald, at Babi Yar, and . . .

What can we say? What can we do? How bear the unbearable, or accept what life has brought to our people? All who are born must die, but how shall we compare the slow passage of our time with the callous slaughter of the innocent, cut off before their time?

They lived with faith. Not all, but many. And, surely, many died with faith; faith in God, in life, in the goodness that even flames cannot destroy. May we find a way to the strength of that faith, that trust, that sure sense that life and soul endure beyond this body's death.

They have left their lives to us: let a million prayers rise whenever Jews worship; let a million candles glow against the darkness of these unfinished lives.

◆ ◆

We recall the loved ones whom death has recently taken from us, those who died at this season in years past, and those whom we have taken into our hearts with our own. . . . The memories of all of them are with us; our griefs and sympathies are mingled as we praise God and pray for the coming of His kingdom.

◆ ◆

MOURNER'S KADDISH

קדיש יתום

יִתְגַּדַּל וְיִתְקַדַּשׁ שְׁמֵהּ רַבָּא בְּעָלְמָא דִּי־בְרָא כִרְעוּתֵהּ,

Yit·ga·dal ve·yit·ka·dash she·mei ra·ba be·al·ma di·ve·ra chi·re·u·tei,

וְיַמְלִיךְ מַלְכוּתֵהּ בְּחַיֵּיכוֹן וּבְיוֹמֵיכוֹן וּבְחַיֵּי דְכָל־בֵּית

ve·yam·lich mal·chu·tei be·cha·yei·chon u·ve·yo·mei·chon u·ve·cha·yei de·chol beit

יִשְׂרָאֵל, בַּעֲגָלָא וּבִזְמַן קָרִיב, וְאִמְרוּ: אָמֵן.

Yis·ra·eil, ba·a·ga·la u·vi·ze·man ka·riv, ve·i·me·ru: a·mein.

יְהֵא שְׁמֵהּ רַבָּא מְבָרַךְ לְעָלַם וּלְעָלְמֵי עָלְמַיָּא.

Ye·hei she·mei ra·ba me·va·rach le·a·lam u·le·al·mei al·ma·ya.

יִתְבָּרַךְ וְיִשְׁתַּבַּח, וְיִתְפָּאַר וְיִתְרוֹמַם וְיִתְנַשֵּׂא, וְיִתְהַדַּר

Yit·ba·rach ve·yish·ta·bach, ve·yit·pa·ar ve·yit·ro·mam ve·yit·na·sei, ve·yit·ha·dar

וְיִתְעַלֶּה וְיִתְהַלַּל שְׁמֵהּ דְּקוּדְשָׁא, בְּרִיךְ הוּא, לְעֵלָּא מִן־כָּל־

ve·yit·a·leh ve·yit·ha·lal she·mei de·ku·de·sha, be·rich hu, le·ei·la min kol

בִּרְכָתָא וְשִׁירָתָא, תֻּשְׁבְּחָתָא וְנֶחֱמָתָא דַּאֲמִירָן בְּעָלְמָא,

bi·re·cha·ta ve·shi·ra·ta, tush·be·cha·ta ve·ne·che·ma·ta, da·a·mi·ran be·al·ma,

וְאִמְרוּ: אָמֵן.

ve·i·me·ru: a·mein.

יְהֵא שְׁלָמָא רַבָּא מִן־שְׁמַיָּא וְחַיִּים עָלֵינוּ וְעַל־כָּל־יִשְׂרָאֵל,

Ye·hei she·la·ma ra·ba min she·ma·ya ve·cha·yim a·lei·nu ve·al kol Yis·ra·eil,

וְאִמְרוּ: אָמֵן.

ve·i·me·ru: a·mein.

עֹשֶׂה שָׁלוֹם בִּמְרוֹמָיו, הוּא יַעֲשֶׂה שָׁלוֹם עָלֵינוּ וְעַל־כָּל־

O·seh sha·lom bi·me·ro·mav, hu ya·a·seh sha·lom a·lei·nu ve·al kol

יִשְׂרָאֵל, וְאִמְרוּ: אָמֵן.

Yis·ra·eil, ve·i·me·ru: a·mein.

Let the glory of God be extolled, let His great name be hallowed, in the world whose creation He willed. May His kingdom soon prevail, in our own day, our own lives, and the life of all Israel, and let us say: Amen.

Let His great name be blessed for ever and ever.

Let the name of the Holy One, blessed is He, be glorified, exalted, and honored, though He is beyond all the praises, songs, and adorations that we can utter, and let us say: Amen.

For us and for all Israel, may the blessing of peace and the promise of life come true, and let us say: Amen.

May He who causes peace to reign in the high heavens, let peace descend on us, on all Israel, and all the world, and let us say: Amen.

◆ ◆

May the Source of peace send peace to all who mourn, and comfort to all who are bereaved. Amen.

FOR SYNAGOGUE AND HOME

The Leader lights the candle and hands it to the youngest person present

הִנֵּה אֵל יְשׁוּעָתִי, אֶבְטַח וְלֹא אֶפְחָד.
כִּי עָזִּי וְזִמְרָת יָהּ יְיָ, וַיְהִי־לִי לִישׁוּעָה.

Behold, God is my Deliverer; I trust in Him, I am not afraid.

For the Lord is my Strength and my Stronghold, the Source of my deliverance.

וּשְׁאַבְתֶּם מַיִם בְּשָׂשׂוֹן מִמַּעַיְנֵי הַיְשׁוּעָה.
לַייָ הַיְשׁוּעָה, עַל־עַמְּךָ בִרְכָתֶךָ, סֶּלָה.

With joy shall we draw water from the wells of salvation.

The Lord brings deliverance, His blessing to the people.

יְיָ צְבָאוֹת עִמָּנוּ, מִשְׂגָּב־לָנוּ אֱלֹהֵי יַעֲקֹב, סֶלָה.
יְיָ צְבָאוֹת, אַשְׁרֵי אָדָם בֹּטֵחַ בָּךְ!

The Lord of Hosts is with us; the God of Jacob is our stronghold.

O Lord of all the universe, happy is the one who trusts in You!

יְיָ, הוֹשִׁיעָה; הַמֶּלֶךְ יַעֲנֵנוּ בְיוֹם־קָרְאֵנוּ.
לַיְּהוּדִים הָיְתָה אוֹרָה וְשִׂמְחָה, וְשָׂשֹׂן וִיקָר; כֵּן תִּהְיֶה לָּנוּ.
כּוֹס יְשׁוּעוֹת אֶשָּׂא, וּבְשֵׁם יְיָ אֶקְרָא.

Save us, O Lord; answer us, O King, when we call upon You. Give us light and joy, gladness and honor, as in the happiest days of Israel's past.

Then we will lift up the cup to rejoice in Your saving power, and call out Your name in praise.

◆ ◆

The Leader raises the cup of wine

בָּרוּךְ אַתָּה, יְיָ אֱלֹהֵינוּ, מֶלֶךְ הָעוֹלָם, בּוֹרֵא פְּרִי הַגָּפֶן.

Blessed is the Lord our God, Ruler of the universe, Creator of the fruit of the vine.

The wine is circulated; the Leader holds up the spice-box

בָּרוּךְ אַתָּה, יְיָ אֱלֹהֵינוּ, מֶלֶךְ הָעוֹלָם, בּוֹרֵא מִינֵי בְשָׂמִים.

Blessed is the Lord our God, Ruler of the universe, Creator of all the spices.

The spice-box is circulated; the Leader holds up the candle

בָּרוּךְ אַתָּה, יְיָ אֱלֹהֵינוּ, מֶלֶךְ הָעוֹלָם, בּוֹרֵא מְאוֹרֵי הָאֵשׁ.

Blessed is the Lord our God, Ruler of the universe, Creator of the light of fire.

◆ ◆

We give thanks for the Sabbath day that now is ending. We are grateful for its many blessings: for peace and joy, rest for the body, and refreshment for the soul. May something of its meaning and message remain with us as we enter the new week, lifting all that we do to a higher plane of holiness, and inspiring us to work with new heart for the coming of the day when Elijah's spirit will herald our redemption from all sadness and every bondage.

◆ ◆

Ei·li·ya·hu ha·na·vi, Ei·li·ya·hu	אֵלִיָּהוּ הַנָּבִיא, אֵלִיָּהוּ
ha·tish·bi; Ei·li·ya·hu, Ei·li·ya·hu,	הַתִּשְׁבִּי; אֵלִיָּהוּ, אֵלִיָּהוּ,
Ei·li·ya·hu ha·gil·a·di.	אֵלִיָּהוּ הַגִּלְעָדִי.
Bi·me·hei·ra ve·ya·mei·nu, ya·vo	בִּמְהֵרָה בְיָמֵינוּ, יָבֹא
ei·lei·nu; im ma·shi·ach ben	אֵלֵינוּ; עִם מָשִׁיחַ בֶּן
Da·vid, im ma·shi·ach ben	דָּוִד, עִם מָשִׁיחַ בֶּן
Da·vid. Ei·li·ya·hu	דָּוִד. אֵלִיָּהוּ . . . .

◆ ◆

בָּרוּךְ אַתָּה, יְיָ אֱלֹהֵינוּ, מֶלֶךְ הָעוֹלָם, הַמַּבְדִּיל בֵּין קֹדֶשׁ לְחוֹל, בֵּין אוֹר לְחֹשֶׁךְ, בֵּין יוֹם הַשְּׁבִיעִי לְשֵׁשֶׁת יְמֵי הַמַּעֲשֶׂה.

בָּרוּךְ אַתָּה, יְיָ, הַמַּבְדִּיל בֵּין קֹדֶשׁ לְחוֹל.

Blessed is the Lord our God, Ruler of the universe, who separates sacred from profane, light from darkness, the seventh day of rest from the six days of labor.

Blessed is the Lord, who separates the sacred from the profane.

The candle is extinguished

הַמַּבְדִּיל בֵּין קֹדֶשׁ לְחוֹל,
חַטֹּאתֵינוּ הוּא יִמְחֹל,
זַרְעֵנוּ וְכַסְפֵּנוּ יַרְבֶּה כַּחוֹל,
וְכַכּוֹכָבִים בַּלָּיְלָה.

Ha·mav·dil bein ko·desh le·chol,
cha·to·tei·nu hu yim·chol,
zar·ei·nu ve·chas·pei·nu yar·beh ka·chol,
ve·cha·ko·cha·vim ba·lai·la.

שָׁבוּעַ טוֹב . . .

Sha·vu·a tov . . .

יוֹם פָּנָה כְּצֵל תֹּמֶר,
אֶקְרָא לָאֵל, עָלַי גֹּמֵר;
אָמַר שׁוֹמֵר, אָתָא בֹקֶר,
וְגַם־לָיְלָה.

Yom pa·na ke·tseil to·mer,
Ek·ra la·eil, a·lai go·meir;
a·mar sho·meir, a·ta vo·ker,
ve·gam lai·la.

שָׁבוּעַ טוֹב . . .

Sha·vu·a tov . . .

צִדְקָתְךָ כְּהַר תָּבוֹר,
עַל חֲטָאַי עָבוֹר תַּעֲבוֹר,
כְּיוֹם אֶתְמוֹל כִּי יַעֲבוֹר,
וְאַשְׁמוּרָה בַלָּיְלָה.

Tsid·ka·te·cha ke·har Ta·vor,
al cha·ta·ai a·vor ta·a·vor,
ke·yom et·mol ki ya·a·vor,
ve·ash·mu·ra va·lai·la.

שָׁבוּעַ טוֹב . . .

Sha·vu·a tov . . .

Hei·a·teir, no·ra ve·a·yom,	הֵעָתֵר, נוֹרָא וְאָיוֹם,
a·sha·vei·a, te·na fid·yom,	אֲשַׁוֵּעַ, תְּנָה פִדְיוֹם,
be·ne·shef, be·e·rev yom,	בְּנֶשֶׁף, בְּעֶרֶב יוֹם,
be·i·shon lai·la.	בְּאִישׁוֹן לָיְלָה.
Sha·vu·a tov ...	שָׁבוּעַ טוֹב . . .

He who separates sacred from profane, may He pardon our sins; may He increase our descendants and prosperity as the sand, and as the stars at night. The day declines as the palm tree's shade; I call to God who is good to me; the lookout says: 'Morning will come, though it still be night.' Your righteousness towers like Mount Tabor; forgive my sins, and let them be as yesterday when it is past, and as a watch in the night. Hear my prayer, revered and awesome God; grant redemption! In the twilight, in the waning of the day, or in the blackness of the night!

◆ ◆

ON A FESTIVAL

Blessed is the Lord our God,	בָּרוּךְ אַתָּה, יְיָ אֱלֹהֵינוּ,
Ruler of the universe,	מֶלֶךְ הָעוֹלָם,
Creator of the fruit of the vine.	בּוֹרֵא פְּרִי הַגָּפֶן.

We thank You, O God, for the Festival we now conclude, and for all the blessings we have received from it. May its influence remain with us from this day until we celebrate it again. May its beauty and its joyful message never fade from our hearts.

Blessed is the Lord our God,	בָּרוּךְ אַתָּה, יְיָ אֱלֹהֵינוּ,
Ruler of the universe,	מֶלֶךְ הָעוֹלָם,
who separates the sacred from the profane.	הַמַּבְדִּיל בֵּין קֹדֶשׁ לְחוֹל.

Havdalah II

The Torah commands:

The Lord spoke to Aaron: "You shall distinguish between the sacred and the profane, the unclean and the clean."

Like Aaron, first of the priests, we who were called at Sinai to be a kingdom of priests are charged to make Havdalah:

We must distinguish between sacred and profane, between holy and common.

We must separate the holy and good from the unholy and evil, from all that stifles the image of God within us.

To this end has Shabbat been set aside.

◆ ◆

Shabbat, most precious of days. Shabbat, the day of holiness.

Shabbat is blessed rest from daily toil. More than rest, Shabbat is freedom:

To reach out to God, to family and friends.

To wash our souls clean, to search and hope to find goodness and beauty, holiness and truth.

Our fathers knew Shabbat as refuge from this world's compromises, from the brutalities and hurts of competition.

It was a refuge, haven, oasis for our mothers: a day of release from earthbound pursuits, from the relentless struggle for daily bread.

A foretaste of heaven which they called: 'Yom she-ku-lo Shabbat,' a time that is all Shabbat.

But our Shabbat is here on earth, this day's earth, and end it does.

With all reluctance we say farewell to this foretaste of heaven.

O let us carry into the coming week some Sabbath hope and joy, and bring them into our souls, our offices and shops, our hours of leisure.

And let the memory of Shabbat past and the anticipation of Shabbat to come lighten our burdens and make us more considerate and generous — determined to make our earthbound world more heavenly.

◆ ◆

VERSES OF THANKS

The ancients took words from Scripture to voice their thanks to God who saves and sustains us during the week as it passes. Within their words of praise was the hint of prayer for life and health in the week to come. May their tranquil faith be ours, as we make their praise our own.

The Leader lights the candle and hands it to the youngest person present

הִנֵּה אֵל יְשׁוּעָתִי, אֶבְטַח וְלֹא אֶפְחָד.
כִּי עָזִּי וְזִמְרָת יָהּ יְיָ, וַיְהִי־לִי לִישׁוּעָה.

Behold, God is my Deliverer; I trust in Him, I am not afraid.

For the Lord is my Strength and my Stronghold, the Source of my deliverance.

וּשְׁאַבְתֶּם מַיִם בְּשָׂשׂוֹן מִמַּעַיְנֵי הַיְשׁוּעָה.
לַייָ הַיְשׁוּעָה, עַל־עַמְּךָ בִרְכָתֶךָ, סֶּלָה.

With joy shall we draw water from the wells of salvation.

The Lord brings deliverance, His blessing to the people.

יְיָ צְבָאוֹת עִמָּנוּ, מִשְׂגָּב־לָנוּ אֱלֹהֵי יַעֲקֹב, סֶלָה.
יְיָ צְבָאוֹת, אַשְׁרֵי אָדָם בֹּטֵחַ בָּךְ!

The Lord of Hosts is with us; the God of Jacob is our stronghold.

O Lord of all the universe, happy is the one who trusts in You!

יְיָ, הוֹשִׁיעָה; הַמֶּלֶךְ יַעֲנֵנוּ בְיוֹם־קָרְאֵנוּ.
לַיְּהוּדִים הָיְתָה אוֹרָה וְשִׂמְחָה, וְשָׂשׂוֹן וִיקָר; כֵּן תִּהְיֶה לָּנוּ.
כּוֹס יְשׁוּעוֹת אֶשָּׂא, וּבְשֵׁם יְיָ אֶקְרָא.

Save us, O Lord; answer us, O King, when we call upon You. Give us light and joy, gladness and honor, as in the happiest days of Israel's past.

Then we will lift up the cup to rejoice in Your saving power, and call out Your name in praise.

◆ ◆

THE WINE
פרי הגפן

The Leader raises the cup of wine

Wine gladdens the heart. In our gladness, we see beyond the ugliness and misery which stain our world. Our eyes open to unnoticed grace, blessings till now unseen, and the promise of goodness we can bring to flower.

בָּרוּךְ אַתָּה, יְיָ אֱלֹהֵינוּ, מֶלֶךְ הָעוֹלָם, בּוֹרֵא פְּרִי הַגָּפֶן.

Blessed is the Lord our God, Ruler of the universe, Creator of the fruit of the vine.

THE SPICES
בשמים

The Leader holds up the spice-box

The added soul Shabbat confers is leaving now, and these spices will console us at the moment of its passing. They remind us that the six days will pass, and Shabbat return. And their bouquet will make us yearn with thankful heart for the sweetness of rest, and the fragrance of growing things; for the clean smell of rainwashed earth and the sad innocence of childhood; and for the dream of a world healed of pain, pure and wholesome as on that first Shabbat, when God, finding His handiwork good, rested from the work of creation.

בָּרוּךְ אַתָּה, יְיָ אֱלֹהֵינוּ, מֶלֶךְ הָעוֹלָם, בּוֹרֵא מִינֵי בְשָׂמִים.

Blessed is the Lord our God, Ruler of the universe, Creator of all the spices.

The spice-box is circulated

THE CANDLE מאורי האש

The candle is raised

The Rabbis tell us: As night descended at the end of the world's first Sabbath, Adam feared and wept. Then God showed him how to make fire, and by its light and warmth to dispel the darkness and its terrors. Kindling flame is a symbol of our first labor upon the earth.

Shabbat departs and the workday begins as we kindle fire. And we, who dread the night no more, thank God for the flame by which we turn earth's raw stuff into things of use and beauty.

The candle's double wick reminds us that all qualities are paired. We have the power to create many different fires, some useful, others baneful. Let us be on guard never to let this gift of fire devour human life, sear cities and scorch fields, or foul the pure air of heaven, obscuring the very skies. Let the fire we kindle be holy; let it bring light and warmth to all humanity.

בָּרוּךְ אַתָּה, יְיָ אֱלֹהֵינוּ, מֶלֶךְ הָעוֹלָם, בּוֹרֵא מְאוֹרֵי הָאֵשׁ.

Blessed is the Lord our God, Ruler of the universe, Creator of the light of fire.

◆ ◆

SEPARATING OURSELVES הבדלה

Havdalah is not for the close of Shabbat alone; it is for all the days.

Havdalah means: separate yourself from the unholy; strive for holiness.

Havdalah means: separate yourself from fraud and exploitation; be fair and honest with all people.

Havdalah means: separate yourself from indifference to the poor and the deprived, the sick and the aged; work to ease their despair and their loneliness.

Havdalah means: separate yourself from hatred and violence; promote peace among people and nations.

May God give us understanding to reject the unholy and to choose the way of holiness.

May He who separates the holy from the profane inspire us to perform these acts of Havdalah.

בָּרוּךְ אַתָּה, יְיָ אֱלֹהֵינוּ, מֶלֶךְ הָעוֹלָם, הַמַּבְדִּיל בֵּין קֹדֶשׁ לְחוֹל, בֵּין אוֹר לְחֹשֶׁךְ, בֵּין יוֹם הַשְּׁבִיעִי לְשֵׁשֶׁת יְמֵי הַמַּעֲשֶׂה.
בָּרוּךְ אַתָּה, יְיָ, הַמַּבְדִּיל בֵּין קֹדֶשׁ לְחוֹל.

Blessed is the Lord our God, Ruler of the universe, who separates sacred from profane, light from darkness, the seventh day of rest from the six days of labor.

Blessed is the Lord, who separates the sacred from the profane.

The candle is extinguished

The light is gone, and Shabbat with it, but hope illumines the night for us, who are called prisoners of hope. Amid the reality of a world shrouded in deep darkness, our hope is steadfast and our faith sure. There will come a Shabbat *without* Havdalah, when the glory of Shabbat, its peace and its love, will endure for ever. Herald of that wondrous Shabbat is Elijah, whom now, in hope and trust, we invoke in song:

Ei·li·ya·hu ha·na·vi, Ei·li·ya·hu	אֵלִיָּהוּ הַנָּבִיא, אֵלִיָּהוּ
ha·tish·bi; Ei·li·ya·hu, Ei·li·ya·hu,	הַתִּשְׁבִּי; אֵלִיָּהוּ, אֵלִיָּהוּ,
Ei·li·ya·hu ha·gil·a·di.	אֵלִיָּהוּ הַגִּלְעָדִי.
Bi·me·hei·ra ve·ya·mei·nu, ya·vo	בִּמְהֵרָה בְיָמֵינוּ, יָבֹא
ei·lei·nu; im ma·shi·ach ben	אֵלֵינוּ; עִם מָשִׁיחַ בֶּן
Da·vid, im ma·shi·ach ben	דָּוִד, עִם מָשִׁיחַ בֶּן
Da·vid. Ei·li·ya·hu	דָּוִד. אֵלִיָּהוּ . . .

◆ ◆

A good week. A week of peace. May gladness reign and light increase . . .

Sha·vu·a tov . . .	שָׁבוּעַ טוֹב . . .

Chanukah

The lights of Chanukah are a symbol of our joy. In time of darkness, our ancestors had the courage to struggle for freedom: freedom to be themselves, freedom to worship in their own way. Theirs was a victory of the weak over the strong, the few over the many, and the righteous over the arrogant. It was a victory for all ages and all peoples.

◆ ◆

אַשְׁרֵי הַגַּפְרוּר שֶׁנִּשְׂרַף וְהִצִּית לְהָבוֹת.
אַשְׁרֵי הַלֶּהָבָה שֶׁבָּעֲרָה בְּסִתְרֵי לְבָבוֹת.
אַשְׁרֵי הַלְּבָבוֹת שֶׁיָּדְעוּ לַחֲדוֹל בְּכָבוֹד.
אַשְׁרֵי הַגַּפְרוּר שֶׁנִּשְׂרַף וְהִצִּית לְהָבוֹת.

Blessed is the match consumed in kindling flame.
Blessed is the flame that burns in the heart's secret places.
Blessed is the heart with strength to stop its beating for honor's sake.
Blessed is the match consumed in kindling flame.

◆ ◆

שָׁמְעָה וַתִּשְׂמַח צִיּוֹן;
וַתָּגֵלְנָה בְּנוֹת יְהוּדָה,
לְמַעַן מִשְׁפָּטֶיךָ, יְיָ.

Zion hears and is glad;
the cities of Judah rejoice, O Lord,
because of Your judgments.

◆ ◆

Within living memory, our people was plunged into deepest darkness. But we endured; the light of faith still burns brightly, and once again we see kindled the flame of freedom. Our people Israel has survived all who sought to destroy us. Now, through love and self-sacrifice, we labor to renew our life.

Let the lights we kindle shine forth for the world. May they illumine our lives even as they fill us with gratitude that our faith has been saved from extinction time and again.

◆ ◆

The candles are placed in the Menorah from right to left,
and kindled from left to right

בָּרוּךְ אַתָּה, יְיָ אֱלֹהֵינוּ, מֶלֶךְ הָעוֹלָם, אֲשֶׁר קִדְּשָׁנוּ בְּמִצְוֹתָיו, וְצִוָּנוּ לְהַדְלִיק נֵר שֶׁל חֲנֻכָּה.

Blessed is the Lord our God, Ruler of the universe, who hallows us with His Mitzvot, and commands us to kindle the Chanukah lights.

◆

בָּרוּךְ אַתָּה, יְיָ אֱלֹהֵינוּ, מֶלֶךְ הָעוֹלָם, שֶׁעָשָׂה נִסִּים לַאֲבוֹתֵינוּ בַּיָּמִים הָהֵם בַּזְּמַן הַזֶּה.

Blessed is the Lord our God, Ruler of the universe, who performed wondrous deeds for our ancestors in days of old, at this season.

◆

On the first night only

בָּרוּךְ אַתָּה, יְיָ אֱלֹהֵינוּ, מֶלֶךְ הָעוֹלָם, שֶׁהֶחֱיָנוּ וְקִיְּמָנוּ וְהִגִּיעָנוּ לַזְּמַן הַזֶּה.

Blessed is the Lord our God, Ruler of the universe, for giving us life, for sustaining us, and for enabling us to reach this season.

◆ ◆

The following verses might be recited after the lights are kindled

1. הָעָם הַהֹלְכִים בַּחֹשֶׁךְ רָאוּ אוֹר גָּדוֹל.

The people who walked in darkness have seen a great light.

2. כִּי נָפַלְתִּי, קָמְתִּי; כִּי־אֵשֵׁב בַּחֹשֶׁךְ, יְיָ אוֹר לִי.

Though I fall, I shall rise; though I sit in darkness, the Lord shall be a light to me.

3. כִּי־אַתָּה תָּאִיר נֵרִי; יְיָ אֱלֹהַי יַגִּיהַּ חָשְׁכִּי.

For You light my lamp; the Lord God makes bright my darkness.

4. זָרַח בַּחֹשֶׁךְ אוֹר לַיְשָׁרִים; חַנּוּן, וְרַחוּם, וְצַדִּיק.

Light dawns in the darkness for the upright; for the one who is gracious, compassionate, and just.

5. יְיָ אוֹרִי וְיִשְׁעִי; מִמִּי אִירָא?

The Lord is my light and my help; whom shall I fear?

6. כִּי נֵר מִצְוָה, וְתוֹרָה אוֹר.

For the Mitzvah is a lamp, and the Torah is light.

7. קוּמִי, אוֹרִי, כִּי בָא אוֹרֵךְ, וּכְבוֹד יְיָ עָלַיִךְ זָרָח.

Arise, shine, for your light has come, and the splendor of the Lord shall dawn upon you.

8. לֹא־יִהְיֶה־לָּךְ עוֹד הַשֶּׁמֶשׁ לְאוֹר יוֹמָם, וּלְנֹגַהּ הַיָּרֵחַ לֹא־
יָאִיר לָךְ; וְהָיָה־לָךְ יְיָ לְאוֹר עוֹלָם, וֵאלֹהַיִךְ לְתִפְאַרְתֵּךְ.

No more shall the sun be your light by day, nor shall the moon give light to you by night; but the Lord will be your everlasting light, and your God your glory.

◆ ◆

הַנֵּרוֹת הַלָּלוּ אֲנַחְנוּ מַדְלִיקִין עַל הַנִּסִּים וְעַל הַנִּפְלָאוֹת וְעַל הַתְּשׁוּעוֹת וְעַל הַמִּלְחָמוֹת, שֶׁעָשִׂיתָ לַאֲבוֹתֵינוּ בַּיָּמִים הָהֵם בַּזְּמַן הַזֶּה.

וְכָל שְׁמֹנַת יְמֵי חֲנֻכָּה הַנֵּרוֹת הַלָּלוּ קֹדֶשׁ הֵם, וְאֵין לָנוּ רְשׁוּת לְהִשְׁתַּמֵּשׁ בָּהֶם אֶלָּא לִרְאוֹתָם בִּלְבָד, כְּדֵי לְהוֹדוֹת וּלְהַלֵּל לְשִׁמְךָ הַגָּדוֹל עַל־נִסֶּיךָ וְעַל־נִפְלְאוֹתֶיךָ וְעַל־יְשׁוּעָתֶךָ.

We kindle these lights because of the wondrous deliverance You performed for our ancestors.

During these eight days of Chanukah these lights are sacred; we are not to use them but only to behold them, so that their glow may rouse us to give thanks for Your wondrous acts of deliverance.

◆ ◆

For Chanukah songs, see page 757.

At a House of Mourning

One of the weekday services is read first

We are assembled with our friends in the shadow that has fallen on their home. We raise our voices together in prayer to the Source of life, asking for comfort and strength.

We need light when gloom darkens our home; to whom shall we look, but to the Creator of light? We need fortitude and courage when pain and loss assail us; where shall we find them, if not in the thought of Him who preserves all that is good from destruction?

Who among us has not passed through trials and bereavements? Some bear fresh wounds in their hearts, and therefore feel more keenly the kinship of sorrow. Others, whose days of mourning are more remote, still recall the comfort that sympathy brought to their sorrowing hearts.

All things pass; all that lives must die. All that we prize is but lent to us; and the time comes when we must surrender it. We are travellers on the same road that leads to the same end.

◆ ◆

Psalm 121

אֶשָּׂא עֵינַי אֶל־הֶהָרִים, מֵאַיִן יָבוֹא עֶזְרִי?
עֶזְרִי מֵעִם יְיָ, עֹשֵׂה שָׁמַיִם וָאָרֶץ.

I lift up my eyes to the mountains: what is the source of my help?

My help will come from the Lord, Maker of heaven and earth.

אַל־יִתֵּן לַמּוֹט רַגְלֶךָ,
אַל־יָנוּם שֹׁמְרֶךָ.

He will not allow your foot to slip;

your Guardian will not slumber.

הִנֵּה לֹא־יָנוּם וְלֹא יִישָׁן שׁוֹמֵר יִשְׂרָאֵל.
יְיָ שֹׁמְרֶךָ, יְיָ צִלְּךָ עַל־יַד יְמִינֶךָ.

Behold, the Guardian of Israel neither slumbers nor sleeps.

The Eternal is your Keeper, the Lord is your shade at your right hand.

יוֹמָם הַשֶּׁמֶשׁ לֹא־יַכֶּכָּה, וְיָרֵחַ בַּלָּיְלָה.
יְיָ יִשְׁמָרְךָ מִכָּל־רָע, יִשְׁמֹר אֶת־נַפְשֶׁךָ.
יְיָ יִשְׁמָר־צֵאתְךָ וּבוֹאֶךָ, מֵעַתָּה וְעַד־עוֹלָם.

The sun shall not harm you by day, nor the moon by night. The Lord will guard you from all evil, He will protect your being.

The Lord will guard you, coming and going, from this time forth, and for ever.

◆ ◆

MEDITATION

As in the world around us, so too in human life, darkness is followed by light and sorrow by comfort. Life and death are twins; grief and hope walk hand in hand. Although we cannot know what lies beyond the body's death, let us put our trust in the undying Spirit who calls us into life and who abides to all eternity.

◆ ◆

O Lord, God of the spirits of all flesh, You are close to the hearts of the sorrowing, to strengthen and console them with the warmth of Your love, and with the assurance that the human spirit is enduring and indestructible. Even as we pray for perfect peace for those whose lives have ended, so do we ask You to give comfort and courage to the living.

May the knowledge of Your nearness be our strength, O God, for You are with us at all times: in joy and sorrow, in light and darkness, in life and death.

◆ ◆

All rise

אֵל מָלֵא רַחֲמִים, שׁוֹכֵן בַּמְּרוֹמִים, הַמְצֵא מְנוּחָה נְכוֹנָה תַּחַת כַּנְפֵי הַשְּׁכִינָה עִם קְדוֹשִׁים וּטְהוֹרִים כְּזֹהַר הָרָקִיעַ מַזְהִירִים אֶת נִשְׁמַת ...... שֶׁהָלַךְ (שֶׁהָלְכָה) לְעוֹלָמוֹ (לְעוֹלָמָהּ). בַּעַל הָרַחֲמִים יַסְתִּירֵהוּ (יַסְתִּירֶהָ) בְּסֵתֶר כְּנָפָיו לְעוֹלָמִים. וְיִצְרוֹר בִּצְרוֹר הַחַיִּים אֶת־נִשְׁמָתוֹ (נִשְׁמָתָהּ). יְיָ הוּא נַחֲלָתוֹ (נַחֲלָתָהּ) וְיָנוּחַ (וְתָנוּחַ) בְּשָׁלוֹם עַל מִשְׁכָּבוֹ (מִשְׁכָּבָהּ), וְנֹאמַר אָמֵן.

O God full of compassion, Eternal Spirit of the universe, grant perfect rest under the wings of Your Presence to our loved one who has entered eternity. Master of Mercy, let him (her) find refuge for ever in the shadow of Your wings, and let his (her) soul be bound up in the bond of eternal life. The Eternal God is his (her) inheritance. May he (she) rest in peace, and let us say: Amen.

All are seated

◆ ◆

אָנָּא, יְיָ, הָרוֹפֵא לִשְׁבוּרֵי לֵב וּמְחַבֵּשׁ לְעַצְּבוֹתָם, שַׁלֵּם נִחוּמִים לָאֲבֵלִים. חַזְּקֵם וְאַמְּצֵם בְּיוֹם אֶבְלָם וִיגוֹנָם, וְזָכְרֵם לְחַיִּים טוֹבִים וַאֲרֻכִּים.

תֵּן בְּלִבָּם יִרְאָתְךָ וְאַהֲבָתְךָ לְעָבְדְךָ בְּלֵבָב שָׁלֵם. וּתְהִי אַחֲרִיתָם שָׁלוֹם. אָמֵן.

O Lord, Healer of the broken-hearted and Binder of their wounds, grant consolation to those who mourn. Give them strength and courage in the time of their grief, and restore to them a sense of life's goodness.

Fill them with reverence and love for You, that they may serve You with a whole heart, and let them soon know peace. Amen.

◆ ◆

Psalm 23

מִזְמוֹר לְדָוִד. יְיָ רֹעִי, לֹא אֶחְסָר. בִּנְאוֹת דֶּשֶׁא יַרְבִּיצֵנִי,
עַל־מֵי מְנֻחוֹת יְנַהֲלֵנִי. נַפְשִׁי יְשׁוֹבֵב. יַנְחֵנִי בְמַעְגְּלֵי־צֶדֶק
לְמַעַן שְׁמוֹ. גַּם כִּי־אֵלֵךְ בְּגֵיא צַלְמָוֶת לֹא־אִירָא רָע, כִּי־
אַתָּה עִמָּדִי; שִׁבְטְךָ וּמִשְׁעַנְתֶּךָ הֵמָּה יְנַחֲמֻנִי. תַּעֲרֹךְ לְפָנַי
שֻׁלְחָן נֶגֶד צֹרְרָי. דִּשַּׁנְתָּ בַשֶּׁמֶן רֹאשִׁי, כּוֹסִי רְוָיָה. אַךְ טוֹב
וָחֶסֶד יִרְדְּפוּנִי כָּל־יְמֵי חַיָּי, וְשַׁבְתִּי בְּבֵית־יְיָ לְאֹרֶךְ יָמִים.

The Lord is my shepherd, I shall not want. He makes me lie down in green pastures, He leads me beside still waters. He restores my soul. He leads me in right paths for the sake of His name. Even when I walk in the valley of the shadow of death, I shall fear no evil, for You are with me; with rod and staff You comfort me. You have set a table before me in the presence of my enemies; You have anointed my head with oil, my cup overflows. Surely goodness and mercy shall follow me all the days of my life, and I shall dwell in the house of the Lord for ever.

◆ ◆

Aleinu, page 615, 617, 618, or 620, may be said here or following the Kaddish below

MOURNER'S KADDISH — קדיש יתום

יִתְגַּדַּל וְיִתְקַדַּשׁ שְׁמֵהּ רַבָּא בְּעָלְמָא דִּי־בְרָא כִרְעוּתֵהּ,

Yit·ga·dal ve·yit·ka·dash she·mei ra·ba be·al·ma di·ve·ra chi·re·u·tei,

וְיַמְלִיךְ מַלְכוּתֵהּ בְּחַיֵּיכוֹן וּבְיוֹמֵיכוֹן וּבְחַיֵּי דְכָל־בֵּית

ve·yam·lich mal·chu·tei be·cha·yei·chon u·ve·yo·mei·chon u·ve·cha·yei de·chol beit

יִשְׂרָאֵל, בַּעֲגָלָא וּבִזְמַן קָרִיב, וְאִמְרוּ: אָמֵן.

Yis·ra·eil, ba·a·ga·la u·vi·ze·man ka·riv, ve·i·me·ru: a·mein.

יְהֵא שְׁמֵהּ רַבָּא מְבָרַךְ לְעָלַם וּלְעָלְמֵי עָלְמַיָּא.

Ye·hei she·mei ra·ba me·va·rach le·a·lam u·le·al·mei al·ma·ya.

יִתְבָּרַךְ וְיִשְׁתַּבַּח, וְיִתְפָּאַר וְיִתְרוֹמַם וְיִתְנַשֵּׂא, וְיִתְהַדַּר

Yit·ba·rach ve·yish·ta·bach, ve·yit·pa·ar ve·yit·ro·mam ve·yit·na·sei, ve·yit·ha·dar

וְיִתְעַלֶּה וְיִתְהַלַּל שְׁמֵהּ דְּקוּדְשָׁא, בְּרִיךְ הוּא, לְעֵלָּא מִן־כָּל־

ve·yit·a·leh ve·yit·ha·lal she·mei de·ku·de·sha, be·rich hu, le·ei·la min kol

בִּרְכָתָא וְשִׁירָתָא, תֻּשְׁבְּחָתָא וְנֶחֱמָתָא דַּאֲמִירָן בְּעָלְמָא,

bi·re·cha·ta ve·shi·ra·ta, tush·be·cha·ta ve·ne·che·ma·ta, da·a·mi·ran be·al·ma,

וְאִמְרוּ: אָמֵן.

ve·i·me·ru: a·mein.

יְהֵא שְׁלָמָא רַבָּא מִן־שְׁמַיָּא וְחַיִּים עָלֵינוּ וְעַל־כָּל־יִשְׂרָאֵל,

Ye·hei she·la·ma ra·ba min she·ma·ya ve·cha·yim a·lei·nu ve·al kol Yis·ra·eil,

וְאִמְרוּ: אָמֵן.

ve·i·me·ru: a·mein.

עֹשֶׂה שָׁלוֹם בִּמְרוֹמָיו, הוּא יַעֲשֶׂה שָׁלוֹם עָלֵינוּ וְעַל־כָּל־

O·seh sha·lom bi·me·ro·mav, hu ya·a·seh sha·lom a·lei·nu ve·al kol

יִשְׂרָאֵל וְאִמְרוּ: אָמֵן.

Yis·ra·eil, ve·i·me·ru: a·mein.

Special Themes

Nature

1

How wonderful, O Lord, are the works of Your hands! The heavens declare Your glory, the arch of sky displays Your handiwork.

The heavens declare the glory of God.

In Your love You have given us the power to behold the beauty of Your world, robed in all its splendor. The sun and the stars, the valleys and hills, the rivers and lakes — all disclose Your presence.

The earth reveals God's eternal presence.

The roaring breakers of the sea tell of Your awesome might; the beasts of the field and the birds of the air bespeak Your wondrous will.

Life comes forth by God's creative will.

In Your goodness You have made us able to hear the music of the world. The raging of the winds, the whisperings of trees in the wood, and the precious voices of loved ones reveal to us that You are in our midst.

A divine voice sings through all creation.

◆ ◆

2

Why should I wish to see God better than this day?
I see something of God each hour of the twenty-four, and each
moment then;
In the faces of men and women I see God, and in my own
face in the glass,

I find letters from God dropt in the street, and every one is sign'd by God's name,
And I leave them where they are, for I know that whereso'er I go,
Others will punctually come forever and ever.

◆ ◆

3

From Psalm 104

בָּרְכִי, נַפְשִׁי, אֶת־יְיָ! יְיָ אֱלֹהַי, גָּדַלְתָּ מְּאֹד! הוֹד וְהָדָר לָבָשְׁתָּ.

Praise the Lord, O my soul! O Lord my God, You are very great!

You are arrayed in glory and majesty.

עֹטֶה אוֹר כַּשַּׂלְמָה, נוֹטֶה שָׁמַיִם כַּיְרִיעָה.

You wrap Yourself in light as with a garment.

You stretch out the heavens like a curtain.

עֹשֶׂה מַלְאָכָיו רוּחוֹת, מְשָׁרְתָיו אֵשׁ לֹהֵט.

The winds are Your messengers,

Flames of fire are Your ministers.

הַמְשַׁלֵּחַ מַעְיָנִים בַּנְּחָלִים, בֵּין הָרִים יְהַלֵּכוּן, יַשְׁקוּ כָּל־חַיְתוֹ שָׂדָי.

You cause streams to spring forth in the valleys;

They run between the mountains, giving drink to all the beasts of the field.

עֲלֵיהֶם עוֹף־הַשָּׁמַיִם יִשְׁכּוֹן, מִבֵּין עֳפָאיִם יִתְּנוּ־קוֹל. מַצְמִיחַ חָצִיר לַבְּהֵמָה.

The birds of the air nest on their banks, and sing among the leaves.

You make grass grow for the cattle.

וְעֵשֶׂב לַעֲבֹדַת הָאָדָם, לְהוֹצִיא לֶחֶם מִן־הָאָרֶץ, וְיַיִן יְשַׂמַּח לְבַב־אֱנוֹשׁ.

And plants for us to cultivate, that bread may come forth from the earth,

And wine to cheer our hearts.

עָשָׂה יָרֵחַ לְמוֹעֲדִים; שֶׁמֶשׁ יָדַע מְבוֹאוֹ. תָּשֶׁת־חֹשֶׁךְ וִיהִי לָיְלָה, בּוֹ־תִרְמֹשׂ כָּל־חַיְתוֹ־יָעַר.

You made the moon to mark the seasons; the sun knows its time of setting.

You make darkness, and it is night, when all the beasts go prowling.

הַכְּפִירִים שֹׁאֲגִים לַטָּרֶף, וּלְבַקֵּשׁ מֵאֵל אָכְלָם. תִּזְרַח הַשֶּׁמֶשׁ, יֵאָסֵפוּן, וְאֶל־מְעוֹנֹתָם יִרְבָּצוּן.

Young lions roar for prey, demanding their food from God.

When the sun rises, they slink away and go to their lairs to rest.

מָה־רַבּוּ מַעֲשֶׂיךָ, יְיָ! כֻּלָּם בְּחָכְמָה עָשִׂיתָ; מָלְאָה הָאָרֶץ קִנְיָנֶךָ.

How manifold are Your works, O Lord!

In wisdom You have made them all; the earth is full of Your creations.

אָשִׁירָה לַיְיָ בְּחַיָּי; אֲזַמְּרָה לֵאלֹהַי בְּעוֹדִי.

I will sing to the Lord all my days;

I will sing praises to my God as long as I live.

◆ ◆

4

כָּל כּוֹכְבֵי בֹקֶר לְךָ יְשִׁירוּ,
כִּי זָהֳרֵיהֶם מִמְּךָ יַזְהִירוּ.
וּבְנֵי אֱלֹהִים עֹמְדִים עַל מִשְׁמְרוֹת
לֵיל וְיוֹם, שֵׁם נֶאְדָּר יַאְדִּירוּ,
וּקְהַל קְדוֹשִׁים קִבְּלוּ מֵהֶם
וְכָל־שַׁחַר לְשַׁחֵר בֵּיתְךָ יָעִירוּ.

To You the stars of morning sing,
From You their bright radiance must spring.
And steadfast in their vigils, day and night,
The sons of God, flooded with fervor, ring
Your praise; they teach the holy ones to bring
Into Your house the breath of early light.

◆ ◆

5

אֵל אָדוֹן עַל כָּל־הַמַּעֲשִׂים, בָּרוּךְ וּמְבֹרָךְ בְּפִי כָּל־נְשָׁמָה.

God is Lord of all creation: every living being sings His praises.

גָּדְלוֹ וְטוּבוֹ מָלֵא עוֹלָם, דַּעַת וּתְבוּנָה סוֹבְבִים אוֹתוֹ.

His greatness and goodness fill the world; knowledge and insight are round about Him.

זְכוּת וּמִישׁוֹר לִפְנֵי כִסְאוֹ! חֶסֶד וְרַחֲמִים לִפְנֵי כְבוֹדוֹ!

Purity and justice before His throne! Love and mercy His foremost glory!

טוֹבִים מְאוֹרוֹת שֶׁבָּרָא אֱלֹהֵינוּ: יְצָרָם בְּדַעַת, בְּרָאָם בְּהַשְׂכֵּל. כֹּחַ וּגְבוּרָה נָתַן בָּהֶם, לִהְיוֹת מוֹשְׁלִים בְּקֶרֶב תֵּבֵל.

Splendid the stars our God has made: He formed them with knowledge, He made them with wisdom, endowed them with power, imbued them with might. He called them to rule in the midst of His world.

מְלֵאִים זִיו וּמְפִיקִים נֹגַהּ, נָאֶה זִיוָם בְּכָל־הָעוֹלָם.

He filled them with splendor: radiant with brightness, their brillance is lovely in all the world.

שְׂמֵחִים בְּצֵאתָם וְשָׂשִׂים בְּבוֹאָם, עוֹשִׂים בְּאֵימָה רְצוֹן קוֹנָם.

They rejoice in their rising, and delight in their setting, obeying in awe the will of their Maker.

פְּאֵר וְכָבוֹד נוֹתְנִים לִשְׁמוֹ, צָהֳלָה וְרִנָּה לְזֵכֶר מַלְכוּתוֹ.

Glory and honor they give to His name, joyfully singing acclaim to their King.

קָרָא לַשֶּׁמֶשׁ וַיִּזְרַח־אוֹר, רָאָה וְהִתְקִין צוּרַת הַלְּבָנָה. שֶׁבַח נוֹתְנִים־לוֹ כָּל־צְבָא מָרוֹם!

He called to the sun, it blazed forth light; He looked to the moon, it circled the earth. All the hosts of heaven proclaim His praise!

◆ ◆

6

"And God saw everything that He had made, and found it very good."

And He said: This is a beautiful world that I have given you. Take good care of it; do not ruin it.

It is said: Before the world was created, the Holy One kept creating worlds and destroying them. Finally He created this one, and was satisfied. He said to Adam: This is the last world I shall make. I place it in your hands: hold it in trust.

◆ ◆

7

Light and splendor
in the sleeping orchards
entering the trees
like a silent movie wedding procession

entering the arches of branches
for the sake of love only
From a hill I watched
the apple blossoms breathe
the silver out of the night
like fish eating the spheres
of air out of the river
So the illuminated night fed
the sleeping orchards
entering the vault of branches
like a holy procession
Long live the Power of Eyes
Long live the invisible steps
men can read on a mountain
Long live the unknown machine
or heart
which by will or accident
pours out with victor's grace
endlessly perfect weather
on the perfect creatures
the world grows

◆ ◆

8

Of all created things the source is one,
Simple, single as love; remember
The cell and seed of life, the sphere
That is, of child, white bird, and small blue dragon-fly,
Green fern, and the gold four-petalled tormentilla
The ultimate memory.
Each latent cell puts out a future,
Unfolds its differing complexity
As a tree puts forth leaves, and spins a fate
Fern-traced, bird-feathered, or fish-scaled.
Moss spreads its green film on the moist peat,
The germ of dragon-fly pulses into animation and takes wing
As the water-lily from the mud ascends on its ropy stem
To open a sweet white calyx to the sky.

Man, with farther to travel from his simplicity,
From the archaic moss, fish, and lily parts,
And into exile travels his long way.

◆

As you leave Eden behind you, remember your home,
For as you remember back into your own being
You will not be alone; the first to greet you
Will be those children playing by the burn,
The otters will swim up to you in the bay,
The wild deer on the moor will run beside you.
Recollect more deeply, and the birds will come,
Fish rise to meet you in their silver shoals,
And darker, stranger, more mysterious lives
Will throng about you at the source
Where the tree's deepest roots drink from the abyss.

◆

Nothing in that abyss is alien to you.
Sleep at the tree's root, where the night is spun
Into the stuff of worlds, listen to the winds,
The tides, and the night's harmonies, and know
All that you knew before you began to forget,
Before you became estranged from your own being,
Before you had too long parted from those other
More simple children, who have stayed at home
In meadow and island and forest, in sea and river.
Earth sends a mother's love after her exiled son,
Entrusting her message to the light and the air,
The wind and waves that carry your ship, the rain that falls,
The birds that call to you, and all the shoals
That swim in the natal waters of her ocean.

Omnipresence

מָה רָאָה הַקָּדוֹשׁ בָּרוּךְ הוּא לְדַבֵּר עִם מֹשֶׁה מִתּוֹךְ הַסְּנֶה?
לְלַמֶּדְךָ שֶׁאֵין מָקוֹם פָּנוּי בְּלֹא שְׁכִינָה, אֲפִילוּ סְנֶה.

Why did the Holy One, blessed be He, choose to speak to Moses out of a thornbush? To teach us that there is no place, not even a thornbush, devoid of the divine Presence.

◆

Earth's crammed with heaven,
And every common bush afire with God!
But only he who sees, takes off his shoes.

◆ ◆

From Psalm 139

יְיָ, חֲקַרְתַּנִי, וַתֵּדָע.
אַתָּה יָדַעְתָּ שִׁבְתִּי וְקוּמִי; בַּנְתָּה לְרֵעִי מֵרָחוֹק.

Lord, You see through me, and You know me.

You know my coming and my going; You understand my every thought.

אָרְחִי וְרִבְעִי זֵרִיתָ, וְכָל־דְּרָכַי הִסְכַּנְתָּה.
כִּי אֵין מִלָּה בִּלְשׁוֹנִי הֵן יְיָ יָדַעְתָּ כֻלָּהּ.

You observe my walking and my lying down, and are acquainted with all my ways.

Lord, there is nothing I can say that You do not know completely.

אָנָה אֵלֵךְ מֵרוּחֶךָ? וְאָנָה מִפָּנֶיךָ אֶבְרָח?
אִם־אֶסַּק שָׁמַיִם, שָׁם אָתָּה! וְאַצִּיעָה שְּׁאוֹל, הִנֶּךָּ!

Whither can I go from Your spirit? Whither can I flee from Your presence?

If I ascend to the heavens, You are there! If I make my home in the lowest depths, behold, You are there!

אֶשָּׂא כַנְפֵי־שָׁחַר, אֶשְׁכְּנָה בְּאַחֲרִית יָם,
גַּם־שָׁם יָדְךָ תַנְחֵנִי, וְתֹאחֲזֵנִי יְמִינֶךָ.

If I take up the wings of the morning and dwell on the ocean's farthest shore,

Even there Your hand will lead me, Your right hand will hold me.

וָאֹמַר: 'אַךְ־חֹשֶׁךְ יְשׁוּפֵנִי, וְלַיְלָה אוֹר בַּעֲדֵנִי,'
גַּם־חֹשֶׁךְ לֹא־יַחְשִׁיךְ מִמֶּךָ, וְלַיְלָה כַּיּוֹם יָאִיר, כַּחֲשֵׁיכָה כָּאוֹרָה!

And if I say: 'Let only the darkness cover me, and the light about me be night.'

Even the darkness is not too dark for You, for whom the night is bright as day!

◆ ◆

Lord, where can I find You?
Your glory fills the world.

Behold, I find You
Where the ploughman breaks the hard soil,
Where the quarrier explodes stone out of the hillside,
Where the miner digs metals out of the reluctant earth,
Where men and women earn their bread by the sweat of their brow,
Among the lonely and poor, the lowly and lost.
In blazing heat and shattering storm, You are with them.

Behold, I find You
In the mind free to sail by its own star,
In words that spring from the depth of truth,
Where endeavor reaches undespairing for perfection,
Where the scientist toils to unravel the secrets of Your world,
Where the poet makes beauty out of words,
Wherever people struggle for freedom,
Wherever noble deeds are done.

Behold, I find You
In the shouts of children merry at their play,
In the mother's lullaby, as she rocks her baby in the cradle,
In the sleep falling on his infant eyelids,
    And in the smile that dances on his sleeping lips.

Behold, I find You
When dawn comes up bearing golden gifts,
And in the fall of evening peace and rest from the Western sea.
In the current of life flowing day and night through all things,
Throbbing in my sinews and in the dust of the earth,
    In every leaf and flower.

Behold, I find You
In the wealth of joys that quickly fade,
In the life that from eternity dances in my blood,
In birth, which renews the generations continually,
    And in death knocking on the doors of life.

O my God,
Give me strength never to disown the poor,
Never before insolent might to bow the head.
Give me strength to raise my spirit high above daily trifles,
Lightly to bear my joys and sorrows,
    And in love to surrender all my strength to Your will.

For great are Your gifts to me:
The sky and the light. This my flesh.
Life and the soul —
Treasures beyond price, treasures of life and of love.

◆ ◆

יָהּ, אָנָה אֶמְצָאֲךָ? מְקוֹמְךָ נַעֲלֶה וְנֶעְלָם.
וְאָנָה לֹא אֶמְצָאֲךָ? כְּבוֹדְךָ מָלֵא עוֹלָם.

Lord, where shall I find You? Your place is hidden and high.
Yet where shall I not find You, Whose glory fills all space?

הַנִּמְצָא בִּקְרָבִים, אַפְסֵי־אֶרֶץ הֵקִים.
הַמִּשְׂגָּב לַקְּרֹבִים, הַמִּבְטָח לָרְחֹקִים.
אַתָּה יֹשֵׁב כְּרוּבִים, אַתָּה שֹׁכֵן שְׁחָקִים.

תִּתְהַלֵּל בִּצְבָאֶךָ, וְאַתְּ עַל־רֹאשׁ מַהֲלָלָם.
גַּלְגַּל לֹא־יִשָּׂאֶךָ, אַף כִּי־חַדְרֵי אוּלָם!

וּבְהִנָּשַׂאֲךָ עֲלֵיהֶם עַל־כֵּס נִשָּׂא וָרָם,
אַתָּה קָרוֹב אֲלֵיהֶם מֵרוּחָם וּמִבְּשָׂרָם.

Far space is Your dominion, yet You dwell in the human heart;

You are the refuge of those close by, the haven of those far off.

You are enthroned in Your house, though unconfined by the heights;

Your hosts adore You, but You transcend their praise.

All space cannot contain You, still less an earthly house!
Yet though exalted above us in high and lonely majesty,

You are closer to us than our own spirit and flesh.

דָּרַשְׁתִּי קִרְבָתְךָ, בְּכָל־לִבִּי קְרָאתִיךָ,
וּבְצֵאתִי לִקְרָאתְךָ לִקְרָאתִי מְצָאתִיךָ!
וּבְפִלְאֵי גְבוּרָתְךָ בַּקֹּדֶשׁ חֲזִיתִיךָ.

I have tried to reach You, I have called with all my heart;

And on my way toward You, You come forth to meet me!

In the wonders of Your creative power, I perceive You.

In the holiness of Your sanctuary, I find You.

מִי יֹאמַר לֹא־רָאָךְ? הֵן שָׁמַיִם וְחֵילָם
יַגִּידוּ מוֹרָאֲךָ בְּלִי נִשְׁמַע קוֹלָם.

Who say they have not seen You?

The heavens and all their host, voiceless declare Your glory.

הַאֻמְנָם כִּי־יֵשֵׁב אֱלֹהִים אֶת־הָאָדָם?
וּמַה־יַּחְשֹׁב כָּל־חשֵׁב אֲשֶׁר בֶּעָפָר יְסוֹדָם?
וְאַתָּה, קָדוֹשׁ, יוֹשֵׁב תְּהִלּוֹתָם וּכְבוֹדָם.

Does God truly dwell in us? Our origin is dust, how can we presume?

O Holy God, we can, for You dwell wherever we sing of Your glory.

◆ ◆

MEDITATION

Here in my curving arms I cup
This quiet dust; I lift it up.
Here is the mother of all thought;
Of this the shining heavens are wrought,
The laughing lips, the feet that rove,
The face, the body, that you love;
Mere dust, no more, yet nothing less.
And this has suffered consciousness,
Passion, and terror, this again
Shall suffer passion, death and pain.

For, as all flesh must die, so all,
Now dust, shall live. 'Tis natural;
Yet hardly do I understand —
Here in the hollow of my hand
A bit of God Himself I keep,
Between two vigils fallen asleep.

◆ ◆

קָדוֹשׁ, קָדוֹשׁ, קָדוֹשׁ יְיָ צְבָאוֹת,	Holy, Holy, Holy is the Lord of Hosts,
מְלֹא כָל־הָאָרֶץ כְּבוֹדוֹ!	the fullness of the whole earth is His glory!

Quest

O incognito god, anonymous lord,
with what name shall I call you? Where shall I
discover the syllable, the mystic word
that shall invoke you from eternity?
is that sweet sound the heart makes, clocking life,
Your appellation? is the noise of thunder, it?
Is it the hush of peace, the sound of strife?

I have no title for your glorious throne,
and for your presence not a golden word, —
only that wanting you, by that alone
I do invoke you, knowing I am heard.

◆ ◆

From Psalms 42 and 43

כְּאַיָּל תַּעֲרֹג עַל־אֲפִיקֵי־מָיִם, כֵּן נַפְשִׁי תַעֲרֹג אֵלֶיךָ, אֱלֹהִים.
צָמְאָה נַפְשִׁי לֵאלֹהִים, לְאֵל חָי; מָתַי אָבוֹא וְאֵרָאֶה פְּנֵי
אֱלֹהִים?

As a deer pants for flowing streams, O God, so does my soul long for You.

My soul thirsts for God, for the living God; when shall I come to see Him?

שְׁלַח־אוֹרְךָ וַאֲמִתְּךָ; הֵמָּה יַנְחוּנִי, יְבִיאוּנִי אֶל־הַר־קָדְשְׁךָ,
וְאֶל־מִשְׁכְּנוֹתֶיךָ.
וְאָבוֹאָה אֶל־מִזְבַּח אֱלֹהִים, אֶל־אֵל שִׂמְחַת גִּילִי, וְאוֹדְךָ
בְכִנּוֹר, אֱלֹהִים אֱלֹהָי!

O send out Your light and Your truth; let them lead me, let them bring me to Your holy mountain, and to Your dwelling.

That I may come to the altar of God, to God my highest joy, and praise You with the harp, O God my God!

◆ ◆

מֵעִמְקֵי כָל־תְּהוֹמוֹת כָּל־מַעְיְנוֹת נִשְׁמָתִי,
לְךָ, אֵל מִסְתַּתֵּר, אֶקְרָא – שְׁמַע תְּפִלָּתִי!
דְּרשׁ, אֵל, מַה־תִּדְרשׁ מֵאִתִּי – הִנֵּנִי!
רַק הַרְאֵנִי פָּנֶיךָ, פָּנֶיךָ הַרְאֵנִי!
מָה עֲתַר הַחַיִּים, אֲצַלְתָּ סָבִיב לִי?

Out of the deep springs of my soul,
To You, O hidden God, I cry — hear my prayer!
Demand of me what You will, O God: here I am!
Only show me Your face, let me see Your face!
You surround me with life's plenty —
what good is it to me?

מַה־כָּל־פְּאֵר עוֹלָמוֹת, בִּלְבָבִי נָתַתָּ?
רַק צְלָלִים הֵם חִוְרִים מֵאוֹרְךָ הַגָּנוּז,
קַוִּים מְטֻשְׁטָשִׁים מִצַּלְמְךָ־אַתָּה,
וַאֲנִי שְׁתוֹת צָמֵאתִי מִמְּקוֹר הַמְּקוֹרוֹת,
וַאֲנִי רְחֹץ אִוֵּיתִי בְּאוֹר הָאוֹרוֹת –
אֶת־פָּנֶיךָ, פָּנֶיךָ שָׁאַפְתִּי לִרְאוֹת!

What use the splendor of the worlds
You have put into my heart?
Pale shadows, these, of Your hidden light,
Blurred outlines of Your true image.
Not for me, these; for I yearn
to drink of the Source of all sources,
to bathe in the Light of all lights,
to see Your face, *Your* face.

◆ ◆

From Psalm 63

אֱלֹהִים, אֵלִי אַתָּה;
אֲשַׁחֲרֶךָּ.

O God, You are my God;
at first light I seek You.

צָמְאָה לְךָ נַפְשִׁי,
כָּמַהּ לְךָ בְשָׂרִי,

My soul thirsts for You,
my flesh longs for You,

as in a dry and weary land,	בְּאֶרֶץ־צִיָּה וְעָיֵף,
where there is no water.	בְּלִי־מָיִם.
So do I look for You in the sanctuary,	כֵּן בַּקֹּדֶשׁ חֲזִיתִיךָ,
to behold Your power and Your glory.	לִרְאוֹת עֻזְּךָ וּכְבוֹדֶךָ.
Your love is better than life;	כִּי־טוֹב חַסְדְּךָ מֵחַיִּים,
my lips will extol You.	שְׂפָתַי יְשַׁבְּחוּנְךָ.
And I will praise You with my life:	כֵּן אֲבָרֶכְךָ בְחַיָּי:
for You have been my help,	כִּי־הָיִיתָ עֶזְרָתָה לִּי,
and in the shadow of Your wings	וּבְצֵל כְּנָפֶיךָ
I sing for joy.	אֲרַנֵּן.

◆ ◆

O God, You are near as the very air we breathe and the light around us, yet our thought's farthest reach falls short of You.

We yearn to reach You. We seek the light and warmth of Your presence, for we are lost without You. Though we say You are near, we are lonely and alone.

O let our desire be so strong that it will tear the veil that keeps You from our sight! Let Your light penetrate our darkness, to reveal to us the glory and joy of Your eternal presence.

As the fish gives himself to the sea, as the bird gives herself to the air, as all life gives itself to life, so may we give ourselves to You, O God.

◆ ◆

From Psalm 84

מַה־יְּדִידוֹת מִשְׁכְּנוֹתֶיךָ, יְיָ צְבָאוֹת!
נִכְסְפָה וְגַם־כָּלְתָה נַפְשִׁי לְחַצְרוֹת יְיָ,
לִבִּי וּבְשָׂרִי יְרַנְּנוּ אֶל אֵל־חָי.

How lovely are Your dwelling places, O Lord of Hosts!

My soul longs and yearns for the courts of the Lord;
my heart and my flesh sing for joy to the living God.

גַּם־צִפּוֹר מָצְאָה בַיִת, וּדְרוֹר קֵן לָהּ אֲשֶׁר־שָׁתָה אֶפְרֹחֶיהָ,
אֶת־מִזְבְּחוֹתֶיךָ, יְיָ צְבָאוֹת, מַלְכִּי וֵאלֹהָי.

As the sparrow finds a home, and the swallow has a nest where she rears her young,

So do I seek out Your altars, O Lord of Hosts, my Sovereign God.

אַשְׁרֵי יוֹשְׁבֵי בֵיתֶךָ, עוֹד יְהַלְלוּךָ. סֶּלָה.
אַשְׁרֵי אָדָם עוֹז־לוֹ בָךְ, מְסִלּוֹת בִּלְבָבָם.

Happy are those who dwell in Your house: they will sing Your praise for ever.

Happy are those who find strength in You: their hearts are highways leading to Your presence.

עֹבְרֵי בְּעֵמֶק הַבָּכָא מַעְיָן יְשִׁיתוּהוּ, גַּם־בְּרָכוֹת יַעְטֶה מוֹרֶה.
יֵלְכוּ מֵחַיִל אֶל־חָיִל, יֵרָאֶה אֶל־אֱלֹהִים בְּצִיּוֹן.

When they pass through the driest of valleys, they find it a place of springs; the rain blesses it with pools.

They go from strength to strength; they behold God in Zion.

כִּי טוֹב־יוֹם בַּחֲצֵרֶיךָ מֵאָלֶף,
בָּחַרְתִּי הִסְתּוֹפֵף בְּבֵית אֱלֹהַי, מִדּוּר בְּאָהֳלֵי־רֶשַׁע.

One day in Your courts is better than a thousand elsewhere.

And better it is to wait at the doorstep of Your house than to be an honored guest among the wicked.

כִּי שֶׁמֶשׁ וּמָגֵן יְיָ אֱלֹהִים, חֵן וְכָבוֹד יִתֵּן יְיָ.

For the Lord God is a sun and a shield;

the Lord gives grace and glory.

לֹא יִמְנַע טוֹב לַהֹלְכִים בְּתָמִים.
יְיָ צְבָאוֹת, אַשְׁרֵי אָדָם בֹּטֵחַ בָּךְ!

No good is withheld from those who walk uprightly.

O Lord of Hosts, happy is the one who trusts in You!

Humanity

וַיִּבְרָא אֱלֹהִים אֶת־הָאָדָם בְּצַלְמוֹ, בְּצֶלֶם אֱלֹהִים בָּרָא
אֹתוֹ: זָכָר וּנְקֵבָה בָּרָא אֹתָם. וַיְבָרֶךְ אֹתָם אֱלֹהִים. וַיִּיצֶר יְיָ
אֱלֹהִים אֶת־הָאָדָם, וַיְהִי הָאָדָם לְנֶפֶשׁ חַיָּה.

When God created us, He made us in His own image, in the likeness of the divine. Both male and female He created; He blessed them, and at the time of their creation He called them Human.

◆ ◆

לְפִיכָךְ נִבְרָא אָדָם יְחִידִי: לְלַמֶּדְךָ שֶׁכָּל הַמְאַבֵּד נֶפֶשׁ אַחַת
מִבְּנֵי אָדָם, מַעֲלֶה עָלָיו הַכָּתוּב כְּאִילוּ אִבֵּד עוֹלָם מָלֵא;
וְכָל־הַמְקַיֵּם נֶפֶשׁ אַחַת מִבְּנֵי אָדָם, מַעֲלֶה עָלָיו הַכָּתוּב
כְּאִילוּ קִיֵּם עוֹלָם מָלֵא.

Therefore was a single human being created: to teach you that to destroy a single human soul is equivalent to destroying an entire world; and to sustain a single human soul is equivalent to sustaining an entire world.

וּמִפְּנֵי שְׁלוֹם הַבְּרִיּוֹת, שֶׁלֹּא יֹאמַר אָדָם לַחֲבֵרוֹ: אַבָּא גָּדוֹל
מֵאָבִיךָ!

And a single human being was created for the sake of peace, that none might say: My lineage is greater than yours!

◆ ◆

Then Isaac asked the Eternal: King of the world, when You made the light, You said in Your Torah that it was good; when You made the expanse of heaven and earth, You said in Your Torah that they were good; and of every herb You made, and every beast, You said that they were good; but when You made us in Your image, You did not say of us in Your Torah that humanity was good. Why, Lord? And God answered him: Because you I have not yet perfected, because through the Torah you are to perfect yourselves, and to perfect the world. All other things are completed; they cannot grow. But humankind is not complete; you have yet to grow. Then I will call you good.

◆ ◆

'וְאַתֶּם עֵדַי', נְאֻם יְיָ, 'וַאֲנִי אֵל.' כְּשֶׁאַתֶּם עֵדַי, אֲנִי אֵל;
וּכְשֶׁאֵין אַתֶּם עֵדַי, אֵין אֲנִי אֵל.

'You are My witnesses,' says the Lord, 'and I am God.' That is: when you are My witnesses, I am God; and when you are not My witnesses, I am, one might almost say, not God.

◆ ◆

The astonishing thing about the human being is not so much his intellect and bodily structure, profoundly mysterious as they are. The astonishing and least comprehensible thing about him is his range of vision; his gaze into the infinite distance; his lonely passion for ideas and ideals . . . for which . . . he will stand till he dies, the profound conviction he entertains that if nothing is worth dying for nothing is worth living for.

◆ ◆

From Psalm 8

Sovereign Lord, how majestic	יְיָ, אֲדֹנֵינוּ,
is Your presence in all the earth!	מָה־אַדִּיר שִׁמְךָ בְּכָל־הָאָרֶץ!
You have stamped Your glory	אֲשֶׁר תְּנָה הוֹדְךָ עַל־הַשָּׁמָיִם.
upon the heavens!	
When I consider Your heavens,	כִּי־אֶרְאֶה שָׁמֶיךָ,
the work of Your fingers;	מַעֲשֵׂה אֶצְבְּעֹתֶיךָ,
the moon and the stars	יָרֵחַ וְכוֹכָבִים אֲשֶׁר כּוֹנָנְתָּה,
that You have established:	

what are we,
  that You are mindful of us?
What are we mortals,
  that You care for us?
Yet You have made us
little less than divine,
and crowned us
  with glory and honor!
You have given us dominion
among the works of Your hands,
setting all things under our feet:
sheep and oxen alike,
and the beasts of the field;
the birds of the air
  and the fish of the sea,
all that traverses
  the paths of the deep.
O Sovereign Lord, how majestic
  is Your presence in all the earth!

מָה־אֱנוֹשׁ כִּי־תִזְכְּרֶנּוּ,
וּבֶן־אָדָם כִּי תִפְקְדֶנּוּ?
וַתְּחַסְּרֵהוּ מְּעַט מֵאֱלֹהִים,
וְכָבוֹד וְהָדָר תְּעַטְּרֵהוּ!
תַּמְשִׁילֵהוּ בְּמַעֲשֵׂי יָדֶיךָ,
כֹּל שַׁתָּה תַחַת־רַגְלָיו:
צֹנֶה וַאֲלָפִים כֻּלָּם,
וְגַם בַּהֲמוֹת שָׂדָי,
צִפּוֹר שָׁמַיִם וּדְגֵי הַיָּם,
עֹבֵר אָרְחוֹת יַמִּים.
יְיָ, אֲדֹנֵינוּ,
מָה־אַדִּיר שִׁמְךָ בְּכָל־הָאָרֶץ!

Loneliness

I have been one acquainted with the night.
I have walked out in rain — and back in rain.
I have outwalked the furthest city light.

I have looked down the saddest city lane.
I have passed by the watchman on his beat
And dropped my eyes, unwilling to explain.

I have stood still and stopped the sound of feet
When far away an interrupted cry
Came over houses from another street,

But not to call me back or say goodbye;
And further still at an unearthly height,
One luminary clock against the sky

Proclaimed the time was neither wrong nor right.
I have been one acquainted with the night.

◆ ◆

Lord, many are tired and lonely;

Teach us to be their friends.

Many are anxious and afraid;

Help us to calm their fears.

Some are tortured in body and mind;

Imbue them with courage and strength.

Others in their emptiness seek only wealth, fame, or power;

Teach them to value other gifts than these.

Some are drained of faith: they are cynical, bored, or despairing;

Let our faith shine forth for them to see, that through us they may come to know Your love.

And some live with death in their souls: they are stunned, violent, and filled with hate.

Give us wisdom to save them from the wastelands of the spirit.

And teach us to show our love; let compassion and knowledge combine for the welfare of all Your children —

That all may know they are not alone.

◆ ◆

There are times when each of us feels lost or alone, adrift and forsaken, unable to reach those next to us, or to be reached by them. And there are days and nights when existence seems to lack all purpose, and our lives seem brief sparks in an indifferent cosmos.

Fear and loneliness enter into the soul. None of us is immune from doubt and fear; none escapes times when all seems dark and senseless. Then, at the ebb-tide of the spirit, the soul cries out and reaches for companionship.

◆ ◆

. . . how strange we grow when we're alone,
And how unlike the selves that meet and talk,
And blow the candles out, and say good night,
Alone. . . . the word is life endured and known.
It is the stillness where our spirits walk
And all but inmost faith is overthrown.

◆ ◆

Could I meet one who understood all . . .
Without word, without search,
Confession or lie,
Without asking why.

I would spread before him, like a white cloth,
The heart and the soul . . .
The filth and the gold.
Perceptive, he would understand.

And after I had plundered the heart,
When all had been emptied and given away,
I would feel neither anguish nor pain,
But would know how rich I had become.

◆ ◆

As the moon sinks on the mountain-edge
The fisherman's lights flicker
Far out on the dark wide sea.

When we think that we alone
Are steering our ships at midnight,
We hear the splash of oars
Far beyond us.

Trust

O God, You have called us into life, and set us in the midst of purposes we cannot measure or understand. Yet we thank You for the good we know, for the life we have, and for the gifts that are our daily portion:

For health and healing, for labor and repose, for the ever-renewed beauty of earth and sky, for thoughts of truth and justice which stir us from our ease and move us to acts of goodness, and for the contemplation of Your eternal presence, which fills us with hope that what is good and lovely cannot perish.

◆ ◆

From Psalm 91

יֹשֵׁב בְּסֵתֶר עֶלְיוֹן, בְּצֵל שַׁדַּי יִתְלוֹנָן.
אֹמַר לַייָ: מַחְסִי וּמְצוּדָתִי, אֱלֹהַי אֶבְטַח־בּוֹ.

The Most High dwells far off, the Mighty One abides in darkness.

Yet I can say: The Eternal is my safe retreat, my God in whom I trust.

בְּאֶבְרָתוֹ יָסֶךְ לָךְ, וְתַחַת־כְּנָפָיו תֶּחְסֶה; צִנָּה וְסֹחֵרָה אֲמִתּוֹ.
לֹא־תִירָא מִפַּחַד־לָיְלָה, מֵחֵץ יָעוּף יוֹמָם.

He will cover you with His pinions; under His wings shall you find refuge; His faithfulness is a shield and buckler.

You need not fear the terror of the night, nor the arrow that flies by day.

כִּי־אַתָּה יְיָ מַחְסִי, עֶלְיוֹן שַׂמְתָּ מְעוֹנֶךָ.
לֹא־תְאֻנֶּה אֵלֶיךָ רָעָה, וְנֶגַע לֹא־יִקְרַב בְּאָהֳלֶךָ.

Because you have made the Lord your refuge, the Most High your dwelling-place,

No evil shall befall you, no plague shall come near your tent.

כִּי בִי חָשַׁק וַאֲפַלְּטֵהוּ. אֲשַׂגְּבֵהוּ, כִּי יָדַע שְׁמִי.
יִקְרָאֵנִי, וְאֶעֱנֵהוּ; עִמּוֹ אָנֹכִי בְצָרָה.

Because they have set their heart on Me, I will rescue them.
I will protect them, because they know My name.

When they call on Me, I will answer; I will be with them in time of trouble.

אֲחַלְּצֵהוּ וַאֲכַבְּדֵהוּ.
אֹרֶךְ יָמִים אַשְׂבִּיעֵהוּ, וְאַרְאֵהוּ בִּישׁוּעָתִי.

I will deliver them and give them honor.

I will satisfy them with long life, and let them witness My deliverance.

◆ ◆

O Lord our God, in our great need for light we look to You. The quick flight of our days impels us to look back with regret or ahead with misgiving. There are times when we are baffled by disorder, and times when we come to doubt life's value and meaning. When suffering and death strike at those we love, our pain and anger embitter us. Our faith fails us; we find it hard to trust in You.

Eternal Spirit, make Your presence felt among us. Help us to find the courage to affirm You and to do Your will, even when the shadows fall upon us. When our own weakness and the storms of life hide You from our sight, teach us that You are near to each one of us at all times, and especially when we strive to live truer, gentler, nobler lives. Give us trust, Lord; give us peace, and give us light. May our hearts find their rest in You.

◆ ◆

Psalm 131

Lord, my heart is not proud,	יְיָ לֹא־גָבַהּ לִבִּי
and my eyes are not haughty;	וְלֹא־רָמוּ עֵינַי,
on things beyond my scope	וְלֹא־הִלַּכְתִּי בִּגְדֹלוֹת
no more I brood.	וּבְנִפְלָאוֹת מִמֶּנִּי.

But I have calmed and quieted my soul,	אִם־לֹא שִׁוִּיתִי וְדוֹמַמְתִּי נַפְשִׁי,
like a child at its mother's breast;	כְּגָמֻל עֲלֵי אִמּוֹ,
my soul is like a comforted child.	כַּגָּמֻל עָלַי נַפְשִׁי.
O Israel, trust in the Lord,	יַחֵל יִשְׂרָאֵל אֶל־יְיָ,
now and for ever.	מֵעַתָּה וְעַד־עוֹלָם.

◆ ◆

הַבֹּטְחִים בַּייָ כְּהַר־צִיּוֹן, לֹא יִמּוֹט, לְעוֹלָם יֵשֵׁב. יְרוּשָׁלַםִ הָרִים סָבִיב לָהּ, וַייָ סָבִיב לְעַמּוֹ, מֵעַתָּה וְעַד־עוֹלָם.

Those who trust in the Lord are like Mount Zion, which cannot be moved, but stands fast for ever. As the mountains surround Jerusalem, so the Lord is round about His people, now and always.

◆ ◆

When evil darkens our world, give us light.
When despair numbs our souls, give us hope.

When we stumble and fall, lift us up.
When doubts assail us, give us faith.

When nothing seems sure, give us trust.
When ideals fade, give us vision.

When we lose our way, be our guide!
That we may find serenity in Your presence, and purpose in doing Your will.

◆ ◆

Psalm 121

אֶשָּׂא עֵינַי אֶל־הֶהָרִים, מֵאַיִן יָבוֹא עֶזְרִי?
עֶזְרִי מֵעִם יְיָ, עֹשֵׂה שָׁמַיִם וָאָרֶץ.

I lift up my eyes to the mountains: what is the source of my help?
My help will come from the Lord, Maker of heaven and earth.

אַל־יִתֵּן לַמּוֹט רַגְלֶךָ,
אַל־יָנוּם שֹׁמְרֶךָ.

He will not allow your foot to slip;
your Guardian will not slumber.

הִנֵּה לֹא־יָנוּם וְלֹא יִישָׁן, שׁוֹמֵר יִשְׂרָאֵל.
יְיָ שֹׁמְרֶךָ, יְיָ צִלְּךָ עַל־יַד יְמִינֶךָ.

Behold, the Guardian of Israel neither slumbers nor sleeps.
The Eternal is your Keeper, the Lord is your shade at your right hand.

יוֹמָם הַשֶּׁמֶשׁ לֹא־יַכֶּכָּה, וְיָרֵחַ בַּלָּיְלָה.
יְיָ יִשְׁמָרְךָ מִכָּל־רָע, יִשְׁמֹר אֶת־נַפְשֶׁךָ.
יְיָ יִשְׁמָר־צֵאתְךָ וּבוֹאֶךָ, מֵעַתָּה וְעַד־עוֹלָם.

The sun shall not harm you by day, nor the moon by night.
The Lord will guard you from all evil, He will protect your being.

The Lord will guard you, coming and going, from this time forth, and for ever.

Sincerity

It is told: Rabbi Chaim of Krosno was once observed watching a rope dancer with great absorption. His disciples wondered why their master found this small thing so full of interest. He explained it thus: This man is risking his life, and I cannot say why. But of this I am certain: while he is walking the rope, he is not thinking of the fact that he is earning money by what he is doing, for if he did, he would fall.

◆ ◆

How may one approach the Holy One?

With sincerity, honesty, and humility.

With what attitude of soul may we seek His presence?

With the purity of a whole heart.

How can we redeem our life from vanity and give it worth?

By seeking holiness through kindness and love.

Know that faithfulness to God gives meaning to your labors and purpose to your life.

Happy are those who observe His decrees,	אַשְׁרֵי נֹצְרֵי עֵדֹתָיו,
who seek Him with all their hearts.	בְּכָל־לֵב יִדְרְשׁוּהוּ.

◆ ◆

What is faithfulness? How does the proper way of life reveal itself? Live with integrity, seeking all the while with sincerity and earnestness to find what you seek. And know what the teachers and prophets sought and found. They left us teachings that call us to righteousness. As it is said: Others have told you what is good; but what does the Lord require of you?

Do justly, love mercy, and walk humbly with your God.

◆ ◆

And now, O Israel, what is it that the Lord your God demands of You?

To revere Him, to walk only in His ways, to love and serve Him with all your heart and soul.

Help me to know Your ways, O Lord; teach me Your paths. Lead me in Your truth, and guide me.

"I desire love, and not sacrifices; the knowledge of God rather than burnt-offerings."

Seek the Lord your God and you will find Him, if you search for Him with all your heart and soul.

I long to do Your will, O my God; Your Torah is in my heart.

With what shall I come before the Lord, and bow down before the High God?

Depart from evil, and do good: so shall you abide for ever, for the Lord loves justice.

◆ ◆

שְׁלַח־אוֹרְךָ וַאֲמִתְּךָ, הֵמָּה יַנְחוּנִי, יְבִיאוּנִי אֶל־הַר־קָדְשְׁךָ וְאֶל־מִשְׁכְּנוֹתֶיךָ.

Send out Your light and Your truth; let them lead me, let them bring me to Your holy mountain, to Your dwelling-place.

◆ ◆

Our rabbis taught: Six hundred and thirteen commandments were given to Moses. Micah reduced them to three Mitzvot: "Do justly, love mercy, and walk humbly with your God."

Isaiah based all the commandments upon two of them: "Keep justice and righteousness."

Amos saw one guiding principle upon which all the Mitzvot are founded: "Seek Me and live."

Habbakuk, too, expounded the Torah on the basis of a single thought: "The righteous shall live by their faith."

Akiba taught: The great principle of the Torah is expressed in the Mitzvah: "You shall love your neighbor as yourself." But Ben Azzai found a principle even more fundamental in the words: "This is the story of humanity: when God created us, He made us in His likeness."

And Hillel summed up the Torah in this maxim: What is hateful to you, do not do to others. The rest is commentary: you must go and study it.

◆ ◆

יְהִי רָצוֹן מִלְּפָנֶיךָ, יְיָ אֱלֹהֵינוּ וֵאלֹהֵי אֲבוֹתֵינוּ, שֶׁלֹּא תַעֲלֶה שִׂנְאָתֵנוּ עַל־לֵב אָדָם, וְלֹא שִׂנְאַת אָדָם תַּעֲלֶה עַל לִבֵּנוּ.

Lord our God and God of ages past, grant that none may hate us, and let hatred for others never enter our hearts.

וּתְיַחֵד לְבָבֵנוּ לְיִרְאָה אֶת־שְׁמֶךָ, וּתְרַחֲקֵנוּ מִכָּל־מַה שֶּׁשָּׂנֵאתָ, וּתְקָרְבֵנוּ לְכָל־מַה שֶּׁאָהַבְתָּ, וְתַעֲשֶׂה עִמָּנוּ צְדָקָה לְמַעַן שְׁמֶךָ.

Unite us in the reverence of Your name; keep us far from the things You hate, and draw us near to the things You love; and treat us with compassion for Your name's sake.

◆ ◆

רִבּוֹנוֹ שֶׁל עוֹלָם, אֲדוֹן כֹּל אֲשֶׁר בְּכָל־מְקוֹמוֹת מֶמְשַׁלְתֶּךָ, כִּי אַתָּה מְקוֹמוֹ שֶׁל עוֹלָם וְאֵין הָעוֹלָם מְקוֹמֶךָ, תֵּן לִי לֵב אֱמֶת, לֵב כָּשֵׁר וְטָהוֹר לַעֲבוֹדָתְךָ וּלְיִרְאָתֶךָ, לֵב יִשְׂרָאֵל בֶּאֱמֶת.

Master of the universe, whose rule is all-pervading, all-transcending, give me a faithful heart, one clean and pure, that I may serve You in reverence: a true Jewish heart.

עַד שֶׁאֶזְכֶּה שֶׁיְּהִי לִבִּי מִשְׁכַּן כְּבוֹדֶךָ; שֶׁיִּהְיֶה נִמְשָׁךְ לְתוֹךְ לִבִּי שְׁכִינַת כְּבוֹדְךָ הַגָּדוֹל וְהַקָּדוֹשׁ הַשּׁוֹכֵן בְּתוֹךְ לְבָבוֹת שֶׁל כָּל־אֶחָד וְאֶחָד מִיִּשְׂרָאֵל עַמְּךָ הַקָּדוֹשׁ.

Make me worthy to be a dwelling-place of Your glory; let Your great and holy presence be drawn into my heart. O let Your glory dwell in the heart of every child of Israel.

וּבְכָל־מָקוֹם וּמָקוֹם שֶׁאָבוֹא לְשָׁם בַּחֲנָיָה וּבִנְסִיעָה כְּפִי רְצוֹנֶךָ, אֶזְכֶּה לִמְצֹא שָׁם אֱלָהוּתְךָ בֶּאֱמֶת, וּלְהִתְקָרֵב אֵלֶיךָ, וּלְהִתְדַּבֵּק בְּךָ בֶּאֱמֶת.

Wherever I make my home, and wherever I journey, give me the grace to find You in truth, to draw near to You, to hold fast to You in truth.

טַהֵר לִבִּי לְעָבְדְּךָ בֶּאֱמֶת. יַחֵד לְבָבִי לְיִרְאָה שְׁמֶךָ. לֵב טָהוֹר בְּרָא לִי, אֱלֹהִים, וְרוּחַ נָכוֹן חַדֵּשׁ בְּקִרְבִּי.

Purify my heart to serve You in truth. Unify my heart to revere Your name. Create in me a pure heart, O God, and renew a willing spirit within me.

◆ ◆

וְטַהֵר לִבֵּנוּ לְעָבְדְּךָ בֶּאֱמֶת.

Purify our hearts to serve You in truth.

Righteousness

May He whose spirit is with us in every righteous deed, be with all men and women who spend themselves for the good of humanity and bear the burdens of others, who give bread to the hungry, clothe the naked, and take the friendless into their homes. May the work of their hands endure, and may the good seed they are sowing bring forth an abundant harvest.

Lord, teach us to use the opportunities for good that each day brings, that at its end we may look back with the joyful knowledge that we have truly sought to serve You.

◆ ◆

We have learned: Say always, 'The world was created for my sake,' and never say, 'Of what concern is all this to me?' Live as if all life depended on you. Do your share to add some improvement, to supply some one thing that is missing, and to leave the world a little better for your stay in it.

◆

And it has been written: "Fire shall be kept burning upon the altar continually; it shall not go out." Our heart is the altar. In every occupation let a spark of the holy fire remain within you, and fan it into a flame.

◆ ◆

Speak to the whole community of Israel, and say to them: "You shall be holy, for I, the Lord your God, am holy."

As God is merciful and gracious, so shall you be merciful and gracious.

When we oppress the poor, we offend their Maker.

But we honor our Maker when we are kind to the needy.

Let your neighbor's property be as dear to you as your own.

And let your neighbor's honor be as dear to you as your own.

You shall not wrong or oppress a stranger, for you were strangers in the land of Egypt.

You shall not insult the deaf, or place a stumbling-block before the blind.

You shall not rejoice when your enemy falls;

You shall not exult when your enemy stumbles.

Never say: I will do to them as they have done to me; I will repay them according to their deeds.

You shall not hate another in your heart; but you shall love your neighbor as yourself.

◆ ◆

וְשֶׁבַע תּוֹעֲבוֹת נַפְשׁוֹ: עֵינַיִם רָמוֹת, לְשׁוֹן שָׁקֶר, וְיָדַיִם שֹׁפְכוֹת
דָּם־נָקִי; לֵב חֹרֵשׁ מַחְשְׁבוֹת אָוֶן, רַגְלַיִם מְמַהֲרוֹת לָרוּץ
לָרָעָה, יָפִיחַ כְּזָבִים עֵד שָׁקֶר, וּמְשַׁלֵּחַ מְדָנִים בֵּין אַחִים.

Seven things are an abomination to the Lord: haughty eyes, a lying tongue, and hands that shed innocent blood; a mind that makes wicked plans, feet that are quick to run to do evil, a false witness who utters lies, and one who sows discord among brothers and sisters.

אֵלֶּה הַדְּבָרִים אֲשֶׁר תַּעֲשׂוּ: דַּבְּרוּ אֱמֶת אִישׁ אֶת־רֵעֵהוּ,
אֱמֶת וּמִשְׁפַּט שָׁלוֹם שִׁפְטוּ בְּשַׁעֲרֵיכֶם. וְאִישׁ אֶת־רָעַת רֵעֵהוּ
אַל־תַּחְשְׁבוּ בִּלְבַבְכֶם, וּשְׁבֻעַת שֶׁקֶר אַל־תֶּאֱהָבוּ, כִּי אֶת־
כָּל־אֵלֶּה אֲשֶׁר שָׂנֵאתִי, נְאֻם־יְיָ.

These are the things that you shall do: speak the truth to one another; render judgments that are true and make for peace;

do not plan evil against your neighbor; and a[illegible]
oath; for all these things I hate, says the Lord.

◆ ◆

ים שֶׁאֵין לָהֶם שִׁעוּר, שֶׁאָדָם אוֹכֵל פֵּרוֹתֵיהֶם
הַזֶּה, וְהַקֶּרֶן קַיֶּמֶת לוֹ לָעוֹלָם הַבָּא, וְאֵלּוּ הֵן׃

These are [illegible]gations without measure, whose reward, too,
is without mea[illegible]

to honor father and moth[illegible]	כִּבּוּד אָב וָאֵם,
to perform acts of love and kindness;	וּגְמִילוּת חֲסָדִים
to attend the house of study daily;	וְהַשְׁכָּמַת בֵּית הַמִּדְרָשׁ שַׁחֲרִית וְעַרְבִית,
to welcome the stranger;	וְהַכְנָסַת אוֹרְחִים,
to visit the sick;	וּבִקּוּר חוֹלִים,
to rejoice with bride and groom;	וְהַכְנָסַת כַּלָּה,
to console the bereaved;	וּלְוָיַת הַמֵּת,
to pray with sincerity;	וְעִיּוּן תְּפִלָּה,
to make peace when there is strife.	וַהֲבָאַת שָׁלוֹם בֵּין אָדָם לַחֲבֵרוֹ.
And the study of Torah is equal to them all, because it leads to them all.	וְתַלְמוּד תּוֹרָה כְּנֶגֶד כֻּלָּם.

◆ ◆

Psalm 15

יְיָ, מִי־יָגוּר בְּאָהֳלֶךָ, מִי־יִשְׁכֹּן בְּהַר קָדְשֶׁךָ?
הוֹלֵךְ תָּמִים וּפֹעֵל צֶדֶק וְדֹבֵר אֱמֶת בִּלְבָבוֹ.

Lord, who may abide in Your house? Who may dwell in Your holy mountain?

Those who are upright; who do justly; who speak the truth within their hearts.

לֹא־רָגַל עַל־לְשֹׁנוֹ, לֹא־עָשָׂה לְרֵעֵהוּ רָעָה, וְחֶרְפָּה לֹא
עַל־קְרֹבוֹ.
בְזֶה בְּעֵינָיו נִמְאָס, וְאֶת־יִרְאֵי יְיָ יְכַבֵּד.

...do not slander others, or wrong them, or bring shame ... them.

...o scorn the lawless, but honor those who revere th...

נִשְׁבַּע לְהָרַע וְ... ר. כַּסְפּוֹ לֹא־נָתַן בְּנֶשֶׁךְ וְשֹׁחַד עַל־נָקִי
לֹא לָקָח.
עֹשֵׂה אֵלֶּה לֹא יִמּוֹט לְעוֹלָם.

Who give their word, and come what may, do not retract.

Who do not exploit others, who never take bribes.

Those who live in this way shall never be shaken.

לֹא־רָגַל עַל־לְשֹׁנוֹ, לֹא־עָשָׂה לְרֵעֵהוּ רָעָה, וְחֶרְפָּה לֹא־נָשָׂא עַל־קְרֹבוֹ.
נִבְזֶה בְּעֵינָיו נִמְאָס, וְאֶת־יִרְאֵי יְיָ יְכַבֵּד.

Who do not slander others, or wrong them, or bring shame upon them.

Who scorn the lawless, but honor those who revere the Lord.

נִשְׁבַּע לְהָרַע וְלֹא יָמִיר. כַּסְפּוֹ לֹא־נָתַן בְּנֶשֶׁךְ וְשֹׁחַד עַל־נָקִי לֹא לָקָח.
עֹשֵׂה אֵלֶּה לֹא יִמּוֹט לְעוֹלָם.

Who give their word, and, come what may, do not retract.

Who do not exploit others, who never take bribes.

Those who live in this way shall never be shaken.

do not plan evil against your neighbor; and approve no false oath; for all these things I hate, says the Lord.

• •

אֵלּוּ דְבָרִים שֶׁאֵין לָהֶם שִׁעוּר, שֶׁאָדָם אוֹכֵל פֵּרוֹתֵיהֶם
בָּעוֹלָם הַזֶּה, וְהַקֶּרֶן קַיֶּמֶת לוֹ לָעוֹלָם הַבָּא, וְאֵלּוּ הֵן:

These are the obligations without measure, whose reward, too, is without measure:

to honor father and mother;	כִּבּוּד אָב וָאֵם,
to perform acts of love and kindness;	וּגְמִילוּת חֲסָדִים
to attend the house of study daily;	וְהַשְׁכָּמַת בֵּית הַמִּדְרָשׁ שַׁחֲרִית וְעַרְבִית,
to welcome the stranger;	וְהַכְנָסַת אוֹרְחִים,
to visit the sick;	וּבִקּוּר חוֹלִים,
to rejoice with bride and groom;	וְהַכְנָסַת כַּלָּה,
to console the bereaved;	וּלְוָיַת הַמֵּת,
to pray with sincerity;	וְעִיּוּן תְּפִלָּה,
to make peace when there is strife.	וַהֲבָאַת שָׁלוֹם בֵּין אָדָם לַחֲבֵרוֹ.
And the study of Torah is equal to them all, because it leads to them all.	וְתַלְמוּד תּוֹרָה כְּנֶגֶד כֻּלָּם.

• •

Psalm 15

יְיָ, מִי־יָגוּר בְּאָהֳלֶךָ, מִי־יִשְׁכֹּן בְּהַר קָדְשֶׁךָ?
הוֹלֵךְ תָּמִים וּפֹעֵל צֶדֶק וְדֹבֵר אֱמֶת בִּלְבָבוֹ.

Lord, who may abide in Your house? Who may dwell in Your holy mountain?

Those who are upright; who do justly; who speak the truth within their hearts.

Justice

עַל־שְׁלֹשָׁה דְבָרִים הָעוֹלָם קַיָּם: עַל־הָאֱמֶת, וְעַל־הַדִּין,
וְעַל־הַשָּׁלוֹם.
צֶדֶק, צֶדֶק תִּרְדֹּף, לְמַעַן תִּחְיֶה.

The world is sustained by three things: by justice, by truth, and by peace.

Justice, justice shall you pursue, that you may live.

זִרְעוּ לָכֶם לִצְדָקָה, קִצְרוּ לְפִי־חֶסֶד.
כִּי־צַדִּיק יְיָ, צְדָקוֹת אָהֵב.

Sow for yourselves righteousness, reap the fruit of steadfast love.

For the Lord is righteous; He loves righteous deeds.

וּקְרָאתֶם דְּרוֹר בָּאָרֶץ לְכָל־יֹשְׁבֶיהָ.
שִׂנְאוּ־רָע וְאֶהֱבוּ טוֹב, וְהַצִּיגוּ בַשַּׁעַר מִשְׁפָּט.

Proclaim liberty throughout the land to all who dwell in it.

Hate evil and love good, and establish justice in the city.

◆ ◆

כֹּה אָמַר יְיָ: אַל־יִתְהַלֵּל חָכָם בְּחָכְמָתוֹ, וְאַל־יִתְהַלֵּל הַגִּבּוֹר
בִּגְבוּרָתוֹ, אַל־יִתְהַלֵּל עָשִׁיר בְּעָשְׁרוֹ; כִּי אִם־בְּזֹאת יִתְהַלֵּל
הַמִּתְהַלֵּל, הַשְׂכֵּל וְיָדֹעַ אוֹתִי, כִּי אֲנִי יְיָ עֹשֶׂה חֶסֶד, מִשְׁפָּט,
וּצְדָקָה בָּאָרֶץ, כִּי־בְאֵלֶּה חָפַצְתִּי.

Thus says the Lord: Let not the wise glory in their wisdom, let not the mighty glory in their might, let not the rich glory in their riches; but let them who glory, glory in this: that they understand and know Me, that I am the Lord who practices kindness, justice and righteousness in the earth, for in these things I delight.

◆ ◆

Our God and Creator, we thank You for the sense of justice You have implanted within us, and which always seeks, though at times haltingly, to express itself in daily life.

Make us, O God, more steadfast in our desire to do Your will. Teach us that the men and women around us are our brothers and sisters, and fill us with such love for our fellow creatures that we will never wrong them, or exploit them, or take advantage of their weakness or ignorance.

Kindle in us a passion for righteousness. Grant us the vision to see that only justice can endure, and that only in being just to one another can we make our lives acceptable to You.

May we by our thoughts and our deeds hasten the time when wrong and violence shall cease, and justice be established in all the earth.

◆ ◆

Let justice roll down like waters,	וְיִגַּל כַּמַּיִם מִשְׁפָּט,
and righteousness like a mighty stream.	וּצְדָקָה כְּנַחַל אֵיתָן.

◆ ◆

It is an easy thing to triumph in the summer's sun
And in the vintage & to sing on the waggon loaded with corn.
It is an easy thing to talk of patience to the afflicted,
To speak the laws of prudence to the homeless wanderer,
To listen to the hungry raven's cry in wintry season
When the red blood is fill'd with wine & with the marrow
of lambs.

It is an easy thing to laugh at wrathful elements,
To hear the dog howl at the wintry door, the ox in the
slaughter house moan;
To see a god on every wind & a blessing on every blast;
To hear sounds of love in the thunder storm that destroys
our enemies' house;
To rejoice in the blight that covers his field, & the sickness
that cuts off his children,
While our olive & vine sing & laugh round our door, & our
children bring fruits & flowers.

Then the groan & the dolor are quite forgotten, & the slave grinding at the mill,
And the captive in chains, & the poor in the prison, & the soldier in the field
When the shatter'd bone has laid him groaning among the happier dead.
It is an easy thing to rejoice in the tents of prosperity.

◆ ◆

לֹא תִּגְנֹבוּ, וְלֹא־תְכַחֲשׁוּ וְלֹא־תְשַׁקְּרוּ אִישׁ בַּעֲמִיתוֹ.
לֹא־תַעֲשֹׁק אֶת־רֵעֲךָ וְלֹא תִגְזֹל.

You shall not steal, and you shall not deceive or lie to one another.

You shall not oppress or rob your neighbor.

לֹא־תָלִין פְּעֻלַּת שָׂכִיר אִתְּךָ עַד־בֹּקֶר.
לֹא־תְקַלֵּל חֵרֵשׁ, וְלִפְנֵי עִוֵּר לֹא תִתֵּן מִכְשֹׁל.

You shall not hold the wage of a laborer beyond its due time.

You shall not insult the deaf, or place a stumbling-block before the blind.

לֹא־תַעֲשׂוּ עָוֶל בַּמִּשְׁפָּט.
לֹא־תִשָּׂא פְנֵי־דָל וְלֹא תֶהְדַּר פְּנֵי גָדוֹל;
בְּצֶדֶק תִּשְׁפֹּט עֲמִיתֶךָ.

You shall do no injustice in judgment.

You shall not be partial to the poor or defer to the powerful; you shall judge your neighbor with fairness.

וְגֵר לֹא תִלְחָץ, וְאַתֶּם יְדַעְתֶּם אֶת־נֶפֶשׁ הַגֵּר,
כִּי־גֵרִים הֱיִיתֶם בְּאֶרֶץ מִצְרָיִם.

You shall not oppress a stranger, for you know the heart of a stranger,

For you were strangers in the land of Egypt.

כְּאֶזְרָח מִכֶּם יִהְיֶה לָכֶם הַגֵּר הַגָּר אִתְּכֶם,
וְאָהַבְתָּ לוֹ כָּמוֹךָ.

The strangers in your midst shall be to you as the native-born,

and you shall love them as yourself.

לֹא תְאַמֵּץ אֶת־לְבָבְךָ וְלֹא תִקְפֹּץ אֶת־יָדְךָ מֵאָחִיךָ הָאֶבְיוֹן,
וְאָהַבְתָּ לוֹ כָּמוֹךָ.

You shall not harden your heart, or shut your hand against the poor, your kin,

but you shall love them as yourself.

חִדְלוּ הָרֵעַ; לִמְדוּ הֵיטֵב;
דִּרְשׁוּ מִשְׁפָּט; אַשְּׁרוּ חָמוֹץ; שִׁפְטוּ יָתוֹם; רִיבוּ אַלְמָנָה.

Cease to do evil; learn to do good;

Seek justice; correct oppression; defend the orphan; plead for the widow.

◆ ◆

כִּי־אָפֵס הַמֵּץ, כָּלָה שֹׁד, תַּמּוּ רֹמֵס מִן־הָאָרֶץ, וְהוּכַן בַּחֶסֶד
כִּסֵּא. וְיָשַׁב עָלָיו בֶּאֱמֶת, בְּאֹהֶל דָּוִד, שֹׁפֵט וְדֹרֵשׁ מִשְׁפָּט,
וּמְהִר צֶדֶק.

When oppression is no more, and exploitation has ceased, and the arrogant have vanished from the land, a throne will be established in steadfast love. And in the tent of David, one who judges and seeks equity, and is swift to do justice, shall sit there in faithfulness.

◆ ◆

The Lord of Hosts is exalted by justice;	וַיִּגְבַּהּ יְיָ צְבָאוֹת בַּמִּשְׁפָּט,
the holy God is sanctified by righteousness.	וְהָאֵל הַקָּדוֹשׁ נִקְדַּשׁ בִּצְדָקָה.

Unity

The day will come when I will make for you a covenant with the beasts of the field, the birds of the air, and the insects of the ground; and I will remove the bow, the sword, and war from the earth, and I will give you a life of peace.

Fear not, O land; be glad and rejoice, for the Lord is doing great things! Have no fear, you beasts of the field, for the pastures of the wilderness are green; the tree bears its fruit, the fig-tree and vine give their full yield.

The wolf shall dwell with the lamb, the leopard shall lie down with the kid, and the calf and the lion shall feed together, with a little child to lead them. The cow and the bear shall feed; their young shall lie down together, and the lion eat straw like the ox. The infant shall play over the cobra's hole; the child shall reach into the adder's lair.

They shall not hurt or destroy in all My holy mountain; for the earth shall be filled with the knowledge of the Lord as the sea-bed is covered by water.

◆ ◆

וַיִּבְרָא אֱלֹהִים אֶת־הָאָדָם בְּצַלְמוֹ; בְּצֶלֶם אֱלֹהִים בָּרָא אֹתוֹ; זָכָר וּנְקֵבָה בָּרָא אֹתָם.

God created us in His own image; in the image of God He created us; male and female He created us.

◆ ◆

Our tradition says that God created us through one human being to teach us that whoever destroys a single human soul has destroyed an entire world.

And whoever sustains a single human soul has sustained an entire world.

And a single human being was created for the sake of peace, that none might say: My lineage is greater than yours.

I call heaven and earth to witness: Gentile or Jew, man or woman, manservant or maidservant — all according to our deeds does the spirit of God rest upon us.

◆ ◆

Eternal God of all peoples and races, may all Your children learn to live together in peace and friendship. Let the day come when oppression, discrimination, and prejudice will be forgotten, and all the world filled with Your spirit, as it has been said: "Turn to Me and be saved, all the ends of the earth!"

May that day come soon, O Lord; the day foretold by our prophets and sages, the day for which we long, when all humanity will recognize that it is one family.

Let the day come proclaimed by Your prophet: "In that day Israel will be the third with Egypt and Assyria, a blessing in the midst of the earth, whom the Lord of Hosts has blessed, saying: Blessed be Egypt My people, and Assyria the work of My hands, and Israel My heritage."

◆ ◆

Laugh, laugh at all my dreams!	שַׂחֲקִי, שַׂחֲקִי עַל הַחֲלוֹמוֹת,
What I dream shall yet come true!	זוּ אֲנִי הַחוֹלֵם שָׂח,
Laugh at my belief in man,	שַׂחֲקִי כִּי בָאָדָם אַאֲמִין,
At my belief in you.	כִּי עוֹדֶנִּי מַאֲמִין בָּךְ.
Freedom still my soul demands,	כִּי עוֹד נַפְשִׁי דְּרוֹר שׁוֹאֶפֶת,
Unbartered for a calf of gold.	לֹא מְכַרְתִּיהָ לְעֵגֶל פָּז,
For still I do believe in man,	כִּי עוֹד אַאֲמִין גַּם בָּאָדָם,
And in his spirit, strong and bold.	גַּם בְּרוּחוֹ, רוּחַ עָז.

אַאֲמִינָה גַּם בֶּעָתִיד,
אַף אִם יִרְחַק זֶה הַיּוֹם.
אַךְ בֹּא יָבוֹא – יִשְׂאוּ שָׁלוֹם
אָז וּבְרָכָה לְאֹם מִלְאֹם.

And in the future I still believe –
Though it be distant, come it will –
When nations shall each other bless,
And peace at last the earth shall fill.

◆ ◆

Lord God of test tube and blueprint,
Who jointed molecules of dust and shook them till their name was Adam,
Who taught worms and stars how they could live together,
Appear now among the parliaments of conquerors and give instruction to their schemes;
Measure out new liberties so none shall suffer from his father's color or the credo of his choice;
Post proofs that brotherhood is not so wild a dream as those who profit by postponing it pretend;
Sit at the treaty table and convoy the hopes of little people through expected straits.

And press into the final seal a sign that peace will come for longer than posterities can see ahead,
That man unto his fellow man shall be a friend for ever.

◆ ◆

הִנֵּה מַה־טּוֹב וּמַה־נָּעִים שֶׁבֶת אַחִים גַּם־יָחַד.

Behold, how good it is, and how pleasant, when brethren live together in unity.

Peace

The young soldiers do not speak.

Nevertheless, they are heard in the still houses: who has not heard them?

They have a silence that speaks for them at night and when the clock counts.

They say: We are young. We have died. Remember us.

They say: We have done what we could but until it is finished it is not done.

They say: We have given our lives but until it is finished no one can know what our lives gave.

They say: Our deaths are not ours; they are yours; they will mean what you make them.

They say: Whether our lives and our deaths are for peace and a new hope or for nothing we cannot say; it is you who must say this.

They say: We leave you our deaths. Give them their meaning.

We were young, they say. We have died. Remember us.

◆ ◆

לֹא מָצָא הַקָּדוֹשׁ בָּרוּךְ הוּא כְּלִי מַחֲזִיק בְּרָכָה לְיִשְׂרָאֵל אֶלָּא הַשָּׁלוֹם, שֶׁנֶּאֱמַר: "יְיָ עֹז לְעַמּוֹ יִתֵּן, יְיָ יְבָרֵךְ אֶת־עַמּוֹ בַשָּׁלוֹם."

The Holy One, blessed is He, found no better vessel to hold Israel's blessings than Peace, for it is written: "The Lord will give strength to His people, the Lord will bless His people with peace."

◆ ◆

Our God, the Guide of humanity, let Your spirit rule this nation and its citizens, that their deeds may be prompted by a love of justice and right, and bear fruit in goodness and peace.

Bless our people with love of righteousness.

Teach us to work for the welfare of all, to diminish the evils that beset us, and to enlarge our nation's virtues.

Bless our people with civic courage.

Bless our striving to make real the dream of Your kingdom, when we shall put an end to the suffering we now inflict upon each other.

Bless our people with a vision of Your kingdom on earth.

For You have endowed us with noble powers; help us to use them wisely, and with compassion.

Bless our people with a wise and feeling heart.

You have given us freedom to choose between good and evil, life and death. May we choose life and good, that our children may inherit from us the blessings of dignity and freedom, prosperity and peace.

◆ ◆

O God, You have called us to peace, for You are Peace itself.
May we have the vision to see that each of us, in some measure,
can help to realize these aims:

Where there are ignorance and superstition,

Let there be enlightenment and knowledge.

Where there are prejudice and hatred,

Let there be acceptance and love.

Where there are fear and suspicion,

Let there be confidence and trust.

Where there are tyranny and oppression,

Let there be freedom and justice.

Where there are poverty and disease,

Let there be prosperity and health.

Where there are strife and discord,

Let there be harmony and peace.

◆ ◆

They shall beat their swords into plowshares,	וְכִתְּתוּ חַרְבוֹתָם לְאִתִּים
and their spears into pruninghooks;	וַחֲנִיתוֹתֵיהֶם לְמַזְמֵרוֹת,
nation shall not lift up sword against nation,	לֹא־יִשָּׂא גוֹי אֶל־גּוֹי חֶרֶב
nor ever again shall they train for war.	וְלֹא־יִלְמְדוּ עוֹד מִלְחָמָה.

◆ ◆

יְהִי רָצוֹן מִלְּפָנֶיךָ שֶׁתְּבַטֵּל מִלְחָמוֹת וּשְׁפִיכוּת דָּמִים מִן הָעוֹלָם, וְתַמְשִׁיךְ שָׁלוֹם גָּדוֹל וְנִפְלָא בָּעוֹלָם. וְלֹא יִשְׂאוּ עוֹד גּוֹי אֶל גּוֹי חֶרֶב, וְלֹא יִלְמְדוּ עוֹד מִלְחָמָה.

May it be Your will to cause war and bloodshed to vanish from the earth, to let a great and wondrous peace prevail in all the world. So never again shall nation lift up sword against nation, nor ever again shall they train for war.

רַק יַכִּירוּ וְיֵדְעוּ כָּל־יוֹשְׁבֵי תֵבֵל הָאֱמֶת לַאֲמִתּוֹ, אֲשֶׁר לֹא בָאנוּ לָזֶה הָעוֹלָם בִּשְׁבִיל רִיב וּמַחֲלוֹקֶת, וְלֹא בִּשְׁבִיל שִׂנְאָה וְקִנְאָה, וְקִנְתּוּר וּשְׁפִיכוּת דָּמִים. רַק בָּאנוּ לָעוֹלָם כְּדֵי לְהַכִּיר וְלָדַעַת אוֹתְךָ. תִּתְבָּרֵךְ לָנֶצַח!

Only let all who dwell on earth clearly see the truth of truths, that we have come into this world not for strife and discord, not for hatred and envy, and not for rivalry and bloodshed. Rather we have come into this world to know and understand You. May You be blessed for ever!

וִימַלֵּא כְבוֹדְךָ אֶת־כָּל־מוֹחֵנוּ וְשִׂכְלֵנוּ וְדַעְתֵּנוּ וּלְבָבֵנוּ, וְאֶהְיֶה מֶרְכָּבָה לִשְׁכִינַת אֱלָהוּתָךְ, עַד שֶׁאֶזְכֶּה לְהַכְנִיס גַּם בַּאֲחֵרִים יְדִיעַת אֲמִתַּת אֱלָהוּתָךְ, לְהוֹדִיעַ לִבְנֵי הָאָדָם גְּבוּרָתְךָ וּכְבוֹד הֲדַר מַלְכוּתָךְ.

May Your glory enter our minds and our hearts, that we may become chariots for the Divine Presence, bringing Your Presence to the world, making known to all who live Your power and the splendor of Your kingdom.

◆ ◆

Keep your tongue from evil, and your lips from deceitful speech.

Depart from evil, and do good; seek peace and pursue it.

Be of the disciples of Aaron:

Loving peace and pursuing it, loving all people, and bringing them to the Torah.

The whole Torah exists only to bring peace, as it is written:

Its ways are ways of pleasantness and all its paths are peace.

Not by might, nor by power, but by My spirit, says the Lord of Hosts.

He will make an end to war throughout the world; He will break the bow and smash the spear; He will make the chariot of war go up in flames.

Justice shall dwell in the wilderness, righteousness in the fruitful field.

Righteousness shall lead to peace; it shall bring quietness and confidence for ever.

I will remove the bow, the sword, and war from the earth, and I will give you a life of peace.

They shall not hurt or destroy in all My holy mountain, for the earth shall be full of the knowledge of the Lord as the sea-bed is covered by water.

All shall sit under their vines and under their fig-trees,

and none shall make them afraid.

◆ ◆

Grant us peace, Your most precious gift, O Eternal Source of peace, and give us the will to proclaim its message to all the peoples of the earth. Bless our country, that it may always be a stronghold of peace, and its advocate among the nations. May contentment reign within its borders, health and happiness within its homes. Strengthen the bonds of friendship among the inhabitants of all lands, and may the love of Your name hallow every home and every heart. Blessed is the Eternal God, the Source of peace.

Revelation

What is Torah? It is what God has revealed to us, and what we have come to understand about God. It is the ideas and ideals, the laws and commandments, that make up our religious heritage. It is the experience of Abraham, the legislation of Moses, the vision of the Prophets, the commentary of the Rabbis, the insight of the Mystics. It is the questions we ask, and the answers we receive, when we seek to understand God, the world, and ourselves.

It is the way of life; the path to self-fulfillment; the design for a better world.

◆ ◆

בָּרוּךְ אֱלֹהֵינוּ שֶׁבְּרָאָנוּ לִכְבוֹדוֹ, וּקְרָאָנוּ לַעֲבוֹדָתוֹ, וְנָתַן לָנוּ תּוֹרַת אֱמֶת, וְחַיֵּי עוֹלָם נָטַע בְּתוֹכֵנוּ.
הוּא יִפְתַּח לִבֵּנוּ בְּתוֹרָתוֹ, וְיָשֵׂם בְּלִבֵּנוּ אַהֲבָתוֹ וְיִרְאָתוֹ, וְלַעֲשׂוֹת רְצוֹנוֹ וּלְעָבְדוֹ בְּלֵבָב שָׁלֵם.

Let us praise God, who has touched us with His glory and called us to serve Him; who has given us a Torah of truth, placing eternity into our lives. May He open our hearts to His Torah, and fill us with love and reverence, that we may learn to do His will and serve Him with a whole heart.

◆ ◆

One event stands out above all others in the memory of our people: When God revealed the Torah, no bird chirped, no fowl beat its wings, no ox bellowed, the angels did not sing, the sea did not stir, no creature uttered a sound. The world was silent and still, and the Divine Voice spoke: 'I am the Lord your God.'

◆ ◆

בָּרוּךְ שֶׁנָּתַן תּוֹרָה לְעַמּוֹ יִשְׂרָאֵל בִּקְדֻשָּׁתוֹ.

Praised be the One who in His holiness has given the Torah to His people Israel!

◆ ◆

The revelation at Mount Sinai is shrouded for us by the mists of antiquity. But this we know: that it released a torrent of spiritual energy that transformed Israel into a people of priests and prophets, bringing enlightenment to humanity.

It inspires and guides us still, and it will redeem the world.

◆ ◆

בָּרוּךְ אַתָּה, יְיָ אֱלֹהֵינוּ, מֶלֶךְ הָעוֹלָם, שֶׁחָלַק מֵחָכְמָתוֹ לִירֵאָיו.

Blessed is the Lord our God, Ruler of the universe, who shares His wisdom with those who revere Him.

בָּרוּךְ אַתָּה, יְיָ אֱלֹהֵינוּ, מֶלֶךְ הָעוֹלָם, שֶׁנָּתַן מֵחָכְמָתוֹ לְבָשָׂר וָדָם.

Blessed is the Lord our God, Ruler of the universe, who gives of His wisdom to flesh and blood.

◆ ◆

Sinai was only the beginning. The Torah has never ceased to grow. In every age it has been purified and enlarged. It has a permanent core and an expanding periphery. It expands as the horizon of our vision grows.

Nor are God's revelations confined to Israel. He has been the inspiration of the great and good among all the families of the earth. His love and guidance reach out to all the world.

Let us then give thanks for the wise and noble of every age and people who, by word and example, have shed light on our way; but above all for the prophets and teachers of Israel, who shine as the brightness of the heavens and, having led many to righteousness, are like the stars for ever.

◆ ◆

The Torah is God's choicest gift to the House of Israel.

Israel without Torah is like a body without a soul.

Like water, it refreshes and purifies.

Like wine, it gladdens the heart.

Like a crown, it exalts us above all creatures.

It is nobler than the crown of priesthood or royalty.

When Torah entered the world, freedom entered it.

The whole Torah exists only to establish peace.

Its first and last aim is to teach love and kindness.

What is hateful to you, do not do to others.

That is the whole Torah; all the rest is commentary; go and learn it.

Those who study Torah are the true guardians of civilization.

When the voice of Jacob is heard, the hand of Esau does not prevail.

Wherever people study Torah, the Presence of God dwells among them.

Honoring parents, performing acts of kindness, and making peace among people, these are among our highest duties;

But the study of Torah is equal to them all, because it leads to them all.

◆ ◆

If you study Torah in order to learn and do God's will, you acquire many merits; and not only that, but the whole world is indebted to you. You will be cherished as a friend, a lover of God and of people. It clothes you with humility and reverence; it enables you to become righteous and saintly, upright and faithful. It keeps you far from sin, and brings you near to virtue. You benefit humanity with counsel and knowledge, wisdom and strength. You become like a never-failing fountain, like a river that grows ever mightier as it flows. You are modest, slow to anger, and forgiving of insults; and it magnifies and exalts you above all things.

◆ ◆

וְכָל־בָּנַיִךְ לִמּוּדֵי יְיָ, וְרַב שְׁלוֹם בָּנָיִךְ.

All your children shall be taught of the Lord, and great shall be the peace of your children.

◆ ◆

All rise

יִתְגַּדַּל וְיִתְקַדַּשׁ שְׁמֵהּ רַבָּא, בְּעָלְמָא דִּי־בְרָא כִרְעוּתֵהּ, וְיַמְלִיךְ מַלְכוּתֵהּ בְּחַיֵּיכוֹן וּבְיוֹמֵיכוֹן, וּבְחַיֵּי דְכָל־בֵּית יִשְׂרָאֵל, בַּעֲגָלָא וּבִזְמַן קָרִיב, וְאִמְרוּ: אָמֵן.

Let the glory of God be extolled, let His great name be hallowed, in the world whose creation He willed. May His kingdom soon prevail, in our own day, our own lives, and the life of all Israel, and let us say: Amen.

יְהֵא שְׁמֵהּ רַבָּא מְבָרַךְ לְעָלַם וּלְעָלְמֵי עָלְמַיָּא.

Let His great name be blessed for ever and ever.

יִתְבָּרַךְ וְיִשְׁתַּבַּח, וְיִתְפָּאַר וְיִתְרוֹמַם וְיִתְנַשֵּׂא, וְיִתְהַדַּר וְיִתְעַלֶּה וְיִתְהַלַּל שְׁמֵהּ דְּקֻדְשָׁא, בְּרִיךְ הוּא, לְעֵלָּא מִן־כָּל־בִּרְכָתָא וְשִׁירָתָא, תֻּשְׁבְּחָתָא וְנֶחֱמָתָא דַּאֲמִירָן בְּעָלְמָא, וְאִמְרוּ: אָמֵן.

Let the name of the Holy One, blessed is He, be glorified, exalted, and honored, though He is beyond all the praises, songs, and adorations that we can utter, and let us say: Amen.

עַל יִשְׂרָאֵל וְעַל רַבָּנָן וְעַל תַּלְמִידֵיהוֹן, וְעַל כָּל תַּלְמִידֵי־תַלְמִידֵיהוֹן, וְעַל כָּל־מָן דְּעָסְקִין בְּאוֹרַיְתָא, דִּי בְּאַתְרָא הָדֵן וְדִי בְּכָל־אֲתַר וַאֲתַר, יְהֵא לְהוֹן וּלְכוֹן שְׁלָמָא רַבָּא,

חִנָּא וְחִסְדָּא וְרַחֲמִין, וְחַיִּין אֲרִיכִין, וּמְזוֹנָא רְוִיחָא, וּפֻרְקָנָא מִן־קֳדָם אֲבוּהוֹן דְּבִשְׁמַיָּא וְאַרְעָא, וְאִמְרוּ: אָמֵן.

God of heaven and earth, grant abundant peace to our people and their leaders, to our teachers and their disciples, and to all who engage in the study of Torah here and everywhere. Let there be for them and for us all, grace, love, and compassion, a joyful life, sustenance, and the hope of Your kingdom, and let us say: Amen.

יְהֵא שְׁלָמָא רַבָּא מִן־שְׁמַיָּא, וְחַיִּים טוֹבִים, עָלֵינוּ וְעַל־כָּל־יִשְׂרָאֵל, וְאִמְרוּ: אָמֵן.

For us, for all Israel, for all men and women, may the blessing of peace and the promise of life come true, and let us say: Amen.

עֹשֶׂה שָׁלוֹם בִּמְרוֹמָיו, הוּא בְּרַחֲמָיו יַעֲשֶׂה שָׁלוֹם עָלֵינוּ וְעַל־כָּל־יִשְׂרָאֵל, וְאִמְרוּ: אָמֵן.

May He who causes peace to reign in the high heavens, let peace descend on us, on all Israel, and all the world, and let us say: Amen.

All are seated

The Ten Commandments עשרת הדברות

From Exodus 20

א אָנֹכִי יְיָ אֱלֹהֶיךָ, אֲשֶׁר הוֹצֵאתִיךָ מֵאֶרֶץ מִצְרַיִם, מִבֵּית
עֲבָדִים.

1. I, THE LORD, AM YOUR GOD who led you out of the land of Egypt, out of the house of bondage.

ב לֹא יִהְיֶה־לְךָ אֱלֹהִים אֲחֵרִים עַל־פָּנָי. לֹא־תַעֲשֶׂה לְךָ
פֶסֶל וְכָל־תְּמוּנָה אֲשֶׁר בַּשָּׁמַיִם מִמַּעַל וַאֲשֶׁר בָּאָרֶץ מִתָּחַת,
וַאֲשֶׁר בַּמַּיִם מִתַּחַת לָאָרֶץ. לֹא־תִשְׁתַּחֲוֶה לָהֶם וְלֹא
תָעָבְדֵם, כִּי אָנֹכִי יְיָ אֱלֹהֶיךָ אֵל קַנָּא, פֹּקֵד עֲוֹן אָבֹת עַל־
בָּנִים, עַל־שִׁלֵּשִׁים וְעַל־רִבֵּעִים לְשֹׂנְאָי, וְעֹשֶׂה חֶסֶד לַאֲלָפִים
לְאֹהֲבַי וּלְשֹׁמְרֵי מִצְוֹתָי.

2. YOU SHALL HAVE NO OTHER GODS BESIDE ME. You shall not carve for yourself an image, the likeness of anything in the heavens above, or on the earth below, or in the waters under the earth. You shall not worship them or serve them, for I the Lord your God am a demanding God, inflicting the sins of the parents upon their children, upon the third and fourth generations of those who hate Me, but showing steadfast love to thousands of generations of those who love Me and keep My commandments.

ג לֹא תִשָּׂא אֶת־שֵׁם־יְיָ אֱלֹהֶיךָ לַשָּׁוְא, כִּי לֹא יְנַקֶּה יְיָ אֵת
אֲשֶׁר־יִשָּׂא אֶת־שְׁמוֹ לַשָּׁוְא.

3. YOU SHALL NOT INVOKE THE NAME OF THE LORD YOUR GOD WITH MALICE; for the Lord does not hold guiltless one who invokes His name with malice.

ד זָכוֹר אֶת־יוֹם הַשַּׁבָּת לְקַדְּשׁוֹ. שֵׁשֶׁת יָמִים תַּעֲבֹד וְעָשִׂיתָ
כָל־מְלַאכְתֶּךָ, וְיוֹם הַשְּׁבִיעִי שַׁבָּת לַייָ אֱלֹהֶיךָ: לֹא תַעֲשֶׂה
כָל־מְלָאכָה, אַתָּה וּבִנְךָ וּבִתֶּךָ, עַבְדְּךָ וַאֲמָתְךָ וּבְהֶמְתֶּךָ,

וְגֵרְךָ אֲשֶׁר בִּשְׁעָרֶיךָ. כִּי שֵׁשֶׁת־יָמִים עָשָׂה יְיָ אֶת־הַשָּׁמַיִם וְאֶת־הָאָרֶץ, אֶת־הַיָּם וְאֶת־כָּל־אֲשֶׁר־בָּם, וַיָּנַח בַּיּוֹם הַשְּׁבִיעִי; עַל־כֵּן בֵּרַךְ יְיָ אֶת־יוֹם הַשַּׁבָּת וַיְקַדְּשֵׁהוּ.

4. Remember the Sabbath day and keep it holy. Six days shall you labor and do all your work, but the seventh day is a sabbath of the Lord your God: you shall do no work — you, your son or daughter, your servants, your domestic animals, or the stranger in your community. For in six days the Lord made heaven and earth, the sea, and all that is in them; then He rested on the seventh day. Therefore the Lord blessed the Sabbath day and called it holy.

ה כַּבֵּד אֶת־אָבִיךָ וְאֶת־אִמֶּךָ, לְמַעַן יַאֲרִיכוּן יָמֶיךָ עַל הָאֲדָמָה אֲשֶׁר־יְיָ אֱלֹהֶיךָ נֹתֵן לָךְ.

5. Honor your father and your mother, that you may long endure in the land that the Lord your God gives to you.

ו לֹא תִּרְצָח.

6. You shall not murder.

ז לֹא תִּנְאָף.

7. You shall not commit adultery.

ח לֹא תִּגְנֹב.

8. You shall not steal.

ט לֹא־תַעֲנֶה בְרֵעֲךָ עֵד שָׁקֶר.

9. You shall not bear false witness against your neighbor.

י לֹא תַחְמֹד בֵּית רֵעֶךָ. לֹא־תַחְמֹד אֵשֶׁת רֵעֶךָ, וְעַבְדּוֹ וַאֲמָתוֹ, וְשׁוֹרוֹ וַחֲמֹרוֹ וְכֹל אֲשֶׁר לְרֵעֶךָ.

10. You shall not covet your neighbor's house. You shall not covet your neighbor's wife, nor his servants, nor his cattle, nor anything that is your neighbor's.

Israel's Mission

Long ago, our ancestors came to believe that they were a people appointed to be God's witnesses to the world. When all others were blinded by idolatry, they alone realized that One God rules the whole universe and that He demands righteousness of all His creatures. And they felt themselves called to proclaim this faith to all the nations.

◆ ◆

אִם־שָׁמוֹעַ תִּשְׁמְעוּ בְּקֹלִי וּשְׁמַרְתֶּם אֶת־בְּרִיתִי, וִהְיִיתֶם לִי סְגֻלָּה מִכָּל־הָעַמִּים.

וְאַתֶּם תִּהְיוּ־לִי מַמְלֶכֶת כֹּהֲנִים, וְגוֹי קָדוֹשׁ.

If you truly listen to Me and keep My covenant, you shall be My treasured possession among the peoples.

You shall be to Me a kingdom of priests, a holy people.

הֵן עַבְדִּי, אֶתְמָךְ־בּוֹ; בְּחִירִי, רָצְתָה נַפְשִׁי.

אַתֶּם עֵדַי, נְאֻם־יְיָ, וְעַבְדִּי אֲשֶׁר בָּחָרְתִּי.

Behold My servant, whom I uphold; My chosen, in whom My soul delights.

You are My witnesses, says the Lord, and My chosen servant.

לִפְקֹחַ עֵינַיִם עִוְרוֹת, לְהוֹצִיא מִמַּסְגֵּר אַסִּיר, מִבֵּית כֶּלֶא יֹשְׁבֵי חֹשֶׁךְ.

נָקֵל מִהְיוֹתְךָ לִי עֶבֶד לְהָקִים אֶת־שִׁבְטֵי יַעֲקֹב, וּנְצוּרֵי יִשְׂרָאֵל לְהָשִׁיב:

To open blind eyes, to bring the captive out of the dungeon, those who sit in darkness out of their prison.

It is not enough that you should be My servant only to re-establish the tribes of Jacob and to restore the survivors of Israel:

וּנְתַתִּיךָ לְאוֹר גּוֹיִם, לִהְיוֹת יְשׁוּעָתִי עַד־קְצֵה הָאָרֶץ.
וְנִבְרְכוּ בְךָ כָּל־מִשְׁפְּחֹת הָאֲדָמָה, וּבְזַרְעֶךָ.

I will make you a light to the nations, that My deliverance may reach to the ends of the earth.

Through you and through your descendants shall all the families of the earth be blessed.

◆ ◆

MEDITATION

The sense of being chosen impressed itself deeply on the soul of our people. And yet they did not consider themselves superior to other nations, for they knew that all humans are God's children. It was not their lineage but the possession of Torah that made them a choice people. For centuries they stood alone in upholding divine truth and the way of Torah in a world steeped in ignorance, superstition, and cruelty. Yet they always believed that others, too, might be chosen, if only they would choose the way of God.

Only one privilege did they claim, that of serving God and His truth. And with that privilege came an exacting responsibility: "You, of all the families of the earth, have known Me best; therefore I will hold you all the more accountable for your iniquities."

Israel gave birth in time to other religions that have brought many to God, but our responsibility continues, for our mission remains unfulfilled. It will continue until the earth is full of the knowledge of the Lord as the sea-bed is covered by water.

◆ ◆

כִּי הֶהָרִים יָמוּשׁוּ וְהַגְּבָעוֹת תְּמוּטֶינָה, וְחַסְדִּי מֵאִתֵּךְ לֹא־
יָמוּשׁ וּבְרִית שְׁלוֹמִי לֹא־תָמוּט, אָמַר מְרַחֲמֵךְ יְיָ.

For the mountains may depart, and the hills be removed, but My steadfast love shall not depart from you, and My covenant of peace shall not be removed, says the Lord, who has compassion on you.

◆ ◆

O God of Israel, teach us to be worthy of the name of Jew. May we do nothing to disgrace it. May our every act bring honor to our faith and glory to Your name. May we understand our responsibility as Jews, to continue the task begun by earlier generations of our people who achieved greatness by their faith in the mission to which You had called them: to serve in Your name, to bring light and blessing to all the families of the earth.

◆ ◆

I am a Jew because the faith of Israel demands of me no abdication of the mind.

I am a Jew because the faith of Israel requires of me all the devotion of my heart.

I am a Jew because in every place where suffering weeps, the Jew weeps.

I am a Jew because at every time when despair cries out, the Jew hopes.

I am a Jew because the word of Israel is the oldest and the newest.

I am a Jew because the promise of Israel is the universal promise.

I am a Jew because, for Israel, the world is not completed: we are completing it.

I am a Jew because, for Israel, humanity is not created; we are creating it.

I am a Jew because Israel places humanity and its unity above the nations and above Israel itself.

I am a Jew because, above humanity, image of the divine Unity, Israel places the unity which is divine.

◆ ◆

To be a Jew in the twentieth century
Is to be offered a gift. If you refuse,
Wishing to be invisible, you choose
Death of the spirit, the stone insanity.
Accepting, take full life, full agonies:
Your evening deep in labyrinthine blood
Of those who resist, fail, and resist; and God
Reduced to a hostage among hostages.

The gift is torment. Not alone the still
Torture, isolation; or torture of the flesh.
That may come also. But the accepting wish,
The whole and fertile spirit as guarantee
For every human freedom, suffering to be free,
Daring to live for the impossible.

◆ ◆

אַשְׁרֵינוּ!
מַה־טּוֹב חֶלְקֵנוּ,
וּמַה־נָּעִים גּוֹרָלֵנוּ,
וּמַה־יָּפָה יְרֻשָּׁתֵנוּ!

How greatly we are blessed!
How good is our portion!
How pleasant our lot!
How beautiful our heritage!

Redemption

אֲנִי מַאֲמִין בֶּאֱמוּנָה שְׁלֵמָה בְּבִיאַת הַמָּשִׁיחַ. וְאַף עַל פִּי שֶׁיִּתְמַהְמֵהַּ, עִם כָּל זֶה אֲנִי מַאֲמִין, עִם כָּל זֶה אֲחַכֶּה לוֹ בְּכָל יוֹם שֶׁיָּבוֹא.

I believe with perfect faith in the Messiah's coming. And even if he be delayed, I will await him.

◆ ◆

And I tell you the good in us will win,
Over all our wickedness, over all the wrongs we have done.
We will look back at the pages of written history, and be amazed, and then we will laugh and sing,
And the good that is in us, children in their cradles, will have won.

Here I stand, the Jew, marked by history, for who can count how long?
Wrapped in compassion as in a Tallith, staring every storm in the face.
Write songs of pain, sing prayers of torment, refresh yourself with suffering.
Too much for one people, small and weak — it is enough to share out among the whole human race.
But God has planted in me goodness, compassion, as a mother loves her children,
So I writhe with pain, weep and sing, sing and weep,
For the blood knows the heart of the world is not made of stone,
The wonderful light of God's face is for all eternity stamped on it firm and deep.

And the heart feels that there is a day and an hour, and a mountain called Zion,
And then all the sufferings will gather there and will all become song,

Ringing out into every corner of the earth, from end to end,
And the nations will hear it, and like caravans in the desert will all to that mountain throng.

◆ ◆

הַרְעִיפוּ, שָׁמַיִם, מִמַּעַל, וּשְׁחָקִים יִזְּלוּ־צֶדֶק; תִּפְתַּח־אֶרֶץ,
וְיִפְרוּ־יֶשַׁע, וּצְדָקָה תַצְמִיחַ יַחַד.

Pour down, O heavens, from above, and let the sky rain righteousness; let the earth open, that deliverance may flourish, and let righteousness too spring up.

◆ ◆

וְאָמַר בַּיּוֹם הַהוּא:
הִנֵּה אֱלֹהֵינוּ זֶה! קִוִּינוּ לוֹ וְיוֹשִׁיעֵנוּ.

And it will be said on that day:
Behold our God! We have waited for Him and His deliverance.

זֶה יְיָ; קִוִּינוּ לוֹ:
נָגִילָה וְנִשְׂמְחָה בִּישׁוּעָתוֹ.

This is the Lord; we have waited for Him:
Let us be glad and rejoice in His deliverance.

כָּל־גֶּיא יִנָּשֵׂא;
וְכָל־הַר וְגִבְעָה יִשְׁפָּלוּ;
וְהָיָה הֶעָקֹב לְמִישׁוֹר,
וְהָרְכָסִים לְבִקְעָה.

Every valley shall be exalted;
Every mountain and hill made low;
The uneven ground shall be made level,
And the rough places a plain.

וְנִגְלָה כְּבוֹד יְיָ,
וְרָאוּ כָל־בָּשָׂר יַחְדָּו.

The glory of the Lord shall be revealed,
And all flesh, united, shall see it.

וְהָיָה אַחֲרֵי־כֵן אֶשְׁפּוֹךְ אֶת־רוּחִי עַל־כָּל־בָּשָׂר,
וְנִבְּאוּ בְּנֵיכֶם וּבְנוֹתֵיכֶם.

זִקְנֵיכֶם חֲלוֹמוֹת יַחֲלֹמוּן,
בַּחוּרֵיכֶם חֶזְיֹנוֹת יִרְאוּ.

And it shall come to pass that I will pour out My spirit on all flesh:
Your sons and daughters shall prophesy.

Your old shall dream dreams,
Your young shall see visions.

לֹא־יִשָּׁמַע עוֹד חָמָס בְּאַרְצֵךְ, שֹׁד וָשֶׁבֶר בִּגְבוּלָיִךְ;
וְקָרָאת 'יְשׁוּעָה' חוֹמֹתַיִךְ, וּשְׁעָרַיִךְ 'תְּהִלָּה.'

Violence shall no more be heard in your land, devastation and destruction within your borders;
But you shall call your walls 'Salvation' and your gates 'Praise.'

לֹא־יִהְיֶה־לָּךְ עוֹד הַשֶּׁמֶשׁ לְאוֹר יוֹמָם, וּלְנֹגַהּ הַיָּרֵחַ לֹא־יָאִיר לָךְ;
וְהָיָה־לָךְ יְיָ לְאוֹר עוֹלָם וֵאלֹהַיִךְ לְתִפְאַרְתֵּךְ.

The sun shall no more be your light by day, nor shall the moon give light to you by night;
But the Lord shall be your everlasting light: your God shall be your glory.

לֹא־יָרֵעוּ וְלֹא־יַשְׁחִיתוּ בְּכָל־הַר קָדְשִׁי, כִּי־מָלְאָה הָאָרֶץ דֵּעָה אֶת־יְיָ כַּמַּיִם לַיָּם מְכַסִּים.

They shall not hurt or destroy in all My holy mountain;
For the earth shall be full of the knowledge of the Lord as the sea-bed is covered by water.

◆ ◆

וְיֶאֱתָיוּ כֹּל לְעָבְדֶךָ, וִיבָרְכוּ שֵׁם כְּבוֹדֶךָ, וְיַגִּידוּ בָאִיִּים צִדְקֶךָ. וְיִדְרְשׁוּךָ עַמִּים לֹא יְדָעוּךָ, וִיהַלְלוּךָ כָּל־אַפְסֵי אָרֶץ, וְיֹאמְרוּ תָמִיד: יִגְדַּל יְיָ.

וְיִזְבְּחוּ לְךָ אֶת־זִבְחֵיהֶם, וְיִזְנְחוּ אֶת־עֲצַבֵּיהֶם, וְיַחְפְּרוּ עִם פְּסִילֵיהֶם, וְיַטּוּ שְׁכֶם אֶחָד לְעָבְדֶךָ. וְיִירָאוּךָ עִם שֶׁמֶשׁ מְבַקְשֵׁי פָנֶיךָ, וְיַכִּירוּ כֹּחַ מַלְכוּתֶךָ, וְיִלְמְדוּ תוֹעִים בִּינָה.

וְיִפְצְחוּ הָרִים רִנָּה, וְיִצְהֲלוּ אִיִּים בְּמָלְכֶךָ, וִיקַבְּלוּ עֹל מַלְכוּתְךָ. וִירוֹמְמוּךָ בִּקְהַל עָם, וְיִשְׁמְעוּ רְחוֹקִים וְיָבוֹאוּ, וְיִתְּנוּ לְךָ כֶּתֶר מְלוּכָה.

All the world shall come to serve You,
And bless Your glorious name,
And Your righteousness triumphant
The islands shall proclaim.
And the peoples shall go seeking
Who knew You not before,
And the ends of earth shall praise You,
And tell Your greatness o'er.

They shall build for You their altars,
Their idols overthrown,
And their graven gods shall shame them,
As they turn to You alone.
They shall worship You at sunrise,
And feel Your kingdom's might,
And impart their understanding
To those astray in night.

With the coming of Your kingdom
The hills shall shout with song,
And the islands laugh exultant
That they to God belong.
And through all Your congregations
So loud Your praise shall ring,
That the utmost peoples, hearing,
Shall hail You crowned King.

Doubt

MEDITATION

Cherish your doubts, for doubt is the handmaiden of truth. Doubt is the key to the door of knowledge; it is the servant of discovery. A belief which may not be questioned binds us to error, for there is incompleteness and imperfection in every belief.

Doubt is the touchstone of truth; it is an acid which eats away the false.

Let none fear for the truth, that doubt may consume it; for doubt is a testing of belief.

For truth, if it be truth, arises from each testing stronger, more secure. Those who would silence doubt are filled with fear; the house of their spirit is built on shifting sands.

But they that fear not doubt, and know its use, are founded on a rock.

They shall walk in the light of growing knowledge; the work of their hands shall endure.

Therefore, let us not fear doubt, but let us rejoice in its help: It is to the wise as a staff to the blind; doubt is the handmaiden of truth.

◆ ◆

צַדִּיק אַתָּה, יְיָ, כִּי אָרִיב אֵלֶיךָ, אַךְ מִשְׁפָּטִים אֲדַבֵּר אוֹתָךְ.
מַדּוּעַ דֶּרֶךְ רְשָׁעִים צָלֵחָה, שָׁלוּ כָּל־בֹּגְדֵי בָגֶד?

You are just, O Eternal One, and so I must contend with You, therefore plead my case before You. Why do the wicked prosper and traitors live at ease?

נְטַעְתָּם, גַּם־שֹׁרָשׁוּ, יֵלְכוּ, גַּם־עָשׂוּ פֶרִי. קָרוֹב אַתָּה בְּפִיהֶם
וְרָחוֹק מִכִּלְיוֹתֵיהֶם.

You have planted them, their roots strike deep, they flourish and bear fruit. You are ever on their lips, yet far from their hearts.

עַד־מָתַי תֶּאֱבַל הָאָרֶץ וְעֵשֶׂב כָּל־הַשָּׂדֶה יִיבָשׁ? מֵרָעַת יֹשְׁבֵי־
בָהּ סָפְתָה בְהֵמוֹת וָעוֹף, כִּי אָמְרוּ ׳לֹא יִרְאֶה אֶת־אַחֲרִיתֵנוּ.׳

How long must the land lie parched and its green grass wither? So wicked are its people who say, 'God does not see the result of what we are doing,' that there are no birds or beasts left!

◆ ◆

From Job 38

וַיַּעַן־יְיָ אֶת אִיּוֹב מִן הַסְּעָרָה וַיֹּאמַר:
מִי זֶה מַחְשִׁיךְ עֵצָה בְמִלִּין בְּלִי־דָעַת?

Then the Eternal answered Job out of the whirlwind:
Who is this whose ignorant words cloud My design in darkness?

אֵיפֹה הָיִיתָ בְּיָסְדִי־אָרֶץ? הַגֵּד, אִם־יָדַעְתָּ בִינָה: מִי־שָׂם מְמַדֶּיהָ? כִּי תֵדָע!
מִי־יָרָה אֶבֶן פִּנָּתָהּ, בְּרָן־יַחַד כּוֹכְבֵי בֹקֶר, וַיָּרִיעוּ כָּל־בְּנֵי אֱלֹהִים?

Where were you when I laid the earth's foundations? Tell me, if you have understanding: Who settled its dimensions? Surely you should know!
Who laid its cornerstone, when the morning stars sang together, and all the sons of God shouted for joy?

וַיָּסֶךְ בִּדְלָתַיִם יָם בְּגִיחוֹ מֵרֶחֶם יֵצֵא? בְּשׂוּמִי עָנָן לְבֻשׁוֹ וַעֲרָפֶל חֲתֻלָּתוֹ, וָאֶשְׁבֹּר עָלָיו חֻקִּי, וָאָשִׂים בְּרִיחַ וּדְלָתָיִם, וָאֹמַר: ׳עַד־פֹּה תָבוֹא וְלֹא תֹסִיף, וּפֹא־יָשִׁיב בִּגְאוֹן גַּלֶּיךָ.׳
הֲנִגְלוּ לְךָ שַׁעֲרֵי־מָוֶת?

Who watched over the birth of the sea when it burst in flood from the womb, when I wrapped it in a blanket of cloud and cradled it in fog, when I established its bounds, fixing its doors and bars in place, and said: 'Thus far shall you come and no farther, and here shall your proud waves be stayed.'
Have the gates of death been revealed to you?

הִתְבֹּנַנְתָּ עַד־רַחֲבֵי־אָרֶץ?
הַתְקַשֵּׁר מַעֲדַנּוֹת כִּימָה אוֹ־מוֹשְׁכוֹת כְּסִיל תְּפַתֵּחַ?

Have you comprehended the vast expanse of the world?
Can you bind the cluster of the Pleiades or loose Orion's belt?

הֲיָדַעְתָּ חֻקּוֹת שָׁמָיִם, אִם־תָּשִׂים מִשְׁטָרוֹ בָאָרֶץ?

Did you proclaim the rules that govern the heavens, or determine the laws of nature on earth?

◆ ◆

From Ecclesiastes 4

וְשַׁבְתִּי אֲנִי, וָאֶרְאֶה אֶת־כָּל־הָעֲשֻׁקִים אֲשֶׁר נַעֲשִׂים תַּחַת הַשָּׁמֶשׁ; וְהִנֵּה דִּמְעַת הָעֲשֻׁקִים, וְאֵין לָהֶם מְנַחֵם. וּמִיַּד עֹשְׁקֵיהֶם כֹּחַ, וְאֵין לָהֶם מְנַחֵם.

Again, I considered all the acts of oppression here under the sun; I saw the tears of the oppressed, and I saw that there was none to comfort them. Strength was on the side of their oppressors, and there was none to comfort them.

וְשַׁבֵּחַ אֲנִי אֶת־הַמֵּתִים שֶׁכְּבָר מֵתוּ, מִן־הַחַיִּים אֲשֶׁר הֵמָּה חַיִּים עֲדֶנָה. וְטוֹב מִשְּׁנֵיהֶם אֵת אֲשֶׁר־עֲדֶן לֹא הָיָה, אֲשֶׁר לֹא־רָאָה אֶת־הַמַּעֲשֶׂה הָרָע אֲשֶׁר נַעֲשָׂה תַּחַת הַשָּׁמֶשׁ.

I counted the dead happy because they were dead, happier than the living who were still in life. And more fortunate than either, the one yet unborn, who had not witnessed the evil deeds done here under the sun.

◆ ◆

MEDITATION

I do not know how to ask You, Lord of the world, and even if I did know, I could not bear to do it. How could I venture to ask You why everything happens as it does, why we are driven from one exile into another, why our foes are allowed to torment us so. But in the Hagadah, the father of him 'who does not know how to ask' is told: "It is for you to disclose it to him." And, Lord of the world, am I not your son? I do not ask you to reveal to me the secret of Your ways — I could not bear it! But show me one thing: show me what this very moment means to me, what it demands of me, what You, Lord, are telling me through my life at this moment. O I do not ask You to tell me *why* I suffer, but only whether I suffer for Your sake!

◆ ◆

הַעִדֹתִי בָכֶם הַיּוֹם אֶת־הַשָּׁמַיִם וְאֶת־הָאָרֶץ: הַחַיִּים וְהַמָּוֶת נָתַתִּי לְפָנֶיךָ, הַבְּרָכָה וְהַקְּלָלָה. וּבָחַרְתָּ בַּחַיִּים, לְמַעַן תִּחְיֶה, אַתָּה וְזַרְעֶךָ, לְאַהֲבָה אֶת־יְיָ אֱלֹהֶיךָ, לִשְׁמֹעַ בְּקֹלוֹ, וּלְדָבְקָה־בוֹ.

I call heaven and earth to witness against you this day: I have put before you life and death, the blessing and the curse. Therefore choose life, that you and your children may live, by loving the Eternal God, heeding His commands, and holding fast to Him.

הֲלוֹא, אִם־תֵּיטִיב, שְׂאֵת, וְאִם לֹא תֵיטִיב, לַפֶּתַח חַטָּאת רֹבֵץ, וְאֵלֶיךָ תְּשׁוּקָתוֹ; וְאַתָּה תִּמְשָׁל־בּוֹ.

Surely, if you do right, there is hope. But if you do not do right, sin is the demon at the door, whose urge is toward you; yet you can be its master.

◆ ◆

רַבִּים אֹמְרִים: מִי־יַרְאֵנוּ טוֹב! נְסָה־עָלֵינוּ אוֹר פָּנֶיךָ, יְיָ! נָתַתָּה שִׂמְחָה בְלִבִּי, מֵעֵת דְּגָנָם וְתִירוֹשָׁם רָבּוּ. בְּשָׁלוֹם יַחְדָּו אֶשְׁכְּבָה וְאִישָׁן, כִּי־אַתָּה, יְיָ, לְבָדָד, לָבֶטַח תּוֹשִׁיבֵנִי.

There are many who say: "O that we might see some good! Bestow Your favor upon us, O Eternal One!" And yet You have put joy in my heart, more than others have when their grain and their wine abound. In peace I will both lie down and sleep, for You alone, Lord, make me live unafraid.

◆ ◆

All rise

יִתְגַּדַּל וְיִתְקַדַּשׁ שְׁמֵהּ רַבָּא בְּעָלְמָא דִּי־בְרָא כִרְעוּתֵהּ,
וְיַמְלִיךְ מַלְכוּתֵהּ בְּחַיֵּיכוֹן וּבְיוֹמֵיכוֹן וּבְחַיֵּי דְכָל־בֵּית
יִשְׂרָאֵל, בַּעֲגָלָא וּבִזְמַן קָרִיב, וְאִמְרוּ: אָמֵן.

יְהֵא שְׁמֵהּ רַבָּא מְבָרַךְ לְעָלַם וּלְעָלְמֵי עָלְמַיָּא.

יִתְבָּרַךְ וְיִשְׁתַּבַּח, וְיִתְפָּאַר וְיִתְרוֹמַם וְיִתְנַשֵּׂא, וְיִתְהַדַּר
וְיִתְעַלֶּה וְיִתְהַלַּל שְׁמֵהּ דְּקוּדְשָׁא, בְּרִיךְ הוּא, לְעֵלָּא מִן
כָּל־בִּרְכָתָא וְשִׁירָתָא, תֻּשְׁבְּחָתָא וְנֶחֱמָתָא דַּאֲמִירָן בְּעָלְמָא,
וְאִמְרוּ: אָמֵן.

Let the glory of God be extolled, let His great name be hallowed in the world whose creation He willed. May His kingdom soon prevail, in our own day, our own lives, and the life of all Israel, and let us say: Amen.

Let His great name be blessed for ever and ever.

Let the name of the Holy One, blessed is He, be glorified, exalted and honored, though He is beyond all the praises, songs, and adorations that we can utter, and let us say: Amen.

All are seated

קדוש

KIDDUSH

For the Eve of Shabbat לליל שבת

The seventh day is consecrated to the Lord our God. With wine, our symbol of joy, we celebrate this day and its holiness. We give thanks for all our blessings, for life and health, for work and rest, for home and love and friendship. On Shabbat, eternal sign of creation, we remember that we are created in the divine image. We therefore raise the cup in thanksgiving:

בָּרוּךְ אַתָּה, יְיָ אֱלֹהֵינוּ, מֶלֶךְ הָעוֹלָם, בּוֹרֵא פְּרִי הַגָּפֶן.

בָּרוּךְ אַתָּה, יְיָ אֱלֹהֵינוּ, מֶלֶךְ הָעוֹלָם, אֲשֶׁר קִדְּשָׁנוּ בְּמִצְוֹתָיו וְרָצָה בָנוּ, וְשַׁבַּת קָדְשׁוֹ בְּאַהֲבָה וּבְרָצוֹן הִנְחִילָנוּ, זִכָּרוֹן לְמַעֲשֵׂה בְרֵאשִׁית. כִּי הוּא יוֹם תְּחִלָּה לְמִקְרָאֵי קֹדֶשׁ, זֵכֶר לִיצִיאַת מִצְרָיִם. כִּי־בָנוּ בָחַרְתָּ וְאוֹתָנוּ קִדַּשְׁתָּ מִכָּל־הָעַמִּים, וְשַׁבַּת קָדְשְׁךָ בְּאַהֲבָה וּבְרָצוֹן הִנְחַלְתָּנוּ. בָּרוּךְ אַתָּה, יְיָ, מְקַדֵּשׁ הַשַּׁבָּת.

Blessed is the Lord our God, Ruler of the universe, Creator of the fruit of the vine.

Blessed is the Lord our God, Ruler of the universe, who hallows us with His Mitzvot and takes delight in us. In His love and favor He has made His holy Sabbath our heritage, as a reminder of the work of creation. It is first among our sacred days, and a remembrance of the Exodus from Egypt.

O God, You have chosen us and set us apart from all the peoples, and in love and favor have given us the Sabbath day as a sacred inheritance. Blessed is the Lord, for the Sabbath and its holiness.

לשחרית של שבת

For the Morning of Shabbat

וְשָׁמְרוּ בְנֵי־יִשְׂרָאֵל אֶת־הַשַּׁבָּת, לַעֲשׂוֹת אֶת־הַשַּׁבָּת לְדֹרֹתָם
בְּרִית עוֹלָם. בֵּינִי וּבֵין בְּנֵי יִשְׂרָאֵל אוֹת הִיא לְעֹלָם, כִּי
שֵׁשֶׁת יָמִים עָשָׂה יְיָ אֶת־הַשָּׁמַיִם וְאֶת־הָאָרֶץ, וּבַיּוֹם הַשְּׁבִיעִי
שָׁבַת וַיִּנָּפַשׁ.

The people of Israel shall keep the Sabbath, observing the Sabbath in every generation as a covenant for all time. It is a sign for ever between Me and the people of Israel, for in six days the Eternal God made heaven and earth, and on the seventh day He rested from His labors.

עַל־כֵּן בֵּרַךְ יְיָ אֶת־יוֹם הַשַּׁבָּת וַיְקַדְּשֵׁהוּ.

Therefore the Lord blessed the seventh day and called it holy.

בָּרוּךְ אַתָּה, יְיָ אֱלֹהֵינוּ, מֶלֶךְ הָעוֹלָם, בּוֹרֵא פְּרִי הַגָּפֶן.

Blessed is the Lord our God, Ruler of the universe, Creator of the fruit of the vine.

For the Eve of Yom Tov לליל יום טוב

בָּרוּךְ אַתָּה, יְיָ אֱלֹהֵינוּ, מֶלֶךְ הָעוֹלָם, בּוֹרֵא פְּרִי הַגָּפֶן.

Blessed is the Lord our God, Ruler of the universe, Creator of the fruit of the vine.

בָּרוּךְ אַתָּה, יְיָ אֱלֹהֵינוּ, מֶלֶךְ הָעוֹלָם, אֲשֶׁר בָּחַר בָּנוּ מִכָּל־עָם, וְרוֹמְמָנוּ מִכָּל־לָשׁוֹן, וְקִדְּשָׁנוּ בְּמִצְוֹתָיו.

Blessed is the Lord our God, Ruler of the universe, who has chosen us from all the peoples, exalting us by hallowing us with His Mitzvot.

וַתִּתֶּן־לָנוּ, יְיָ אֱלֹהֵינוּ, בְּאַהֲבָה [שַׁבָּתוֹת לִמְנוּחָה וּ] מוֹעֲדִים לְשִׂמְחָה, חַגִּים וּזְמַנִּים לְשָׂשׂוֹן, אֶת־יוֹם [הַשַּׁבָּת הַזֶּה וְאֶת־יוֹם]

In Your love, O Lord our God, You have given us (Sabbaths of rest,) feasts of gladness and seasons of joy: this (Sabbath day and this) festival of

Pesach—season of our freedom,	חַג הַמַּצּוֹת הַזֶּה – זְמַן חֵרוּתֵנוּ,
Shavuot—season of revelation,	חַג הַשָּׁבֻעוֹת הַזֶּה – זְמַן מַתַּן תּוֹרָתֵנוּ,
Sukkot—season of thanksgiving,	חַג הַסֻּכּוֹת הַזֶּה – זְמַן שִׂמְחָתֵנוּ,
Atzeret-Simchat Torah—season of our gladness,	הַשְּׁמִינִי חַג הָעֲצֶרֶת הַזֶּה – זְמַן שִׂמְחָתֵנוּ,

מִקְרָא קֹדֶשׁ, זֵכֶר לִיצִיאַת מִצְרָיִם.

כִּי־בָנוּ בָחַרְתָּ וְאוֹתָנוּ קִדַּשְׁתָּ מִכָּל־הָעַמִּים, [וְשַׁבָּת] וּמוֹעֲדֵי קָדְשְׁךָ [בְּאַהֲבָה וּבְרָצוֹן,] בְּשִׂמְחָה וּבְשָׂשׂוֹן הִנְחַלְתָּנוּ.

בָּרוּךְ אַתָּה, יְיָ, מְקַדֵּשׁ [הַשַּׁבָּת וְ] יִשְׂרָאֵל וְהַזְּמַנִּים.

to unite in worship and recall the Exodus from Egypt. For You have chosen us from all peoples, consecrating us to Your service, and giving us (the Sabbath, a sign of Your love and favor, and) the Festivals, a time of gladness and joy.

Blessed is the Lord, who hallows (the Sabbath,) the House of Israel and the Festivals.

This blessing is not recited on the last day of Pesach

בָּרוּךְ אַתָּה, יְיָ אֱלֹהֵינוּ, מֶלֶךְ הָעוֹלָם, שֶׁהֶחֱיָנוּ וְקִיְּמָנוּ וְהִגִּיעָנוּ לַזְּמַן הַזֶּה.

Blessed is the Lord our God, Ruler of the universe, for giving us life, for sustaining us, and for enabling us to reach this season.

In the Sukkah

בָּרוּךְ אַתָּה, יְיָ אֱלֹהֵינוּ, מֶלֶךְ הָעוֹלָם, אֲשֶׁר קִדְּשָׁנוּ בְּמִצְוֹתָיו וְצִוָּנוּ לֵישֵׁב בַּסֻּכָּה.

Blessed is the Lord our God, Ruler of the universe, who hallows us with His Mitzvot, and commands us to celebrate in the Sukkah.

For food

בָּרוּךְ אַתָּה, יְיָ אֱלֹהֵינוּ, מֶלֶךְ הָעוֹלָם, הַמּוֹצִיא לֶחֶם מִן הָאָרֶץ.

Blessed is the Lord our God, Ruler of the universe, who causes bread to come forth from the earth.

לשחרית של יום טוב

For the Morning of Yom Tov

ON SHABBAT

וְשָׁמְרוּ בְנֵי־יִשְׂרָאֵל אֶת־הַשַּׁבָּת, לַעֲשׂוֹת אֶת־הַשַּׁבָּת לְדֹרֹתָם בְּרִית עוֹלָם. בֵּינִי וּבֵין בְּנֵי יִשְׂרָאֵל אוֹת הִיא לְעֹלָם, כִּי שֵׁשֶׁת יָמִים עָשָׂה יְיָ אֶת־הַשָּׁמַיִם וְאֶת־הָאָרֶץ, וּבַיּוֹם הַשְּׁבִיעִי שָׁבַת וַיִּנָּפַשׁ.

The people of Israel shall keep the Sabbath, observing the Sabbath in every generation as a covenant for all time. It is a sign for ever between Me and the people of Israel. For in six days the Eternal God made heaven and earth, and on the seventh day He rested from His labors.

עַל־כֵּן בֵּרַךְ יְיָ אֶת־יוֹם הַשַּׁבָּת וַיְקַדְּשֵׁהוּ.

Therefore the Lord blessed the seventh day and called it holy.

◆ ◆

אֵלֶּה מוֹעֲדֵי יְיָ, מִקְרָאֵי קֹדֶשׁ, אֲשֶׁר תִּקְרְאוּ אֹתָם בְּמוֹעֲדָם.

וַיְדַבֵּר מֹשֶׁה אֶת־מוֹעֲדֵי יְיָ אֶל־בְּנֵי יִשְׂרָאֵל.

These are the appointed seasons of the Lord, the sacred days, that you shall proclaim at their appointed times.

And Moses declared the appointed seasons of the Lord to the people of Israel.

בָּרוּךְ אַתָּה, יְיָ אֱלֹהֵינוּ, מֶלֶךְ הָעוֹלָם, בּוֹרֵא פְּרִי הַגָּפֶן.

Blessed is the Lord our God, Ruler of the universe, Creator of the fruit of the vine.

◆ ◆

In the Sukkah

בָּרוּךְ אַתָּה, יְיָ אֱלֹהֵינוּ, מֶלֶךְ הָעוֹלָם, אֲשֶׁר קִדְּשָׁנוּ בְּמִצְוֹתָיו, וְצִוָּנוּ לֵישֵׁב בַּסֻּכָּה.

Blessed is the Lord our God, Ruler of the universe, who hallows us with His Mitzvot, and commands us to celebrate in the Sukkah.

◆ ◆

For food

בָּרוּךְ אַתָּה, יְיָ אֱלֹהֵינוּ, מֶלֶךְ הָעוֹלָם, הַמּוֹצִיא לֶחֶם מִן הָאָרֶץ.

Blessed is the Lord our God, Ruler of the universe, who causes bread to come forth from the earth.

שירים וזמירות

SONGS AND HYMNS

Index to Songs and Hymns

Adon Olam 729
Al Hanisim 759
Al Shelosha Devarim 751
All the World 710
Amar Rabbi Akiva 751
Amar Rabbi Elazar 751
America the Beautiful 763
Ani Maamin 753
Anim Zemirot 745
Ashreinu 746
Ata Echad 747
Baruch Eloheinu 747
Come, O Holy Sabbath Evening 738
Come, O Sabbath Day 737
Could We with Ink 755
David Melech 750
Deror Yikra 743
Early Will I Seek You 332
Eileh Chameda Libi 742
Eili Eili 267
Ein Adir 756
Ein Keiloheinu 730
Esa Einai 748
Father, Hear the Prayer 761
From Heaven's Heights the Thunder Peals 755
God of Might 754
God of our People 764
Halleluhu, Praise Him 379
Hatikva 765
Hoshia Et Amecha 752
How Good It Is 739
If Our God Had Not Befriended 753
Im Ein Ani Li Mi Li 751
In the Wilderness 755
Ivedu 749
Ki Eshmera Shabbat 742
Lecha Dodi 736
Lo Yisa Goi 748
Magein Avot 744
Ma Navu 750
Maoz Tsur 758
Menucha Vesimcha 741
Mi Ha-ish 749
Mi Yemaleil 757
O God, Our Help 762
O Holy Sabbath Day 738
O Lord, Where Shall I Find You? 761
O Worship the King 762
Pitechu Li 750
Queen Sabbath 733
Rad Halaila 752
Rock of Ages 758
Sachaki, Sachaki 690
Shachar Avakeshecha 745
Shalom Aleichem 735
Shomeir Yisraeil 747
Shoshanat Yaakov 760
Song of the Partisans 574
Spring-Tide of the Year 754
Sweet Hymns and Songs 364
Take Unto You 757
The Lord of All 730
The National Anthem 764
There Lives A God 763
Tov Lehodot 744
Utsu Eitsa 760
Vatik 742
Vehaeir Eineinu 746

Veheishiv Leiv Avot 749
Vetaheir Libeinu 743
We Praise the Living God 732
When This Song of Praise 761
Yah Ribon 740
Yedid Nefesh 742
Yerushalayim 592
Yigdal 731
Yismechu Hashamayim 261
Yom Zeh Leyisraeil 734
Yom Zeh Mechubad 740

A NOTE ON TRANSLITERATION

The system employed in this Prayerbook is, with minor deviations, the "Proposed Standard Romanization of Hebrew" prepared for the American National Standards Institute.

Vowels and Consonants for Special Notice

a	as in 'papa' (short) or 'father' (long)
e	as in 'get' or 'the' (sheva)
eh	as in 'get' (used only at the end of a word)
i	as in 'bit' (short) or 'machine' (long)
o	as in 'often'
u	as in 'pull' (short) or 'rule' (long)
ai	as in 'aisle'
oi	as in 'boil'
ei	as in 'veil'
g	as in 'get' (hard 'g')
ch	as in Scottish 'loch' or German 'ach'

1

ADON OLAM	אדון עולם
A·don o·lam, a·sher ma·lach	אֲדוֹן עוֹלָם, אֲשֶׁר מָלַךְ
be·te·rem kol ye·tsir niv·ra,	בְּטֶרֶם כָּל־יְצִיר נִבְרָא,
le·eit na·a·sa ve·chef·tso kol,	לְעֵת נַעֲשָׂה בְחֶפְצוֹ כֹּל,
a·zai me·lech she·mo nik·ra.	אֲזַי מֶלֶךְ שְׁמוֹ נִקְרָא.
Ve·a·cha·rei ki·che·lot ha·kol,	וְאַחֲרֵי כִּכְלוֹת הַכֹּל,
le·va·do yim·loch no·ra,	לְבַדּוֹ יִמְלוֹךְ נוֹרָא,
ve·hu ha·ya, ve·hu ho·veh,	וְהוּא הָיָה, וְהוּא הֹוֶה,
ve·hu yi·he·yeh be·tif·a·ra.	וְהוּא יִהְיֶה בְּתִפְאָרָה.
Ve·hu e·chad, ve·ein shei·ni	וְהוּא אֶחָד, וְאֵין שֵׁנִי
le·ham·shil lo, le·hach·bi·ra,	לְהַמְשִׁיל לוֹ, לְהַחְבִּירָה,
be·li rei·shit, be·li tach·lit,	בְּלִי רֵאשִׁית, בְּלִי תַכְלִית,
ve·lo ha·oz ve·ha·mis·ra.	וְלוֹ הָעֹז וְהַמִּשְׂרָה.
Ve·hu Ei·li, ve·chai go·a·li,	וְהוּא אֵלִי, וְחַי גּוֹאֲלִי,
ve·tsur chev·li be·eit tsa·ra,	וְצוּר חֶבְלִי בְּעֵת צָרָה,
ve·hu ni·si u·ma·nos li,	וְהוּא נִסִּי וּמָנוֹס לִי,
me·nat ko·si be·yom ek·ra.	מְנָת כּוֹסִי בְּיוֹם אֶקְרָא.
Be·ya·do af·kid ru·chi	בְּיָדוֹ אַפְקִיד רוּחִי
be·eit i·shan ve·a·i·ra,	בְּעֵת אִישַׁן וְאָעִירָה,
ve·im ru·chi ge·vi·ya·ti:	וְעִם־רוּחִי גְּוִיָּתִי:
A·do·nai li, ve·lo i·ra.	יְיָ לִי, וְלֹא אִירָא.

He is the eternal Lord, who reigned before any being had yet been created; when all was done according to His will, already then His name was King.

And after all has ceased to be, still will He reign in solitary majesty; He was, He is, and He shall be in glory.

And He is One; none other can compare to Him, or consort with Him; He is without beginning, without end; to Him belong power and dominion.

And He is *my* God, my living Redeemer, my Rock in time of trouble and distress; He is my banner and my refuge, my benefactor when I call on Him.

Into His hands I entrust my spirit, when I sleep and when I wake; and with my spirit, my body also: the Lord is with me, I will not fear.

2

THE LORD OF ALL

The Lord of all, who reigned supreme,
Ere first creation's form was framed;
When all was finished by His will,
His name Almighty was proclaimed.

When this, our world, shall be no more,
In majesty He still shall reign,
Who was, who is, who will remain,
His endless glory we proclaim.

Alone is He, beyond compare,
Without division or ally,
Without initial date or end,
Omnipotent He rules on high.

He is my God, my Savior He,
To whom I turn in sorrow's hour —
My banner proud, my refuge sure,
Who hears and answers with His pow'r.

Then in His hand myself I lay,
And trusting sleep, and wake with cheer;
My soul and body are His care;
The Lord does guard, I have no fear.

3

EIN KEILOHEINU

אין כאלהינו

Ein kei·lo·hei·nu, ein ka·do·nei·nu,

ein ke·mal·kei·nu, ein ke·mo·shi·ei·nu.

Mi chei·lo·hei·nu? Mi cha·do·nei·nu?

Mi che·mal·kei·nu? Mi che·mo·shi·ei·nu?

No·deh lei·lo·hei·nu, no·deh
la·do·nei·nu,
no·deh le·mal·kei·nu, no·deh
le·mo·shi·ei·nu.
Ba·ruch E·lo·hei·nu, ba·ruch
A·do·nei·nu,
ba·ruch Mal·kei·nu, ba·ruch
Mo·shi·ei·nu.

אֵין כֵּאלֹהֵינוּ, אֵין כַּאדוֹנֵינוּ,
אֵין כְּמַלְכֵּנוּ, אֵין כְּמוֹשִׁיעֵנוּ.
מִי כֵאלֹהֵינוּ? מִי כַאדוֹנֵינוּ?
מִי כְמַלְכֵּנוּ? מִי כְמוֹשִׁיעֵנוּ?
נוֹדֶה לֵאלֹהֵינוּ, נוֹדֶה לַאדוֹנֵינוּ,
נוֹדֶה לְמַלְכֵּנוּ, נוֹדֶה לְמוֹשִׁיעֵנוּ.
בָּרוּךְ אֱלֹהֵינוּ, בָּרוּךְ אֲדוֹנֵינוּ,
בָּרוּךְ מַלְכֵּנוּ, בָּרוּךְ מוֹשִׁיעֵנוּ.

A·ta hu E·lo·hei·nu,	אַתָּה הוּא אֱלֹהֵינוּ,
a·ta hu A·do·nei·nu,	אַתָּה הוּא אֲדוֹנֵינוּ,
A·ta hu Mal·kei·nu,	אַתָּה הוּא מַלְכֵּנוּ,
a·ta hu Mo·shi·ei·nu.	אַתָּה הוּא מוֹשִׁיעֵנוּ.

There is none like our God; there is none like our Lord; there is none like our King; there is none like our Savior.

Who is like our God? Who is like our Lord? Who is like our King? Who is like our Savior?

We will give thanks to our God; we will give thanks to our Lord; we will give thanks to our King; we will give thanks to our Savior.

Blessed is our God; blessed is our Lord; blessed is our King; blessed is our Savior.

You are our God; You are our Lord; You are our King; You are our Savior.

4

YIGDAL — יגדל

Yig·dal E·lo·him chai ve·yish·ta·bach,	יִגְדַּל אֱלֹהִים חַי וְיִשְׁתַּבַּח,
nim·tsa ve·ein eit el me·tsi·u·to.	נִמְצָא וְאֵין עֵת אֶל־מְצִיאוּתוֹ.
E·chad ve·ein ya·chid ke·yi·chu·do,	אֶחָד וְאֵין יָחִיד כְּיִחוּדוֹ,
ne·lam ve·gam ein sof le·ach·du·to.	נֶעְלָם וְגַם אֵין סוֹף לְאַחְדוּתוֹ.
Ein lo de·mut ha·guf ve·ei·no guf,	אֵין לוֹ דְמוּת הַגּוּף וְאֵינוֹ גוּף,
lo na·a·roch ei·lav ke·du·sha·to.	לֹא נַעֲרוֹךְ אֵלָיו קְדֻשָּׁתוֹ.
Kad·mon le·chol da·var a·sher niv·ra,	קַדְמוֹן לְכָל־דָּבָר אֲשֶׁר נִבְרָא,
ri·shon ve·ein rei·shit le·rei·shi·to.	רִאשׁוֹן וְאֵין רֵאשִׁית לְרֵאשִׁיתוֹ.
Hi·no a·don o·lam, le·chol no·tsar	הִנּוֹ אֲדוֹן עוֹלָם, לְכָל־נוֹצָר
yo·reh ge·du·la·to u·mal·chu·to.	יוֹרֶה גְדֻלָּתוֹ וּמַלְכוּתוֹ.
She·fa ne·vu·a·to ne·ta·no,	שֶׁפַע נְבוּאָתוֹ נְתָנוֹ,
el a·ne·shei se·gu·la·to ve·tif·ar·to.	אֶל־אַנְשֵׁי סְגֻלָּתוֹ וְתִפְאַרְתּוֹ.
Lo kam be·yis·ra·eil ke·mo·sheh od	לֹא קָם בְּיִשְׂרָאֵל כְּמֹשֶׁה עוֹד
na·vi u·ma·bit et te·mu·na·to,	נָבִיא וּמַבִּיט אֶת־תְּמוּנָתוֹ,
To·rat e·met na·tan le·a·mo Eil,	תּוֹרַת אֱמֶת נָתַן לְעַמּוֹ אֵל,
al yad ne·vi·o ne·e·man bei·to.	עַל יַד נְבִיאוֹ נֶאֱמַן בֵּיתוֹ.

Lo ya·cha·lif ha·eil, ve·lo ya·mir	לֹא יַחֲלִיף הָאֵל, וְלֹא יָמִיר
da·to, le·o·la·mim le·zu·la·to.	דָּתוֹ, לְעוֹלָמִים לְזוּלָתוֹ.
Tso·feh ve·yo·dei·a se·ta·rei·nu,	צוֹפֶה וְיוֹדֵעַ סְתָרֵינוּ,
ma·bit le·sof da·var be·kad·ma·to.	מַבִּיט לְסוֹף דָּבָר בְּקַדְמָתוֹ.
Go·meil le·ish che·sed ke·mif·a·lo,	גּוֹמֵל לְאִישׁ חֶסֶד כְּמִפְעָלוֹ,
no·tein le·ra·sha ra ke·rish·a·to.	נוֹתֵן לְרָשָׁע רַע כְּרִשְׁעָתוֹ.
Yish·lach le·keits ya·min pe·dut o·lam,	יִשְׁלַח לְקֵץ יָמִין פְּדוּת עוֹלָם,
kol chai ve·yeish ya·kir ye·shu·a·to.	כָּל־חַי וְיֵשׁ יַכִּיר יְשׁוּעָתוֹ.
Cha·yei o·lam na·ta be·to·chei·nu,	חַיֵּי עוֹלָם נָטַע בְּתוֹכֵנוּ,
ba·ruch a·dei ad sheim te·hi·la·to.	בָּרוּךְ עֲדֵי עַד שֵׁם תְּהִלָּתוֹ.

Magnified and praised be the living God; His existence is eternal. He is One and unique in His unity; He is unfathomable, and His Oneness is unending. He has no bodily form, He is incorporeal; His holiness is beyond compare. He preceded all creation; He is the First, and He Himself has no beginning.

Behold the eternal Lord, who reveals His greatness and sovereignty to every creature. He inspired with the gift of prophecy those whom He chose to make known His glory.

Never has there been a prophet like Moses, whose closeness to God is unmatched. A Torah of truth did God give to His people, through His prophet, His faithful servant.

God does not change; His teaching will not be supplanted; He will always be the same. He watches us and knows our secret thoughts; He perceives the end of every matter before it begins.

He deals kindly with those who merit kindness, and brings upon the wicked the evil consequences of their deeds. At the end of days He will send an everlasting redemption; all that lives and breathes shall witness His deliverance.

He has implanted eternal life within us. Blessed is His glorious name to all eternity.

5

YIGDAL (*A Metrical Version*)

We praise the living God,
For ever praise His name,
Who was and is and is to be
For e'er the same;

The One eternal God
Before our world appears,
And there can be no end of time
Beyond His years.

Without a form is He,
Nor can we comprehend
The measure of His love for us —
Without an end.
For He is Lord of all,
Creation speaks His praise.
The human race and all that grows
His will obeys.

He knows our every thought,
Our birth and death ordains;
He understands our fervent dreams,
Our hopes and our pains.
Eternal life has He
Implanted in our soul.
We dedicate our life to Him —
His way, our goal!

6

QUEEN SABBATH

שבת המלכה

Ha·cha·ma mel·rosh ha·i·la·not nis·tal·le·ka,	הַחַמָּה מֵרֹאשׁ הָאִילָנוֹת נִסְתַּלְּקָה,
Bo·u ve·nei·tsei lik·rat Sha·bat ha·mal·ka.	בֹּאוּ וְנֵצֵא לִקְרַאת שַׁבָּת הַמַּלְכָּה.
Hi·nei hi yo·re·det, ha·ke·do·sha ha·be·ru·cha,	הִנֵּה הִיא יוֹרֶדֶת, הַקְּדוֹשָׁה הַבְּרוּכָה,
Ve·i·ma mal·a·chim, tse·va sha·lom u·me·nu·cha.	וְעִמָּהּ מַלְאָכִים, צְבָא שָׁלוֹם וּמְנוּחָה.
Bo·i, bo·i ha·mal·ka!	בֹּאִי, בֹּאִי הַמַּלְכָּה!
Bo·i, bo·i ha·ka·la!	בֹּאִי, בֹּאִי הַכַּלָּה!
Sha·lom a·lei·chem, mal·a·chei ha·sha·lom.	שָׁלוֹם עֲלֵיכֶם מַלְאֲכֵי הַשָּׁלוֹם.

The sun on the treetops no longer is seen,
Come gather to welcome the Sabbath, our queen.
Behold her descending, the holy, the blessed,

And with her the angels of peace and of rest.
Draw near, draw near, and here abide,
Draw near, draw near, O Sabbath bride.
Peace also to you, you angels of peace.

7

YOM ZEH LE·YISRA·EIL

יום זה לישראל

Yom zeh le·yis·ra·eil o·ra ve·sim·cha,
Sha·bat me·nu·cha.

יוֹם זֶה לְיִשְׂרָאֵל אוֹרָה וְשִׂמְחָה,
שַׁבַּת מְנוּחָה.

Tsi·vi·ta pi·ku·dim be·ma·a·mad Si·nai,
Sha·bat u·mo·a·dim lish·mor be·chol sha·nai,
la·a·roch le·fa·nai mas·eit va·a·ru·cha,
Sha·bat me·nu·cha.

צִוִּיתָ פִּקּוּדִים בְּמַעֲמַד סִינַי,
שַׁבָּת וּמוֹעֲדִים לִשְׁמוֹר בְּכָל־שָׁנַי,
לַעֲרוֹךְ לְפָנַי מַשְׂאֵת וַאֲרוּחָה,
שַׁבַּת מְנוּחָה.

Yom zeh le·yis·ra·eil o·ra ve·sim·cha,
Sha·bat me·nu·cha.

יוֹם זֶה לְיִשְׂרָאֵל אוֹרָה וְשִׂמְחָה,
שַׁבַּת מְנוּחָה.

Chem·dat ha·le·va·vot le·u·ma she·vu·ra,
li·ne·fa·shot nich·a·vot ne·sha·ma ye·tei·ra,
mi·ne·fesh me·tsei·ra ya·sir a·na·cha,
Sha·bat me·nu·cha.

חֶמְדַּת הַלְּבָבוֹת לְאֻמָּה שְׁבוּרָה,
לִנְפָשׁוֹת נִכְאָבוֹת נְשָׁמָה יְתֵרָה,
מִנֶּפֶשׁ מְצֵרָה יָסִיר אֲנָחָה,
שַׁבַּת מְנוּחָה.

Yom zeh le·yis·ra·eil o·ra ve·sim·cha,
Sha·bat me·nu·cha.

יוֹם זֶה לְיִשְׂרָאֵל אוֹרָה וְשִׂמְחָה,
שַׁבַּת מְנוּחָה.

Ki·dash·ta bei·rach·ta o·to mi·kol ya·mim,
be·shei·shet ki·li·ta me·le·chet o·la·mim,
bo ma·tse·u a·gu·mim hash·keit u·vit·cha,
Sha·bat me·nu·cha.

קִדַּשְׁתָּ בֵּרַכְתָּ אוֹתוֹ מִכָּל־יָמִים,
בְּשֵׁשֶׁת כִּלִּיתָ מְלֶאכֶת עוֹלָמִים,
בּוֹ מָצְאוּ עֲגוּמִים הַשְׁקֵט וּבִטְחָה,
שַׁבַּת מְנוּחָה.

Yom zeh le·yis·ra·eil o·ra ve·sim·cha,
Sha·bat me·nu·cha.

יוֹם זֶה לְיִשְׂרָאֵל אוֹרָה וְשִׂמְחָה,
שַׁבַּת מְנוּחָה.

This is Israel's day of light and joy, a Sabbath of rest. You bade us, standing assembled at Sinai, that all the year through we should keep Your behest: To set out a table full-laden to honor the Sabbath of rest. *This is . . . .*

Treasure of heart for the broken people, gift of new soul for the souls distressed, soother of sighs for the prisoned spirit: the Sabbath of rest. *This is . . . .*

When the work of creating the world was done, You chose this day to be holy and blessed, that those heavy-laden find safety and stillness, a Sabbath of rest. *This is . . . .*

8

SHALOM ALEICHEM — שלום עליכם

Sha·lom a·lei·chem, mal·a·chei ha·sha·reit, mal·a·chei El·yon,	שָׁלוֹם עֲלֵיכֶם, מַלְאֲכֵי הַשָּׁרֵת, מַלְאֲכֵי עֶלְיוֹן,
mi·me·lech ma·le·chei ha·me·la·chim,	מִמֶּלֶךְ מַלְכֵי הַמְּלָכִים,
ha·ka·dosh ba·ruch Hu.	הַקָּדוֹשׁ בָּרוּךְ הוּא.
Bo·a·chem le·sha·lom, mal·a·chei ha·sha·lom, mal·a·chei El·yon,	בּוֹאֲכֶם לְשָׁלוֹם, מַלְאֲכֵי הַשָּׁלוֹם, מַלְאֲכֵי עֶלְיוֹן,
mi·me·lech ma·le·chei ha·me·la·chim,	מִמֶּלֶךְ מַלְכֵי הַמְּלָכִים,
ha·ka·dosh ba·ruch Hu.	הַקָּדוֹשׁ בָּרוּךְ הוּא.
Ba·re·chu·ni le·sha·lom, mal·a·chei ha·sha·lom, mal·a·chei El·yon,	בָּרְכוּנִי לְשָׁלוֹם, מַלְאֲכֵי הַשָּׁלוֹם, מַלְאֲכֵי עֶלְיוֹן,
mi·me·lech ma·le·chei ha·me·la·chim,	מִמֶּלֶךְ מַלְכֵי הַמְּלָכִים,
ha·ka·dosh ba·ruch Hu.	הַקָּדוֹשׁ בָּרוּךְ הוּא.
Tsei·te·chem le·sha·lom, mal·a·chei ha·sha·lom, mal·a·chei El·yon,	צֵאתְכֶם לְשָׁלוֹם, מַלְאֲכֵי הַשָּׁלוֹם, מַלְאֲכֵי עֶלְיוֹן,
mi·me·lech ma·le·chei ha·me·la·chim,	מִמֶּלֶךְ מַלְכֵי הַמְּלָכִים,
ha·ka·dosh ba·ruch Hu.	הַקָּדוֹשׁ בָּרוּךְ הוּא.

The translation of Shalom Aleichem is on page 178.

9

LECHA DODI

לכה דודי

לְכָה דוֹדִי לִקְרַאת כַּלָּה,
פְּנֵי שַׁבָּת נְקַבְּלָה.

Le·cha do·di lik·rat ka·la,
pe·nei Sha·bat ne·ka·be·la.

1 שָׁמוֹר וְזָכוֹר בְּדִבּוּר אֶחָד,
הִשְׁמִיעָנוּ אֵל הַמְיֻחָד.
יְיָ אֶחָד וּשְׁמוֹ אֶחָד,
לְשֵׁם וּלְתִפְאֶרֶת וְלִתְהִלָּה.

לְכָה דוֹדִי. . .

Sha·mor ve·za·chor be·di·bur e·chad,
hish·mi·a·nu Eil ha·me·yu·chad.
A·do·nai e·chad u·she·mo e·chad,
le·sheim u·le·tif·e·ret ve·li·te·hi·la.

Le·cha do·di . . .

2 לִקְרַאת שַׁבָּת לְכוּ וְנֵלְכָה,
כִּי הִיא מְקוֹר הַבְּרָכָה.
מֵרֹאשׁ מִקֶּדֶם נְסוּכָה,
סוֹף מַעֲשֶׂה, בְּמַחֲשָׁבָה תְּחִלָּה.

לְכָה דוֹדִי. . .

Lik·rat Sha·bat le·chu ve·nei·le·cha,
ki hi me·kor ha·be·ra·cha.
mei·rosh mi·ke·dem ne·su·cha,
sof ma·a·seh, be·ma·cha·sha·va te·chi·la.

Le·cha do·di . . .

3 מִקְדַּשׁ מֶלֶךְ, עִיר מְלוּכָה,
קוּמִי צְאִי מִתּוֹךְ הַהֲפֵכָה.
רַב לָךְ שֶׁבֶת בְּעֵמֶק הַבָּכָא —
וְהוּא יַחֲמֹל עָלַיִךְ חֶמְלָה.

לְכָה דוֹדִי. . .

Mik·dash me·lech, ir me·lu·cha,
ku·mi tse·i mi·toch ha·ha·fei·cha.
rav lach she·vet be·ei·mek ha·ba·cha —
ve·hu ya·cha·mol a·la·yich chem·la.

Le·cha do·di . . .

4 הִתְנַעֲרִי! מֵעָפָר קוּמִי!
לִבְשִׁי בִּגְדֵי תִפְאַרְתֵּךְ, עַמִּי!
עַל־יַד בֶּן יִשַׁי, בֵּית הַלַּחְמִי,
קָרְבָה אֶל נַפְשִׁי גְאָלָהּ.

לְכָה דוֹדִי. . .

Hit·na·a·ri! mei·a·far ku·mi!
li·ve·shi bi·ge·dei tif·ar·teich, a·mi!
al yad ben yi·shai, beit ha·lach·mi,
ka·re·va el naf·shi ge·a·la.

Le·cha do·di . . .

5 הִתְעוֹרְרִי, הִתְעוֹרְרִי,
כִּי בָא אוֹרֵךְ! קוּמִי, אוֹרִי,
עוּרִי עוּרִי, שִׁיר דַּבֵּרִי;
כְּבוֹד יְיָ עָלַיִךְ נִגְלָה.

לְכָה דוֹדִי. . .

Hit·o·re·ri, hit·o·re·ri,
ki va o·reich! ku·mi, o·ri,
u·ri u·ri, shir da·bei·ri;
ke·vod A·do·nai a·la·yich nig·la.

Le·cha do·di . . .

6 לֹא תֵבֹשִׁי וְלֹא תִכָּלְמִי;
מַה תִּשְׁתּוֹחֲחִי, וּמַה תֶּהֱמִי?
בָּךְ יֶחֱסוּ עֲנִיֵּי עַמִּי,
וְנִבְנְתָה עִיר עַל תִּלָּהּ.

Lo tei·vo·shi ve·lo ti·ka·le·mi;
ma tish·to·cha·chi, u·ma te·he·mi?
bach ye·che·su a·ni·yei a·mi,
ve·niv·ne·ta ir al ti·la.

לְכָה דוֹדִי. . .

Le·cha do·di . . .

7 וְהָיוּ לִמְשִׁסָּה שֹׁאסָיִךְ,
וְרָחֲקוּ כָּל־מְבַלְּעָיִךְ;
יָשִׂישׂ עָלַיִךְ אֱלֹהָיִךְ,
כִּמְשׂוֹשׂ חָתָן עַל כַּלָּה.

Ve·ha·yu li·me·shi·sa sho·sa·yich,
ve·ra·cha·ku kol me·va·le·a·yich;
ya·sis a·la·yich E·lo·ha·yich,
ki·me·sos cha·tan al ka·la.

לְכָה דוֹדִי. . .

Le·cha do·di . . .

8 יָמִין וּשְׂמֹאל תִּפְרֹצִי,
וְאֶת יְיָ תַּעֲרִיצִי:
עַל יַד אִישׁ בֶּן פַּרְצִי,
וְנִשְׂמְחָה וְנָגִילָה!

Ya·min u·se·mol tif·ro·tsi,
ve·et A·do·nai ta·a·ri·tsi:
al yad ish ben par·tsi,
ve·nis·me·cha ve·na·gi·la!

לְכָה דוֹדִי. . .

Le·cha do·di . . .

9 בּוֹאִי בְשָׁלוֹם, עֲטֶרֶת בַּעְלָהּ;
גַּם בְּשִׂמְחָה וּבְצָהֳלָה.
תּוֹךְ אֱמוּנֵי עַם סְגֻלָּה.
בּוֹאִי כַלָּה! בּוֹאִי כַלָּה!

Bo·i ve·sha·lom, a·te·ret ba·a·la;
gam be·sim·cha u·ve·tso·ho·la.
toch e·mu·nei am se·gu·la.
bo·i cha·la! bo·i cha·la!

לְכָה דוֹדִי. . .

Le·cha do·di . . .

The translation of Lecha Dodi is on page 123.

10

COME, O SABBATH DAY

Come, O Sabbath day and bring
Peace and healing on thy wing;
And to every weary one
Let God's word of blessing come:
Thou shalt rest, Thou shalt rest.

Welcome Sabbath, let depart
Every care of troubled heart;

Now the daily task is done,
Let God's word of comfort come:
Thou shalt rest, Thou shalt rest.

Wipe from ev'ry cheek the tear,
Banish care and silence fear;
All things working for the best,
Teach us the divine behest:
Thou shalt rest, Thou shalt rest.

11

COME, O HOLY SABBATH EVENING

Come, O holy Sabbath evening,
Crown our toil with well earned rest;
Bring us hallowed hours of gladness,
Day of days beloved and blest.

Weave your mystic spell around us
With the glow of Sabbath light:
As we read the ancient wisdom,
Learn its laws of truth and right.

Come, O holy Sabbath spirit,
Radiant shine from every eye;
Lending us your benediction,
Filling every heart with joy.

12

O HOLY SABBATH DAY

O holy Sabbath day, draw near,
You are the source of bliss and cheer;
The first in God's creative thought,
The final aim of all He wrought.

Welcome, welcome, day of rest,
Day of joy the Lord has blessed.

Let all rejoice with all their might,
The Sabbath, freedom brings and light;

Let songs of praise to God ascend,
And voices sweet in chorus blend.

Welcome, welcome, day of rest,
Day of joy the Lord has blessed.

Now come, O blessed Sabbath-Bride,
Our joy, our comfort, and our pride;
All cares and sorrow now bid cease,
And fill our waiting hearts with peace.

Welcome, welcome, day of rest,
Day of joy the Lord has blessed.

13

HOW GOOD IT IS

לְכָה דוֹדִי לִקְרַאת כַּלָּה,
פְּנֵי שַׁבָּת נְקַבְּלָה.

Le·cha do·di lik·rat ka·la
pe·nei Sha·bat ne·ka·be·la [2]

How good it is to thank the Lord,
To praise Your name, O God Most High;
To tell Your kindness through the day,
Your faithfulness when night draws nigh.

Le·cha do·di . . .

With joyous psalms and with the harp,
Will I Your marvels gladly sing;
Your works have made my heart rejoice;
I triumph in Your work, my King!

Le·cha do·di . . .

Like stately palm the righteous thrive,
As cedar fair they flourish free
In God's own house; His courts alone
Their dwelling-place and home shall be.

Le·cha do·di . . .

Still, in old age, ripe fruit they bear,
Verdant and fresh they still remain
To prove that God, my Rock of Help,
His righteousness does e'er maintain.

Le·cha do·di . . .

14

YAH RIBON

יה רבון

Yah ri·bon a·lam ve·al·ma·ya,
ant Hu mal·ka, me·lech mal·cha·ya.
O·vad ge·vur·teich, ve·tim·ha·ya,
she·far ko·da·mai, le·ha·cha·va·ya.

יָהּ רִבּוֹן עָלַם וְעָלְמַיָּא,
אַנְתְּ הוּא מַלְכָּא, מֶלֶךְ מַלְכַיָּא.
עוֹבַד גְּבוּרְתֵּךְ, וְתִמְהַיָּא,
שְׁפַר קֳדָמַי לְהַחֲוָיָה.

Yah ri·bon . . .

יָהּ רִבּוֹן עָלַם וְעָלְמַיָּא,
אַנְתְּ הוּא מַלְכָּא מֶלֶךְ מַלְכַיָּא.

She·va·chin a·sa·deir, tsaf·ra ve·ram·sha,
lach, E·la·ha ka·di·sha, di ve·ra chol naf·sha.
I·rin ka·di·shin, u·ve·nei e·na·sha,
chei·vat ba·ra, ve·o·fei she·ma·ya.

שְׁבָחִין אֲסַדֵּר, צַפְרָא וְרַמְשָׁא,
לָךְ, אֱלָהָא קַדִּישָׁא דִּי בְרָא כָל־נַפְשָׁא.
עִירִין קַדִּישִׁין, וּבְנֵי אֱנָשָׁא,
חֵיוַת בָּרָא, וְעוֹפֵי שְׁמַיָּא.

Yah ri·bon . . .

יָהּ רִבּוֹן עָלַם וְעָלְמַיָּא,
אַנְתְּ הוּא מַלְכָּא מֶלֶךְ מַלְכַיָּא.

Rav·re·vin o·ve·dach, ve·ta·ki·fin,
ma·cheich ra·ma·ya ve·za·keif ke·fi·fin,
Lu ye·chei ge·var she·nin a·le·fin,
la yei·ol ge·vur·teich be·chush·be·na·ya.

רַבְרְבִין עוֹבְדָיךְ, וְתַקִּיפִין,
מָכֵךְ רָמַיָּא וְזָקֵף כְּפִיפִין,
לוּ יְחֵא גְבַר שְׁנִין אַלְפִין,
לָא יֵעֹל גְּבוּרְתֵּךְ בְּחֻשְׁבְּנַיָּא.

Yah ri·bon . . .

יָהּ רִבּוֹן עָלַם וְעָלְמַיָּא,
אַנְתְּ הוּא מַלְכָּא מֶלֶךְ מַלְכַיָּא.

The translation of Yah Ribon is on page 220.

15

YOM ZEH MECHUBAD

יום זה מכבד

Yom zeh me·chu·bad mi·kol ya·mim,
ki vo sha·vat tsur o·la·mim.

יוֹם זֶה מְכֻבָּד מִכָּל־יָמִים,
כִּי בוֹ שָׁבַת צוּר עוֹלָמִים.

Shei·shet ya·mim a·sei me·lach·te·cha,
ve·yom ha·she·vi·i lei·lo·he·cha,

שֵׁשֶׁת יָמִים תַּעֲשֶׂה מְלַאכְתֶּךָ,
וְיוֹם הַשְּׁבִיעִי לֵאלֹהֶיךָ,

Sha·bat lo ta·a·seh vo me·la·cha,	שַׁבָּת לֹא תַעֲשֶׂה בוֹ מְלָאכָה,
ki chol a·sa shei·shet ya·mim.	כִּי כֹל עָשָׂה שֵׁשֶׁת יָמִים.
Yom zeh . . .	יוֹם זֶה. . .
Ha·sha·ma·yim me·sa·pe·rim ke·vo·do,	הַשָּׁמַיִם מְסַפְּרִים כְּבוֹדוֹ,
ve·gam ha·a·rets ma·le·a chas·do,	וְגַם הָאָרֶץ מָלְאָה חַסְדּוֹ,
re·u kol ei·leh a·se·ta ya·do,	רְאוּ כָּל־אֵלֶּה עָשְׂתָה יָדוֹ,
ki Hu ha·tsur po·o·lo ta·mim.	כִּי הוּא הַצּוּר פָּעֳלוֹ תָמִים.
Yom zeh . . .	יוֹם זֶה. . .

This is the day most blessed of all, this is the day of the Creator's rest. Six are your days of labor, the seventh devote to your God; on Shabbat refrain from work for gain: celebrate rather the work of creation. *This is the day* . . . . The heavens declare His glory, earth is full of His love; See it all — His handiwork, the Rock whose work is pure. *This is the day* . . . .

16

MENUCHA VESIMCHA — מנוחה ושמחה

Me·nu·cha ve·sim·cha or la·ye·hu·dim,	מְנוּחָה וְשִׂמְחָה אוֹר לַיְּהוּדִים,
yom sha·ba·ton yom ma·cha·ma·dim.	יוֹם שַׁבָּתוֹן יוֹם מַחֲמַדִּים.
Sho·me·rav ve·zo·che·rav hei·ma me·i·dim,	שׁוֹמְרָיו וְזוֹכְרָיו הֵמָּה מְעִידִים,
ki le·shi·sha kol be·ru·im ve·o·me·dim.	כִּי לְשִׁשָּׁה כֹּל בְּרוּאִים וְעוֹמְדִים.
She·mei sha·ma·yim e·rets ve·ya·mim,	שְׁמֵי שָׁמַיִם אֶרֶץ וְיַמִּים,
kol tse·va ma·rom ge·vo·him ve·ra·mim.	כָּל־צְבָא מָרוֹם גְּבוֹהִים וְרָמִים.
ta·nin ve·a·dam ve·cha·yat re·ei·mim,	תַּנִּין וְאָדָם וְחַיַּת רְאֵמִים,
ki ve·yah A·do·nai tsur o·la·mim.	כִּי בְּיָהּ יְיָ צוּר עוֹלָמִים.

Rest and gladness, a light for the Jew, the Sabbath day is a day of delight. Those who keep and remember it give witness to the story of creation. All things were made: the highest heavens, earth and sea, the high and exalted host of heaven, sea-monster and human, the wild beast — the Lord God is the Creator of all worlds.

17

YEDID NEFESH — ידיד נפש

Ye·did ne·fesh, av ha·ra·cha·man,
me·shoch av·de·cha el re·tso·ne·cha.
Ya·ruts av·de·cha ke·mo a·yal,
yish·ta·cha·veh el mul ha·da·re·cha.

יְדִיד נֶפֶשׁ, אָב הָרַחֲמָן,
מְשׁוֹךְ עַבְדְּךָ אֶל רְצוֹנֶךָ.
יָרוּץ עַבְדְּךָ כְּמוֹ אַיָּל,
יִשְׁתַּחֲוֶה אֶל מוּל הֲדָרֶךָ.

Heart's delight, Source of mercy, draw Your servant into Your arms: I leap like a deer to stand in awe before You.

18

EILEH CHAMEDA LIBI — אלה חמדה לבי

Ei·leh cha·me·da li·bi
chu·sa na ve·al na tit·a·leim.

אֵלֶּה חָמְדָה לִבִּי
חוּסָה נָּא וְאַל נָא תִּתְעַלֵּם.

This is my heart's desire: have pity, do not hide Yourself!

19

VATIK — ותיק

Va·tik, ye·he·mu na ra·cha·me·cha,
ve·chu·sa na al bein a·hu·ve·cha.
Ki zeh ka·ma nich·sof nich·saf·ti
lir·ot be·tif·e·ret u·ze·cha.
Ei·leh cha·me·da li·bi,
ve·chu·sa na ve·al na tit·a·leim.

וָתִיק, יֶהֱמוּ נָא רַחֲמֶיךָ,
וְחוּסָה נָא עַל בֵּן אֲהוּבֶךָ.
כִּי זֶה כַּמָּה נִכְסוֹף נִכְסַפְתִּי
לִרְאוֹת בְּתִפְאֶרֶת עֻזֶּךָ.
אֵלֶּה חָמְדָה לִבִּי,
וְחוּסָה נָא וְאַל נָא תִּתְעַלֵּם.

God our Reliance, let Your pity be stirred up for Your beloved child. I have yearned so long to see Your glorious might. This is my heart's desire; have pity: hide Yourself no more.

20

KI ESHMERA SHABBAT — כי אשמרה שבת

Ki esh·me·ra Sha·bat
Eil yish·me·rei·ni.

כִּי אֶשְׁמְרָה שַׁבָּת
אֵל יִשְׁמְרֵנִי.

Ot hi le·o·le·mei ad	אוֹת הִיא לְעָלְמֵי עַד
bei·no u·vei·ni.	בֵּינוֹ וּבֵינִי.

If I keep Shabbat, God keeps me. It is a sign for ever between Him and me.

21

DEROR YIKRA — דרור יקרא

De·ror yik·ra le·vein im bat,	דְּרוֹר יִקְרָא לְבֵן עִם בַּת,
ve·yin·tso·re·chem ke·mo va·vat.	וְיִנְצָרְכֶם כְּמוֹ בָבַת.
Ne·im shi·me·chem ve·lo yush·bat,	נְעִים שִׁמְכֶם וְלֹא יֻשְׁבַּת,
she·vu ve·nu·chu be·yom Sha·bat.	שְׁבוּ וְנוּחוּ בְּיוֹם שַׁבָּת.
De·rosh na·vi ve·u·la·mi	דְּרשׁ נָוִי וְאוּלָמִי
ve·ot ye·sha a·sei i·mi.	וְאוֹת יֶשַׁע עֲשֵׂה עִמִּי.
Ne·ta so·rek be·toch car·mi,	נְטַע שׂוֹרֵק בְּתוֹךְ כַּרְמִי
she·ei shav·at be·nei a·mi.	שְׁעֵה שַׁוְעַת בְּנֵי עַמִּי.
E·lo·him tein ba·mid·bar har	אֱלֹהִים תֵּן בַּמִּדְבָּר הָר
ha·das, shi·ta, be·rosh, tid·har.	הֲדַס, שִׁטָּה, בְּרוֹשׁ, תִּדְהָר.
Ve·la·maz·hir ve·la·niz·har	וְלַמַּזְהִיר וְלַנִּזְהָר
she·lo·mim tein ke·mei na·har.	שְׁלוֹמִים תֵּן כְּמֵי נָהָר.

May He proclaim freedom for all His sons and daughters, and keep you as the apple of His eye. Pleasant is your name; it will not be destroyed. Repose, relax, on the Sabbath day. Revisit my holy temple. Give me a sign of deliverance. Plant a vine in my vineyard. Look to my people, hear their laments. Place, O God, in the mountain waste, fir and acacia, myrtle and elm. Give those who teach, and those who obey, abundant peace, like the flow of a stream.

22

VETAHEIR LIBEINU — וטהר לבנו

Ve·ta·heir li·bei·nu le·ov·de·cha be·e·met.	וְטַהֵר לִבֵּנוּ לְעָבְדְּךָ בֶּאֱמֶת.

Purify our hearts to serve You in truth.

23

MAGEIN AVOT — מגן אבות

Ma·gein a·vot bi·de·va·ro,	מָגֵן אָבוֹת בִּדְבָרוֹ,
me·cha·yei ha·kol be·ma·a·ma·ro.	מְחַיֵּה הַכֹּל בְּמַאֲמָרוֹ.
Ha·eil ha·ka·dosh she·ein ka·mo·hu.	הָאֵל הַקָּדוֹשׁ, שֶׁאֵין כָּמוֹהוּ,
ha·mei·ni·ach le·a·mo be·yom Sha·bat kod·sho,	הַמֵּנִיחַ לְעַמּוֹ בְּיוֹם שַׁבַּת קָדְשׁוֹ,
ki vam ra·tsa le·ha·ni·ach la·hem.	כִּי בָם רָצָה לְהָנִיחַ לָהֶם.
Le·fa·nav na·a·vod be·yir·a va·fa·chad,	לְפָנָיו נַעֲבוֹד בְּיִרְאָה וָפַחַד,
ve·no·deh li·she·mo be·chol yom ta·mid	וְנוֹדֶה לִשְׁמוֹ בְּכָל־יוֹם תָּמִיד,
mei·ein ha·be·ra·chot.	מֵעֵין הַבְּרָכוֹת.
Eil ha·ho·da·ot, A·don ha·sha·lom,	אֵל הַהוֹדָאוֹת, אֲדוֹן הַשָּׁלוֹם,
me·ka·deish ha·sha·bat u·me·va·reich she·vi·i,	מְקַדֵּשׁ הַשַּׁבָּת וּמְבָרֵךְ שְׁבִיעִי,
u·mei·ni·ach bi·ke·du·sha le·am me·du·she·nei o·neg,	וּמֵנִיחַ בִּקְדֻשָּׁה לְעַם מְדֻשְּׁנֵי עֹנֶג,
zei·cher le·ma·a·sei ve·rei·shit.	זֵכֶר לְמַעֲשֵׂה בְרֵאשִׁית.

The translation of Magein Avot is on page 141.

24

TOV LEHODOT — טוב להודות

Tov, tov, tov le·ho·dot,	טוֹב, טוֹב, טוֹב לְהוֹדוֹת,
tov le·ho·dot la·a·do·nai.	טוֹב לְהוֹדוֹת לַייָ.
U·le·za·meir le·shi·me·cha, El·yon,	וּלְזַמֵּר לְשִׁמְךָ עֶלְיוֹן,
le·shi·me·cha El·yon.	לְשִׁמְךָ עֶלְיוֹן.
Tov, tov	טוֹב, טוֹב. . . .
Le·ha·gid ba·bo·ker chas·de·cha	לְהַגִּיד בַּבֹּקֶר חַסְדֶּךָ
ve·e·mu·na·te·cha ba·lei·lot.	וֶאֱמוּנָתְךָ בַּלֵּילוֹת.
Tov, tov	טוֹב, טוֹב. . . .

It is good to give thanks to the Lord, to sing praises to Your name, O Most High!

25

ANIM ZEMIROT	אנעים זמירות
An·im ze·mi·rot ve·shi·rim e·e·rog,	אַנְעִים זְמִירוֹת וְשִׁירִים אֶאֱרוֹג,
ki ei·le·cha naf·shi ta·a·rog.	כִּי אֵלֶיךָ נַפְשִׁי תַעֲרוֹג.
Naf·shi chi·me·da be·tseil ya·de·cha,	נַפְשִׁי חִמְּדָה בְּצֵל יָדֶךָ,
la·da·at kol raz so·de·cha.	לָדַעַת כָּל־רָז סוֹדֶךָ.
Mi·dei da·be·ri bi·che·vo·de·cha,	מִדֵּי דַבְּרִי בִּכְבוֹדֶךָ,
ho·meh li·bi el do·de·cha.	הוֹמֶה לִבִּי אֶל־דּוֹדֶיךָ.
Ye·e·rav na si·chi a·le·cha,	יֶעֱרַב־נָא שִׂיחִי עָלֶיךָ,
ki naf·shi ta·a·rog ei·le·cha.	כִּי נַפְשִׁי תַעֲרוֹג אֵלֶיךָ.

I make pleasant songs, and weave verses, because my soul longs for You. To know Your deepest secret, to be in Your hand's shade, is my soul's strongest wish. My heart yearns for Your love, whenever I speak of Your glory. So may my thought be sweet to You, for whom my soul longs.

26

SHACHAR AVAKESHECHA	שחר אבקשך
Sha·char a·va·ke·she·cha, tsu·ri	שַׁחַר אֲבַקֶּשְׁךָ, צוּרִי
u·mis·ga·bi,	וּמִשְׂגַּבִּי,
e·roch le·fa·ne·cha shach·ri	אֶעֱרוֹךְ לְפָנֶיךָ שַׁחְרִי
ve·gam ar·bi.	וְגַם עַרְבִּי.
Lif·nei ge·du·la·te·cha e·mod	לִפְנֵי גְּדֻלָּתְךָ אֶעְמֹד
ve·e·ba·heil	וְאֶבָּהֵל,
ki ei·ne·cha tir·eh kol	כִּי עֵינְךָ תִרְאֶה כָּל
mach·she·vot li·bi.	מַחְשְׁבוֹת לִבִּי.
Ma zeh a·sher yu·chal	מַה־זֶּה אֲשֶׁר יוּכַל
ha·leiv ve·ha·la·shon	הַלֵּב וְהַלָּשׁוֹן
la·a·sot, u·ma ko·ach ru·chi	לַעֲשׂוֹת, וּמַה כֹּחַ רוּחִי
be·toch kir·bi?	בְּתוֹךְ קִרְבִּי?
Hi·nei le·cha ti·tav zim·rat	הִנֵּה לְךָ תִּיטַב זִמְרַת
enosh. Al kein	אֱנוֹשׁ. עַל כֵּן

o·de·cha be·od ti·he·yeh	אוֹדְךָ בְּעוֹד תִּהְיֶה
nish·mat E·lo·ah bi.	נִשְׁמַת אֱלוֹהַּ בִּי.

At dawn I seek You, my Rock and Stronghold; I place before You my morning and evening prayers. Before Your greatness I stand afraid, for Your eye sees all my thoughts. What can heart and tongue do, and what is my spirit's strength within me? Behold, our human song will gain Your favor. Therefore I will affirm You while yet Your spirit lives within me.

27

ASHREINU — אשרינו

Ash·rei·nu! Ma tov chel·kei·nu!	אַשְׁרֵינוּ! מַה־טּוֹב חֶלְקֵנוּ!
U·ma na·im go·ra·lei·nu!	וּמַה־נָּעִים גּוֹרָלֵנוּ!
U·ma ya·fa ye·ru·sha·tei·nu!	וּמַה־יָּפָה יְרֻשָּׁתֵנוּ!

How greatly we are blessed! How good is our portion! How pleasant our lot! How beautiful our heritage!

28

VEHA·EIR EINEINU — והאר עינינו

Ve·ha·eir ei·nei·nu be·to·ra·te·cha,	וְהָאֵר עֵינֵינוּ בְּתוֹרָתֶךָ,
ve·da·beik li·bei·nu be·mits·vo·te·cha,	וְדַבֵּק לִבֵּנוּ בְּמִצְוֹתֶיךָ,
ve·ya·cheid le·va·vei·nu	וְיַחֵד לְבָבֵנוּ
le·a·ha·va u·le·yir·a et she·me·cha.	לְאַהֲבָה וּלְיִרְאָה אֶת־שְׁמֶךָ.
Ve·lo nei·vosh	וְלֹא נֵבוֹשׁ
ve·lo ni·ka·leim	וְלֹא נִכָּלֵם
ve·lo ni·ka·sheil	וְלֹא נִכָּשֵׁל
le·o·lam va·ed.	לְעוֹלָם וָעֶד.

Enlighten our eyes in Your Torah, cause our hearts to cling to Your Mitzvot, and unite our hearts to love and revere Your name. Then we shall not be shamed, nor humiliated, nor shall we ever stumble.

29

BARUCH ELOHEINU — ברוך אלהינו

Ba·ruch E·lo·hei·nu	בָּרוּךְ אֱלֹהֵינוּ
she·be·ra·a·nu li·che·vo·do,	שֶׁבְּרָאָנוּ לִכְבוֹדוֹ,
ve·hiv·di·la·nu min ha·to·im,	וְהִבְדִּילָנוּ מִן־הַתּוֹעִים,
ve·na·tan la·nu To·rat e·met	וְנָתַן לָנוּ תּוֹרַת אֱמֶת
[ve·cha·yei o·lam na·ta be·to·chei·nu].	(וְחַיֵּי עוֹלָם נָטַע בְּתוֹכֵנוּ).

Blessed is our God, who has touched us with His glory, separated us from error and given us a Torah of truth [implanting within us eternal life].

30

ATA ECHAD — אתה אחד

A·ta e·chad ve·shi·me·cha e·chad	אַתָּה אֶחָד וְשִׁמְךָ אֶחָד
u·mi ke·a·me·cha Yis·ra·eil, [2]	וּמִי כְּעַמְּךָ יִשְׂרָאֵל, (2)
goi e·chad ba·a·rets?	גּוֹי אֶחָד בָּאָרֶץ?
Tif·e·ret ge·du·la va·a·te·ret ye·shu·a,	תִּפְאֶרֶת גְּדֻלָּה וַעֲטֶרֶת יְשׁוּעָה,
yom me·nu·cha u·ke·du·sha le·a·me·cha na·ta·ta.	יוֹם מְנוּחָה וּקְדֻשָּׁה לְעַמְּךָ נָתָתָּ.
A·ta e·chad ve·shi·me·cha e·chad	אַתָּה אֶחָד וְשִׁמְךָ אֶחָד
u·mi ke·a·me·cha Yis·ra·eil [2]	וּמִי כְּעַמְּךָ יִשְׂרָאֵל, (2)
goi e·chad ba·a·rets . . .	גּוֹי אֶחָד בָּאָרֶץ.

You are One, Your name is One, and there is none like Your people Israel, a unique people on earth. A garland of glory have You given us, a crown of salvation: a day of rest and holiness. You are One . . . .

31

SHOMEIR YISRA·EIL — שומר ישראל

Sho·meir, sho·meir Yis·ra·eil,	שׁוֹמֵר יִשְׂרָאֵל,
she·mor she·ei·rit Yis·ra·eil;	שְׁמוֹר שְׁאֵרִית יִשְׂרָאֵל,
Sho·meir, sho·meir Yis·ra·eil,	
she·mor she·ei·rit Yis·ra·eil.	

Ve·al yo·vad, ve·al yo·vad Yis·ra·eil,
ve·al yo·vad, ve·al yo·vad Yis·ra·eil;
ha·o·me·rim, ha·o·me·rim,
ha·o·me·rim She·ma Yis·ra·eil.

וְאַל־יֹאבַד יִשְׂרָאֵל,
הָאוֹמְרִים שְׁמַע יִשְׂרָאֵל.

Sho·meir, sho·meir goi e·chad,
she·mor she·ei·rit am e·chad;
Sho·meir, sho·meir goi e·chad,
she·mor she·ei·rit am e·chad.

שׁוֹמֵר גּוֹי אֶחָד,
שְׁמוֹר שְׁאֵרִית עַם אֶחָד,

Ve·al yo·vad, ve·al yo·vad goi e·chad,
ve·al yo·vad, ve·al yo·vad goi e·chad;
ha·me·ya·cha·dim, ha·me·ya·cha·dim shi·me·cha
A·do·nai E·lo·hei·nu, A·do·nai e·chad.

וְאַל־יֹאבַד גּוֹי אֶחָד,
הַמְיַחֲדִים שִׁמְךָ,
יְיָ אֱלֹהֵינוּ,
יְיָ אֶחָד.

Guardian of Israel, guard the remnant of Israel. Let not Israel perish, the people that proclaims: Hear, O Israel. Guardian of a unique people, guard the remnant of that people. Let them not perish, who proclaim You the One God.

32

LO YISA GOI

לא ישא גוי

Lo yi·sa goi el goi che·rev,
lo yil·me·du od mil·cha·ma.

לֹא יִשָּׂא גוֹי אֶל גּוֹי חֶרֶב,
לֹא יִלְמְדוּ עוֹד מִלְחָמָה.

Nation shall not lift up sword against nation, nor ever again shall they train for war.

33

ESA EINAI

אשא עיני

E·sa ei·nai el he·ha·rim,
mei·a·yin ya·vo ez·ri.
Ez·ri mei·im A·do·nai,
o·seh sha·ma·yim va·a·rets.

אֶשָּׂא עֵינַי אֶל־הֶהָרִים,
מֵאַיִן יָבוֹא עֶזְרִי.
עֶזְרִי מֵעִם יְיָ,
עוֹשֵׂה שָׁמַיִם וָאָרֶץ.

I lift up my eyes, unto the mountains,
From whence does my help come?
My help will come from the Lord,
Maker of heaven and earth.

34

MI HA·ISH	מי האיש
Mi ha·ish he·cha·feits cha·yim,	מִי הָאִישׁ הֶחָפֵץ חַיִּים,
o·heiv ya·mim, lir·ot tov?	אֹהֵב יָמִים, לִרְאוֹת טוֹב?
Ne·tsor le·sho·ne·cha mei·ra,	נְצֹר לְשׁוֹנְךָ מֵרָע,
u·se·fa·te·cha mi·da·beir mir·ma;	וּשְׂפָתֶיךָ מִדַּבֵּר מִרְמָה;
sur mei·ra va·a·sei tov,	סוּר מֵרָע וַעֲשֵׂה טוֹב,
ba·keish sha·lom ve·rod·fei·hu.	בַּקֵּשׁ שָׁלוֹם וְרָדְפֵהוּ.

Who among you loves life, and longs to enjoy good for many days? Then guard your tongue from evil, and your lips from deceitful speech; turn away from evil, and do good; seek peace and pursue it.

35

VEHEISHIV LEIV AVOT	והשיב לב אבות
Hi·nei a·no·chi sho·lei·ach la·chem	הִנֵּה אָנֹכִי שֹׁלֵחַ לָכֶם
Ei·li·ya·hu ha·na·vi	אֵלִיָּהוּ הַנָּבִיא
li·fe·nei bo yom A·do·nai;	לִפְנֵי בּוֹא יוֹם יְיָ:
Ve·hei·shiv leiv a·vot al ba·nim	וְהֵשִׁיב לֵב אָבוֹת עַל בָּנִים
ve·leiv ba·nim al a·vo·tam.	וְלֵב בָּנִים עַל אֲבוֹתָם.

Behold, I am sending to you Elijah the prophet, before the coming of the day of the Lord: and he will cause the hearts of the parents to turn to the children, and the hearts of the children to the parents.

36

I·VE·DU	עבדו
I·ve·du et Ha·shem be·sim·cha,	עִבְדוּ אֶת־ה׳ בְּשִׂמְחָה,
bo·u le·fa·nav bi·re·na·na.	בֹּאוּ לְפָנָיו בִּרְנָנָה.

Serve the Lord with gladness! Come into His presence with singing!

37

PITECHU LI

פתחו לי

Pi·te·chu li
sha·a·rei tse·dek
a·vo vam, o·deh Yah.

פִּתְחוּ־לִי
שַׁעֲרֵי־צֶדֶק
אָבֹא־בָם, אוֹדֶה יָהּ.

Open for me the gates of righteousness; I will enter them and give thanks to the Lord.

38

MA NAVU

מה־נאוו

Ma na·vu al he·ha·rim
ra·ge·lei me·va·seir
mash·mi·a sha·lom,
mash·mi·a ye·shu·a.
Kol tso·fa·yich na·se·u kol,
yach·dav ye·ra·nei·nu.
Ki a·yin be·a·yin yir·u
be·shuv A·do·nai tsi·yon.

מַה־נָּאווּ עַל־הֶהָרִים
רַגְלֵי מְבַשֵּׂר
מַשְׁמִיעַ שָׁלוֹם,
מַשְׁמִיעַ יְשׁוּעָה.
קוֹל צֹפַיִךְ נָשְׂאוּ קוֹל,
יַחְדָּו יְרַנֵּנוּ.
כִּי עַיִן בְּעַיִן יִרְאוּ
בְּשׁוּב יְיָ צִיּוֹן.

How beautiful upon the mountains are the feet of the herald, the one who proclaims peace, who brings tidings of good and proclaims deliverance. All your sentries raise their voices and shout together in triumph. For clearly they see the return of the Lord to Zion.

39

DAVID MELECH

דוד מלך

Da·vid me·lech Yis·ra·eil
chai ve·ka·yam.

דָּוִד מֶלֶךְ יִשְׂרָאֵל
חַי וְקַיָּם.

David, king of Israel, lives and endures.

40

AMAR RABBI AKIVA	אמר רבי עקיבא
A·mar Ra·bi A·ki·va [3]	אָמַר רַבִּי עֲקִיבָא
Ve·a·hav·ta le·rei·a·cha ka·mo·cha:	וְאָהַבְתָּ לְרֵעֲךָ כָּמוֹךָ:
zeh ke·lal ga·dol ba·to·rah.	זֶה כְּלָל גָּדוֹל בַּתּוֹרָה.

Said Rabbi Akiva: "You shall love your neighbor as yourself" — this is the great principle of the Torah.

41

AMAR RABBI ELAZAR	אמר רבי אלעזר
A·mar Ra·bi El·a·zar,	אָמַר רַבִּי אֶלְעָזָר,
a·mar Ra·bi Cha·ni·na:	אָמַר רַבִּי חֲנִינָא:
Tal·mi·dei cha·cha·mim	תַּלְמִידֵי חֲכָמִים
mar·bim sha·lom ba·o·lam.	מַרְבִּים שָׁלוֹם בָּעוֹלָם.

Rabbi Elazar said, quoting Rabbi Chanina: "The disciples of the wise (students of Torah) add peace to the world."

42

IM EIN ANI LI MI LI	אם אין אני לי מי לי
Im ein a·ni li mi li?	אִם אֵין אֲנִי לִי מִי לִי?
U·che·she·a·ni le·ats·mi	וּכְשֶׁאֲנִי לְעַצְמִי
ma a·ni?	מָה אֲנִי?
Ve·im lo ach·shav ei·ma·tai,	וְאִם לֹא עַכְשָׁו אֵימָתַי,
ei·ma·tai?	אֵימָתַי?

If I am not for myself, who will be for me? But if I am for myself alone, what am I? And if not now, when?

43

AL SHELOSHA DEVARIM	על שלשה דברים
Al she·lo·sha de·va·rim	עַל־שְׁלֹשָׁה דְבָרִים
ha·o·lam o·meid:	הָעוֹלָם עוֹמֵד:

al ha·torah,	עַל הַתּוֹרָה,
ve·al ha·a·vo·da,	וְעַל הָעֲבוֹדָה,
ve·al ge·mi·lut cha·sa·dim.	וְעַל גְּמִילוּת חֲסָדִים.

The world depends on three things: on Torah, on worship, and on loving deeds.

44

RAD HALAILA — רד הלילה

Rad ha·lai·la rav shi·rei·nu,	רַד הַלַּיְלָה רַב שִׁירֵנוּ,
ha·bo·kei·a la·sha·ma·yim.	הַבּוֹקֵעַ לַשָּׁמַיִם.
Shu·vi shu·vi ho·ra·tei·nu	שׁוּבִי שׁוּבִי הוֹרָתֵנוּ
me·chu·de·shet shiv·a·ta·yim.	מְחוּדֶּשֶׁת שִׁבְעָתַיִם.
Shu·vi shu·vi ve·na·sov	שׁוּבִי שׁוּבִי וְנָסוֹב
ki dar·kei·nu ein la sof,	כִּי דַרְכֵּנוּ אֵין לָהּ סוֹף,
ki od nim·she·chet ha·shal·she·let,	כִּי עוֹד נִמְשֶׁכֶת הַשַּׁלְשֶׁלֶת,
ki li·bei·nu leiv e·chad	כִּי לִבֵּנוּ לֵב אֶחָד
mi·ni az va·a·dei ad	מִינִי אָז וַעֲדֵי עַד
ki od nim·she·chet ha·shal·she·let.	כִּי עוֹד נִמְשֶׁכֶת הַשַּׁלְשֶׁלֶת.
La, la la, la la la la la la	ל, ל, ל, ל, ל, ל, ...

Night descends, and great is our song which breaks through to the heavens. Again, again our Hora, renewed sevenfold. Again, again, and let us go around. For our path has no end; for the chain still continues. For our heart is one heart, now and always, for the chain still continues.

45

HOSHIA ET AMECHA — הושיעה את עמך

Ho·shi·a et a·me·cha	הוֹשִׁיעָה אֶת־עַמֶּךָ
u·va·reich et na·cha·la·te·cha	וּבָרֵךְ אֶת־נַחֲלָתֶךָ
u·re·eim ve·na·se·eim ad ha·o·lam.	וּרְעֵם וְנַשְּׂאֵם עַד־הָעוֹלָם.

Help Your people, bless Your heritage, tend them and exalt them for ever.

46

ANI MAAMIN | **אני מאמין**

A·ni ma·a·min be·e·mu·na she·lei·ma	אֲנִי מַאֲמִין בֶּאֱמוּנָה שְׁלֵמָה
be·vi·at ha·ma·shi·ach.	בְּבִיאַת הַמָּשִׁיחַ.
Ve·af al pi she·yit·ma·he·mei·a,	וְאַף עַל פִּי שֶׁיִּתְמַהְמֵהַּ,
im kol zeh a·ni ma·a·min,	עִם כָּל זֶה אֲנִי מַאֲמִין,
im kol zeh a·cha·keh lo	עִם כָּל זֶה אֲחַכֶּה לוֹ
be·chol yom she·ya·vo.	בְּכָל יוֹם שֶׁיָּבוֹא.

I believe with perfect faith in the Messiah's coming. And even if he be delayed, I will await him.

47

IF OUR GOD HAD NOT BEFRIENDED

If our God had not befriended,
Now may grateful Israel say,
If the Lord had not defended
When with foes we stood at bay,
Madly raging, madly raging,
Deeming our sad lives their prey:

Then the tide of vengeful slaughters
O'er us had been seen to roll,
And their pride, like angry waters,
Had engulf'd our struggling soul,
Those loud waters, those loud waters,
Proud and spurning all control.

Praise to God, whose mercy token
Beam'd to still that raging sea;
Lo, the snare is rent and broken,
And our captive souls are free.
Lord of glory, Lord of glory,
Help can come alone from Thee.

48

SPRING-TIDE OF THE YEAR

Behold, it is the spring-tide of the year!
Over and past is winter's gloomy reign.
The happy time of singing-birds is here,
And clad in bud and bloom are hill and plain.

And in the spring, when all the earth and sky
Rejoice together, still from age to age
Rings out the solemn chant of days gone by,
Proclaiming Israel's sacred heritage.

For as from out the house of bondage went
The host of Israel, in their midst they bore
The heritage of law and freedom, blent
In holy unity for evermore.

And still from rising unto setting sun
Shall this our heritage and watchword be:
"The Lord our God, the Lord our God is One,
And law alone it is that makes us free!"

49

GOD OF MIGHT

God of might, God of right,
Thee we give all glory;
Thine all praise in these days,
As in ages hoary,
When we hear, year by year,
Freedom's wondrous story.

Now as erst, when Thou first
Mads't the proclamation,
Warning loud ev'ry proud,
Ev'ry tyrant nation,
We Thy fame still proclaim,
Bow'd in adoration.

Be with all who in thrall
To their tasks are driven;
By Thy power speed the hour
When their chains are riven;
Earth around will resound
Joyful hymns to heaven.

50

IN THE WILDERNESS

In the wilderness no wind blew,
In the heavens no bird flew,
In the meadows no cow was lowing,
In the rivers the water stopped flowing.
Camel bells were nowhere ringing,
Even the angels ceased their singing.
Over the whole world silence was falling,
Only the voice of the shofar calling.
At the foot of the mountain we stood,
And received the Torah!

51

COULD WE WITH INK

Could we with ink the ocean fill,
Were every blade of grass a quill,
Were the world of parchment made,
And every one a scribe by trade,
To write the love of God above
Would drain the ocean, drain it dry.
Nor would the scroll contain the whole,
Though stretched from sky to sky.

52

FROM HEAVEN'S HEIGHTS THE THUNDER PEALS

From heaven's heights the thunder peals,
The trumpets sound with might;
In storm and clouds the Lord reveals
The glory of His light.
The Lord of Hosts proclaims His Word,
To us He speaks, Creation's Lord.

The idols reel, their temples shake,
Despotic pow'rs rebound;
With awe the mountain summits quake,
Before the awful sound.
From Horeb's height descends the word,
To us He speaks, Creation's Lord.

Let Judah's harp intone His praise,
Our Maker's glory sing;
For truth and light, for heav'nly grace,
Reveal'd by God, our King.
Extol His name in one accord,
To us He speaks, Creation's Lord.

53

EIN ADIR	אין אדיר
Ein a·dir ka·a·do·nai	אֵין אַדִּיר כַּיְיָ
ve·ein ba·ruch ke·ven Am·ram.	וְאֵין בָּרוּךְ כְּבֶן עַמְרָם.
Ein ge·do·lah ka·to·rah	אֵין גְּדוֹלָה כַּתּוֹרָה
ve·ein dar·sha·ne·ha ke·yis·ra·eil.	וְאֵין דַּרְשָׁנֶיהָ כְּיִשְׂרָאֵל.
Mi·pi Eil u·mi·pi Eil	מִפִּי אֵל וּמִפִּי אֵל
ye·vo·rach kol Yis·ra·eil.	יְבֹרָךְ כָּל יִשְׂרָאֵל.
Ein ha·dur ka·a·do·nai	אֵין הָדוּר כַּיְיָ
ve·ein va·tik ke·ven Am·ram.	וְאֵין וָתִיק כְּבֶן עַמְרָם.
Ein za·ka ka·to·rah	אֵין זַכָּה כַּתּוֹרָה
ve·ein cha·cha·me·ha ke·yis·ra·eil.	וְאֵין חֲכָמֶיהָ כְּיִשְׂרָאֵל.
Mi·pi Eil	מִפִּי אֵל. . .
Ein ta·hor ka·a·do·nai	אֵין טָהוֹר כַּיְיָ
ve·ein ya·chid ke·ven Am·ram.	וְאֵין יָחִיד כְּבֶן עַמְרָם.
Ein ka·bi·ra ka·to·rah	אֵין כַּבִּירָה כַּתּוֹרָה
ve·ein lam·da·ne·ha ke·yis·ra·eil.	וְאֵין לַמְדָנֶיהָ כְּיִשְׂרָאֵל.
Mi·pi Eil	מִפִּי אֵל. . .
Ein po·deh ka·a·do·nai	אֵין פּוֹדֶה כַּיְיָ
ve·ein tsa·dik ke·ven Am·ram.	וְאֵין צַדִּיק כְּבֶן עַמְרָם.
ein ke·do·sha ka·to·rah	אֵין קְדוֹשָׁה כַּתּוֹרָה
ve·ein to·me·che·ha ke·yis·ra·eil.	וְאֵין תּוֹמְכֶיהָ כְּיִשְׂרָאֵל.
Mi·pi Eil	מִפִּי אֵל. . .

None is mighty as the Lord; none so blessed as Amram's son; nothing is as great as the Torah; none can interpret it as Israel can. *From the mouth of God, the mouth of God, let all Israel be blessed.*

None is glorious as the Lord; none so pious as Amram's son; nothing is as pure as the Torah; none so wise as Israel. *From the mouth ....*

None is pure as the Lord; none can match Amram's son; nothing is as mighty as the Torah; none so learned as Israel. *From the mouth ....*

None can redeem like the Lord; none is as righteous as Amram's son; nothing is as holy as the Torah; none who hold fast to it as Israel. *From the mouth ....*

54

TAKE UNTO YOU

"Take unto you the boughs of goodly trees,
Branches of palm, and willows of the brook,
And build you booths in which to dwell with these."
So it was written in the sacred book.

Thus kept they harvest in the years gone by,
And blessed the Lord for all His bounteous store,
And songs of praise and prayer arose on high
To Him whose mercies are for evermore.

Afield no longer as in ancient days
We go to gather corn and wine and oil;
Yet still, O Lord, we come with prayer and praise,
To seek Your blessing on our harvest toil.

For toilers in the field of life are we;
Whether amidst green meadows smooth and fair,
Or tracks of barren land our portion be,
You, Lord, have bidden us to labor there.

Hear, then, our prayer this day, and deign to bless
The precious seed we scatter far and wide,
That with rejoicing and with thankfulness,
We may bring home our sheaves at harvest-tide.

55

MI YEMALEIL

מי ימלל

Mi ye·ma·leil ge·vu·rot Yis·ra·eil,
o·tan mi yim·neh?

מִי יְמַלֵּל גְּבוּרוֹת יִשְׂרָאֵל,
אוֹתָן מִי יִמְנֶה?

Hein be·chol dor ya·kum ha·gi·bor,	הֵן בְּכָל דּוֹר יָקוּם הַגִּבּוֹר,
go·eil ha·am.	גּוֹאֵל הָעָם.
She·ma! Ba·ya·mim ha·heim ba·ze·man ha·zeh,	שְׁמַע! בַּיָּמִים הָהֵם בַּזְּמַן הַזֶּה
Ma·ka·bi mo·shi·a u·fo·deh.	מַכַּבִּי מוֹשִׁיעַ וּפוֹדֶה.
U·ve·ya·mei·nu kol am Yis·ra·eil	וּבְיָמֵינוּ כָּל עַם יִשְׂרָאֵל
yit·a·cheid, ya·kum le·hi·ga·eil!	יִתְאַחֵד יָקוּם לְהִגָּאֵל!

Who can retell the things that befell us,
Who can count them?
In every age a hero or sage
Came to our aid.

Hark! In days of yore, in Israel's ancient land,
Brave Maccabeus led his faithful band.
And now all Israel must as one arise,
Redeem itself through deed and sacrifice!

56

MA·OZ TSUR — מעוז צור

Ma·oz tsur ye·shu·a·ti,	מָעוֹז צוּר יְשׁוּעָתִי,
le·cha na·eh le·sha·bei·ach;	לְךָ נָאֶה לְשַׁבֵּחַ;
ti·kon beit te·fi·la·ti,	תִּכּוֹן בֵּית תְּפִלָּתִי,
ve·sham to·da ne·za·bei·ach.	וְשָׁם תּוֹדָה נְזַבֵּחַ.
Le·eit ta·chin mat·bei·ach,	לְעֵת תָּכִין מַטְבֵּחַ,
mi·tsar ha·me·na·bei·ach,	מִצָּר הַמְנַבֵּחַ,
az eg·mor, be·shir miz·mor,	אָז אֶגְמוֹר, בְּשִׁיר מִזְמוֹר,
cha·nu·kat ha·miz·bei·ach.	חֲנֻכַּת הַמִּזְבֵּחַ.

57

ROCK OF AGES

Rock of ages, let our song
Praise Your saving power;
You, amid the raging foes,
Were our sheltering tower.

Furious, they assailed us,
But Your arm availed us,
  And Your word
  Broke their sword,
When our own strength failed us.

Kindling new the holy lamps,
Priests approved in suffering,
Purified the nation's shrines,
Brought to God their offering.
And His courts surrounding
Hear, in joy abounding,
  Happy throngs,
  Singing songs,
With a mighty sounding.

Children of the Maccabees,
Whether free or fettered,
Wake the echoes of the songs,
Where you may be scattered.
Yours the message cheering,
That the time is nearing,
  Which will see
  All men free,
Tyrants disappearing.

58

AL HANISIM	על הנסים
Al ha·ni·sim ve·al ha·pur·kan,	עַל הַנִּסִּים, וְעַל הַפֻּרְקָן,
ve·al ha·ge·vu·rot, ve·al ha·te·shu·ot,	וְעַל הַגְּבוּרוֹת, וְעַל הַתְּשׁוּעוֹת,
ve·al ha·mil·cha·mot,	וְעַל הַמִּלְחָמוֹת,
she·a·si·ta la·a·vo·tei·nu,	שֶׁעָשִׂיתָ לַאֲבוֹתֵינוּ
ba·ya·mim ha·heim, ba·ze·man ha·zeh.	בַּיָּמִים הָהֵם, בַּזְּמַן הַזֶּה.
Bi·mei Ma·tit·ya·hu ben Yo·cha·nan	בִּימֵי מַתִּתְיָהוּ בֶּן־יוֹחָנָן
ko·hein ga·dol Chash·mo·na·i u·va·nav,	כֹּהֵן גָּדוֹל חַשְׁמוֹנָאִי וּבָנָיו,
ke·she·a·me·da mal·chut Ya·van	כְּשֶׁעָמְדָה מַלְכוּת יָוָן
al a·me·cha Yis·ra·eil,	עַל עַמְּךָ יִשְׂרָאֵל,

le·hash·ki·cham To·ra·te·cha,	לְהַשְׁכִּיחָם תּוֹרָתֶךָ,
u·le·ha·a·vi·ram mei·chu·kei re·tso·ne·cha.	וּלְהַעֲבִירָם מֵחֻקֵּי רְצוֹנֶךָ.
Ve·a·ta be·ra·cha·me·cha ha·ra·bim,	וְאַתָּה בְּרַחֲמֶיךָ הָרַבִּים,
a·mad·ta la·hem be·eit tsa·ra·tam.	עָמַדְתָּ לָהֶם בְּעֵת צָרָתָם.

The translation of Al Hanisim is on page 45.

59

UTSU EITSA — עוצו עצה

U·tsu ei·tsa ve·tu·far;	עוּצוּ עֵצָה וְתוּפָר;
da·be·ru da·var ve·lo ya·kum:	דַּבְּרוּ דָבָר וְלֹא יָקוּם:
ki i·ma·nu Eil.	כִּי עִמָּנוּ אֵל.

Make your plans — they will be annulled; scheme against us — it will not avail — for God is with us.

60

SHOSHANAT YAAKOV — שושנת יעקב

Sho·sha·nat Ya·a·kov, tsa·ha·la ve·sa·mei·cha,	שׁוֹשַׁנַּת יַעֲקֹב, צָהֲלָה וְשָׂמֵחָה,
bi·re·o·tam ya·chad, te·chei·let Mor·de·chai.	בִּרְאוֹתָם יַחַד, תְּכֵלֶת מָרְדְּכָי.
Te·shu·a·tam ha·yi·ta la·ne·tsach,	תְּשׁוּעָתָם הָיִיתָ לָנֶצַח,
ve·tik·va·tam be·chol dor va·dor.	וְתִקְוָתָם בְּכָל דּוֹר וָדוֹר.
Le·ho·dia she·kol ko·ve·cha lo yei·vo·shu	לְהוֹדִיעַ שֶׁכָּל קֹוֶיךָ לֹא יֵבֹשׁוּ
ve·lo yi·ka·le·mu la·ne·tsach kol ha·cho·sim bach.	וְלֹא יִכָּלְמוּ לָנֶצַח כָּל הַחוֹסִים בָּךְ.
A·rur Ha·man a·sher bi·keish le·a·be·di,	אָרוּר הָמָן אֲשֶׁר בִּקֵּשׁ לְאַבְּדִי,
ba·ruch Mor·de·chai ha·ye·hu·di.	בָּרוּךְ מָרְדְּכַי הַיְּהוּדִי.

The Jews of Shushan shouted with joy when they all saw Mordechai robed in purple. You have always been their deliverance, their hope in every generation: to show that those who rest their hope in You will never be shamed, that those who trust in You will never be humiliated. Cursed is Haman, who sought to make me perish; blessed is Mordechai the Jew!

61

FATHER, HEAR THE PRAYER

Father, hear the prayer we offer,
Not for ease that prayer shall be,
But for strength that we may ever
Live our lives courageously.

Be our strength in hours of weakness,
In our wanderings be our guide;
Through endeavor, failure, danger,
Be for ever at our side.

62

WHEN THIS SONG OF PRAISE

When this song of praise shall cease,
Let Your children, Lord, depart,
With the blessing of Your peace,
And Your love in every heart.

Oh, where-e'er our path may lie,
Father, let us not forget,
That we walk beneath Your eye,
That Your care upholds us yet.

63

O LORD, WHERE SHALL I FIND YOU?

O Lord, where shall I find You? Hid is Your lofty place;
And where shall I not find You, whose glory fills all space?
Who formed the world, abiding within the soul alway;
Refuge to them that seek Him, ransom for them that stray.

O, how shall mortals praise You, when angels strive in vain —
Or build for You a dwelling, whom worlds cannot contain?
I find You in the marvels of Your creative might,
In visions in Your temple, in dreams that bless the night.

Who say they have not seen You, Your heavens refute their word;
Their hosts declare Your glory, though never voice be heard.
And You, transcendent, holy, delight in Your creatures' praise,
And descend where we are gathered to glorify Your ways.

64

O GOD OUR HELP

O God, our help in ages past, our hope for years to come,
Our shelter from the stormy blast, and our eternal home.

Before the hills in order stood, or earth received her frame,
From everlasting You are God, to endless years the same.

Beneath the shadow of Your throne Your children dwell secure;
Sufficient is Your arm alone, and our defence is sure.

O God, our help in ages past, our hope for years to come,
Be now our guide while troubles last, and our eternal home.

65

O WORSHIP THE KING

O worship the King, all glorious above!
O gratefully sing His pow'r and His love!
Our Shield and Defender, the Ancient of Days,
Pavilioned in splendor and girded with praise.

O tell of His might, O sing of His grace,
Whose robe is the light, whose canopy space!
His chariots of wrath the deep thunderclouds form,
And dark is His path on the wings of the storm.

The earth, with its stores of wonders untold,
Almighty, Your power has founded of old;
Has 'stablished it fast by a changeless decree,
And 'round it has cast, like a mantle, the sea.

Your bountiful care what tongue can recite?
It breathes in the air, it shines in the light,
It streams from the hills, it descends to the plain,
And sweetly distils in the dew and the rain.

Frail children of dust, and feeble as frail,
In You do we trust, nor find You to fail;
Your mercies how tender, how firm to the end,
Our Maker, Defender, Redeemer and Friend!

66

THERE LIVES A GOD!

There lives a God! Each finite creature
Proclaims His rule on sea and land;
Throughout all changing forms of nature
Is clearly shown His mighty hand.
In ev'ry place is heard the call:
"The Lord of Hosts has made us all."

There lives a God! Though storms are sweeping
Across our pilgrim paths of life,
More bright the morn that ends the weeping
Through nights of elemental strife.
Wherever God does choose my way,
I follow Him without dismay.

There is a God! When life is waning,
His love is near from dread to save;
My years are all of His ordaining
He only taketh what He gave.
The grave shall not end all for me,
Thou livest, God, I live in Thee.

67

AMERICA THE BEAUTIFUL

O beautiful for spacious skies,
For amber waves of grain,
For purple mountain majesties,
Above the fruited plain!
America! America!
God shed His grace on thee,
And crown thy good with brotherhood,
From sea to shining sea.

O beautiful for pilgrim feet,
Whose stern, impassioned stress,
A thoroughfare for freedom beat,
Across the wilderness!
America! America!
God mend thy every flaw,
Confirm thy soul in self-control,
Thy liberty in law!

O beautiful for heroes proved
In liberating strife,
Who more than self their country loved,
And mercy more than life!
America! America!
May God thy gold refine
Til all success be nobleness,
And ev'ry gain divine!

O beautiful for patriot dream,
That sees beyond the years,
Thine alabaster cities gleam,
Undimmed by human tears!
America! America!
God shed His grace on thee,
And crown thy good with brotherhood,
From sea to shining sea!

68

THE NATIONAL ANTHEM

O say, can you see
By the dawn's early light,
What so proudly we hailed
At the twilight's last gleaming?
Whose broad stripes and bright stars,
Through the perilous fight,
O'er the ramparts we watched
Were so gallantly streaming!
And the rockets' red glare,
The bombs bursting in air,
Gave proof through the night
That our flag was still there!
O say, does that star-spangled banner yet wave
O'er the land of the free, and the home of the brave?

69

GOD OF OUR PEOPLE

God of our people, whose almighty hand
Leads forth in beauty all the starry band
Of shining worlds in splendor through the skies,
Our grateful songs before Thy throne arise.

Thy love divine hath led us in the past,
In this free land by Thee our lot is cast;
Be Thou our ruler, guardian, guide and stay,
Thy word our law, Thy paths our chosen way.

From war's alarms, from deadly pestilence,
Be Thy strong arm our ever sure defense;
Thy true religion in our hearts increase,
Thy bounteous goodness nourish us in peace.

Refresh Thy people on their toilsome way,
Lead us from night to never ending day;
Fill all our lives with love and grace divine,
And glory, laud and praise be ever Thine.

70

HATIKVAH

HATIKVAH	התקוה
Kol od ba·lei·vav pe·ni·ma,	כָּל עוֹד בַּלֵּבָב פְּנִימָה
ne·fesh Ye·hu·di ho·mi·ya.	נֶפֶשׁ יְהוּדִי הוֹמִיָּה,
U·le·fa·a·tei miz·rach ka·di·ma,	וּלְפַאֲתֵי מִזְרָח קָדִימָה
a·yin le·tsi·yon tso·fi·ya.	עַיִן לְצִיּוֹן צוֹפִיָּה.
Od lo a·ve·da tik·va·tei·nu,	עוֹד לֹא אָבְדָה תִּקְוָתֵנוּ,
ha·tik·va she·not al·pa·yim,	הַתִּקְוָה שְׁנוֹת אַלְפַּיִם,
li·he·yot am chof·shi be·ar·tsei·nu,	לִהְיוֹת עַם חָפְשִׁי בְּאַרְצֵנוּ,
be·e·rets tsi·yon vi·ru·sha·la·yim.	בְּאֶרֶץ צִיּוֹן וִירוּשָׁלַיִם.

So long as still within the inmost heart a Jewish spirit sings, so long as the eye looks eastward, gazing toward Zion, our hope is not lost — that hope of two millennia, to be a free people in our land, the land of Zion and Jerusalem.

Transliterations of Recurring Passages

1

READER'S KADDISH

Yit·ga·dal ve·yit·ka·dash she·mei ra·ba	יִתְגַּדַּל וְיִתְקַדַּשׁ שְׁמֵהּ רַבָּא
be·al·ma di·ve·ra chi·re·u·tei,	בְּעָלְמָא דִּי־בְרָא כִרְעוּתֵהּ,
ve·yam·lich mal·chu·tei be·cha·yei·chon	וְיַמְלִיךְ מַלְכוּתֵהּ בְּחַיֵּיכוֹן
u·ve·yo·mei·chon u·ve·cha·yei	וּבְיוֹמֵיכוֹן וּבְחַיֵּי
de·chol beit Yis·ra·eil,	דְכָל־בֵּית יִשְׂרָאֵל,
ba·a·ga·la u·vi·ze·man ka·riv,	בַּעֲגָלָא וּבִזְמַן קָרִיב,
ve·i·me·ru: a·mein.	וְאִמְרוּ: אָמֵן.
Ye·hei she·mei ra·ba me·va·rach	יְהֵא שְׁמֵהּ רַבָּא מְבָרַךְ
le·a·lam u·le·al·mei al·ma·ya.	לְעָלַם וּלְעָלְמֵי עָלְמַיָּא.
Yit·ba·rach ve·yish·ta·bach,	יִתְבָּרַךְ וְיִשְׁתַּבַּח,
ve·yit·pa·ar ve·yit·ro·mam ve·yit·na·sei,	וְיִתְפָּאַר וְיִתְרוֹמַם וְיִתְנַשֵּׂא,
ve·yit·ha·dar ve·yit·a·leh ve·yit·ha·lal	וְיִתְהַדַּר וְיִתְעַלֶּה וְיִתְהַלָּל
she·mei de·ku·de·sha, be·rich hu,	שְׁמֵהּ דְּקוּדְשָׁא, בְּרִיךְ הוּא,
le·ei·la min kol bi·re·cha·ta ve·shi·ra·ta,	לְעֵלָּא מִן כָּל־בִּרְכָתָא וְשִׁירָתָא,
tush·be·cha·ta ve·ne·che·ma·ta	תֻּשְׁבְּחָתָא וְנֶחֱמָתָא
da·a·mi·ran be·al·ma, ve·i·me·ru: a·mein.	דַּאֲמִירָן בְּעָלְמָא, וְאִמְרוּ: אָמֵן.

2

BARECHU

Ba·re·chu et A·do·nai ha·me·vo·rach!	בָּרְכוּ אֶת־יְיָ הַמְבֹרָךְ!
Ba·ruch A·do·nai ha·me·vo·rach	בָּרוּךְ יְיָ הַמְבֹרָךְ
le·o·lam va·ed!	לְעוֹלָם וָעֶד!

3

MA·ARIV ARAVIM

Ba·ruch a·ta, A·do·nai E·lo·hei·nu,	בָּרוּךְ אַתָּה, יְיָ אֱלֹהֵינוּ,
me·lech ha·o·lam, a·sher bi·de·va·ro	מֶלֶךְ הָעוֹלָם, אֲשֶׁר בִּדְבָרוֹ
ma·a·riv a·ra·vim. Be·choch·ma	מַעֲרִיב עֲרָבִים. בְּחָכְמָה

po·tei·ach she·a·rim,	פּוֹתֵחַ שְׁעָרִים,
u·vi·te·vu·na me·sha·neh i·tim,	וּבִתְבוּנָה מְשַׁנֶּה עִתִּים,
u·ma·cha·lif et ha·ze·ma·nim,	וּמַחֲלִיף אֶת־הַזְּמַנִּים,
u·me·sa·deir et ha·ko·cha·vim	וּמְסַדֵּר אֶת־הַכּוֹכָבִים
be·mish·me·ro·tei·hem ba·ra·ki·a	בְּמִשְׁמְרוֹתֵיהֶם בָּרָקִיעַ
ki·re·tso·no.	כִּרְצוֹנוֹ.
Bo·rei yom va·lai·la,	בּוֹרֵא יוֹם וָלָיְלָה,
go·leil or mi·pe·nei cho·shech	גּוֹלֵל אוֹר מִפְּנֵי חֹשֶׁךְ
ve·cho·shech mi·pe·nei or,	וְחֹשֶׁךְ מִפְּנֵי אוֹר,
u·ma·a·vir yom u·mei·vi lai·la,	וּמַעֲבִיר יוֹם וּמֵבִיא לָיְלָה,
u·mav·dil bein yom u·vein lai·la,	וּמַבְדִּיל בֵּין יוֹם וּבֵין לָיְלָה,
A·do·nai tse·va·ot she·mo.	יְיָ צְבָאוֹת שְׁמוֹ.
Eil chai ve·ka·yam, ta·mid	אֵל חַי וְקַיָּם, תָּמִיד
yim·loch a·lei·nu, le·o·lam va·ed.	יִמְלוֹךְ עָלֵינוּ לְעוֹלָם וָעֶד.
Ba·ruch a·ta, A·do·nai,	בָּרוּךְ אַתָּה, יְיָ,
ha·ma·a·riv a·ra·vim.	הַמַּעֲרִיב עֲרָבִים.

4

SHEMA

שְׁמַע יִשְׂרָאֵל: יְיָ אֱלֹהֵינוּ, יְיָ אֶחָד!

She·ma Yis·ra·eil: A·do·nai E·lo·hei·nu, A·do·nai E·chad!

בָּרוּךְ שֵׁם כְּבוֹד מַלְכוּתוֹ לְעוֹלָם וָעֶד!

Ba·ruch sheim ke·vod mal·chu·to le·o·lam va·ed!

5

VE·AHAVTA

Ve·a·hav·ta eit A·do·nai E·lo·he·cha, be·chol	וְאָהַבְתָּ אֵת יְיָ אֱלֹהֶיךָ בְּכָל־
le·va·ve·cha, u·ve·chol naf·she·cha, u·ve·chol	לְבָבְךָ וּבְכָל־נַפְשְׁךָ וּבְכָל־
me·o·de·cha.	מְאֹדֶךָ.

Ve·ha·yu ha·de·va·rim ha·ei·leh, a·sher a·no·chi
me·tsa·ve·cha ha·yom, al le·va·ve·cha. Ve·shi·nan·tam
le·va·ne·cha, ve·di·bar·ta bam be·shiv·te·cha
be·vei·te·cha u·ve·lech·te·cha va·de·rech,
u·ve·shoch·be·cha u·ve·ku·me·cha. U·ke·shar·tam le·ot
al ya·de·cha, ve·ha·yu le·to·ta·fot bein ei·ne·cha.
U·che·tav·tam al me·zu·zot bei·te·cha
u·vish·a·re·cha.

וְהָיוּ הַדְּבָרִים הָאֵלֶּה, אֲשֶׁר אָנֹכִי
מְצַוְּךָ הַיּוֹם, עַל־לְבָבֶךָ. וְשִׁנַּנְתָּם
לְבָנֶיךָ, וְדִבַּרְתָּ בָּם בְּשִׁבְתְּךָ
בְּבֵיתֶךָ, וּבְלֶכְתְּךָ בַדֶּרֶךְ,
וּבְשָׁכְבְּךָ וּבְקוּמֶךָ. וּקְשַׁרְתָּם לְאוֹת
עַל־יָדֶךָ, וְהָיוּ לְטֹטָפֹת בֵּין עֵינֶיךָ.
וּכְתַבְתָּם עַל־מְזֻזוֹת בֵּיתֶךָ,
וּבִשְׁעָרֶיךָ.

Le·ma·an tiz·ke·ru, va·a·si·tem et kol
mits·vo·tai vi·he·yi·tem ke·do·shim
lei·lo·hei·chem. A·ni A·do·nai E·lo·hei·chem, a·sher
ho·tsei·ti e·te·chem mei·e·rets Mits·ra·yim,
li·he·yot la·chem lei·lo·him. A·ni A·do·nai
E·lo·hei·chem.

לְמַעַן תִּזְכְּרוּ וַעֲשִׂיתֶם אֶת־כָּל־
מִצְוֹתָי, וִהְיִיתֶם קְדֹשִׁים
לֵאלֹהֵיכֶם. אֲנִי יְיָ אֱלֹהֵיכֶם, אֲשֶׁר
הוֹצֵאתִי אֶתְכֶם מֵאֶרֶץ מִצְרַיִם
לִהְיוֹת לָכֶם לֵאלֹהִים. אֲנִי יְיָ
אֱלֹהֵיכֶם.

6

MI CHAMOCHA

Mi cha·mo·cha ba·ei·lim, A·do·nai?
Mi ka·mo·cha, ne·dar ba·ko·desh,
no·ra te·hi·lot, o·sei fe·leh?

מִי־כָמֹכָה בָּאֵלִם, יְיָ?
מִי כָּמֹכָה, נֶאְדָּר בַּקֹּדֶשׁ,
נוֹרָא תְהִלֹּת, עֹשֵׂה פֶלֶא?

Mal·chu·te·cha ra·u va·ne·cha,
bo·kei·a yam li·fe·nei Mo·sheh;
"Zeh Ei·li" a·nu ve·a·me·ru.
"A·do·nai yim·loch le·o·lam va·ed."

מַלְכוּתְךָ רָאוּ בָנֶיךָ,
בּוֹקֵעַ יָם לִפְנֵי מֹשֶׁה;
"זֶה אֵלִי!" עָנוּ וְאָמְרוּ:
"יְיָ יִמְלֹךְ לְעֹלָם וָעֶד!"

Ve·ne·e·mar: "Ki fa·da A·do·nai et Ya·a·kov,
u·ge·a·lo mi·yad cha·zak mi·me·nu."
Ba·ruch a·ta, A·do·nai, ga·al Yis·ra·eil.

וְנֶאֱמַר: "כִּי־פָדָה יְיָ אֶת־יַעֲקֹב,
וּגְאָלוֹ מִיַּד חָזָק מִמֶּנּוּ."
בָּרוּךְ אַתָּה, יְיָ, גָּאַל יִשְׂרָאֵל.

7

TSUR YISRAEIL

Tsur Yis·ra·eil, ku·ma be·ez·rat
Yis·ra·eil, u·fe·dei chi·ne·u·me·cha
Ye·hu·dah ve·yis·ra·eil.

צוּר יִשְׂרָאֵל, קוּמָה בְּעֶזְרַת
יִשְׂרָאֵל, וּפְדֵה כִנְאֻמֶךָ
יְהוּדָה וְיִשְׂרָאֵל.

Go·a·lei·nu A·do·nai tse·va·ot she·mo, ke·dosh
Yis·ra·eil. Ba·ruch a·ta, A·do·nai, ga·al
Yis·ra·eil.

גֹּאֲלֵנוּ יְיָ צְבָאוֹת שְׁמוֹ, קְדוֹשׁ
יִשְׂרָאֵל. בָּרוּךְ אַתָּה, יְיָ, גָּאַל
יִשְׂרָאֵל.

8

VESHAMERU

Ve·sha·me·ru ve·nei Yis·ra·eil et ha·sha·bat,
la·a·sot et ha·sha·bat le·do·ro·tam, be·rit
o·lam. Bei·ni u·vein be·nei Yis·ra·eil ot
hi le·o·lam. Ki shei·shet ya·mim a·sa A·do·nai
et ha·sha·ma·yim ve·et ha·a·rets, u·va·yom
ha·she·vi·i sha·vat va·yi·na·fash.

וְשָׁמְרוּ בְנֵי־יִשְׂרָאֵל אֶת־הַשַּׁבָּת,
לַעֲשׂוֹת אֶת־הַשַּׁבָּת לְדֹרֹתָם בְּרִית
עוֹלָם. בֵּינִי וּבֵין בְּנֵי יִשְׂרָאֵל אוֹת
הִיא לְעֹלָם, כִּי שֵׁשֶׁת יָמִים עָשָׂה יְיָ
אֶת־הַשָּׁמַיִם וְאֶת־הָאָרֶץ, וּבַיּוֹם
הַשְּׁבִיעִי שָׁבַת וַיִּנָּפַשׁ.

9

AVOT

A·do·nai, se·fa·tai tif·tach, u·fi
ya·gid te·hi·la·te·cha.

אֲדֹנָי, שְׂפָתַי תִּפְתָּח, וּפִי
יַגִּיד תְּהִלָּתֶךָ.

Ba·ruch a·ta, A·do·nai, E·lo·hei·nu vei·lo·hei
a·vo·tei·nu, E·lo·hei Av·ra·ham, E·lo·hei
Yits·chak, vei·lo·hei Ya·a·kov: ha·eil ha·ga·dol,
ha·gi·bor ve·ha·no·ra, Eil el·yon,
go·meil cha·sa·dim to·vim, ve·ko·nei ha·kol,
ve·zo·cheir cha·se·dei a·vot, u·mei·vi ge·u·lah
li·ve·nei ve·nei·hem, le·ma·an she·mo, be·a·ha·va.
Me·lech o·zeir u·mo·shi·a u·ma·gein.
Ba·ruch a·ta, A·do·nai, ma·gein Av·ra·ham.

בָּרוּךְ אַתָּה, יְיָ אֱלֹהֵינוּ וֵאלֹהֵי
אֲבוֹתֵינוּ, אֱלֹהֵי אַבְרָהָם, אֱלֹהֵי
יִצְחָק, וֵאלֹהֵי יַעֲקֹב: הָאֵל הַגָּדוֹל,
הַגִּבּוֹר וְהַנּוֹרָא, אֵל עֶלְיוֹן,
גּוֹמֵל חֲסָדִים טוֹבִים, וְקוֹנֵה הַכֹּל,
וְזוֹכֵר חַסְדֵי אָבוֹת, וּמֵבִיא גְאֻלָּה
לִבְנֵי בְנֵיהֶם, לְמַעַן שְׁמוֹ, בְּאַהֲבָה.
מֶלֶךְ עוֹזֵר וּמוֹשִׁיעַ וּמָגֵן.
בָּרוּךְ אַתָּה, יְיָ, מָגֵן אַבְרָהָם.

10

GEVUROT

A·ta gi·bor le·o·lam, A·do·nai,
me·cha·yei ha·kol a·ta,
rav le·ho·shi·a.

אַתָּה גִּבּוֹר לְעוֹלָם, אֲדֹנָי,
מְחַיֵּה הַכֹּל אַתָּה,
רַב לְהוֹשִׁיעַ.

Me·chal·keil cha·yim be·che·sed,	מְכַלְכֵּל חַיִּים בְּחֶסֶד,
me·cha·yei ha·kol be·ra·cha·mim ra·bim.	מְחַיֵּה הַכֹּל בְּרַחֲמִים רַבִּים.
So·meich no·fe·lim, ve·ro·fei cho·lim,	סוֹמֵךְ נוֹפְלִים, וְרוֹפֵא חוֹלִים,
u·ma·tir a·su·rim, u·me·ka·yeim	וּמַתִּיר אֲסוּרִים, וּמְקַיֵּם
e·mu·na·to li·shei·nei a·far.	אֱמוּנָתוֹ לִישֵׁנֵי עָפָר.
Mi cha·mo·cha, ba·al ge·vu·rot,	מִי כָמְוֹךָ, בַּעַל גְּבוּרוֹת,
u·mi do·meh lach,	וּמִי דּוֹמֶה לָּךְ,
me·lech mei·mit u·me·cha·yeh	מֶלֶךְ מֵמִית וּמְחַיֶּה
u·mats·mi·ach ye·shu·a?	וּמַצְמִיחַ יְשׁוּעָה?
Ve·ne·e·man a·ta le·ha·cha·yot ha·kol.	וְנֶאֱמָן אַתָּה לְהַחֲיוֹת הַכֹּל.
Ba·ruch a·ta, A·do·nai,	בָּרוּךְ אַתָּה, יְיָ,
me·cha·yei ha·kol.	מְחַיֵּה הַכֹּל.

11

YISMECHU

Yis·me·chu be·mal·chu·te·cha sho·me·rei Sha·bat	יִשְׂמְחוּ בְמַלְכוּתְךָ שׁוֹמְרֵי שַׁבָּת
ve·ko·re·ei o·neg. Am me·ka·de·shei she·vi·i	וְקוֹרְאֵי עֹנֶג. עַם מְקַדְּשֵׁי שְׁבִיעִי
ku·lam yis·be·u ve·yit·a·ne·gu mi·tu·ve·cha.	כֻּלָּם יִשְׂבְּעוּ וְיִתְעַנְּגוּ מִטּוּבֶךָ.
Ve·ha·she·vi·i ra·tsi·ta bo ve·ki·dash·to,	וְהַשְּׁבִיעִי רָצִיתָ בּוֹ וְקִדַּשְׁתּוֹ.
chem·dat ya·mim o·to ka·ra·ta, zei·cher	חֶמְדַּת יָמִים אוֹתוֹ קָרָאתָ, זֵכֶר
le·ma·a·sei ve·rei·shit.	לְמַעֲשֵׂה בְרֵאשִׁית.

12

RETSEI VIMENUCHATEINU

E·lo·hei·nu vei·lo·hei a·vo·tei·nu,	אֱלֹהֵינוּ וֵאלֹהֵי אֲבוֹתֵינוּ,
re·tsei vi·me·nu·cha·tei·nu.	רְצֵה בִמְנוּחָתֵנוּ.
Ka·de·shei·nu be·mits·vo·te·cha,	קַדְּשֵׁנוּ בְּמִצְוֹתֶיךָ,
ve·tein chel·kei·nu be·to·ra·te·cha.	וְתֵן חֶלְקֵנוּ בְּתוֹרָתֶךָ.
Sa·be·ei·nu mi·tu·ve·cha,	שַׂבְּעֵנוּ מִטּוּבֶךָ,
ve·sa·me·chei·nu bi·shu·a·te·cha,	וְשַׂמְּחֵנוּ בִּישׁוּעָתֶךָ,
ve·ta·heir li·bei·nu le·ov·de·cha be·e·met.	וְטַהֵר לִבֵּנוּ לְעָבְדְּךָ בֶּאֱמֶת.

Ve·han·chi·lei·nu, A·do·nai E·lo·hei·nu,	וְהַנְחִילֵנוּ, יְיָ אֱלֹהֵינוּ,
be·a·ha·va u·ve·ra·tson	בְּאַהֲבָה וּבְרָצוֹן
Sha·bat kod·she·cha,	שַׁבַּת קָדְשֶׁךָ,
ve·ya·nu·chu va Yis·ra·eil	וְיָנוּחוּ בָהּ יִשְׂרָאֵל
me·ka·de·shei she·me·cha.	מְקַדְּשֵׁי שְׁמֶךָ.
Ba·ruch a·ta, A·do·nai,	בָּרוּךְ אַתָּה, יְיָ,
me·ka·deish ha·sha·bat.	מְקַדֵּשׁ הַשַּׁבָּת.

13

MA TOVU

Ma to·vu o·ha·le·cha Ya·a·kov,	מַה־טֹּבוּ אֹהָלֶיךָ, יַעֲקֹב,
mish·ke·no·te·cha, Yis·ra·eil!	מִשְׁכְּנֹתֶיךָ, יִשְׂרָאֵל!
Va·a·ni, be·rov chas·de·cha a·vo vei·te·cha,	וַאֲנִי, בְּרֹב חַסְדְּךָ אָבֹא בֵיתֶךָ,
esh·ta·cha·veh el hei·chal kod·she·cha	אֶשְׁתַּחֲוֶה אֶל־הֵיכַל קָדְשְׁךָ
be·yir·a·te·cha.	בְּיִרְאָתֶךָ.
A·do·nai, a·hav·ti me·on bei·te·cha,	יְיָ, אָהַבְתִּי מְעוֹן בֵּיתֶךָ,
u·me·kom mish·kan ke·vo·de·cha.	וּמְקוֹם מִשְׁכַּן כְּבוֹדֶךָ.
Va·a·ni esh·ta·cha·veh ve·ech·ra·a,	וַאֲנִי אֶשְׁתַּחֲוֶה וְאֶכְרָעָה,
ev·re·cha li·fe·nei A·do·nai o·si.	אֶבְרְכָה לִפְנֵי־יְיָ עֹשִׂי.
Va·a·ni te·fi·la·ti le·cha, A·do·nai, eit ra·tson.	וַאֲנִי תְפִלָּתִי לְךָ, יְיָ, עֵת רָצוֹן.
E·lo·him, be·rov chas·de·cha,	אֱלֹהִים, בְּרָב־חַסְדֶּךָ,
a·nei·ni be·e·met yish·e·cha.	עֲנֵנִי בֶּאֱמֶת יִשְׁעֶךָ.

14

YOTSEIR

Ba·ruch a·ta, A·do·nai E·lo·hei·nu,	בָּרוּךְ אַתָּה, יְיָ אֱלֹהֵינוּ,
me·lech ha·o·lam, yo·tseir or	מֶלֶךְ הָעוֹלָם, יוֹצֵר אוֹר
u·vo·rei cho·shech,	וּבוֹרֵא חֹשֶׁךְ,
o·seh sha·lom u·vo·rei et ha·kol.	עֹשֶׂה שָׁלוֹם וּבוֹרֵא אֶת־הַכֹּל.
Ha·mei·ir la·a·rets	הַמֵּאִיר לָאָרֶץ
ve·la·da·rim a·le·ha be·ra·cha·mim,	וְלַדָּרִים עָלֶיהָ בְּרַחֲמִים,
u·ve·tu·vo me·cha·deish be·chol yom	וּבְטוּבוֹ מְחַדֵּשׁ בְּכָל־יוֹם

ta·mid ma·a·sei ve·rei·shit.
תָּמִיד מַעֲשֵׂה בְרֵאשִׁית.

Ma ra·bu ma·a·se·cha, A·do·nai!
מָה רַבּוּ מַעֲשֶׂיךָ, יְיָ!

Ku·lam be·choch·ma a·si·ta,
כֻּלָּם בְּחָכְמָה עָשִׂיתָ,

ma·le·a ha·a·rets kin·ya·ne·cha.
מָלְאָה הָאָרֶץ קִנְיָנֶךָ.

Tit·ba·rach, A·do·nai E·lo·hei·nu,
תִּתְבָּרַךְ, יְיָ אֱלֹהֵינוּ,

al she·vach ma·a·sei ya·de·cha,
עַל־שֶׁבַח מַעֲשֵׂה יָדֶיךָ,

ve·al me·o·rei or she·a·si·ta:
וְעַל־מְאוֹרֵי־אוֹר שֶׁעָשִׂיתָ:

ye·fa·a·ru·cha. Se·la.
יְפָאֲרוּךָ. סֶּלָה.

Ba·ruch a·ta, A·do·nai,
בָּרוּךְ אַתָּה, יְיָ,

yo·tseir ha·me·o·rot.
יוֹצֵר הַמְּאוֹרוֹת.

15

RESPONSES TO THE KEDUSHAH

Ka·dosh, ka·dosh, ka·dosh
קָדוֹשׁ, קָדוֹשׁ, קָדוֹשׁ

A·do·nai tse·va·ot,
יְיָ צְבָאוֹת,

me·lo chol ha·a·rets ke·vo·do.
מְלֹא כָל־הָאָרֶץ כְּבוֹדוֹ.

Ba·ruch ke·vod A·do·nai mi·me·ko·mo.
בָּרוּךְ כְּבוֹד יְיָ מִמְּקוֹמוֹ.

A·ni A·do·nai E·lo·hei·chem!
אֲנִי יְיָ אֱלֹהֵיכֶם!

Yim·loch A·do·nai le·o·lam,
יִמְלֹךְ יְיָ לְעוֹלָם,

E·lo·ha·yich Tsi·yon,
אֱלֹהַיִךְ צִיּוֹן,

le·dor va·dor. Ha·le·lu·yah!
לְדֹר וָדֹר. הַלְלוּיָהּ!

16

TORAH BLESSINGS

Before the reading

Ba·re·chu et A·do·nai ha·me·vo·rach!
בָּרְכוּ אֶת־יְיָ הַמְבֹרָךְ!

Ba·ruch A·do·nai ha·me·vo·rach le·o·lam va·ed!
בָּרוּךְ יְיָ הַמְבֹרָךְ לְעוֹלָם וָעֶד!

Ba·ruch a·ta, A·do·nai E·lo·hei·nu, me·lech
בָּרוּךְ אַתָּה, יְיָ אֱלֹהֵינוּ, מֶלֶךְ

ha·o·lam, a·sher ba·char ba·nu mi·kol
הָעוֹלָם, אֲשֶׁר בָּחַר־בָּנוּ מִכָּל־

ha·a·mim, ve·na·tan la·nu et To·ra·to.	הָעַמִּים וְנָתַן־לָנוּ אֶת־תּוֹרָתוֹ.
Ba·ruch a·ta, A·do·nai, no·tein ha·to·rah.	בָּרוּךְ אַתָּה, יְיָ, נוֹתֵן הַתּוֹרָה.

After the reading

Ba·ruch a·ta, A·do·nai E·lo·hei·nu, me·lech	בָּרוּךְ אַתָּה, יְיָ אֱלֹהֵינוּ, מֶלֶךְ
ha·o·lam, a·sher na·tan la·nu To·rat e·met,	הָעוֹלָם, אֲשֶׁר נָתַן־לָנוּ תּוֹרַת אֱמֶת
ve·cha·yei o·lam na·ta be·to·chei·nu.	וְחַיֵּי עוֹלָם נָטַע בְּתוֹכֵנוּ.
Ba·ruch a·ta, A·do·nai, no·tein ha·to·rah.	בָּרוּךְ אַתָּה, יְיָ, נוֹתֵן הַתּוֹרָה.

17

HAFTARAH BLESSINGS

Before the reading

Ba·ruch a·ta, A·do·nai E·lo·hei·nu, me·lech	בָּרוּךְ אַתָּה, יְיָ אֱלֹהֵינוּ, מֶלֶךְ
ha·o·lam, a·sher ba·char bi·ne·vi·im	הָעוֹלָם, אֲשֶׁר בָּחַר בִּנְבִיאִים
to·vim, ve·ra·tsa ve·di·ve·rei·hem	טוֹבִים, וְרָצָה בְדִבְרֵיהֶם
ha·ne·e·ma·rim be·e·met.	הַנֶּאֱמָרִים בֶּאֱמֶת.
Ba·ruch a·ta, A·do·nai, ha·bo·cheir ba·to·rah	בָּרוּךְ אַתָּה, יְיָ, הַבּוֹחֵר בַּתּוֹרָה
u·ve·mo·sheh av·do, u·ve·yis·ra·eil a·mo,	וּבְמֹשֶׁה עַבְדּוֹ, וּבְיִשְׂרָאֵל עַמּוֹ,
u·vi·ne·vi·ei ha·e·met va·tse·dek.	וּבִנְבִיאֵי הָאֱמֶת וָצֶדֶק.

After the reading (*short form*)

Ba·ruch a·ta, A·do·nai E·lo·hei·nu, me·lech	בָּרוּךְ אַתָּה, יְיָ אֱלֹהֵינוּ, מֶלֶךְ
ha·o·lam, tsur kol ha·o·la·mim,	הָעוֹלָם, צוּר כָּל־הָעוֹלָמִים,
tsa·dik be·chol ha·do·rot, ha·eil ha·ne·e·man,	צַדִּיק בְּכָל־הַדּוֹרוֹת, הָאֵל הַנֶּאֱמָן
ha·o·meir ve·o·seh, ha·me·da·beir u·me·ka·yeim,	הָאוֹמֵר וְעוֹשֶׂה, הַמְדַבֵּר וּמְקַיֵּם,
she·kol de·va·rav e·met va·tse·dek.	שֶׁכָּל־דְּבָרָיו אֱמֶת וָצֶדֶק.
Al ha·to·rah, ve·al ha·a·vo·dah,	עַל־הַתּוֹרָה, וְעַל־הָעֲבוֹדָה,
ve·al ha·ne·vi·im, ve·al yom ha·sha·bat	וְעַל־הַנְּבִיאִים, וְעַל־יוֹם הַשַּׁבָּת
ha·zeh, she·na·ta·ta la·nu, A·do·nai E·lo·hei·nu,	הַזֶּה, שֶׁנָּתַתָּ לָּנוּ, יְיָ אֱלֹהֵינוּ,
li·ke·du·sha ve·li·me·nu·cha, le·cha·vod	לִקְדֻשָּׁה וְלִמְנוּחָה, לְכָבוֹד
u·le·tif·a·ret, al ha·kol, A·do·nai E·lo·hei·nu,	וּלְתִפְאָרֶת, עַל־הַכֹּל, יְיָ אֱלֹהֵינוּ,

a·nach·nu mo·dim lach, u·me·va·re·chim o·tach.	אֲנַחְנוּ מוֹדִים לָךְ וּמְבָרְכִים אוֹתָךְ.
Yit·ba·rach shi·me·cha be·fi kol chai ta·mid	יִתְבָּרַךְ שִׁמְךָ בְּפִי כָּל־חַי תָּמִיד
le·o·lam va·ed. Ba·ruch a·ta, A·do·nai,	לְעוֹלָם וָעֶד. בָּרוּךְ אַתָּה, יְיָ,
me·ka·deish ha·sha·bat.	מְקַדֵּשׁ הַשַּׁבָּת.

18

PASSAGES RELATED TO THE TORAH RITUAL

I.

Av ha·ra·cha·mim, hei·ti·va vi·re·tso·ne·cha	אַב הָרַחֲמִים, הֵיטִיבָה בִרְצוֹנְךָ
et Tsi·yon, tiv·neh cho·mot Ye·ru·sha·la·yim.	אֶת־צִיּוֹן, תִּבְנֶה חוֹמוֹת יְרוּשָׁלָיִם.
Ki ve·cha le·vad ba·tach·nu, me·lech Eil ram	כִּי בְךָ לְבַד בָּטָחְנוּ, מֶלֶךְ אֵל רָם
ve·ni·sa, a·don o·la·mim.	וְנִשָּׂא, אֲדוֹן עוֹלָמִים.

II.

Ba·ruch she·na·tan To·rah le·a·mo Yis·ra·eil	בָּרוּךְ שֶׁנָּתַן תּוֹרָה לְעַמּוֹ יִשְׂרָאֵל
bi·ke·du·sha·to.	בִּקְדֻשָּׁתוֹ.

III.

Ki mi·tsi·yon tei·tsei To·rah	כִּי מִצִּיּוֹן תֵּצֵא תוֹרָה
u·de·var A·do·nai mi·ru·sha·la·yim.	וּדְבַר־יְיָ מִירוּשָׁלָיִם.

IV.

Le·cha, A·do·nai, ha·ge·du·la, ve·ha·ge·vu·ra	לְךָ, יְיָ, הַגְּדֻלָּה וְהַגְּבוּרָה
ve·ha·tif·e·ret, ve·ha·nei·tsach, ve·ha·hod, ki chol	וְהַתִּפְאֶרֶת וְהַנֵּצַח וְהַהוֹד, כִּי כֹל
ba·sha·ma·yim u·va·a·rets, le·cha, A·do·nai, ha·mam·la·cha	בַּשָּׁמַיִם וּבָאָרֶץ, לְךָ יְיָ הַמַּמְלָכָה
ve·ha·mit·na·sei le·chol le·rosh.	וְהַמִּתְנַשֵּׂא לְכֹל לְרֹאשׁ.

V.

Ho·do al e·rets ve·sha·ma·yim, ve·ya·rem ke·ren	הוֹדוֹ עַל־אֶרֶץ וְשָׁמָיִם, וַיָּרֶם קֶרֶן
le·a·mo, te·hi·la le·chol cha·si·dav, li·ve·nei	לְעַמּוֹ, תְּהִלָּה לְכָל־חֲסִידָיו, לִבְנֵי
Yis·ra·eil, am ke·ro·vo. Ha·le·lu·yah!	יִשְׂרָאֵל, עַם קְרוֹבוֹ. הַלְלוּיָהּ!

VI.

Ki le·kach tov na·ta·ti la·chem,	כִּי לֶקַח טוֹב נָתַתִּי לָכֶם,
To·ra·ti al ta·a·zo·vu.	תּוֹרָתִי אַל תַּעֲזֹבוּ.

Eits cha·yim hi la·ma·cha·zi·kim ba,
ve·to·me·che·ha me·u·shar. De·ra·che·ha da·re·chei
no·am, ve·chol ne·ti·vo·te·ha sha·lom.

עֵץ־חַיִּים הִיא לַמַּחֲזִיקִים בָּהּ,
וְתֹמְכֶיהָ מְאֻשָּׁר. דְּרָכֶיהָ דַרְכֵי־
נֹעַם, וְכָל־נְתִיבֹתֶיהָ שָׁלוֹם.

VII.

Ha·shi·vei·nu, A·do·nai, ei·le·cha ve·na·shu·va;
cha·deish ya·mei·nu ke·ke·dem.

הֲשִׁיבֵנוּ, יְיָ, אֵלֶיךָ וְנָשׁוּבָה;
חַדֵּשׁ יָמֵינוּ כְּקֶדֶם.

VIII.

Ye·ha·le·lu et sheim A·do·nai,
ki nis·gav she·mo le·va·do.

יְהַלְלוּ אֶת־שֵׁם יְיָ,
כִּי־נִשְׂגָּב שְׁמוֹ לְבַדּוֹ.

IX.

Va·a·ni zot be·ri·ti o·tam, a·mar A·do·nai:
Ru·chi a·sher a·le·cha, u·de·va·rai a·sher
sam·ti be·fi·cha, lo ya·mu·shu mi·pi·cha,
u·mi·pi zar·a·cha, u·mi·pi ze·ra zar·a·cha, a·mar
A·do·nai, mei·a·ta ve·ad o·lam.

וַאֲנִי זֹאת בְּרִיתִי אוֹתָם, אָמַר יְיָ:
רוּחִי אֲשֶׁר עָלֶיךָ, וּדְבָרַי אֲשֶׁר־
שַׂמְתִּי בְּפִיךָ, לֹא־יָמוּשׁוּ מִפִּיךָ
וּמִפִּי זַרְעֲךָ וּמִפִּי זֶרַע זַרְעֲךָ, אָמַר
יְיָ, מֵעַתָּה וְעַד־עוֹלָם.

X.

Ve·zot ha·to·rah a·sher sam Mo·sheh li·fe·nei
be·nei Yis·ra·eil, al pi A·do·nai be·yad Mo·sheh.

וְזֹאת הַתּוֹרָה אֲשֶׁר־שָׂם מֹשֶׁה לִפְנֵי
בְּנֵי יִשְׂרָאֵל, עַל־פִּי יְיָ בְּיַד־מֹשֶׁה.

XI.

Se·u she·a·rim ra·shei·chem,
ve·hi·na·se·u pi·te·chei o·lam,
ve·ya·vo me·lech ha·ka·vod!
Mi hu zeh me·lech ha·ka·vod?
A·do·nai tse·va·ot —
hu me·lech ha·ka·vod! Se·la.

שְׂאוּ שְׁעָרִים רָאשֵׁיכֶם,
וְהִנָּשְׂאוּ פִּתְחֵי עוֹלָם,
וְיָבוֹא מֶלֶךְ הַכָּבוֹד!
מִי הוּא זֶה מֶלֶךְ הַכָּבוֹד?
יְיָ צְבָאוֹת —
הוּא מֶלֶךְ הַכָּבוֹד! סֶלָה.

19

ALEINU

A·lei·nu le·sha·bei·ach la·a·don ha·kol,
la·teit ge·du·lah le·yo·tseir be·rei·shit,
she·lo a·sa·nu ke·go·yei ha·a·ra·tsot,

עָלֵינוּ לְשַׁבֵּחַ לַאֲדוֹן הַכֹּל,
לָתֵת גְּדֻלָּה לְיוֹצֵר בְּרֵאשִׁית,
שֶׁלֹּא עָשָׂנוּ כְּגוֹיֵי הָאֲרָצוֹת,

ve·lo sa·ma·nu ke·mish·pe·chot ha·a·da·mah;	וְלֹא שָׂמָנוּ כְּמִשְׁפְּחוֹת הָאֲדָמָה;
she·lo sam chel·kei·nu ka·hem,	שֶׁלֹּא שָׂם חֶלְקֵנוּ כָּהֶם,
ve·go·ra·lei·nu ke·chol ha·mo·nam.	וְגֹרָלֵנוּ כְּכָל־הֲמוֹנָם.
Va·a·nach·nu ko·re·im u·mish·ta·cha·vim u·mo·dim	וַאֲנַחְנוּ כּוֹרְעִים וּמִשְׁתַּחֲוִים וּמוֹדִים
li·fe·nei me·lech ma·le·chei ha·me·la·chim,	לִפְנֵי מֶלֶךְ מַלְכֵי הַמְּלָכִים,
ha·ka·dosh ba·ruch Hu.	הַקָּדוֹשׁ בָּרוּךְ הוּא.

20

ALEINU (Conclusion)

Ve·ne·e·mar: "Ve·ha·ya A·do·nai le·me·lech	וְנֶאֱמַר: "וְהָיָה יְיָ לְמֶלֶךְ
al kol ha·a·rets; ba·yom ha·hu yi·he·yeh	עַל־כָּל־הָאָרֶץ; בַּיּוֹם הַהוּא יִהְיֶה
A·do·nai e·chad u·she·mo e·chad."	יְיָ אֶחָד וּשְׁמוֹ אֶחָד."

21

HAVDALAH BLESSINGS

Ba·ruch a·ta, A·do·nai E·lo·hei·nu,	בָּרוּךְ אַתָּה, יְיָ אֱלֹהֵינוּ,
me·lech ha·o·lam, bo·rei pe·ri ha·ga·fen.	מֶלֶךְ הָעוֹלָם, בּוֹרֵא פְּרִי הַגָּפֶן.
Ba·ruch a·ta, A·do·nai E·lo·hei·nu,	בָּרוּךְ אַתָּה, יְיָ אֱלֹהֵינוּ,
me·lech ha·o·lam, bo·rei mi·nei ve·sa·mim.	מֶלֶךְ הָעוֹלָם, בּוֹרֵא מִינֵי בְשָׂמִים.
Ba·ruch a·ta, A·do·nai E·lo·hei·nu,	בָּרוּךְ אַתָּה, יְיָ אֱלֹהֵינוּ,
me·lech ha·o·lam, bo·rei me·o·rei ha·eish.	מֶלֶךְ הָעוֹלָם, בּוֹרֵא מְאוֹרֵי הָאֵשׁ.
Ba·ruch a·ta, A·do·nai E·lo·hei·nu,	בָּרוּךְ אַתָּה, יְיָ אֱלֹהֵינוּ,
me·lech ha·o·lam,	מֶלֶךְ הָעוֹלָם,
ha·mav·dil bein ko·desh le·chol,	הַמַּבְדִּיל בֵּין קֹדֶשׁ לְחוֹל,
bein or le·cho·shech,	בֵּין אוֹר לְחֹשֶׁךְ,
bein yom ha·she·vi·i	בֵּין יוֹם הַשְּׁבִיעִי
le·shei·shet ye·mei ha·ma·a·seh.	לְשֵׁשֶׁת יְמֵי הַמַּעֲשֶׂה.
Ba·ruch a·ta, A·do·nai,	בָּרוּךְ אַתָּה, יְיָ,
ha·mav·dil bein ko·desh le·chol.	הַמַּבְדִּיל בֵּין קֹדֶשׁ לְחוֹל.

22

CHANUKAH BLESSINGS

בָּרוּךְ אַתָּה, יְיָ אֱלֹהֵינוּ,
מֶלֶךְ הָעוֹלָם, אֲשֶׁר קִדְּשָׁנוּ
בְּמִצְוֹתָיו, וְצִוָּנוּ
לְהַדְלִיק נֵר שֶׁל חֲנֻכָּה.

Ba·ruch a·ta, A·do·nai E·lo·hei·nu,
me·lech ha·o·lam, a·sher ki·de·sha·nu
be·mits·vo·tav, ve·tsi·va·nu
le·had·lik neir shel Cha·nu·ka.

בָּרוּךְ אַתָּה, יְיָ אֱלֹהֵינוּ,
מֶלֶךְ הָעוֹלָם, שֶׁעָשָׂה נִסִּים
לַאֲבוֹתֵינוּ בַּיָּמִים הָהֵם
בַּזְּמַן הַזֶּה.

Ba·ruch a·ta, A·do·nai E·lo·hei·nu,
me·lech ha·o·lam, she·a·sa ni·sim
la·a·vo·tei·nu ba·ya·mim ha·heim
ba·ze·man ha·zeh.

בָּרוּךְ אַתָּה, יְיָ אֱלֹהֵינוּ,
מֶלֶךְ הָעוֹלָם, שֶׁהֶחֱיָנוּ
וְקִיְּמָנוּ וְהִגִּיעָנוּ
לַזְּמַן הַזֶּה.

Ba·ruch a·ta, A·do·nai E·lo·hei·nu,
me·lech ha·o·lam, she·he·che·ya·nu
ve·ki·ye·ma·nu ve·hi·gi·a·nu
la·ze·man ha·zeh.

23

KIDDUSH FOR THE EVE OF SHABBAT

וַיְהִי עֶרֶב, וַיְהִי בֹקֶר,
יוֹם הַשִּׁשִּׁי. וַיְכֻלּוּ הַשָּׁמַיִם וְהָאָרֶץ
וְכָל צְבָאָם, וַיְכַל אֱלֹהִים בַּיּוֹם
הַשְּׁבִיעִי מְלַאכְתּוֹ אֲשֶׁר עָשָׂה;
וַיִּשְׁבֹּת בַּיּוֹם הַשְּׁבִיעִי מִכָּל
מְלַאכְתּוֹ אֲשֶׁר עָשָׂה. וַיְבָרֶךְ
אֱלֹהִים אֶת־יוֹם הַשְּׁבִיעִי וַיְקַדֵּשׁ
אֹתוֹ, כִּי בוֹ שָׁבַת מִכָּל־מְלַאכְתּוֹ
אֲשֶׁר בָּרָא אֱלֹהִים לַעֲשׂוֹת.

Va·ye·hi e·rev, va·ye·hi vo·ker,
yom ha·shi·shi. Va·ye·chu·lu ha·sha·ma·yim ve·ha·a·rets
ve·chol tse·va·am, va·ye·chal E·lo·him ba·yom
ha·she·vi·i me·lach·to a·sher a·sa;
va·yish·bot ba·yom ha·she·vi·i mi·kol
me·lach·to a·sher a·sa. Va·ye·va·rech
E·lo·him et yom ha·she·vi·i va·ye·ka·deish
o·to, ki vo sha·vat mi·kol me·lach·to
a·sher ba·ra E·lo·him la·a·sot.

בָּרוּךְ אַתָּה, יְיָ אֱלֹהֵינוּ, מֶלֶךְ
הָעוֹלָם, בּוֹרֵא פְּרִי הַגָּפֶן.

Ba·ruch a·ta, A·do·nai E·lo·hei·nu, me·lech
ha·o·lam, bo·rei pe·ri ha·ga·fen.

בָּרוּךְ אַתָּה, יְיָ אֱלֹהֵינוּ, מֶלֶךְ
הָעוֹלָם, אֲשֶׁר קִדְּשָׁנוּ בְּמִצְוֹתָיו

Ba·ruch a·ta, A·do·nai E·lo·hei·nu, me·lech
ha·o·lam, a·sher ki·de·sha·nu be·mits·vo·tav

ve·ra·tsa va·nu, ve·sha·bat kod·sho be·a·ha·va	וְרָצָה בָנוּ, וְשַׁבַּת קָדְשׁוֹ בְּאַהֲבָה
u·ve·ra·tson hin·chi·la·nu, zi·ka·ron le·ma·a·sei	וּבְרָצוֹן הִנְחִילָנוּ, זִכָּרוֹן לְמַעֲשֵׂה
ve·rei·shit. Ki hu yom te·chi·la	בְרֵאשִׁית. כִּי הוּא יוֹם תְּחִלָּה
le·mik·ra·ei ko·desh, zei·cher li·tsi·at	לְמִקְרָאֵי קֹדֶשׁ, זֵכֶר לִיצִיאַת
Mits·ra·yim. Ki va·nu va·char·ta ve·o·ta·nu	מִצְרָיִם. כִּי בָנוּ־בָחַרְתָּ וְאוֹתָנוּ
ki·dash·ta mi·kol ha·a·mim, ve·sha·bat kod·she·cha	קִדַּשְׁתָּ מִכָּל הָעַמִּים, וְשַׁבַּת קָדְשְׁךָ
be·a·ha·va u·ve·ra·tson hin·chal·ta·nu. Ba·ruch	בְּאַהֲבָה וּבְרָצוֹן הִנְחַלְתָּנוּ. בָּרוּךְ
a·ta, A·do·nai, me·ka·deish ha·sha·bat.	אַתָּה, יְיָ, מְקַדֵּשׁ הַשַּׁבָּת.

24

KIDDUSH FOR THE EVE OF YOM TOV

Ba·ruch a·ta, A·do·nai E·lo·hei·nu,	בָּרוּךְ אַתָּה, יְיָ אֱלֹהֵינוּ,
me·lech ha·o·lam,	מֶלֶךְ הָעוֹלָם,
bo·rei pe·ri ha·ga·fen.	בּוֹרֵא פְּרִי הַגָּפֶן.
Ba·ruch a·ta, A·do·nai E·lo·hei·nu,	בָּרוּךְ אַתָּה, יְיָ אֱלֹהֵינוּ,
me·lech ha·o·lam, a·sher	מֶלֶךְ הָעוֹלָם, אֲשֶׁר
ba·char ba·nu mi·kol am,	בָּחַר בָּנוּ מִכָּל־עָם,
ve·ro·me·ma·nu mi·kol la·shon,	וְרוֹמְמָנוּ מִכָּל־לָשׁוֹן,
ve·ki·de·sha·nu be·mits·vo·tav.	וְקִדְּשָׁנוּ בְּמִצְוֹתָיו.
Va·ti·ten la·nu, A·do·nai E·lo·hei·nu,	וַתִּתֶּן־לָנוּ, יְיָ אֱלֹהֵינוּ,
be·a·ha·va (Sha·ba·tot li·me·nu·cha u·)	בְּאַהֲבָה (שַׁבָּתוֹת לִמְנוּחָה וּ)
mo·a·dim le·sim·cha, cha·gim u·ze·ma·nim	מוֹעֲדִים לְשִׂמְחָה, חַגִּים וּזְמַנִּים
le·sa·son, et yom (ha·sha·bat ha·zeh	לְשָׂשׂוֹן, אֶת־יוֹם (הַשַּׁבָּת הַזֶּה
ve·et yom)	וְאֶת־יוֹם)
On Pesach	
chag ha·ma·tsot ha·zeh— ze·man chei·ru·tei·nu,	חַג הַמַּצּוֹת הַזֶּה—זְמַן חֵרוּתֵנוּ,
On Shavuot	
chag ha·sha·vu·ot ha·zeh—	חַג הַשָּׁבֻעוֹת הַזֶּה—
ze·man ma·tan To·ra·tei·nu,	זְמַן מַתַּן תּוֹרָתֵנוּ,
On Sukkot	
chag ha·su·kot ha·zeh— ze·man sim·cha·tei·nu,	חַג הַסֻּכּוֹת הַזֶּה—זְמַן שִׂמְחָתֵנוּ,